June 1985
Public defender investi-
gator Jerry Justine
finds, in attic of
deceased police detec-
tive's home, audiotapes
of Tony DiLisio's 1975
hypnotism sessions
with police; clemency
petition filed

November 22, 1985
Oral argument in state
trial court; all relief
denied

:h 1984
argument in
Supreme Court

1985

ourt;

June 1984
U.S. Supreme Court
rules against Spaziano,
affirming his death sen-
tence; postconviction
investigation kicks into
high gear

death
two more
preme
s

4
5.

Novembe
First death
execution
7:00 A.M.,
1985

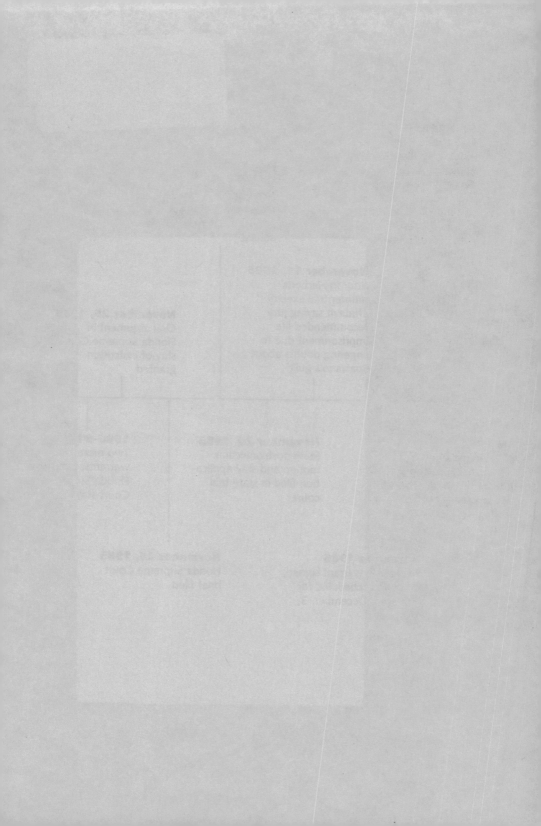

The Wrong Man

FLA DOR
A049 043
JULY 19 1976

The Wrong Man

A
True
Story
of
Innocence
on
Death Row

MICHAEL MELLO

Foreword by Mike Farrell

University of Minnesota Press
Minneapolis • London

Published by the University of Minnesota Press
111 Third Avenue South, Suite 290
Minneapolis, MN 55401-2520
http://www.upress.umn.edu

Library of Congress Cataloging-in-Publication Data

Mello, Michael.
   The wrong man : a true story of innocence on death row / Michael Mello ; foreword by Mike Farrell.
      p.   cm.
   Includes index.
   ISBN 0-8166-3783-0 (hard : alk paper)
   1. Spaziano, Joe.   2. Death row inmates—Florida—Case studies.
   3. Spaziano, Joe—Trials, litigation, etc.   4. Mello, Michael.   5. Trials
   (Murder)—Florida—Case studies.   6. Trials (Rape)—Florida—Case
   studies.   7. Judicial error—Florida—Case studies.   8. Capital
   punishment—Florida.   I. Title.
      HV8699.U5 M45 2001
      364.15'23'0975924—dc21

                                                                00-011589

Printed in the United States of America on acid-free paper

The University of Minnesota is an equal-opportunity educator and employer.

12 11 10 09 08 07 06 05 04 03 02 01   10 9 8 7 6 5 4 3 2 1

For Gene Miller,

Warren Holmes,

and Lori Rozsa,

and for

the loving memories

of Beauty,

Tommy,

and

Scotty Mello

Contents

Foreword   **ix**
   Mike Farrell

Author's Note   **xiii**

Acknowledgments   **xv**

Introduction   **xix**

1.   Watching Two Lives Converge:
     The Biker and the Nerd   **1**

2.   Prisoner No. 049043:
     Letters from Death Row   **41**

3.   Lawyers for the Dead   **83**

4.   Hurricane Season:
     The First Death Warrant   **98**

5.   The Outlaw Bikers' Clubhouse   **127**

6.   Outlaw Judiciary:
     Giving Up on the Courts   **178**

7.   Death's Witness:
     Tony DiLisio Redux   **204**

8.   "Dear Governor Chiles . . ."   **211**

9.   The Secret Police Report   **226**

10.   Acoustic Shadow   **247**

11.   Exquisite Chaos:
      The Final Death Warrant
      (August 1995)   **273**

12. Checkmate **303**

13. Hell in a Very Small Place **332**

14. I'm Fired by the Court:
"Crazy Michael" and "Crazy Joe" **345**

15. "I Won't Debate My Soul with Strangers":
Outlaws against All Odds **357**

16. The Police Detective, the Psychic,
and the Skull **383**

17. The Fires of Jubilee:
Florida's Malfunctioning Electric Chair **402**

18. Judgment Day **428**

19. To Bedlam and Partway Back **453**

20. An Absence of Malice **479**

21. Life Itself **487**

22. Why the "Crazy Joe" Case Matters **501**

Appendix Execution Guidelines
for the State of Florida **517**

Index **565**

*A timeline of the events of this case appears
inside the front and back covers of this book.*

Foreword

Mike Farrell

"Abandon hope, all ye who enter here." Dante's admonition is appropriate at this juncture, it seems to me, because those who choose to go beyond these portals risk exposure to the "sorrowful city" of American jurisprudence.

Believers in justice, proceed at your own risk. The "eternal suffering" of which Dante warned can result when those taught that fairness, honor, and a search for truth undergird our legal system are confronted with the ugly reality so vividly captured in the pages that follow.

Little you will find in these pages has been taught in any law school, ergo this book should be required reading in all of them. Note the operative word: it is not only proper reading for present and future practitioners of the law, it should be a *requirement* for same. And more; judges, politicians—Lord, especially politicians!—should be forced to read this book.

And, of course, let me not leave out you, the innocent in all this. You who may have been in a bar but not before one, you to whom a suit means clothing, you for whom charges are credit card matters and a cell a modern telephone. If you know, somewhat vaguely, that people are dying, but they're bad and it doesn't disturb you; if you think that somewhere a judge (white, of course, and male) sits awaiting the chance to do good for our land; if you think that our leaders, the experts, the pros, can be trusted to do the right thing, that virtue is its own reward and innocence will ultimately prevail—read on at your peril.

The author of this work is a madman. He is that quite literally in the eyes of some, mostly those who have opposed him, who have stood against his resolute—no, absolute—unwillingness to bend in the face of laziness, cowardice, dishonesty, and hypocrisy. For others he is a mad man, one whose rage at a system so in love with itself, its customs, and its practices that the humane is drowned in the process, is palpable. Noting that "the ludicrous element of a human life overshadowed by a procedural detail was, at times, overwhelming," this man is *not* only not overwhelmed, he is so offended that he becomes maniacally intent on pouring in light to prevent the overshadowing of that life. And that light is blinding. It is searing. Its searching beams peer through the fabric of our system, exposing the comfortable, if putrid and self-righteous, rot beneath.

A lawyer—a professor of constitutional law and legal ethics at one of our nation's law schools—the author of this work is no Don Quixote, no romantic with broken-down nag and pointless lance. This lethal enemy of mendacity possesses a hunger for justice that requires the full and ferocious use of every weapon in his arsenal—and they are many, proved, sharpened, and ready. Witness:

> Lawyers are powerful because the law is powerful, and because lawyers have a monopoly on access to the law's power. Kafka calls us "gatekeepers," and it's an apt metaphor. If the law is a labyrinth, then we are the only guides with the clue of thread essential for admittance into, navigation through, and safe return from the maze. We know the maze because we designed and built it. Only we know the secret language of the maps, because we wrote the maps. Only we know where the land mines and their trip wires are buried, because we buried them. . . . And we mean to keep it that way. Without the labyrinth of our own creation, without our high priests and hermeneutic mysteries, why would the laity pay us two hundred dollars per hour for our services?

This is a simple book. It is the story of a lawyer using his skills to achieve justice for an innocent man wrongly convicted. This is also a complex and deeply profound book. It is the literary equivalent of a whore in church, a bad joke in good company, and picking one's nose in public. These pages should be hot to the touch as they smoke with the rage of a principled man made a juggernaut of fury by a stupid, deaf, hidebound system that purports to do justice as it blithely sweeps the detritus of "insignificant" lives under the rug of legal conformity.

Consider: an unsolved murder; a social outcast; a largely circumstantial Tinkertoy case; a hurried, harried, unsure jury; and a sentence of death for an innocent, if unlovely, man. This case, under the usual circumstances, goes unnoticed and the condemned dies, along with his—and our—innocence. He dies because the system will not, cannot, admit an error. It would rather kill wrongly than admit wrong. This much-vaunted criminal justice system of ours wants everyone to play the game; dot the i's, cross the t's, bow, scrape, nod, and genuflect in all the right times and places, and those of us who brush our teeth after eating can sleep the sleep of virtue.

But put a madman in the equation, a mad man fired by a belief in the ultimate value of human life and an undying commitment to a system of justice unsullied by cronyism and self-righteousness, arm him with a quiver full of severely barbed, ego-piercing arrows, and the result is chaos—out of which, life.

Read on, brave soul, as the effort to save an innocent man exposes the moral bankruptcy of the death system in America. But protect your eyes as a human blowtorch scours the legal countryside, unmasks the perversion of fatuous, black-robed pomposity, reveals the Pilatesque contortions of butter-wouldn't-melt politicians, and lays waste contemptible pretenders of the Fourth Estate, all the while giving scorched-earth policy a new meaning.

Watch as Michael Mello burns away the curtain covering the nakedness, the wheels, pulleys, whistles, and tricks of the Wizards of Florida.

Los Angeles, California
November 1999

Author's Note

What follows is a true story—in the sense that it is a narrative. As such, it has no footnotes. So let me say at the outset that virtually all of the witness interviews quoted in this book, as well as the rest of the gumshoe investigation done since 1995, was done by a brilliant investigative reporter, Lori Rozsa of the *Miami Herald,* guided by Warren Holmes and Gene Miller. Virtually all witness quotations, particularly in the later chapters, are attributed to Lori Rozsa and the *Herald*; I am deeply grateful for their generous permission to draw upon their superb work.

I have chosen not to include footnotes or other citation paraphernalia in this book for two reasons. First, this book is based on personal experience, case files, and journals. Most footnotes would therefore cite myself or my own files, and this seems to me unnecessary and tacky. Second, my decision to avoid footnotes is driven by aesthetics: I do not want to interrupt the narrative flow with small numbers in the midst of the text, and I do not want to lengthen an already long book with endnotes. In my experience, general readers often find footnotes distracting.

Acknowledgments

The story this book tells could not have been written without the people who fought so hard to save the real "Crazy Joe" Spaziano's life after the legal system had failed: Gene Miller, Warren Holmes, Lori Rozsa, John Pancake, Deanna Mello, Nell Joslin Medlin, Jerry Justine, Steve Gustat, Mike Farrell, Beth Grossbard (and her mom in Miami), Eric Freedman, Rosie Merrill and Mark, Fuzzy Miller, Smitty, Speedy, Stella Madden, Wildman, Rocky, Linda Harrell, Bob Trebilcock, Tony Proscio, Martin Dyckman, Colman McCarthy, James Jackson Kilpatrick, Colin Wentworth, Rich Bard, John McKinnon, Tom Fielder, Tom Blackburn, Bruce Shapiro, Jeffrey Rosen, Peter Katel, David Von Drehle, Nina Alvarez, Mark Potter, Laura Gillen, Judy Hilts, Virginia Fifield, Micki Dickoff, Christie Webb, Sonny Jacobs, Mike and Lisa Radelet, Jeff Robinson, Mike and Sally Millemann, Harry Weiner, Mike Lehmann, Richard Capozzola, Paul Basille, Toni Apel, Rose Marie Boniello, Richard Ofshe, Dottie Irwin, Sandra Dickson, Linda Gibson, David Greenburg, Larry Kaplow, Beth Curnow, Ian Ridlon, Dawn Poland, Tanja Shipman, Elyse Ruzow, Doug Gould, Brad Powers. Deanna Mello was a genuine partner in the 1995–96 events described in this book.

I am deeply grateful to Joe Spaziano for his permission to use his letters in this book. I first got to know Joe Spaziano through his letters, and it is appropriate for the reader to see how this slow process unfolded. Joe's letters can be powerful, and they are honest and direct. Their power is not diminished by their misspellings and grammatical errors; indeed, these give the letters a Faulkneresque quality.

I owe a special debt to Emily Kucer, my partner in crime on this project; Emily was involved in most stages of this book, and her thoughtfulness is reflected throughout. A quartet of extraordinarily gifted and hardworking Vermont Law School students adopted this enterprise as something personal and devoted themselves to it accordingly: Paul Perkins, Ian Ridlon, Emily Kucer, and Dawn Seibert. Their thoughtful, honest, direct, and wise attention to this project is visible on virtually every page. So are the ideas of many, many people who read and commented helpfully on the manuscript, beginning with Kent Araldi, Ray Adams, and a number of the folks named above.

I want especially to thank Mike Farrell for his foreword, Lloyd Steffan and Margaret Vandiver for their incisive comments on the manuscript, and Carrie Mullen and the other folks at the University of Minnesota Press for their outstanding work on this project. Many other people also read and commented helpfully on at least one version of this manuscript, including Fuzzy Miller, Joe Spaziano, Warren Holmes, Gene Miller (who read three drafts), Lori Rozsa, Emily Kucer, Ellen Swain, Michael Millemann, and Lisa (Eberly) Mossor. Thank you all. Any remaining errors in this book are solely my own.

The Florida Outlaws motorcycle club members with whom I have dealt over the years have allowed me to glimpse that they are truly a brotherhood and not merely a gang as depicted by the journalists at newspapers like the *Orlando Sentinel*; not all bikers are outlaws, and not all "suits" possessing press credentials, law degrees, or police shields are sincerely respectful of the truth.

The wizards at the West Palm Beach, Florida, Public Defender's Office were always there for Joe Spaziano, even long after Joe was no longer their client: Dick Jorandby, Craig Barnard, Richard Green, Jerry Schwarz, Flo Wilson, Lee Currie, and Mike Lehman. Ditto as to the first generation of CCR: MO, Scharlette, Lissa, Tim, Steve, Eloise, Barbara, and the "Wookies."

This book is based loosely on several models, none of which was written by a legal academic. For storytelling structure and tone, I have taken some cues from Gene Miller's *Invitation to a Lynching* (1975), David Von Drehle's *Among the Lowest of the Dead* (1995), Anthony Lewis's *Gideon's Trumpet* (1966), Roger Parloff's *Triple Jeopardy* (1996), Michael Radelet, Hugo Bedau, and Constance Putnam's *In Spite of Innocence* (1992), Richard Kluger's *Simple Justice* (1974), and

Phillip Shaw Paludan's *Victims: A True Story of the Civil War* (1981). I have based the structure and use of primary historical documents here on Henry Steele Commager's *Documents of American History* and the collected works of the historian Theodore Draper.

This book is not intended for scholars alone, although I think it meets the rigors of scholarship. It is intended for the general educated reader who, as Draper puts it, is "no longer merely interested in the daily or even weekly ration of the news," who "wants to understand present events in some organized form and in some historical perspective."

Also, I want to mention the nickname of this book's subject. For the past thirty years, Joseph Spaziano has carried the nickname "Crazy Joe." I discuss the source of the moniker later in this book, but for now I want to explain why I use Joe's nickname in these pages. Many people use the nickname as a sign of derision of Joe Spaziano. For years, I objected loudly when anyone other than Joe or his family referred to my friend and client as "Crazy Joe." Then Joe took me aside and told me to lighten up. He liked the label, he told me, because, in today's America, only the crazy are sane, and vice versa. He saw the name as something of an ironic, inside joke—and not a joke told only at his own expense.

We made a deal, Joe and I. I'd call him "Crazy Joe." He'd call me "Crazy Mike." In 1995 and afterward, that's how Joe and I signed our letters to each other.

In the end, though, it was Dick Gregory who convinced me to refer in this book to "Crazy Joe" Spaziano. So, to paraphrase the dedication of Gregory's book *Nigger*: Joe, whenever some asshole reporter or cop or politician calls you "Crazy Joe," his voice dripping with loathing and fear, remember this: He's advertising this book. He's advertising our book. He's advertising *your* book.

Introduction

Capital punishment is to law what Surrealism is to Realism in art.

Norman Mailer

Innocent people are sentenced to death and executed in the United States. It's as inevitable as the law of averages and the fallibility of legal institutions devised and administered by humans. As of this writing, eighty-three condemned prisoners have been exonerated and released since 1973 under current death penalty statutes. The state of Illinois freed ten wrongfully condemned prisoners between 1973 and 1994—two fewer than it put to death. Florida has freed nineteen for the forty-three it has put to death. Nationally, one innocent person has been released for every five executed. *One in five.*

On Christmas Day 1998, retiring Florida Chief Justice Gerald Kogan was quoted in the *Washington Post* as saying he had "grave doubts" about the guilt of some of the people executed in Florida in recent years: "There are several cases where I had grave doubts as to the guilt of a particular person." Chief Justice Kogan is no bleeding-heart, soft-on-crime liberal. He had been both a homicide detective and a prosecutor before he was appointed to the Florida Supreme Court.

I want to be clear at the outset what I mean by *innocence*. I mean the person on death row didn't do the crime; I mean they got the wrong guy; I mean innocence the old-fashioned way. I don't mean "innocence" by some legal technicality; I don't mean he did it but he was crazy; I don't mean he was there but didn't pull the trigger. I mean he wasn't there at all. I mean he didn't do it—period. *I mean they got the wrong person.*

Sometimes a person's innocence is not proven until after that person has been executed. In 1990, the state of Florida executed Jesse Tafero. Tafero, his wife Sonia (Sonny) Jacobs, and a man named Rhodes had been found guilty of killing a policeman at an interstate rest stop in south Florida. Rhodes turned state's evidence and testified against Tafero and Jacobs. Tafero was sentenced to death and executed. Jacobs was sentenced to life imprisonment and was later freed when it was proven that Rhodes—not Jacobs or Tafero—had killed the police officer. But Jesse Tafero was already dead by the time the truth came out. The execution was botched, because Florida's 1923, three-legged execution stool malfunctioned, and Tafero's head burst into flames.

By 1995 I'd had enough. After twelve years of working, full- or part-time, on behalf of death row prisoners, I decided that I could no longer, in good conscience, continue to work as a defense lawyer in the American system of capital punishment. This book is the story of the case that drove me from deathwork, the "Crazy Joe" Spaziano case. Spaziano was innocent of the crimes for which he was scheduled to die, but in the spring of 1995 he was on the verge of being executed for other men's crimes, and there didn't seem to be much that I—or any other defense lawyer following the rules laid down—could do to stop it.

"Crazy Joe" Spaziano was innocent. When we first met, he had been on death row for seven years for a crime he did not commit. I had recently graduated law school. That was in 1983. Thirteen years later, "Crazy Joe" Spaziano was the last death row prisoner I represented as a lawyer. He was still on death row for that same crime. You might say we grew up together.

This book tells a true story about how justice can miscarry over a period of decades. It describes how the system was saved from committing the most hideous sort of injustice possible under our Constitution— the electrocution of an absolutely innocent man—only by virtue of the endgame intervention of a staunchly pro–capital punishment newspaper, the *Miami Herald*.

Only in 1995 did we understand how the criminal justice system had gotten it so wrong two decades earlier. Today we can construct an almost seamless narrative of how Joseph Spaziano came to be condemned for crimes he did not commit. What you must understand, however, is that this narrative became possible only at the end of a twenty-year process of dogged factual investigation.

"Crazy Joe" Spaziano was a member of the Orlando Outlaws motorcycle brotherhood. He was sentenced to death in 1976 for the rape and murder of Laura Lynn Harberts, whose body was found in a Seminole County, Florida, trash dump. The dump was not far from Spaziano's trailer, and Spaziano often hid drugs there. One important factor separated "Crazy Joe" Spaziano from virtually all of my other clients: Spaziano was innocent. Not that Spaziano was a boy scout—far from it. But he was innocent of the crime for which he was convicted. I had known it to a virtual certainty since 1985, when the investigator on Joe's case discovered a set of audiotapes in the attic of the widow of the lead police detective who had investigated the Harberts case. The tapes were made by the police during sessions in which they hypnotized and coached the state's chief witness against Spaziano, Anthony DiLisio.

At the time of his testimony, DiLisio was an eighteen-year-old with a troubled life; he was often high on drugs. At the trial, DiLisio told the jury that Spaziano had driven him to the dump to show him the bodies of two women Spaziano had raped and tortured. What neither the jury nor the judge knew at the time was that DiLisio had told a dramatically different story about the dump when he first met with the police. Prior to repeated police interrogation and hypnosis sessions, he had said nothing about Spaziano driving him to the dump or about seeing the bodies of women.

When our investigator discovered the tapes of these sessions, I believed we had exculpatory evidence that would lead to a new trial; in 1985, Florida had become one of the states in which hypnotically produced testimony is not admissible. Moreover, nine years after Spaziano's murder trial, a former juror swore in an affidavit that the jury had not been sure that Spaziano was guilty, hadn't trusted DiLisio's testimony, and would not have convicted had they known DiLisio had been hypnotized. Although the jury had found Spaziano guilty, it recommended against the death penalty because of concerns about the credibility of DiLisio's testimony. The judge overrode the jury's life sentence verdict and sentenced Spaziano to die in the electric chair.

For twelve years, I played the role of the polite, play-by-the-rules lawyer. And for those twelve years, "Crazy Joe" Spaziano's case headed steadily toward the electric chair. No one in authority would listen. I lost in court after court. In fact, in the Eleventh Circuit Court of Appeals, Judge Ed Carnes refused to review my new evidence. Judge

Carnes, whose appointment to the bench I had opposed publicly, had held only one legal job prior to his being appointed to the federal bench: capital prosecutor in Alabama. In May 1995, twelve years after I had first become involved in the Spaziano case, the governor of Florida signed Joe Spaziano's fourth death warrant. An execution date was set for 7:00 A.M. on June 17, 1995.

In June 1995, with less than a month to go before Spaziano's execution, I gave up on the legal system and became, in a way, an "outlaw lawyer." I took Spaziano's case to the *Miami Herald,* pleading with reporters to listen to me and review the case. I burned my bridges in Florida, blasting the police, the governor, the trial judge, and the state and federal appeals court judges in the media. The *Miami Herald* assigned investigative reporter Lori Rozsa, who concluded that Spaziano was innocent, and the *Herald* began covering the case. DiLisio recanted. Spaziano's story was picked up by ABC News, nationally syndicated columnists James Kilpatrick and Colman McCarthy, and national publications including the *Washington Post, New York Times, Nation, New Republic,* and *National Law Journal.* At the last minute, Governor Chiles backed down and withdrew the death warrant he had signed three weeks earlier. He would sign a new death warrant weeks later.

This is a story about failure—about failure of our legal system, and about my own personal failure as an attorney. It is a story of friendship and love against all odds. It is also a story about lost causes that are still worth fighting like hell to win. This is a story about moral advocacy against overwhelming odds and about turning the power of the law against the law itself. In the end, this is a story about the transcendence of the truth—the truth is still the truth, even in our postmodern, deconstructed age of irony. Even when the legal system defines it as false, the truth remains true.

In this book I tell a story; I don't make an argument. This book is not a polemic on capital punishment; I use capital punishment as a frame of reference and as a window into how the human spirit responds to extreme circumstances. What interests me is not the moral issue of the death penalty, but the world of capital punishment as it exists as a legal system. Joe Spaziano's case is a microcosm of everything that is wrong with capital punishment as a legal institution: rogue cops, rabid prosecutors, inept defense lawyers, cowardly, tunnel-visioned judges, and politicians who play the politics of death with perfect pitch.

Looking back on the mountains of paper on the "Crazy Joe" Spaziano case, I have found it very tempting to superimpose order and coherence on the sprawling narrative I tell in this book. To some extent I have done so, while still keeping in mind what the historian Michael Bernstein has called "foreshadowing"—the feeling of historical inevitability, the tendency to read the past in terms of the future, to see our history as moving toward a predetermined goal or as controlled by fate. Foreshadowing distorts the haphazardness, randomness, and contingency of human life.

This book was written long after the events described here occurred. Because I knew the outcome, some essential qualities of those events are compromised in the telling of this story. Thus I chose not to write this book as a straight, linear narrative, telling the whole two-decade story of the "Crazy Joe" case from beginning to end, based on all the facts and information I now possess. For me, the process of the slow accumulation of facts—and some of the most fascinating facts (having to do with necrodentistry, the police detective, the psychic, and the skull, for instance) did not become known to me until near the end of the "Crazy Joe" saga—is as important as the facts themselves.

I don't tell this as a nice, neat story because it *wasn't* a nice, neat story. The events described in this book did not occur in a well-ordered sequence, as though one mind controlled the outcome.

Besides, I'm not just trying to tell a story; I'm trying to describe a world, the world of deathwork. Essential qualities of that world are chaos, uncertainty, and luck.

Chaos and uncertainty. At every critical juncture in this epic story, events could easily have gone differently: a war really *can* be lost for want of a nail. For this reason, I present here primary, historical materials, litigation documents, letters, and diary entries. Reproducing these documents seems to me the best way to capture the contingency, and some of the verisimilitude, of the events I am trying to capture. These materials were written at the time without knowledge of the future, and such uncertainty is an essential quality of the world of deathwork I am trying to describe. By presenting litigation documents, journal entries, and other artifacts, I hope to restore some of the chaos and uncertainty of daily life in deathwork.

Luck—good luck and bad. My life in deathwork has made me a great believer in luck. If I had to choose between good luck and great skill as a capital defense lawyer, I'd take good luck every time. In my representation of Joe Spaziano, we've had some good luck and some bad luck, but on balance our luck has been bad. This story does not have a happy ending.

Also, as Larry Daniel puts it in his wonderful book *Shiloh: The Battle That Changed the Civil War,* I have "attempted to avoid lengthy biographical vignettes. The reader learns about the principal characters throughout the text. This, after all, is how we meet people in real life; everything is not learned at first acquaintance."

One of the things that makes this book unique is my vantage point on capital punishment as a legal system. There is a vast literature on death as a punishment; histories and philosophies have been written. There have been memoirs of death row prisoners and their jailers and their counselors. But this book is one of the only real reports, from the inside, of what *Washington Post* editor David Von Drehle calls the "real" capital punishment: "The guts of our American death penalty are not to be found in prison. Death row—with its prisoners and wardens and pastors—is a dull, slow hell of waiting and despair. The real death penalty enterprise is a bustling, frantic mill of investigation, litigation, brief drafting, strategy, written and oral argument, a Rube Goldberg contraption kept clanking perpetually by the fuel of caffeinated lawyers and their cousins, the poll-driven politicians. It is a madhouse." That madhouse—and the qualities of chaos and uncertainty that typify it—is an essential part of the world I am trying to capture in this book. My description of that world is built around the Spaziano case, but capturing that world is as important to me as telling the Spaziano story.

In fall 1995, when Joe Spaziano was at the lip of the grave, days away from death, when Joe, his family, and I were making his funeral arrangements, I was sometimes asked, "What if you got him released from prison—where would he go then?" When I'd reply that he would come to live in my home in Vermont, some people thought I was kidding. But I wasn't. I'd trust Joe with my life as he trusted me with his.

Wilder, Vermont
December 17, 1999

1

Watching Two Lives Converge: The Biker and the Nerd

This ["Crazy Joe" Spaziano execution] is one of those choices that tests a civilization's soul. Out of all the static about defining moments and public morality that crowds the narrow bandwidth of modern politics, here, finally, is a real defining moment for a real public. It will tell what morality, if any, guides Florida government. The issue is life or death, and the choice will be made in the next 12 days.

The question is whether the state of Florida will kill a man for committing a crime to which utterly no evidence links him.

Tony Proscio, "'Memory' of Murder, Mockery of Justice,"
Miami Herald, *June 14, 1995*

My name is Michael Mello. I'm forty-two years old. I married for the first time only three years ago. For the past eleven years, I have been a professor at Vermont Law School. In the early and mid-1980s, I was a capital public defender in Florida. I have been involved in about seventy capital cases, including Ted Bundy's, Ted Kaczynski's, and Paul Hill's. But Joe Spaziano was my first and my last capital client. In a way, his case made me crazy—at any rate, it landed me in the hospital. Or perhaps Joe's case simply forced me to see clearly the brutal truths of capital punishment in America. In the end, Joe's case made me see that I'm not the one who's crazy.

I oppose capital punishment. However, those who know me well know that I'm not "soft" on crime. I don't sentimentalize criminals, including my clients. When I was in college, my significant other was raped at knifepoint. In 1989, a man I loved as a father was murdered

1

by a terrorist who sent a mail bomb to his home a few days before Christmas. The bomb detonated in the man's kitchen, killing him and nearly killing his wife. I wanted to find these bastards and kill them myself.

My last book was about the case of "the Unabomber," Theodore Kaczynski. There, I argue that Kaczynski was unlawfully denied his day in court, that constitutional corners were cut to nail the obviously guilty Unabomber. On more radio talk shows than I like to remember, I was asked—quite properly and fairly—why we should care that the law was bent to get the Unabomber. My answer was always the same: we should care that the Unabomber's rights were violated because of "Crazy Joe" Spaziano. If constitutional corners can be cut to convict the guilty Unabombers, then they can be—and, as I show in this book, are—cut to convict, condemn, and execute the innocent Spazianos.

Unlike the Unabomber, Joe Spaziano isn't a celebrity serial killer. Joe Spaziano is an obscure member among the some three thousand persons on death rows in the United States. But, as the poet Sam Hazo has noted, obscurity also has its tale to tell.

David Von Drehle, the leading historian concerning Florida's modern experience with capital punishment, has written that not long ago capital punishment may have been a "liberal" versus "conservative" issue, but no longer. Today the great divide is between those who understand how the legal machinery of death works and those who don't. I understand capital punishment because, in addition to having studied and researched it, I lived at its center for four years.

Although at the moment my day job is as a tenured professor of constitutional law at Vermont Law School, my professional life has been devoted to deathwork. In the early 1980s, I was the "death clerk" for Judge Robert S. Vance, an appellate judge on the U.S. Court of Appeals for the Eleventh Circuit, who was assassinated by a letter bomb in 1989. As the death clerk, I conducted preliminary reviews of the death sentence appeals that came through Vance's chambers and drafted the opinions in the cases of many who were subsequently executed. At the end of my clerkship, Judge Vance urged me to go to Wall Street and make some money. Instead, I went to Florida and became a public defender representing death row inmates.

I thought twelve years would have been long enough. I thought that after twelve years I could read the letters from my old clients and the other men on death row in Florida whom I had tried to help during the mid-1980s. Some of these men had been executed—James Adams, James Dupree Henry, Bob Sullivan, David Leroy Washington, Freddy Goode, David Funchess, Dan Thomas, Ronnie Straight, Nollie Lee Martin, Ed Kennedy, Dennis Adams, Ted Bundy, Willie Jasper Darden, Larry Joe Johnson, Buford White, Jerry White. Many more were saved, but it's funny—I have a harder time remembering their names. It's the names and faces and histories of my dead I can summon from memory—what Lincoln called the "mystic chords of memory"—without effort. I still get letters from clients I was able to save. Still, it's the letters from clients I was unable to save that are burned into my memory. Those are the people and the cases I feel compelled to write about. The cases I lost. The people I lost. The people like "Crazy Joe" Spaziano.

When I left Florida and full-time deathwork in 1987, I threw the letters into a file folder, and there they remained, unread, until the summer of 1996, when I began writing this book. Most of the letters were from Joseph Spaziano. My innocent client. My unlikely friend.

By 1995 I was willing to stake my license to practice law on my belief that Joe was innocent. But twelve years earlier I thought otherwise. For my first year or so as Spaziano's lawyer, I thought he was guilty.

I first read Spaziano's trial transcript in 1983. The same transcript that years later persuaded an experienced *Miami Herald* investigator of Spaziano's innocence confirmed my belief in his guilt. The difference was experience. The *Herald* investigator (an ex-cop) knew what to look for in a murder trial transcript. He knew how to interpret the evidence missing from the record. He knew how to connect the dots. I didn't have a clue. In September 1983, when I was first assigned to work on Spaziano's case, I was a brand-new lawyer. I had taken the Florida bar exam just a couple of months earlier. I had graduated law school the year before, and during that year I was the death clerk for Judge Vance.

Judge Vance was a genuine hero of the 1960s civil rights wars in Alabama; he was George Wallace's principal political nemesis within the Democratic Party of Alabama. The judge despised the death penalty because of its arbitrariness and its disproportionate impact on racial minorities and the poor. Had Vance been in the legislature, he would have voted against capital punishment; had he sat on the U.S. Supreme Court, he would have held the death penalty unconstitutional. But Judge Vance wasn't a legislator or a Supreme Court justice. He was an intermediate appellate judge, and he refused to allow his personal loathing of capital punishment to interfere with his duty to follow the Supreme Court's decisions upholding the constitutionality of the punishment. (His one attempt to clear Alabama's death row was resoundingly reversed by the Supreme Court.)

The judge also never sentimentalized the killers who populate death rows. Robert Vance's philosophy was chiseled out of raw experience. His philosophy of law was *about* life and *for* life in the real world.

"No innocent people are on death row," Judge Vance had said again and again when I was working for him. Now that I was a public defender, I was determined to approach my own capital clients with Judge Vance's sort of cold realism. I expected all my clients to be guilty. My job would be to attack the death sentence. And I'd do that not because the inmates deserved sympathy, but because I believed that the legal machinery that exists for the purpose of executions diminishes all of us and warps our law. By deciding who dies, the state is making intensely subjective moral decisions that cannot conform to the narrow categories set out by positive law. It is simply not possible to classify these decisions according to existing legal pigeonholes, and attempts to do so ultimately warp the law and result in the political polarization of the legal system. In addition, decisions regarding who deserves to die involve moral issues that lawyers and judges are not especially competent to address.

Maybe, I thought, after ten or twenty years as a public defender, I might represent an innocent person who had been railroaded onto death row. But my *first* client? Give me a break. So the fact that Joe Spaziano said he was innocent carried no weight with me; if anything, it set off my skeptic's warning bells. Especially when the capital crime described by the prosecutor in the trial transcript was the harrowing rape, torture, and killing of a young woman by an Outlaw biker. If ever a case was a candidate for capital punishment, this seemed to be it.

When I first read the trial transcripts, Spaziano had been on death row for seven years. The legal papers in the case file were weathered and obviously well used, and the whole thing had about it the air of a period piece. Spaziano's case was tried in the seventies, and the crime took place in south Florida. Biker "gangs" were feared and hated by the police and condemned by the local newspaper, the *Orlando Sentinel*. In the mid-seventies the *Sentinel* brought the Florida Outlaws to national attention. In 1995, the *Orlando Sentinel* described the members of this motorcycle brotherhood:

> Like ogres in a fairy tale they are part of a legend that reaches across decades to seed the sleep of innocents with nightmares.
>
> These are grim brothers, all right: rugged, hairy men in black leather and chains, roaring across 1970's Florida on motorcycles.
>
> The bikers nailed one woman to a tree. They chained another to a ceiling for an afternoon of rape and torture. They snatched teen-age girls from sidewalks, took them to dark clubhouses and raped them repeatedly.
>
> Tales of motorcycle gangs were so potent in the 1970s that even today, 20 years after Outlaws member Joe Spaziano was sentenced to death for killing an Orlando woman, many people familiar with the case still are too terrified to talk about it publicly.

At the time of Spaziano's arrest in 1975, he was a member of the local Outlaws club.

To hear the prosecutor tell it in the trial transcript, Spaziano's crimes were especially vile: the gang rape and mutilation of one young woman and the torture, rape, and murder of another. The murder was particularly grisly.

The jury in the murder trial had found Spaziano guilty, so they must have found the prosecutor's evidence at least somewhat persuasive. And the jury knew Joe was an Outlaw biker, because his club brothers showed up for every day of the trial, in their Outlaw regalia. Yet there was a puzzle: Why would a jury that had found Spaziano guilty of this brutal killing then recommend that he not be put to death for it? Part of the reason may lie in the fact that the jury didn't know about Spaziano's prior rape conviction. Still, Florida juries are not known for their mercy to bikers who slaughter young women. All strong opponents of capital punishment had been removed from the jury at the start of the case, so the jurors' imposition of a life sentence (which the judge overrode, imposing the death sentence) couldn't have been based on opposition to capital punishment. It was all quite odd.

Joseph Spaziano was convicted of the rape of Vanessa Dale Croft and the murder of Laura Lynn Harberts in two separate trials. The long and tortuous history of Spaziano's murder case actually began in February 1974, with the rape of Vanessa Dale Croft. Although Spaziano was convicted of the two separate crimes, the rape case and the murder case were crucially related. Spaziano was targeted as Harberts's killer solely because the police assumed that he had attacked Croft.

Although related, the two crimes were not similar—but the two trials were. The prosecution's star witness against Spaziano in both trials was one Anthony Frank DiLisio. Further, Spaziano's 1975 rape conviction was *the* reason he was sentenced to death in 1976. Spaziano's 1976 sentencing jury convicted him of the first-degree murder of Harberts but shied away from a death sentence, based on Tony DiLisio's lack of credibility. However, the judge overrode the jury's life sentence decision and sentenced Spaziano to death because of Spaziano's 1975 conviction of the brutal rape and mutilation of Vanessa Dale Croft. The murder trial jury did not know about Spaziano's 1975 rape conviction or about Tony DiLisio's role as key witness in that trial, but the judge knew about both and used this information to justify sentencing Spaziano to death as a punishment for the 1976 murder.

In 1975, Joseph Spaziano went on trial for the rape of Vanessa Dale Croft. In June 1975, I graduated from Wakefield High School. Despite rather mediocre grades, I managed to get myself admitted to Mary Washington College in Fredericksburg, Virginia, as part of the college's affirmative action plan. (Mary Washington College had just gone coed and was admitting pretty much any person with a penis. I qualified.) While Joe Spaziano was riding Harley motorcycles, I was listening to Bruce Springsteen singing about cars, motorcycles, and outsiders on *Born to Run*.

While I was adjusting to college in Virginia, "Crazy Joe" Spaziano was on trial in Florida for the rape and mutilation of Vanessa Dale Croft. The rape victim testified that on February 9, 1974, while she was walking on 38th Street in Orlando, she was approached by a man who emerged from some bushes and asked her if she knew anyone who would be interested in purchasing marijuana. The man called himself "Dennis" and was wearing jeans, no shirt, and a sleeveless jean jacket. Dennis had "long, black, skaggly *[sic]* hair" and a full beard and was slightly taller than Croft. He invited her to smoke marijuana with him and suggested that they go to his truck to smoke because it was so cold outside. Croft followed Dennis into a dark truck with a camper on the back. A second man, who called himself "Ronnie," also got into the truck. Croft became frightened and wanted to leave, but Dennis and Ronnie wouldn't let her. Croft testified that while Dennis drove the truck, Ronnie shoved her onto the floor of the truck's cab and forced her to perform oral sex on him at knifepoint.

Their destination was a small, white, wood frame house in the woods with lots of graffiti on the walls and a motorcycle in the kitchen, Croft said. She testified that at the house, Ronnie forced oral sex on her and then Dennis forced her to perform oral sex on him. Ronnie later took her to the bedroom, made her take off her clothes and beat and raped her.

Croft testified that eventually she was taken back to the truck, where she was pushed onto the floor and was again forced to perform oral sex on Ronnie while Dennis drove. After they had driven for approximately forty-five minutes, Dennis stopped the truck on a small dirt road. Croft testified that the two men then forced her to her hands and knees, and Dennis choked her with her belt until she lost consciousness.

When she regained consciousness, she was unable to open her eyes because they were covered with blood. Her eyelids had been slashed with a weapon as sharp as a surgeon's scalpel. Croft found her way to a road and flagged down a car; the driver dropped her off at the first house they came to, where she stumbled, half naked and bleeding, into the front yard. The woman who lived in the house called an ambulance and the police.

Croft's testimony was problematic. As a male writer, I find it particularly difficult to question the validity of her rape experience. I try to presume the truthfulness of all women's claims of rape. But in this case, although she was brutally slashed, I'm not at all certain Croft was raped. Furthermore, I am convinced that Joseph Spaziano had nothing whatsoever to do with the attack on Croft.

Crucial aspects of Croft's account have changed dramatically over time. Before her testimony, Croft gave at least four different versions of how Ronnie and Dennis first approached her, as well as conflicting descriptions of the men. Croft was confused about whether she voluntarily got into the truck or was forced in at knifepoint. At one point she said that one man had raped her in the house, and later she said that both men had raped her there. In one account she said that she had been choked in the house, but later she stated that she had been choked outside, in a weedy area. The medical doctor who examined Croft the morning following her assault found no evidence of rape and no evidence of recent sexual intercourse.

Although the name of "Ronnie" never varied in Croft's accounts, the other assailant's name changed from "Steve" to "Dennis." Finally, Croft identified Joe Spaziano as one of her attackers. She initially described "Dennis" as about twenty-four years old, with long, dark hair and a beard. Later she said that his hair was red. Croft's descriptions of "Dennis" did not come close to fitting Spaziano.

The Orlando police, skeptical about Croft's truthfulness, did something highly unusual for a rape case: they had Croft take a lie detector test. She flunked it. The police polygrapher concluded that "a careful review of the charts . . . indicated deception. It is my opinion that [Croft] left willingly with two men to a house that she had visited previously. Sexual relations were indicated to be freely given and that she knows the men involved."

The Orlando police were certainly not protecting Joe Spaziano, or the Outlaws. In fact, Spaziano had been targeted as a suspect in the Croft case because the police assumed from the outset that the attack had occurred at the Orlando Outlaws' clubhouse (although Croft said that she didn't know where the assault took place) and therefore that the assailants were Outlaws.

Why the police made these early assumptions was never explained publicly, but it is not too difficult to understand. At this time, during the early to mid-1970s, Outlaw club members were all over central Florida and had been charged with everything from rape to prostitution and murder. Florida bikers terrorized innocent bystanders and warred among themselves. The day before the Croft attack, the *Orlando Sentinel* had reported a story about crimes attributed to a motorcycle brotherhood.

South Florida spawned biker brotherhoods like the Outlaws for the same reason California spawned the Hells Angels. As Hunter Thompson puts it in his 1966 classic *Hell's Angels: The Strange and Terrible Saga of the Outlaw Motorcycle Gangs*: "The California climate is perfect for bikers, as well as surfboards, convertibles, swimming pools and abulia. Most cyclists are harmless weekend types, no more dangerous than skiers or skin divers. But ever since the end of World War II the west coast has been plagued by gangs of wild men on motorcycles, roaming the highways in groups of ten to thirty and stopping whenever they get thirsty or road-cramped to suck up some beer and make some noise."

Thompson traces the origins of the California Hells Angels to the postwar culture of the late 1940s. Most ex-soldiers wanted peace and quiet and home and family and steady jobs in Levittown. But not all. "Like the drifters who rode west after Appomattox, there were thousands of veterans in 1945 who flatly rejected the idea of going back to their prewar pattern," Thompson writes. "They didn't want order, but privacy—and time to figure things out. It was a nervous, downhill feeling, a kind of *Angst* that always comes out of wars . . . a compressed sense of time on the outer limits of fatalism." These World War II vets "wanted more action, and one way to find it was on a big motorcycle. By 1947 (California) was alive with bikes, nearly all of them powerful American-made irons from Harley-Davidson and Indian."

Two and a half decades later, and in the wake of another American war, the Outlaws and other clubs came to south Florida. But because this war was in Vietnam, and because this was a war that America lost, the postwar angst Thompson mentions was magnified in both intensity and depth. Like the World War II vets who founded the California Hells Angels in the 1940s, many of the original Florida Outlaws were combat vets. One Outlaw had trained Green Berets in long-range reconnaissance patrols. Another was up for the Medal of Honor, but his candidacy was squelched, someone who would know told me recently, "because they were afraid of what he'd say to the president, face-to-face."

At the time Vanessa Dale Croft was attacked, in February 1974, motorcycle brotherhoods—the Outlaws, the Warlocks, the Pagans—were all over central Florida and had been charged with everything from rape to prostitution and murder. Florida bikers terrorized innocent bystanders and warred among themselves. In 1975, the central Florida police were eager to solve what the press dubbed "the Garbage Dump Murders"—the bodies of five women had been found in and around a rural Altamonte Springs dump—and investigators were taking a hard look at the Outlaws as suspects. Given yet another violent crime to deal with, police assumptions regarding the Outlaws' clubhouse were understandable. Despite all the public pressure to solve the Croft case, however, it was never established that the assault happened at the clubhouse. No link with Spaziano was ever established.

As of this writing, it is not clear precisely who came up with the idea that the Croft attack might have occurred at the Outlaws' clubhouse. One intriguing possibility is a man named Hoover. Hoover was an undercover cop working out of the Outlaws' Orlando clubhouse, and he encountered Croft shortly after the attack—while her wounds were still fresh. Perhaps Hoover gave Croft the idea that the clubhouse had been the site of her assault, and Croft went along with Hoover's suggestion. We don't know for certain that Hoover planted that possibility in Croft's mind, but we do know that *someone* did.

In any event, in February 1974, shortly after the Croft incident was publicized, a woman named Keppie called the Orlando sheriff's office and claimed that she knew who had assaulted Croft. She said that an Outlaw had, indeed, raped Croft and that she, too, had been raped by that very same Outlaw. The Outlaw was Joe Spaziano, a former family friend. Based on what Keppie said, the police issued a warrant for Spaziano's arrest for the rape of Croft.

Days after the assault, police showed Croft a photo of Spaziano. She didn't recognize him. On May 13, 1974, the police conducted a lineup with Spaziano as man number two. Spaziano was twenty-nine years old at the time. Croft again failed to identify him. She didn't pick anyone out until a police officer told her the suspect was there. "She was scared," Croft's mother later recalled. "She didn't identify him, but then she went to church, she got saved, and she went back and identified him." The next day Croft told the police that her assailant *had* been in the lineup—he was man number two.

In a deposition taken by Spaziano's defense attorney, Edward Kirkland, three months after the lineup and before the trial, Croft admitted that, after she had failed to identify Spaziano in the lineup, Detective JoAnn Hardee, who supervised the lineup, "said something" to her about Spaziano's being number two. Kirkland questioned, "Isn't it true, Vanessa, that you did in fact discuss this matter after you failed to recognize him with Detective Hardee, and she, in fact told you the names of the persons in the lineup, more particularly, as Joe Spaziano was the one?" Croft replied, "She said that, yes."

But by the time of the trial, Croft was certain that Spaziano was one of her attackers. She admitted that she had seen him on television before. She testified that although Spaziano had changed his appearance, she still recognized him because of his eyes. "They are evil," she told the jury.

In light of Croft's uncertain accounts and identifications, the police officers investigating the rape case needed another witness to corroborate Croft's inculpating Spaziano. They came up with Anthony Frank DiLisio, the stepson of Keppie, the woman who had called the sheriff's office claiming she knew who had attacked Croft. DiLisio was the sole witness to corroborate Croft's testimony that Spaziano was one of her attackers. DiLisio testified that Spaziano was "bragging to me" that "he raped a young girl . . . stabbed her and slashed her eyes."

Because of Croft's vague and conflicting descriptions, DiLisio's testimony was particularly powerful. In his rebuttal to the defense's closing argument, the prosecutor said of DiLisio's testimony: "He is the strongest reason in this case, outside the facts and the physical evidence and the emotional evidence that the victim has given. Tony DiLisio's testimony corroborates her story. I know it's a one-on-one situation, the victim versus the defendant, saying he did it, but we have a second person who can say he did it. That's very strong evidence."

There was no physical evidence linking either Joe Spaziano or the Outlaws' clubhouse to the attack on Croft—no fingerprints, no blood tests, no sperm tests, no hair match, no weapon. Detective Hardee came up with a knife for the prosecution to present to the rape jury, but it didn't belong to Spaziano. Hardee had borrowed it from a knife store at the local mall, because Spaziano supposedly owned a similar knife.

One of the pivotal issues in the rape trial concerned tattoos. Croft had told the police officer who questioned her the night of the attack that "Dennis" was wearing a sleeveless denim jacket and a T-shirt and that he had no tattoos or distinguishing marks. Spaziano's arms are colorfully tattooed with elaborate dragons, a parrot, and a drawing of "my Geisha girl"—his fiancée at the time of his arrest in 1974. Joe's tattoos are what I remember most clearly about his appearance when we first met in 1984.

At trial, Judge Peter deManio repeatedly instructed the jury not to consider the tattoo issue because the defense had not established that Spaziano had acquired the tattoos before the rape. Initially, the jury ignored the judge's instruction. The jurors began deliberating at

4:05 P.M., and after six hours, they requested to hear the tattoo testimony again. According to the trial transcript, a juror gasped when the clerk reread the testimony. The jurors resumed their deliberation, and then, moments later, the bailiff announced that they had reached a verdict. The judge refused to accept the verdict and reissued the instruction, this time in writing, that whether the defendant had any tattoos on his arms at the time of the alleged offense should not be considered in any way. The jurors trooped out silently and three minutes later, at 11:55 P.M., August 13, 1975, they found Spaziano guilty of rape. Judge deManio sentenced Spaziano to life imprisonment. He later described Spaziano as "the lowest form of human life. He is the scum of the earth."

Photographs of Spaziano establish that he had his tattoos more than two years before Croft's assault. He got his first tattoo when he was sixteen years old. His draft card noted his tattoos—so did his rap sheet. In the late 1980s, more than twelve years after his conviction, Spaziano's mother, Rose, gave me a photo of a twenty-six-year-old Spaziano lying on a carpet next to his baby daughter, Mary Noel. The tattoos on his left arm are clearly visible in the photo. All Spaziano's defense attorney had needed to do was obtain a photograph of Spaziano to demonstrate that the tattoos existed before February 9, 1974.

Orange County sheriff's deputy Herb Tillman remembers picking up Spaziano for the rape charge. Spaziano had run to Chicago because, Spaziano said, a friend had used his truck in a robbery and he knew the police would trace it to him. "For all the meanness in him, there was a strange side to him that you wouldn't have expected," Tillman said. "You would have expected a hard shell, for him to be a cold-hearted individual, but I didn't see that."

Before the rape and murder charges, Spaziano had served time in prison for beating up a rival gang member. His rap sheet—which, as I've noted, mentioned his tattoos—listed numerous assaults and thefts. His ex-wife, Linda, said that although she wouldn't be surprised if Spaziano had committed many other crimes, she is certain that he would never rape anyone. "He treated women so well, and he always had women coming after him," she said. "Out of all the times we fought and he hit me, he even took a shot at me once, he never attacked me in a sexual way. Never." Linda said that the police interviewed her after they arrested Spaziano for the rape. "I told them

there's no way he was a rapist," she said. "One of them sai
think he did it either but he damn well knows who did.' Bu
never tell on a brother. He told me later when he was i
knew who did the rape. I said, 'Why don't you tell and sa . . .
He said, 'I'd be dead five minutes after I got out of the gates.'"

On August 5, 1973, six months before Vanessa Dale Croft was raped
and slashed in Orlando, Laura Lynn Harberts disappeared from nearby Seminole County. Her roommate reported Harberts missing. Sixteen
days later, a swimming pool worker discovered Harberts's remains at
an illegal dump site in Altamonte Springs in Seminole County.

Laura Lynn Harberts worked as a records clerk at Orlando Hospital, and police suspicion soon focused on one of her coworkers, Joe
Suarez, who was later arrested for indecent exposure. Harberts had
dated him. After Suarez, the police's suspicions centered on a second
suspect, Lynwood Tate, a job applicant at the hospital. Tate was a convicted rapist. A witness placed Tate near the Altamonte Springs dump
site. Eventually, the homicide investigators lost interest in Tate and
Suarez and targeted Joseph Spaziano, a biker with no apparent ties to
Harberts. I wondered for twelve years why the police shifted their inquiry from Tate and Suarez to Spaziano. In 1995, the *Miami Herald*'s
Lori Rozsa found an answer: the Seminole County homicide detective
in charge of the Harberts case had identified the Outlaw based on a tip
from a psychic.

When Laura Lynn Harberts disappeared on August 5, 1973, she
was a year out of high school, living on her own for the first time and
working as a hospital records clerk. In her job, as she had been in high
school, Harberts was a conscientious worker. She had plans. She was
about to enter nursing school, and when she was killed, she was just a
day away from owning her first car, a used powder-blue Pinto, bought
with five hundred dollars borrowed from her aunt and uncle.

A friend described Harberts as "always bubbly, happy. She was the
kind of person who would bring you a rose to work for no reason at
all, just because she felt happy and good today, and she wanted you to
feel good, too." Her friend said that Harberts had a risky habit—she
liked to hitchhike. In the early 1970s a lot of teenagers hitchhiked—to
save money, to meet new people, or just for the hell of it.

In 1995, twenty-two years after her disappearance, the *Orlando*

Sentinel published a photo of Laura Harberts. It depicted a blonde, blue-eyed, smiling young woman, hair parted in the middle, wearing a thin gold necklace and an off-the-shoulder evening dress. The photo could easily have been a high school yearbook or senior prom photo.

In 1976, just as I was beginning the second semester of my freshman year at college, "Crazy Joe" Spaziano was on trial for his life in Seminole County, Florida, for the murder of Laura Lynn Harberts.

The most striking characteristic of the prosecution's case against Spaziano was the total lack of physical evidence linking him to the murder. No DNA. No fingerprints. No fiber comparisons. No blood. No eyewitnesses. No confession. The prosecution's case rested almost entirely on hearsay testimony that came from people who seemed to have reasons to hate Spaziano and to want to see him in prison or executed.

On August 21, 1973, the decomposing remains of two humans were discovered at the Altamonte city dump in the southeast section of Seminole County, Florida. One corpse was piled on top of the other amid the garbage. The body on top, which had been torn apart by animals, was identified through dental records as that of Laura Lynn Harberts.

The other body has never been explained or identified. Even its gender is questionable. Police and the Seminole County medical examiner have said they believe the remains to be those of a man, because of the size of the skull. However, an anthropologist at the Smithsonian Institution who was later consulted was of the opinion that the skeleton was that of a nineteen-year-old female.

The first witness to testify at trial about the discovery of Harberts's body was Johnny Broner. While traveling off State Road 436 around August 21, 1973, at 5:00 to 6:00 P.M., he saw a body that he said was positioned facedown and was covered with fruit-box tops. Broner stated that he reported the incident to the Eatonville police the next morning. Otha Lee Abgney, chief of the Eatonville Police Department, went with Broner to the scene on August 22, 1973, at approximately 11:25 A.M. Chief Abgney testified that he observed human remains, and described the area as wooded and containing discarded debris. By the time he left the area at approximately 1:10 P.M., Seminole County sheriff's investigators were on the scene.

Charles Wehner was an evidence technician with the Seminole County Sheriff's Department. He testified that upon arriving at the dump, he saw what appeared to be human remains with basket lids and cardboard lying on top. Wehner could smell the decomposed bodies; decomposition would be very rapid in August in central Florida. Although the bodies were in an advanced state of decomposition and there was a great deal of maggot activity, there was still some flesh left on the bone structure. Wehner took several series of photographs. The Seminole County medical examiner assembled the remains and performed a brief on-site examination. Wehner then organized a team to rope off and search the surrounding area. A partial lower jawbone was found thirty feet from where the bodies were located, and a complete lower jawbone was found thirty-five feet away. Mr. Wehner also indicated there were no signs of a struggle and that there was no evidence to indicate whether the bodies had been brought there from some other place.

The medical examiner testified that he conducted an autopsy on one of the bodies the morning after it was found. The body was that of a young adult female and was in an advanced stage of decomposition, with half of the jaw separated from the skull. The doctor's examination of the body revealed no trauma. He matched the partial lower jawbone found at the dump to the skull he was examining. The medical examiner estimated the time of death to be two to four weeks prior to the examination; he could not give an opinion as to the cause of death.

Dr. Carson Kendall was a practicing general dentist who had seen Laura Harberts four times in April and May 1973. He testified that he had examined a skull at his office and, based on his dental records, concluded that both the upper skull and lower jaw portion were those of his patient, Laura Harberts.

Beverly Fink was Laura Harberts's roommate in Orlando. Fink testified that the last time she saw Harberts was around noon on Sunday, August 5, 1973. The previous night, as Fink and her boyfriend, Jack Mallen, were preparing to leave the apartment Fink and Harberts shared, Harberts was on the phone. As Fink and Mallen were leaving, Harberts said into the phone, "Hold on a minute, Joe," and then waved good-bye to Fink and Mallen. Fink testified that Harberts had been dating a person named Joe Suarez shortly before she disappeared. Suarez worked at the hospital with Fink and Harberts; he was also a sex offender known to the police. Fink was not sure whether Harberts was, indeed, talking to Joe Suarez the night before she was last seen. Fink stated that when she and Mallen returned to the apartment at about 2:30 or 3:00 A.M., Harberts was asleep on the couch. The prosecution introduced into evidence that Fink heard Harberts speaking to a "Joe" on the night before she disappeared. What the police and prosecutors knew, but didn't disclose at the trial, was that Harberts was talking to Joe Suarez. Later, as the result of an undocumented interview they conducted with Suarez, the police concluded that Suarez was with Harberts the night before her disappearance.

That same night, at around 3:00 A.M., someone knocked at the door of Fink and Harberts's apartment. Harberts asked Jack Mallen to go to the door and, without opening it, tell whoever it was to go away; it was too late at night, and she did not want to talk to anyone. Mallen complied with her request and the person went away.

A week prior to her disappearance, Harberts had told Fink about some people she was afraid of, Ann and Walter Garris. Harberts and Fink had met these people when Harberts and a friend, Gordon Butters, had been involved in a car accident with the Garrises in another car. Butters and Harberts brought the Garrises to Harberts's home with them after the accident, and when they arrived at the apartment, Fink and Mallen were there. Then Mallen and Butters left, leaving Harberts and Fink with the Garrises. Fink recalled that the couple began talking about group sex, and that this disturbed her and Harberts.

Fink further recalled that Harberts had later gone to Rock Springs with the Garrises. Although Fink had advised Harberts not to go with them because they were so "weird," Harberts went anyway. After that trip, Harberts told Fink that when the group got to Rock Springs she became frightened when the couple began driving down back roads and talking about sex. She got spooked and told them she wanted to go home. After she came back from Rock Springs, she agreed with Fink that the Garrises were weird. She said she had been frightened and had ended up staying with them longer than she had wanted. As a result of that trip, Harberts refused to go out with them again when they called and tried to convince her to do so.

Jack Mallen testified that Beverly Fink was his girlfriend, and his testimony substantially corroborated Fink's. As to the knock at the door on the night before Harberts disappeared, Mallen testified that

Harberts asked him not to open the door, but to tell the person to go away. She told Mallen that she was frightened and he said that she acted scared. Mallen observed the silhouette of a person through the translucent jalousied door. He described the individual as short, with slightly bushy hair, a denim jacket, and a crooked mouth. After Mallen told the person to leave, the individual muttered obscenities and banged down the steps. According to Mallen, the person at the door was neither the man Harberts had met during the car accident (Walter Garris) nor Joe Suarez, who was tall and lanky and had light skin.

William Coppick and Michael Ellis, two acquaintances of Joseph Spaziano, testified that approximately two years prior to Harberts's disappearance, Spaziano lived in a trailer in the same general area where Harberts's body was found. Coppick testified that Spaziano told him about finding some bones, but Coppick did not say where or exactly when this alleged conversation took place. Ellis stated that Spaziano took him to the general area where the human remains had been found. He concluded that Spaziano went to get some marijuana he had stashed there. Ellis was unsure of the date when this took place.

The state's star witness was sixteen-year-old Anthony Frank DiLisio. DiLisio testified that he and Spaziano were friends. He stated that around his sixteenth birthday (August 16) in 1973, he saw something unusual at a dump in Forest City. The trip began at Spaziano's place in Casselberry. Spaziano suggested that DiLisio and another person take a ride with him, and they drove around Seminole County and then went to the dump in Spaziano's two-tone pickup truck.

DiLisio testified that Spaziano said, "I am going to show you some of my girls." DiLisio said that a couple of days before the trip to the dump, Spaziano and some other people were at Spaziano's place in Casselberry, smoking marijuana, when Spaziano told DiLisio that he was going to "show him some of his girls that he had raped, stabbed, and cut their tits and cunts out." According to DiLisio, Spaziano said that he had showed their vaginas to them and tortured them. DiLisio said that he had heard Spaziano talk like that several times before, and that he had not believed him.

DiLisio testified that at the dump, he saw two bodies lying beside some trees. He said that they were completely naked and that the smell was very bad. He saw trash in the area, including cardboard, a lot of newspaper, orange crates, tar paper, and round lids of baskets. The body closest to him was more decomposed than the other one. The least decomposed of the bodies had light brown hair and was covered with blood. DiLisio said that there was lot of blood on the upper part of the body and the face. He could tell that it was a female body by the breasts. He said he saw cuts in the breasts, stomach, and chest.

DiLisio testified that he started walking back to the truck and Spaziano walked to the bodies. DiLisio remembered asking Spaziano if they could leave and Spaziano responding, "Go back to the truck and take some acid, take some drugs." DiLisio said he took some purple microdot acid and sat in the truck. He looked through the back window and saw Spaziano and the other person talking over the bodies. They then got back in the truck and drove around. DiLisio said that Spaziano said, "Now you believe me when I tell you about my girls." (DiLisio further testified that he was not able to recall this incident when the police first interrogated him because he just wanted to forget it and put it out of his mind since he had enough problems and was "into drugs really heavy.")

What made DiLisio's account sound believable to Spaziano's south Florida jury was the fact that Spaziano was an Outlaw. The jurors were never told, officially, that Spaziano belonged to the hated motorcycle brotherhood. They didn't need to be told officially. Spaziano's club brothers attended the trial in full biker regalia.

Because Spaziano was an Outlaw, his jury of Florida citizens must have believed him capable of all manner of depravity. Members of the jury would have equated the Outlaw Spaziano with the outlaw Charles Manson. Even if Spaziano's jury didn't make the Manson parallel, others did. About sixteen months after the trial, a writer named Sam Roen published an article about the Croft and Harberts cases in *True Police* magazine. The piece was titled "Manson Would Have Been Real Proud of Crazy Joe and the Boys . . . ," and it was accompanied by a black-and-white photograph of Joe Spaziano with a flowing mane of black hair, beard, and droopy mustache. With his beady black-and-white eyes peering out from under all that hair, Joe did look a little bit like Manson.

The Spaziano/Manson theme was interlarded throughout the fifteen pages of text and photos that *True Police* magazine devoted to the Spaziano story. The article's subtitle and running head was, "Florida's Cult Leader Left Nothing but Bones." The article described Joe Spaziano as a "long-haired, bearded man with beady eyes who looked enough like the infamous Charles Manson to be his brother." According to one police theory, this Manson look-alike had taken Laura Harberts to see a movie: *Jesus Christ Superstar.* The *True Police* story explained the movie's significance to the police investigation into the Harberts homicide: homicide police detective George Abbgy "felt that there was an ominous significance in the fact that the featured movie was *Jesus Christ, Superstar.* As Abbgy thought about the description of the bearded man with beady eyes and of this movie serving as a bridge to Christ, the coincidence struck him that he was trailing another Charles Manson." Also, according to Roen, despite Laura Lynn Harberts's all-American appearance, her "penchant for the motorcycle came to the fore" of Detective Lieutenant Abbgy's investigation: "With not much else for a handle on the case," Abbgy "decided to zero in on motorcycles and motorcyclists."

With these composite views of his target—sort of a Charles Manson meets *The Wild One*—Detective Abbgy found his man in the form of Vanessa Dale Croft's attacker, whom Roen described in *True Police* as having a "weird charm," a "small, long-haired, Christ-like man." Because Croft's description of her attacker "was so concise, her information so complete, so accurate and so reliable, the investigators were able to establish that her assailants were members of the notorious Outlaws gang [and] . . . were able to establish the identity of the petite Manson-like attacker as Joseph Robert Spaziano."

But before the jury in Spaziano's capital murder trial could find him guilty of killing Laura Lynn Harberts, the jurors had to decide to believe the graphically horrific testimony of Tony DiLisio. The prosecutor himself told them so. In a pretrial motion, the trial prosecutor told the judge: "If we can't get in the testimony of Tony DiLisio, we'd absolutely have no case here whatsoever. . . . So either we're going to have it through Tony, or we're not going to have it at all."

The prosecutor's final argument urging the jury to recommend, and the judge to impose, the death penalty depended entirely on DiLisio's trip to the dump. The prosecutor argued that "this case is bottomed on the testimony of Anthony DiLisio" and that the alleged trip to the dump with Spaziano is "what makes DiLisio's testimony more than just idle gossip. The defendant was actually bragging and showing him his handiwork. . . . [It's] not someone sitting in a bar somewhere, the defendant is not telling this in a bar, he's not bragging."

In the closing arguments, the prosecutor told the jury that Anthony DiLisio was "the most important witness in this case"; he stated, "If you don't believe DiLisio, then find the defendant . . . not guilty in 5 minutes." This closing argument proved prophetic. After considerable deliberation, the jurors informed the judge that they couldn't agree on a verdict. The jury's only choices were an acquittal or a conviction for first-degree murder. The jury was then given a "dynamite charge." The judge told them that it was their duty to try to agree upon a verdict. They tried again and reported that they did not believe they could reach a verdict. The court gave a more emphatic charge, after which, late in the evening, a verdict of guilty was returned within minutes. The only evidence that could have possibly convicted Spaziano was Tony DiLisio's testimony, and the reason for the jurors' uncertainty was accurately portrayed by the state: they "struggled so diligently with Mr. DiLisio's testimony."

As it turned out, for reasons not revealed at the trial, virtually all of the state's evidence against Joseph Spaziano was either misleading or downright wrong. Some of this would be documented over the next thirteen years by the fact investigators working with Spaziano's defense lawyers. But the crucial evidence discrediting the state's case against Joe Spaziano would not be unearthed by Spaziano's lawyers or investigators. It would be discovered by reporters for the *Miami Herald* more than a decade later. Among these crucial facts were the factual, historical, and legal connections between the 1973 murder of Laura Lynn Harberts and the 1974 attack upon Vanessa Dale Croft, as well as the fact that the police initially targeted Spaziano because he was an Outlaw biker; Spaziano was presumed guilty of killing Harberts because he was presumed guilty of attacking Croft because he was an Outlaw. This was the chain of assumptions the police used to nail Joe Spaziano for the murder of Laura Harberts. But, as I will set out later in this book, this chain of assumptions had many missing links. The most obvious was this: Laura Lynn Harberts was murdered in early or mid-August 1973, but Joe Spaziano did not even join the Outlaws until September or October 1973. At the time Harberts disappeared and when her remains were found in the Altamonte Springs dump, *"Crazy Joe" Spaziano was not an Outlaw.*

Spaziano's sentencing jury recommended a sentence of life imprisonment for the murder of Laura Lynn Harberts. The jurors' recommendation suggests that they weren't completely convinced of Spaziano's guilt. If they were certain that he had committed this brutal crime, they probably would have sentenced him to death. The trial judge, Robert McGregor, who, unlike the jury, knew about Spaziano's conviction for the rape of Vanessa Dale Croft, invoked a quirk in Florida's capital punishment statute and overrode the jury's life verdict. Finding the crime "heinous and atrocious," the judge sentenced "Crazy Joe" Spaziano to die in the electric chair.

Tony DiLisio had ample reason to be angry and to lie in his testimony against Joe Spaziano. At the time of the 1976 murder trial, the teenage DiLisio's life was coming apart at the seams. He was into drugs, was a biker gang wanna-be, and was in trouble with the law—a volatile combination anywhere, but especially in south Florida in the 1970s.

On the surface, the DiLisios were a close-knit Italian American family. Ralph DiLisio sold insurance and later owned and ran a marina; his wife, Irene, stayed home with Tony and their other five kids. The children were raised on the catechism, and the family had a reserved pew at St. Mary Magdalene Church.

Beneath the surface, the DiLisio family was dysfunctional. Tony said that he had a devastating childhood. Ralph frequently beat his wife and children and regularly flogged Tony with a razor strop. When he was in seventh grade, there were times when Tony did not want to go to school because he was afraid that in gym class others would see the bruises he had on his body from beatings.

Ralph eventually dumped Irene for the beautiful twenty-five-year-old boat-show model Keppie Epton. During Irene and Ralph's eighteen-month-long rancorous divorce, Irene had to get a restraining order to prevent him from breaking into her house and beating her. Two months after the divorce became final, Ralph married Keppie. Ralph was obsessively jealous of his attractive young wife. Years later, Keppie told the *Miami Herald* that Ralph beat her just as he beat his children and that he "would call five times a day to check up on me. . . . My life was hell."

After Ralph and Keppie's wedding, Tony was kicked out of his father's house because of his drug use. He went to his mother's house, but he was kicked out of there, too. Tony then stayed temporarily with friends. He said that in the early winter and spring of 1974, he was dealing drugs and that he used all kinds of drugs as often as he could get them. During this time, he lived on the streets, sleeping under park benches.

Keppie knew Joseph Spaziano well. She and Ralph had double-dated with Spaziano and his girlfriend, Spaziano had attended Ralph and Keppie's wedding, and Joe had bought a boat from Ralph's marina. Keppie claimed that Spaziano helped her husband run drugs from the Bahamas. Tony said that his father was involved in "organized crime" and that Spaziano helped his father blow up boats for insurance money.

Shortly after Ralph and Keppie's marriage, Keppie and Spaziano began an affair that lasted six weeks. After Ralph found out and confronted her, Keppie said it wasn't an affair and that Spaziano had raped her at knifepoint around Christmas 1973. According to Tony, when his father found out about Keppie and Spaziano, "he went nuts" and got a gun. Spaziano said Ralph confronted him about the affair: "He took a gun out and said he was going to blow my brains out if I didn't quit messing with his wife. So I said fine, and I quit seeing her." Ralph told Tony that Spaziano had raped Keppie. Tony said his father called Spaziano "Crazy Joe" and demanded, "Didn't he tell you he used to pick up niggers hitchhiking and cut off their dicks and pick up girls and cut off their tits?" In 1995, nineteen years after Spaziano's murder trial, Tony admitted that he had never heard Spaziano talk like this. Tony also said that after his father found out about Keppie and Spaziano, he never saw Spaziano at his father's house or at the marina or with Keppie anymore.

To this day, Joseph Spaziano emphatically denies ever raping Keppie. He maintains that their affair was totally consensual and that it started out as guilty sex on the side with the wife of a good friend. As early as Keppie and Ralph's wedding day, "she was flirting with me" Spaziano said. "She was a real looker, too, you know. A really good-looking lady."

In February 1974, Keppie read a front-page newspaper headline describing the Vanessa Dale Croft rape and slashing, which was attributed to the Outlaws. She called the Orlando sheriff's office and claimed that she knew who did it. She told the police that Spaziano the Outlaw biker was the culprit and that he had raped her, too. She also told the police that Spaziano liked to rape women and cut them up. Her husband had told her so.

Keppie told the police that her stepson Tony knew Spaziano and could tell them all about his crimes. It was easy for Keppie to manipulate Tony—when Tony was fourteen years old, she had been secretly seducing him five months before she married his father. According to Tony, his sexual relationship with Keppie continued up to and including the afternoon of her wedding to his father. Tony said that he was emotionally attached to Keppie and that he thought he loved her.

When the cops investigating the Croft rape case questioned Tony about that crime, he did indeed attribute it to "Crazy Joe" Spaziano. During the course of police interrogations, Tony also attributed the Harberts murder to Spaziano. At the time of his initial interrogation, Tony was in the Seminole County Juvenile Detention Center for drug possession. According to Tony, his father had turned him in to the police when he found marijuana that Tony had stashed at his house. Tony was interrogated twice at the juvenile hall, and he claims that his father told him to cooperate with the officers. On October 7, 1974, Tony told the detectives that he was a friend of Spaziano and that Spaziano had bragged to him about raping a young girl in Orange County and cutting her eyes. Tony told the detectives that he had asked Spaziano about the bodies of the girls at the Altamonte dump and Spaziano had told him, "Man, that's my style." The next day, Tony was interrogated again and reiterated what he had said the day before. The police felt that Tony was holding back information and doubted that he would fully cooperate with them.

Subsequent to his interviews with the police, Tony was assigned to the Door, a drug rehabilitation center. After a short time, he ran away with two other boys and was apprehended in New Jersey. He was then sent to the Volusia House in Orlando for drug treatment. On May 13, 1975, at the Volusia House, Tony was again interrogated by the police. Tony later testified that his father had alerted him to the interrogation and told him to cooperate. It was just before this interview that Keppie had filed a rape charge against Spaziano for the alleged December 1973 rape. The detectives questioned Tony about Spaziano. Tony later said that the detectives offered to get him out of the house if he would cooperate with them. Tony also later spoke of his willingness to do anything to please his abusive father. Tony told the detectives that he did not remember Spaziano specifically telling him about a dump murder, and he gave a confusing account of Spaziano's having mentioned two girls he had killed, cut up, and put in an orange grove. The evening of the May 13 interrogation, Tony wrote out a sworn statement that Spaziano told him he had stabbed a good-looking girl's eyes out and raped her and that Spaziano had told him she was dead.

Tony's account of what Spaziano supposedly told him was incredibly muddled and not particularly incriminating. The police made arrangements for Tony to undergo hypnosis.

Neither Joseph Spaziano's jury nor his judge was told—by the prosecutor, defense lawyer, or anyone else—that there was a strong likelihood that the singularly devastating DiLisio testimony was hypnotically manufactured. Not only that, but the manufacturing was flawed. The hypnosis sessions, administered months after DiLisio was allegedly taken to the dump, were conducted in such a suggestive and unprofessional manner that the resulting "recall" and testimony are not credible. The Florida police used a self-styled "ethical hypnotist" to spoon-feed the cops' version of the facts into Tony DiLisio's brain. In 1995, two decades after the hypnosis sessions took place, Tony DiLisio would characterize these sessions as "brainwashing."

Some of the hazards of using hypnosis and other suggestive procedures to "recover hidden memories" were known at the time of Spaziano's trial. Much more is known today. Courts have increasingly recognized that testimony extracted by hypnosis is untrustworthy and should be treated with skepticism. The scientific consensus is that a subject's reactions while under hypnosis are characterized by suggestibility arising from even slight nuances in the hypnotist's words or manner, a desire to please the hypnotist, and the subject's later inability to distinguish between memories existing before hypnosis and false memories that came into existence because of it.

There is a public misconception that hypnosis acts as a form of truth serum, preventing a witness who has been hypnotized from lying under hypnosis and later in court. However, hypnosis experts are united in the view that hypnotized subjects can and occasionally do prevaricate while under hypnosis. It is now well established that hypnotized subjects often engage in "confabulation," the invention of details concerning unremembered events in order to make their accounts complete, logical, and acceptable to the hypnotist. This tendency to "fill in the gaps" of memory is extremely difficult to detect, particularly when combined with other dangers of hypnosis. Although the exact nature of the hypnotic state is still not understood, scientists have observed that hypnosis is characterized by loss of initiative, redistribution of attention and tolerance for reality distortion, increased suggestibility, and amnesia about what happened while in the hypnotic state.

Subsequent to Spaziano's trial and direct appeal, the Florida Supreme Court decided in Ted Bundy's case that hypnotically refreshed testimony, such as Tony DiLisio's, would be per se inadmissible. In reaching this conclusion, the court recognized several problems with hypnosis: (1) hypnosis is not widely accepted by psychiatrists and psychologists as a reliable method of refreshing or enhancing memory of past perceptions and experiences; (2) hypnosis subjects are often so susceptible to suggestion and so receptive to the hypnotist's verbal and nonverbal cues that they respond in accordance with what they perceive to be desired responses in order to please the hypnotist; (3) subjects confabulate, or fill in the gaps in their memories; (4) the recall induced by hypnosis may be totally incorrect; (5) the subject can willfully lie; (6) the subsequent opportunity for cross-examination at trial of a hypnotized witness is virtually ineffective because hypnotically created memories become "frozen" in the subject's mind; and (7) no set of procedural safeguards is effective in eliminating these problems. All of these problems undermined the credibility of Tony DiLisio's testimony.

One job of a postconviction lawyer is to expose lies. In "Crazy Joe" Spaziano's capital case, both the police and the state insisted that audiotapes of Tony DiLisio's police hypnosis sessions had been lost or destroyed. Such tapes were essential to any meaningful evaluation of whether the hypnosis sessions created or warped the testimony that sent Joe Spaziano to death row. Hypnotically manufactured testimony is tantamount to fabrication of evidence.

As of March 1985, Joe's postconviction lawyers, (of which I was one), working out of the West Palm Beach Public Defender's Office, possessed nothing more than typed transcriptions of DiLisio's sessions with the police hypnotist a decade previously. When we sought the audiotapes themselves, the police said they had none. The police said they had no idea of the tapes' location. They'd love to help us find the tapes, but what could they do? Without the audiotapes, no hypnosis expert we could hire would be able to say for certain whether Tony DiLisio had been hypnotically brainwashed; definitive evaluation of the reliability of any hypnosis session requires subtle information not contained in typewritten transcripts of the sessions—nuances of voice inflection, volume, cadence, phrasing, and the like.

Enter Jerry Justine, the West Palm Beach public defender's chief capital investigator. Justine was tall, husky, silver-haired, and gruff; he had a rapid-fire interrogation style, but also a singular charm and a heart of gold. He had the bearing of a Marine drill sergeant, and he intimidated the hell out of me.

Many people, including many attorneys, think that lawyers and the law they know are what get stays of execution. This is a myth. Clever legal arguments by clever lawyers don't get stays—new facts get stays.

If I had to triage the importance of the various players that compose a winning capital postconviction team, the fact investigators like Jerry Justine would be at the apex. Without the new evidence and new witnesses and new facts unearthed by these investigators, the lawyers have nothing to say to the judges who decide whether the client lives or dies. No new facts, no stay of execution.

Investigator Justine's job in Joe Spaziano's case was to find everything that Joe's trial lawyer didn't find and that therefore never came in at trial. Justine was to investigate and document "Crazy Joe" Spaziano's life from embryo to death row. Beginning with painstaking interviews with Joe—in some respects the only source of information about his own life—Justine's search would proceed outward in ever-widening concentric circles, to include Joe's entire life. This investigation took the better part of a year and led Justine from Rochester, New York, where Joe was born and grew up, to California, where Tony DiLisio was then living, to the Outlaws' clubhouse in Orlando.

Justine also had a more immediate task: to find out everything there was to know about the police's hypnotism of Tony DiLisio. Joe's defense lawyer at the murder trial knew a little about the hypnotism of the prosecutor's star witness, but he didn't follow up on leads that would have helped him to understand exactly what happened behind those locked police doors in 1975, when Tony DiLisio was being hypnotized at the direction of the police. A logical place for Justine to start was with the police hypnotist himself, Joe McCawley. Justine found him in Orlando.

McCawley is a showman. It soon became clear to Justine that this police hypnotist knew nothing of interest to us. The only reason McCawley met with Justine at all was because Justine agreed to pay him at his "usual" hourly rate. But McCawley did mention one tantalizing fact: *he had made audiotapes of the hypnosis sessions and recalled having given them to the police.* Joe's trial lawyer had known about transcripts of the hypnosis sessions, but this was the first indication that the sessions had been audiotaped as well.

Our next step was to contact Joe's trial lawyer to find out what he knew about these hypnosis tapes. On March 6, 1985, I wrote a letter to Ed Kirkland, Joe's trial lawyer, inquiring about the tapes that McCawley said were given to the police. Did any of that sound familiar to the trial attorney? No, Kirkland stonewalled. Did he ever ask for the tapes? Can't remember. Any idea how we might extricate the tapes from the police, assuming they still exist? Sorry.

While I dealt with Kirkland, Justine tore the state of Florida apart looking for the tapes. He talked to every living person he could find with some connection to the case. Then he started working on the dead.

George Abbgy had been the lead detective on the Harberts murder investigation in the mid-1970s. He died while Spaziano was waiting to be executed. In June 1985, Justine tracked down Abbgy's last known address and met the detective's widow, who still lived there. Justine charmed his way into her home. The widow told Justine that she didn't know anything about any tapes, but that Justine was welcome to poke through her late husband's old files in the attic. In the attic, Justine found a box labeled "Spaziano," and in the box he found the hypnosis tapes.

There were three audiotapes: a May 13, 1975, interrogation of Tony DiLisio, a June 15 hypnosis session with McCawley, and a second session with the hypnotist the next day. The tapes were a gold mine.

Spaziano's postconviction counsel hired Dr. Bernard Diamond and Dr. Robert Buckhout, two of the nation's foremost experts on hypnotism, to analyze the audiotapes and transcripts of DiLisio's pretrial hypnosis sessions and to compare the stories DiLisio told before the sessions, during the sessions, after the sessions, and at trial.

In discussing the May 13 prehypnosis interrogation of Tony Di-Lisio, Dr. Buckhout reported:

> I received a tape recording of an interview with Mr. DiLisio by the police a few days before the hypnosis session. This tape gives some insight into the state of knowledge of the instant case of the witness. However, it is also a remarkable example of pre-conditioning by the witness to a future hypnotic session by implying that his memory would be better and that he need not fear being named as an accomplice. The interview begins with some vagueness of memory and frequent denials that certain conversations between the witness and the defendant had ever taken place. It is clear from the tape that the police had other conversations with Mr. DiLisio prior to this interview. It is also clear that many of the details under discussion had been part of the prior news media coverage. After a very brief period of time, the officer sought the witness's agreement to be hypnotized and only then reads him his rights. The witness's statement: "You'll find out when I am under hypnosis," is remarkable in that he is in the process of negotiating the conditions under which he will give evidence. The officer conducting the interview then meets every vague answer by giving more information, asking leading questions, providing details about another suspect, showing the witness a map of where the body was found, etc. . . .
>
> . . . The entire interview is characterized by excessive use of leading questions. The witness keeps promising that he will be able to give more details and then separates this information from the newspaper coverage. Meanwhile, the witness appears to use the language in his answers which had been previously fed to him in the form of leading questions. In my opinion, the substance of what the witness provided in the later hypnosis session had already been discussed in his earlier police interview.

In discussing the actual hypnosis sessions themselves, Buckhout observed:

> In the instant case, the transcripts and the recently found tapes of the hypnosis of the key witness appear to be incomplete; indicating that critically important conversations before and after

the sessions (which could have influenced the witness) remain as a source of doubt. A competent expert witness could well have pointed out the importance of these missing elements to a jury. For example, it is clear from the record that the hypnotist had obtained a great deal of advance information about the facts of the case and some speculations about the character of the defendant. . . .

. . . By interjecting names and ages of victims, conclusions about the alleged behavior of the defendant, and assumptions about event sequences, the hypnotist signals a clear line of expected answers and scenarios without waiting for the witness to freely volunteer information. This pattern violates the standards for conducting any type of hypnotic interview and resembles more the interrogation of a witness by an investigator who thinks he knows more about the crime than the witness. . . .

It is my opinion that the leading and suggestive manner of questioning Mr. DiLisio by the hypnotist raises the possibility that the so-called memories generated by this process could have been a mixture of real facts, fantasies, confabulations and outright fabrications owing to the numerous violations of standard professional practice evidenced in the transcript. The process was such that one cannot tell the difference between fact and fantasy since no effort was made to even determine whether the witness was hypnotized nor was the questioning conducted in an objective manner. Such a process as shown here also tends to encourage an exaggerated sense of confidence in a witness which makes cross-examination virtually useless.

Dr. Diamond also performed an extensive analysis of the tapes and transcripts of the hypnosis sessions. He concluded that Anthony DiLisio's recollections may well have been drug-induced fantasies and hallucinations: "[A] habitual abuser of . . . drugs would be expected to have greater difficulty than the average individual in distinguishing truth from fantasy. If some of the events claimed to be recalled occurred while the subject was under the influence of . . . drugs, it is almost certain that memory distortions will occur."

A remarkable feature of hypnosis is its ability to resolve doubts and uncertainties in the subject. Hypnosis can generate an artificial confidence so great that it can withstand the most vigorous cross-examination. This raises serious constitutional problems. Most people, when uncertain while being cross-examined, will communicate their uncertainty by hesitance, expressions of doubt, and body language indicating lack of self-confidence. Juries rely on this "demeanor evidence" in evaluating the truthfulness of the testimony.

Defendants have a constitutional right to confront witnesses against them through cross-examination. When a witness is absolutely convinced he is telling the truth and yet his account is not the truth, there may be no way to test his subjective belief to ascertain the objective truth. Although the witness may be prepared "to tell the whole truth and nothing but the truth" as he sees it, what the witness honestly believes to be the truth is a purely fictitious creation. When the right to effective cross-examination is subverted in this way, the defendant is deprived of his Sixth and Fourteenth Amendment rights.

In a rational world, the discovery of the secret tapes the police had succeeded in hiding for almost a decade would have been more than sufficient to convince an appeals court to order a retrial of the Harberts murder case. But the appeals courts ignored the tapes and the tapes' significance to the reliability of Joe Spaziano's capital murder conviction and death sentence. They ignored the tapes by relying upon a legal technicality: in essence, the judges said we should have found the tapes earlier. Because the state succeeded in hiding the tapes for a decade, we could not convince the courts to consider them at all.

Nine years had gone by since Tony DiLisio's testimony sent Joseph Spaziano to death row. On April 17, 1985, investigator Jerry Justine tracked DiLisio from Seminole County, Florida, to Vista, California, a small town near San Diego. Justine arrived unannounced. When Justine told Tony that he was working on Joe Spaziano's case, Tony paled and told him to leave. "I don't want any fucking thing to do with it," he told Justine. When Justine returned to DiLisio's house the next morning, Tony was gone.

Joseph Spaziano's lawyers appealed his murder conviction to the Florida Supreme Court. The court on direct appeal affirmed the conviction but remanded the case for a pro forma hearing. Following the pro forma hearing, the Florida Supreme Court upheld Spaziano's death sentence.

While Spaziano's case was bouncing back and forth between the trial court and the state supreme court, I was finishing up college and going to law school. I graduated law school in 1982 and was hired for a one-year clerkship with Judge Robert S. Vance of the U.S. Court of Appeals for the Eleventh Circuit in Birmingham, Alabama.

On the first day of my clerkship, Judge Vance called his three clerks into his private office and pointed to three piles of case files. He said, "I need one of you to take charge of the civil rights cases, another to take the death cases, and the third to do the business law cases." I wasn't quick enough to snag the civil rights cases, and I sure wasn't doing the business cases, so I pounced on the death cases. I didn't think before I jumped; I hadn't thought much about capital punishment before that time, but I thought the capital cases sounded interesting. For the next year, from summer 1982 to summer 1983, I served as Judge Vance's "death clerk."

Meanwhile, Spaziano's lawyers were investigating his case for further appeals and postconviction proceedings. There was a lot to discover.

Physically, Joseph Robert Spaziano is a slightly built man; short and whippet thin, his nickname, other than "Crazy Joe," was "Little Joe." But, like "Crazy Joe," the "Little Joe" moniker carried with it a strong dose of irony. Other than his stature, nothing about Joe Spaziano is slight. He has what actors call presence, and that presence has filled every room Joe and I have been in together. His muscular body always seems poised, and his eyes almost never stop moving—when they do, they can cut through tempered steel. When not under death warrant, he's constantly chatting, cracking jokes, laughing, trying to make his visitors feel at ease in the alien surroundings of Florida State Prison. I have never met with Joe in any setting other than Florida's maximum security prison.

Joe Spaziano was born in Rochester, New York, on September 12, 1945, shortly after the Japanese surrendered in World War II. He was the fourth of five children, growing up with an older sister, two older brothers, and a younger brother.

In many ways, Joe's was a stereotypical rough-and-tumble working-class Italian American family; times were rough, money was scarce, the father drank too much, but for the most part the mother, Rose, held the family together. As a teenager, Joe was handsome and charming, and, to put it delicately, he was smooth and popular with the ladies. Rochester in the mid-1960s was a hard town, and Joe adapted. He smoked dope and committed petty crimes against property. Sometime in his teenage years Joe found the love of his life: motorcycles, bikes that were heavy and fast and loud. Then, in May 1966, when Joe Spaziano was twenty years old, life as he knew it ended.

What is Spaziano's alibi? Where was he on the day Laura Lynn Harberts was murdered? He doesn't know.

It would be difficult for anyone to verify his or her whereabouts on a particular day two years after that day. It is particularly difficult for Spaziano, because he was living the nomadic and chaotic life of an Outlaw biker. South Florida bikers in the mid-1970s spent most of their days on the road, riding their Harleys from clubhouse to clubhouse, run to run, state to state.

And there is another reason Joe Spaziano can't remember. On May 29, 1966, he was run over by an automobile as he was walking across a street. Rushed to Rochester General Hospital, he was diagnosed with a "fracture of the skull in the right parietal area, contusion of the brain with accompanying coma, contusion of the urinary bladder, a fracture of the right ulna, a right peripheral facial paralysis, a 4" laceration of the scalp, and a 1" laceration of the right wrist." His brain damage and paralysis were permanent. He was in a coma for three weeks, and after he was discharged from the hospital, his family was unable to take care of him.

Hospital records indicate that within two weeks of his discharge, on July 2, 1966, Spaziano "began to have odd feelings as if he were dreaming. Since then they have recurred every day. In some of them he feels as if he were going to die and wants to have his mother close to him. He has also felt as if his father didn't like him, for the past few days." Because of this reaction, Spaziano returned to Rochester General Hospital, where examination by a neurosurgeon, Dr. Leonard Zinker, revealed that he "was very unsure of himself and constantly looked to his mother to help him answer simple questions." In addition to complaining of dreamlike states, Spaziano demonstrated memory impairment: "He did recall being at a bar shortly before his injury [but] claimed he had no recall of ever having been in the hospital or having left the hospital. Apparent recall started about 1 wk. ago." In light of these symptoms, as well as the history of his head injury and the continuing facial paralysis caused by that injury, Dr. Zinker wrote up the following diagnosis: "Patient apparently developing post-traumatic temporal lobe seizures. Also to consider an intracranial hematoma in the right middle cranial fossa as a result of a serious head injury associated with a right facial paralysis and loss of hearing on the right."

In 1984, Joe's postconviction attorneys at the West Palm Beach Public Defender's Office hired Dr. Harry Krop and Dr. James Vallely to conduct neuropsychological and neuropsychiatric exams on him to determine whether he had ever been mentally competent to stand trial. The significance of this injury in relation to the recent evaluations made by Drs. Krop and Vallely cannot be overstated. Closed head injuries such as the one Joe suffered are the most common cause of organic personality syndromes in peacetime. Further, the temporal lobe seizures, classically manifested as the dreamlike states that Spaziano began to experience after his head injury, augmented the original damage and aided in the development of an organic personality syndrome.

Spaziano's history also revealed to Drs. Krop and Vallely another hallmark of the organic personality syndrome: significant changes in personality in the months following the accident. On December 30, 1967, nearly two years after his injury, Spaziano voluntarily admitted himself to a mental institution, the Rochester State Hospital. The admission note observed: "This 22-year old white single male was admitted to this hospital today on a Voluntary Application. He was accompanied by his mother and father, who stated that *since he was run over by a car two years ago and suffered extensive head injuries and brain concussion, he underwent personality changes characterized by quarrelsome temper and frequent fights with other siblings.*" A subsequent examination, on January 5, 1968, described Spaziano's stream of mental activity as "incoherent," "flighty," and "blocked," and his emotional mood and affect as "depressed" and "flattened." The evaluation mentioned that the accident had caused a "personality change."

Dr. Krop's and Dr. Vallely's diagnoses of organic personality disorder are also supported by their mental status examination of Spaziano. After conducting his examination, Dr. Krop observed:

Speech was clear and well-modulated with no articulation deficits noted. Some pressuring of speech was observed as it appears that Spaziano had difficulty monitoring the flow and content of his verbalizations. He was found to be alert and well-oriented to person, place and time. From the onset of the interview, Spaziano exhibited marked suspiciousness regarding the evaluation, despite being introduced to this examiner by one of his attorneys. Although the inmate attempted to relate in a friendly manner, marked suspiciousness pervaded the interview. Anger and resentment were evinced and overtly expressed following the examiner's refusal to permit the inmate to smoke in the office. His affect was labile, as he openly cried when discussing certain emotionally laden events such as his daughter's current drug treatment. Anxiety was exhibited throughout the evaluation, but increased when we discussed the aspect of administering some psychological tests. During that portion of the interview, Spaziano became markedly upset and his thinking was increasingly looser and paranoid in content. He exhibited a number of gestures and mannerisms consistent with his paranoia as he consistently looked around the room and even inspected the air conditioning vent. He became visibly upset at times and had difficulty concentrating and remaining on task. The inmate had considerable difficulty presenting an organized chronological history, particularly as related to events prior to his automobile accident. He had difficulty recalling the exact number of siblings and even had a problem providing his age ("I'm either 39 or 40.").

The picture of mental status observed by Dr. Vallely eight days earlier was quite similar:

Spaziano related in manner indicative of borderline intellectual abilities. Long term memory was generally adequate for personal and historical fact but short term memory was impaired upon informal inspection. He recalled 1 of 3 objects in five minutes. Verbal auditory attention was within the impaired range as he recalled only 4 digits forward and 3 digits backward. Verbal insight was minimal but social judgment was very poor. Reality contact appeared to be within normal limits relative to intellectual abilities. No indication of psychotic processes was noted either in the client's behavior or expression of ideas. He denies ever experiencing hallucinations, delusions, or paranoid ideation. Suspiciousness and mild paranoia were noted during portions of the evaluation. Spaziano also exhibited odd behavior in that he would spontaneously stop talking and stare off for a while during conversation. This behavior is suggestive of possible petit mal seizure activity.

Spaziano's family members and friends have verified the lifelong impact of the damage to his brain. After the accident, life for this previously good-looking, easygoing young man was never again the same. Upon discharge from the hospital, Spaziano went to his parents' home to recover. He could not walk. He could not remember the names or identities of friends and family members. He could not care for his own physical needs. He could remember neither recent nor remote events from his past. Because of the paralysis on the right side of his face, which remains to this day, he would never again be able to eat or drink normally.

This twenty-year-old man, whose primary assets had been his good looks and friendly personality, regressed to the state of a disfigured, helpless child. Adding to the emotional trauma, the young woman to whom Joe had been engaged left him, apparently unable to withstand the uncertainties and tribulations of a long recovery process. Physically, psychologically, and emotionally, Joe Spaziano was devastated.

His family, friends, and acquaintances are unanimous in their statements that after the accident "Crazy Joe" Spaziano was never the same. He became quarrelsome, hot tempered, difficult to live with. Once confident of his good looks, he came to have a very poor self-image. He would often stare into space or forget what he was talking about in the middle of a conversation. Speaking with him became a test of patience and endurance because of his disorganization and forgetfulness; this remains true today. He developed an extreme need to be surrounded by friends and approval, often compensating for his facial disfigurement by making funny faces and exaggerated body movements in order to make people laugh. It was then that friends began calling him "Crazy Joe."

His family's own words, as provided in affidavits first presented to the courts in 1985, speak most poignantly about the changes that overcame Joseph Spaziano. His mother recalls:

When Joe had the car accident, we thought he would die. He was in bed for months at home after they let him go from the hospital. After the accident, he just never was the same. He was always a good boy and a hard worker. But after the accident, he just seemed to be picking fights all the time and [could] not re-member things and got angry and depressed very easily. I took him to doctors and we took him even to a mental hospital to get help. . . .

After the accident Joe was always conscious of how he looked and would often ask his father or me if we thought he was ugly. Joe was engaged before the accident, but his girlfriend dropped him when he got hurt. Joe had a lot of headaches after the acci-dent and blurred vision. He wasn't confident of himself any-more. His friends started calling him "Crazy Joe" because he would act so "spacy."

Barbara Spaziano Walker, Joe's sister, is certain that the accident left permanent injury. In her affidavit, she reports:

After Joe's car accident, we were told that he was not expected to live and that he might never walk again. After the accident, Joe was very hard to live with. He was always very good looking be-fore the accident and was very easy going. But it was never the same after he came home from the hospital. He would always ask me whether I thought he was ugly because the right side of his face was paralyzed. His head was shaved because of his in-juries. He always had beautiful dark curly hair and he really looked terrible after the accident. . . .

After the accident, Joe couldn't recognize his good friends or even his aunts and uncles and cousins. It was very hard to talk to him. He wouldn't remember anything from our past at all. He seemed not to know anything. We would tell him things that had happened and show him places like the schools that he had gone to give him back his history. Bobby [Joe and Barbara's brother] stayed with him a lot then. He had to have everything done for him. He couldn't even feed himself for a long time.

Robert Spaziano, one of Joe's three brothers, helped Joe recover from the accident. As he tells the story:

The accident that Joe had really changed his life. He seemed to be confused all the time and he always needed to have friends around for support. At the time of the accident, I was the youngest one at home. Tommy was born, but he was still just a baby. I would take Joe for walks. He was paralyzed. His memory was lost. He couldn't remember anything from our past, the things we did as kids. He thought he was very funny looking because of his face. He had to drink on one side of his mouth. He still does. . . .

After the accident, Joe seemed to pick fights with us for nothing. I would spend a lot of time with him, trying to teach him how to walk again. When you would talk to him, he would just gaze off. He was never like that before the accident, but he is still like that today. He just seems "spacy" a lot of the time.

After the accident, Joe started hanging out with bikers. He really needed friends and people who accepted him the way he looked and acted.

Spaziano had a difficult family life, which probably exacerbated the effects of his brain damage. Robert Spaziano remembers in his affidavit that

[our father] also drank a lot. When he was home, it seemed that [he] was always screaming and yelling about something or hitting us. We were all afraid of him. He never hit our sister Barbara, but he would never let her out of the house. Even on weekends, she would have to stay home and do housework.

It's hard to explain how we were all affected by this constant yelling and turmoil. Each of us left home as soon [as] we could. Barbara got married very young. I don't think all children react in the same way to a situation. Some of my brothers learned to react in the same way that my father did, while I became extremely passive. Each of us just had to find a way to cope.

Barbara Walker recalls:

The problem was that [our father] did not have much patience with us when he would come home from work. He drank a lot and he seemed to yell at us all of the time. We were all terrified of him. My mother tried to protect us as much as she could, but this was thirty years ago and my parents had an old fashioned, traditional Italian marriage with the husband being the total head of the household. It is very difficult to talk about these things in public because now we are older and our father is very ill and he cannot harm us any more. And my mother still lives with him. But it is true that it was really terrible for us as children and each of us left home as soon as we were old enough. I myself got married as a young teenager to escape the tyranny of my father. To say that we left home is accurate, but it is also that our father kicked the boys out of the house and made them be self supporting as soon as they were teenagers. He never showed us kindness or affection. Although he never physically hit me, he would hit the boys with whatever was available. . . .

Our father drank all the time it seemed. He drank everywhere, at work and at home. He would even have wine with his eggs for breakfast. As an adult I know how his alcoholism was a disease, but as a child the yelling and screaming really terrorized all of us.

Life as Joseph Spaziano knew it ended at age 20, leaving him with devastating and disfiguring injuries. He turned to the Hells Angels motorcycle brotherhood to take him in and care for him.

Before and after. The car accident described above is the signal event in Joseph Spaziano's life. It explains why Joe had no alibi for the night Laura Lynn Harberts disappeared. More fundamentally, however, that cataclysmic experience explains Spaziano's lifetime allegiance to motorcycle brotherhoods.

One aspect of this case I've always had trouble getting my mind around is the role that motorcycle brotherhoods—first the Hells Angels and then the Outlaws—have played in Spaziano's life. I have become increasingly convinced that the defining moment for Joe on this subject— as with so many others—is the car accident that nearly killed him. After the accident, he needed constant physical, emotional, and psychological support. His need for approval and acceptance became almost an obsession. His father's verbal and physical abuse made life at home impossible. When members of a local motorcycle club offered support, Spaziano accepted.

"Crazy Joe" Spaziano came home from the hospital not alive or dead but in between, boxed and crated in braces. He was reduced, at age 20, to a second infancy. He had to be taught, all over again, how to eat, how to bathe himself, how to use a toilet by himself, how to walk by himself. His biological family was utterly unable to care for him, much less rehabilitate him. His parents couldn't do it, and his siblings wouldn't.

As soon as he was able to leave his family's home after the accident, Spaziano escaped, turning to the family of the motorcycle gang, who accepted his physical and psychological disfigurement. Given Spaziano's impaired judgment, limited coping skills, and need for support, his seeking the fellowship of the motorcycle brotherhood is completely understandable. He saw nowhere else to turn.

After about two years with the Hells Angels, Joe left the club for love. He had met a woman named Linda, and he wanted to (and eventually did) marry her. After they were married, Linda insisted that Joe extricate himself from the club. He did so, but one does not simply quit the Hells Angels. For this traitorous act, he was severely punished—tortured, beaten, and left for dead. A friend took him home. His sister and her husband came to help him. In an affidavit Barbara Walker prepared for a defense investigator in 1985, she says:

> I saw Joe the night he tried to leave the motorcycle club and they beat him up. It was really terrible. Joe's wife called my husband and me and we went to their house. Joe was almost lifeless. They had beaten his legs and arms and all over his body. They had used a branding iron or something hot to burn off a tattoo on his arm. He had cigarette burns everywhere, even on his private areas. His whole body was bloody. Joe's wife called her parents in Florida and they left very quickly, leaving everything, including their clothes and furniture and home behind. My husband helped carry Joe from the house to get them out of there as quickly as possible.

The beating was bad, but it could have been much worse, and Joe knew it. He was one of relatively few men ever to resign from the Hells Angels and live. I think the Angels didn't kill him because they understood that he would continue to keep the vows of loyalty he had made to them even after he left. He did. To this day, Joe refuses to criticize the Hells Angels or to provide any information about his involvement with them. That is why all of the information about the club given above was provided by people other than Joe.

Joe and his bride drifted to Florida, where, at first, Joe remained free of the lure of the biker life. In time, however, he hooked up with the Florida Outlaws. The connection forged between Joe and the Outlaws would withstand prison, death row, and the passage of decades. It remains unbroken today.

Joe's bond with his Outlaw biker brothers was at work a decade later in 1995, when both Joe and I fully expected him to be killed in a matter of days. He insisted that, if he was about to be executed, a thousand Outlaws would amass themselves just beyond the prison's perimeter. I argued that such a display of force would make it harder for any court or governor to stay the execution. But my client was firm: the Outlaws had to be there, on Harleys and flying their club colors.

Lurching toward recovery from the auto accident and later nursed back to relative health by the Outlaws after nearly being killed by the Hells Angels, Joe had been to places very few people go. The bikers had become his family. They wanted to bear public witness to their brother's execution for a crime he did not commit. Who was I to argue?

2

Prisoner No. 049043: Letters from Death Row

[Eichmann's prosecutors] knew, of course, that it would have been very comforting indeed to believe that Eichmann was a monster, even though if he had been Israel's case against him would have collapsed or, at the very least, lost all interest. Surely, one can hardly call upon the whole world and gather correspondents from the four corners of the earth in order to display Bluebeard in the dock. The trouble with Eichmann was precisely that so many were like him, and that the many were neither perverted nor sadistic; that they were, and still are, terribly and terrifyingly normal. From the viewpoint of our legal institutions and of our moral standards of judgment, this normality was much more terrifying than all the atrocities put together, for it implied—that this new type of criminal, who is in actual fact *hostis generis humani,* commits his crimes under circumstances that make it well-nigh impossible for him to know or to feel that he is doing wrong.

Hannah Arendt, Eichmann in Jerusalem:
A Report on the Banality of Evil, *1963*

In Florida, the litigation stages from imposition of death sentence to execution can be diagrammed as shown in Exhibit 2.1. As the exhibit illustrates, the capital appeals assembly line can be divided into three clusters of stages: the trial and direct appeal stage (column A in the exhibit), the state postconviction stage (column B), and the federal habeas corpus stage (column C).

At the beginning of the first cluster of steps, there is a traditional trial to determine guilt or innocence (Step 1). This is followed by a

A	B	C
Step 1 Trial and sentence in Florida state trial court	Step 4 State postconviction motion in state trial court (Rule 3.850 motion)	Step 7 Federal habeas corpus petition in federal district court
Step 2 Affirmance of conviction and sentence on direct/plenary appeal to Florida Supreme Court	Step 5 Appeal to Florida Supreme Court of state postconviction motion (Rule 3.850 motion); filing of original proceedings	Step 8 Appeal to Eleventh Circuit Court of Appeals Step 9 Request for plenary review (cert) in U.S. Supreme Court
Step 3 Request for plenary review (cert) in U.S. Supreme Court	Step 6 Request for plenary review (cert) in U.S. Supreme Court	Step 10 Executive clemency

Exhibit 2.1. Stages of litigation in Florida from death sentence to execution.

penalty phase, which constitutes, in essence, a separate trial on the issue of sentencing (Step 1). Following conviction of a capital offense and imposition of the death penalty, the condemned person in Florida has a right to a direct (plenary) appeal to the Florida Supreme Court (Step 2). On direct appeal, the inmate argues that legal errors at trial require a retrial or resentencing. Only legal issues appearing within the trial record can be raised on direct appeal.

If the Florida Supreme Court rules against the prisoner on direct appeal, he or she may attempt to convince the U.S. Supreme Court that his or her case is worthy of the Court's consideration by filing a certiorari (cert) petition (Step 3) and then, if unsuccessful, may seek postconviction relief in state court (Step 4).

The prisoner then moves into the steps shown in column B of the exhibit, the state postconviction cluster of steps. Filing a state postconviction motion (Step 4)—in Florida called a Rule 3.850 motion—provides a procedural mechanism for raising claims that were not or could not have been raised at trial or on the direct appeal. These Rule 3.850 motions typically raise claims that are outside of the trial record (record-based claims must be raised earlier, on direct appeal). The quintessential Rule 3.850 motion claim is a claim of ineffective assistance of trial counsel—an argument that trial counsel should have conducted a more thorough pretrial factual investigation into the defendant's background and life history. Because presentation of evidence that trial counsel did *not* investigate (and therefore present at trial) requires postconviction counsel to go *outside* the trial record, such extra-record-based claims are properly presented in a Rule 3.850 motion.

Such a motion must be initiated in the state trial court and, if denied, appealed to the Florida Supreme Court (Step 5). State postconviction litigation may also be initiated in the state appellate court (Step 5). Following Florida Supreme Court affirmance of the trial court's denial of the Rule 3.850 motion and denial of any litigation initiated directly in the Florida Supreme Court, the prisoner may seek cert in the U.S. Supreme Court (Step 6).

Following exhaustion of state postconviction litigation and denial of cert in the U.S. Supreme Court, the Florida inmate moves into the steps shown in column C of the exhibit and is entitled to petition the federal district court for a writ of habeas corpus mandating retrial or resentencing (Step 7). Think of a federal habeas corpus petition as a combination of all direct appeal (column A) issues + state postconviction (column B) issues (or, Step 7 = column A trial-record-based issues and column B outside-the-trial-record issues). If the habeas petition is denied in federal district court, the prisoner then appeals to the Eleventh Circuit Court of Appeals (Step 8). Then, if the inmate loses in the appellate court, he or she may seek cert in the U.S. Supreme Court (Step 9). At any time following direct appeal, a condemned prisoner may file an application for executive clemency or pardon. In Florida, a grant of clemency requires the votes of the governor and a majority of the executive cabinet.

At any point beyond the plenary direct appeal (Step 2), an execution date may be set by the governor. In most states—Louisiana and Texas, for example—execution dates are set by the state courts. In other states, an execution date is set when the governor signs the prisoner's death warrant; this is the case in Florida and New Hampshire. Once a death warrant has been signed and a date is set, the condemned inmate must obtain a stay of execution in order to remain alive to pursue postconviction remedies in state and federal courts.

While Joe Spaziano's case was wending its way through the capital appeals process, the governor signed several death warrants on Joe, and so his case was litigated "under death warrant." Such litigation is fairly rough-and-tumble, with the defense lawyers flying from court to court in search of a stay as the case moves down the assembly line of the appeals process: from state trial court to Florida Supreme Court, to the U.S. Supreme Court, to federal district court, to the Eleventh Circuit, to the U.S. Supreme Court, sometimes in a matter of days. The Ted Bundy case, for example, was decided by three different courts in one day.

The logistics of litigating cases under warrant—where cases can move rapidly from the state trial court in Miami to the Florida Supreme Court in Tallahassee to the federal district court and back again to the Eleventh Circuit in Atlanta to the U.S. Supreme Court in Washington, D.C.—have led to some unique procedural customs and practices. For instance, stay papers can be "lodged" in courts well in advance of when the cases actually reach those courts; later, if all the courts earlier along the assembly line deny a stay, an attorney can place a phone call to "activate" the papers previously lodged.

For example, assume a hypothetical death row prisoner who was tried and sentenced to death (Step 1 in the process) three years ago. His direct appeal was denied two years ago (Step 2). His request for U.S. Supreme Court review of his case was denied last year (Step 3). The governor and executive cabinet have denied clemency. Assume further that the governor signs a death warrant on our hypothetical prisoner today. The prison will schedule the execution for 7:00 A.M. twenty-eight days hence. Our prisoner will file a Rule 3.850 motion and an application for stay in the Florida trial court in which he was originally tried and sentenced (Step 4). If the trial court denies the Rule 3.850 motion and stay, then the prisoner appeals to the Florida Supreme Court for a stay (Step 5). If he loses there, then it's on to the U.S. Supreme Court for a stay (Step 6), then on to the federal district court (Step 7), the Eleventh Circuit Court of Appeals (Step 8), and finally back to the U.S. Supreme Court (Step 9). If all of these courts refuse to stay the execution, then our hypothetical inmate will be put to death on schedule.

When I first became involved in Joe Spaziano's case in 1983, he had been on death row for seven years, and his case had been to the Florida Supreme Court on direct appeal (Step 2). The court had affirmed the murder conviction and death sentence. The case had not yet moved into the postconviction (Rule 3.850 and federal habeas corpus) stages of litigation. It seemed he had all the time in the world.

During the year following my graduation from law school, near the end of my clerkship with Judge Vance, I applied to work for about seventy-five capital public defender organizations. I got one interview, with the West Palm Beach, Florida, Public Defender's Office. The office offered me a job, and I accepted on the spot.

I couldn't believe my good luck; in the world of capital litigation, West Palm Beach was at the center of the universe. This was so due to the work of one man: Richard Jorandby, the elected public defender for Palm Beach County. Jorandby was patrician and a prominent fixture in Florida's conservative circles; he tirelessly devoted his life to ensuring that every citizen accused of crime, no matter how guilty, would be guaranteed the best possible legal aid. While other public defenders' offices were slaughtered by budget cuts, ours survived—in fact, our capital appeals division thrived and became the best in the nation. This was because of Dick Jorandby's political acumen. Richard Greene, a graduate of the University of Texas Law School, was our guide through the maze of Florida politics. Richard Burr was the other lawyer. His manner was self-deprecating, that of the southern gentleman—Jimmy Stewart with a law degree. Jorandby, Greene, and Burr—the three Dicks, as it were. They were the team. I was the kid. I felt like a high school student working at the Manhattan Project.

Jorandby hired Craig Barnard to be creator and coach of his capital appeals unit. Nothing rattled Craig. In spite of the onslaught and chaos of death warrants, briefs, oral arguments, and deadlines, Craig remained serene as Buddha in his office overlooking the intercoastal waterway, puffing on his pipe—the mastermind of our team.

The West Palm Beach Public Defender's Office team had been "Crazy Joe" Spaziano's appellate lawyers since he was first sentenced to death, in 1976. When I first read Spaziano's trial transcripts, in the fall of 1983, the case had already been to the Florida Supreme Court on direct appeal. The court had affirmed the murder conviction and death sentence. This meant that the case would be appealed to the U.S. Supreme Court, and, if it lost there, it would move into the postconviction stages of litigation.

The heart of a capital postconviction case is fact investigation. The discovery of new facts that never came out at the original trial can win a case. Jerry Justine was the chief fact investigator of the capital appeals division of the West Palm Beach Public Defender's Office. His project in 1983 was to find Tony DiLisio and see what DiLisio had to say about his pivotal testimony in Spaziano's murder and rape cases. Justine's travels in aid of Joe's case would take him from a small town in California to the attic of the late chief detective on Joe's murder case.

While Justine reinvestigated the facts, Craig Barnard and I would ask the U.S. Supreme Court to agree to consider and decide a vexing issue of federal constitutional law that was crucial to Joe's case: May a state's capital punishment statute include a "jury override" procedure authorizing a trial judge to override a sentencing jury's verdict of life imprisonment and impose the death sentence? My job was to research and draft a petition seeking U.S. Supreme Court review of the judge's override of the jury's life imprisonment sentence in Joe Spaziano's case. These petitions seeking Supreme Court review are routinely filed and almost never granted. For years, Barnard had been unsuccessfully trying to convince the Court to decide his death cases. Now, for the first time, the Court said yes.

Although in the end we lost Joseph Spaziano's case in the U.S. Supreme Court, it was heady for a legal tadpole like me to be involved in such a case. In the course of helping Barnard write Joe's briefs and prepare for oral argument before the justices in D.C., I gained my first personal experience with the mysteries of capital litigation in the nation's highest court. The world of the U.S. Supreme Court—and the forces within it that drive the tactical and strategic decisions made by the few veteran lawyers familiar with its topography and minefields—was brand new to me at the time.

Barnard and I had Anthony Amsterdam, the best possible guide a novice like me could hope for. Amsterdam was, after all, the architect of the national campaign to use the courts and the Constitution to abolish capital punishment. From the beginnings of his litigation efforts in the early 1960s, Amsterdam was in the thick of the fight, often successfully writing the briefs and presenting the oral arguments in landmark capital cases in the U.S. Supreme Court. Amsterdam is, quite simply, the most magnificent human being with whom I have ever worked as a lawyer. He is brilliant and decent and generous.

A couple of days before the oral argument in D.C., Craig Barnard,

Dick Jorandby, Flo Wilson (Barnard's secretary), and I flew from West Palm Beach to Washington National Airport. The night before the argument I was a wreck, and I think Jorandby was, too.

That night, as Craig paced his hotel room while I fired off questions to him, Jorandby casually asked me about the suit I planned to wear to court the next morning. Preoccupied, and knowing next to nothing about the nomenclature of men's fashions, I said the suit was "madras." I don't know why that word popped into my head just then, because my suit was actually an understated brown pinstripe. I forgot my offhand comment as soon as it was out of my mouth, but Jorandby (a study in sartorial elegance) had nightmares of sitting next to me in the Supreme Court with me dressed in a flamboyant, vivid madras plaid suit.

My parents, who lived just outside of D.C., were able to see me sitting at counsel table in the U.S. Supreme Court, wearing a very nice (nonmadras) suit, carrying the briefcase they had given me as a law school graduation present. They were so proud. I was twenty-seven. Neither they nor I ever thought I'd go to college, much less act as a defense attorney before the U.S. Supreme Court.

What surprised me most about the oral argument was how close we were to the justices. Sitting beside Dick Jorandby at counsel's table while Barnard fielded the justices' questions, I could almost reach out my hand and touch Justice John Paul Stevens. The low point in the argument came when the prosecutor argued that Spaziano "is lucky he wasn't tried by a jury in one of those [Ku Klux] Klan counties in north Florida." When the prosecutor said this, Justice Lewis Powell (the courtly Virginian whose own racial politics had become an issue when he was appointed to the Supreme Court) seemed to pale and rock back in his swivel chair.

We lost Joe's case in the U.S. Supreme Court by a vote of six to three. It wasn't even close. Florida judges could continue to override jury verdicts of life imprisonment and impose the death penalty. Joe's death sentence would stand.

I always wanted to meet my clients at the outset. Yet, in Spaziano's case, Craig Barnard kept postponing my meeting Joe. Because capital postconviction cases take many years to work their way through the state and federal court systems, any single death row prisoner may expect to have a series of different lawyers: one attorney at trial, another on the first appeal to the Florida Supreme Court, still another for executive clemency, and another for state postconviction, federal habeas corpus, and so on. This serial lawyering can cause death-sentenced prisoners great anxiety, and Barnard attempted to maintain as much continuity in representation as possible. While he and I were working on Joe's case in the U.S. Supreme Court, Barnard alone kept in contact with Joe and kept him informed and up-to-date on developments. For a little over a year, Joe Spaziano might have noticed my name on his briefs, but as far as he was concerned, Barnard continued to be his lawyer. Keeping me anonymous made sense because I was so new, inexperienced, and untested at the beginning of my work on Joe's case; if I bombed out of deathwork, there would be no reason for Joe Spaziano—or anyone else outside our office—to know I had ever worked on his case in the first place.

I got to know Joe from his letters. The first thing one notes when receiving a letter from Joe Spaziano is his artwork on the envelope, typically a full-color painting of Donald Duck, Goofy, or some other Disney animated character. Joe paints and draws, and he sends his paintings to his lawyers and their secretaries. He sends them also to his friends, family members, and other inmates. Mail sent from Florida State Prison inmates is supposed to conform to certain requirements: written on standard-issue paper denoting the prisoner's number and cell block location at the top of each page. Otherwise, the wide-ruled paper could have come from anywhere, written by anyone.

Joe wrote to me frequently, except when he was under death warrant, when we could talk on the phone at least once a day. He almost always wrote in ink, crossing out words as necessary. The handwriting itself was carefully and neatly printed. Writing was a very painstaking process for him. Joe wrote about his daughter, his mother, and his Outlaw brothers. He almost always asked after my family and friends. He wrote about his fears of living on death row. Joe's letters were punctuated with smiley faces and paintings and sketches of Disney characters. He seldom complained in his letters. He never trashed the prison or the corrections officers.

I wanted to bring myself up to speed on Joe's case before we met for the first time. I had hoped to finish reading and mastering Joe's trial transcript by the end of January 1985, but the case turned out to be more complicated than I'd anticipated. The murder trial transcripts were fairly straightforward, but the Vanessa Dale Croft rape case didn't seem to fit.

On January 12, 1985, I wrote Joe to tell him that I wouldn't be able to meet with him until mid-February. On January 14, Joe wrote back on a card he had illustrated on both sides. One side was devoted to two *Peanuts* characters: a smiling and kneeling Linus, patting the head of Woodstock the bird. In purple ink within a black inked border, Joe had written in script, "Just Thinking of You." The flip side of the card was illustrated by a rainbow that seemed dissonant with the tone of the message Joe had written across the rainbow.:

Hi Mike, are you still coming this month ☺ I'm waiting to see you. I got them paintings out there. I just hoping to hear from you, got something for you to let me know the day your coming so I can give it to you ok.

Write Back
Sincerely
Your Friend Joe

I finally wrote back on February 7, a short, stiff, and pompous letter that thanked him for the *Peanuts*/rainbow card. I said I was working on his trial transcript, and I closed by saying, "I hope to meet you soon. Take care and stay in touch." I didn't say when we might meet.

Sure, I'd been busy with other cases. I'd filed an Eleventh Circuit brief in one case, and Craig Barnard and I had filed a fifty-page brief for the full Eleventh Circuit Court of Appeals in Jim Hitchcock's case (raising an issue Barnard would eventually win, in a unanimous decision, in the U.S. Supreme Court in 1987). We finalized Hitchcock's brief on February 7, the same day I wrote my prissy letter to Joe. Looking back on it now, my other cases didn't justify my sending such a wooden letter to Joe Spaziano. But if the letter bothered Joe, he showed no sign (after all, in early 1985 I was the inexperienced one; he had been doing this stuff for nine years, since being sentenced to death in 1976).

Joe gave me a few days to stew, and then on February 12 he sent me a cheerfully illustrated card in a cheerfully illustrated envelope. The envelope had a delicately drawn bunny rabbit popping up out of a tree stump to find spring flowers, below an orange quarter moon and yellow stars connected by a blue ribbon of velvet. And that was just the envelope.

A full quarter of the card was given to a cartoon bumblebee wearing blushing orange cheeks and sporting a red beanie that somehow didn't seem to interfere with his antennae. The bee was kneeling, his round face tight with concentration or concern, picking up an empty soda can, a straw, paper, and other debris, and putting it all in a brown garbage bag already packed full of soda cans and papers. Joe's caption: "Keep whatever is around you clean." I'm certain today that when I received this card, it didn't occur to me that Joe's illustration was a lambent commentary on my previous snippy letter. Today, I wonder.

The card included a note and a poem:

Mike [I]n your book on legal History it has a was sentenced to life and 5 years for first degree murder. It was a rape case I was sentenced on that. Just to let you know ok. It is wrong ok see you next week.

> Sincerely
> Joe

> *As you lie or work, on a*
> *Summer's day in a warm*
> *And sunny place, don't*
> *Look up at the clouds*
> *Or sky:*
> *Instead look down and*
> *Squint your eyes.*
> *That if you look with all*
> *Your might you'll fine*
> *The land of Murethansmal*
> *And in this land are*
> *Buggs that's all.*
> *Joseph Spaziano 1985*

That very day, February 16, I wrote Joe to tell him that I'd be at the prison to meet him in three days, on February 19. He received my February 16 letter on February 17, and once again he got a letter off to me that same day—this time it was just a letter on prison-issue stationary, with the lines for the requisite information at the top—institution, name, cell/dorm and bunk, prisoner number and date—left blank. No artwork, either. Joe wrote:

Feb. 17, 1985

Hi Mike,

I just got your letter and glad to hear from you.

Glad you like my art work. Be honest this is play around stuff, I got lot's better stuff I do.

Did Craig get that and letters I sent to him this week.

About that Magazine and, Stella [a woman affiliated with the Outlaws and a good friend of Joe's] why they refused to put her onto my list?

I like to get a copy of my trial transcript to. Not the Brief.

The hole case is a buck of shue. That Delisio is lying. He's a punk.

Well I'll close I'll be waiting for you to drop by. I know the clemscie is in March I forget what day.

Some way the cops put it to him what to say.

I'll tell you what I saw while in Sanford getting rea-sentence. No everybody but a feau people the cops corts'n ones that were bringing in guys on drunk charges or stoned, they be telling the guy his rights and after he guy wold say he wants to call his lawyer the cops would kick trow and put the guy in his cell or an empty scell and beat him and mean it the cops in Sanford, some are jerks, some are ok. That cold be why Tony said it. Mike I don't know I sentence to die pel and I never killed nobody.

Sincerely

Joe

Because I was scheduled to meet Joe on February 19, I didn't write back right away. There was also a matter I wanted to discuss with him only in person, as I have always suspected that inmate mail is read by prison authorities before it reaches my clients. The topic I wanted to discuss with Joe was delicate—it concerned an alleged serial killer named Gerald Stano.

Stano had been convicted of raping and murdering many young women in Florida. One of Joe Spaziano's West Palm Beach lawyers had read newspaper accounts of Stano's capital trial, and there seemed to be interesting similarities between Spaziano's alleged crime and the murders to which Stano had reportedly confessed. Laura Lynn Harberts's body had been found in August 1973 at an Altamonte Springs trash dump site. Stano was in the south Florida area around that time, and reportedly he had confessed to leaving the bodies of his female victims in dump areas. Most intriguingly, Stano had described himself as a "traveling cook," and Harberts's roommate Beverly Fink and Fink's boyfriend, Jack Mallen, had said that Harberts had known a "traveling cook." No one would describe Joe Spaziano as a "cook," much less as a "traveling cook."

The possibility that Stano had murdered Harberts and left her body in a trash dump area was promising news for Joe Spaziano's lawyers. One contextual and atmospheric weakness in Joe's innocence claim had always been our inability to identify any person who might have been Harberts's real killer; when you are claiming your client didn't do it, it's always nice if you can point to the person who did. And for our purposes, Stano seemed a promising possibility. Stano lacked Bundy's telegenic appearance, poise, and personality, and he had already confessed to dozens of murders of young women in Florida. Maybe he would confess to the Harberts homicide as well. It was worth a shot.

I wished I could have met with Stano myself to question him about the Harberts murder. The problem was, Stano was represented by a public defender office entirely unrelated to my West Palm Beach office. Before I could meet with Stano, I would need to get permission from his lawyer. Of course, Stano's lawyer said no—as I would have done had I been Stano's lawyer rather than Spaziano's. Stano's lawyer surmised—absolutely correctly—that no good could come to Stano if he allowed his client to meet with me. When Stano's attorney turned me down, I couldn't have known that in only two years the same public defender's office—the Office of Capital Collateral Representative, or CCR—would simultaneously represent both Stano and Spaziano. This joint representation raised what we in the ethics dodge call a conflict of interest.

Although I couldn't talk with Stano about Spaziano, I certainly could talk with Spaziano about Stano. When I finally met with Joe on February 19, I did just that. Joe said he'd never heard of Stano.

During my first two years as a capital public defender, I had never visited death row itself. I thought I could imagine it; my clients had described it in detail. But when I finally saw death row, I realized how incomplete my image had been.

The Florida State Prison, where Joe was on death row, is in the small rural town of Starke. There is no commercial airport in Starke. To get there from West Palm Beach, you have to fly into Jacksonville or Gainesville and then drive to the prison along Route 301. When you turn off Route 301 and pass the "Florida State Prison" sign, you might think that you've arrived. Actually, you still have about eleven miles to go, on a two-lane road past modest houses and trailers where the corrections officers live. Most of their parents and grandparents also live in and around the town of Starke. The prison is the only real industry in town, and corrections is a family tradition.

Just when you're beginning to think you made a wrong turn off 301, the prison comes into view. You follow the signs to visitor parking. Then you follow the signs to the administration building, where you're told you're in the wrong place. You are instructed to go to the guard tower, pick up the phone at the base of the tower, call the guard at the top, and tell him your name. If you're on his list of authorized visitors for the day, the guard will buzz you through a pair of massive, barred gates. When the first gate closes behind you, you know you're in a prison.

You now enter the prison building. Directly in front of you is a Plexiglas-enclosed booth behind which sit corrections officers monitoring the comings and goings at the prison. At this booth you sign in, giving the date, time, and reason for your visit. Your right wrist is stamped with a mark visible only under ultraviolet light. To the left of the booth are two more sets of barred gates, leading into the part of the facility where prisoners are housed. To the right of the booth are two doors leading to administrative offices. There is a lone public bathroom in this entry area, as well as a glass-encased detailed model of the prison complex. Death row used to be on R wing; it then expanded to include R wing and Q wing. Finally, a few years ago the state of Florida constructed a high-tech death row, a self-contained prison within a prison.

Your next step is to pass through the metal detector from hell. Your watch sets it off; your belt sets it off; your shoes set it off; your jewelry (tie tack, earrings) sets it off. Once you've removed all offending items and passed through successfully, a uniformed escort arrives from the other side of the bars and waits impassively while you hurry to put them all back on.

Uniformed escort at your side, you pass through more barred doors and walk down a long corridor toward "grand central station" and the control room. "Grand central" is the principal crossroads in the prison, and the heavily fortified control room governs the flow of prison traffic through that thoroughfare. From the safety of the control room, guards can seal off portions of the prison from the rest.

Death row is where condemned people live. When you are an attorney visiting a condemned client in Florida State Prison, you don't meet on death row—you meet in a cubicle adjoining the "colonel's (i.e., warden's) office." When Joe and I met for the first time, it was my first trip to Florida State Prison, and I wasn't certain what I was supposed to do once I was actually inside the visitor's cubicle, meeting my client face-to-face for the first time. The cubicle had a small table and two plastic chairs. Eventually, Joe Spaziano arrived; his arms and legs were shackled. The arm chains were removed by a corrections officer, and Joe shook my hand. He then sat down on one side of the table. Joe was the opposite of the Outlaw biker I had expected to meet. He was slight of build and wiry, and his hair was dark and cut very short, according to prison regulations. He wore black, thick-framed prison-issue glasses and a regulation death row–issue orange T-shirt. He had complicated tattoos on both arms. After an hour, a guard rapped on the visitor booth's door to signal that our time was up. It was time for me to return to the world and for Joe to return to death row.

When Joe and I met that first time, we didn't talk much about Stano or any other aspect of Joe's case. According to my journal entry for that day, we spent "most" of our two-hour visit talking about "his art and his daughter. He gave me a hand-drawn card for [my son Larkin] and promised a painting; gave ok for our checking into Stano." My journal says I found Joe "slim, short, and wiry," a man who "spits out energy that just stops now and then, and he says 'I'm lost,' with a quizzical look."

Back in my office in West Palm Beach the next day, I wrote Joe a thank-you note:

February 20, 1985
Dear Joe,

I really enjoyed meeting you on Tuesday. Ruthann (my "wife"; we're not actually married, though "wife" is OK as short-hand) and Larkin (our son) both loved the card. I don't know if I mentioned this when we met, but they enjoy your art as much as I do. In fact, as I'm writing this, I'm looking at a rabbit peeking out of a stump, a moon connected to stars by a string of velvet, and a marvelously pissed-off duck smoking a cigarette in a holder. They are the most interesting and colorful things on my desk. And, now that we've met, I can connect the art to a face and a person.

Best, Michael

Over the next week I drafted Joe's application for executive clemency. The principal argument was the same one Joe had been making since his trial: he is innocent; they got the wrong guy. After much thought I decided to include the Stano argument, but only as an area requiring further investigation.

In addition to the clemency petition, I drafted a postconviction motion challenging the legality of Joe's 1975 conviction of the rape and slashing of Vanessa Dale Croft. In a February 28 letter to Joe I laid out why I thought we should go after the rape conviction. His death sentence in the Harberts case was largely based on the rape conviction; that is, the rape case was the reason the sentencing judge in the homicide case overrode the jury's recommendation of life imprisonment and sentenced Joe to death for killing Laura Lynn Harberts. If we could knock out the rape case—especially if we could prove Joe's total innocence in that case—then the death sentence would become more vulnerable to attack. I planned to raise only one issue in habeas on the rape conviction: that of the tattoos. Neither of Croft's attackers had prominent tattoos on his arms. Joe did.

Once again, my preoccupation with Joe's case led me to neglect Joe the person. On February 26, Joe sent a card:

Mike,

Mike can you let me know if you received the (2) paintings I sent (2) weeks ago and haven't heard nothing from you.

So what has been going on with you Mike.

I myself keep pretty busy paint every day ☺. I love it, Mike. Well let me know what them people think of my work and I'll close, tell everybody I said hello.

Write Back
Your friend Joe

On the envelope, Joe had drawn Mickey Mouse in a pale blue drum major's uniform, carrying a baton. My address appeared in a banner held aloft by two little yellow birds who obviously were panting from the effort. The artwork on the card itself is difficult to describe. On the ground of the drawing are puffy pink and blue mushrooms. Hanging from a tree by its ratlike tail, which is coiled around the tree's upper branches, is an opossum in black-and-white-striped prison garb, eyes tightly closed. Two ratlike buckteeth protrude from its mouth; they are so long they extend almost to the collar of the opossum's striped suit. Or maybe it's not an opossum—maybe it's a rat (in prison parlance, an informer; rats are the bottom feeders of prison culture).

On March 1, Craig Barnard marched into my office to tell me that I must respond to clients' letters quickly. He'd just gotten a letter from Joe in which he wrote that he'd met with me and the rest of the "crew." "Looks and sounds like you got a good crew. They like my art work, at [least]," Joe had written. Still, Joe was concerned that Barnard himself had abandoned him; he wrote "Sometimes I thought you left me but I understand what is going on" with our "crew." The portion of Joe's letter that chilled my blood was this: "I'm not looking forward to that clemicie, Craig. But what can I say. They just clowning arround with my life."

Barnard was absolutely correct in chiding me for allowing Joe—*my* client now—to feel abandoned. I again resolved to answer every client letter the day it arrived. But again I let it slide, and I heard from Joe before he'd heard from me:

March 3, 1985

Hi ~~Mike, Machell~~ Michael.

I got my spelling book here so I don't spell to wrong. Ya I enjoyed seeing you to. I had some more cards and envolopes made out to show youes. Glad they liket the pictures I done on the card and envolope. I'm so hung up into cartoon art. ☺

Oh I send Ed a card and envolope. I don't understand all tha law stuff you sent. But it sounds good ☺. What I know ☺.

I hope you believe me that I never killed nobody or know nothing about it. Oh that Duck is Dafy Duck. I usely put him in fron of a bike ☺. I keep the bike out. I want to get back into painting. I just sent Craig another letter. That girl that said she was rapet is a lier. I never seen that girl before only in court I think. Could of saw her someplace but I don't know. I didn't have to rape no chick out there in them streets. I had a feau honeys. Ya I done ok Pel ☺.

Somebody up stairs sent this artical today or just now that is, so I'm going to send it to you ok.

Joe

This letter arrived in the midst of my frantic efforts to prepare for my first capital oral argument in the Eleventh Circuit Federal Court of Appeals, where I had clerked for Judge Vance during 1982–83. The argument was in Nollie Lee Martin's case, the most infamous Palm Beach County capital case in recent memory ("Palm Beach County's Ted Bundy case," Barnard called it). Lee Martin had confessed twice to the kidnap, rape, and murder of a young woman who was supplementing her college tuition by working at the convenience store from which Martin abducted her. Most of my Eleventh Circuit brief was spent arguing that Martin's two confessions should not have been admitted into evidence at his capital trial. Until a few days before my oral argument in Atlanta, the confessions claims had been slam-dunk winners. I'd even written to Martin: "I am now spending every waking minute either working on, talking about or worrying about the [oral] argument on Wednesday. It's all coming together, Lee. I *never* say or even think this, but I really do feel like we may win. You have a strong case. You have three [Eleventh Circuit] judges who should be sympathetic. God is watching, I feel. . . . I hope to visit you soon after the argument. You are constantly in my thoughts and my prayers."

Then, right before the argument, the U.S. Supreme Court decided an Oregon case that smashed my argument in the Martin case to bits. I read the Oregon case quickly before the argument, but when the Eleventh Circuit judges spent almost the entire argument time grilling me about that case, I was caught flat-footed. When the judges ruled, Martin lost. I was so shaken by this experience that when I returned from Atlanta to West Palm Beach and sent Joe a copy of the clemency petition we were about to file, I didn't even include a cover letter. But when I was able to visit Joe (and Lee Martin, too), Joe was cool:

March 6, 1985

Hi Mike

This is quick I read that thing you gave me. I love you people and know you trying to save my life.

Can I ask you a favor my Mom I get word is in the hospital had an oparation. Can you give her a fast call for me and let me know how she is Chris or Rose Spaziano

ok hope you like my card ☺

Your Friend

Joe

I called Joe's Outlaw brother Chris, who told me that Joe's mom was fine; she'd only had some gallstones. She had been in the hospital for a short time, but she was home already. The family hadn't wanted to tell Joe about her hospitalization for fear he'd worry. I put all this in a March 11 letter that crossed in the mail with one Joe sent me that same day:

March 11, 1985

Hi Mike,

I hate to bother you again. But can I ask you something.

Did Stano know Tony De Lisio or his father. Would you let me know that its important to me.

I think I know what happened not happened but who and whats its about.

I believe that you all know now that I didn't do no rape or murder. I wasn't no angle but I goofed off. I thank all you again. I hope the other courts see it or Stano tells the truth: I see it Mike everybody I let see it feels it to.

Ok I'll close and be exspecking you after clemicie thanks all of you.

Sincerely, Joe

Then, a couple of days later, after Joe had received my letter telling him his mom was fine, Joe wrote again:

March 14, 1985, Wed.

Dear Mike,

I just got your letter and really glad about my mom, that it wasn't ceriest. Thank you Mike, I worry more when they think I don't know.

You tell Ruthann that I promiss when and I say when because I see what is going on, and I can't ask for better lawyers then what I got and investigator to. I thank all of you. Anyway you tell Ruthann that where ever you like I promiss to paint the hole livingroom of your house with the pretiest painting. I got neat idia's with my head that you would really like.

See Mike I got a certain party that is going to open a rib place for me all mine. I'm going to be around their till I get good help to leave and let them handle it. Don't think I know about cooking I do't eggs ☺ frie stake ☺ but that is it. This friend open fire rib place is the hit. See this person is a friend thinks the world of me and can't do it hiself but want's much to help me, he's a friend like really all you are.

So anyway I can have income from that and do my art work. Mike I can make it and can go anywhere in the U.S. once the people can see what I mean. All that wall paper stuff they got isn't nothing. I put good prices on stuff I'll get the work. Not to friends who helped me as I was down.

Can you tell Jerry that I didn't and won't forget him on that painting for his wife. I got everything now but I painting pads and the lady has got them for me just I'm waiting for my per-mite. He probley though I forgot but I got it writtin down so I don't forget ☺.

All you'es going to be proud of me in time ☺.

I know one thing you all believe me I can tell it. I wanted to ask how is Susan doing is she ok. That lady is a hard worker I can tell you that. [Susan Cary is a lawyer and counselor to many Florida death row prisoners.]

Well Mike don't want to burn you out ☺.

Ok can't waite to hear what is going on, in clemicie. Can't waite to see you again eather. I hope to have a painting for you and Ruth to same time as Jerry.

Sincerely, Joe

In late March, Edward Kirkland, Joe's trial attorney, argued Joe's application for executive clemency. After the argument, the ball of

Joe's life was in Governor Graham's court. Graham could grant clemency and commute Joe's death sentence to life, but no one expected that to happen; Graham was far too politically motivated. Graham could deny clemency by signing Joe's death warrant and scheduling his execution for twenty-eight days hence at 7:00 A.M. That was most likely—the question was when. When would the death warrant come? Knowing Graham, it was only a matter of time.

But time was what we needed: time to investigate, time to do legal research, time to draft the legal papers that might win Joe Spaziano a stay of execution once the warrant came. The more time we lawyers and fact investigators had, the more ready we could be when the warrant was signed.

For Joe himself, time was life. Between early January and the end of March 1985, my correspondence with Joe settled into a comfortable groove. He was the more faithful letter writer, but by now he'd come to know that my silences meant nothing more than that there was no word on clemency. Our silences had become companionable ones—or so I had convinced myself.

March 17, 1985

Hi Everybody,

Just a little depresset so I wrote everybody today I even wrote Ed Kirkland, so I figure I wrote him I better write you ☺.

I think you all are the best. I couldn't ask for no better people that is helping me.

I got so depess I packet all my stuff that I'll be going over to Q wing. Just call me fast thinker Joe ☺. I'm so goofet up in the head. Got word Stano had a visit today. I won't do nothing to fine out nothing or say a word to him. I seen what I needed to see.

Can't waite to hear what happened Wed. Let's see nothing new hope to see you soon. Susan I wanted to ask you I got a Birthday card from Gainsville said Susan on it I didn't answer it because it wasn't my birtday and didn't know who it was.

Ok let me close and you all take care.

Sincerely, Joe

P.S. Mike, can I get a copy of my Medical Record. When you ant busy or just thinking ☺. Ok Buddy catch you later. From the Acident one

Joe

Monday, March 21, 1985
Hi Mike,

Mike you guy done a good job in my investigation. Now I see a hole new light already. I thought so wrong and very confussed. But no more.

Everybody said so far that my case is in good hands that my lawyers are doing a good job. Thank you all very much.

Let me know if Stano knew Delisio ok. Just to finish my thoughts.

Ok to I hear from you after clemencie. I didn't understand it after 30 days additional but must be good so I want worry ☺.

Can't waite to see you again.

Sincerely, Joe

Wed, March 21, 1985
Hi Mike & Ruthann,

Ruthann I'll do a slick painting for you, and Mike.

Glade your a big fan of my work ☺. I need fans ☺.

Can I hold onto the picture of Larkin till you come up. I want to try something.

Ok a couple guys trew me a shot like I myself trying to pin it on Stano. They goof with me but I get mad because of how cops set me up or whoever. You all know more then I do anyway.

What I wanted to say is what do you personally think Mike. And again a feau people talk about that clemicie that if you get clemicie that means the rest of your life in here no parole. You can exsplain that stuff to me when I see you.

Mike I got a chance to live a perfick life with my own busness I want my little girl with me. Not to much a little girl no more but she can hang around me as long as she wants.

Ok Mike till I see you. You take care tell Ruthann I said hi. And tell Susan I'll see her next week.

Your friend, Joe

March 22, 1985
Hi Mike,

Can I ask you something, I had to go to the clinick today to get put someplace else to see a docter about my head and suicidal tendencies, it's a lie Mike it happed to me when their hospital in N.Y. gave me that medication I thought I was in a dream world. Se I ant going to do nothing on less I talk to you's and I don't want to show no disrepeck for the Govenor. I don't want to be put in a trick bag that is why I'm in here. So till I talk to you'es I don't want to see nobody, ok.

Ok have a good Easter for all of you.

Sincerely, Joe

I gathered from this letter that the prison had forced Joe to undergo a neurological exam, even though Governor Graham's clemency aide had promised Craig Barnard that no psychiatric exams would be done on Joe. Joe was adamant, to Barnard and to me, that he wasn't mentally ill—he's not a "bug," as he put it. By doing the exam behind our backs, the governor's office had jeopardized the trust between Joe and his defense team.

More troubling was the fact that some of the inmates were giving Joe a hard time over the Stano matter. On March 25, I wrote Joe asking him to "try to stay cool about the Stano thing. . . . Just tell [the other guys on the row] that your lawyers feel that the facts just can't be ignored. Feel free to trash me on this. I realize how tense it can get in there." Like hell I did.

Rather than trash me, Joe thanked me. In an April Fool's Day letter:

April Fool's Day 1985
Hi Mike,

Hay Mike I conceder all you my friends, and no matter if even I was back on the streets you'es are my friends and hope we can be friends out there.

I owl you all. See we all know I didn't do no murder. As now I know who it was. I can see of what I read.

I got lot's of faith in you and belive you's will be getting me out.

That coloring book is neet but it isn't all of my work I'll be doing. And you all can alway's have a peace of what I got.

I'm going to be an Artice pel ☺. I worket all these years at it, to do it.

I hope to see you soon so I can give you a copy of the book.

Your friend, Joe

On April 16, I learned that I'd be able to visit Joe on April 26. When I wrote him to make our date, he wrote back:

Hi Mike

That is great next fri April 26. I'll have 2 pictres out there for you one is for Jerry Justine, I promisset his wife Gloria one.

I can't waite to see you got lots to ask you. Not really inportent just want to know a feau things.

Ok let me close and you all take care, tell Susan I said Hi.

Sincerely, Joe

P.S. I'll have your book done to ☺.

Prison life is mundane. When nine years have been drained from a life with scant hope, a life-or-death decision is a blessing or a curse—or worse, both. So, I was relieved when, for the first time in a while, I was at least able to give Joe some concrete news about when he could expect a death warrant. Craig Barnard had received an off-the-record commitment from Governor Graham's clemency aide that no warrant would be signed on Spaziano for ninety days. That meant that mid-June would be the earliest a warrant would come. Graham signed twenty-eight-day warrants, which meant the earliest Joe would likely be killed would be mid-July, soon before the Florida Supreme Court justices left Tallahassee for the August recess. Four months. If the governor's aide really could keep the promise he'd made, for at least four months Joe could count on uncertainty.

April 22, 1985
Hi Mike,

Did you ever receive your painting? Let me know ok.

I done a lot of thinking on this and I see them courts are by passing me and don't give a dame.

So I decides if you ok it to do that interview with 60 minutes or 20/20 whatever.

I don't want to do it when it's to late because I see this state wants to kill me.

Well I haven't heard from you in awhile, don't know if you'll give up on me don't know shit. But at times get mad as what the courts do.

Ok I'll close hope to hear from you soon.

Your friend, Joe

My April 26 visit with Joe was satisfying, albeit marred by prison bureaucracy at the end of the visit. My April 26 journal notes: "Joe was great; gave me a coloring book for Larkin; very close talk about the club" (that is, the Outlaws). And: Joe "asked me point blank if he was going to die; I told him I didn't think so, but who could tell?"

Under Florida State Prison rules, Joe was not permitted to hand me bulky packages—such as his paintings—during our visits. During this visit, he told me to pick up two paintings that would be waiting for me at the final security checkpoint before I left the prison. However, when I asked at the checkpoint, I was told the guard had no packages for me; he also wouldn't allow me back into the visiting area to ask Joe what had gone wrong, because Joe was already in transit back to death row.

To me this was a petty inconvenience, but it really pissed Joe off. I tried to smooth things over in a May 1 letter to him by telling him an anecdote from my trip from the prison back home to West Palm Beach. On the plane I'd been flipping through the coloring book Joe had given me to give Larkin, and "the person in the seat next to me (a grey pinstripe suit businessman type) gave me some curious looks. I loved it." The biker and the nerd revisited? Or the nerd using the biker's coloring book to convince another nerd that he's not really such a nerd after all?

Meanwhile, U.S. Supreme Court justices Brennan and Marshall had just issued a stinging dissent from the Court's refusal to hear a Louisiana inmate's claim that execution by electrocution violates the Constitution. Did this mean that the two dissenters were trying to telegraph a message to lawyers in states with the electric chair—like Florida—that someday soon the Court might grant full review to his legal issue, and that therefore we ought to be raising it in every Florida capital case? Who knew? But to be on the safe side, we should raise it in our cases.

This was on my mind because I was writing Joe's postconviction papers. In a letter to Joe, I wrote: "The 90 day grace period the Governor has given us runs out in the middle of June, and after that you will be vulnerable to a warrant. I want to have papers filed in court to decrease that vulnerability," because Governor Graham sometimes didn't sign warrants in cases with litigation pending in the postconviction courts. I wrote that letter on May 1—Mayday.

Tuesday, May 3, 1985
Hi Mike,

Just wondering how you liket the pencil drawing. I'm not use to the pencil drawing but I done my best ☺.

Did them cards get mailed out and what did you think of them? I'll start your painting this week with Donald Duck and the rug rats ☺. Your going to love that painting, your wife will for sure ☺.

I'm thinking of doing up Christmas card for people for Christmas. I could have a good start.

I'll be honest with you what happened to me. Friday after I got done seeing you I got real down and out. I felt that we are going to lose and they going to kill me. But I got over it I'm in good hands ☺.

I can't do nothing about me proving Tony is lying or I didn't do it. So what can I say. Hope them big shots can see he's lying.

Lets see ok next month you said you'll be back I'll have that painting.

Tell Susan if she's got a problem, she didn't want to talk to me.

How do you like my hand writting. I got it pretty well under control. Still got little troble with the spelling but I'll have that pretty well under control ☺.

I got some book that are pretty to learn how to spell.

Well let me close tell everybody I said hello.

Oh I forgot to ask you Friday. Did you ever file that rape conviction yet. Or what is going on that?

Ok I'll close.

Sincerely, Joe

I shouldn't have mentioned the impending end of the governor's ninety-day grace period. On May 4, Joe wrote:

Fri May 4

Hi Mike,

Ya it was good seeing you to, I sure wanted to hear them tapes [the DiLisio hypnosis tapes]. But next time I'll have that painting for you. I'll bring it out myself ☺.

You might of ask the wrong people about the cards ad envolopes and your pictures, I haven't got them back yet.

Ya I try not to think of June 12th but I do every day.

That is funny about the plain trip back. But some people don't understand art.

Your a good man Mike I know you try to help me. I get so depress at times thinking of a certain person.

Ok let me close and let me know when you'll be up and I'll have that painting for you. Take care tell everybody I said hi.

Your friend Joe

This letter and the envelope containing it were both illustrated with salivating, pink, green-eyed werewolves, tongues hanging out through their fangs, droplets of saliva spewing from their mouths, claws out and knotty limbs curled in anticipation of the kill. I wish I could report that I wrote back immediately to calm Joe's escalating panic. But before I did, Joe wrote again:

5-9-85

Dear Mike,

Mike I got a problem and I hope you can help me on it before I go to court.

Ok I got a D.R. [prison disciplinary infraction] for yelling at my [corrections] counselor and whoever else thinks it ok to take stuff from me.

See ever since you didn't get the 60 cards and envolops the consalor keep telling me different stuff of why they cant fine them and the 2 pictures to that where yours and Jerrys.

So yesterday I got realy mad because they feel they or he's got me and I'm going to say it's ok.

Well I yelled for him to come talk to me because the day before that he wouldent talk to me a brush off. So yesterday after he did talk to me he said he gav them to McCrag package room man and for a hole week and 3 days couldn't fine him, that was bull. Then he said McCraig gave them to somebody else who they can't fine for that same week and 3 day nobody got the keys all lies. So I got wrote up I don't know what the D.R. saids yet but what could I have done when they take something from me. What I like you to do can you get hold of the superintendent and let him know what is going on so I know somebody will lisen to me and not keep giving me a brush off to one guy to the next. I have to much going on in my head and can't handle all the pre-ture. I don't want no problems more on my mine was 5-5-85 I got a visit they said new rules that Tom [Joe's brother] could only have a visit for 1 hour. My folks come all this ways to see us and only see Tom for am hour. The Guards I said the classifica-tion just come up with that. It bothered me to but I couldn't say nothing. Another thing is my consalor after they denied Stella on my list. I was going out to see Susan or you I forgot think Susan. Well he stopet me and said hay Joe Mr. Dan [Joe's corrections counselor] wanted to put her on the list but because she lied about her arest record. But he said to waite 2 weeks and do it again for her to tell the truth ok we waited 3 weeks and done it 5-6-85 Dan said they refused her because I get to many visits and that she lied. So I was mad then walket away didn't say nothing.

My consalor lied again used on excuss. I excepted it the first time talket to try and get her on but couldn't. Oh let it go buy but then they pull that on me all this stuff comming at me at one time I couldn't handle it. Thinking of Gram what he trying to do to me, not him as yet but what I feel.

I hope you understand this and can call the superintendent to exsplain to him my problem. ·

I need somebody to talk for me. I get to excited and I'm mad yet. I got to count on a consalor who is a lier. I was mad yes be-cause the day before he wouldn't come see me. He was on the wing most of the day to. I didn't and wont have them steel from me. I put lots of work into them 2 pictures and 60 cards and en-volopes. You all seen what I can do and the work. People can ask me not to take from me and laught behind my back. Can you see about getting that D.R. scoutch.

Your friend Joe

Finally, more than a day late and much more than a dollar short, I wrote:

May 10, 1985

Dear Joe,

Sorry for not writing sooner, but I've been out with a cold. Thanks for the card and letter, but I was a little concerned that you were down.

I want to stress that June 12 is only the day after which Graham *might* sign a warrant. You really do have a strong clemency argument, and by the way it was made stronger by the opinion yesterday in Ted Bundy's case (dealing with hypnotism); we'll be filing something with the Governor on this. We're also preparing papers to file in state court; this is another way to ward off a warrant.

Even if he does sign a warrant, we'll get a stay. No first-time warrant in Florida has been carried out. I have no intention of permitting you to be the first.

I know that none of this helps much. The ordeal experienced by the defendants and their families, friends and loved ones is one of the worst barbarities of this inhuman process we call a criminal justice system. It must be doubly brutal on someone who is going through it for a crime they did not commit. All I can tell you is that there are people out here who care very deeply about you and who will leave no stone unturned in seeking justice in your case.

Thank you again for the painting—you're right, next time bring it out yourself. Take care, Joe. And stay in touch.

Sincerely,
Michael A. Mello
Assistant Public Defender

Just when our ninety-day grace period was nearing its end, I was able to write to Joe with good news from the least likely source. In Ted Bundy's case, the Florida Supreme Court had ruled that hypnotically influenced testimony would be per se inadmissible in Florida criminal trials. But this new rule wouldn't be applied retroactively to trials— like Joe's—that occurred prior to the *Bundy* ruling. In cases like Joe's, the court would examine hypnosis on a case-by-case basis. The court's retroactivity ruling was such an arid technicality that I couldn't believe the justices would let Joe's capital murder conviction stand. All the reliability problems with hypnosis identified in *Bundy* had been present in spades in Joe's case. The state's star witness didn't even concoct his story until after at least two sessions with a police hypnotist.

When Joe wrote back, on May 18, the salivating pink werewolves had been replaced by placid white ducks strolling along green pasture-land, with intertwined strands of ivy held in place by two bluebirds and two bumblebees, spelling out the legend, "Friendship, Love and Truth." Joe wrote:

> Hi Everybody,
>
> Just wanted you to know Mike that I got your 2 letters today. All sounds good to me.
>
> Well Susan explained to me more and I love all of you people. Susan after you talked to me I seen a shrink doctor. They said Tallahassee told them to run a report on me. So I had to answer a few questions.
>
> OK now did I do right I hope so I don't want to cause no stink.
>
> Let's see well I'll have some cards for you Susan and I got 90 days I can relax. Can't really relax but I sure hope they see I'm not guilty.
>
> I will close got quite a few letters in the head right now to write. Susan your good people. I'm going to write Ed too.
>
> Your friend, Joe

I think I conveyed my naive enthusiasm to Joe. On May 20 he wrote back:

> Dear Mike,
>
> Hi buddy, I seen Susan Monday and went straight to D.R. court. I got 30 days.
>
> I still haven't got the 2 pictures back or the 60 cards or 60 stamps. But what can I say they got me. I hear I don't have to do the whole 30 days so that is ok.
>
> I got too mad about it anyway. I should of just let them take my stuff.
>
> Well Mike in your letter I can't remember all you said but you thank me for the pictures. What pictures you talking about?
>
> And you was saying something about Bundy's case a new rul-ing. They got all my stuff so I'll read it when I see it.
>
> I got to get myself together. I get so much stuff on my mind I

blow up when something goes wrong. But I can handle it hope they could. . . .

I got another coloring book for you no marks on it. I'll let you get that one. The kid can have the other one to mess with. You know how the rug rats are they enjoy tearing stuff up. Kids are great, ain't they. They can do a bunch of funny stuff just watching them.

OK, I'm going to write Mr. Dan a nice letter. The 12th of May. He let Stella come up and visit me. Mike I felt so good it was nice of him to do that. He gave me the 30 days the next day but he didn't and still don't know the whole story about my 60 cards and 60 envelopes and pictures that were for you that are still missing.

Hi Mike, hay I think it's straighten out about what happened with the envelopes and cards. They gave the package from you to my brother by mistake. Because they brought the one for him back again. So ya I'm still on D.C. don't know how much longer but what the counselor said less than 30 days. So I won't be painting or drawing till I get off they got all my stuff. I read the clemency paper that Ed wrote up. I just realize to that is what you meant I think. I wanted to say something else about that. I don't think that I read that right before. Anyway I wanted to say Tony's mom was never raped, she was more than willing to have a relationship. She went down on Tony to what she told me. And about any crimes I done on the street, ya, I wasn't no angel. I was only into marijuana. I use to like to smoke. But other crime no I don't rob people or places. I'm not into that stuff. I just didn't want people to bother me or my friends. Let's see oh ya I wanted to ask, hope I ain't a bother but did that rape charge ever get filed. I read in the newspaper the guy next store let me see of Stano was denied, no that the Florida court's denied to hear his case. He is an ass hole.

Hay I wanted to tell you something real great that happened to me. Ya for a change well last Sunday the day before I went to court on that D.R. well they called Stella that Friday afternoon and told her they'll let her come up to see me that weekend. So she was up Sunday for the whole day. I got so ok. So I'll close you take care and tell everybody I said hello.

Sincerely, Joe

No ducks or bluebirds or bumblebees. Not even any werewolves. No artwork at all, just ballpoint pen handwriting on yellow legal paper.

The last week of May, I took off for San Francisco, to attend the American Booksellers Association meeting (the other ABA, the fun ABA). Larkin and I wandered around Berkeley while Ruthann attended a conference. On May 30, three days before we were to head back to West Palm Beach, Craig Barnard called to tell me that Marvin Francois had been executed that morning at Florida State Prison.

Joe Spaziano's ninety-day grace period officially ended on Tuesday, June 11. On the day before, Barnard got an off-the-record extension of the off-the-record grace period. I immediately wrote Joe:

June 10, 1985
Dear Joe,

It was great to get your card. I just got back from visiting Ed Kirkland in Orlando, and I've been working on your case.

The word from the Governor's office is that we're safe on warrants at least until the end of July. That should give us time to get papers filed in state court. Those papers are what I'm working on now; you're right that Ted Bundy's case should help us, but the Florida Supreme Court played many games in Bundy's case so I'm not really sure. As soon as I get a working draft of what I want to file in your case, I'll send a copy up to you.

There is a law student from New York, working here for the summer, who has been putting in great time and effort on your case. Would it be OK if I bring him up to meet you, the next time I'm in your neighborhood? I know he'd really like to meet you.

I hope to see you soon, Joe. I can hardly wait to see the pictures. Take care and stay in touch.

Sincerely,
Michael Mello
Assistant Public Defender

Joe wrote back the day he received my June 10 letter:

June 13, 1985
Dear Mike

Hi Mike I just got your letter.

Let me know when you'll be up give me a week in advance so I can have the picture out there ok.

Sure I'll meet that law student. But really don't want no new people working on my case. I don't know no more. So many people and ant gone no place in court don't know what is going to happen.

Well I'll close till I see you. Make sure you let me know in time to let me know when you come ok tell everybody I said hay.

Sincerely, Joe

Now that the warrant heat was off of Joe, I felt almost giddy. I wrote to Joe with a special request:

Dear Joe,

Could you do me a favor if you get the chance? Garry Trudeau, who does the comic strip *Doonesbury,* is doing a series on Palm Beach, which is where I live. One frame of the strip is especially good. Is there any way you could do a painting or sketch of this frame, which I enclose? I would insist on paying you for this.

Take care, Joe, and stay in touch. See you soon.

Sincerely,
Michael A. Mello
Assistant Public Defender

Joe's June 28 reply was decorated with Florida summer themes: a purple sailboat under a smiling yellow sun, birds chirping tunes, and Snoopy the magician pulling a dazed Woodstock out of a blue hat on a pink table. The card said:

Hi Mike,

I just got your letter and made me feel extra good Mike.

I thought you'll like Uncle Sam.

OK now some good news I'll wait to I see you in person to give it to you. But to let you know I just got a copy of my coloring book, not the one Susan was doing another one. Anyway I like your kid to have it. OK pal, if you like when Susan come back I'll let her get it to give to you? But I rather give it to you in person.

OK I'll close hope it all goes good at clemency, myself I haven't got no play on nothing. But maybe this time I hope.

Tell everybody I said hello and you're going to love this coloring book. I think a lot of you all and the help you've giving me. Thank you all and I love you.

Sincerely, Joe

Along with this card Joe had written a letter:

Hi Mike,

Well just got your 2 letters and glad you liked the painting.

Yes I can do that for you Mike but let me know what color the cops clothes are, ok? Does he have light blue shirt dark blue pants and light blue stripes? let me know ok? Might as well do it right. You said or a sketch if it's going to be in a frame I'll paint it but if it to use for show down Palm Beach I'll do a sketch. But no matter no problem. I can do it. I only need some stamps Mike, I need nothing else.

Well let me close you all take care.

Sincerely, Joe

By July 8, Joe wrote that the *Doonesbury* painting was finished:

Hi Mike,

I got your picture done. I'll give it to Susan or you when I see you. Here is something somebody gave me to let you look at. I don't understand it. OK. I wanted to ask what statement did Tony give when I got indicted on murder.

Sincerely, Joe

As it happened, I received the *Doonesbury* painting before I got Joe's July 8 letter. I wrote:

Dear Joe,

Thanks again for doing the *Doonesbury* frame. I think the Palm Beach cops wear light blue shirts and dark blue pants with a light blue stripe. Do you think a painting would look better, or a sketch? I just don't want to put you to too much trouble. In either case, I'll frame it right away. This, you see, will settle a small dispute between Ruthann and I: I want the painting in my office, and she likes it for the house. This way the "hear, see, speak no evil" painting can hang in one place, and the "local cops hassling outsiders" work can hang in the other.

But I insist on paying you, one way or another, for the "cop" work. This is because I *asked* you to do it. So it's like a commission, right? I'll be glad to pay in stamps, but I wouldn't feel right asking you to do it for nothing.

I am still drafting papers from the next round of litigation. As soon as Susan winds up some investigation she's doing and as soon as Ed Kirkland gets some papers in to me, we should be set. I have sent the transcripts of DiLisio's hypnotism session to a Professor in San Francisco named Bernard Diamond, who is an expert in hypnosis. We also need his report because we'll be ready to file in court.

Take care, Joe. Mike Lehman, Susan, Craig and Dick all say "hi."

See you soon.

Sincerely,
Mike Mello

On July 10, Joe replied:

Hi Mike,

I just got them stamps from you. Can't believe it sure is a big help. But I goofed. This weekend that just past I had you painting sent out. But it only was on a 9×12 or something like that. I should of done it on a 16×20. The colors are bout right and ask some guys what cops dress like in Palm Beach. Thanks for the stamps. I only was short them stamps now I'm back in shops. I got a couple of these other stamps left. I hate to use these. They look slick. I hope something good comes up. On that stuff you filing. I'm very nervous. What can I say. Mike I worry about everything. OK let me close. You take care. Tell Ruthann I'll get her or you a painting, ok.

Sincerely, Joe

On July 15, Joe mailed me a card captioned "Thinking of you." The main character reminded me of Herblock's 1950s cartoons of the bomb, but Joe's sketch was actually of a joint, with the legend "Keep on tokin'." He wrote:

Hi Mike,

Hay buddy I come up with a good idea. I feel bad that I done that 9×14 or whatever it was. I didn't realize it was going in your frame and you was going to send that many stamps. So I come up with a good idea ok. I'll send or let Susan pick up 8 painting real slick ones everybody in the office can get a painting for 10.00 and worth every cent 12×20. It'll help me and keep everybody happy. Let me know if ok because I got them already. If they can't go you can send them to an address of mine. But they'll go I know. Mike you will love these. Just let me know the day Susan can pick them up and I'll have them for her.

I just ordered more supplies so many people want some stuff done. I love it. Maybe if I get this cap off me I can work for Disney World. Be neat wouldn't it. I got so many good ideas, Mike.

I still feel bad about that other painting. Did you get it? OK, catch you later, Mike.

Sincerely, Joe

Then I did it again. I got so absorbed with writing Joe's postconviction papers that I fell out of touch with him. Then I spent a week visiting my parents in northern Virginia. While I was there, Joe wrote:

July 22, 1985

Hay buddy tell me you mad at me. I didn't do that painting right? Or maybe you didn't get it let me know ok I had that painting sent to you before I got the 50 stamps.

But I'll make it up. Have you'es been getting my letters Mike? Did you get the picture. Let me know if I done something wrong I don't like the cold shoulders.

I don't need a lawyer of mine mad at me. I done nothing wrong.

Susan comes up here every week to see a certain nigar every week and don't call me out but it's ok I don't want to see her anyway. She's in a different world then me.

Ok I'll close let me know something ok.

Sincerely, Joe

P.S. Why people get mad at me I don't know it ant wright I didn't do nothing or mess with anybody.

Hay Mike I got 8 real slick painting I'll sent to you all to pick out you a painting you get one on the house if you didn't get that other one. Just took a shower. Mike I don't want my friends mad at me. If it is because of my art I'll give it up as much as I don't want you.

I get so disapointed in what is going on.

I like to hear from you.

Sincerely, Your friend Joe

Even when I'd returned to Florida I didn't write. I don't know why. I don't know if there was any reason. Joe wrote:

July 29, 1985
Hi Mike,

One more letter and this will be it you got me feeling like an ass hole. I don't want a friend to feel I done something wrong. But hay if that how you feel ok with me. Wish I knew what I done wrong. Don't fuck with my head I got enought problem.

Sincerely, Joe

On July 25, I wrote:

July 25, 1985
Dear Joe,

Sorry I haven't written, but I was out of town (in Virginia and D.C.) at a conference of death penalty lawyers. Then I took a week off to visit my parents and some old friends from school.

But what a wonderful surprise to come back to: your marvelous rendition of *Doonesbury*. It's a great piece of work, Joe. I'll ask the other people here (Craig, Dick and others) if they want one too; thank you for the kind offer. I'm getting mine framed, though I have not yet decided whether to hang it here or in my study at home.

Anyway, please don't think I was mad at you or snubbing you, Joe. You're my friend, and I value that friendship very much. I could never be mad at you.

Take care and stay well, Joe. Hope to see you soon.

Sincerely,
Michael A. Mello
Assistant Public Defender

Joe wrote back:

Dear Mike:

Hi buddy, sure glad to hear from you Mike. I got this neat painting in my cell for you. You're going to love it for sure.

But let me know about when you'll be here so I can have it out there for you.

Ya I don't know if it is good or not how slow they are. Sure hope they do something for me and see I'm telling the truth. Ok let my folks and Stella know but please don't forget about me. I'll send my mom the letter.

Oh ya I paint and do card and envelopes every day all day. Get a little burnt out at times, thing of my daughter but she is ok now. Linda bought a new house on the lake or ocean, I'm not sure, and Marynoel is doing ok. Did Lee [Currie, my secretary] ever get that painting of the unicorn. Nobody let me know?

Ya Stella should be up in a week or so.

OK I'll close and glad you're still with me. I haven't heard from you in so long.

Your friend, Joe

This card was illustrated with a drawing of President Ronald Reagan, scrawny, veined neck popping out of his too-large suit and too-bright green tie, ears the size of Chevy doors, and a rainbow descending into his jet-black pompadour. For some reason, Joe's Reagan looked like a stereotype gay, as in homosexual gay; it was something about the hooded blue eyes or the oversized pink lips of the same hue as the aforementioned rainbow. Reagan as Rorschach blot?

Joe wrote again on July 30:

Hi Mike,

Sure was worried buddy. I was, thought you was mad, but I'm not the best thinker in the world.

At less you got the Doonesbury painting and didn't know.

Hay Mike I got some real slick painting a good price for the people there then all of us can be happy. $10.00 a picture isn't bad 16×20 I can send you 8 or 10 you can pick out what you want and send the rest to an address I send. If you want Susan to pick them up I'll have them out there just let me know when. But looks like you might be up so let me know ok.

Sorry I thought you was mad ok.

Sincerely, Joe

To which I wrote on July 31:

Dear Joe,

Your last couple of letters sound like you're mad at me. I think those letters were written before you received my letter of July 25, a copy of which I enclose. Are we OK now? I PROMISE I'm not mad at you. Cool?

I also enclose a draft of legal papers I plan to file this month. This isn't in final form, but it's generally what I think it will look like.

Take care and stay well, Joe. And remember that I care about you very much and that I am fighting, and will continue to fight, for you.

Sincerely,
Michael Mello
Assistant Public Defender

And then:

August 4, 1985
Mike, ☺

I just got the draft whatever☺.

Hay no not at all am I mad at you no, no. I thought you was mad at me so I got mad for you getting mad☺. Hay pel I'm not the best thinker in the world☺.

Hay Mike for sure we are friends.

Ya Mike I worry a hole lot trying to get things togeather so I can have something for my kid moving right along☺.

I read some of what is wrote but got lost on some stuff will go back to reread because I forgot what I mosely read in the beginning☺. No problem but☺

Wish I had people like you for friends on the street. I belive in you. You ended up a pretty nice guy. You like my Art which I like☺. I'm going to have some Art stuff in a show in VA in Sept. and again in Oct or Nov not sure yet of that day. You know I got that lady friend of mine in VA. She is stone country lady real nice person. Next time your up that way if you like I'll let you meet her. She is a great artice to sure is here is a picture of one of my paintings on her wall in the kitchen of her home but send it back it is the only one I got. ok.

Ok I'll close thank you Mike. I feel like your going to get me out of this. I know I get depresset but I love you all.

Your friend, Joe

August 9, 1985
Dear Joe,

Many thanks for your recent card, with the enclosed photo (which you asked me to return). I very much enjoyed the photo, and the next time I'm in that part of Virginia I must look up your friend. She obviously cares about you very much.

Things are very hectic here right now, Joe. We represent Bill Harvard. So if I'm slow in writing to you, that's why. It's not that I'm not thinking of you.

Take care, Joe. And stay in touch.

Sincerely,
Michael A. Mello
Assistant Public Defender

August 18, 1985
Hi Mike,

Ya Pel don't pay attention to me when I lose myself in thoughts. I got down on everybody last month, this month back to me ☺.

I got where I think wrong ☺.

I'm back into working out found out how weak I was getting no exercise just bulling around, so now I work out get myself feeling better ☺.

I'll be seeing Mary Nel this weekend or next sure can't waite ☺.

Well I know you'es are pretty bussey so I'll take off. Tell everybody I said hello.

Sincerely, Joe

August 19, 1985
Hi Mike,

Been lying up thinking what is going on.
So what you's been up to.

Well next week we will see what Gov. does. Hope some of them up there can see it's all lies.

I've been doing cards and a feau paintings but slowed up quite a bit. doing lots of thinking ☺. Ya I think ☺.

Mike I don't get to upset at time ☺. But I get treated pretty good here. I got carred away because of the cards and pictures that where missing but I got 2 for you now. When I see one of you I'll get it out there. can't help myself for blowing up so easy now. Lots of preture on me.

A couple weeks ago I had a call out to see Jerry and he never showed.

About Bundys case some of the guys where telling me it will help my case quite abit is that true.

Well I'll close pel and still got a picture for you and a coloring book ☺. I a nut but love it ☺.

Get over these bad times. I'll be ok again.

Sincerely, Joe

On August 25, Joe wrote:

Hi Mike,

Hay pal my head is really moving pal.

I'm so mix up can't think right.

Let's see now I'm just going to mail these 2 paintings to you personal ok. I got them packaged already and just waiting for the man to pick them up. So you'll probably get them this week. Do me a favor on 10 of that 30 you get can you send me stamps ok. I need stamps again bad.

Mike I try my best to see the wrong way society said I live in the club and stuff. But Mike I can't believe how some people can be.

Joe

Sept. 9

Hi Mike,

I just got your letter and got the 2 already done. I was getting ready to mail them to Orlando but I took these 2 out. The one with Garfield has got the Pink Panther and him roler skating with lots of flowers around the picture. They'll love it. Ok. Susan can pick it up if you can tell her it's out there and to call me out to talk a little bit. I want to tell her something, ok. Mike let me know when you get these and what you think.

Sincerely your friend, Joe

I didn't write back. On September 21, Joe sent me a card with a note:

Hi Mike,

Hay, I don't know why you won't answer my letter Mike but I sent the 2 paintings that you said somebody wanted to buy in the office. What is going on.

Joe

The illustrations on the other card and its envelope reflected Joe's anxiety, although I probably didn't pick up on them at the time. The envelope had a woman (the mom from the *Family Circus* cartoon strip?) staring perplexed and gape-jawed at her fishing pole and its empty, wormless, fishless hook. The caption of the card art read, "jitterbuggs," and the card showed several bumblebees doing the jitterbug. Joe also included this:

All week long, at school, Jitterbugg would plan and plan for Saturday night. Fridays were very special. He would whirl his way to school, dance through his classes and then tango down Bugg Street to get home. School work was always a snap on Friday night, because tomorrow would be Saturday and Saturday night was Jitterbugg's night to get down and boogie.

It was clear I needed to visit Joe, and on September 24 I did. I told him then that I had decided to accept a job with the newly created CCR, which would open its doors on October 1. I told Joe that I would be taking his case with me to CCR, that I'd still be his lawyer ("until the last dog dies"), and that at CCR his case would receive the benefit of the ferocious brilliance of Mark Olive and Scharlette Holdman. My journal records it was a "very pleasant visit with Joe," but another of my clients, Nollie Lee Martin, had just been placed on suicide watch.

The same day as our visit, Joe wrote:

September 24, 1985
Hi Mike,

Hay Pel real glad to see you today. But hay Mike I was in another world ☺ really tell you the truth I had write down stuff but couldn't bring it out but I had most of it to the point☺.

Hay you ok Mike next time I'll have cigaretts. I don't think to good with out a smoke ☺. I think if I can't smoke I'll lose my hair ☺. Ok Mike, hay I'm going to write Mary Nel and tell her about getting hold of you in case she's got problems.

I'll close thank you all.

Sincerely, Your friend, Joe

The day after our visit, Joe wrote again:

September 25, 1985
Hi Mike,

Just got your letter, and will send Mary Noel the numbers.

OK Pel was good seeing you to but I was floating. Had some cards and stuff to bring out and I couldn't, I go into a fog at stupit stuff we can't do, but I know this is their way, but very stupit.

I sent Lee the permite, I put it in your name at the time I sent it out I didn't have her name. But it's no problem. Hope to meet her some time.

Oh Mike I know what else I had to say I never heard Ed's tape from clemicie. But no problem.

I'll close and hope to see you again some tiem in the future. Got a hell of a tooth ake right now ☺.

Tell everybody I said hello.

Sincerely,
Your friend, Joe

During all this time, our fact reinvestigation of Joe's case was chugging along. The more we learned about the facts and circumstances leading up to Joe's capital murder trial, the more Joe looked like the victim of a law enforcement community utterly determined to nail him because they were determined to destroy the Outlaws motorcycle brotherhood.

3

Lawyers for the Dead

A judge yesterday reprimanded a lawyer for claiming that a prosecutor "wants to kill my client."

"Judge Scolds Lawyer for His Choice of Words,"
Rochester Democrat and Chronicle, *January 31, 1997*

In 1985, the Florida State Legislature, governor, and attorney general endorsed the creation of the Office of Capital Collateral Representative, a new statewide public defender office to represent everyone on Florida's death row who didn't have a lawyer. Virtually everyone on Florida's death row was a candidate. The legislature, governor, and attorney general were all passionately in favor of capital punishment and against the postconviction judicial process that can result in delays of a decade or more between the imposition and execution of death sentences. The idea was that if all condemned prisoners were given lawyers, the chaotic and time-consuming system of postconviction appeals would become more routinized and efficient, and thus delays between sentencing and execution would be reduced.

From the mid-1970s until the creation of CCR in October 1985, the only institutionalized mechanism for locating pro bono lawyers for Florida death row inmates was a small, nonprofit community organization called the Florida Clearinghouse on Criminal Justice. The Clearinghouse, which received no government funds and relied for financial support on contributions from private citizens, religious groups, and foundations, consisted of a director, Scharlette Holdman, and a one- or two-person staff. Neither Holdman nor any of her staff were attorneys.

The primary responsibility of the Clearinghouse was to attempt to recruit and assist volunteer counsel for condemned inmates whose convictions and sentences had been affirmed by the Florida Supreme Court. Although Holdman described the nature of the recruitment work as "pretty informal," David Von Drehle describes it this way in his book *Among the Lowest of the Dead*:

> All day, every day, Holdman sat at her telephone in her shabby office at the FOG Building, chain-smoking Benson and Hedges cigarettes with one hand and dialing with the other. Quite a sight she was: Hair frizzed, feet bare, body rocking in a cheap swivel chair, face lost in a cloud of smoke. She called the heads of local bar associations and asked for recommendations. She called managing partners at big law firms and inquired about their pro bono programs. She got rosters of various liberal organizations and cross-indexed them with the state legal directory, targeting potentially friendly lawyers for calls. She haunted law conferences, scouting for likely prospects. Holdman spent so much time on the telephone in search of lawyers that one Christmas her secretary gave her a cushion for the receiver to prevent cauliflower ear.

In Florida, as I've mentioned, an execution date is set by the governor's signing of a death warrant. During the 1980s, the number of death warrants signed increased dramatically at the same time the pool of available volunteer counsel decreased. Between 1979 (when Florida inmate John Spenkellink became the first nonconsensual execution—that is, an execution for which the condemned prisoner did not volunteer—in the modern era of capital punishment) and December 1983, the Florida governor signed sixty-five warrants. Fifty-one (78 percent) of those cases required volunteer counsel. Six warrants were issued in 1979; twenty were issued in 1983. Of the six inmates scheduled for execution in 1979, five (83 percent) were continuously represented by volunteer counsel; all six had counsel at the time their warrants were signed. By 1982, when twenty-three warrants were signed, fifteen (65 percent) were without counsel at the time their warrants were signed.

During the summer of 1985, after CCR had been created but before the new agency opened its doors on October 1, I applied for a job there. As very few Florida attorneys with real capital appellate experience wanted to work at CCR, I guess I looked attractive. After two years working with Craig Barnard and Richard Greene in Dick Jorandby's West Palm Beach Public Defender's Office, at least I had some experience. And Craig Barnard was one of the best teachers in Florida or anywhere else. CCR offered me a job as a senior assistant, at a salary of thirty thousand dollars per year.

There was a catch, though. In 1983 I had committed to work for Dick Jorandby and Craig Barnard for three years. When I asked Dick and Craig to let me leave a year early to work at CCR, they would have been well within their rights to hold me to my three-year contract. After all, they'd invested two years in training me; now, just when they were beginning to see some return on their investment, I was asking to abandon ship. West Palm Beach had its own capital clients to consider. By summer 1985 I was one-half of the full-time capital appeals division.

In the end, Dick and Craig left the decision up to me. I decided to go to CCR—decided to go for a range of reasons, some of which I'm proud and others of which I'm not so proud (for example, I *enjoyed* the adrenaline rush of litigating cases under death warrant). From the day CCR opened its doors, the agency became the front lines—in the Western Front, World War I sense—and it was the front not only in Florida but nationally as well. Capital punishment states from Texas to California to Pennsylvania were watching Florida's experiment in creating a state agency to provide legal aid to death row. CCR was the first entity of its kind in a state serious about carrying out executions.

CCR thus had no models; we would be making it up as we went along. Actually, that was part of the agency's attractiveness to me in the summer of 1985. Until CCR became operational in October 1985, the West Palm Beach Public Defender's Office had been the front lines, the epicenter of the newest and most sophisticated litigation strategies and constitutional theories. Thereafter, that center of gravity shifted to CCR in Tallahassee. I went to CCR because, to paraphrase Willie Sutton, that's where the cases were. CCR was where the action would be, and I didn't want to miss any of it. I was twenty-eight years old when I started working at CCR.

At West Palm Beach, my two supervisors and I had a dozen cases. I was lead counsel in three—the cases of Joe Spaziano, Butch Sireci, and Nollie Lee Martin. At Craig Barnard's suggestion, I took these three cases with me when I relocated to CCR in Tallahassee. Plus, I became responsible for thirty or so other capital cases. I had been practicing law for two years.

On September 30, I packed all my stuff into my blue 1972 VW Beetle (nicknamed Bluebird by my father). My significant other and son would remain in South Florida until Ruthann could find a legal aid or legal teaching job in Tallahassee. If I had any real foreboding about the legal and political hurricane I was driving into, speeding up I-95 with the windows open and rock and roll blasting from the boom box on the seat beside me, I don't really remember it today.

As I drove, I hear a radio news report that Governor Bob Graham had signed twenty-eight-day death warrants on two men whose names I didn't recognize at all. Both would be CCR clients. One of them was Robert Preston, my brand-new client. Two weeks later, the governor signed two new warrants on two other CCR clients. Two weeks after that, two more warrants. And that became the pattern. At any given time—except over the Christmas holiday and during the three weeks in August when the Florida Supreme Court justices took their summer vacation—four CCR clients would be under death warrant.

Everyone at CCR in those days worked extraordinarily long hours and shared a deep commitment to the office's mission. But what made the office work in the early years was the presence of two certifiable geniuses: Scharlette Holdman and Mark Olive. Precision and soul—that's what they had: precision and soul.

Olive and Holdman made the CCR of the mid-1980s a dangerous law firm; dangerous to the powerful, the dishonest, and the deceitful—dangerous to the prosecutorial state that had created CCR and that paid our salaries. It's hard to find the words to describe what made CCR dangerous, but I do know that it had little to do with levels of funding or resources; we were a hungry army. Perhaps it was a matter of attitude. What Olive and Holdman brought to CCR, in addition to skills and experience, was a fearless will. I asked Olive once what it was that stopped executions from occurring. He told me that it wasn't good facts (although those helped), it wasn't good law (although that helped), it wasn't even having an innocent client (which didn't help at all, it just made the state actors more determined not to admit they had made a mistake). What stopped executions was will: an iron determination that *this killing will not happen.*

Sometimes stopping an execution requires taking risks, and taking risks requires courage—what Plato defined as wise endurance. Taking *wise* risks isn't being reckless; it's the difference between Oskar Schindler and Evel Knievel. For a deathwork law firm, living safely is dangerous—dangerous and deadly to its clients.

The Florida State Legislature set the size of the CCR staff and its budget with the expectation that the office would handle about 30 cases in its first year of operation. Instead, it handled about 150 cases. Even though CCR attorneys were routinely working sixty- to ninety-hour weeks, and some private attorneys remained available as volunteers, CCR was having trouble keeping up with the increase in Florida's death row population. CCR's crushing caseload raised serious ethical dilemmas—dilemmas that have led courts and commentators to find that staggering caseloads can result in ineffective representation.

Despite the caseload, CCR did not fulfill Attorney General Smith's expectations and speed up the execution process, at least in its early years. In its first year and a half of existence, only three executions occurred in Florida. CCR or CCR-assisted volunteer counsel won retrials or resentencings in several cases. Further, stays of execution were usually obtained in state court far earlier in the postconviction process than had been true previously. Ironically, once CCR had become operational and had succeeded in preventing a string of executions, some legislators complained that CCR had violated the legislative intent behind its creation.

William Faulkner, in *Intruder in the Dust,* says that it's always within the reach of every southern boy to imagine that it is 1:00 P.M. on July 3, 1863, in Gettysburg, and the guns are laid, the troops are lined up, the flags are already out of their cases and ready to be unfurled—but it hasn't happened yet. He can go back to the moment before the war was irretrievably lost, and he can always have that moment for himself. Every southern boy can imagine that he is a soldier in Robert E. Lee's army on the morning of the third day of Gettysburg—before Pickett's charge, before the war was lost, when, after Fredericksburg and Chickamauga and the Seven Days, and even after Antietam, it was possible to *imagine* southern victory, notwithstanding the impossible odds and the inexorable math of manpower and combined industrial and economic firepower.

When I began doing deathwork in summer 1983, there had been only one Florida execution in seventeen years, that of John Spenkellink. Of course, I knew the odds; I'd done the math—we all had. Still, we hadn't lost yet. It was still possible, for me, at least, to imagine winning the war for judicial abolition of capital punishment as a legal system.

The other side had the resources and the power those resources could buy. But there are ways a tiny army can defeat a large army— ways, indeed, to use the larger army's strengths against it. Lee and Jackson, Mosby and Stuart, Longstreet and Forrest had taught that lesson all across the Virginia of my childhood. And our side had the best generals: Anthony Amsterdam, Craig Barnard, Mark Olive, Scharlette Holdman. I thought a lot about that passage from Faulkner during the early days of CCR. We had that same sense of fragile optimism.

Given the amount of work and soul and emotional energy that capital postconviction litigation requires, CCR's caseload was staggering. I have never worked so hard in my life, and I never will again. The office's lawyers, support staff, and investigators routinely worked eighty-hour weeks and fifteen-hour days, and longer hours were required in (frequent) crises. During an especially frenetic five weeks in 1986, one CCR lawyer seldom left the office except to shower. Three people represented by CCR were put to death during this period: Daniel Thomas (executed April 15, 1986), David Funchess (executed April 22, 1986), and Ronald Straight (executed May 20, 1986). Maniacal commitment to the clients, and not nearly enough time in the day or night to fulfill that commitment, was the essence of the job. If this description gives you the feeling that working at CCR was like being in a madhouse, it is the right feeling. It was like living a M*A*S*H script, or maybe M*A*S*H meets L.A. Law in an ER.

Extensive posttrial reinvestigation must be undertaken in every capital postconviction case. At the time CCR commenced operations on October 1, 1985, approximately two hundred people lived on Florida's death row. About half of these had not reached the state postconviction litigation stage, and therefore they were not yet represented by CCR. Of the approximately one hundred cases that were in the postconviction stages of litigation, thirty or so inmates were represented by volunteer, pro bono counsel. CCR was not directly responsible for those prisoners, although the agency did what it could to help the pro bono attorneys. That left about seventy inmates whose cases were divided among three comparatively experienced and several less experienced CCR lawyers.

At any given time, execution dates were scheduled for two to four of these prisoners, triggered by the governor's signing of death warrants. Unless a stay is obtained prior to a specified execution date, the subject of the warrant will be put to death, even though his conviction may rest upon legal or factual error of constitutional magnitude.

On November 4, 1985, it was Joe Spaziano's turn. His execution was scheduled for 7:00 A.M. December 3. When his death warrant was signed, I had been working at CCR for slightly more than four weeks.

Joe's black-bordered death warrant was accompanied by a press release from the governor's office.

FOR IMMEDIATE RELEASE: CONTACT: Art Wiedinger
November 4, 1985   Assistant General Counsel
Jill Chamberlin, Press Secretary

GRAHAM SIGNS TWO DEATH WARRANTS

TALLAHASSEE—Governor Bob Graham today signed death warrants in the cases of Joseph Robert Spaziano and David Walter Trodel. Spaziano's case was heard by Governor Graham and the Cabinet members, sitting as the Board of Executive Clemency, on March 13, 1985. Trodel's case was heard by the Board on September 12, 1985.

The Governor's Assistant General Counsel, speaking on behalf of the Governor, stated that the Governor has determined that there is no basis to alter the court-imposed sentence in either of these cases.

Pursuant to Section 922.11, Florida Statutes, Governor Graham has designated the executions for the week beginning noon, Wednesday, November 27, 1985 and ending noon, Wednesday, December 4, 1985. In accord with the same statute, Superintendent Richard L. Dugger has set the executions for commencement at 7:00 A.M., Tuesday, December 3, 1985.

At Florida State Prison, the airplane was the sound of danger and death. In the days before fax machines, when the governor signed a death warrant, the document was flown by single-engine plane to the prison so that it could be read to the man who had been selected by the governor to die. The prison would be locked down, and the prisoner named in the warrant would be escorted from death row to the assistant superintendent's office, where the warrant would be read to him. He would then be allowed to speak to a lawyer and family member by telephone, before being escorted to the deathwatch cells. When the inmates on the row heard the approaching airplane on warrant days, they knew the governor had made a selection. Stomachs clenched, the private betting began: Who would it be this time? That was the lore, anyway.

The death chamber at Florida State Prison is about the size of two living rooms in an average house; it is divided by a wall highlighted by three large windows and a door to the side. The walls are white, the floor is white linoleum, and the ceiling consists of the undistinguished white dropped tiles common to many state offices. On the observers' side of the windows, color is provided by brown folding metal chairs and pale-yellow wooden chairs with backs reminiscent of tulip profiles. There is a wall-mounted air conditioner.

On the other side of the windows, observers can see to the left a small room with a glassless slit in one wall. That's where the executioner throws the switch. The prisoner is brought in from a special holding cell through a curtain behind that cubicle. A gray metal box about five feet high stands against the far wall and serves as the backdrop for the room's main feature—the brown oak chair where capital sentences are carried out. It looks like a slightly oversized, regular wooden chair with arms, except for two vertical stakes at the top center of the chair's back. That is where the inmate's head rests.

The prisoner is brought in from the special holding cell and allowed to say any final words. Most are brief, resigned to their fate. The inmate is then strapped to the chair. An electrode is attached to his leg, and a metal hat with a second electrode is placed on his head, which has been shaved. A wet sponge is placed between the upper electrode and the inmate's head to help conduct the electricity and to offset the heat it generates. A leather shield covers the inmate's face.

A switch is thrown on the electrical box behind the chair, activating the electronics. The power for the chair is generated internally at the prison. The superintendent, who has been maintaining an open phone line with the governor's office, checks to make sure there is no last minute stay, and then nods to the executioner in his room. The executioner throws the final switch, sending the electrical charge through the inmate. There is a two-minute program for the execution, and the voltage and amperage vary. The maximum charge delivered is about two thousand volts at thirteen amps. The charge is usually turned off after thirty to forty-five seconds.

After the execution there is a period during which the attending physicians wait for a cessation of all body functions before declaring the inmate dead. It usually takes several minutes for the heart to stop beating and all digestive sounds to stop. The longest wait in recent memory was for Ted Bundy, who was not declared dead for ten or eleven minutes. The usual wait is four or five minutes.

Although the legal history may be important for a full understanding of the capital sentencing process in Florida, it perhaps obscures the banal bureaucratic mechanics of how a condemned person is put to death by that state. Dostoyevski, who as a young man had been condemned to die, wrote that "the chief and the worst pain is perhaps not inflicted by wounds, but by your certain knowledge that in an hour, in ten minutes, in half a minute, now, this moment your soul will fly out of your body, and that you will be a human being no longer, and that that's certain—the main thing is that it is *certain.*" Prisons, being bureaucracies, promulgate procedural protocols and guidelines for such things (deliciously skewered by John Grisham's Colonel Nugent character in *The Chamber*; one strength of *The Chamber* is its portrayal of Nugent as the exception among death squad personnel—too often prison guards are portrayed in cartoonish terms). The protocol is drained of emotion and humanity for a reason, according to Wayne Scott, a chip off the Texas prison system. Father Mike Keppler, a former Episcopal prison chaplain who has counseled members of the death chamber staff, has been quoted as explaining: "We adhere to the schedule and we put all our focus on the schedule and not what's actually happening. Therefore, we don't have to come to grips with what's actually happening. They do, and that's when they get to talk to a chaplain, not all of them, but some of them do. And it's as if they were on a stage and the emphasis is on correct performance, not carrying out the death of an individual."

In Florida, the protocols include a section titled "Execution Guidelines for Week of Active Death Warrant." The protocols were first issued on May 1, 1979, and were revised in 1983 by the superintendent of

Florida State Prison. They are deemed "confidential" by the prison; they were generously provided to me by Michael Radelet. This singular historical document, which is reproduced in full as the appendix to this book, possesses an unsettling quality reminiscent of Hannah Arendt's phrase, which originated in a quite different context, "the banality of evil." Arendt, the political historical and social philosopher who covered the Jerusalem trial of Nazi Adolf Eichmann for the *New Yorker,* found Eichmann terrifyingly normal, monstrous precisely because he was an ordinary man, a civil servant doing his job, capable of mass murder. Execution detail is just part of the job. Note the words of Texas prosecutor John Holmes Jr.: "The best way to repeal bad law is to enforce it. I take no great pride in the fact that we are No. 1 in death penalty cases. I don't like being called a killer. But I have a job to do. Everyone who got death out of Harris [County] has gotten it from a jury." The photograph accompanying this quotation in a Texas newspaper article is of a doe-eyed gentleman wearing a flower in his suit lapel and sporting an impressive handlebar mustache and what appears to be an unlit meerschaum pipe: a picture of normality itself.

The reading of the death warrant to the prisoner starts a period officially designated as the first phase of "deathwatch," in which the prisoner is moved to a cell that is closer to the electric chair and isolated from other inmates. Most of his possessions are taken away, his visitations are limited, and a guard constantly sits outside his cell, ready to intervene should the prisoner attempt suicide. The second phase of deathwatch begins five days before the scheduled date of the execution. During this time, the "execution squad" is identified, the electrical equipment to be used in the execution is tested, and the condemned person specifies the disposition of his property and makes funeral arrangements. On the day before the execution date, the prison chef takes the inmate's order for his last meal and the inmate is measured for his funeral suit. By this time, the prison guard stationed outside the inmate's cell must record what the condemned is doing every fifteen minutes.

The prisoner is usually allowed a final "contact visit" at about midnight on the night before the planned 7:00 A.M. execution. At 4:30 A.M. the prisoner is served the last meal, which must be eaten with a spoon from a paper plate. By 5:30, the twelve official witnesses to the execution are assembled at the main prison gate, and at 5:50 the twelve media witnesses are gathered; all of the witnesses are then escorted to the witness room of the execution chamber. The electric chair itself is remarkably close to the front row of witness chairs; my experience is that one cannot appreciate the claustrophobic proximity caused by these spatial relationships without actually sitting in that electric chair. Until a few years ago, by informal custom the prison superintendent would have a drink of Wild Turkey bourbon with the condemned in his cell; Michael Radelet told me that "the Wild Turkey was available only to [Robert] Sullivan and [Anthony] Antone," but in any event public outcry was so great when the practice became known that it was discontinued. At about 6:00 A.M., "the condemned inmate has his head and right calf shaved (the better to conduct electricity), takes a shower under the supervision of a high-ranking prison official, and is dressed in his new burial clothes. . . . At 6:50 'conducting gel' is applied to the person's head and leg. The superintendent reads the death warrant to the condemned a final time."

At 6:56 A.M., the condemned inmate is escorted to the death chamber by the prison superintendent and two other prison officials. After being strapped into the electric chair, the condemned is permitted to make a last statement at 7:00 A.M. One execution witness, a journalist for a Florida newspaper, has given this account of the next few minutes:

> The electrician places the sponge and cap on the inmate's head. The assistant superintendent engages the circuit breaker. The electrician activates the panel, the superintendent signals the executioner to throw the switch, and the "automatic cycle will begin." . . . Once the automatic cycle has run its course, the superintendent invites the doctor to conduct the examination. If all has gone well, the condemned is pronounced dead and the time recorded. . . . By custom, someone in attendance waves a white cloth just outside the prison to signal the crowd assembled in a field across from it—reporters, death penalty opponents and proponents, and any others—that the deed is done.

As soon as the prisoner is pronounced dead, ambulance attendants remove him from the chair and take the body to the medical examiner's office for an autopsy. The executioner, whose identity is kept secret, is returned to a prearranged point and compensated. Finally, there is a debriefing at the prison of all the other participants in the execution, save one.

My first encounter with Florida's method of execution came soon after I began working in the capital appeals division of the West Palm Beach Public Defender's Office. On the eve (literally) of Robert Sullivan's execution, in November 1983, my office had drafted an eleventh-hour constitutional challenge to electrocution as cruel and unusual punishment.

In 1983, executions weren't nearly so commonplace as they are today. The execution guidelines earlier were first issued in preparation of John Spenkellink's execution in 1979. They were revised in 1983, in preparation for the execution of Robert Sullivan. Sullivan's would be only the second Florida execution since 1967.

After Sullivan had been denied a stay by the U.S. Supreme Court, in the early evening before his 7:00 A.M. scheduled execution, my supervisors and colleagues in West Palm Beach decided we had to do *something*. So the members of the capital appeals division—deathbusters—assembled back at the office and paced around in circles until one of us came up with the idea of challenging the use of the electric chair itself as unconstitutional. States had been killing people by electrocution since New York executed William Kemmler in 1890; even when Louisiana's portable electric chair malfunctioned, the U.S. Supreme Court did not really question the legality of electrocution as a method of execution. But in 1983, only a few weeks before Bob Sullivan was scheduled to die in Florida's electric chair, U.S. Supreme Court Justice Thurgood Marshall had published a dissenting opinion, in a Louisiana case, doing precisely that. Marshall's dissenting opinion suggested to us in the trenches that perhaps the time was approaching when the Court as a whole might decide to take a hard look at the constitutionality of execution by electrocution. I found a law journal article setting out the constitutional argument. Craig Barnard, the office's chief litigator, word-processed the papers as he, Dick Burr, and I drafted and edited them. We finished about 1:00 A.M., six hours before the scheduled execution.

Because those were the days before law offices (ours, anyway) had fax machines, there was only one way to get our legal briefs from West Palm Beach in south Florida to federal district court in Jacksonville, where the lawsuit needed to be filed: we had to drive them. So that's what Dick Burr and I did. With music blasting from the car's cassette player, and loaded with supplies of caffeine and snack food, we tore up I-95. Meanwhile, Barnard called an attorney friend in Jacksonville, Bob Link, who, once he woke up, said he'd be happy to file our little lawsuit on Bob Sullivan's behalf. Barnard detailed our legal arguments, which took a good portion of the night. By the time Link and Barnard got off the phone, it was almost dawn, and Burr and I were rolling into Jacksonville.

Actually, *flying* into Jacksonville would be more accurate. Pumped up with adrenaline and caffeine, we met Link at his law office at about 6:00 A.M., one hour before Sullivan's scheduled electrocution. We handed the paperwork to him, and the three of us drove to the federal courthouse to file. When we filed the stay application, the clerk's office told us to sit and wait. We did—until around 6:45.

Fifteen minutes before the scheduled time of execution, the clerk told us that the judge wanted us in open court at once.

But it wasn't to be for long. Link argued for maybe three minutes before the judge denied the stay. The judge ruled against us and asked if we wanted to appeal to the Eleventh Circuit Court of Appeals in Atlanta. Uh, sure, we said.

The fact of it was that I hadn't thought that far ahead. I had been a licensed lawyer for only a few weeks; I'd been out of law school for little more than a year. No problem, though. Dick Burr was an old hand at this stuff. We filed the one-paragraph notice of appeal.

But where the hell was Burr? The Eleventh Circuit had three judges, in three different cities, standing by for a telephone conference call. The execution was five minutes away, and in the dash from the courtroom to the judge's chambers on another floor of the building, somehow we had lost Burr. As 7:00 A.M. approached, with Link on the phone with the three (increasingly impatient) judges, it became clear to us all that he'd have to wing it. I tried to help, but panic had turned my mouth into a desert. Link did a great job outlining our legal argument. Still, the three appellate judges denied the stay. That decision came about two minutes after 7:00 A.M. Sullivan probably was already dying, if not dead.

I later heard that our last-minute lawsuit delayed Sullivan's execution by about five minutes. Maybe; maybe not. It didn't matter to me;

at about 7:10 Burr and I heard, over the car radio, that Sullivan was dead. A five-minute reprieve was less than worthless; most likely it only upset whatever equanimity and dignity he had been able to muster for his appointment with the electric chair.

The electric chair. When I was working full time as a Florida death-worker, in the 1980s, it seemed that every year someone or other in the state legislature would raise the possibility of introducing a bill to change Florida's method of execution from the electric chair to the more "humane" method of lethal injection. I never knew whether to support such technological innovations. On the one hand, I was acutely aware that some of my clients would die by Florida's execution method of choice. Ought I not therefore work for the most painless, dignified, and humane method?

On the other hand, lethal injection felt to me too closely akin to "putting a dog to sleep," as a friend of mine put it once. As Robert Sapolsky wrote in an article titled "Measures of Life," which appeared in *Harper's* magazine in July 1994:

> The days of the electric chair are almost over; the method of choice among modern executioners is the lethal-injection machine. The cosmetic benefits of this $30,000 contraption are obvious—no smoke, no sudden jolts, no unpleasant smell. But the real reason for the machine's growing popularity, one suspects, is not its effect on the prisoner but its effect on the executioner. The machine, as stipulated by law in some States, is outfitted with dual sets of syringes and dual stations, with switches for two people to throw at the same time. A computer with a binary-number generator randomizes which syringe is injected into the prisoner—and then erases the decision. No one will ever know who really killed the prisoner—not even the computer.
>
> Such rites of execution are part of a subtle cognitive game. When a member of the two-man lethal-injection team goes home on the night of the execution, he does not think, "I am a murder-er," or "Today I contributed to a murder." More likely, he will try to frame the issue in terms of statistical innocence; as half the team, he can imagine that he has been responsible for only half of the act. Or, more concretely, he might conclude: "I have a 50 percent chance of *not* having helped kill someone today."

And as Judge Alex Kozinski wrote in the February 10, 1997, *New Yorker*:

Lethal injection, which has overtaken the electric chair as the execution method of choice, is favored because it is sure, painless, and nonviolent. But I find it creepy that we pervert the instruments of healing—the needle, the pump, the catheter, F.D.A.-approved drugs—by putting them to such an antithetical use. It also bothers me that we mask the most violent act that society can inflict on one of its members with such an antiseptic veneer. Isn't death by firing squad, with mutilation and bloodshed, more honest?

4

Hurricane Season:
The First Death Warrant

Nothing stops the conversation at a dinner party quite like the half-whispered explanation "I have to take this call. It's a stay in a death case. Don't hold dessert."

Judge Alex Kozinski, "Tinkering with Death,"
New Yorker, *February 10, 1997*

Florida's death row housing has changed a good bit between today and 1985, when Joe Spaziano's first death warrant was signed. Death row today is a high-tech prison-within-a-prison at the Union Correctional Institution (UCI); death row a decade ago consisted of a wing or two within the medieval fortress of Florida State Prison (FSP). Even the addresses are different: Florida State Prison is in Starke, and Union Correctional Institution is just across the county line in Union County.

Florida's death row and the electric chair used to be located in the same building on the grounds of FSP. Death row consisted of tiers of cells connected by catwalks. Each cell was about the size of an average bathroom, about two paces wide and three paces deep, and housed one inmate. The prisoner slept on a thin mattress about thirty inches wide, situated on a metal bunk. Each cell had three concrete walls, a concrete floor, and a concrete ceiling. The fourth wall consisted of bars that opened onto the corridor and catwalk, which were about eight feet wide. In addition to the steel bunk, each cell contained a sink-and-toilet combination and a small steel locker for the prisoner's personal possessions.

The prisoner spent an average of twenty-three hours a day in this cell. He did his laundry in his sink or toilet and hung it overhead to dry. In this cell he exercised, slept, watched TV, wrote, read, and shouted messages to his friends or enemies living nearby in the same sorts of cells.

In November 1985, when Joe's first death warrant was signed by Governor Graham, Joe called me. I promised him we'd get a stay; no one had ever been executed in Florida on a first warrant. I had recently joined CCR, and I knew that the agency's chief investigator, Scharlette Holdman, and chief litigation attorney, Mark Olive, were the best in the business.

I've often wondered whether Joe believed me as he was escorted to the deathwatch cells to begin the twenty-eight-day countdown. I wasn't sure I believed myself. I wasn't at all certain I'd be able to keep my promise. Paradoxically, at the same time I was certain of one thing: Holdman and Olive would not permit Joe to be killed on a first warrant.

The juror took it personally. That much was clear. When she spoke of the judge who, nine years earlier, had overridden the sentencing jury's verdict of life imprisonment in "Crazy Joe" Spaziano's case, the juror constantly referred to the court as "*that* Judge McGregor." Not just "Judge McGregor, but "*that* Judge McGregor." As in "How could *that* Judge McGregor ignore our life verdict" and impose the death penalty?

On the day Joe's first death warrant was signed, Mark Olive decided it was time to test the Craig Barnard Hypothesis: the theory that Joe's jury recommended life imprisonment, rather than death, because it wasn't certain that Joe had committed the Harberts murder at all. Barnard's theory rested on several assumptions: (1) The crime, according to the prosecution, was especially brutal—a rape-torture-slashing murder-for-the-hell-of-it. (2) The victim, Laura Lynn Harberts, was a sympathetic figure, a teenager with her whole life ahead of her. (3) The already convicted killer was an especially frightening-looking man—an Outlaw biker whose club colleagues' presence during the trial served as a graphic reminder (if the Seminole County jury needed any reminder) of the company kept by the man at defense table. (4) The jury had taken hours, and pressure from the court to reach a verdict, before they found Joe guilty of first-degree murder; by contrast, their sentencing verdict came quickly and, to all outside appearances, easily. (5) The jury's only choice at the guilt/innocence stage of Joe's trial was outright acquittal or conviction of first-degree, capital murder. Thus, Barnard concluded, when the jurors found him guilty of murder one but recommended a sentence of life imprisonment rather than death, they signaled a lack of confidence in their own verdict. If ever a death sentence could be expected, this was such a case. The possibility that Joe might actually be innocent of the murder of Laura Lynn Harberts must have seemed remote given the evidence the jury was shown, but something seemed wrong—something was missing.

It was an elegant theory, yet at the end of the day it was merely that: a theory. The only way we could prove (or disprove) the theory was to go to the source of the verdicts—in other words, to the jurors themselves.

I thought this was a bad idea. We already had Barnard's theory. Why risk disproving it by finding a juror who said that the jury had no doubt whatsoever about Joe's guilt? Olive's instincts told him that we should track down as many jurors as possible. He assigned a CCR investigator to comb Joe's trial transcripts for information that might lead to the identities and locations of Joe's jurors. This was something of a long shot. The population of the greater Orlando metropolitan area is fluid, and the trial had taken place nine years earlier.

But we got lucky. CCR's investigators located the names and then-current addresses of three individuals who had served as jurors in Joe's 1976 murder trial.

Florida law limits the ability of defense attorneys to contact and question former jurors. The law required us to have reasonable cause—which we had in spades. It also required us to provide notice of our intentions (by U.S. mail or other means) to the prosecutor and judge. This I did by letter. I placed the notifications in the U.S. mail at 6:00 P.M. on a Friday evening, walked back to my office, and called the first former juror on the list. She was still living outside of Orlando.

I placed the call and, when the former juror answered the phone, I identified myself as Joe's attorney and requested permission to ask her a few questions about her experiences as a juror nine years ago. She said yes, in a crisp, sure voice. Then she said she remembered the case very well; that was the one where "*that* Judge McGregor" disregarded "our verdict against the death penalty." What did I want to know?

Did she recall that the trial had two stages, a guilt/innocence phase followed by a penalty phase? "Of course I remember that." Did she re-member the jury's deliberations during the guilt/innocence stage of trial? "Yes. I didn't think we'd ever reach a decision. I thought we'd be a hung jury." Why did they have so much trouble? "The kid. We weren't sure about believing the kid." Tony DiLisio? "Yes." Why, if you weren't sure about Tony's credibility, didn't the jury simply acquit Joe outright? Pause. "Some of the jurors were afraid of the motorcycle gang." Were they there in court? "Every day. They were there every day of the trial. They put flyers on some of our cars, threatening us if we didn't acquit him." Was the jury told that Tony DiLisio had been hypnotized? "No." Might that have made a difference in the murder one verdict? "It might." And finally: So is it fair to say that the jury voted against the death penalty because you weren't so certain that Joe was guilty at all of killing Laura Lynn Harberts? Her response was clipped, impatient, as though I were a slightly dense child (which is how I felt): "Yes, that's what I'm saying." Could I visit her tomorrow morning? "Yes."

The following morning was atypically gorgeous, even for Florida in November. As we sat on Adirondack chairs on the wraparound porch of the juror's home, sipping iced tea she'd made fresh that morning, I got my first good look at this woman who might save Joe Spaziano's life. I knew from the trial transcript that she was now eighty-one years old, but she neither looked nor sounded her age. She wore a blue print dress and sensible black pumps. Her gray hair was loose, but looked severe nonetheless. Although she had an Italian surname, she was every inch the southern lady. Her face was all angles. Her brown eyes seldom left mine, and those eyes missed nothing.

As we talked, she smiled easily, but she wasn't smiling as she repeat-ed all that she had told me over the phone. Her eyes narrowed when she spoke of "*that* Judge McGregor." I remembered something I'd read once: never make war on women—they have the longest memories.

I asked the former juror if she would be willing to repeat what she had told me in a sworn affidavit, and she said she would. I thanked her profusely, and we sat there for a few moments, looking at each other. It was about that time I realized I had not brought an affidavit. Or a type-writer on which to produce an affidavit. Or a notary to sign off on the affidavit I didn't have and couldn't produce. I felt my face growing red. I felt utterly incompetent, stupid, and *young*.

Perhaps because she could see or feel or smell my rising panic, the juror asked me what was wrong and whether I was okay. I explained my dilemma. Not a problem, she assured me. She owned a typewriter and knew how to use it. She also knew someone who was a notary and who worked in a local real estate office.

So this guardian juror dictated her affidavit. I wrote down what she said and suggested a few minor edits. After she typed up the affidavit, she called her notary friend, who came down and opened the real estate office. Fifteen minutes later I had my affidavit signed, sealed, and ready for filing in the court. On the drive home to Tallahassee, I had to pull my VW over to the shoulder of I-10 to read it again. Yup. It really said it. It really said:

> One of the major reasons for [nine or ten] of us favoring a life sentence was our doubts about whether Spaziano was guilty of the crime as charged. I distinctly remember this being expressed as a factor in many of the jurors' minds.
>
> One of our major concerns was the testimony of the 16-year-old boy, Tony DiLisio, which we didn't entirely believe at the time of the trial. Had we known his testimony was prompted by hypnosis, I believe it would have made a difference.

The signing of a client's death warrant triggered a controlled frenzy of activity at CCR. Investigators and lawyers would investigate facts and incorporate those facts into applications for stays of execution and postconviction motions for substantive relief (retrial or resentencing). In Joe's case, the postconviction motion we filed on November 20, 1985, was 143 pages long—plus voluminous appendices.

A state postconviction motion (in Florida called a Rule 3.850 motion) is filed in the same courthouse where the original trial took place. If the original judge is still on the bench and available, the state postconviction motion and stay application are assigned to that same judge. Thus our judge in 1985 was Robert McGregor—the same judge who had presided over Joe's 1976 murder trial and who had overridden the sentencing jury's verdict of life imprisonment rather than death. *That* Judge McGregor, as Joe's juror had put it.

State postconviction proceedings are designed to address new facts and arguments unknown or overlooked during trial and direct appeal. The postconviction legal papers filed on Joe's behalf raised a number of matters that were never raised or developed at trial, and thus were never considered by the Florida Supreme Court on direct appeal. Taken as a whole, the revelations *were* compelling.

First, the motion summarized everything Joe's postconviction investigators had discovered about the police's hypnotism of Tony DiLisio. Relying on the audiotapes that investigator Justine had found in Detective Abbgy's widow's attic, as well as the expert analysis of the hypnosis sessions conducted by Drs. Diamond and Buckhout, we argued that had the jurors known about the actual circumstances surrounding the creation of Tony's testimony, they never would have found Joe guilty of capital murder. They would never have convicted Joe based on Tony's hypnosis-warped word—as evidenced by the affidavit from the juror. Second, we argued that Joe's trial attorney should have investigated, researched, and raised the facts and circumstances of Tony's pretrial police hypnotism. Third, we claimed that, based on the investigation of Joe's medical, psychiatric, and family histories, Joe had been mentally incompetent to stand trial.

The first issue, impeaching Tony DiLisio, was really nothing more than a different way of framing the foundational reason Joe's execution would be lawlessness at its most grotesque: Joe Spaziano was innocent. The remaining two constitutional issues—and other claims we raised in the state postconviction motion—offered various explanations of *why* the legal system failed so completely here, failed to the point of bringing an innocent man to the brink of electrocution for a crime he didn't commit. The unifying narrative theme that cut across all of the legal arguments was a very simple and basic proposition of fact: the state of Florida was about to execute the wrong man.

The best way I can convey the frenzy of activity during that period when Joe was first under death warrant is through my journal entries from the time. The entries that follow refer also to people and events unrelated to Joe Spaziano's case. I have left such references in because they illustrate clearly that at no time during my tenure as Joe's lawyer was his my only case. At CCR I was responsible for thirty-five or so capital clients, including Joe. The journal entries are overwhelmingly about Joe, however, and the reason is simple: Joe had an execution date and time.

Since 1983, I have kept a private and personal journal. Until 1993 I kept it in War Resistors League calendars, the formats of which allowed me only a tiny space (roughly one inch by six inches) per day in which to record the day's events. That limitation was essential, because any more space would have been too intimidating and therefore paralyzing. No matter how chaotic my daily life became, I could always find time to jot down a few daily notes in my War Resistors League calendar. The calendars became my memory books.

The Joe Spaziano story, as told in this book, is written and presented in isolation from the rest of the chaotic world of capital postconviction litigation within which the story occurred. By including material from my journals, I hope to restore some sense of the chaotic daily life of capital litigation during the mid-1980s, when Florida was the capital of capital punishment.

My second reason for including my journal entries has to do with the fact that this book is being written long after the events it describes occurred. Because I know the outcome, an essential quality of those events is compromised in the telling. That essential quality is uncertainty. The journals, by contrast, were written without knowledge of the future. The singular characteristic of Florida deathwork in the mid-1980s, along with chaos and randomness, was uncertainty. This uncertainty hangs over every page of my journals. Reading them now, I'm struck by the freshness and shock of experience immediately recorded.

You likely won't recognize the names of most of the condemned prisoners mentioned in the journal, nor are you likely to recognize the legal issues referred to in shorthand. You don't need to. All you need know is that each name refers to a man on death row, and that each issue refers to a challenge to the legality of that man's capital murder conviction or death sentence—and perhaps that those legal issues, about which my journals reflect such optimism, were in the end almost always lost.

Monday, November 4, 1985

10:30 AM: Art [the governor's clemency aide] called: Warrants in *Spaziano* and *Trodel* (he says *Trodel* has lawyer; Scharlette says no); executions set for Dec. 3—probably no warrants until end of year, but maybe; I called Joe, but Col. Mathis said he's being transferred to Deathwatch; called Craig, and *he* was on phone with Joe; set up conference call—Joe sounds like he's ready to explode—set up visit for tomorrow; called Ed Kirkland. I can go through his files; will do that later in week or next week; called Tom Horkan and set up meeting with he and former Fla. Supreme Court Chief Justice Ervin for Wed. morning; talked about strategy on when to file 3.850.

Tuesday, November 5, 1985

Spaziano: In office at 8:00; at 8:30, a FedEx from Craig arrived: *Spaziano* memo and letter from J. Letts of 4th DCA: decided to get judges to testify this year in legislature; left at 9:00 for Florida State Prison with Gail and Terry, driving; met with Joe for 2 hours—went over issues, strategy, timing for filing, etc.—he same spirits as ever; visited Lee Martin: very withdrawn and depressed and talking about dropping his appeals if we lose in the 11th Cir; left office at 1:00 AM.

Wednesday, November 6, 1985

Spaziano: Met with Tom Horkan of Florida Catholic Conference: he'll do whatever we need: gave him copies of papers (Rule 3.850 Motion came in today); no one has talked with Justice Ervin—I'll do that today or tomorrow; talked with Dick and Craig about timing: They think we need to file ASAP, to increase Judge McGregor's chances of reading the papers and granting a stay; Called Judge McGregor's office and state attorney—said I'm counsel for *Spaziano*; at office until 11:30.

Thursday, November 7, 1985

Spaziano: Long talk with Craig about *Spaziano* issues—we will not do Fed *habeas* pleadings on *Allen* charge (dead issue in 11th Cir., only argued in state court as due process issue); Justice Ervin called; He'll do Fla Sup Ct argument on override; called Tanya Carroll at Fla Sup Ct.: tentative oral argument date is Nov. 26th—talked about our problems with last 4 death warrants and *Trodel* (told her Rineman is looking for a lawyer for *Trodel*); took break from *Spaziano* stay memo to work on *Straight*; left office at 2:00 AM.

Friday, November 8, 1985

. . . My mother to arrive in Ft. Lauderdale at 10:50 A.M., NY Air #143; drove from Tallahassee to West Palm Beach (drove from Tallahassee, after Mark told me that Larry was bitching about my travel expenses); left Tallahassee at midnight and arrived in West Palm Beach at 8:00AM, then drove to Ft. Lauderdale to get mom); Scharlette: Fla Sup Ct. set oral argument for the 25th at 2:00 P.M.

Saturday, November 9, 1985

Home at West Palm Beach.

Sunday, November 10, 1985

Mother to leave—Ft. Lauderdale 1:20 in afternoon; drove her to airport and then drove back to West Palm Beach.

Monday, November 11, 1985

Spaziano: Drove to Orlando to meet with juror—met her at home and talked on her porch—she very angry at judge for overriding jury ("why have a jury . . .")—not want to come into court, but got her to sign affidavit—found notary at real estate office; drove to Tallahassee; called Joe: he in good spirits—talked about artwork—excited about the juror's affidavit—he invited me for Thanksgiving dinner with his family; worked on stay memo until midnight.

Tuesday, November 12, 1985

Spaziano: called Craig: went over *Spaziano* issues; researched juror issues and state law on override; did form motions; Mark wants to edit *Spaziano* 3.850; worked until 11:30 PM.

Wednesday, November 13, 1985

Spaziano: Tried to fly to Orlando to go through Ed Kirkland's trial files—flight canceled due to fog—rescheduled for tomorrow; Mark editing *Spaziano*; he and I edited Larry's draft of petition on Rule 3.850 change; Joe called: invited me to his house for Thanksgiving—his brother did some legal research for him and is sending it to me, on *Beck* issue; Mark and Larry had a spat about Larry's refusal to let Mark rewrite the 3.850 proposal; Eloise printed out *Spaziano* memo; I added in new state constitution and jury override stuff; picked up Kirkland's files at bus station at midnight; at office until 3:00 AM, going through Kirkland's files and researching.

Thursday, November 14, 1985

Spaziano: Meet Tom Horkan here at 10:00 AM to go over issues: went over issues; in office at 8:00 AM left at 1:00 AM; James Johnson, lawyer from Pensacola, called: he has penalty phase coming up and wanted to talk about doubt about guilt—turns out he has same *Beck* issue as in *Spaziano*, but there was no personal waiver of lessers, no objection—he wants me to testify as expert on death penalty; Sid White called Larry, saying Florida Supreme Court Chief Justice Boyd asked us to file early and not interfere with the justices' Thanksgiving.

Friday, November 15, 1985

Spaziano: Rosemary Barkett starts as justice on Fla Sup Ct; I met with former Justice Ervin at 10:00, after xeroxing for him override cases—he seemed frail and had recently had a stroke, but was very willing to argue the override issue; Joe called to see how things were going—talked about family and about the rib place he'll open up when he gets out; very little progress on *Spaziano*: clear we're not filing on Monday; called Joe, talked for 1½ hours—he read me letters from Outlaw Brothers; wrote all day; left office at 1:30 AM.

Saturday, November 16, 1985

Spaziano: Mark now talking about filing Tuesday or Wed; Craig called: *Esquire Magazine* did a story on Scharlette as a "leader in America"; . . . Mark will edit *Spaziano* 3.850 and memo—may file Wed or Thurs; called Dr. Harry Krop, Dr. Bernard Diamond—very hard to come to hearing next week—worked on *Spaziano* until 1:30 A.M.

Sunday, November 17, 1985

Spaziano: Went over sentencing hearing record: If *Gardner* hearing wasn't limited, then *Cooper/Lockett/Songer* issue may evaporate; talked with Mark on and off all day about issues; Scharlette: 55 cases have been affirmed by Fla Sup Ct and don't have lawyers; Mark wants to challenge Joe's rape conviction—resurrected my old fed habeas draft on tattoos issue—Mark wants to challenge other stuff and maybe allege that West Palm Beach was ineffective; left office at 2:30 A.M.

Monday, November 18, 1985

Spaziano: target date to file *Spaziano* 3.850 in trial court: not even close; Tom Horkan in Mobile, Alabama—will call . . . Called Joe and he depressed. "My life is in your hands"—chilling; Rhonda Kibler called: wants me to testify before Fla Bar Bd of Governors on jury override; called Joe's mother—she worried, but in good spirits—invited me for Thanksgiving; worked until 6:00 AM; Mark doing what I'd call a light style edit and he'd call and edit to make it into a persuasive litigation document, but I accept all changes—we joke, but it has an edge; in office until 2:30 AM, but state papers almost done.

Tuesday, November 19, 1985

Spaziano: in office at 10:00 A.M.: working on federal *habeas* and stay papers: Mark wants to reorder appendices (pull them apart and re-order) Mark has *Esquire* article: Among other things, Scharlette said that repealing the override would bring the whole statute down; problem with Joe's 3.850 verification—Susan says she can't get it to us until tomorrow night; called Judge McGregor's office: OK to give unverified 3.850 motion to him tomorrow and file Thursday morning—hearing Fri afternoon; Called Craig to tell about hearing: rehearing denied in *Hitchcock* and lost *Aldridge*; worked all night on *Spaziano*—slept for 2 hours on couch.

Wednesday, November 20, 1985

Spaziano: Called Judge McGregor's secretary at 9:30 A.M. and told her we'd probably get there a little after 5:00—she said someone would be there to take the papers; Fla. Sup. Ct. Chief Justice Boyd called Scharlette—wanted to know why Malone wasn't filing *Trodel* earlier ("I told him to be here Mon")—Scharlette thinks Boyd is setting Steve up to be held in contempt; spent morning and afternoon rushing to get *Spaziano* printed and copied; while at lunch (with Sarah Bleakley), Judge McGregor's secretary called and talked to Scharlette—No need to rush to file in Orlando: tomorrow is fine.

Thursday, November 21, 1985

Spaziano: Scharlette and Mark picked me up to go to airport—picked me up at 8:15 to catch an 8:20 plane—Scharlette said she called the airport and the plane was an hour late, but it took off on time, so I missed it; I rented car and drove, just ahead of the hurricane hitting Tallahassee; Mark and I talked on the way down about office politics, power and gossip: Mark suggested I run an appellate division within the office, taking cases not under warrant, filed *Spaziano* at 2:30 and served State Attorney; went to Holiday Inn and waited in room; planes and phones out in Tallahassee—same in South Florida—couldn't get office, or Stella or Joe's family on phone—finally got Joe's mom; I went over issues and did outline—worked until 1:00 A.M.; talked with Tom Horkan—where he is, the Hurricane has killed the power, so he read our papers by candlelight.

Friday, November 22, 1985

Spaziano: Woke up at 7:00 and finished oral argument outline in hotel dining room; Mark moot courted me; called Tom—no planes out of Tallahassee, and decided not to drive, hearing started at 2:00—Mark did opening on CCR, but Judge McGregor only wanted to know why it took us 10 years to file, bad faith, etc—then I got up to argue merits, but McGregor kept at it—I went over my involvement with the case, from law school to present—judge gave us *Songer/Harvard* issue and doubt abut guilt issue, but clear he's going to stomp us—and he did, in a nasty little order; called Joe from pay phone in court—he expected it; I talked to his parents, who were there in court; Tallahassee has no power and 7:00 P.M. curfew, due to Hurricane, drove to Gainesville and stayed with Mike Radelet.

Saturday, November 23, 1985

Spaziano: left Gainesville about 10:30 A.M. and drove to Tallahassee: Scharlette told me my house and car are OK—much of city hit hard by Hurricane; called Sid White (Fla Sup Ct clerk) at home—oral argument still on for Mon, but may be moved to Tues—no need to get trial court papers in tomorrow—he not know that Judge McGregor had ruled until I called; spent rest of day writing Fla Sup Ct papers.

Sunday, November 24, 1985

Spaziano: Finished drafting Fla Sup Ct issues: Scharlette got appendices bound and delivered to Fla Sup Ct.; called Dad—voice hoarse again—last time, when I was in college, this meant cancer—tests not in until Tues; called mom and she very, very upset; Scharlette angry about *Spaziano* footnotes, and she stomped off in a huff; Mark increasingly concerned about scope of *Gardner* remand as killing the *Harvard/Songer* issue—long talks about dealing with it—record came in at 6:30 P.M.—sent it to Fla Sup Ct; Florida Supreme Court brief being edited, etc.; worked at office until 2:30 AM—others still working on papers when I left; listened to *Harvard* oral argument tape before going to sleep.

Monday, November 25, 1985

Fla Sup Ct set oral argument for *Spaziano*. 2:00 P.M: came in at 9:00 A.M.: State's answer brief in—our brief almost finished being copied; Jim and Terry asleep on floor; called J. Ervin, to suggest he not do arguments, but he was so up for it that I didn't; called Sid White and he said its OK to split argument; moot courted with Mark and Scharlette and went over at 1:30 P.M.; met Ervin in lounge and we chatted until Tom and Sid White came in; Sid said we had 30 min for argument—I went first and stressed hypnotism—court seemed very concerned about it in *Bundy*—many questions from all sides—my yellow light was on before I was into *Harvard/Songer* issue; they not seem concerned about it—Ervin was great: folksy, simple justice—they loved him; State was OK—delay, bad faith, etc.—court not seem to be buying it—I got fired up on rebuttal; met clerks for Justices Shaw and Boyd after; good reviews from Tim and Jimmy; went back to office to wait and by 4:00 P.M. decided we'd lost; at 4:15, Sid White called: stay, 4-2; called Joe, his mom, clubhouse—cheers.

Tuesday, November 26, 1985

Slept in and arrived at office at 1:30; cleaned up; Talked to Roger Lowenthal of *Wall St. Journal* about override; called mom: Dad is OK; I'll fly home tomorrow to Virginia, for Thanksgiving with parents.

Wednesday, November 27, 1985

Housekeeping stuff at work; will catch 1:40 P.M. flight to DC; changed flight to 6:30, because Malone is in trouble on *Trodel*: state is agreeing we have a hearing, but wants it today, so Mark wants to play hardball: as a state agency, we just won't do a hearing now, only 3 weeks after getting the case—we'll all resign before we do that; as of 11:00 A.M., Larry had done his intro argument on why CCR wasn't ready and Steve was arguing the merits of the issues on phone with Craig on strategy when Scharlette came running down hall, looking for Mark: Judge denied *Trodel* at 12:15 P.M.; conference call with Steve: no hearing; Craig said that Mon is traditionally a big hearing day in US Sup Ct—Expect *Ford* denial. 2:00 P.M.: Sid White called: transcript can't be done, so I did application for stay application for *Trodel* on that basis; stay denied ½ hr later—Sid called; flew from Talle to Virginia.

Thursday, November 28, 1985, Dumfries, VA

Thanksgiving: spent last night and today relaxing with Dad, slept until 1:00 PM; mop-up in *Spaziano*.

Friday, November 29, 1985

At Dad's in Virginia; *Trodel* Fla Sup Ct argument this morning; called office at 10:30: Sid watched argument and said it was a disaster—justices not scream about delay in the argument itself, but clearly they were hostile to the merits, especially Steve's argument that they improperly considered the record of co-defendant Hawkins on *Trodel's* appeal: Justice McDonald, who went out on a limb in *Hawkins*, accused Steve of insulting the court and demanded an apology, which he got; Sid also told me about a letter Justice Boyd sent to Larry, saying unreasonable delays won't be tolerated, that we're expected to be in Fla Sup Ct 10 days before execution date, that we're presumed to represent everyone on death row: reminded us of 3.850 rule charge which means they've decided to deny our petition; called later: *Trodel* lost: Scharlette and Jimmy agreed the argument was awful; *Spaziano* mop up.

Saturday, November 30, 1985, D.C.

Ruthann and Larkin arrive in DC: I meet them at Shorham hotel; mop up *Spaziano*; Scharlette wants me to pick up *Trodel* US Sp Ct papers at airport—good panel in 11th Cir. Dist Ct judge is Kehoe: they filed today, in Miami.

Sunday, December 1, 1985

I took Larkin to mom's for day; Scharlette calls dad's: *Trodel* stay from Federal District Judge Kehoe.

Mark Olive and I divided the oral argument before Judge McGregor. Mark argued first, explaining why we hadn't been able to file earlier. Then I argued that the juror's affidavit required a stay of execution and an evidentiary hearing on whether Joe Spaziano was actually guilty of the crime for which he was scheduled to be killed in eight days. All this was prologue, because my real strategy in the argument was to bait a trap for the judge.

The plan was to goad the judge into admitting that, at the time of

Joe's sentencing in 1976, the judge had limited his consideration only to those mitigating factors listed in the Florida capital statue. The law in Florida, in 1976, was that sentencing judges couldn't consider mitigating circumstances that didn't fit within the statutory list. The problem with this constricted view of the scope of mitigating factors was that two years after Joe's sentencing, in 1978, the U.S. Supreme Court (in Sandra Lockett's case) ruled that such restrictions are unconstitutional.

If we could persuade Judge McGregor to admit—on the record, in open court—that his view of Florida law in 1976 violated the rule the U.S. Supreme Court set out in 1978, then Joe's death sentence would be unconstitutional. The strategy couldn't have worked better. In fact, before I'd really had a chance to bait the hook, Judge McGregor chomped down on it and wouldn't let go. The judge defended his view of the law in 1976, and he blamed any confusion on the Florida Supreme Court.

This is how the argument went:

MELLO: If I could, I'd like to leave the hypnotism series of issues and move on to the second issue, which is the limitation on mitigating [factors issue] the issue which I know Your Honor is very familiar with from the [Bill Harvard] case. And I'd like to just reiterate at the outset that the only issue here today is whether to grant a stay of execution.

And we submit that that issue, as a practical matter, was resolved in the *Harvard* case, because the Florida Supreme Court granted a stay in [the Bill Harvard case]. . . . And we submit that *Harvard* now stands for the authority that Your Honor should grant a stay of execution in Mr. Spaziano's case which raises the identical issue. And I won't—since I know Your Honor—

THE COURT: You're talking about non-statutory mitigation, are you not?

MELLO: Yes.

THE COURT: The case law refers to the ambiguity. There was no ambiguity. *Lockett,* I guess, speaks of it in that fashion. The statute was very plain.

MELLO: I agree.

THE COURT: And, you know, I—[those were] the rules we were working under at that time, and, you know, Mr. Kirkland's only incompetence in that respect was his lack of clairvoyance.

MELLO: I didn't raise a traditional ineffective assistance. I didn't mean to interrupt, Your Honor.

THE COURT: You did raise it, though, in your motion, that it was a—

MELLO: As to the hypnotism issue and as a failure to move for a competency hearing, but the limitation on the mitigating issue, I view is different from what I call the traditional ineffective assistance of counsel claim, which basically says the attorney messed up. This kind of claim argues that the attorney was being reasonable and that the Court was being reasonable in following the very clear Florida law at the time of this trial. And that the unconstitutionality of the death sentence flows not from errors on the part of—or unreasonableness, rather, on the part of counsel or the judge, but rather flows more from the Florida Supreme Court's limitation on capital sentence consideration of mitigating circumstances.

So, the claim really is that Your Honor was reasonable given the state of Florida law at that time. And that's—

THE COURT: Well, but you continue to urge the error of our ways, and it's just so hard for me to accept the responsibility when the plain reading of the statute said that I should exclude that, and, of course, [Sandra Lockett's case] came along, what, a couple of years later or something. I can't anticipate that. And if, you know, if that's error, so be it, but I'm not going to find it. Some Appellate Court is going to have to tell me that, as I said in *Harvard*, that, you know, I just—they expect too much for a Court to anticipate, to foresee.

MELLO: But the Florida Supreme Court, in granting a stay in *Harvard*, necessarily held that that's an important enough question that an imminent execution shouldn't take place. That's the question before the Court today, and we rely on *Harvard*. . . .

THE COURT: Okay, thank you.

MELLO: I would just very briefly like to go through the non-statutory mitigating circumstances which were present before the Court, which given the constraints imposed upon the Court by the Florida Supreme Court's decisions, wouldn't have been considered. And these were factors that Justice McDonald identified in his dissent on direct appeal . . . , and I won't go through all of them; I'll just go through very briefly.

The first was a statement that was in the confidential portion of the PSI that Mr. Spaziano was a very attentive father and that he felt that the sun rose and set over his daughter, Mary Noel; that's at Page 2 and Page 5. Clearly something not listed in the statute, but which would, under *Lockett,* have been extremely relevant in deciding life or death.

Secondly, a statement also in the confidential section of the PSI at Page 5 from Joe's—from Mr. Spaziano's exwife, that he had a good outgoing personality, and that even within the context of the motorcycle brotherhood which he was affiliated, he stopped fights and prevented violence from happening.

The second series of mitigating features in this case which fall without—fall outside of the statutory list is—are really in many ways the fundamental core of this case and of this thirty-eight fifty, and that's reasonable doubt about guilt; doubt not rising to the level of doubt beyond a reasonable doubt, but real, genuine doubt about guilt. And as we argue—

THE COURT: [Interposing] What's the difference?

MELLO: If you visualize certainty as being a continuum, no certainty at all over here and absolute certainty on this end, beyond a reasonable doubt goes to here, but there's a gap between here, beyond a reasonable doubt, and absolute doubt. And that's the kind of doubt that ought to be—that's the kind of doubt that isn't relevant in deciding guilt or innocence. Doubt doesn't need to go that—

THE COURT: [Interposing] I'm sorry, I can't accept that.

MELLO: But juries are routinely instructed—and this jury was—and that's part of the Florida standard jury instructions, that guilt only need be proven beyond a reasonable doubt. And we submit that doubt beyond a reasonable doubt is relevant in deciding whether to impose an irrevocable sanction.

THE COURT: Absolutely not. It can't be. If the standard of proof beyond a reasonable doubt, you know, is necessary for the determination of guilt—

MELLO: Your Honor, Your Honor's position is entirely consistent with the decisions of the Florida Supreme Court in the *Buford* case and recently in the *Charlie Burr* case, as well, of course, as Your Honor's position . . . at the original trial. However, a number of authorities which we discuss, again, probably at too much length in the memo, have recognized that doubt about guilt is a very relevant factor in setting penalty. The U.S. Court of Appeals for the Eleventh Circuit has recognized what it called whimsical doubt about guilt. I don't know about the term, the word "whimsical." But what they mean is what I'm talking about.

In two cases, *Smith v. Balcom* out of Georgia and Smith, *Dennis Wayne Smith v. Wainwright* out of Florida, the U.S. Court of Appeals for the Eleventh Circuit has recognized that doubt about guilt not rising to the level of doubt beyond—guilt beyond a reasonable doubt is relevant in deciding whether to impose death.

The model penal code upon which, in part, Florida statute is based recognizes doubt about guilt not rising to the level of reasonable doubt to be a mitigating factor of such power that the death penalty is precluded. You can't—under the model penal code, you can't even consider imposing death unless there is doubt—unless there is absolute certainty. Unless that gap is filled up. And in a lot of death cases, it is filled up. In a lot—in most cases, there's no question but that the defendant did it. But once again, Mr. Spaziano's case is different.

THE COURT: I hear your words. I don't—I just can't fathom that concept. Go ahead, please.

MELLO: This is particularly—in many cases, the argument that I've just made is very hypothetical. In this case, we have the unique advantage of having the affidavit from the juror who said very clearly, "the reason we recommended life imprisonment was we had doubt about guilt." And that has to be read in conjunction with the fact that the jury wasn't instructed on lesser included offenses. And when all of that is read together, what comes out is that the jury's ultimate verdict in this case wasn't really just guilty of first degree murder, but rather was guilty of first degree murder, but life. And the "but life" reflects genuine doubt about whether Mr. Spaziano was guilty of involvement in this case at all. And part of the evidentiary—

THE COURT: That's your interpretation, but I—you know—

MELLO: That was what the juror said in her affidavit.

THE COURT: One.

MELLO: The only one that—true, one. But the only one that we know of so far. The only one that we know of.

THE COURT: I have to pre—all right, go ahead.

MELLO: Even without the juror's affidavit, it—in litigating Mr. Spaziano's case—in the United States Supreme Court, this came up in the hypothetical sense. And we were asked—I believe it came up at oral arguments, "how do you know that—you know, you got some circumstantial evidence that the jury's life recommendation was based on doubt about guilt, but how can you know for sure?" And, of course, we couldn't know for sure until now. But now we do. And now we know that the—from the only juror who has said one way or the other that their verdict in this trial was guilty by life and that the "but life" reflects doubt about guilt.

Part of the showing that we ask to put on at the evidentiary hearing that we request would be the testimony of Michael Radelet of the—a sociology professor at the University of Florida and/or the testimony of Hugo Bedau, a professor at Tufts who recently completed a study of individuals—of cases in this century who were convicted of capital offenses and sentenced to death, and in some cases actually executed, but who turned out to be actually innocent. And what we believe—and their—the Radelet and Bedau study as well as the voluminous appendices are included as in the appendices that we've submitted.

But what they would show, what they would testify to is that this concern about doubt about guilt isn't just an academic theoretical hypothetical concern. That it really happens in the real world, and that would provide, we submit, some perspective suggesting that it really happened in this case.

THE COURT: Thank you. Phil, we got any coffee? Excuse me, but you kept me up last night.

MELLO: I apologize. It's winding down. These next two issues are—I'll be brief. Briefer.

We now had our stay issue. If the Florida Supreme Court wouldn't stay the execution, then the federal courts would. Between the judge's admission and the juror affidavit, I was guardedly nonpessimistic that Joe wouldn't be killed on schedule.

We still had a choreographed dance to complete, however. After hearing oral arguments from Mark, me, and the prosecutor, Judge McGregor sat on the bench, shuffling his papers and reviewing his notes. Then, ruling from the bench (and only two days after the state postconviction motion was filed in Judge McGregor's court), he denied all requested relief. No stay of execution. No retrial. No resentencing. No nothing—from Judge McGregor, anyway.

Several members of Joe's family were in the courtroom during the oral argument before Judge McGregor, and after he ruled against Joe, the family consoled the lawyers while the lawyers consoled the family. It was the first time I'd met Joe's parents, and his mom seemed to me to be the Italian counterpart to my own Jewish mother. Her son was scheduled to die in one week and one day, he had just been denied a stay of execution, and she was mostly concerned that I was upset and that I looked unhealthily thin. I assured her I'd eaten breakfast (Mark Olive and I had moot-courted the oral argument over breakfast in the Holiday Inn dining room), and I explained why I thought Joe had a pretty good shot at a stay from the Florida Supreme Court and a real shot at a stay from the federal courts.

Our mantra was, No Florida prisoner has ever been executed on a first death warrant—and this case has real issues that should get a stay. What I didn't say then was that there's always a first time. Joe and his case still had all the problems that had led him to be convicted and condemned for a murder he did not commit. It was still an especially heinous murder. He was still an Outlaw.

In denying the stay and postconviction motion, Judge McGregor employed an intellectual maneuver that court after court would later use to avoid even considering the newly discovered evidence of innocence unearthed by CCR's investigation: he invoked a series of procedural technicalities. We had found the new evidence too late. The 1985 court decision on hypnotism could not be applied retroactively to Joe's case. And so on. The ludicrous element of a human life overshadowed by a procedural detail was, at times, overwhelming.

Courts use such technicalities all the time to avoid considering the factual and legal challenges raised by death row prisoners. Judge McGregor, however, had invoked the wrong technicalities in denying some of Joe's claims. Because Judge McGregor didn't recite the correct magic words, it seemed likely that the Florida Supreme Court justices would stay the execution.

So it was on to Tallahassee and the Florida Supreme Court. Actually, there was some chance that the court might issue a stay based on hurricane. While Mark Olive and I were arguing before that Judge McGregor in Orlando, Tallahassee was being hammered by a hurricane. The city had taken a hard hit and was under curfew.

But death in Florida doesn't wait for hurricanes. The oral argument in the Florida Supreme Court went on as planned.

The prosecutor screeched procedural technicalities, but Joe had an ace in the hole: Former Florida Supreme Court Chief Justice Richard Ervin did part of the oral argument for Joe. I did the rest, but it was Ervin who got the stay. It was an indefinite stay, to give the court time to consider our constitutional claims, and that meant Joe was safe for the time being. But a few months later, the court denied all of Joe's claims for retrial or resentencing. We all understood that a new death warrant could be signed at any time. For the moment, however, Joe was safe. He was transferred from the deathwatch cells back onto death row, where he could paint and socialize and wait for the next warrant to come. It was a victory, of sorts.

As my journal entries show, during the height of the frenzy caused by Joe's first warrant, both Joe and his mother invited me several times to join the Spazianos at her table for Thanksgiving. I demurred, but she insisted that no one should be alone for Thanksgiving. Only when I promised her that I would be spending Thanksgiving with my parents in Virginia did Mrs. Spaziano let me off the hook.

There is one aspect of Joe's first death warrant that unsettles me to this day: I wasn't honest with him.

Lawyers are powerful because the law is powerful, and because lawyers have a monopoly on access to the law's power. Kafka calls us "gatekeepers," and it's an apt metaphor. If the law is a labyrinth, then we are the only guides with the clue of thread essential for admittance into, navigation through, and safe return from the maze. We know the maze because we designed and built it. Only we know the secret language of the maps, because we wrote the maps. Only we know where the land mines and their trip wires are buried, because we buried them—or if not we personally, people whose hieroglyphics we've been trained to translate and to understand. And we mean to keep it that way. Without the labyrinth of our own creation, without our high priests and hermeneutic mysteries, why would the laity pay us two hundred dollars per hour for our services?

In the United States lawyers are especially powerful because the law is especially powerful. Ours is a nation under law, which also makes us a nation under lawyers. Social conflicts and disputes that in other countries are resolved within the family or by religious institutions, or through community or political processes, are solved in America by the courts: we sue.

Traditional legal representation involves professional distance and role compartmentalization. Lawyers have their predefined role to play in this dance—which, keep in mind, has been choreographed by lawyers or people trained to "think like lawyers"—and so do their clients. And along with our role differentiation comes a specialized set of moral norms and values particular to members of the profession. Such role morality includes duties of loyalty and confidentiality; lawyers must do things most nonlawyers would deem wrong or immoral—give undivided loyalty to killers who we know to be guilty, keep the secrets and confidences of our clients, no matter their character.

Capital postconviction defense representation tends to shorten the professional distance that separates the traditional lawyer from the traditional client. (It also tends to blur the lines between advocates and judges.) Given the stakes (life itself) and the nature of the litigation (to decide whether a fellow human being has lost the moral entitlement to live, whether that person deserves to die), this blurring of professional lines is perhaps inevitable. Like the 1863 atrocity that is the subject of Phillip Shaw Paludan's superb book *Victims,* the stories at the heart of capital postconviction litigation—including Joe Spaziano's—involve "primary emotions that are less a part of a certain moment in history and more a part of the human personality."

When a lawyer and a client disagree about certain courses of action, whose choices should prevail? If you are a nonlawyer, you probably would say the client's views should prevail. If you are an attorney, you probably would say the same thing. If you are a realistic attorney, however, you also have to acknowledge that, as a practical matter of how things work in the real world, lawyers—especially public defenders with death row clients—pretty much call the shots because they have the education, experience, and communication skills that are essential to navigate the labyrinthine byways of the law. As a law school professor who teaches legal ethics and professional responsibility—a field of study that addresses and attempts to conceptualize the appropriate allocation of decision-making power between lawyers and their clients—I know it is essential to tell my students that such questions in the abstract can't be answered categorically. Some decisions are clearly the client's to make (whether to testify or to plead guilty), whereas others (those under the broad rubrics of "tactics" and "strategy") fall within the attorney's orbit of professional expertise and judgment. Attorneys are, after all, paid for their expertise and empowered to advocate. In the midst of war, swift judgments are essential to victory.

My job as attorney is to empower my clients so that they can make their decisions with their eyes open, and my knowledge *is* power. When I was a capital public defender in Florida, my goal was to provide client-centered representation. By this I mean that the client set the goals, but my role was to provide factual and legal information about the risks and potential benefits involved, so that the client could make informed, lifesaving decisions.

In capital litigation, feelings are fine, but strategy saves lives. When the two conflict, it is a lawyer's task to resolve the problem. In the end, the client usually follows his lawyer's recommendations. "Crazy Joe" Spaziano, however, did not. When we disagreed on issues at the core of my ability to represent him effectively, the subject of strategy was more than a mere academic exercise. The configuration of my client's feelings threatened his defense, and his loyalties jeopardized his life.

A word of explanation: When an attorney undertakes the post-conviction representation of a death-sentenced person in Florida, two lines of factual investigation are basic. First, the new client's history is investigated and documented—from embryo to death row. Second, an experienced mental health and status professional, trained in forensics, evaluates the client, using state-of-the-art techniques and knowledge. Ideally, both areas of investigation will already have been conducted by the client's trial lawyers.

In Joe Spaziano's case, neither his personal history nor his mental status had been investigated by his trial attorney. This was not just an oversight on the attorney's part; it also had something to do with Spaziano himself. Joe didn't think he was crazy, and he didn't want any "shrinks" to testify at his trial and question his sanity. He also didn't want to put his family or the Outlaws through the anguish of testifying at his trial in support of a life sentence rather than the death penalty. He knew how an aggressive prosecutor would savage his family and friends on cross-examination. He decided he would rather die in Florida's electric chair than put his loved ones through that crucible.

Joe Spaziano was adamant with me, as he had been with his trial lawyer: no family and no shrinks. I tried to explain to him the reasons for my conviction that we *really needed* this information. I pointed out that Governor Graham would likely sign Joe's death warrant before I would be able to investigate and write a motion for state post-conviction relief. If the family and psychiatric histories were not fully investigated and mapped out and documented in that postconviction motion, the motion wouldn't be strong enough to secure a stay of the death warrant. We would probably win a stay further on down the capital postconviction assembly line, in federal court, but by then it would be too late to raise the family and psychiatric evidence. If this information wasn't in the *first* postconviction motion filed in *state* court, then that evidence would be forever waived; on this score Florida's procedural rules were clear and were enforced by the Florida courts with a vengeance. Thus it was now or never. If, a year or two down the line, Joe changed his mind and decided that it was okay for me to investigate his family background and psychiatric history, it would be too late. Florida's procedural default rules would bar me from raising these matters.

I tried to persuade Joe by framing the issue in terms of his keeping his options open. At least let us *investigate* these areas, I pleaded with him. If you decide later not to let me present them in the state post-conviction motion, that's fine. If I don't do the investigation, we won't know how strong these issues might be—and you need to know and understand exactly how strong an issue you're waiving before you decide to waive it. And these kinds of exacting investigations are extremely labor-intensive; they take time—time we won't have if we wait until a twenty-eight-day death warrant is signed before we even *begin* to investigate these matters.

I explained, cajoled, and argued, but Joe still said no. Even to do the investigation would be too hurtful for his family, and Joe was determined to spare his family any more pain. And he was *innocent,* not crazy. Go out and prove my innocence, Joe Spaziano told me. Present *that* to the state postconviction courts. Forget this he-had-a-bad-childhood stuff, and forget the even-if-he-did-the-crime-he-was-nuts crap. He was *innocent.* Raising sideshow issues like family history and psychiatric status only muddied the waters.

Actually, Joe was both innocent *and* crazy. It was obvious even to someone with no medical or psychiatric training that something was broken inside the head of "Crazy Joe" Spaziano. You could see it in his crooked smile and partial paralysis of his face. You could hear it in his speech patterns and in the way he periodically "checked out" of conversations in mid-thought or mid-sentence. Was it fair to him, his family, or his Outlaw brothers for him to play the martyr?

But Joe was my client, and he had given me clear directions limiting the scope of my investigation. That raised both moral and tactical issues. Would it be wrong for me to disregard the instructions of my client, even if my client was possibly really *crazy* Joe? And, as a practical matter, could my investigators conduct the investigation without Joe's finding out about it? Surely he would hear from his family if I started asking them intimate questions about the family history. It is also fairly impossible to conduct a psychiatric evaluation on a condemned man without his being able to figure out that that's what you're doing.

Joseph Spaziano may have been crazy, but he was by no means stupid; far from it—he could be frighteningly intuitive and perceptive. If I tried to conduct the investigation behind his back, he'd find out. And his finding out would obliterate his trust in me, which would also obliterate any possibility of a meaningful attorney-client relationship developing between us. Then I'd become just another in the long series of lawyers who had lied to him and otherwise abused his trust and faith. That would mark the end of my role as Joe Spaziano's defense attorney.

This was the scenario I dreaded most: My investigator manages to conduct the necessary investigation without Joe's detection of it. I get terrific affidavits documenting his horrific family background and his profound mental illness—the kind of evidence that convinces Florida postconviction courts to grant stays of execution. Against Joe's wishes, I incorporate all this wonderful (for Joe's legal case, that is) information into a kick-butt motion for state postconviction relief. Assume, however, that I can't get all this done and filed before the governor signs Joe's death warrant. No problem: the information in the postconviction motion should be ample enough to convince the state trial judge or Florida Supreme Court to stay the execution to allow the courts sufficient time to evaluate the claims in a deliberate and careful manner. So I file the postconviction motion along with a boilerplate application for stay of execution based on the facts and law set out in the motion. Piece of cake.

But now comes the tricky part of my doomsday scenario. Joe must *sign* the postconviction motion, verifying that to the best of his knowledge the facts set out in the motion are true and accurate. Such motions routinely run two hundred pages in length, and I could probably get away with snookering him into signing the motion without reading it. However, that would be an act of fraud that could jeopardize my license to practice law as well as Joe Spaziano's life—probably not a good idea. On the other hand, if I am straight with him about the content of the motion, he will know that I lied to him and misled him about the scope of the investigation. He could refuse to sign the motion, and he might even fire me as his lawyer. He might even become so stressed that he could decide to drop his appeals altogether and become a "volunteer for execution." So long as the state trial judge—in this instance Judge Robert McGregor, who presided over Joe's original 1976 murder trial—finds Spaziano sufficiently mentally competent to decide to acquiesce in the state's wish to execute him, neither Joe's family nor I could stop the execution. I had no doubt that Judge McGregor would confirm Joe Spaziano's decision to die. He had, after all, already ignored the jury's sentencing recommendation of life imprisonment by sentencing Joe to Florida's electric chair. It's doubtful he would suddenly be gripped by humanitarian concern.

My clever deception could backfire and result in Joe's execution. He might refuse to sign the verification of the postconviction motion, so no motion could be filed, so there would be no basis for a stay of execution, so he'd be killed. Or he might fire me, and no stay application or postconviction motion would be filed, so he'd be executed. Or he might fire me and volunteer for execution, so he'd be executed.

The crush-depth pressure of the death warrant might well have caused Joe to fire me, or at a minimum, to refuse to sign the essential verification. Or it might have pressured him into signing it, into ratifying post hoc and retrospectively the investigative fait accompli with which I presented him. The investigation had in fact been done; I had already put his family through the emotional wringer—and they didn't mind at all, because they love him and want to do everything within their power to help keep him alive, even though they knew he didn't want them to go through that horror show. They wanted to help him. In any event, the damage had been done. I already had the family's affidavits.

Then there was the psychiatric evaluation. It would be even harder to finesse. It was clear that neither Judge McGregor nor "Crazy Joe" would cooperate with a mental evaluation for these purposes. So I lied to Joe. I told Joe that the purpose of the psychiatric evaluation was to explain why he had no alibi for his whereabouts the day Laura Lynn Harberts disappeared in 1973.

On the basis of my selective communication, Joe agreed to the family history and psychiatric evaluation. The psychiatrist who conducted the evaluation found that Joe was mentally incompetent to stand trial or to receive the death penalty. Joe signed and verified the state postconviction motion that included the evaluation, and that motion won him a stay of execution.

Although my lying to Joe worked, it doesn't justify my actions. I'm ashamed of what I did. The truth remains that I lied to and manipulated a man who had entrusted me with his life. I only risked having my deception unmasked at the time when my client hardly could have tagged me for it—when his only realistic choices were to ratify my previous actions or die in the electric chair in a matter of weeks for a crime he did not commit. I used the death warrant to strong-arm Joe into endorsing my duplicity. Imminent death concentrates a man's mind wonderfully, Samuel Johnson wrote. It also makes that man highly susceptible to coercion by his attorney.

I have no doubt that had this investigation not been done in 1984–85, Joe Spaziano would have been executed years ago. However, I'm still uncomfortable with the means I employed to make that end possible. By what right did I override my client's instructions? How could I allow his family to pass through the pain of reconstructing, and swearing to under penalty of perjury, the horror of their lives so long ago? Once I had laid out for Joe the risks and potential benefits, should I not have respected his wishes? It was, after all, his life.

Lawyers for death row prisoners possess enormous power over their clients, and given the power imbalance in this relationship, there is a tremendous temptation for attorneys to make whatever decisions they deem to be in their clients' best interests, to control their clients. This temptation is strongest when a client suffers from mental or psychiatric impairment, as many condemned men and women do.

Today I teach courses in legal ethics and professional responsibility. I often present my students with these issues in the context of a Joe Spaziano "hypothetical." My students usually agree with my actions back in 1984–85 (law school classrooms, of course, have their own power dynamics and disparities). On this score, they are more certain than I.

As 1985 ended and 1986 began, the fledgling CCR was bursting its rivets: far too many clients with far too frequent execution dates set by the governor, far too few experienced defense attorneys and investigators. It was like bailing out the *Queen Mary* with a teaspoon.

CCR in 1986 was a madhouse. Three of our clients were executed within six weeks during spring 1986. By the time the Florida Supreme Court denied Joe Spaziano's appeal—in late 1986—I was making plans to relocate to Washington, D.C., or northern Virginia for good. I accepted a job with the D.C. firm of Wilmer, Cutler & Pickering. When I left Florida, in early 1987, I left Joe's case in the care of Ed Stafman, a Tallahassee criminal defense attorney. I promised to get involved in Joe's case again if it ever reached the U.S. Court of Appeals for the Eleventh Circuit—the next-to-last stop on the capital punishment assembly line. It was a promise I never expected to have to keep.

When I left Florida for private practice in D.C. and, later, to teach law in Vermont, Joe and I kept in touch through letters and through Stafman. Surely, I told Joe, the Florida Supreme Court or the federal district court would consider the evidence on innocence. Surely the case would never even reach federal court.

5

The Outlaw Bikers' Clubhouse

Which of us has known his brother? Which of us has looked into his father's heart? Which of us has not remained forever prison-pent? Which of us is not forever a stranger and alone?

Thomas Wolfe, Look Homeward, Angel, *1929*

There is an unbridgeable gulf between those condemned to die and the rest of us—including the lawyers who represent the condemned. Virtually all death row prisoners in the United States come from backgrounds of extreme poverty and family dysfunction. And virtually all are ashamed of their backgrounds and reluctant to let their lawyers raise their histories as legal issues, even when such claims would get them off death row. They'd rather die than let their lawyers tell the world about how they were raped by their parents or how their families lived in tar-paper shacks and subsisted on dog food. In Joe's case, I didn't have to try to understand issues of race and extreme poverty—instead, I had to try to understand the Outlaws.

Sublime is the word I'm looking for, I think. Pleasurable, but also with a faint but unmistakable edge of danger. Sublime—that's what I felt the first time I visited the clubhouse of the Orlando Outlaws.

The visit wasn't planned ahead of time, which probably was just as well. The Florida Supreme Court had stayed Joe Spaziano's death warrant, so he was safe for the moment. But another of my CCR clients, Butch Sireci, was still under warrant and scheduled to be killed in less than two weeks. Sireci's capital murder trial had been in Orlando, so that's where CCR filed the application for stay of the impending execution. The judge had decided he wanted to hear oral argument on Sireci's stay application, so I'd flown from Tallahassee to Orlando to take part in the argument. The argument lasted much of the day, which was unusual. Even more unusual, in the end the judge issued a stay of execution. After calling Sireci's family to give them the good news, I made plane reservations for my trip back to Tallahassee (another client of mine, Nollie Lee Martin, was also under death warrant).

My flight wouldn't leave for a few hours, so after taking a cab to Orlando's airport I did something I'd been meaning to do since I began working on Joe Spaziano's case in 1983: I phoned the Outlaws' clubhouse in Orlando and told them I was in town. If they wanted, I could catch a cab from the airport to the clubhouse, and I could finally put faces to the phone voices I'd been dealing with for years. (I also needed to talk with the club leadership about money; during my time as Joe's lawyer until that point, money had never been an issue, because my salary was paid by state-funded public defender's offices; my successor counsel would need to work out the money issues with Joe and the club.) Unfailingly polite and direct, the person with whom I spoke that day—Wildman, I think—invited me for a visit. The clubhouse is located in a rural area outside of town, so I was told someone would pick me up.

When my ride arrived—in an old Chevy, not on a Harley, as I'd sort of secretly hoped—I couldn't have looked, or acted, like the kind of attorneys the club was used to dealing with. My suit, such as it was, was rumpled and drenched with sweat from the Butch Sireci argument and its preparation. I was exhausted from the adrenaline crash that followed the unexpected stay in Sireci's case ("execution interruptus," Mark Olive called it). I was worried about my other client's scheduled execution; I was running on caffeine and stress, which aggravates a facial tick about which I am always self-consciously aware. Add to this my owlish glasses and my quiet, soft-spoken demeanor, and I couldn't have looked like much of a lawyer to them.

And in a way I wasn't. Florida bikers tend to be fairly savvy consumers of legal services; that comes from the fact that bikers in general, and Orlando Outlaws in particular, are subjected to almost continuous harassment from law enforcement. When bikers think of lawyers—as when most Americans think of lawyers—they think of *trial* lawyers, lightening-quick litigators who are adept at swaying juries and judges with their oratorical skills and withering cross-examinations. In fact, Joe's trial lawyer fit that bill quite nicely: He was quick on his feet, he shot from the hip, he used all his Perry Mason tricks in court. Joe's trial lawyer put on quite a show, and he almost pulled it off: the jurors were hesitant to convict Joe of murder, and their recommended sentence was life imprisonment rather than death.

I'm not quick on my feet, and I'm surely not any kind of showman, which partly explains why I was an appellate public defender rather than a trial lawyer. I have enormous admiration (and some envy, I must admit) for the great trial attorneys, such as Clarence Darrow, Millard Farmer, Mark Olive, David Bruck, Judy Clarke, Edward Bennett Williams, F. Lee Bailey, Dennis Balske, Johnnie Cochran, Deanne Siemer—but that ain't me.

When I was a Florida appellate public defender, I was most happy reading and writing briefs and the like, in my office, surrounded by books and piles of paper and notes—far away from any courtroom. On those frequent occasions I did have to go to court, I was making my clients' cases to panels of judges, not juries. Appellate judges—at least those sitting on the courts I was actually in, the Florida Supreme Court and the U.S. Court of Appeals for the Eleventh Circuit—like their lawyers to be polite, quiet, dignified, deferential, respectable, and, above all, reasonable. Appellate judges don't want showmanship; they want straightforward attorneys who have done their homework and who know the law and the record cold. It was always interesting for me to watch trial lawyers performing in appeals cases; most of them seemed as awkward as I would have been trying to make a closing argument to a jury. The skills are different and the requisite temperaments are different.

Still, if the Outlaws found me as alien as I felt, they gave no sign of it. As I said, the brothers were unfailingly polite and otherwise respectful of me and my quirks. When I arrived at the clubhouse, the brothers greeted me with a handshake and a beer. They sat patiently, in companionable silence, as I searched my briefcase for some paper or another. They allowed me to set the agenda and conversational cadence during our meeting, which took place in the clubhouse living room, with two or three brothers and me pitched on various couches. The tone of the meeting was serious and businesslike—in other words, professional. There were no verbal pyrotechnics on either side. All this was especially interesting to me because I had arrived with so little advance notice and because the topics I was there to talk with them about were not easy ones: money and information. It clearly was okay for us to disagree, and we did.

At the clubhouse I was impressed with their self-control, as I had been in the past when I'd met club members during crisis moments in Joe's case, times of tremendous tension. What always struck me was the dissonance, the total and utter disconnect, between the actual flesh-and-blood Outlaws with whom I was dealing and the hysterically paranoid view of the biker organization portrayed in the *Orlando Sentinel* newspaper. So these were the notorious bikers of whom Orlando and its newspapers were so terrified? These were the big, bad devils on bikes who, it was feared, would turn Orlando into a scene of citywide hysteria and lawlessness? These were the *Outlaws*? Sure, I was on Joe's side, which meant that I was on their side. But I doubt they were on their best behavior during our meeting. These were not the type of men who needed to put on "best behavior" for anyone—and certainly not for an owlish-looking chap in a gray pinstriped suit. In fact, I think that their transparency and independence were the reasons we got along so well together. They were what they were, and if you didn't like it you could take a hike. I like to think of myself as being much the same way. Deal with me honestly and directly, and we'll all get along just fine. So we did—the bikers and the nerd.

The Outlaws I met at the Orlando clubhouse in 1986 were nothing if not honest and direct. Unlike most people I encountered during my Florida deathwork days, the Outlaws never lied to me. They never bullshitted me, and I always tried to return the courtesy. Yes, they were courteous, and not in a fake, quintessentially southern way. Emily Kucer, one of my students at Vermont Law School, has described Joe Spaziano as "chivalrous," and, in their own quirky way, most of the Outlaws I've come to know over the years have indeed been chivalrous—as I hope I am, in my own quirky way.

The Outlaws' chivalry is impossible for me to define without coming across as patronizing or condescending. It's a rare quality that I have found only in people who really know who they are, what they're about, and what they believe is worth fighting for. They've decided who they are. They've sorted through the endless stream of cultural and societal messages about who they're supposed to be, who they're expected to be, and they haven't simply rejected all of straight society's norms; rather, they've chosen, for themselves, a code of values and conduct by which they will live their lives. That's the first point: they've made a conscious choice about how they'll live and under what rules. They actually live by that code; that's the second point. And they're ready to accept the consequences of the choices they have made, be they ostracism and fear and loathing by the dominant culture and its adjuncts and enforcers, the police; that's the third point.

What I felt in the Orlando clubhouse that day in 1986, what I've always felt from the Outlaws, is the serenity of individuals who have selected a code of values to live by—a code of honor. As I've said, it's a quality I have encountered only rarely. Perhaps unsurprisingly, I've seen it mostly in people who are society's rejects—outcasts, outlaws.

Who are the Outlaws I've met over the years? Some of them are Marine Corps veterans who saw combat in Vietnam—they're men who feel they've earned the right to live their lives as free men in America, to wear their hair long and to ride Harleys and, most of all, to be *let alone* by the government they defended with their blood. They're roofers and electricians and mechanics and construction workers. They don't pick fights, either with the locals or with the cops, but when someone has the poor judgment to pick a fight with them, they fight back; and, because so many people seem to feel threatened by, or jealous of, the Outlaws, such fights are not infrequent. They make the best of friends and the most fearsome of enemies. They are, in Rilke's phrase, guardians of one another's solitude.

Perhaps because I'd read his 1966 book on the Hells Angels shortly before my first visit to the Outlaws' clubhouse, Hunter Thompson's observations of biker culture resonated with me before and after that day. Today, more than ten years after my visit (and thirty years after Thompson's *Hell's Angels* was published), and after having read a fair amount of the literature on motorcycle brotherhoods in the United States, I believe that Thompson's 1966 book remains the best on this subject.

Another book that resonates with me in regard to my experiences with the Outlaws is Phillip Shaw Paludan's *Victims: A True Story of the Civil War*. Paludan focuses on a moment in American history long before motorcycle brotherhoods, or motorcycles, or internal combustion engines, for that matter: the 1863 massacre at Shelton Laurel, North

Carolina, of a community of mountaineers in southern Appalachia by forces of the Confederate Army. Paludan's insights into what happened at Shelton Laurel can be applied to the events at My Lai or Auschwitz, or to the two decades Joe Spaziano has lived on Florida's death row for crimes he didn't commit. That is not why I mention his book here, however. I mention it because Paludan's descriptions of the people of Shelton Laurel capture, for me at least, the social dynamics of the Outlaws as I have experienced them and explain how the Outlaws are perceived and treated by mainstream America. Indeed, the Shelton Laurel mountaineers were called outlaws by the Confederate authorities.

What typified the Shelton Laurel "outlaw"? His qualities were those of most mountain men: he valued isolation and individualism, and he had the courage and the attitude of self-assuredness that came from knowing "exactly who he was and where he fit in the scheme of things, even though he was limited by his physical and intellectual isolation. This limited viewpoint, because it was *his,* was frequently exalted into truth. He did what was right, and it was right because he did it."

Fearlessness, courage, individualism and isolation might have "foster[ed] pride and devotion to heritage" in these mountaineers, but it "also nurtured a primitive and potentially dangerous emotionalism. Although their emotionalism could provide a release from the pains of life, it could also erupt into a violence linked with self-righteousness." The same could be said of the Outlaws. On the other hand, the Outlaws, like the mountain men Paludan describes, possess a remarkable capacity for tenderness, kindness, and generosity of spirit. I have seen this quality again and again in my encounters with them over the years. Recall that it was a biker "gang"—the Hells Angels, not the Outlaws—that literally nursed "Crazy Joe" Spaziano back to life following his nearly fatal car accident in 1966. To recognize in bikers the capacity to be tender and kind—sometimes arrestingly so—is not sentimentality. It is simply accurate and honest.

Paludan observes that among the mountain men, the combination of perceived self-preservation and self-righteousness, independence, and isolation "often encouraged brutality rather than restraining it. Men who would feel conscience-stricken over something like breaking the sabbath or swearing could commit murder and feel that their souls somehow remained unblemished." The code of retribution was strict and strictly followed: the "capacity to judge others and find them wanting seems to have been one that many mountain killers possessed. Some folks deserved killing, and a man had the right, and maybe even the obligation, to determine who those folks might be." Like the mountain men, the Outlaws pass sentences of life or death. Justice is *personal*. Whether these sentences are driven by self-righteousness, self-preservation, or simple meanness, the results are always the same.

Paludan writes:

> More than simple self-righteousness was involved in the personal views of justice held by the mountaineers. The power of kinship, the isolation . . . and a highly developed individual sense of right and wrong all contributed to private justice and did so in a complex way. At issue was not a simple balancing of personal vendettas against the rule of law represented by the judicial system. The local courts—located sixteen twisted, rugged miles away . . . did not necessarily dispense an impersonal justice.

Residents of Shelton Laurel didn't trust juries to be impartial, and such distrust was grounded in the reality of experience and history. The outlaws of Shelton Laurel knew what they could expect from the "law"— as Outlaws today know what they can expect from the judges and juries of south-central Florida. Paludan could be referring to the Outlaws in mid-1970s Florida when he writes: "Juries in county seats could and did ignore the law and evidence to acquit or convict people they liked or disliked, people whose values or kin they did or did not respect." Thus Shelton Laurel was ruled by one principle:

> Private justice could be more just than the verdicts of a court. This principle existed when community standards could be applied to members of a community, when the rules of a way of life in a particular place were factors in decisions to punish or not. When people shared values and shared lives, justice outside the courts might claim to be at least as just as that which courts dispersed. The order of custom might be preferable to the rule of law.

This doesn't work when cultures collide, however. When strangers encounter each other, "a man might not be judged by a jury of his peers—by men who shared values about the ends and means of justice.

In fact, he might be judged by people who thought his values and his style of living did not deserve respect."

I think the Outlaws and I get along so well together because, in part, we share common views (some would call them character flaws) about the fragility of life and the mystery of death. It's not a fear of death—far from it. The closer my proximity to my own death—and, in 1994 and early 1995, through health problems, car wrecks, pneumonia, and a mistaken diagnosis of tongue cancer, I was faced with the clear and present actuality of my own death—the more serene I feel about the fact that I don't think I've ever really feared death. The taste of my own death in my mouth has given me perspective as well as courage, and both of those have given me the voice I needed to write this book and its predecessor, *Dead Wrong*.

Just as the Orlando Outlaws are not demons, their clubhouse seemed to me an unlikely Gomorrah. It was quite different from the clubhouse where Vanessa Dale Croft wasn't raped in 1974. The clubhouse I visited in 1986 was a pleasant, albeit dilapidated, ranch house alongside a river—cozy, almost, with fake wood paneling, threadbare carpet, overstuffed chairs, and a pair of couches. All the talking was done by the men. The few women I saw that day passed through the house like ghosts, trying to remain invisible and never making eye contact with me. I tried not to worry about these women; they seemed healthy and maybe even somewhat content, in a sullen sort of way, and, besides, my business that day was with Joe's brothers.

Our meeting completed, the Outlaws and I sat for a while, sipping our Budweisers and chatting about the local judges and the like. They weren't surprised that the Orlando trial judge had stayed Butch Sireci's execution. The Outlaws knew the local judges far better than I.

After leaving Florida in early 1987, I settled comfortably into life as a private practitioner of civil law. Even when the work itself was morally neutral to me (representing Amtrak against Conrail, for example), it was intellectually challenging and, thanks to the generosity of litigation supervisors like Deanne Siemer, John Payton, Stephen Sachs, and James Coleman, civil practice was never dry, dull, or boring. These Wilmer partners were magnificent teachers and, like all great teachers, they taught by example: they rode us associates hard and long, but they didn't push us any harder than they pushed themselves. When Siemer asked me to work all night or all weekend doing Amtrak research on degrees of negligence or punitive damages, she was there, too.

Wilmer, Cutler & Pickering is often referred to as "Lloyd Cutler's law firm," but for me the soul and conscience of the place was Cutler's contemporary, John Pickering. Pickering personified the citizen lawyer, and his law firm reflected Pickering's bedrock commitment to public service and pro bono work. Most large Washington, D.C., law firms take on some clients pro bono, because it's good public relations and because it gives their young lawyers some on-the-job, hands-on experience; not all firms treat their pro bono clients as they treat their paying clients. At Wilmer, Cutler & Pickering, pro bono clients are not second-class citizens; when Ted Bundy's case heated up, for instance, Wilmer, Cutler & Pickering associate Polly Nelson worked virtually full-time on behalf of the alleged serial killer. The firm also shied away from promoting itself by publicizing its tremendous commitment to pro bono work; it just did the work, and did it brilliantly, and let the work speak for itself.

The firm was extraordinarily generous and indulgent of my own commitment to pro bono representation of condemned prisoners in Florida. I worked with partner James Coleman on Steve Booker's case, a Wilmer, Cutler & Pickering client since 1983. Coleman and I also wrote a U.S. Supreme Court amicus brief in an Oklahoma death case raising the question of whether a state can, consistent with the U.S. Constitution, execute a person who had not turned age eighteen at the time he or she committed a capital crime. The firm allowed me to argue Roy Harich's case before the U.S. Appeals Court for the Eleventh Circuit, and it sent me to Florida to assist Pat Doherty during the capital representation of Paul Magill. In addition, Wilmer, Cutler & Pickering had developed a reputation as a "feeder" firm into law teaching; alumni of the law firm had gone on to become professors at law schools from Yale to Michigan to the University of Virginia. This was partly due to the fact that the firm tended to hire the kind of recent law graduates (top of their class, law review, clerkship with a federal appellate judge or justice) who end up in full-time law teaching. It was also partly due to the firm's encouraging its young lawyers to write and publish scholarly articles in law journals. During my time at Wilmer, Cutler & Pickering, I wrote a longish article about the counsel crisis in

Florida that led to the creation of CCR. I held up CCR as a model for other states encountering the same sort of counsel crises.

Joe kept in touch:

January 19, 1987
Hi Mike,

What to bussy to write a friend

I was talking to Stella last week and she called you she said they took the call but you never called back. I wrote you a letter and you never got back to me.

So anyway how you doing and how is your dad. What you been up to Mike.

I hear that the U.S.S.C. is going to decide on Hipnosis sometime in June or July. What you think help my case at all?

Write back Mike let me know you ok.

Sincerely
Joe

May 5, 1987
Hi Mike,

Oh I have to write you to understand this better. I heard on the new that Supreme Court is going to decide on 12 cases on that Hitchcock case you was telling about this week and over turn them. They say cases before 78 am I in there with that?

A feau of us was talking about it in the yard today, they told me to write you.

Mike pel sounds good but. Wish you was still in Fla. Hope you come back Mike

I got so much faith in you. Does Ed Stafman know about it. Just one more thing am I still in the Supreme Court? Ok Mike hope to hear from you.

Sincerely
Joe

Private practice in D.C. was satisfying and fun. The work was challenging and interesting. The people were great. I had a terrific secretary, Lisa Eberly. Still, I knew (I'd always known) that eventually I wanted to teach at a law school. In fall 1987, mainly for the hell of it and for the experience, I threw my hat into the law teaching ring. I was happy at Wilmer, Cutler & Pickering, and I did it mainly to test the waters and to have a dress rehearsal where the personal stakes wouldn't be high. After the law teachers' job fair (meat market) in Chicago, I visited a few schools for full days of on-campus interviews. I fell in love with Vermont Law School before my plane even landed. I took the job the moment it was offered to me.

In May 1988 I piled all my possessions into my VW Rabbit and moved to Vermont. (Ruthann and I had split up in 1987, so I went to Vermont alone.) Over the next few years I tried to learn to be a law teacher. And I wrote—traditional law review articles, for the most part, then, after being given tenure in 1991, more experiential and autobiographical pieces drawing upon my time in Florida. Because of the agency's case overload, I answered CCR's plea that I take over two capital cases, those of Bennie Demps and Davidson James. There also was the occasional amicus brief, testimony before the U.S. Senate Judiciary Committee and ABA task force, academic conferences, and the like.

Joe still wrote, even when the governor signed another death warrant on him:

April 18, 1988
Hi Mike,

Ya me ☺. I just got a letter from the people who are checking on you to get you into the Bar ☺. [When I applied to join the D.C. Bar, I needed a reference from a "typical" client. As all my clients had been death row prisoners, I gave Joe's name, and the Bar Association sent him a form to fill out in which he could attest to my good character.] Trash [another death row inmate] has got it and is filling it out for me so it will be good writting and lookes good for you ☺. Your a good lawyer ☺. Wish I still had you hear ☺.

Hay Mike you ant mad at me are you.

Is Lisa still working for you. She is a nice girl if she don't have a boy friend and got time tell her to drop me a letter. Ok. Everybody cut me short on mail ☺. Oh Trash just sent me down the thing he fill out for me to help you out.

Ok Mike drop me a letter and let me know how you doing and let me know if this is for you ok.

Sincerely
Your Friend Joe

Write Back ☺.

May 1, 1988

Hi Mike,

Ya sure was good hearing from you to Mike. You probley didn't hear the news but the Circuit court turned me down same day I got your letter ☹. Mike I'll get a message to everybody where you are pel ☺. Your good people Mike. Sure be nice to see you Mike. Hay Mike what is going to happen to me. How can I ever prove I'm not guilty.

Well I'll close you take care, what ever happened to your secatary she quite writting?

Sincerely
Joe

State of Florida
Office of the Governor
Legal and Legislative Affairs
The Capitol
Tallahassee, Florida
Bob Martinez, Governor
Peter M. Dune, General Counsel

August 29, 1989

Honorable Sid J. White, Clerk
Florida Supreme Court

Dear Mr. White:

Enclosed are copies of the death warrants signed by Governor Martinez in the cases of Joseph Robert Spaziano, Angel Diaz, Bryan F. Jennings, J. B. Parker, Gregory Scott Engle and Rickey Bernard Roberts.

Sincerely,
Andrea Smith Hillyer
Assistant General Counsel

September 10, 1989

Dear Mike,

Hi buddy, just wanted to let you know it was good hearing your voice. Mike budy I'm not to much in a writting mude just can't think to good got a lot on my mine. Lisen pel thanks a hole lot your help means a lot to me hope you'll see me in the future sure like to see you.

Dame Mike buddy can's think love you and will start writting after I get the stay ok ☺. Your on my mine pel.

Your Friend Joe

Opinions written and issued by the U.S. Supreme Court often are difficult to decipher, even—especially—by attorneys and legal commentators who follow closely the Court's evolving law of death. One of the Court's most astute watchers, Anthony Amsterdam, once compared Court watchers to the eminences of ancient Greece. When the citizens of ancient Greece wanted to know the will of the gods, they sent emissaries to the Temple at Delphi, where the priestess Pythia sat on a tripod making ambiguous pronouncements calculated to obscure the truth and confuse the Greeks; when citizens in the United States want to know how to conduct themselves in accordance with the Constitution, they must send emissaries to consult another Delphic oracle: the U.S. Supreme Court.

Sometimes, however, the Court's commands are explicit. One such clear directive was handed down in 1992; it involved the ways in which death row claims of factual innocence are to be treated by the federal courts. "The execution of a person who can show that he is innocent comes perilously close to simple murder," wrote Supreme Court Justice Harry Blackmun in a dissenting opinion. He wasn't writing about Joe Spaziano; he was writing about Leonel Herrera, a Texas death row prisoner who, like Joe Spaziano, was attempting to persuade the Supreme Court to consider newly discovered evidence proving his innocence. A majority of the justices said no to Leonel Herrera and, by implication, to Joe Spaziano as well. The Court held that executing an innocent person does not violate the U.S. Constitution. Electrocuting or hanging or gassing or shooting a totally innocent man does not violate the Constitution's guarantees of "due process of law" and "equal protection" under the law. Hanging or injecting or gassing a totally innocent woman does not constitute "cruel and unusual punishment."

In other words, to the federal courts innocence is constitutionally irrelevant. Factual innocence is just another legal technicality, like a cop's failure to read a suspect his *Miranda* rights or a search of a suspect's apartment without a valid search warrant. If you're innocent, the justices reasoned in Herrera's case, then you must look to the state courts and the state governor and pardon board to sort things out. Leonel Herrera did just that; he took his innocence claim to the Texas governor and courts. The Texas executive and judiciary did what any sentient observer must have expected them to do: they ignored Herrera's evidence. He was put to death a few months after the U.S. Supreme Court ruled that Herrera must stop wasting the justices' valuable time.

One chapter of the Leonel Herrera story is not widely known, and it is a chapter that occurred in the days and hours leading up to the U.S. Supreme Court justices' decision to grant full review to Herrera's case. Shortly before Herrera was scheduled to be put to death, his attorney, Mark Olive—my boss from the old days of CCR in Florida and my principal adviser when Joe Spaziano's case later got very weird—asked the U.S. Supreme Court to stay Herrera's execution and grant plenary review (certiorari) to his innocence claim. Granting certiorari requires the votes of four Supreme Court justices; a stay requires five votes. One might think that a vote for certiorari would imply a stay of execution—otherwise, the prisoner would be killed before the justices would have time to receive briefs and oral argument on the constitutional claims upon which the court had granted certiorari. If the prisoner is dead, the Court won't decide his constitutional claims. In the Court's nomenclature, those claims would be moot.

Herrera had four votes for certiorari, but he didn't have a fifth vote for a stay. In effect, the court was telling Olive: Your client's innovative claim is important enough to warrant our full review. But we're not going to allow your client to remain alive long enough to give us the time to give him that review. Since your client will be dead by the time we even consider the merits of his innocence claim, your certiorari petition will be dismissed as moot.

Olive asked the justices to reconsider. They refused.

By now it was late into the night, and Herrera had a certiorari grant by the U.S. Supreme Court, but no stay. So Olive went off in search of a *lower court* willing to stay Herrera's execution long enough to give the U.S. Supreme Court time to hear his innocence claim. Close to dawn, Olive found one: a Texas Court of Criminal Appeals judge was willing to grant the stay. Herrera would live long enough for the U.S. Supreme Court to receive briefs and hear oral argument in Herrera's case—a process that ended up taking several months. In the meantime, Olive recruited Sandy D'Alemberte to represent Herrera in the U.S. Supreme Court. In the end, of course, Herrera lost on a five to four vote in the U.S. Supreme Court, and soon thereafter he was executed. The Olive/D'Alemberte tag team would play a crucial role later in Joe Spaziano's case, during the time when Joe was under his final death warrant in August–September 1995.

Leonel Herrera was dead before Joe Spaziano's case had worked its way through the state postconviction and federal habeas corpus systems. By then, Justice Blackmun had retired from the Court. The *Herrera* ruling that innocence is irrelevant in federal court was old news. Not a single justice voted to grant plenary consideration of my claim about Joe's innocence. To appreciate what happened in Joe's case, you need to understand some of the background.

In 1993, the Supreme Court in Herrera's case instructed the lower federal courts how to analyze death row claims of factual innocence. The Court in *Herrera* did pay some lip service to the repugnance of the idea of executing the innocent. The justices assumed for the sake of argument "that in a capital case a truly persuasive demonstration of actual innocence made after trial would render the execution of a defendant unconstitutional and warrant federal habeas corpus relief if there were no state avenue open to process such a claim." The key word here is "process," as in rubber-stamp.

Notwithstanding the justices' desultory reference to claims of innocence, the rhetorical thrust of the *Herrera* decision is that federal courts are to treat such claims with a great deal of skepticism. Evidence of factual innocence does not in and of itself provide a basis for throwing out a death sentence. As the Court explained, a claim of innocence "would have to fail unless the federal habeas court is itself convinced that those new facts [suggesting innocence] unquestionably establish (the prisoner's) innocence." Innocence is not totally irrelevant, however. For instance, if a death row prisoner's trial lawyer didn't object in exactly the right way at exactly the right time, such procedural technicalities won't bar federal court review of the claim if the prisoner is actually innocent. Thus, the justices explain, a claim of total innocence is "not itself a constitutional claim, but instead a gateway through which a habeas petitioner must pass to have his otherwise [procedurally] barred constitutional claims considered on the merits."

This is crazy, of course. But it's what a majority of the U.S. Supreme Court did and said. The federal Constitution does not forbid the government from electrocuting, gassing, hanging, shooting, or lethally injecting men and women who are *totally innocent* of the crimes for which they pay with their lives. Unless the innocence claim "unquestionably establishes" the prisoner's innocence, the federal courts cannot intervene to stop the execution. "Unquestionably establish." That's not my phrase. It's the Supreme Court's phrase, which makes it the law of the land—a law that children of an enlightened and decent epoch will in time condemn as pornographically unjust, much as today we condemn the nineteenth-century Supreme Court's handiwork in *Dred Scott* and *Plessy v. Ferguson.*

During the oral argument in Leonel Herrera's case, Justice Harry Blackmun presented the lawyer representing the state of Texas with a hypothetical situation: What if the new evidence of innocence included an alibi videotape—a videotape proving beyond dispute that the death-sentenced prisoner was somewhere else at the precise moment of the murder? Was the government really arguing that the federal courts could not even *consider* this piece of evidence that definitively proved the inmate's innocence? The answer the state's lawyer gave was yes. The state was arguing that the federal courts couldn't intercede. The federal judiciary must rely upon the state executive clemency process to identify and correct death row claims of actual innocence.

Justice Blackmun's *Herrera* hypothetical materialized in a case that the Court decided in 1995, the year that Joe Spaziano's innocence claim appeared to be slouching toward oblivion. Lloyd Schlup had the piece of evidence that Leonel Herrera lacked: an alibi videotape proving Schlup was somewhere else at the precise moment of the murder of which he had been convicted. Easy case, one might think; the unanimous justices would at least order a new trial for Schlup, if not order his immediate release from death row. One would be wrong.

Like Herrera before him, Lloyd Schlup wasn't asking for immediate release. He wasn't even really asking for a retrial based on the alibi videotape. All Schlup expected was a *hearing* in federal court. The federal district court and circuit court of appeals refused to give Schlup his hearing, as they were required to do according to the binding precedent of Leonel Herrera's case.

A bare majority of the Supreme Court decided to give Schlup his hearing. The justices split five to four, even on this. Justice John Paul Stevens's opinion for the majority spoke of "the paramount importance of avoiding the injustice of executing one who is actually innocent. . . . the individual interest in avoiding injustice is most compelling in the context of actual innocence. The quintessential miscarriage of justice is the execution of a person who is entirely innocent. Indeed, concern about the injustice that results from the conviction of an innocent person has long been at the core of our criminal justice system."

Maybe this was true once upon a time, but not under the regime of the Rehnquist/Thomas/Scalia Court. With this Court it's important to watch what the justices *do* as well as what they say. What the Court did, by the razor-thin margin of five to four, was give Lloyd Schlup his hearing—and he had a *videotape*. What the Court did was empower the state of Texas to kill Leonel Herrera without a hearing, which the state promptly did.

Ditto in Jesse Jacobs's 1995 case in Texas. As described by Justice Stevens, the prosecutor admittedly made inconsistent arguments at Jacobs's capital trial and at the trial of Jacobs's sister about whether Jacobs or his sister actually committed the capital murder, and "if prosecutor's statements at the [sister's] trial were correct, then Jacobs is innocent of capital murder." Justices Stevens and Ruth Bader Ginsburg thus wrote that Jacobs's case presented a "self-evident" and "deeply troubling" instance of "injustice." Those two justices said they would have stayed Jacobs's execution to consider his claim of innocence. The Court majority, however, was not deeply troubled. No stay. No reason for the federal courts to prevent the state of Texas from mainlining lethal chemicals into Jacobs's veins. Texas obliged, and Jacobs was executed on schedule.

The message the Supreme Court sent in Leonel Herrera's case was that the lower federal courts should deny most death row innocence claims without holding hearings on newly discovered evidence of innocence. The lower federal courts got the message: if the condemned prisoner doesn't have an alibi videotape, then he or she doesn't get a hearing. That's exactly what the federal courts did in Joe Spaziano's case hearing on the new evidence of innocence.

When Alice stepped through the looking glass, the world that greeted her was inverted, whimsical, and surreal. Her life and surroundings took on new shapes and colors, and for as long as she lived there, she believed it was all real. The legal world of capital punishment is much like Alice's looking-glass world.

As discussed earlier, Governor Graham signed Joe Spaziano's first death warrant in 1985. On November 20, 1985, Joe's CCR lawyers filed a motion to vacate his judgment and sentence in the trial court. Two days later, that court denied Spaziano a stay, a hearing, and all requested relief. The Florida Supreme Court granted a stay, but later affirmed the denial of postconviction relief.

Among the issues raised in Spaziano's first motion to vacate judgment and sentence was his claim that he had been denied the opportunity to present mitigating evidence at his original penalty phase proceeding. The Florida Supreme Court held that, without regard to whether he was denied such opportunity, he was provided that opportunity at the limited remand hearing. However, Spaziano's attorney had failed to conduct any investigation or present any mitigating evidence at that hearing. Accordingly, on December 24, 1986, Spaziano filed in the state trial court a second state postconviction motion, alleging that his attorney's failure to investigate and present the substantial mitigating evidence that existed at this resentencing proceeding was an unreasonable failure that amounted to the ineffective assistance of counsel. The state trial court summarily denied relief, and the Florida Supreme Court affirmed. Justice McDonald, although concurring with the majority, "strongly adhered" to his previously stated view that the jury override was improper. Justices Kogan and Barkett agreed.

Before the Florida Supreme Court resolved the issues of Spaziano's second postconviction motion, the U.S. Supreme Court decided Jim Hitchcock's case, holding that Florida capital sentencers must be permitted to hear and consider mitigating circumstances even if such mitigating circumstances are not enumerated in the capital statute. Spaziano filed a petition in the Florida Supreme Court seeking to raise his *Hitchcock* claims in that pending proceeding, but the motion was denied without prejudice to raising the claim in a successive state postconviction motion.

Spaziano thus initiated a third state postconviction proceeding raising his *Hitchcock* claims. While that petition was pending, Governor Bob Martinez signed Joe's second death warrant. The state trial court denied the postconviction motion without a hearing, and Spaziano simultaneously appealed and filed a state habeas corpus petition in the Florida Supreme Court. Ultimately all relief was denied. Justices Kogan and Barkett continued to dissent. Curiously, in its ruling rejecting Spaziano's claim, the Florida Supreme Court noted: "The presentence investigation report specifically considered by the judge at sentencing contains *substantial* evidence concerning Spaziano's mental condition. The judge declined to view such evidence as constituting a *statutory* mitigating circumstance." This language stands in stark contrast to the earlier opinion, in which the Florida Supreme Court affirmed the trial court finding of *no* mitigating circumstances—statutory or otherwise.

During the pendency of the death warrant, Spaziano's postconviction counsel discovered exculpatory evidence in the police files that had never been revealed to the defense and that cast substantial doubt upon the reliability of Spaziano's conviction. When the third state postconviction motion was resolved, Spaziano filed a fourth motion for postconviction relief in the state trial court, alleging that the prosecutor at trial had failed to disclose exculpatory information to the defense. While this petition was pending, Governor Martinez signed another death warrant. The trial court and the Florida Supreme Court denied a hearing and relief on the pending postconviction petition. Two justices, however, continued to oppose Spaziano's death sentence.

While Joe's case was pending in the Florida Supreme Court, the U.S. Supreme Court decided Robert Parker's case, a case dealing with Florida's jury override. *Parker* indicated that Justices Barkett, Kogan, and McDonald had been correct in believing that the jury override was improperly applied to Spaziano. Spaziano filed a habeas corpus petition in the Florida Supreme Court explaining that *Parker* required that Spaziano's jury override be set aside. With no attempt to distinguish *Parker,* but simply because Spaziano's case had once been before the U.S. Supreme Court on other issues, the Florida Supreme Court denied relief. Justices Kogan and Barkett continued to dissent.

Following completion of state postconviction litigation, Spaziano filed a petition for writ of habeas corpus in federal district court.

On to the Eleventh Circuit Court of Appeals.

It was 1993 when I learned that Joe Spaziano, my old client, had just lost in federal district court in Orlando. The next step would be an appeal to the U.S. Court of Appeals for the Eleventh Circuit. I learned that Joe Spaziano's case had, finally, reached the federal court of appeals level. My 1986 promise to Joe had thus come due; this was the stage at which I had agreed to come back into Joe's case.

In early 1987, when I'd left Florida deathwork, I'd left Joe's case in the capable and experienced hands of Ed Stafman, a Tallahassee criminal defense attorney. When I called Stafman in Tallahassee, I hoped he wouldn't hold me to my seven-year-old promise. No chance. He wanted me back in.

In his representation of Joe Spaziano, Stafman had been aided by the Volunteer Lawyers Resource Center (VLRC) of Florida. Congress had created such centers to provide logistical, investigative, and resource help to lawyers, like Stafman, who represent death row prisoners in state and federal postconviction litigation. Stafman and VLRC had done a good job of keeping Joe's case bouncing around the state courts for years. More important, their ongoing factual investigation had uncovered significant exculpatory evidence that the state had theretofore managed to keep hidden: Joe Spaziano had not been the cops' first—or their best—suspect in the Harberts murder case. Also, the Stafman/VLRC tag team had located Tony DiLisio. As earlier, however, DiLisio stonewalled. By 1993, Stafman seemed burned out on Joe's case. At one point, Stafman wrote to VLRC that he would not be able to appeal Joe's case to the Florida Supreme Court; unless VLRC would write the appellate briefs, no appeal would be taken. Stafman had been arguing with Joe and the Outlaws about payment of his fees. When I saw that important parts of the habeas corpus petition Stafman had filed in federal district court were strikingly similar to the first state postconviction motion CCR and I had written and filed during Joe's first death warrant in 1985, I tentatively decided to join Stafman on the Eleventh Circuit appeal.

If there was to be an appeal. Federal District Judge G. Kendall Sharp hadn't simply denied Joe's habeas corpus petition, he had also denied Joe permission to appeal his decision to the Eleventh Circuit. Judge Sharp denied the petition; he also summarily denied a certificate of probable cause to appeal, as he has done in every capital habeas to come before him (he has also never granted a stay of execution). Stripped of its legalese, this means that in his decade on the federal bench, Judge Sharp has never found a single issue in any capital case to be nonfrivolous—not even arguable, not even debatable among jurists of reason. In a June 19, 1995, opinion in a noncapital criminal case, the Eleventh Circuit gave Judge Sharp a stinging and unprecedented rebuke. The appellate court said:

> Judge Sharp's cryptic handwritten notation that [the defendant] owes full restitution because he once had physical possession of the money is more than irresponsible, it is defiant. Far from performing the assessment that he explicitly was instructed to conduct in [in this case], Judge Sharp's cursory handwritten notation dashed at the top the motion to correct his sentence evidences Judge Sharp's disregard for this court's instruction and mandate.

The court continued:

> Regrettably, this case is not an aberration. We previously have reversed and/or remanded cases to Judge Sharp for failing to provide factual and legal explanations for his rulings. . . . We have gently chided Judge Sharp for his failure to provide reasoning for dismissing a claim "without prejudice and without leave to amend" by stating. . . . We also have used the severe remedy of reassigning a case when Judge Sharp abused his discretion by refusing to grant an evidentiary hearing.

And:

> We are greatly troubled that Judge Sharp continues to ignore or to circumvent specific directives and mandates from this court in his adjudication of cases before him. His deliberate defiance of our mandate in [this case], however, not only shows a disregard for our explicit instruction, complete with our quoting the governing statute to him, but also disregard for [the defendant], who is before Judge Sharp for a just resolution of his case. Further, the third sentencing appeal in this case exemplifies the judicial inefficiency that results from such obstinate conduct. Apparently, the only way we can obtain compliance from Judge Sharp in this case is to reverse or vacate his rulings outright with the instruction that he cannot rule in a particular way. . . . Judge Sharp stubbornly persisted in his questioned decision without reasonable explanation or justification. We again hold that Judge Sharp abused his discretion . . . specifically defied our mandate . . . we

have no confidence that he will perform the appropriate evaluation of [the defendant's] financial condition on another remand concerning the same restitution issue.

In order to receive permission to appeal, a prisoner must obtain leave to appeal by making a "substantial showing of the denial of a constitutional right." Until the enactment of the federal Antiterrorism and Effective Death Penalty Act of 1996, the mechanism for making the requisite "substantial showing" was an application for certificate of probable cause to appeal (CPC).

In Judge Sharp's courtroom, however, no one has ever yet made a substantial showing. Other federal district courts have routinely granted such permission to appeal, at least in first-time habeas petitions. Judge Sharp's court is the one exception; during his first decade on the federal bench, he never granted CPC in a death case, no matter how obviously deserving the case might be. For Judge Sharp, substance has never been the issue, nor would the granting of CPC free a guilty party; all a CPC does is allow the prisoner to make an appeal. Federal district judges are permitted to deny CPC to appeal if every claim in the habeas petition is patently frivolous, but they are directed to permit appeal based on substantial evidence of a legal defect. Judge Sharp's rejection of the constitutional questions presented in the habeas petition was irresponsible, but unassailable—or so Judge Sharp believed.

As a matter of justice, however, denial of CPC by a federal district court doesn't make appeal impossible. For Joe, it only meant that he would have to ask the Eleventh Circuit for the CPC. By 1993, the appellate court had become familiar with Judge Sharp's habitual pattern of denying CPC even in cases where CPC should have been granted. The appellate judges had become quite used to granting CPC in cases arising out of Judge Sharp's court. I had little doubt that the Eleventh Circuit Court of Appeals would reverse Judge Sharp on this score and grant Joe a CPC to appeal, as the appellate court had properly done so often in the past.

Our plan was for me to apply to the court to be appointed as Stafman's cocounsel. First, however, we needed to apply to the Eleventh Circuit for a CPC to appeal; otherwise, there would be no appeal. Stafman and I agreed that I would write the CPC application. The CPC became a joint venture by several of my Vermont Law School students, Laura Gillen (my secretary), and me.

In July 1993 I flew from Vermont to Florida, where I was to conduct a training session for CCR's attorneys and to visit Joe Spaziano at the prison. I flew from Vermont to Tallahassee, where my lady friend, Nell Medlin, met me at the Tallahassee airport. The following day Nell and I drove our rental car across the top of Florida, east from Tallahassee to Starke, where I met with Joe.

I had seen Joe last in 1986, when I was still working at CCR, but the seven years since our last visit meant nothing. The time evaporated the moment we shook hands. Thirty seconds later we were chuckling, then laughing, then guffawing, as we traded news and gossip. We mostly talked about other people. Joe talked about his mother's health and his daughter's future. I talked a lot about Nell.

It was a lovely visit with a friend from my past life as a full-time capital public defender. Our old connection was still there. Why, then, did I leave the prison feeling so sad? Maybe it was the weather; by the time Nell steered the rental car onto the interstate as we drove away from the prison, rain was sheeting down with a power that seemed almost violent. Maybe it was Nell, or maybe it was talking with Joe about Nell; until then I'm not sure I'd realized how much I was falling in love with her. Maybe it was having to leave Joe behind while I left the prison. Maybe it was how little had really changed in Joe's case—and therefore in Joe's life—in the seven years since I had seen him last. Maybe it was nostalgia for deathwork in the trenches—being hundreds of miles away and disconnected from the nurturing deathwork family at CCR and West Palm Beach. Maybe it was being in a different climate zone from my old clients—letters and phone calls were enough up to a point, but they weren't the same as being there.

Sometime during the drive from the prison to Tallahassee, I realized that coming to Florida had felt like coming home. Couldn't be— Florida *home*? The South, *home*? I realized I had been homesick for the food and the people and the culture and the language and the land. I missed the work and the people who do the work, and even the politicians and judges who hate the people who do the work. I finally understood the final lines of Faulkner's *Absalom, Absalom!* Asked by his Harvard roommate, "Why do you hate the South?" the novel's pro-tagonist shoots back, "I *don't* hate it! I don't hate the South."

I had missed it, all of it: the pressure cooker of the death warrants, the all-night marathons of writing briefs and skull sessions about legal issues and tactics and politics, all fueled mostly by adrenaline and caffeine and fear; watching the true masters of our game at work—Mark Olive, Scharlette Holdman, Craig Barnard, Tony Amsterdam, Millard Farmer.

Of course, the world I was missing no longer existed. Craig Barnard was dead. Judge Vance was dead. Scharlette Holdman and Mark Olive were gone from CCR, the former fired and the latter forced to resign in protest of Holdman's firing. The CCR that Holdman and Olive created in 1985 and infused with their brilliance, heart, and courage was already in decline.

And then there was me—a deserter from the death wars, safe and warm in my tenured sinecure amid the mountains of New England. Who was I to criticize CCR or anyone else who was on the front lines? For a lot of years—until Joe Spaziano's case came apart in 1995—I didn't criticize CCR, publicly or privately. This, in retrospect, was a mistake, because it blinded me to the reality of what CCR was becoming. Olive saw it; Holdman saw it; many others saw it long before I saw it, long before I'd allow myself to see it.

Maybe my mixed feelings about Florida being home explained why, when I returned to Vermont a few days after visiting Joe, I neglected to write to him. He called me on it, of course.

July 5, 1993
Hi Mike,

I haven't heard from you since you left the prison. You didn't like the painting? Well I hook you up something better Mike. You ok Pel. Sorry I'm so dame lost half the time Mike. Ok just a short not to see if you're ok.

Sincerely
Joe

July 6, 1993
Hi Mike,

Hay pel that little painting I done for you wasn't nothing just play around stuff. Lisen I'm going to do up you and your son a real slick painting ok. I'll waite to hear from you. I never heard from the lady you said was going to write? I'm sorry I freeze up so much when I see you, I haven't heard from you in so long or seen you and get frooze a little ☺. Ok I'll close to I hear from you I'm must getting back painting the way I want so pel I got you a couple neat painting comming ☺. Your good people Mike and thanks.

Your Friend Crazy Joe

P.S. Send me a book of stamps and your son's first name ok I need his first name to put it into the cartoon painting.

July 12, 1993
Dear Joe:

I just received your letter. I apologize for not writing to you sooner, but things have been a little hectic here. It is not because I'm not thinking about you or working on your case.

I thought the painting was terrific. The problem was that my friend Nell, the woman who is working on your case with me, really fell in love with it and made me give it to her. I hope it was OK for me to give it to her. She will be writing soon to thank you for the painting. Her life is very crazy these days, because she is studying for the bar exam.

It was wonderful to see you again, although I wish we could have spent more time together. As of right now your brief is due on July 31, but I expect to request and to receive an extension of time. If not, then I will file it on the 31st. Anyway, take care and stay well. And keep in touch. I love to hear from you.

Sincerely yours,
Michael Mello

July 14, 1993
Dear Joe:

It was great to hear from you again. Don't ever worry about "freezing" when we meet; I appreciate that at our most recent visit we did have some somewhat awkward things to sort out regarding Ed and I. I just really needed to be clear that you were totally comfortable with my taking over the 11th Circuit portion of your case. It was terrific seeing you again and catching up in person.

The new painting sounds slick. My son's name is Larkin. I know he'll love the painting. Enclosed are all of the stamps I have in my house. Anyway, hang in there, my friend. Write soon.

Sincerely,
Michael Mello

P.S. Enclosed is a draft of a motion for an extension of time that I plan to file in the next day or so. The state has agreed to 30 extra days, but I (being greedy) am requesting 60 days. If the court denies this motion then your brief will remain due on July 30.

August 2, 1993
Dear Joe:

Just a quick letter in between drafts of your brief. Nell and I are working steadily on the brief.

I got the two paintings today and they look fabulous. Thank you! Thank you! I know Larkin will love his painting.

As always, it was great to hear from you. Take care and stay well.

Sincerely yours,
Michael Mello
Professor of Law

August 9, 1993
Dear Joe:

The brief is progressing. Here is the latest version. Nell is being very helpful.

Here is something for you to think about. I got an unexpected phone call last week from Governor Chiles's clemency aide, whom I have never met. He (and Chiles) appear interested in asking the Florida legislature to repeal the jury override. It's a long shot, but I told him I would do what I could to help.

We didn't talk about your case specifically, but it made me think: If Chiles has problems with the override, then maybe we should apply for clemency *now*, rather than waiting until the end of the federal habeas case. My concern is that if we wait, and if Chiles is not re-elected (and there is a good change he won't be) then we may have to seek clemency from a Governor who has no problem with the override. Jim Smith, for example.

Anyway, I'm drafting a clemency memorandum, just in case we decide not to wait. Let me know what you think.

Sincerely,
Michael Mello

P.S. The paintings are absolutely BEAUTIFUL.

August 9, 1993
Hi Mike

Mike have you received the 2 paintings as yet. I never got 2 receit back from them I think they are still in the package room. They have been moving more people over here. I'll write him another letter.

Hay Mike thanks for interducing me to Nell she is a real nice lady. She send me some pictures of her kids they look supper and very healthy. I got 2 letter from one of the twins she wanted me to do her if a painting if I would. I hooket her up a supper one ☺. Thanks Mike for letting her write to me. She even sent me stamps she's on the ball Mike ☺.

Well I'll check on the paintings in case they haven't sent them out as yet.

How is the new Brief comming along? Sure hope you got it all in there. 65 pages don't sound much from over 170, 180 whatever. Ok I'll close Mike and your great people.

Your Friend Joe

August 17, 1993
Dear Joe:

I just got your letter postmarked August 10. You have probably received my earlier letter, but, just in case, I wanted to say how much I loved the 2 new paintings. Larkin will really enjoy them.

The brief and clemency application are coming along well. The brief will be ready to file on August 30, although some more time would be nice.

I need to raise two things with you, both of which involve money and which are therefore awkward. We have always been straight with each other, and I think that's the best way to be now.

First, I'm afraid that Nell will not be able to make business arrangements concerning the marketing of your artwork. Those sorts of business relationships could be seen as a conflict of interest, which could hurt your case and get Nell in hot water with the bar. Your case can be our only priority now. We have to keep our eyes on that ball.

Second, I am leaning towards filing a clemency application in your case. I drafted out a memorandum, but plan to wait a bit before filing it. I am also inclined *not* to ask the courts or Governor to cover my expenses or fee for the clemency; I'm afraid that asking for money from the government could hurt our chances for clemency. So I will be doing the clemency pro bono, which is a fancy legal way of saying I'll be doing it for free. That's OK with me, although any money you could send for expenses would be appreciated.

Anyway, Joe, I hope things are well with you. And I'm glad you and Nell are getting along. Write soon.

Sincerely,
Michael Mello

August 24, 1993
Dear Joe:

Thanks for your letter of August 17. It was great to hear from you.

The brief is going well. I still plan to file it Monday, August 30.

As soon as the brief is filed, I want to start mapping out a clemency application. Clemency is not usually sought while the case is still moving through the courts, but I'm afraid that if we wait, Jim Smith rather than Lawton Chiles will be Governor. That would not be good.

You asked about going back to state court if things don't go well in the Eleventh Circuit. You certainly *could* go back to state court with new evidence or legal arguments, *but* the state courts would *not* be likely to listen very carefully. Their view would be that you've had all the "bites" at the state court apple you're entitled to.

So, I think that our energy is best spent on clemency and in the Eleventh Circuit. If we lose in the Eleventh Circuit, I will ask the U.S. Supreme Court to hear your case again.

Anyway, my friend, I hope this answers your questions. Let me get back to the brief. Write soon.

Sincerely,
Michael Mello

August 27, 1993
Dear Joe:

The court denied my motion for extra time to file the brief as well as my motion to exceed the 55 page limit. But after a frantic week, and with the invaluable assistance of Mike Millemann, Nancy Levit, Nell, Laura Gillen, Ian Ridlon and Dawn Poland, we got the brief filed on time. I think it looks good. Let me know what you think.

The state now has 30 days to file its brief, and then we will have 2 weeks to file a reply brief. After we rest a bit, I will start drafting and circulating the reply brief as well as a clemency memorandum. I'll keep you posted. I hope you are doing well.

Sincerely,
Michael Mello

August 31, 1993
Dear Joe:

I received your letter postmarked August 27. I fear that I was confusing when I wrote you earlier.

You do NOT need to pay me to represent you, either on the Eleventh Circuit brief or on the clemency application. I have never asked you for money, and I'm not doing so now. My services are FREE. OK?

My only intent was to let you know that no one will be paying for my work on your clemency application. As I hoped to make clear, that's totally OK. I'll still do the application. I'll still spend whatever time and money I need to make it perfect. I'll still fly to Florida to meet with the Governor's staff.

Joe, if I were in the business for the money I would not represent death row inmates. Are we cool? OK?

Sincerely yours,
Michael Mello

P.S. So what do you think of the brief?

September 8, 1993

Federal Express Corp.
Memphis, TN 38194
Re: Ms. Cynthia Bueller,
W. Lebanon, N.H.

Dear Sir or Madam:

Recently we had an extraordinary encounter with your West Lebanon, New Hampshire office. A package which "absolutely, positively had to be there overnight" was perilously close to not making it to the office by closing. The package contained legal papers to be filed on behalf of a death row prisoner. He is a prisoner whom we believe to be innocent, so you can imagine our concern that the documents arrive the next day.

On our arrival at your Lebanon office, Ms. Cynthia Bueller was extremely helpful in expediting the administrative procedures involved. She was extraordinarily courteous under the high pressure circumstances.

Our past dealings with the office have been more than satisfactory. Federal Express is the most reliable way of getting materials from the provinces of Vermont to the various courts in Georgia and Florida before which capital litigators practice. People like Ms. Bueller make it so. Thanks.

We wanted to take this opportunity to both thank and commend Ms. Bueller for her help in getting our package to its destination on time.

Sincerely,

Michael Mello   Ian Ridlon
Professor of Law   Law Student

September 16, 1993
Dear Joe:

Thank you for your kind words about the brief. I'm glad that you like it and that you are feeling better.

While waiting for the state's answer brief (due in two weeks or so), Nell and I have drafted a clemency memo and reply brief.

They're still *very* rough, but we have no time limit (or page limit) on clemencies. Let me know what you think.

Anyway, stay well, my friend. Let me hear from you.

Sincerely yours,
Michael Mello

September 21, 1993
Hi Mike,

I got the 2 briefs and the Birthday card thanks Mike. I have 2 painting for the package room man to pick up to mail to you. Hope you like them ☺.

Ok haven't read these yet but don't matter? Wont understand it anyway.

Haven't heard from Nell lately think she maybe mad at me What the hell can I say ☺. Ok pel I'll close get a couple sketches I want to do while they are on my mine. I love art work ☺. As you can tell.

Your Friend Joe

October 11, 1993
Dear Joe:

I am enclosing the state's answer brief and a draft of our reply. Please let me know your thoughts. Anyway, take care and stay well. And keep in touch. I love to hear from you.

Sincerely yours,
Michael Mello

October 22, 1993
Dear Joe:

As always, it was terrific to hear from you. I got two paintings from you a couple of weeks ago, and I thought that I had written to tell you how much I loved them. I even shared them with my students, and they were the hit of the semester.

Of course I'm not mad at you. Thank you again for the paintings and for keeping in touch. Nell sends her regards, and is working around the clock at her dad's law firm.

Now that all of the 11th Circuit briefs are in, the court should schedule oral argument in Atlanta. I will let you know when that happens. As always, if you have any questions or thoughts please let me know.

Take care, my friend, and stay well.

Sincerely yours,
Michael Mello

October 28, 1993

Hi Mike,

I got the brief and lookes good to me. I let some of the guys red it to so they exsplain things to be ☺. Ok thanks Mike. glad you got the paintings ok. Will have some more to you soon. Fill up your office and house ☺. Whats up pel ☺. Well ok sure hope we get good news in the 11th Circuit Court. Who will be in the Arguments in the 11th Circuit court? Ok I'm going Mike. You take care did your son like his painting? Hope he did. Ok I'll close.

Your Friend
Crazy Joe

November 1, 1993

Dear Joe:

Thank you for your recent letter. I'm glad you thought the brief looked OK.

I will be doing the oral argument on your behalf in the 11th Circuit. I assume that Margene Roper, the Assistant Attorney General who wrote the Answer Brief for the state in the 11th Circuit will be representing the prosecution. As of now, the court has not scheduled an oral argument date. So far we only know the identity of one 11th Circuit judge: Ed Carnes, who is very bad news. We will not learn the identities of the other two judges until 7 days before the oral argument.

Take care, my friend. As always it was terrific to hear from you. Take care and stay well.

Sincerely,
Michael Mello

February 2, 1994

Dear Joe:

Thank you for the lovely painting. Your art just gets better and better.

I was so sorry to hear about your daughter [who had had a fire in her home]. But at least material possessions can be replaced. The important thing is that *she* is intact.

Still no word on an oral argument date. I'm plodding ahead on clemency.

Anyway, It was great to hear from you. Take care and stay well, my friend.

Sincerely,
Michael Mello
Professor of Law

The Eleventh Circuit granted permission to appeal. Now we knew there would be an appeal, complete with written briefs and oral argument, in Atlanta, the Eleventh Circuit's base of operations. We were in business.

Or so we thought. When Ed Stafman filed a motion for me to be appointed cocounsel, the court denied it. The Eleventh Circuit said it would not appoint me cocounsel, but it would entertain a motion for me to *substitute* for Stafman as Joe's sole appellate counsel. Ominously, the court's order was signed by Judge Ed Carnes. Carnes was a former capital prosecutor in Alabama, and I had opposed his appointment to the U.S. Court of Appeals for the Eleventh Circuit. Joe's was the first capital case to come before the neophyte Judge Carnes.

Judge Carnes's denial of the cocounsel motion required Joe, Stafman, and me to decide whether Stafman or I would represent Joe on this, most likely his last, appeal. Joe wanted me. Stafman wanted me. I wanted to do it, but I would need help. Laura, my secretary, promised to word-process the briefs. Friends also offered to pitch in: Michael and Sally Millemann, Jeff Robinson, Mark Olive, and Nell.

Judge Carnes applied the Eleventh Circuit's procedural rules with a vengeance: not an extra page for the briefs; no extra time in which to file them. It was a nightmare, but due to the tireless assistance of Laura Gillen and a group of law students, the briefs were filed on time and within the prescribed page limits.

Then things fell apart. The stress of Joe's case proved too much for me. I was overcome with a sense of hopelessness and despair that, no matter what I did, Joe was going to be executed for crimes he didn't commit; that the courts—and I—were just going through the motions before killing him. And that wasn't all there was to my meltdown. I was in two automobile wrecks. I had a seizure. I was drinking too much. My health went to hell. My health problems caused me to miss a few of my law school classes, and the dean threatened me with the loss of my job. After a fight with Nell, I drank a bottle of vodka and a bottle of wine. A friend, worried that she hadn't heard from me, came to my home, found me dead drunk, and called 911.

My employer emphatically suggested that I take disability leave, and I agreed. I also agreed to spend a month at the Hanley-Hazelden Center for alcoholic treatment in West Palm Beach, Florida, thus bringing my life as a lawyer full circle. I decided to quit drinking and put my life back in order, and, with some backsliding on both fronts, I have succeeded in doing both.

Reconfiguring my relationships with people was relatively easy; it was a process of discarding a few people and clinging to others, particularly my mother. Far harder was sorting out my relationship to work. Work has always been at the center of my life—whether I was doing search and rescue work for the Civil Air Patrol in high school, writing for and editing the school newspaper in college, drafting opinions for Judge Vance, representing death row prisoners, teaching law school, writing, or taking on capital cases.

I decided that Joe's would be my last capital case. I had become convinced, after so many years in the madhouse of capital punishment as a legal system, that I had become an enabler of executions. The government was going to kill Joe Spaziano, an innocent man, regardless of what I or any lawyer did. Worse, I would be the state's alibi; the system could feel okay about killing him because he'd had a lawyer—me. And this was how an *innocent* man was treated. I decided I could no longer, in good conscience, participate in such a system.

I firmly believe that but for my meltdown—and the process I underwent in working through and out of it—in the spring of 1994, I would not have had the serenity and strength to do what I had to do a year later to save Joe Spaziano's life. What I did in the fall of 1995—taking Joe's case to the *Miami Herald,* and then taking on the governor, CCR, the attorney general's office, and, in the end, the Florida Supreme Court—was the most frightening thing I've ever done as a lawyer. Only a fool wouldn't have been frightened, and I knew what I was risking in Joe's case: his life, my license to practice law, my job, and my freedom. It has been said that what doesn't kill us makes us stronger. My meltdown made me stronger. My health precluded my doing the oral argument in Joe's case. In a decision I came to regret, I asked Marty McClain, CCR's chief assistant, if CCR would do the oral argument in my stead. McClain said that was no problem, and he assigned the task to Gail Anderson, CCR's chief appellate litigator.

I didn't write to Joe about any of this, of course. I did write this:

May 1, 1994
Dear Joe:

This is a difficult letter for me to write. I'm afraid that at the moment I am ill. My illness will prevent me from doing the Eleventh Circuit oral argument in your case. But an excellent oral advocate—Gail Anderson of CCR—will do it instead.

The Eleventh Circuit has scheduled the oral argument for June 1. As you know, I had planned to do the argument. But in December I was in a fairly serious car crash; that led to complications, which, combined with other stuff going on in my life, led to more complications—which, among other reasons, led to my being placed on disability leave by the law school, for at least a month, beginning May 1. I had to cancel classes and to get a colleague to grade my exams; for the month of May (at least) I will be in the hospital. I have been in a local hospital for about a week; on May 2 I'll be transferred to a hospital in Florida (ironically, in West Palm Beach).

Under the circumstances, I attempted to identify the lawyers who could pinch hit for me in your June 1 argument. I came up with three lawyers, one of whom was Gail Anderson at CCR. I know Gail's work very well; I helped train her in the mid-1980s; I have seen videotapes of some of her recent arguments before the Florida Supreme Court. In short, she's terrific.

At my request, Gail agreed to do your argument. She will ask the court for an extension of time, but regardless she will do the argument. I will send her your case files and will work with her. Please don't worry about this development: Your oral argument is in good hands.

Be clear: you need to understand that I am **NOT** dropping your case; we've been through too much together over the past 10 years for me to cut you loose now. Except for the oral argument, I will remain your attorney. My doctors tell me that my prognosis is good. Nell, Tom Horkan (Executive Director of Florida Catholic Conference) and I are working on a clemency application; enclosed is the most recent draft of the petition and supporting appendices. I will deal with whatever we need to do beyond the Eleventh Circuit panel level. Please understand that I REMAIN YOUR LAWYER, if you wish.

Joe, I wish I were able to do your oral argument. But you are in good hands with Gail.

Very truly yours,
Michael Mello

May 27, 1994

Dear Joe:

Thank you so much for your card and your kind words. As always, your painting did bring a smile to my face. I will be back in Vermont in early June. I am recuperating well. I have been in touch with CCR and everything is cool.

Thomas Horkan, Executive Director of Florida Catholic Conference (the Florida Catholic Church's chief lobbyist in the legislature), has agreed to hand deliver the clemency materials to the Governor and Cabinet, and to advocate for clemency on your behalf. I am enclosing the most recent draft of the application.

It was great to hear from you. Take care, keep the faith and stay well.

Sincerely,
Michael Mello
Professor of Law

July 18, 1994

Dear Joe:

Thank you for your recent letter; it was good to hear that you are doing well.

Here is the supplemental brief as filed, along with the state's brief. Since the briefs were filed on the same day, neither brief refers to the other. Let me know your thoughts.

Now we wait for the court's decision. That could come in a month or a year or longer; there's really no way to predict. It will depend on whether the three judges can all agree on a result and an opinion, whether there will be a dissenting judge, how occupied the judges are with other cases, and so on. Also, they could wait to see what the U.S. Supreme Court does in *Schlup v. Delo,* which we refer to in our brief; because *Schlup* may give some guidance about how federal courts ought to deal with claims of innocence, the Eleventh Circuit may want to wait to see what the Supremes have to say on the matter. I'll let you know as soon as I hear anything.

Anyway, let me know if you have any questions. And keep your fingers crossed.

Sincerely,
Michael Mello
Professor of Law

It felt good to be back on Joe's case, back to writing to him, and even better visiting with him. It was like coming home.

When a capital habeas appeal reaches the Eleventh Circuit, it is assigned to a panel of three judges; of the three, the junior judge in seniority is designated the "orders" judge, which means he or she rules on preliminary, routine, and administrative matters. On Joseph Spaziano's appeal, the Eleventh Circuit orders judge for the panel was Carnes. We have a history, Judge Carnes and I, which I will get to in a moment and which perhaps explains his unjudgelike behavior in this case. I opposed his appointment by President Bush to the Eleventh Circuit (to replace the semiretiring Judge Frank Johnson, a legend of the civil rights struggles; it was sort of like replacing Justice Thurgood Marshall with Clarence Thomas). I had hoped our disagreements were all in the past; after all, we're both professionals. But Judge Carnes started making rulings that can only be called petty: denial of motion to appoint me as cocounsel, denial of motion to exceed the court's rather stingy page limits for briefs, and denial of motion for extension of time. In addition, out of the blue, I received a condescending lecture from the judge about how to write, provided for "the guidance of counsel." It did not look promising.

In our briefs before Judge Carnes, we argued that Joe Spaziano's death sentence violated the Florida Constitution, because the sentencing judge did not consider nonstatutory mitigating evidence and because existing Florida precedent precluded Joe's counsel from presenting nonstatutory mitigating evidence. Further, we argued that the Florida Supreme Court acted arbitrarily and capriciously in failing to credit the mitigating evidence in the record in considering the validity of Joe's jury override.

We also claimed that trial counsel was ineffective. Counsel's unreasonable failure to inform the jury (1) that the testimony of the state's star witness was the product of sessions with a police hypnotist and (2) that the hypnosis sessions destroyed the reliability of the "testimony," as well as counsel's unreasonable failure to attempt to exclude the tainted testimony, undermined any reasonable confidence in the outcome of Spaziano's trial and sentencing. Also, the state's hypnotically generated testimony yielded a constitutionally unreliable conviction and death sentence. Further, we argued that Joe's due process rights were violated by the state's withholding of exculpatory evidence—that the "Joe" with whom the victim spoke before her disappearance was *not* Joe Spaziano, contrary to the state's position at trial. Another person was identified as the assailant and had admitted that he possibly had committed the crime.

We also argued that he was denied due process of law because he was tried, convicted, and sentenced when he was mentally incompetent. Finally, trial counsel's unreasonable failure to petition the trial court for evaluation and hearing on Joe's competency to stand trial, and that counsel's blind following of Spaziano's instructions not to present "shrinks" on his behalf, undermines any reasonable confidence in the outcome of Spaziano's trial and sentencing.

Judge Carnes's opinion for the Eleventh Circuit panel began with a complaint about the length of the petition for writ of habeas corpus:

> Although the habeas rules require more than notice pleading, and some factual specificity will often be helpful, or even necessary, a habeas petition should not resemble a treatise. Effective writing is concise writing. Attorneys who cannot discipline themselves to write concisely are not effective advocates, and they do a disservice not only to the courts but also to their clients.

Earlier in the Eleventh Circuit proceedings of this case, Judge Carnes had entered an order stating:

The court, having read appellant's application for a Certificate of Probable Cause, believes that it is unlikely that the court will look with favor upon a motion to exceed the 55 page limitation applicable to appellant's initial brief by more than 10 pages. The requirement of Eleventh Circuit's Rule 29-1, that any motion for leave to file briefs in excess of the page requirements must be filed at least 7 days in advance of its due date, will be strictly enforced in any event. This information is provided for the guidance of counsel.

As noted above, Judge Carnes thereafter denied our motions to exceed the court's briefing page limits. Perhaps Judge Carnes's preoccupation with brevity explains why his forty-four page opinion ignored several of our principal constitutional claims.

The Eleventh Circuit's opinion endorsed the district court's finding that "at the time of the initial sentence proceeding the trial judge believed that the Florida sentencing statute, which explicitly limited the trial court's consideration of mitigating circumstances to those enumerated in the statute, precluded consideration of nonstatutory mitigating circumstances." Judge Carnes reasoned that the issue of whether *Hitchcock* error occurred in this case "is a legal one, it is almost entirely dependent upon the answer to a question of fact: did the sentencing judge consider any and all nonstatutory mitigating circumstance evidence that was presented to him?" The court noted that Joe's initial death sentence was vacated and the case remanded for a limited resentencing and "what matters is what the trial judge thought and did at that resentencing proceeding, not the initial sentencing." Judge Carnes then engaged in a selective discussion of the question of whether the resentencing was a full-blown resentencing proceeding or a limited remand. Applying a clearly erroneous standard, the Eleventh Circuit concluded that "the district court did not clearly err in finding that at Spaziano's resentencing proceeding Judge McGregor knew he was bound to consider, and he did actually consider, all nonstatutory mitigating circumstance evidence presented to him. . . . The factual premise of Spaziano's *Hitchcock* claim involving the sentencing judge fails." Judge Carnes's opinion ignored the presumptively correct fact-finding made by Judge McGregor—the judge both at the original sentencing and the remand proceeding—that the resentencing was not a full-blown resentencing proceeding; it was no more than a limited proceeding.

Further, although Judge Carnes recognized that "defense counsel argued as nonstatutory mitigating circumstances residual doubt," he lumped residual doubt—an issue irrelevant as a matter of law under Florida law—with all other sorts of clearly relevant nonstatutory mitigating circumstances and concluded that "all nonstatutory mitigating circumstance evidence presented" to Judge McGregor was considered at the resentencing proceeding. The factor nowhere mentioned in the Eleventh Circuit's opinion is that lingering doubt about guilt is today— and was at the time of Joe Spaziano's original sentencing as well as at the time of his resentencing—legally irrelevant as a matter of state law. Spaziano aggressively raised this residual doubt issue in his Eleventh Circuit briefs. As to our argument that the Spaziano case was indistinguishable from *Parker v. Dugger*—which also involved an Eighth Amendment limitation upon the power of the Florida Supreme Court to uphold a death sentence imposed following a jury recommendation of life imprisonment when mitigating circumstances, statutory and nonstatutory, were present in the case—Judge Carnes reasoned that "the square peg of this case will not fit into *Parker*'s round hole . . . although Spaziano has gone to great lengths to disguise his contention as a *Parker* claim, stripped to its essentials the claim is that the Florida Supreme Court erred in its application of the *Tedder* rule."

The Eleventh Circuit also dismissed our claim that Joe was entitled to an evidentiary hearing (to prove that trial counsel rendered ineffective assistance of counsel in two crucial respects) related to the fact that the state's "key witness," Tony DiLisio, had been hypnotized before trial. Trial counsel, who knew that DiLisio had been hypnotized by the police, had failed to object to DiLisio's being allowed to testify, and even if counsel could not have excluded DiLisio's testimony he was ineffective for failing to present and develop the hypnosis facts in order to impeach DiLisio before the jury. Although no court has granted Joe Spaziano's request for an evidentiary hearing to prove the factual basis for this claim, the Eleventh Circuit found that trial counsel's decisions "involve[d] a matter of trial strategy." Trial counsel "decided to pursue the strategy he did because he had abundant information to use in impeaching DiLisio, and he did not want to risk having the jury think that DiLisio's testimony was more reliable because it had been hypnotically refreshed." The Eleventh Circuit did not address the core of Spaziano's claim of ineffective assistance of counsel: that trial counsel's "strategic" decision not to challenge the hypnotically influenced testimony of the state's star witness was meaningless, because that "tactical" decision was made in the absence of any investigation whatsoever by trial counsel into the dangers of hypnosis. Joe Spaziano's habeas corpus petition detailed, and his Eleventh Circuit briefs summarized, a vast amount of information about the unreliability of hypnosis, information that would have been easily available at the trial—had trial counsel bothered to look for it.

In addressing our claim that the use of the hypnotically created testimony of the prosecution's star witness violated Joe's rights under the Eighth and Fourteenth Amendments, the Eleventh Circuit held that it need not address the merits, because the court concluded the claim was barred under the technical doctrine of retroactivity. The opinion did not mention that retroactivity was raised by the state neither in the district court nor in its brief nor at oral argument; retroactivity became an issue in the case only when the court, *sua sponte* (that is, on its own), invited the parties to brief it.

Finally, the Eleventh Circuit rejected the merits of our contention that the state at trial unconstitutionally withheld exculpatory evidence. The district court had found this claim (called a *Brady* claim because it is based on the U.S. Supreme Court's ruling in *Brady v. Maryland,* 1963) to be procedurally defaulted, but, as the Eleventh Circuit opinion noted, the district court "did not explicitly address the actual innocence exception" to the procedural default doctrine. The Eleventh Circuit noted that "the precise contours of that exception as it applies to guilt stage claims is unsettled at the present time. When the legal dust settles in this area, which could happen after the Supreme Court issues its opinion in *Schlup v. Delo,* it may be that the actual innocence exception will overlap substantially with the materiality component of a *Brady* claim." The court determined that it "need not speculate about that, however, because Spaziano's *Brady* claim lacks merits." Without any discussion of the evidence presented by the prosecutor at trial—specifically the weakness of the evidence—Judge Carnes's opinion concluded that the evidence suppressed was not sufficiently "material."

The decision by Judge Ed Carnes of the Eleventh Circuit Court of Appeals was predictably mean spirited; the surprise was that it was also rife with errors. The errors made it more than usually likely that the U.S. Supreme Court would agree to accept the case for plenary consideration, which put me in an exquisite dilemma. Should I ask Judge Carnes to reconsider his opinion, and run the risk that he would clean it up and so reduce the chances of interesting the Supreme Court justices in the case? (The possibility that Carnes might amend his opinion to make it more fair to Joseph Spaziano seemed out of the question.) Or should I go directly to the Supreme Court and hope to get Joe's case bound up with the other innocence-based capital cases already before the Court, including a case challenging the constitutionality of the Alabama jury override? Also, the Court had requested the record in Raleigh Porter's case (another Florida jury override case), suggesting that the justices remained interested in the override. Indeed, my research into Thurgood Marshall's papers confirmed that interest; in a series of internal memoranda, the justices and their clerks had argued that some of the very issues presented by Joe's case had in the past grabbed the attention of the Court. (But could I use the papers themselves, directly, in the petition, or, given that at least Chief Justice Rehnquist had been outraged by the release of the papers to the public, would it be in bad taste, or would it be bad tactics, to rely on them now? Now that I had the papers, how could I not use them?) Further, Justice John Paul Stevens, who wrote a dissenting opinion in Spaziano's case back in 1984, was still on the Court and had rebuked his colleagues, urging them to grant plenary review in more cases; Justice Harry Blackmun, who wrote the Court's opinion against Joe Spaziano, had since retired. Carnes's opinion for the Eleventh Circuit was issued on October 7, 1994. If the petition for Supreme Court review could be filed by October 19, then the justices would consider it at their December 9 conference—two days after hearing oral argument in the Alabama jury override case.

This, then, was the quandary: Should we take the full ninety days we were allowed to file the petition for Supreme Court review, or should we file early, so that the case could be heard as a companion to the other three innocence cases then under plenary review by the Court? Even if we increased the odds of actually securing plenary Supreme Court review by filing quickly, those odds were still not hopeful: less than 5 percent of petitions for review are granted by the Court. And even if the Court agreed to hear Joe's case, there was certainly no guarantee that in the end he would win a new trial or new sentencing; this was still the Rehnquist/Scalia/Thomas Court. And who decides? Me, the lawyer, or Joe Spaziano, the man whose life hangs in the balance? In the end, I decided to file the petition early, so that the Court could consider it at the December 9 conference. So, after eighteen years on death row for a crime he did not commit, Joseph Spaziano waived the guaranteed three months of delay and filed directly in the Supreme Court. The petition requesting plenary review was filed in Washington twelve days after the Eleventh Circuit issued its judgment, before the court's opinion had even been published.

But the petition was not considered at the December 9 conference. Why not? Because the prosecutor—after almost two decades of whining at every turn about how "all these capital defense lawyers try to do is delay, delay, delay"—needed an extra month to respond to our certiorari petition. This was fine with us, because the state's delay meant that Joe would certainly live throughout the 1994–95 Christmas and New Year's holiday season. One day at a time, as they say in the recovery industry. The exquisite irony of the poor, overworked prosecutor needing extra time was not lost on me—or on my client.

When the U.S. Supreme Court decides that a case isn't worth the justices' time, there isn't a lot of fanfare. At 10:00 A.M. on the Court's "orders day," you can call the Court's clerk's office to learn whether the justices have made your case one of the tiny percentage selected as sufficiently worthy. The office follows up with a form letter.

In Joe Spaziano's case, the Supreme Court's decision denying review was unanimous: nine to zero. The denial of review meant several things for Joe's short-time future. First, he was eligible (if that's the right word) for the governor to sign a new death warrant on him—his fourth. Second, the court's denial meant that any new warrant would likely be carried out. This was so not because Joe had had three warrants already, but because of where Joe's case was situated within the postconviction appellate process. The January 1995 denial marked the end of Joe's completion of the obstacle course that is the legal system: he had been through all the steps in both the state and federal postconviction legal systems.

In other words, Joe Spaziano had already had his one bite at the postconviction apple. By January 1995 the law pretty much prohibited a second bite. Only one Florida prisoner had survived a fourth death warrant, Willie Jasper Darden. Darden was executed on his seventh warrant.

One implication of the Supreme Court's denial of review had to do with who, in the future, would serve as Joe's attorney. When I had come back to Joe's case in 1993, we had all agreed that, if the U.S. Supreme Court denied review, CCR would replace me as Joe's counsel. After some confusion, that's exactly what happened. Once again, I was Joe Spaziano's former lawyer. This new reality hit home for me when I sent my case files to CCR. Joe's case was to have been my last. As of late January 1995 I was officially retired as a capital appeals attorney.

From the time I left CCR in early 1987 until June 1995, I remained one of CCR's most consistent and vocal supporters outside of Florida; for years, I defended CCR against accusations of incompetence and timidity. I represented CCR (pro bono) as amicus curiae in a handful of cases in the U.S. Supreme Court. I agreed to take over the representation of some of CCR's clients when the agency's underfunding and too-large caseload began to impair its attorneys' ability to provide quality legal representation to its condemned clients. I tried to act as intermediary between CCR (which shunned the outside world) and the outside world (which returned the favor).

In the future I would write about capital punishment rather than practice it. On and off during 1994, I had been working on a book about capital punishment as a legal system. I'd thought about devoting a chapter to Joe's case, but I couldn't write it while I was still Joe's attorney. Now that CCR had replaced me as Joe's lawyer, I was free to write. I fully expected that Joe wouldn't live long enough to read a draft of the book chapter about his case.

January 26, 1995
Dear Mike,

Hi Mike I thought about . . . Ed Stafman. I wrote Ed to see what he feels. Anyway I think I like to see what Ed saids to you and me on if he feels he can handle it and knows what to do. Your the one who nterrduced me to Ed. And at the time you felt he is a great lawyer in court. I don't know shit about law. But I don't want to be used by nobody as a ginny pig. I got fealings and care. But don't want people to use me or bull shit me. Mike

I'm as you know in big troble why they can't get togeather and help Ed. I haven't heard from nobody, but you what is going on and you ant going to handle it. Let me know if you and Ed talk and you can let me know. Dame Mike what the hell I know. That saw I think of all day is my case and what is going on.

Mike do what you feel is right. I seen Susan Cary today hope she gave you the message about Ed Prevazono the federal Judge in New York. [Ed Provenzono was Joe's lawyer following his near-fatal accident when he was twenty. Provenzono later became a judge, and Joe had some vague hope that Provenzono might somehow be of help in his case, but this never panned out.]

Sincerely,

Joe

January 30, 1995

Dear Joe:

It was terrific hearing from you. I'm relieved that you seem to be doing OK, all things considered.

Let me try to set out where we are, as I understand it. You have a choice about who will represent you from here on out: *either* (1) Gail Anderson and the folks at CCR, who worked on your case before and after I got Ed Stafman involved, *or* (2) the Resource Center and Ed. It is up to you to decide which lawyers you want. It's your choice. Whomever you choose, I will, of course, do everything I can to help them long distance, from Vermont.

As I said in my letter to Matthew Lawry of the Resource Center (I sent a copy of the letter to you and to CCR), my very strong personal choice is that CCR take over your case. I'm sure the Resource Center would do its best on your case, but I *know* that CCR will do an excellent job for you. I've never done much work with the Resource Center, but my little contact with their lawyers has left me unimpressed (with the exception of Matthew Lawry, who is very competent and truthful and non-petty). By contrast, I have worked closely with CCR for 10 years now. I trust their work, because I know their work.

I don't make this suggestion lightly, Joe. I care very deeply about you and your case; that's why I got back into your case at the Eleventh Circuit level. It's extremely important to me that you have the *best* and most experienced lawyers fighting for you this time around. That's why CCR should serve as your lawyers.

As I said in my letter to Matthew, I am angry that the Resource Center has created this idiotic confusion at this critical time in your case. Your new lawyers—regardless of whether they are CCR or the Resource Center—need to be working on your case now, because there are decisions that need to be made now—decisions that might hold off a death warrant. Wasting everyone's time—yours, mine and CCR's—with intrigues about who will represent you is more than irresponsible; it's actionable, and it might even be criminal. If not, it should be.

I hope this clarifies things a bit. Hopefully, the confusion will be cleared up before you even get this letter. Keep well, my friend.

Sincerely,
Michael Mello
Professor of Law

February 2, 1995
Dear Mike,

Hi pel I got your letter and you know best. You know I wrote Gail [Anderson], to tell her I'm sorry the missuderstanding abut my paintings. But I think I address it VLRC But I don't know. Whoever it is I won't talk to them onless word from you Mike. Can't think to good lately well never could to good anyway ☺. Seen Susan Cary the other day She was suppose to get hold of you did she? I found out that Ed Prevazone died a feau years ago my mom wrote me and told me. Well I got only you'es now. Dam Mike I can't prove nothing on my case.

Sincerely
Your Friend Joe

3-12-95
Hi Mike,

I want to ask you a question on what I heard. Some of the guy'es on the roul where telling me that people who had C.C.R. not the one's now but when C.C.R. where first started, that they some where busted for Coke, and Crack where on dope. And that they are fileing stuff on onafical asistent of consal on their case I like to know is that true? And if so can I do something like that. See Mike be honest I don't know anymore who to trust. I got so fucket around so many ways. Do you know what is going on now in my case how long before we hear something. Is Tom Horkan [my cocounsel during parts of Joe's case] doing anything. See I never seen him or heard from him at all. I don't even know if there is a Tom Horkan or just bull shit. I went trew the Fedaral courts so fast. They never seem like they looket at my case. What is going on Mike? Can't know Judges see the bull shit in my case. I don't know if I told you but Ed. Privasano the federal Judge in new york died a few years back. So I got nobody to speak up for me. Well let me know something Mike I don't know what to think.

Sincerely,

Joe

After I received this letter, I wrote to Joe and told him that as long as I was alive, he would always have someone to speak up for him. I also told him that I was ill at the moment (I had been diagnosed with cancer), but I was on the mend.

3-24-95

Hi Mike,

First Mike I trust you a hole buch never think I have no doughts. I know you worket hard on my case for me.

What I hear about Tom Horkan I hear he is trying to talk and help me with the cabanet and Governor's office.

I haven't been doing no art work Mike I'm pretty depress and worry about the state that will leagaly murder me. Mike your my pel I like you Mike. And feel in my heart you'll never hurt me.

Mike feel bad you getting so sick now cansor dam Mike I've been smoking so long figure I get cansor but only problem I have is my heart blood not going trew it to well but they got me on a diet and medication.

Mike I'm scared shit so much I want to do to help out and can't do nothing and and maybe die like this. Glad I had you for a lawyer Mike get tell your to young to be sick Pel and need lawyers like you in this world ☺.

> Your Pel
> Crazy Joe 1%er
> A.O.A.

Joe's signature on this letter reaffirms his identification with the Outlaws. Members of the Outlaws often refer to themselves as "1 percenters," meaning they are among the 1 percent of Americans who are truly free. The A.O.A. stands for Association of Outlaws America.

I wrote back to Joe and told him that I would do all I could to help CCR with his case, that I had been misdiagnosed with cancer, and that I was clearing my decks to give his case my undivided attention. I soon heard from him again.

4-7-95
Hi Mike,

Me again ☺. I just got your nice letter Mike, thanks. I feel the same with you Mike.

I heard about Raleigh Porter. And heard about Justice John Paul Stevens.

I don't know what is going to happen to me. Yes Mike I worry but lookes like I got some of the best trying to save me ☺.

Well sure hope you get better your good people. OK I'll close and take <u>CARE</u>, I'm think of you.

> your friend
> CRAZY JOE

4-22-95
Hi Mike,

Was thinking you and wonder'en if your ok, are you Mike. Hay pel want to tell you as long as you haven't smoket I feel you shouldn't. You never know if their will be a cure some day. Them cirgarett's ant shit. Well noothing new on my case seen Leslie [Delk] Thur 4-20-95. To sing some papper's. Well hope your ok Mike and hell with them cirgarett. Your good people Mike. You take caer and I'm thinking of you.

> Your Friend
> Crazy Joe

5-17-95

Dear Mike,

Hi Mike. I just received your letter. Gail Anderson was here today to tell me about the same Miami Herold. Mike whatever you want to do is ok with me. Nothing worket so far I'm with you Mike.

Now how you still messet up I see. Sure hope you'll be ok. Your real good people. Nobody hard nothing in Telahassee on my case or nothing on nothing. Don't know if that is good or bad. Nobody but a couple will believe an Outlaw, but what can I say. Well Mike I try to keep bussy thats all I want to do is Art ☺. Thats all I thik about ☺. Try to keep away from these people to murder me. Ok I'll close you take care Mike. I think of you a lot pel.

Your Friend
Crazy Joe

Tenured teachers at Vermont Law School are granted a semester-long sabbatical at full pay every seventh year. My first sabbatical was in the spring of 1995. I spent it in bed, first with pneumonia and then recovering from tongue surgery. I had been diagnosed with tongue cancer, part of my tongue was removed, and the recovery period was slow, excruciatingly painful, and unnecessary—it turned out I didn't have cancer after all.

Soon after my cancer scare, Deanna Peterson, a law student, decided to take a leave of absence from the law school. We then began dating.

While down with pneumonia, in early January 1995, I agreed to represent Paul Jennings Hill on his direct appeal to the Florida Supreme Court. Hill was on death row for the shotgun slayings of a Pensacola, Florida, doctor who performed abortions and the doctor's escort. I am strongly pro-choice, but I wrote a brief arguing that Hill's homicides were justified. Hill fired me before the brief was filed, because he thought (erroneously) that I planned to argue that he was mentally ill.

In spring 1995, Joe's new lawyers at CCR filed an application to Governor Lawton Chiles for clemency. They also planned for a new round of postconviction litigation that would commence when Governor Chiles signed Joe's death warrant—which would be Joe's fourth. CCR tracked Tony DiLisio to Pensacola, Florida. He stonewalled CCR as he had stonewalled Joe's previous lawyers when they found him.

In evaluating the quality—both legal and moral—of the judiciary's treatment of death penalty cases, details matter. Virtually all relevant objective indicia are misleading, in that the purported precision is false. U.S. Supreme Court opinions since 1983 have evinced a sensibility of hostility toward death row prisoners (and their attorneys), but tone is hard to quantify. The Court's recent enforcement of rules regarding page limits (for briefs, petitions, and the like) provides a clue, it seems to me. It's a petty thing, but its very pettiness is precisely my point. Small things matter. They provide clues to larger, less tangible attitudes. Page limits tell death row prisoners—and their lawyers—that the justices' law clerks can't be bothered to read why the death sentence at issue might offend the Constitution. Very few of the justices themselves read any certiorari petitions, anyway.

Many folks think that criminals "get off" on legal technicalities. Some do, but in my experience the law's technicalities work most often *against* people condemned to die. People are executed because of such legal technicalities.

Time limits are a good example. A few years ago, a Virginia death row inmate's lawyer missed a filing date by three days. The Virginia courts held that the late filing constituted a procedural default. And because the state courts had applied a procedural bar, the federal courts refused to consider the prisoner's constitutional claim: that he was innocent of the crime for which Virginia wanted to kill him. The man lost and was executed on schedule, without the federal courts ever considering his evidence of innocence—and all because his lawyer filed court papers three days late.

Joe's case is filled with examples of the courts—both state and federal—deploying legal technicalities to avoid even considering Joe's evidence of innocence. Hypnotically warped testimony is per se inadmissible in Florida courts today—but not for cases decided prior to 1985. Exculpatory evidence hidden by the state from the defense at trial was found too late. Joe's prominent tattoos—not present on the arms of her attacker, according to the rape victim—couldn't be considered by the jury because defense counsel failed to jump through some procedural hoops, and courts further down the capital punishment assembly line couldn't consider the tattoos for the same reason.

For me, the enforcement of arbitrary page limits amounts to procedural artifice and gives away the courts' game. It's a contemptuous slap at any condemned person coming before the court. It says, "We, the busy and important court, just don't have the time and energy to listen to you complain about why the state shouldn't kill you."

It doesn't much matter anyway. No one who is familiar with the appellate courts needs to know about the page limits to understand the judges' contempt for the people who are litigating for their lives. Their contempt shines through in their tone and affect, and in the outcomes of the cases. To paraphrase Abraham Lincoln, for death row prisoners—in and outside of the South—there is no North.

6

Outlaw Judiciary:
Giving Up on the Courts

Always mystify. Mislead and surprise the enemy if possible. And when you strike and overcome him, never let up in pursuit so long as your men have strength to follow, for an army routed, if hotly pursued, becomes panic-stricken, and can then be destroyed by half their number.

Another rule—never fight against heavy odds, if by any possible maneuvering you can hurl your own forces on only a part, and that the weakest part, of your enemy and crush it. Such tactics will win every time, and a small army may thus destroy a large one in detail, and repeated victory will make it invincible.

Stonewall Jackson, describing his tactics in the Valley campaign of 1862

Joe Spaziano was no longer my client, but I couldn't stop thinking about him. Joe's time was just about up. One more death warrant would be the end of him. CCR would go through the choreographed dance, dashing from court to court. The courts would rely on procedural technicalities to deny a stay. To save Joe's life, we would have to come up with a new dance, a dance that the governor and the courts had never seen before.

Despite—or maybe because of—my experiences as a reporter for my college newspaper, when I was a capital public defender I hated talking to reporters about my clients' cases. In particular, I hated talking with anyone from the pro-capital punishment newspaper the *Miami Herald*. Although I wrote a few op-ed pieces for the *Herald,* and I sometimes spoke with reporters about legal *issues* raised in death penalty cases, for the most part I treated newspapers the same way I treated most judges—as entities institutionally predisposed to support the execution of my clients and unwilling to engage the complexities and nuances of the constitutional claims I was trying to raise on behalf of my condemned clients. But circumstances were about to change my usual practice.

May 9, 1995
Ogunquit, Maine

In retrospect, it was only fitting that I was on the coast of Maine when I got the phone call from Karen. Ogunquit is where I go when people I care about die, be they former clients (Ed Kennedy, Johnny Garrett, Nollie Lee Martin), colleagues, or mentors (Craig Barnard, Judge Robert Vance). So it was appropriate that I was in Ogunquit when Karen Gottlieb, a friend from my days as a Florida public defender, left a message on my Vermont home answering machine: "Gene Miller is open to a phone call from you on Joe Spaziano." I was delighted, of course, but delight was leavened with terror, along with a queasy vertigo akin to motion sickness—that moment when despair gives way to possibility.

Gene Miller is an editor with the *Miami Herald*. Twenty years previously, Miller had published a series of articles for the *Herald* (later synthesized into a magnificent book, *Invitation to a Lynching*) that resulted in the pardon and release of two African American men, Freddie Pitts and Wilbert Lee, who had been railroaded onto death row for crimes they did not commit. Pitts and Lee were wrongly convicted and condemned in 1963 for the murders of two gas station attendants in the Florida panhandle. Both men spent twelve years in prison—nine on death row—before another man's confession (and the galleys of *Invitation to a Lynching*) caused Governor Reubin Askew to grant them a full pardon and release from prison in 1975.

My hope in contacting Miller was that he and the *Herald* would do for Joe Spaziano what they had done for Pitts and Lee. I had never met Miller, and I was thoroughly intimidated by his reputation in Florida as a skeptic of death row claims of innocence. After his book was published in 1975, he was contacted by countless prisoners who attempted to enlist his aid in their causes. Miller stated at the time that he would never again become involved in a capital case. He did not want to become the arbiter of all death row claims of innocence. Miller's skepticism of prisoners' claims of innocence is legendary nationwide.

Karen knew Miller's daughter from high school and at my behest she had persuaded the daughter to convince Miller to accept a short telephone call from me so long as it occurred at a specific date and time. When she called, Karen emphasized that the chances that Miller would be interested in "Crazy Joe" Spaziano's case were minuscule. Even though I had no hope that Miller and the *Herald* would champion Joe's claim of total innocence, what did Joe and I have to lose? The state and federal courts were done with Joe's case. Governor Chiles might sign Joe's death warrant—Joe's fourth—any day now.

Two necessary conditions had to be met before I could even *consider* taking Joe's case to Gene Miller and the *Herald*. First, I had to conclude that Joe's chances of winning anything in the courts had dropped to around zero. On this score, I had more than consensus. CCR's Marty McClain and Gail Anderson joined in unanimous agreement that Joe's legal case was far beyond hope. None of the evidence that Joe's advocates had uncovered over the years—the gross unreliability of testimony elicited through hypnotism, the juror's affidavit, the jury override, the other suspects—had succeeded in convincing any court anywhere to give so much as a hearing to the innocence evidence. It would be harder to get the courts to look the second time around, when even more procedural technicalities barred consideration of Joe's evidence. And CCR had recently tracked Tony DiLisio, but to no effect. Tony had rebuffed CCR as he had rebuffed Jerry Justine in 1985.

The second essential precondition had to do with the *Herald*: I had to be convinced that there was at least a reasonable probability that the newspaper (1) would approach Joe's case with a clear eye and an open mind, and (2) would have the guts to take on the governor and prosecutors if the *Herald*'s own investigation confirmed my belief that Joe was, in fact, innocent. Here, my friends Karen Gottlieb and Elliot Scherker made the difference for me. I had trusted their experience, judgment, and intuition many times in the past; they shared my own instinctive distrust of newspapers in general and the pro-capital punishment *Herald* in particular.

By early May 1995, Joe's CCR attorneys (grudgingly) and I (not quite so grudgingly) agreed that both conditions had been met—indeed, had been exceeded. After Joe's CCR lawyers discussed things with Joe, they gave their blessing for me to contact Gene Miller and the *Herald*.

I would be acting on my own. I wouldn't be acting as Joe's lawyer because I no longer *was* Joe's lawyer. CCR was Joe's lawyer, and the agency would retain public deniability. Still, Joe's CCR lawyers endorsed my approach enthusiastically; had CCR instructed me not to take Joe's case to the *Herald,* I never would have done so.

The risks were high; in fact, had I been Joe's attorney in May 1995, I'm not at all certain *I* would have authorized a third party to take Joe's case to the *Herald.* For this reason, I made certain that CCR appreciated both the risks and the small likelihood of success.

In particular, I made sure Joe's CCR lawyers understood that the *Herald*'s investigation would be totally independent—independent of CCR and independent of me. That meant that if Joe was in fact guilty, the *Herald* would find that out. The *Herald* would print what it had found and crucify Joe. Not only would that doom any legal claim based on factual innocence, but Joe's whole world, including his blood family, would know for certain that Joe had been guilty all along, that Joe's (and my) innocence argument had been a nineteen-year-old lie. (That is precisely what happened in another case not long ago: a media investigation into a death row miscarriage-of-justice case was converted into a media investigation into the way clever defense lawyers were running a bogus innocence claim.)

The chairman of my college philosophy department told a story. Once he took a final exam that asked only one question: "What is risk?" All the students, save one, answered with page after page of arguments on all sides from the semester's assigned readings. The only answer that received an A, however, consisted of one sentence: "This is risk."

This was risk.

May 12, 1995
Wilder, Vermont

I knew that my initial call to Miller would be the riskiest telephone call of my professional life. I was beyond nervous. If I took Joe's case files to the pro-capital punishment *Herald,* and if the newspaper read those files, concluded that Joe was guilty, and published its findings (as it must), then Joe surely would be executed on his next death warrant—and I would be burned in effigy by my community of capital punishment abolitionists for my reckless decision to entrust Joe's innocence claim to the *Miami Herald.* I was so nervous, in fact, that I wrote myself an outline of what I hoped to cover during the call.

But I chickened out. Rather than call Miller, I decided to write him instead:

Dear Mr. Miller:

Thank you for taking the time to read this letter. I'm writing about one of my former clients, Joseph Spaziano. I expect you receive these sorts of special pleas all the time, but this is a first for me. Karen Gottlieb suggested I contact you.

I am convinced that Mr. Spaziano is innocent, but I can't prove it with the certainty you did for Pitts and Lee. I have no compelling physical or testimonial evidence proving that Mr. Spaziano did not commit the crime for which he is condemned to die. I do know, and want you to know at the outset, that Mr. Spaziano is no Boy Scout; he was at the time of his arrest (and is today) an Outlaw; he has been convicted of rape, and he has done some bad things. What I think my investigators and I *have* done is more a matter of vaporizing the state's case of guilt than proving his innocence, which, I know, isn't the same thing.

I have a juror affidavit that says that the jury recommended life imprisonment rather than death because *they* weren't so certain that he was guilty at all; their only choices at the guilt/innocence stage were acquittal or conviction of first degree murder; they knew he was an Outlaw (his club colleagues attended the trial, in full regalia), and they were squeamish about letting him loose on the streets of Orlando. So the jury split the difference, and found him guilty of first degree murder but voted (9–3 or 10–2), according to the juror's affidavit) against the imposition of death. But there was a catch: the trial judge didn't know the reason for the jury's life recommendation—the jurors' lingering doubt about whether he was guilty at all—and, anyway, Florida law does not permit a judge to factor such lingering doubt into a capital sentencing decision ("You can't be a little bit guilty," in the memorable words of Florida Supreme Court Justice Joe Boyd).

But it gets worse. The trial prosecutor told the jury that if they didn't believe the testimony of one Anthony DiLisio—a sixteen-year-old acidhead who had been an acquaintance of Mr. Spaziano's—the jury should vote to acquit Mr. Spaziano. As the juror told me, they had doubts about Mr. DiLisio's believability at the time of trial. But what the jury *wasn't* told at trial was that Mr. DiLisio's damning testimony did not exist until he had undergone two sessions with police hypnotists. My investigator tracked down the audio tapes of the hypnosis sessions (he found them in the dusty attic of the then-deceased police detective who led the investigation of this crime, but that's another story). I hired two experts to evaluate the tapes, and both concluded that the sessions were hideously suggestive and therefore unreliable.

The problem is that I have failed utterly to convince a court to look at any of this. They let me file briefs and listen politely to my oral arguments. My opinion is that the judges ignore Mr. Spaziano's arguments because he's an Outlaw. So stop wasting our time.

The matter has some urgency to me. There will likely be a death warrant signed soon.

Enclosed are chapters from my forthcoming book that discuss the case in some detail. I could also send you a copy of the cert. petition filed with the United States Supreme Court last December.

Thank you for your time.

Sincerely,

Michael

I faxed my handwritten draft of the letter from the coast of Maine to Laura Gillen, my Vermont Law School secretary and friend. Laura word-processed the letter, photocopied the relevant chapters from my book manuscript, and got the whole mess ready to send to Miller via Federal Express.

Later that afternoon, I began to feel cowardly for not just picking up the phone and calling Miller. So, at 6:00 P.M., on the appointed hour, I called him. The phone call was brief, and Miller was charmingly direct. We chatted about our mutual admiration for David Von Drehle's then recently published book, *Among the Lowest of the Dead*. Miller wisecracked, "Aren't you the guy [death row prisoner and former client] Paul Hill denounced in our pages a few months ago?" I was. Great: Miller had heard of me.

Miller was polite but firm about what he was willing to read, and, specifically, what he was *not* willing to read: "I want the trial transcripts, the police reports, the transcripts of the hypnosis sessions of the state's star witness, the audiotapes of those hypnosis sessions, *and nothing more*. I don't want briefs. I don't want legal memoranda. I don't want anything else written by any of Spaziano's defense lawyers— especially not anything written by you." Fair enough.

Miller appreciated Spaziano's dilemma and, although my desperation appeared genuine, it was extremely unlikely that he or the *Miami Herald* would get involved in Spaziano's case.

That same day I wrote Joe a letter:

Dear Joe:

I hope this finds you well, my friend. I need to talk with you about a matter of some delicacy. I would much prefer to discuss this with you in person, but I'm still fairly bedridden and very broke financially. So a letter will have to do.

Here's the deal: A while back you and I discussed the possibility of getting the media to take up your case, or at least to focus on it. I generally think that's a bad idea, because reporters seldom do their own homework, and because they'll turn on you viciously if they think you're bullshitting them (*60 Minutes* recently did that to a Nevada death row prisoner).

The key is to find an experienced reporter who is honorable enough to work through a complicated case of innocence. . . . I know of only one such reporter: Gene Miller of the *Miami Herald*. Miller is *only* interested in factual innocence of the homicide. He's not interested in legal or technical arguments against the legality of the death sentence. When he's on your side, he's hell-on-wheels: His 1975 book, *Invitation to a Lynching*, was what sprung Pitts and Lee from death row to freedom.

What you absolutely must understand is that Gene Miller gets requests for his help all the time, and that most of them are phony claims of innocence. So he is *very* skeptical, to put it mildly, about such claims. He is a *very* tough man to convince. He's *not* a man to bullshit. And he does his own homework. He has investigated several death row claims of innocence, and, in the end, he has rejected them—but never in public. And, as I said, he's *only* interested in innocence "the old fashioned way; the guy didn't do it, period."

A friend of a friend of mine knows Gene Miller's daughter, and she set up a phone call between Mr. Miller and I. He was interested in *taking a look at* your case, although, as I say, he's a hard man to convince. He asked me to send him the book chapter I've written setting out why *I* think you're innocent. I did so; the thing will be published in December anyway, and all the arguments in the book are ones we've been making since 1985.

If Gene Miller decides, on the basis of what I sent him, that he *does* want to pursue his own investigation of your case, the next thing he'll want to see is the trial transcript. I sent all of that stuff to CCR in January. I haven't spoken to CCR about any of this. You and CCR will need to decide whether Gene Miller is something worth pursuing. I think he is.

I won't do anything further with Mr. Miller until I hear back from you. I hope this is helpful to you. You are constantly in my thoughts and prayers. Take care and keep well, my friend. And *write*.

Sincerely,
Michael

In this letter I tried to strike the right balance between realistic hope and realistic despair. In fact, I expected never to hear from Gene Miller again.

May 16, 1995
Wilder, Vermont

Miller called. My memory is that the telephone conversation went something like this. Miller asked, "What aren't you telling me in your book chapter? You can't be telling me the whole story here, because no case, not even a Florida capital case tried twenty years ago, could possibly be as bad as you describe in your chapter." I replied that the book chapter I had written was as close as I was capable of coming to objective reporting. I bent over backward to construe every piece of evidence and every single logical inference that could reasonably be drawn from that evidence in favor of the prosecution and against Spaziano's claim of innocence. After letting me speak my piece, Miller politely insisted that there must be *something* I was leaving out of the chapter, such as credible evidence that my client was guilty of murder. I then suggested to Miller that there really was only one way that he could determine whether I had left anything out. I offered to send him the trial transcripts in Spaziano's murder case.

May 19, 1995
Washington, D.C.

Dear Mr. Miller:

I'm still in DC, but I've found a morbidly interesting piece of Spaziano trivia buried in Thurgood Marshall's papers. In 1983, the cert. petition I wrote seeking plenary U.S. Supreme Court review of Mr. Spaziano's case was scheduled to be denied—and Justice Harry Blackmun had drafted an opinion dissenting from the Court's denial of plenary review. But the Court reconsidered, and Blackmun's dissent never got published. The justices ordered the case to be fully briefed and orally argued in early 1984. When they finally released their opinions in *Spaziano v. Florida,* in spring 1984, we had lost, by a vote of 6–3. The majority opinion was written by Justice Harry Blackmun.

Thus did I snatch defeat from the jaws of victory. Shit.

Sincerely,
Michael Mello
Professor Law

On May 24, 1995, Governor Lawton Chiles signed Joe Spaziano's death warrant. The prison scheduled the execution for approximately four weeks hence, at 7:00 A.M., June 27, 1995. Both Spaziano and I fully expected that he would be killed on schedule.

I called Miller. He told me I hadn't given the *Herald* nearly enough lead time; had I come to him a year ago, maybe the *Herald* could have been ready for the warrant. But twenty-eight days from today? No. I had waited too long.

Still—Miller did want to know if I knew Tony DiLisio's location today. In 1985, Jerry Justine had tracked DiLisio down to a small town in California, and DiLisio had refused to talk about the case. In March 1995, CCR's investigator, Mike Hummell, tracked DiLisio down to Pensacola, Florida. Hummell not only also struck out with DiLisio, but his heavy-handed approach made it extremely unlikely that DiLisio would now be willing to talk to *anyone* about Spaziano's case. Miller said he wanted Warren Holmes and Martin Dardis to talk with

DiLisio. Holmes was a former cop and expert polygrapher. Dardis had been Miami state's attorney's chief investigator; in the early 1970s, it was Dardis who "followed the money" from the Watergate burglars to President Nixon's Committee to Reelect the President. Miller trusted Holmes's and Dardis's judgment implicitly.

I told Miller I didn't know Tony DiLisio's present whereabouts, but I would try to find out. It didn't take long for Jerry Justine to find out that DiLisio was still in Pensacola. But Tony was stonewalling. CCR was willing to let Miller and Holmes take a pass at DiLisio, but not until CCR's investigators had again approached him. I asked Joe's CCR lawyers if they would at least permit Miller's investigators to accompany their investigators when they next met DiLisio. No.

When I reported to Miller that Justine had located DiLisio, but that CCR first wanted another shot at him, Miller was skeptical. CCR had already tried and failed to persuade Tony to talk about the events of nineteen years ago. Holmes and Dardis were Joe's best shot, and whoever did the first interrogation would have the greatest chances of success. All true, I said, but CCR was planning to approach DiLisio within the next few days. After that, Miller would have Tony to himself.

I then did what I always did when confronted with impossible tactical choices. I called Mark Olive, my boss when I had worked at CCR in 1985–86, and Karen Gottlieb. Olive's "Do it" reassured me about telling Miller how to get in touch with Tony. Karen reassured me that Holmes and Dardis are the best in the business. Both men have reputations for being honest.

I wanted to learn all I could about Warren Holmes, but I didn't want him (or Miller) to learn that I was investigating the *Herald*'s investigator. As it turned out, I didn't even need to leave my house in Vermont to find about who Warren Holmes is and how he works. I found it all right there in Gene Miller's book about the Pitts and Lee case.

Holmes's skepticism of claims of innocence is, if such is possible, greater than Gene Miller's.

On the Friday of Memorial Day weekend, Miller dropped the trial transcripts, police reports, and other material on Holmes's desk and asked him, as a personal favor, to glance through them. As Holmes told me later, he was not pleased. He hoped, and fully expected, to spend about half an hour reading through the trial transcript of the murder case and conclude as he has concluded in virtually every other capital case he has investigated, that Spaziano is, in fact, as guilty as the prosecution argued he was at trial. But a half an hour became ten hours.

The first red flag that Spaziano's case might be different was the name of the police hypnotist who had hypnotized Tony DiLisio: the same man had "hypnotized" (in open court, no less) a witness in the famous Pitts and Lee case. That got Holmes's attention, and he really dug into the Spaziano transcripts. What he found shocked him: there just was not any evidence of Spaziano's guilt. Holmes knew that Spaziano had also been convicted of the rape and mutilation of Vanessa Dale Croft, and so he dug into the trial transcript of the rape case. And, *mirabile dictu,* Holmes concluded that Spaziano did not commit the rape, either.

I wish I had a tape recording of the first conversation I had with Warren Holmes in connection with Joseph Spaziano's case. It went something like this: Holmes asked me whether I was a defense lawyer. I answered in the affirmative. There was a *long* pause. Holmes then asked me whether I happened to have any doubts, based on the case files, about whether Joe raped Vanessa Dale Croft. I told him that I thought the evidence against Joe in the Croft rape case was as flimsy as the evidence against him in the Harberts murder case. He asked me whether I had mentioned those problems to Miller. I told him that I had not. Incredulous, he asked me why not. I confessed that I was afraid that if I had told Miller that I thought that the police had framed Joseph Spaziano for the rape, in addition to framing him for the homicide, he would dismiss me as a flake. What else, I visualized Miller asking me at the time, did the state frame your client for? JFK? Jimmy Hoffa? Elvis?

I then had one of those dialogues with Warren Holmes that is of the sort that a defense lawyer has maybe once in a lifetime. In essence, Holmes laid out for me why *he* thought Spaziano was innocent of both the homicide and the rape. He told me that he had reviewed between twelve hundred and fourteen hundred trial transcripts in his time as a law enforcement officer and as a private investigator. Out of all of those transcripts, he had thought three men were innocent: Pitts, Lee, and Joseph Robert Spaziano.

I thought we were home free. Surely, now that the legendary skeptic Gene Miller *and* the even more legendarily skeptical Warren Holmes were convinced there was significant doubt about Spaziano's guilt on the homicide, the *Miami Herald* would jump into the case. Eventually, the *Herald* did jump in, with both feet and with both guns blazing. But, even with the vociferous advocacy of Gene Miller and Warren Holmes, for a time the powers that be at the *Herald* remained unconvinced. Miller and Holmes fought like wildcats to persuade the newspaper's editors to assign a team of reporters to conduct a top-down reinvestigation of the factual circumstances of Joseph Spaziano's conviction and condemnation, but there did not seem to be enough time. The scheduled killing was only weeks away. I had come to them too late.

May 25, 1995
Wilder, Vermont
(27 days to execution)

Gene Miller called me with a proposition. The *Herald* was willing to publish, in its "Viewpoint" section, an opinion piece that I would write and that would appear under my byline. The *Miami Herald* would not insert itself into Spaziano's case, and the paper would not assign a group of reporters to investigate the crimes unless I wrote the opinion piece and allowed the paper to publish it. I tried to bargain. Let me write it, but let it appear under someone else's byline—any name other than my own. No. It had to be written by me. It had to be written in the first person. It had to appear under my name.

Miller then followed up on a point that I had made in my first telephone conversation with him. Had I really meant it when I told him that, of the seventy or so condemned prisoners I have been involved with over the past twelve years, Spaziano was my only innocent client? I told him yes. He told me that I needed to say that, explicitly and forcefully, in the first paragraph of the opinion piece that the *Herald* was willing to publish.

I told Miller that there were seventy reasons why I could not write such an opinion piece for publication in the pages of Florida's flagship newspaper: seventy other clients. How would they feel, how would their families feel, to read in the pages of the *Miami Herald* that their former lawyer believed, at least implicitly, that they were in fact guilty all along? Such an action would be unethical, according to the rules and regulations governing the behavior of lawyers admitted to practice before the courts of Florida. More important, it would be wrong.

Miller said he understood and appreciated my reticence. He would fully understand if I chose not to write the opinion piece. All he was doing was informing me of the factual reality.

Given the situation, I finally decided to agree to write the piece, and to write it in time for it to appear in the Sunday, June 4, 1995, edition of the *Miami Herald*. Over the next few days, I tried to write it as best I could, with the critical help of my friends Deanna Peterson and Bob Trebilcock.

May 26, 1995
Wilder, Vermont
(26 days to execution)

My law school secretary and friend Laura, my friend Deanna, and I worked around the clock to get Miller his op-ed piece on time. At 4:00 A.M., I was halfway through faxing my latest round of edits from my home to Laura at the law school when the electricity in my house went dead. Resetting the circuit breakers failed to restore the power, and I finished editing by the dancing light of a hurricane lamp.

May 27, 1995
South Royalton, Vermont
(25 days to execution)

We worked all day at Vermont Law School, trying to craft an op-ed draft we weren't embarrassed to send to Gene Miller. We quit around midnight.

May 28, 1995
Wilder, Vermont
(24 days to execution)

The news from Florida kept getting worse. Governor Chiles didn't care about claims of innocence; he'd leave them to the courts to sort out. But the courts were leaving it to the *governor* to sort out innocence claims. Thus, when Joe is executed, the governor can blame the courts and vice versa.

May 29, 1995
Wilder, Vermont
(23 days to execution)

Memorial Day. We worked all day at the law school, trying to condense the nineteen-year-long Spaziano saga into a newspaper op-ed piece. Every edit felt like I was cutting off a piece of my own history; it *all* seemed necessary to me. By the end of this very long day, I was feeling cranky, depressed, and defeated.

I was also frightened—for Joe but also for myself. Neither the Florida Supreme Court nor the Florida Bar would think well of me for trying Joe's case in the press. The people in the governor's office already didn't like me, and they'd go ballistic over this. And what if, after my piece was published, the *Herald* found evidence suggesting Joe was guilty? Joe would be dead, and I knew I would feel that I'd caused it. A lot of other people would believe it, too.

May 30, 1995
Wilder, Vermont
(22 days to execution)

By 7:00 A.M. the draft was ninety-six pages—about eighty-five pages too long. Throughout the day I axed into the fat, but I only succeeded in cutting about twenty pages. Joe's case has an incredibly complicated—and lengthy—history, and it was almost physically painful for me to eliminate whole sections of evidence and argument. I hated even reading through the thing, especially the part where I sold all my other former capital clients down the river. Around noon, I asked Deanna to take over the cutting, which she did, wonderfully, and I wish I could say I was gracious about her thoughtful suggested edits, but I wasn't. I took out my frustrations on her because I couldn't take them out on the *Herald* or the governor or the courts.

Finally, I faxed my pitiful excuse for an op-ed piece to Gene Miller. Miller not only reworked, edited, and polished the piece, but he arranged for it to appear simultaneously, on Sunday, June 4, in the *Miami Herald,* the *St. Petersburg Times,* and the *Orlando Sentinel.*

Before faxing the final draft of the piece to Miller, I called Joe's lawyers at CCR. They told me to fax the draft to Miller without faxing it to them first. CCR had to retain its deniability. It was critical that everyone, the *Herald* in particular, understand with crystal clarity that I was acting on my own—not in concert with CCR. By working with Miller and the *Herald*, I was off on my own separate frolic—I was not acting as Joe's lawyer. The *Herald* approach could blow up in my face, and I needed to insulate Joe and CCR from any possible fallout.

May 31, 1995
Wilder, Vermont
(21 days to execution)

Joe's CCR lawyers called. Five days ago, their pass at Tony DiLisio had failed, so I could give Miller a chance. They finally gave me Tony's address in Pensacola, along with their blessing to pass it on to Miller. I did so at once.

In Florida, it was officially the first day of hurricane season 1995.

June 1, 1995
Wilder, Vermont
(20 days to execution)

Miller had been contacting people he knew at the *New York Times,* the *Washington Post,* and *Newsweek*. He'd also called James Jackson Kilpatrick, a conservative columnist from my own native Commonwealth of Virginia.

June 2, 1995
Wilder, Vermont
(19 days to execution)

When Joe called, he asked me to call his mom and niece. Could they visit him in three days, on Monday?

He also mentioned that a *Miami Herald* reporter named Lori Rozsa had written him requesting an interview. Did I know her? Nope. Never heard of her. Should he agree to meet with her? No. She must be the reporter assigned to investigate the case. I asked Joe to meet with no one other than Miller or Holmes. And before he met with any reporters, he needed to talk with his CCR attorneys; I couldn't give him legal advice, because I was no longer his lawyer. I didn't say that CCR seemed to have ceased returning my phone calls; Joe's CCR lawyers might demand to be present when Joe met with the *Herald*. That would chill the meeting. After CCR's insistence that it make a last pass at Tony DiLisio before allowing Holmes to meet with him, I was afraid the *Herald* would decide that Joe's case wasn't worth the hassle.

Now, looking back on it, I can see that there were two pivotal moments in Joe Spaziano's two-decade effort to prove his innocence, and both events occurred in the offices of the *Miami Herald*. First, Warren Holmes read Joe's files and decided the case didn't feel right. Second, after Holmes had read Joe's case files, he told Gene Miller that the *Herald* had a moral obligation to assign a reporter to investigate Joe's claim of innocence. Miller agreed, but it wasn't his call. Miller was the *Herald*'s local editor, and his editorial jurisdiction was limited to Miami and Dade County. Because Joe's case fell outside Dade County, the decision about whether the *Herald* should jump in fell within the jurisdiction of the state editor, John Pancake. So, when Holmes told Miller that the *Herald* needed to investigate Joe's case, Miller set up a conference with Holmes and Pancake.

The meeting became spirited, boisterous, and passionate. Pancake shared Miller's skepticism about timing: I had simply waited too long before contacting Miller initially about getting the *Herald* into Joe's case. Holmes agreed, but he insisted that this case was "a matter of conscience." The verbal fusillades stopped for a long moment; during that cease-fire, Pancake looked Holmes hard in the eye. Then Pancake said okay. The *Herald* was in.

In describing this scene, Warren Holmes is emphatic that John Pancake was the one who made the decision, and that, had Pancake gone the other way, the chances of the *Herald*'s intervening in Joe's case would have ended with the meeting: "Pancake gave the go-ahead, and he made that decision unilaterally. Joe's life hung in the balance at that meeting, and it was Pancake who set the machinery in motion that led to the *Herald*'s involvement. . . . Pancake's decision was one of the . . . key events that decided the course of the *Herald*'s involvement in the case."

A bit later, Pancake made a second decision that proved critical. He assigned the task of investigating and reporting Joe's case to a reporter named Lori Rozsa. When Miller called to tell me that the *Herald* was in and that Lori Rozsa would be the point person, I objected. Gene Miller patiently explained to me that he's an editor, not a reporter. Even if he wanted to meet with Joe and jump into the *Herald*'s nascent investigation—and he didn't—newspaper politics made that impossible. He was busy editing. Warren Holmes was out of town.

I wasn't sure. I didn't even really know Miller at that time, let alone Rozsa, and I sure didn't want to entrust Joe's life to another reporter. Miller suggested a compromise. Perhaps Rozsa and Holmes might meet Joe together. He said I should call Rozsa and suggest it. She's a superb reporter and human being, Miller assured me.

Miller was right. What struck me initially about Lori Rozsa was her kindness and her respect for how awkward it was for Joe and me to be seeking the *Herald*'s help. She said she didn't want to take advantage of a man who was both scared and crazy. She said she had no problem with Holmes participating in her first meeting with Joe; she'd contact Holmes and Miller to make the arrangements for the following Tuesday, five days away. In the meantime, she would read every piece of paper on the case. She also mentioned that the cop who had originally arrested Joe, in Chicago, didn't think Joe seemed like a cold-blooded killer; indeed, the arresting officer was struck by Joe's main concern: How would his family react to his arrest? I hadn't known that. Lori Rozsa had already done her homework.

I needed to know how all of this would sit with Joe, so I phoned him. When he wondered how he should act with the *Herald* folks, I told him he shouldn't act at all. He just needed to be himself and, most important, to be honest—totally honest—with them. Joe seemed to breathe a sigh a relief. "I don't want to bullshit these people, Mike. I want to tell them how I feel. I want to trust them, and, if you do, I will." I told him I did.

June 3, 1995
Wilder, Vermont
(18 days to execution)

The op-ed draft was, under Gene Miller's craftsmanship, evolving into something perhaps worthy of appearing in Florida's flagship newspaper. Draft after draft burned up the fax wires between Miami and Vermont.

Rozsa finalized plans for she and Holmes to meet Joe on Tuesday. They'd fly into Jacksonville early Tuesday morning, rent a car, and drive Route 301 south to Starke.

June 4, 1995
Wilder, Vermont
(17 days to execution)

My (and Gene Miller's and Rich Bard's and Deanna Peterson's and Bob Trebilcock's and Margaret Vandiver's) op-ed piece was published.

Mark Olive phoned at 9:00 A.M. "You're splattered all over the newspapers, the operative word being *splattered*." In addition to the *Herald* and the *Orlando Sentinel*, the *St. Petersburg Times* ran the piece, along with a strong editorial and column by Martin Dyckman.

Olive saw the essay for the first time when it appeared in print. "All of your other former clients may be either dead or no longer litigating innocence claims. But how would they feel to have their former lawyer telling the world that they were guilty all along? How would *you* feel?" Angry. Betrayed. It was the only way for me to get the *Herald* into Joe's case, but the decision to write the piece was mine and mine alone. The responsibility was mine alone, too.

Miller and Holmes had put themselves on the line. Based on Holmes's reading of the trial files, Miller had been spreading the word that this was an honest-to-God case of innocence. For Holmes and Miller, this fight was a matter of conscience.

But it could all disappear when Holmes and Rozsa met with Joe on Tuesday. Holmes insisted on questioning Joe himself. "I wish I'd never seen this record. I've been desperately looking for a hook ever since I first read the transcripts over Memorial Day weekend. But it's just not there. The evidence isn't there. Miller has put his job in jeopardy over this. Well, Mello, you're getting *everyone* in trouble. But don't worry about CCR or the Florida Bar coming down on you. By the time this is over, you won't be able to practice law in Hawaii."

But I was in it now, and I had to see it through.

June 4, 1995
Gene Miller
Miami Herald

Dear Mr. Miller:

The more I think about it, the more I think this is a case for clemency. As David Von Drehle points out, the Florida Supreme Court's refusal to apply its 1985 *Bundy* decisions retroactively means that Spaziano will be killed because of a legal technicality. Most folks are offended when killers "get off" on a "technicality." Here we have the opposite.

If Spaziano's trial were held today, the *Bundy* decision would mandate the *per se* exclusion of DiLisio's hypnotically-warped testimony. However, the *Bundy* Court explicitly made its ruling prospective only. It did so to avoid a "flood" of cases challenging hypnotism, most of which would have been frivolous. But the non-retroactivity of the *Bundy* rule, while a good idea from the standpoint of judicial economy, is disastrous to the few cases, such as Joe Spaziano's, where hypnotism wrought a substantial injustice. Despite the fact that experts have concluded that the testimony which convicted Spaziano was thoroughly and unacceptably tainted, Spaziano seems to have no recourse in the Florida courts.

This situation presents a classic case for clemency. It is similar to the case of Clifford Hallman. Hallman was tried, convicted, and sentenced to death for the murder of Eleanor Groves. The Florida Supreme Court affirmed. Approximately two years later, Hallman filed a three-part motion to mitigate sentence with the sentencing circuit judge. The motion alleged that in 1975 the administrator of Groves' estate had filed suit against Tampa General Hospital contending that Mrs. Groves had died as a result of the negligence of the hospital rather than from the injuries inflicted by Hallman; that Hallman's acts were therefore not the cause of Groves' death; and that if in a new trial a jury found that the hospital's negligence was an intervening cause of death, that jury could not find Hallman guilty of homicide. The trial court denied all relief, and the Florida Supreme Court affirmed.

Hallman received executive clemency. There, as here, subsequent developments cast a conviction and sentence of death in doubt. The same principles of justice and equity which supported Hallman's clemency call for clemency for Joe Spaziano. As Governor Graham himself has been quoted as saying:

> The purpose of clemency is to allow consideration of special circumstances that might not be available to a court applying strict laws and strict precedents.
>
> *Cabinet to Hear 'Mercy Killing' Arguments,* The (Palm Beach) Post, August 8, 1985 at B9.

One aspect of this case I've always had trouble getting my mind around is the role that motorcycle brotherhoods—first the Hell's Angels, and now the Outlaws—have played in Spaziano's life. I'm becoming increasingly convinced that the defining moment for Joe on this subject—as with so many others—was the car accident that nearly killed him. After the car accident, Joe Spaziano needed constant physical, emotional and psychological support. His need for approval and acceptance became almost an obsession. His father's verbal and physical abuse made life at home impossible. When members of a local motorcycle club offered support, Joe accepted.

As soon as he was able to leave the house after his accident, Joe escaped, turning to the family of the motorcycle gang who accepted his physical and psychological disfigurement. With Joe's impaired judgment, limited coping skills and need for support, his seeking the fellowship of the motorcycle brotherhood is completely understandable. He saw nowhere else to turn.

At one point, Joe attempted to extricate himself from the motorcycle gang. For this traitorous act, he was severely punished—tortured, beaten and left for dead. A friend took him home. His sister, Barbara, and her husband came to help him. Barbara recalls, in an affidavit she prepared for my investigator in 1985, that:

> I saw Joe the night he tried to leave the motorcycle club and they beat him up. It was really terrible. Joe's wife called my husband and me and we went to their house. Joe was almost lifeless. They had beaten his legs and arms and all over his body. They had used a branding iron or something hot to burn off a tattoo on his arm. He had cigarette burns everywhere, even on his private areas. His whole body was bloody. Joe's wife called her parents in Florida and they left very quickly, leaving everything, including their clothes and furniture and home behind. My husband helped carry Joe from the house to get them out of there as quickly as possible.

Finally—and not for the last time—I want to thank you for doing what I have failed for so long to do: to get people to *listen* to the facts of this case. Naively, I never dreamed Joe would ever get this close to being destroyed—or that Lawton Chiles, of all governors, would be the one who signed Joe's last warrant.

Anyway, if Chiles asks, I'll beg one final time for—at a minimum—commutation of sentence through executive clemency. He has adjusted to life in prison. He does not receive disciplinary reports, and he spends his time improving his considerable talents as an artist. Under these circumstances, there would be no purpose served in taking his life. And extinguishing his life will not extinguish the very real doubt about his guilt.

Sincerely,
Michael Mello

June 5, 1995
Wilder, Vermont
(16 days to execution)

Lori Rozsa and Warren Holmes planned to meet with Joe at 3:00 in the afternoon on June 6. Their meeting was to follow a six-hour meeting with Joe and his family. It didn't happen. A hurricane in the Florida panhandle backed up over much of north Florida, and many of the Florida State Prison workers had gone home for the day. The *Herald* would try again the following day, on Wednesday. But it might be Rozsa solo: the prison refused to permit Holmes to accompany her because he wasn't a reporter. Rozsa tried to reclassify Holmes as a paralegal, but ultimately she decided to meet Joe alone.

So far, so good. The Florida newspapers had exploded with Joe's story on Sunday, June 4, sparking national interest and television attention. By next Sunday, June 11, the Florida press would be getting tired of a (to them) week-old story. That's when the national press, the *Washington Post* and *New York Times,* would jump into it, thus giving the Florida media its second wind and validation of their earlier news judgment the weekend before.

My handwritten notes:

The plan

A. We're in place: (1) St. Pet Times and Herald (and Orlando Sentinel and Talle Dem?) jump this Sun; (2) I've offered [. . . over?]

B. Between this Sun and next Sun, Fla papers go nuts

— 2nd tier papers jump, following Herald and SPT

— Meanwhile (1) our Fla A team of Herald and SPT maintain their leads, requiring the others in Fla to get their info from Miller & Holmes

— (2) TV picks up on it. I ignore them, sending them to Tom Horkan

C. On Tues, Holmes and Lori meet with Joe, the only 2 reporters I'll authorize. This keeps Miller and Holmes in front of the story, and in control of any new info from me and Joe.

D. Next Sun, Von Drehle Wash Post piece appears, resulting in (1) nationalization of the story, with NYT, LA Times, Boston Globe, getting their info from Von Drehle, who's getting his info from Miller & Holmes; (2) Von Drehle's piece will re-energize the Fla media (who will have had the story for a week), and validate and confirm their initial decision to make this a big story in the first place

E. After next Sun, who the fuck can predict? Hopefully:

1. Miller and Holmes will (a) still be on our side (b) will be the sole source of info from Joe and me

2. Other media will need to rely on Miller and Holmes for their direct info from Joe and I

3. Tom Horkan will be the sole source of info for reporters

F. The key for me: knowing when to relinquish control or, more precisely, making a conscious *decision* to give up control of info, before events carry the control out of my hands, as they inevitably will

1. Now, by controlling info and access to Joe, I still *can* control Miller and Holmes, sort of

2. But that will end soon, if it hasn't happened already. I certainly can't control lots of newspapers and TV

3. So: At the right time, I need to pass the baton to Tom H. and hope that the reporters don't turn up any nasty surprises

When I called Martin Dyckman at the *St. Petersburg Times* to thank him for his column the day before, he said he had received calls from two citizens, including "a housewife who's strongly pro capital punishment but is so outraged over this she's calling national media. I've never had a reaction like this from anything I've written in thirty-five years as a columnist."

The editor of the *Orlando Sentinel* called to say thanks for the op-ed piece. "The more I read in the case file, the more it seems that Spaziano was railroaded by the hypnotized word of this . . . drug addict [Tony DiLisio]," he told me. He also had an interesting story. The day before, he'd made a call in response to an ad for a used car, and guess who picked up the phone? Joe McCawley—the self-styled "ethical hypnotist" who had hypnotized Tony DiLisio in the Harberts homicide investigation. Orlando is a city of 1.5 million people. What were the odds of that?

When I spoke with Joe that evening, he wanted to talk about the Outlaws. The brotherhood wanted to put on a display of solidarity, and so did Joe. "I go on Phase II [of deathwatch] at 8:00 A.M. on June 20. That's when I want the guys to come to show the world I'm not alone. . . . I want them to see that people care. What'll people think of a thousand Outlaws, arriving on the 27th to watch me die?"

"I really think they'll kill me on the 27th," Joe said. So did I.

June 6, 1995
Wilder, Vermont
(15 days to execution)

The prison still refuses to allow Warren Holmes to accompany Lori Rozsa when she meets Joe tomorrow at 9:30. Today she received a gracious letter from Joe; she seemed prepared for their meeting.

I wasn't. The frenzy of the past few days let up enough to give me time to panic. Deep breaths, I told myself. There was nothing more I could *do*. That was the point. Now it would be up to Joe and Lori. I knew Joe was armed with the truth, and I had faith that his direct and unadorned way of telling his story would allow Rozsa to glimpse his truth—if she was looking for it.

I was used to having faith in Joe; I'd been trusting Joe for so many years that it had the comfortable familiarity of an old leather jacket. But trusting reporters was brand new for me. I'd come to trust Gene

Miller, in part because of his history and in part because I didn't have much choice. I wanted to trust Rozsa because Miller trusted her, but it was all happening too fast.

This all had something to do with power and control. When I was Joe's lawyer I could control events by controlling the case. This felt decidedly different—but not in terms of stress and weight and responsibility. It mattered as much as it would if I had been doing legal work, but it mattered differently. Rather than doing my job, all I was doing here was providing accurate information to others so they could do their jobs. This felt liberating, but it was an existential freedom that was as terrifying as it was freeing.

This may be nothing more than a self-serving rationalization for abdication of my responsibility for this genie I had set loose. If the *Herald* turned on Joe, nothing could save him.

June 7, 1995
Wilder, Vermont
(14 days to execution)

Miller checked in mid-afternoon. Rozsa did meet with Joe this morning, and James J. Kilpatrick's column runs tomorrow. "You don't get any better than this."

Joe called around 5:00 P.M. It had been a very long day for him, and he was feeling especially close to death. "I'm just lying here under the bright lights. They're going to kill me. I've only got a few hours left to visit my family before Phase II of deathwatch begins. Who's going to save *them*, Mike?"

And the closer Joe got to the electric chair, the more he talked about the Outlaws. "I'm ready to bring my people in. These others are all cops and politicians. . . . My brothers want it to be a full Outlaw funeral." What "I've got to tell my people is 'Forgive them, for they know not what they do.' Didn't someone else say that?"

He was able to meet with Rozsa only for an hour. It wasn't a contact visit; she met him "behind the glass." The prison wouldn't let her use her tape recorder. Still, Joe thought she had been listening to him. She asked where he was when Laura Harberts disappeared. "I told her I don't *know* where I was. If I wanted to make up a story, I could have had 100 brothers take the stand. . . . I'm an Outlaw. It was 1976. What jury would have believed an Outlaw in 1976? They'd have just cut my brothers down. But I trusted [my trial lawyer]. *I don't know where I was*" when Harberts was killed. She "does seem to understand that I'm a stone Outlaw. . . . I want a charly tombstone. I want you to be there at the funeral, Mike. It'll be like fucking *Daytona*. . . . "They're going to murder me, Mike. Twenty days. Only twelve hours more with my family."

June 8, 1995
Wilder, Vermont
(13 days to execution)

Lori Rozsa called from Pensacola. Tony DiLisio had had nothing to say to her.

Her interview with Joe was satisfying. Joe seemed lucid, chatty, and forthright. He didn't deny his past sins. "The most scary thing was how resigned he was," she said. "He's just not a rapist. I believed him, especially his die-hard allegiance to the Outlaws. He *could* have had ten witnesses that Joe was someplace else, but he didn't want them to be embarrassed during cross-examination. He gets choked up about his family."

Joe also told Lori that his ex-wife had documentary evidence placing him in New York at the time Vanessa Croft was raped. "Wives aren't credible. But *ex*-wives, well . . ."

Joe called around 8:00 P.M. "I woke up this morning mad at everyone, so I took my razor and cut my hair bald. I don't want them bastards to touch my hair.

"I'm mad inside. They're going to murder me. If I die, I die. I don't want anyone hurt. I don't want trouble, and the brothers will do what I want.

"The Superintendent will let me be electrocuted wearing my [Outlaw] colors. . . . They'll turn my body over to my brothers. I'll have a real Outlaw funeral."

Joe had asked his ex-wife to witness his electrocution. She promised she would. It was the first time he had made this request of her. It meant he was truly frightened. Joe and I talked, as we often did, about my belief that an Outlaw show of numbers would decrease his chances of winning a stay from the courts or the governor. Over the years, I'd succeeded in convincing him and his brothers that a low profile was in Joe's best legal interest.

I still thought that, but I didn't push him on it now. For thirteen years, I had been telling him that the courts would listen. I'd been wrong. Now he and his families needed to focus not on litigating to live but preparing to die.

The law and its enforcers and its judges hadn't let Joe alone to live his life, but by God they weren't going to take away his death, too. If Joe wanted an Outlaws rally, then I wasn't going to say no.

7

Death's Witness:
Tony DiLisio Redux

Furthermore, all correspondence referring to the matter [of the final so-
lution] was subject to rigid "language rules." . . . It is rare to find documents in which such bold words as "extermination," "Liquidation,"
or "killing" occur. The prescribed code names for killing were "final
solution," "evacuation" and "special treatment."

> *Hannah Arendt,* Eichmann in Jerusalem:
> A Report on the Banality of Evil, *1963*

June 9, 1995
Wilder, Vermont
(12 days to execution)

Gene Miller: Lori Rozsa's second pass at Tony was interesting but un-
productive. He didn't exactly retract his trial testimony, but pretty
close.

Miller hoped to get Warren Holmes to interview Tony within the
next few days.

June 10, 1995
Wilder, Vermont
(11 days to execution)

The *Herald* hit paydirt. Miller telephoned around 4:30 P.M. "We're
running a page-one story tomorrow. On her fifth try, Lori got him
to talk. He retracted to Lori." Tony also spoke to Warren Holmes by
phone.

On June 8, 1995, Lori Rozsa had first knocked on DiLisio's front door. She told him that she wanted to talk to him about the Spaziano case. DiLisio still wasn't ready to deal with it. He got rid of her, with some difficulty. She put her foot in his door and wouldn't take no for an answer. He threatened to call 911 and she finally removed her foot so he could shut the door and lock it. DiLisio later described her as "a real bitch." Rozsa came back again the same day and bothered him a second time. She did not get her foot in the door, as he stepped outside. She returned yet a third time later that afternoon, but he still would not talk to her. The next day, Rozsa knocked on DiLisio's door again. He sent her away without talking to her. Rozsa returned a fifth time. He let her in. She showed him a book containing his statements and testimony. She explained to him there were loopholes in the case. She also told him that she felt that the police had manipulated him in May 1975. She started to bring doubt to his mind. DiLisio later testified (at an evidentiary hearing in January 1996) that he still didn't want to come clean with what he had done and take the full blame, so he agreed with Rozsa's statements that the police had manipulated him. He testified that at that point he remembered more than he revealed to Rozsa at the time. Rozsa was at his house for two to three hours. DiLisio told Rozsa he couldn't "remember" Spaziano taking him to the dump to see the corpse, the hypnosis sessions, or even the trial. According to Rozsa, DiLisio said, "How do I know what I said back then was reliable? Especially if it came out under hypnosis?" DiLisio, testifying later, did not deny saying that. DiLisio admitted that it was true, as Rozsa reported, that he remembered being married at twenty-one, but the years before that were a void.

Rozsa learned that day that Tony today preaches the gospel to death row inmates in Alabama. His nickname is Brother Nitro. Brother Nitro was stunned that Joe was about to be executed on the strength of his testimony nineteen years ago. Tony said to the reporter, "Surely they're not going to kill Spaziano based on the testimony of a scared kid." He thought that Chiles should at least hold a hearing. Tony was angry that "Joe might be killed based on my testimony."

Rozsa spoke with Tony DiLisio for three hours. Tony told her he couldn't "believe they'd hypnotize a kid. . . . I doubt that *I* would take the word of a sixteen-year-old kid. . . . I'm all for staying the execution. . . . I want to talk to the governor."

Tony also had harsh words for CCR, which he felt had been trying to strong-arm him. CCR's people had told him, "You'll have Joe's blood on your hands." Tony was convinced that one of the men CCR had sent to interrogate him was an Outlaw. Still, Tony tried reaching CCR by telephone soon after the CCR interrogation. No one answered.

Warren Holmes and I spoke later that evening, and he, like Lori, believed that Tony was telling the truth now, albeit perhaps not the whole truth. He told me, "Regardless of how this case comes out, whenever anyone asks me about the death penalty from now on, 'Crazy Joe's' case will be at the forefront of my mind."

When Joe called, I downplayed the day's miraculous developments. He spoke of his gratitude to the *Herald*. "I wrote a letter to Lori, thanking her for believing me, whatever happens on the 27th. . . . I got a feeling you think I'm coming home, Mike. You've never thought that before."

It's no accident that hope was at the bottom of Pandora's box of terrors unleashed upon the world.

On June 13, 1995, two agents of the Florida Department of Law Enforcement (FDLE) contacted DiLisio. FDLE is Florida's state-level equivalent of the FBI; FDLE agents seem to view themselves as the elite of Florida's law enforcement community, at any rate. The FDLE agents informed DiLisio that he could not be charged with perjury because of the seven-year statute of limitation on that offense. DiLisio agreed to speak with them in their office.

On June 14, DiLisio went to the FDLE office with a lawyer and met with the agents. DiLisio claimed that Spaziano never took him to the dump site to show him the bodies. He claimed that the police gave him information prior to his being placed under hypnosis. He was then asked, "So from the time the police came in contact with you, they started feeding you information about what took place during this crime?" DiLisio responded, "Well, I don't know if you could say they fed me anything. You know, I can't—I can't recall what they said to me. But I know that what I said had to come from somewhere."

June 15, 1995
Wilder, Vermont
(6 days to execution)

A CCR lawyer called with news about the Vanessa Dale Croft rape case. CCR's investigators had discovered that Croft had flunked a police polygraph. For almost two decades, the state had succeeded in keeping this secret. Now, not only had the investigators unearthed the fact that the polygraph had occurred, they had obtained a copy of the polygrapher's report. CCR faxed me a copy.

The polygraph was a tasty appetizer. Gene Miller then called with the main course. FDLE had interrogated Tony DiLisio on the record. Tony told the FDLE agents that he had told the police that Joe never took him to the dump site. The cops, not Joe, had taken Tony to the dump.

Miller phoned at 3:36 P.M. There was going to be a stay issued at 5:00. Chiles himself would issue the stay.

Lori Rozsa called at 3:45. It was still only a rumor, but the word was that it would be a real stay, not a temporary reprieve that could evaporate after a few days. Governor Chiles would be making some sort of final decision by the end of the day. And there was more. Not only had Joe never taken Tony to the dump site, but Joe had never bragged to Tony about the inflammatory twaddle Tony testified to at Joe's murder trial.

Gail Anderson at CCR phoned at 4:30. An Associated Press story was saying the execution had been stayed. Her boss was on the phone with the governor's clemency aide as we spoke. While we waited for official word, Anderson said to me that the stay was "all your doing, you know." No, I replied—as I had replied to Gene Miller, Lori Rozsa, Martin Dyckman, and others who had made similar remarks—this wasn't my doing at all. If there was to be a stay, it would be Rozsa's and Miller's and Holmes's doing.

If there was a stay—in a moment, we knew that there was. While I stayed on the phone, Anderson's CCR boss told us that there was a stay of execution. Sort of, anyway. Governor Chiles had stayed the death warrant; he had not withdrawn it. Thus Chiles could reinstate the warrant, although CCR's director thought that reinstatement was "highly unlikely." Further, the lawyers at CCR didn't know whether the prison would take Joe off deathwatch and return him to death row.

Criminologist Mike Radelet in Gainesville brought me back to earth: "Mello, get off the floor. Remember Larry Joe Johnson?" Larry Joe Johnson had been scheduled to be killed in Florida's electric chair. Public protests and media heat arose because Johnson was a Vietnam vet with posttraumatic stress disorder. The governor issued a temporary stay, but only until the pressure died down, which it soon did. The governor signed a new death warrant, and Larry Joe Johnson was executed on schedule. Oh, yes, I remembered Larry Joe Johnson.

Radelet doubted Joe would be taken off deathwatch given that, by its own terms, the warrant wouldn't expire until June 30. After that, the governor would have to sign a new death warrant before the prison could set a new execution date.

Another wrinkle: reporters were now saying that Chiles intended to order a police investigation into whether Tony DiLisio's recantation was truthful. What the hell did that mean? Maybe it was bad news; how likely was it that a police investigation into the police actions that put Joe on death row would find anything that would hurt the police? Maybe it was good news; any credible investigation would take a month or more, which would take Joe past the magic date of June 30, when the existing death warrant would expire.

Joe's family was wonderful, as always. His mother told me her "prayers were answered. . . . I had a gut feeling you'd get it stayed. . . . Mike, you worked so hard and believed in him all these years. . . . when he gets out, we all *party*. . . . Prepare yourself for a big party. I love you, honey, and god bless you." Joe's daughter: "We can start breathing normally again, at least for now." Joe's ex-wife called me "the jumper cables; none of this would have happened without you. I can't thank you enough."

Around 8:00 P.M., Joe called. "I'm happy, but where do we go next? . . . Mike, if it wasn't for you and Lori, none of this would have happened. . . . You're the one who was out there, when no one else was listening; man, you *believed* in me."

And Joe answered the central question of how fragile the stay might be: "After I get off the phone with you, they're taking me off of deathwatch and moving me back to UCI."

That meant the prison thought the stay would hold. It was the strongest sign yet that the stay *would* hold.

Joe asked me that night, "How would you feel about taking my case over again?" Joe's family had already requested that I come back on board as Joe's lawyer. They didn't want CCR, but CCR and I were not the only options. I had spent much of that morning trying to find an attorney other than me to take Joe's case over from CCR.

To the surprise of us both, Deanna thought I ought to come back into Joe's case as counsel. "As strange as this sounds, I have reservations about your getting out of it completely. You have the next eight steps mapped out in your mind. . . . If this ends badly for Joe, you'll need to know that you've done all you could do. I've seen you when you've had control over Joe's case (before January) and now, when you don't. Don't take this the wrong way, but you're crazier when you don't."

A phone call to Joe and another to CCR, and it was a done deal. I was again Joe's lawyer.

My first official act was to call Kelly McGraw, Tony DiLisio's attorney in Pensacola. She was appalled about how the cops had manipulated her client in 1976. After twelve years of despising Tony DiLisio for his lies in 1976, it felt entirely unnatural for me to think of Tony as an "ally." That was the word Kelly used, as in "We're allies on this. . . . We're all on the same side on this; I'm convinced now he's telling the truth." So was I.

Gene Miller's sights were set far beyond this stay of execution. "There's a *distinct* possibility that, down the line, that you'll spring him from prison. I'm really beginning to believe that. It's been a pretty good week."

Miller was right, of course. It had been a good week. But it was only the beginning. This stay was a good first step, but it was no more than that. Joe is *innocent,* and his reward for proving his innocence ought not be spending the rest of his life in Florida's maximum-security prison, rather than being subject to electrocution at the whim of whoever happens to be governor at any given moment. He deserves to be freed. He deserves an apology from the state that stole the last twenty years of his life.

Every additional day Joe spends in prison is an outrage. Every state actor whose hands touched this case ought to be out of a job. Every cop or prosecutor who sanctimoniously railroaded Joe Spaziano to death row, every judge—state and federal—who rubber-stamped this conviction and death sentence should be dusting off his résumé.

Chiles's stay was like the passage of a hurricane's eye: a tranquil moment after the fury, a serene interruption before the storm begins anew. Joe and I knew another death warrant would come. We knew that even as we celebrated the stay. This time, Joe didn't even try to pretend he wasn't afraid a new warrant would come. He was afraid of the dark, because he had been there before.

The *Miami Herald* was responsible for obtaining the stay of execution. During my years as a capital postconviction litigator, I swore that I would never try any of my cases in the media. Now, I swear that I will never again try one in court.

Joe said, "I grew up with you, Mike. You're like a brother out on the streets. We're the little people, Mike. We're garbage, and no one listens to us. You're the only one who's believed in me all these years."

Thus did I again become Joe Spaziano's attorney. It was a comfortable and familiar place for me to be. Like coming home.

State of Florida
Office of the Governor
The Capitol
Tallahassee, Florida

June 15, 1995

Michael Minerva
Capital Collateral Representative
Tallahassee, Florida

Dear Mr. Minerva:

This letter confirms that on Thursday, June 15, 1995 I issued a stay of execution of indefinite duration for Joseph Robert Spaziano. The underlying death warrant established the week of June 23, 1995 through June 30, 1995 for the sentence to be carried out. The Superintendent of Florida State Prison thereupon set the execution for Tuesday, June 27, 1995 at 7:00 a.m. To repeat, the execution of Joseph Spaziano has been stayed indefinitely.

I shall advise you of any further developments.

With kind regards, I am

Sincerely,
Lawton Chiles

8

"Dear Governor Chiles . . ."

Out in the mountains, therefore, these [outlaw mountain] men were suspicious, cautious and usually well armed. . . . They were walking arsenals. . . . They wanted to be left alone, they told [New York reporter Albert] Richardson, but "when the Rebels come to hunt us, we hunt them. They know that we are in earnest, and that before they can kill any one of us he will break a hole in the ice large enough to drag two or three of them along with him."

Phillip Shaw Paludan, Victims: A True Story of the Civil War, *1981*

June 18, 1995
Martin McClain
Office of the Capital Collateral Representative
Tallahassee, FL

Dear Marty:

As I discussed with Gail on Friday, I am delighted that CCR will remain involved in Joe's case. As you know, I am without a secretary, investigator or research assistant. I hope CCR can do a few things sooner rather than later (I'm still treating the stay as fragile).

First, I understand that CCR filed a 119 request on Tony DiLisio's videotape. Can you fax me a copy? Any action? Any attempts, through informal FDLE contacts or DiLisio's lawyer, to get the videotape?

Second, what has CCR done about FDLE's intention to polygraph DiLisio? Objections? Alternative polygraphers?

Third, what is the status of the baby 3.850 on the rape conviction? Can you FedEx a draft, along with any other CCR work products that might help me come up to speed? Might there be *Brady* material on the FDLE videotape?

Fourth, has CCR followed up on its initial contact with Joe's ex-wife, Linda? Any follow-up on the names of the two cops who questioned her about the rape, or on the materials she passed on to Joe's lawyer in the rape case?

Fifth, what about the four other bodies found at the Altamonte dump site?

Sixth, any attempts to track down Lynwood Tate and Joe Suarez? What about Tall Paul, the Outlaw who may have committed the rape?

Seventh, any research on Florida law on repressed memory?

Eighth, any follow-up on Dr. Toni Apel's willingness to nail down the connection between closed head trauma and deficits in short and long term memory? Any update on my 1985 reports on Joe's brain damage?

Ninth, exactly what happened when Mike Hummell met with DiLisio twice? Did Hummell go alone? Why was the *Herald* (and FDLE) able to get such great stuff from him?

Tenth, any attempts to meet with Joe McCawley? What has he been doing since he sent Pitts, Lee and Joe to death row?

Eleventh, could CCR make four copies of all your files on Joe and send (1) the originals to me, and copies to (2) Pat Doherty, . . . ; (3) Dr. Toni Apel, . . . ; (4) Jeff Robinson, Nussbaum & Wald, . . . ; and (5) Tom Equels, . . . ?

Finally, did Minerva really tell a reporter that all CCR has ever wanted in this case is a life sentence? Joe's family read that in the newspaper and they asked me to explain it. If it was a misquote, I'd like to be able to pass that on to Joe and to his people.

Thanks for your help.

Sincerely,
Michael Mello

I never heard back from CCR on these questions. But I did get an answer, of sorts, when CCR sent me all its files on Joe Spaziano's case. The answer was chilling. Only a few weeks prior to the scheduled execution of CCR's factually innocent client, CCR had done virtually none of the investigation set out in the above letter. And as I would soon discover, whatever flaccid investigation CCR *had* conducted was either botched or useless. Whether CCR had given up on Joe's case or had simply conducted an inept investigation was rather beside the point. CCR was going to let Joe die without a fight.

June 19, 1995
Wilder, Vermont

I had found cocounsel. Pat Doherty, an old friend from my Florida deathwork days, let himself be badgered by me and by his wife, Marlene, into joining me on the bridge of the *Titanic*. Pat's a brilliant trial lawyer, and he's a master at divining the currents in Florida politics.

"This case isn't legal; it's political, and under death warrant there are no courts," Doherty said. "We have to treat this as a *purely* political matter."

I wondered what his instincts told him about an idea I'd been playing with for a week or so: What if, in order to keep the pressure on Chiles, we announced that we had decided *not* to take Joe's case back into court? The *courts* wouldn't bail Chiles out. If he signed a new warrant, Chiles alone would bear responsibility for the execution of this innocent man. Of course, the strategy depended on the conscience of Lawton Chiles, and on Chiles's belief that Doherty and I didn't have the time or investigative resources to conduct another round of postconviction litigation in the courts. The courts have had their chance to do right in this case, and they've blown it. They've been blowing it for nineteen years. It was entirely possible the governor's sense of duty would prevail.

Pat agreed: "It would take a fucking lot of balls, but you can't fall out of a ditch. If we file in court, then the heat is off of Chiles, and Mello and Doherty run like rabbits, from court to court, and in the end they kill Joe anyway—they kill him, and no one is to blame."

It was spooky how well Pat articulated my own thoughts on this score. He found it jarring as well: "We are dangerously similar in our thinking." An Art Spiegelman line: "Damaged minds travel in the same ruts."

On the other hand, CCR had decided that I was no longer competent to be Joe's lawyer. In a fax from Martin McClain, CCR's chief assistant, I was informed: "You should not be Spaziano's counsel. . . . Your decision is unwise for Joe Spaziano. It will feed the notion that this has all been a game."

The next day McClain called to say he was sorry about his fax. "You've *made* the judgment call; I disagree with that call, but you and I are cool." Once CCR sent me its files on Joe's case, it was out of the case and I would be on my own. Michael Minerva, CCR's director, told me that "Once we're out of the case, I can't have our people working on it." I asked whether CCR would cocounsel the case with me. No. CCR had "143 clients; 20 more in the next two months; we've doubled our caseload since 1991. I'm scared, Mike," McClain concluded. End of session.

Next, I spoke with Joe's mom about some investigative leads. I wanted to get her thoughts on my not taking Joe's case back to court. She was frightened by the strategy. "I want him out so badly, Mike. . . . You're not as tough as you seem, Mike; neither is Joe, and I think that's one thing he recognized in you." She wanted me to give the courts one last shot. Joe wanted that, too. So Pat Doherty and I decided to file one final motion directly in the Florida Supreme Court. First, however, we decided to file a new application for executive clemency.

June 20, 1995
Governor Lawton Chiles
The Capitol
Tallahassee, FL 32399-0001

Dear Governor Chiles:

Members of your administration have been intimating to reporters that you might lift your stay of Joseph Spaziano's execution or, in the alternative, that you might sign a new death warrant altogether. In light of this possibility, I want to clarify my letter to you of June 16, 1995.

In my previous letter, I wrote that I am investigating the *possibility* of initiating future litigation on behalf of Spaziano. If given a reasonable time to investigate and craft constitutional claims on Spaziano's behalf, I may do so. However, I will *not* breach my ethical duty to fully investigate and research any claims prior to raising them in a lawsuit. Specifically, there is insufficient time to present an effective motion for post conviction relief between now and June 30, when the present warrant expires. Critical expert witnesses are about to leave the country on business; crucial fact witnesses—such as Lynwood Tate and Joe Suarez—have not yet been located; I am trying to determine why the rape victim flunked a polygraph; I understand that the FDLE videotape of DiLisio—which you have *still* refused to provide, either to CCR or to me—contains newly discovered evidence of exculpatory information unlawfully withheld from the defense at trial, documentary and other evidence that Spaziano could not have committed the rape; pursue leads that might identify the dirtbag who committed the rape and mutilation of Vanessa Dale Croft; and the like.

What this means, as a practical matter, is that should you lift your stay and reschedule the execution for prior to noon on June 30—and if you enter no stay between now and then—Spaziano will be electrocuted on schedule. Unless the courts act *sua sponte* to stay the execution, or unless you do, the execution will be carried out.

Ten years ago, Governor "Bob" Graham extorted me into rushing to investigate and file a state postconviction motion under warrant. He and I knew the courts would stay the scheduled execution, and they did. But the papers I was forced to file—at the barrel of a warrant—were based on an investigation I now believe was inadequate and, therefore, unethical; once I filed in court, and was therefore locked into my pleadings, the courts could reject those pleadings *as* inadequate, and they did. I teach legal ethics now, and my students are not shy about calling my decision to file pleadings I *knew* were based on inadequate investigation by its real name—cowardice.

As I said in my earlier letter, because I want the petition and motions to be thorough—and because I want to include all appropriate legal issues suggested by my ongoing investigation into the complex legal and factual dimensions of this case—I presume you will allow me reasonable time to investigate and craft the motion and its supporting materials. None of us want piecemeal litigation, do we?

In other words, you ought not to count on the judiciary to correct the monstrous injustice in your again scheduling Spaziano to die. I have been litigating Spaziano's innocence claims in the courts for eleven years, and they have said, in effect, take your case to the governor. So we have. If you lift your stay, Spaziano's destruction will be *your* responsibility and yours alone. For the first time in the two-decade sorry history of this case, responsibility rests with one man and one man alone. Sequential courts have evaded their own responsibility for the killing of this innocent man. They've passed the buck to you, but clemency *is* your job. The buck stops here.

Finally, you should know my ultimate goals in this case. They are (1) invalidation of both convictions—the rape as well as the homicide; (2) an apology by the State of Florida for the two decades it has stolen from my client—including four death warrants; and (3) reparations. I am, at the moment, negotiable on (3), if you are negotiable on (1) and (2). Should you succeed in rushing to execute my innocent client, I will pursue an action for wrongful death. My understanding is that sovereign immunity does not insulate governmental officials from causes of action grounded in intentional homicide committed by state actors who are in full possession of the facts of their intentional conduct.

One must wonder why three serial governors have signed four death warrants, in light of the vulnerability of the case against my client. I don't know why you and your predecessors keep trying to kill my client. But it isn't because you were not told—and told again—why killing this man would be a grotesque injustice. The *Miami Herald, St. Petersburg Times,* and others have done your homework for you, and you ought to be grateful to them—rather than impugning their motives.

You and I both know that Governors Graham and Martinez signed warrants in order to manipulate defense lawyers into rushing into court with pleadings that were often inadequate. But let me suggest a more honorable and honest precedent: Governor LeRoy Collins. Governor Collins once told me why he had a policy of meeting—face to face—with every person upon whom the governor signed a death warrant. He told me that he did so because he wanted to look into the eyes of each man for whose killing he was responsible. *He* was responsible, and he had the courage to say so.

Should you have the bad judgment to think that this is some kind of bluff on my part, you should ask around. I don't bluff.

Sincerely,
Michael Mello
Counsel for Joseph Robert Spaziano

Within the Florida death row defense community, this letter has become known as my "You are the murderer" letter to Governor Chiles.

6-20-95
Dear Mike & D,

Hi folks me CRAZY JOE back at U.C.I. Darn Mike everything you done this time worket. You all don't know how happy I am. Going to miss talking to you all. If you hear from Lori I got a couple paintings going to her and you to. Don't know when I'll be getting more supplies but in a few weeks. I need to catch up on all the letters I didn't write while on death watch. Thank Lori for all the support she gave me and believing me about the murder and the rape charge. Made so many happy and think different then all the bad news I use to get. I feel much different about news paople and if wasn't for Miami Herald I would of been dead and if Tony Jr. died dearing this 20 years I would of been dead. He finely told the truth and I believe him that the cops made him do it. Thank you to Mike for takeing my case back I owe you & D so much you are going to enjoy having me for a friend. Your welcome in our nation Mike. You don't realize how everybody is going to respect you. I know my heart your going to get me back out in the streets. You believed what I told you since I meet you. If not to much troble can I get every news storys you have. Oh Rosie & Mark got some new newspaper clipping to. Hay D. Hi ya pretty close I'm going to be proud to be Mike's best man. You got a hell of a man there. I know you 2 are going to be a great couple, thanks for likeing me makes me feel good really good. I'm going to make your place look so neat I mean it real slick no place will look like it not even a church. So proud of you all love the hell out of you. And a bunch of other people. You'es don't know but you'es gonig to have a special party you never had before.

Ok write back ok. I love you.

CRAZY JOE A.O.A.

June 21, 1995
Wilder, Vermont

I sent out an SOS to Volunteer Lawyers Resource Center of Florida. Since 1988, the federally funded VLRCs had provided assistance to lawyers representing death row prisoners in postconviction proceedings. The VLRCs recruited lawyers for condemned prisoners and provided those lawyers with research, logistical, and investigative support; in some instances, they provided direct representation for death row inmates. By the mid-1990s, Congress had become disenchanted with the VLRCs and was in the process of defunding them and shutting them down. Florida's VLRC was scheduled to shut down on October 1, 1995.

Still, the Florida VLRC's codirectors, Jenny Greenburg and Matthew Lawry, were ready to help me with Joe's case. They assigned one of their most experienced investigators, Steve Gustat, to work on the case full-time.

I worked on drafting and editing the clemency application for most of the day. Meanwhile, Lori Rozsa was in Georgia, interviewing Lynwood Tate, an early suspect in the Harberts homicide. Tate is very smart. Tony DiLisio was recanting to ABC's Nina Alvarez and Mark Potter; it was reassuring that Tony had now recanted to someone other than the *Herald*.

According to one of my Florida sources: "The governor is taking this investigation very seriously. He's looking into it personally."

Tom Horkan, executive director of Florida Catholic Conference, was getting similar intelligence from Dexter Douglass, Governor Chiles's general counsel. Horkan met with Douglass this morning, and "Douglass mentioned Joe's case; Douglass has taken the matter over himself," replacing the governor's clemency aide as the point man in the investigation. "He has given carte blanche to FDLE, and he'll be immersing himself in the record" sooner rather than later.

I wanted to believe that the FDLE investigation was indeed a good-faith effort to find the truth about Tony DiLisio's recantation. Still, I had seen no evidence so far that the cops or the governor's office could be trusted, that the stay and the police probe were something other than an exercise in political damage control.

There were other political developments that I hoped would support Joe's case for clemency based on factual innocence. As the police investigation of Tony DiLisio proceeded, the federal Antiterrorism and Effective Death Penalty Bill was progressing through the U.S. Senate. The bill would sharply limit federal habeas corpus, but it would also enhance the importance of executive clemency, especially clemency based on new evidence of innocence. Thus, the pitch went, Chiles's signing a new warrant on Joe would hurt U.S. Senator Bob Graham's push for the federal statute. Clemency for Joe would be consistent with the ethos of the proposed federal legislation: governors, not courts, should consider and act upon new evidence of factual innocence.

My letter to Governor Chiles was being panned by the reviewers. Gene Miller blasted me for sending the letter. Others said much the same thing, only not quite as loudly.

Actually, our strategy was nothing more than a variation on the good cop/bad cop technique used in obtaining confessions from suspected criminals. Pat Doherty was the good cop, talking nicely and quietly with the governor's office. I was the bad cop, the one who makes you confess to the good cop so you won't have to deal with me.

This new information wasn't the only gift Joe received from Pensacola that day. Kelly McGraw, Tony DiLisio's attorney, agreed to my adding her name and Tony's to the clemency application. Thus the clemency petition would be filed on behalf of both Joe and the state's star witness against him at the 1976 murder trial.

These happy developments were counterweighted by news from CCR and the *Orlando Sentinel*. The March 1995 clemency petition CCR had written waived Joe's release in exchange for a life sentence. Amazingly, Joe's former lawyers had said in writing that their client would settle for spending the rest of his life in Florida State Prison. There may have been tactical reasons for such a concession, but Joe got nothing in return: Governor Chiles signed his death warrant a few weeks later anyway.

The *Orlando Sentinel* brought us information that was truly chilling. Members of the governor's staff were saying that they'd seen

FDLE's videotape of its recent interrogation of Tony DiLisio, and that on the tape Tony *didn't* recant. All he said was that he couldn't remember what he did or said nineteen years ago in Joe's case. No recantation. If this were true, I inferred, then Joe would be finished. No matter that he had recanted to the *Herald* and ABC News. If he didn't recant when he met with FDLE, then it would be over.

But Kelly McGraw was emphatic that Tony *had* recanted the trip to the dump when he met with FDLE. She had been there as Tony's attorney, and she remembered the recantation clearly. The *Herald*'s Lori Rozsa was equally certain that Tony had recanted to her. So was ABC's Nina Alvarez.

This was reassuring, but not enough. I needed to see the videotape myself. The word went out to everyone working for Joe that getting ahold of that videotape was now our top priority. In the meantime, I asked McGraw whether Tony would be willing to sign an affidavit reiterating his recantation. She said he would and promised to draft the affidavit for Tony to sign.

I strongly suspected that if anyone outside the governor's office had a copy of the videotape, it would be the *Orlando Sentinel*. So I called Mike Griffin, the *Sentinel*'s point man on the Spaziano story. Griffin said his newspaper didn't have the videotape, but he seemed to be looking for dirt to throw at Tony DiLisio. "Old cop talk is that they thought DiLisio was lying [back in 1975 and 1976]. . . . He might even have been involved himself in the murder." If true, then the cops let the capital prosecutor put on a star witness the *police themselves* believed to be a liar.

Griffin also said he knew what FDLE was looking for and how they were going about finding it. The police were questioning Tony's friends and associates, with the obvious intent of undercutting the credibility of Tony's recantation. Griffin said he didn't know who, exactly, FDLE was talking to.

By 9:30 P.M., Laura Gillen had completed word processing on a semifinal draft of the clemency petition. She FedExed it to Pat Doherty and Mark Olive. I double-checked with Doherty to verify that he was still solid on our decision not to return to court if a new warrant came. He was. "If a warrant comes on July 4, we hang tough. . . . If we take the heat off of Chiles and Chiles *alone* [by filing in court], we're *fucked*. . . . The only chance of getting something *real* is from a retiring politico, a sixty-two-year-old guy who served his state honorably for thirty years and is leaving office with an eye to how he'll be remembered in the history books. . . . This is his *moment*." Pat quoted George Patton: "We're in the right place at the right time with the right instrument. God willing." And: " 'It's not important whether the generals know whether I'm kidding. *I* need to know when I'm kidding.' Mike, we're not kidding about this. Any judicial action takes the pressure right off Chiles and puts it *nowhere*."

And if Chiles signs a fifth warrant, and the time winds down, and it's one minute until Joe is electrocuted for a crime he didn't commit—could Pat and I really *not* petition the courts for a stay? Yes. Chiles would back down. Wouldn't he?

June 25, 1995
Wilder, Vermont

Finalized the clemency petition. Double-checked that Tony DiLisio and his lawyer were still on board. Ditto Pat Doherty.

We'd file the clemency petition tomorrow. Tonight, I'd fax it to Lori Rozsa. It seemed only fair.

June 26, 1995
Wilder, Vermont

I delayed filing the clemency petition with the governor's office because I wanted to make certain Tony and his lawyer were okay with the wording. McGraw phoned: "Nothing controversial here. . . . It looks great. . . . The Tony quote was straight out of what he told FDLE; I read it to Tony, and he has no problem with it."

Today was a Monday. Mike Griffin of the *Orlando Sentinel* told me that on Friday, Governor Chiles's general counsel, Dexter Douglass, would brief Chiles on Joe's case. Also, FDLE had expanded its inquiry to include past friends and associates of Tony DiLisio.

One of my most reliable spies tells me his contacts say that Douglass is the "fulcrum; Chiles will take his recommendation." Douglass is "smart and working hard on this," but he's troubled by DiLisio's *pre-hypnosis* statement to the police. This is not a good sign. All Tony said in that statement that mattered was that Joe had bragged to Tony about what he had done to unnamed and unidentified women. Not even *Tony* believed Joe's braggadocio; without Tony's trip to the dump with Joe, Tony was telling the cops nothing more than hearsay that not even the teenaged doper biker wanna-be Tony believed himself.

June 27, 1995
Interstate 89 (Vermont)

At 3:15 P.M., while in Montpelier on an errand with Deanna, I learn from my spies that Dexter Douglass will indeed brief Chiles this Friday, and that Chiles is expected to make a decision at that time.

Jeffrey Robinson, a close friend in D.C., might be able to photocopy the clemency application and three-volume appendix and get the whole mess on a plane tonight, to be filed tomorrow morning. But that won't work. Jeff doesn't have the application. Deanna and I could try to copy it at a Staples Office Supply and FedEx it to Tallahassee, but there probably isn't time to do that and get it into FedEx by 5:00 P.M. Maybe I should just fax it to Chiles tonight, all 250 pages of it. But then, as I flip through the application, I see errors I've made in the document. They need to be corrected.

I call Laura Gillen at the law school and ask her to make those and other corrections. At last, at 10:30 P.M., the clemency application is finished. Laura leaves it at the law school, and Deanna and I drive in to make ten photocopies (one for Governor Chiles, one for Dexter Douglass, one each for the seven executive cabinet members, one for us). We get home around 1:30 A.M. I fax the pages to Chiles and go to sleep.

June 28, 1995
Wilder, Vermont
(Yesterday, Joe would have been dead.)

3:10 P.M.: A reporter called to tell me that the FDLE investigation and report are done, and they're devastating to my innocence claim. The reporter told me that according to his source, "they've got new stuff on Joe that'll leave the *Herald* and that bleeding-heart attorney with egg on their faces. . . . This is brand new stuff."

When I phoned Dexter Douglass's office to check his fax number, his assistant told me, "Dexter Douglass is in charge of this one, so you have the right number." But minutes later I heard from Mike Griffin at the *Orlando Sentinel*. Chiles's clemency aide, Mark Schlakman, had just told the *Sentinel* that *he* (Schlakman) was now in charge of the

Spaziano matter—not Dexter Douglass. Who's on first? Griffin also said he'd heard "they've come up with corroborative evidence of Joe's guilt."

Around 6:00 P.M., Lori Rozsa called. "Mike, how much do you *really* believe he didn't do it?" In my bone marrow. The state's evidence was smoke and mirrors, but it's more a feeling I've had all these years I've known Joe. He has a big mouth and horrible judgment about who to befriend and trust, but he's just not a killer. He's not *that kind* of criminal. Joe wouldn't do those things to women. "Would he snitch on his club brothers who would do these things to women?" No. Never. He would die in the electric chair for a crime he didn't commit before he'd inform on his brother who *did* do the crime. "Mike, I don't think he did the murder. So why do they *think* he did it?" They have to. Bureaucratic inertia. Cops investigating other cops. Most of all he's an Outlaw. Legal niceties—like proof beyond a reasonable doubt—don't apply to Outlaws in south Florida. Not in 1976. Not today.

Mike Griffin phoned at 9:30 P.M. "FDLE will brief Chiles at 11:30 A.M. on Friday. The FDLE report will be made public next week. . . . It's not likely the governor will sign [a warrant] on Friday."

As if things weren't zany enough, it seemed that Tony DiLisio was furious at CCR. A reporter told me that a CCR investigator "threatened Tony: If you talk to us, none of your family will be hurt. . . . Mike Hummell showed up at Tony's with someone Tony was certain was an Outlaw biker." A few years earlier, FDLE had looked into allegations that CCR's investigators employed strong-arm tactics to "persuade" reluctant witnesses to recant. It seemed that Tony had talked about CCR's pressure tactics—on the still-secret (to me) FDLE videotaped interrogation of Tony.

All roads seemed to lead me back to that phantom videotape. Did Tony recant on the tape? Did Tony describe CCR's strong-arm tactics? I didn't know. It was a secret I couldn't find out, because the state wouldn't release a copy of the videotape. Not to me, at any rate.

Because we didn't know what was on the secret police videotape or in the secret police report, we needed to plan for any contingency. If FDLE"s agenda was to smear Tony DiLisio as a flake and a liar, that might not hurt Joe's case: Tony may be a flake, but he's the *state's* flake. (He was your star witness at Joe's 1976 capital trial, remember? And if you think he's a flake now, when he's relatively clean and sober and law-abiding, imagine the flake he must have been when he was your star witness—then, he was a teenage doper biker hanger-on who was fucking his stepmother and who hated Joe because Joe was also fucking his stepmother.)

The world was inside out; the law was upside down. For twelve years, before twenty-six judges, I had been arguing that Tony DiLisio was a flake whose linchpin trial testimony shouldn't be believed. During the same twelve years, the state had been arguing that Tony *wasn't* a flake. Now, I'm arguing for Tony's believability, and the state is arguing he's a flake.

I'm ready to retire again from deathwork, now, please.

6-28-95

Dear Mike & D.

Hi folks. I haven't heard from you all since I've been over here. Oh ya I have just haven't heard but from Susan and guest you and her will keep up. I keep getting letters from people that want to interview me. Here is one I got last night. The Documentary Institute Sandra H. Dickerson. She told me she talket to you an ok'ed it. Is it true Mike?

D. and you mike you sure gained friends on my side. D. thanks for being so nice to my family. Mike pal got a good lady their don't know her yet. But is ok in my book. You know we are friends the rest of our lives. You ever need me I'm going to be their pal. Well I'll be painting your hole house up. It's going to be so slick pal when I'm done nobody is going to have a house lke it and when they see it they'll wish the could. The way it look's I'll be their. Owe you so much. D.you got a hell of a man their. You know it. Ok hope to hear from you tomorrow I'll be interviewing with A.B.C. I'll look funny if you see me because I cut all my hair on my head when I was on death watch. Mike pal I was suppose to be dead yesterday and you done it. Love ya Mike.

Your friend CRAZY JOE

I just got the nettest letter from my best club brother we go back years and years Mike. Anyway he talket so good about and said Joe the club owes you a hell of a party. Hay Mike they mean it Mike. Waite to the rest understand. Pal you done something that my people going to look out for you. Can't wait to you can meet everybody you'll see. Love you Mike. You'll be getting a letter from him Speedy. He's a supper bro.

Michael Griffin from Orlando Sentinel let me know if ok for interview.

Your pal, Crazy Joe

June 29, 1995
Wilder, Vermont

The *Orlando Sentinel*'s Mike Griffin, my own little ray of sunshine, phoned early with a hot news flash: "Douglass is going to be pushing Chiles to sign [a warrant] again." No kidding. Griffin asked whether Joe would let Griffin interview him. I said probably not. Griffin got testy. "Why will Joe talk to ABC but not to us?" Maybe it's because Joe *reads* the *Orlando Sentinel*.

The day brightened, however, when a fellow named Richard Capozzola called. Richard lives in Florida, is active in Italian American organizations, and sounded as though he believed Joe Spaziano was about to become a latter-day Sacco and Vanzetti. In rapid-fire staccato, he said I needed to contact the president-elect of the Florida Sons of Italy, the Italian-American Association, *Fra Noi* newspaper, and a dozen other folks who might want to help. By the time we rang off, I was a believer. I knew that Joe, and especially his mom, would love this sort of support. And who knows? Chiles is a politician, and these folks are very organized, which meant they could be mobilized. Mobilized for exactly what, I had no idea.

What was intriguing about Capozzola's call was the possibility of converting Joe's case from simply a death penalty story into something in addition to that. The Italian American aspect was a vehicle to do that, to broaden our base of support for the campaign to save Joe's life beyond the minuscule core community of capital punishment abolitionists. I had no illusion that Joe's case could be used as a wedge with which to convert the Italian American community into abolitionists. But if they could identify at all with Joe as a person, and as a member of groups viewed with suspicion by the dominant culture—the Outlaws are often compared to the Mafia—then perhaps that recognition might spark a willingness to rethink capital punishment as a social issue. The issue would become not "capital punishment," the abstract issue, but rather Joe Spaziano, an innocent man on death row. Joe would thus humanize the issue of capital punishment.

9

The Secret Police Report

The state's case [of capital murder against weatherman Dixon Bell] was like bad journalism. First you reach a conclusion. Then you go out and find the facts to support that conclusion. The facts that don't fit, you simply ignore.

Steve Thayer, The Weatherman, *1995*

Criminals shun reporters, more than they do cops, because reporters are smarter and less merciful.

Clarence Darrow

June 30, 1995
Wilder, Vermont

FDLE was supposed to brief Chiles at 11:30 A.M., but it didn't happen. Lori Rozsa called to tell me that the FDLE report would not be delivered to Governor Chiles today. FDLE had decided to expand its investigation. The *Tampa Tribune*'s Kevin Metz confirmed it: "FDLE is telling me it's taking longer than expected. . . . No report to the governor today. . . . We're in a couple-of-weeks-mode, from today." ABC's Mark Potter called at 11:50 A.M.: "Chiles has told FDLE to do it *right,* with signed statements, all very legal. . . . Nothing will happen this weekend, and maybe not for a couple of weeks. . . . The word seems to have come down from on high that FDLE had better do it *right* this time." Joe's fourth death warrant would expire at noon.

Just like the army—hurry up and wait. Not that I was complaining about the respite, no matter how brief.

At 12:10 P.M., Joe's fourth death warrant officially expired.

At 12:15, Fed Ex delivered seventeen boxes of Joe's case files from CCR.

God, how a day can turn around. This morning, I expected Joe to have a seven-day death warrant by now. As the AA bumper sticker says: One day at a time.

July 2, 1995
Wilder, Vermont

As Woodrow Wilson might say, it was a time of watchful waiting. Taking stock. And noodling.

Pat Doherty thought, "This is going *well*. The *St. Petersburg Times* is running a column calling for an independent investigation. Would you trust *your* life or liberty to this FDLE investigation?"

We were still searching for a strategy that would set Joe free without the government's having to admit it was wrong. Pat had been through this drill before, with Jent and Miller. Jent and Miller were bikers who were sentenced to die in Florida for another man's crime; after their innocence was proven, they were released from prison. Pat: "No Florida government official has *ever* admitted to being wrong. Not in Pitts and Lee. Not in Jent and Miller. Not in Richardson. Last year I voir dired a hundred jurors in a case, and every one of them said, 'Yes, I make mistakes; even government officials can make mistakes.' But government officials never *admit* their mistakes. They brush them under the rug, or they bury them."

No matter the angle from which we approached it, Pat and I kept finding no realistic alternative to our forgoing-the-courts strategy. "This is a high-risk strategy, but after nineteen years on death row, do you know of a *low*-risk strategy?" I said I didn't.

There's a world of difference between a risky strategy and a *reckless* strategy. I define recklessness as the taking of a risk that is both (1) substantial and (2) unjustifiable. When an experienced and wise cancer surgeon performs a procedure with a 2 percent likelihood of success, she is running a substantial risk. But it may well not be an unjustifiable risk. Whether the substantial risk is unjustifiable can be gauged only by the surgeon, who must apply her experience and wisdom to each case.

Joe in May and June 1995 was that cancer patient with the 2 percent likelihood of survival. He was an Outlaw; the murder was especially vicious; he had been litigating for nineteen years; twenty-six judges had ruled against him; he had survived three death warrants. After the fourth warrant was signed in May, Joe's chances dropped from 2 percent to 1 percent. Only one other Florida death row prisoner has survived four death warrants, and he was killed on his seventh.

Thus we knew that our strategy of keeping the pressure on Governor Chiles and forgoing the courts was a substantial risk. Was it also an unjustifiable risk, rendering the strategy reckless? Neither Pat nor I thought so, and most of the capital punishment experts we talked with about it didn't think so either.

July 3, 1995
Wilder, Vermont

The *Orlando Sentinel* strikes again. Mike Griffin's front-page story blared that Joe is the "best suspect" in "two other murders and five other rapes." Griffin also trashed Tony DiLisio pretty thoroughly. Reading the story, I got the distinct feeling I was reading a first draft of FDLE's secret report.

Griffin's story relied upon unidentified "court files." This was striking, because in his conversations with me, Griffin had been severely critical of the *Herald* in general and Lori Rozsa in particular for "not coming to the Sanford Courthouse and looking through the court files." Only the *Orlando Sentinel*, Griffin boasted, had spent "two weeks going through the court files."

What "court files" was the *Sentinel*'s ace reporter talking about? I called Griffin and asked. He coyly refused to tell me. He also refused to send copies to me.

But the more I read Griffin's article based on the "court files," the more familiar Griffin's information sounded. Where had I seen all of this before? It came to me in a flash: I'd read it in the trial transcripts. The "court files" of which the *Orlando Sentinel* was so proud were nothing more than the trial transcripts and files—the same files I sent to Gene Miller at the outset; the same files Miller had dumped on Warren Holmes's desk on the Friday of Memorial Day weekend; the same files the *Herald* had for two months. This had taken the *Sentinel* two weeks?

In an overabundance of caution, Lori Rozsa did eventually wade through all of the "case files" in the Sanford County Courthouse. It took her two days rather than two weeks—because she had seen it all months before, in the boxes I had sent to Miller way back when. Rozsa found nothing new in those "court files."

Someone I trust a great deal gave me a chilling warning. "Chiles *hates* withdrawing warrants. This is *all* cover. Be ready for a new death warrant as soon as the Florida Supreme Court returns from their summer vacation in late August."

That wasn't the chilling part. The chilling part was "CCR is out to nail you. CCR isn't above sabotage. They're incompetent, but they also have malice beyond incompetence."

A friend who still worked at CCR was even more explicit: "You're being trashed big time at CCR. . . . 'Mello is going to kill Spaziano, and as soon as a warrant comes down he'll dump it back on us [at CCR]. . . . We actually had an office party to celebrate the stay CCR got last month.

"During Joe's warrant, no one here seemed to be doing anything. . . . Marty [McClain, the chief assistant at CCR] is never in the office, and that ethos trickles down. . . . No lawyer here is busting his ass. . . . By 4:30 on Friday this place is a ghost town. . . . CCR is always complaining about overwork, but all someone would need to do is subpoena our time records."

Rozsa and I chatted about Claude van Hook, who prosecuted Joe's 1976 murder trial and was now in private practice. I'd neither met nor spoken with him. Rozsa had: "He strikes me as a man of integrity. He stands by the prosecution but *not* the police investigation, which he had no role in; he got the case when the evidence [collection] was all done and put in a neat package" by the police. Perhaps Pat Doherty could persuade van Hook to sign an affidavit useful to Joe?

I don't know many people who are close to generals counsel to governors, but I did know someone who was close to Dexter Douglass, Chiles's general counsel. I asked my source whether I was being too rough on Douglass in public, and the answer I got was emphatic: "No! Keep the heat on him. He'll do the right thing, but only if its his path of least resistance. . . . What you need to do is use the media to create a political context, a political environment in which, for him, it is the path of least resistance to do the right thing.

"What you need to understand about Dexter is that his overriding goal is publicity, even if it's bad. Not justice; not even political benefits for his boss the governor. If Dexter thinks he'll get maximum publicity by Lawton [Chiles] signing Joe's warrant and having him executed, that's what Dexter will push Lawton to do—even if it destroys Lawton politically, and even if it robs Lawton of his place in history."

My thoughts kept returning to CCR, though, and what my mole had said my old public defender office had become. He had said: "It's been so vicious and horrible here. . . . You're going to kill him, or you'll get sick again and dump Joe's case back on CCR. . . . And CCR today has an *awful* reputation on the row; it's like being [the worst kind of] public defender."

Hi Mike & D.

I seen you on T.V. Mike you looket good Mike healthy great. D You got to be proud of him. I am D. I got a letter here from a broghter thought you might want to read it. He writes so the prison people have a hard time reading it. But I tell you this he sure respects you Mike and you got a friend their he's a great brother and has a great head for brotherhood.

Ya Friday Susan told me not to do no more interviews. I don't do none Mike on less you or susan ok's it. You are the boss.

I was called to classification a couple days ago, and was asked to sign a paper, to agree to be interviewed as three Broward county detectives. I told my class[ification] officer I'll let em interview me when we meet in hell. I wrote down the cops names, and I called south rep to find out what's going on down that way. I talked with Houston and he says the three cops that want to talk with me heads the south rep organized crime task force. The cops must be planning something new again and are looking for some weak links. They're sure pissing up a rope if they think I'm one.

I'm going to close here Joe. So know my brother, that you're in my thoughts, and will forever be in my heart. Know too, that I haven't forgotten my promise to you.

I love you my brother!

Anything new going on Mike. I write you but don't hear from you? Just let me know you and D. are ok and I'm happy. Well I'll close. As yet I haven't received my money from F.S.P. that I had into my account. I ask Susan to look into it no answer as yet.

Don't have no cigarettes or coffee don't have shit, but am alive today.

Well I'll close looking forward to the wedding.

Love you all,
Crazy Joe

Dear Joe:

I'm so sorry for not writing sooner, but I've been scrambling to get the new clemency filed. Here it is. Let me know what you think.

As to interviews you wrote to me about: I would *not* talk with Mike Griffin or anyone else from the *Orlando Sentinel*. For whatever reason, their agenda seems to be to provide Chiles with political cover to justify his signing another warrant. The *Sentinel* to date has published—uncritically—whatever gossip, rumor and innuendo about you and Tony that the cops feed to them. Their most recent hatchet job is a lovely display of integrity worthy of another Joe—"Tailgunner Joe" McCarthy—that relied upon anonymous police sources and unspecified "court records." Dexter Douglass told the *Sentinel* to look in the "court records," and after spending weeks doing that, I guess the reporters would have felt silly saying "oops; there's nothing here except innuendo, gossip, and testimony so unreliable that the judge wouldn't even let the jury *hear* it." They also rely upon their secret sources to accuse you as being the "best suspect" in other cases. The *Herald* saw this for what it was—cops circling their wagons and trying to close old cases by blaming them on the big, bad Outlaw—but the *Sentinel*, performing its function as bulletin board for the ~~merry trolls~~ local police, for FDLE, and for Douglass, went ahead and published it uncritically as fact. The *Sentinel*'s idea of an "investigation" is to read the trial transcripts and to embroider the obvious with the self-serving statements by the cops—no matter that the "information" they regurgitate as fact was so laughably unreliable that not even a gung ho prosecutor determined to nail the club even *tried* to get it into evidence. I've asked the *Sentinel* reporters why, if the garbage they're dredging up now was so great, why the prosecutor didn't even *attempt* to get it in. I don't know why the *Sentinel* is doing this; maybe they're jealous that the *Herald* scooped them on a story in their own backyard, or maybe they're in the tank with their local law enforcement folks. The *Sentinel* will write whatever it wants, and, if another warrant comes, your blood will be on *their* hands. But we shouldn't waste our time with those sorts of lazy journalistic hacks.

As to the Documentary Institute, I *would* meet with them. Sandra and I have spent a good deal of time on the phone; she's a very solid journalist who does her own homework, and who is working on a full-length treatment of your case. I've spoken with several people who have worked with her on other projects, and she knows her stuff.

I'm delighted with the way the ABC story—which ran last Friday—came out. Mark Potter is a superb journalist; I worked with him in 1986, when *Nightline* did a story on Dennis Adams' case and on killing crazy people. I sent them about 1,300 pages of materials, and they read it all *before* talking with me on the phone about it. I thought your hair looked fine, and I thought you came across quite well. Your mom did, too, by the way; she called me right after the broadcast.

And, of course, I would continue to meet with—and to be totally honest and open with—Lori Rozsa and the other folks at the *Miami Herald*. Their investigation is chugging along, and, as always, they're light years ahead of the *Sentinel*. (The "court files" trumpeted by the *Sentinel* were materials the *Herald* has had for months—they didn't write about it, not because they didn't know about it, but rather because the stuff is worthless and unreliable.) My complete files will remain open to the *Herald*, as always.

Anyway, it was terrific to hear from you, my friend. Deanna sends her love, as do your people. Take care, bro. And *write me*.

Sincerely,
Michael

July 5, 1995
Hi Mike,

I got your paper work for clemencie. Today Chiles had a heart atack or something, doe's that mess anything up? Hay you looket good on t.v. to bro. You sure got a greate party comjing up if I can this case or cases. I now know who put Tony up to it, his dad and the cops. It was you'es who found all that out. Ya the way it looks I'm still not out of hot water, Mike did Chiles ask for the new clemic paper? I'm still not sure what is going on. I'll ask Susan as soon as I see her. I just got my slip I got my money from F.S.P. today now I can get some smokes I love you all Mike I owe you. Told you what I was going to do and more. So my man seen us on t.v. They didn't even have me talk but you all done a good job. I'm waiting on stamps. Oh Mike do you think they will mine if you have 2 cases of mine going to clemicie. What I know just asking. OK I'll close told D. to drop me a line now and then to see you'es are ok.

I love you, your friend, Crazy Joe

July 5, 1995
Wilder, Vermont

Florida Governor Lawton Chiles had a stroke and had been hospitalized.

I prayed for his speedy and complete recovery. In the meantime, we needed to know whether Chiles's incapacitation changed the political calculus regarding clemency for Joe. Does the Florida Constitution have a counterpart to the Twenty-fifth Amendment to the U.S. Constitution? If the governor is incapacitated, does the lieutenant governor automatically assume the full powers and responsibilities of the government—including clemency and pardon power? Was Chiles even incapacitated? Who *was* the lieutenant governor? Someone told me it was Buddy McKay. So who was Buddy McKay?

Most important, might Chiles's stroke alter *Dexter Douglass*'s importance in the clemency calculus? If Chiles was out, and Lieutenant Governor McKay was in, perhaps this might reduce Douglass's outcome-determinative role as fulcrum of the clemency decision under Chiles? I'd heard that McKay and Chiles are still feuding over something or other from the last campaign cycle. So if McKay is peeved at Chiles, maybe he'll take it out on Chiles's clemency *consiglieri*, Douglass.

Keeping Joe alive as political retribution against Douglass would be poetic justice. Hey, you never know.

July 5, 1995

Dear Joe:

I hope this finds you well, my friend. The stay seems solid, at least for the next couple of weeks, until FDLE finishes its investigation.

This is a difficult letter for me to write, and I want to preface it at the outset by telling you that, *whatever* happens, I will be your lawyer. I may work with other lawyers on your case, but *I* will remain as lead counsel. I will never again give your case to *anyone* else: not to Stafman, and certainly not to CCR. I was wrong when I advised you, back in January, that CCR would be the best law firm to take your cases back over.

This is the hard part to write. CCR opposed my taking your case back over from them, and they opposed it so strongly that they refused to co-counsel it with me; CCR told me they can't co-counsel cases, which is not true, since CCR has been co-counseling Jerry Stano's case for some time. CCR also refused to provide me with any investigative or logistical support.

CCR has disagreed—stridently—with just about every decision I've made in your case over the past six months. CCR thought it was a mistake not to ask the full Eleventh Circuit to hear your case; to file the cert. petition early; to take your case to the *Herald*; to ask the Governor for more than a life sentence without possibility of parole; to file the clemency in the way I did. Rumors within CCR have included that my approach in your case will get you killed; that if a new warrant comes, I'll dump your case on CCR; that I'll become "ill" again—CCR seems to put the word in quotes—and use that as an "excuse" to get out of your case.

The distrust between CCR and me is mutual. In my view CCR's "investigation" in your case was lazy, inept, and, to the extent it happened at all, they botched it badly—their heavy-handed attempts to strong-arm Tony DiLisio into changing his testimony, for instance. Reporters hated to call CCR, because it was too depressing and because CCR never seemed to be *doing* anything.

I've been hearing for years that CCR had devolved into a hack public defender's office, a 9 to 5 operation staffed with grey bureaucrats who whine about how *hard* they work but who must *pray* that no one will ever subpoena their time sheets. I've always defended CCR against its many critics, but the way CCR handled your case has led me to the painful conclusion that Office of Capital Collateral Representative's critics have been right about what the agency has become.

The bottom line is that I will never entrust your case—or anyone else's, for that matter—to CCR. Come what may, I'm your lawyer.

You're stuck with me, my friend.

Sincerely,
Michael

At long last, someone friendly to me had acquired a copy of Tony DiLisio's June interrogation with FDLE. It was a bootleg copy of a copy of the original FDLE videotape, but I didn't care. My friend would send me the videotape.

Now, finally, amid all the governmental manipulation and deceit, a nugget of truth had appeared. My obtaining the FDLE's secret videotape of its secret interrogation of Tony DiLisio shook Governor Lawton Chiles's world. And yet this nugget of truth was treated by the governor's chief lawyer, general counsel Dexter Douglass, as if it were radioactive. Now that *I* had the videotape, none of the governor's men wanted to get near it. In the debate over whether Tony DiLisio had or had not recanted during his interrogation by FDLE—Tony and his lawyers saying he had, Douglass saying he hadn't—truth was a dangerous commodity.

Was Douglass misquoted by several newspapers? When Douglass thought I'd never see the FDLE videotape, he represented that, on the tape, Tony DiLisio did not recant his crucial testimony at trial. Now, recall that the heart of DiLisio's trial testimony was his trip to the dump site *with Joe*.

This is what Tony DiLisio said on my bootleg copy of the FDLE videotape:

INTERVIEWER: Okay, going back to that same time when you were with the police officers. Did at some point in time before hypnosis did you take them to a place where the body of this young lady that was killed . . .

DILISIO: They took me there.

INTERVIEWER: They took you there?

DILISIO: They took me there, . . .

INTERVIEWER: All right . . .

DILISIO: The cops brought me there. The cops brought me there. I had never been there in my life until they brought me there. And they made it look like that a guy that they arrested, Crazy Joe, brought me there. They are the ones that showed me where the dump was, they were the ones that brought me to the dump. And I remember that I didn't do something right the first time that they brought me back to that office, and that doctors, and so they left, and they brought me back to the dump. And then brought me back to the office and I did really good.

INTERVIEWER: Do you recall what you told them after that experience?

DILISIO: No, I don't remember . . . that experience . . . no, it was almost like buddy, buddy, you know, they played me then.

INTERVIEWER: Do you recall Spilanzo [sic] ever taking you to the dump?

DILISIO: No, never.

INTERVIEWER: If that in fact, did happen, do you think that you would recall that?

DILISIO: Most definitely.

Chiles and Douglass managed to keep the rest of the police investigation into Tony DiLisio's recantation a secret (secret from Joe's lawyers, I mean; not secret from the *Orlando Sentinel*). To this day, the bootleg video remains the only piece of the police investigation I have been able to extract from the government of Florida. Both the Florida Supreme Court and the U.S. Supreme Court refused, unanimously, to allow me access to the rest of the FDLE "investigation."

July 7, 1995
Wilder, Vermont

Crisis of conscience. Going through the seventeen boxes of paper CCR had sent me, I ran across a file from a rape case I knew nothing about. Although Joe had been a suspect, the victim decided not to prosecute.

This was the problem. I was pretty sure that the *Herald*'s Lori Rozsa didn't know about this file; she had never mentioned it to me, at any rate. I had given Rozsa and Gene Miller my word that I would not withhold any information from them. But I had made that promise in May and early June, before I again became Joe's lawyer.

I decided to give the file to Rozsa, but I shouldn't have worried. She already had it. She'd read it in the court files.

In fact, she knew much more about the case than I did. "The social context was so different then [in the mid-1970s]. . . . It's really hard to tell where group sex ended and rape began. . . . During my last meeting with Joe, he was very open about group sex; he did it, but only if [the women] agreed.

"Joe and you are the only two people in this case who have never lied to me."

July 7, 1995
Somewhere on the road in Michigan

Road trip. Deanna, her sister Beth, and I are driving from Vermont to their parents' home on Spooner Lake, Wisconsin. It's a two-day drive, including a ferry trip across Lake Michigan.

Maybe it was the Tom Paxton and *Forrest Gump* soundtrack tapes blasting as we drove, but somewhere in Michigan I decided we should give the Florida Supreme Court one last chance to do right in Joe's case. That's what Joe and his mother wanted. Some experienced capital litigators agreed. If we clearly stated that we would not go into federal court, that might not relieve too much of the pressure on Governor Chiles.

We didn't want to file a *new* lawsuit; we wanted the Florida Supreme Court to take another look at the first lawsuit I had filed in Joe's case, during his first warrant in 1985. Then and thereafter, the state courts had invoked procedural technicalities to avoid even considering Joe's new evidence of factual innocence. The goal was to give the Florida courts a final opportunity to eschew their legalistic technicalities and to consider—for once—Joe's innocence claim.

I wanted to concede candidly in our motion that a plethora of procedural devices bar what I'm trying to do here: time limits, retroactivity principles, claim and issue preclusion doctrines. The technicalities are all available, if the Florida Supreme Court wants to use them. But it shouldn't want to use them in this instance. Factual innocence ought to trump time limits and the like.

The biggest problem wasn't the technical rules of preclusion, however. In Florida all of these rules are discretionary. Trial judges have latitude to disregard them in the interests of justice. The biggest problem was that our trial judge would have been Judge McGregor—*that* Judge McGregor. The judge had a long history of invoking legal technicalities to avoid even considering Joe's claims of innocence. I had no reason to think he would act any differently here.

In a worst-case scenario, Governor Chiles could sign a new, fifth warrant. I would then be forced to file in Judge McGregor's court. He would dismiss the innocence claim as procedurally defaulted, forcing us to appeal to the Florida Supreme Court. For Joe to win a stay, the Florida Supreme Court would need to, in effect, reverse Judge McGregor's procedural rulings. That would be dicey, because Judge McGregor's procedural rulings would have been proper under Florida law. We would then be too late and thus time barred. The unlikeliness of the higher court overturning Judge McGregor might even *diminish* because the case would be reaching the Florida Supreme Court under a death warrant. The path of least resistance for the Florida Supreme Court would be to affirm Judge McGregor's procedural rulings. That way McGregor, not the justices themselves, would be responsible for Joe's execution. Even with the raising of a reasonable doubt, it would involve tremendous courage to admit a ten-year oversight and place technicality aside. Thus I wanted to file the postconviction motion directly in the Florida Supreme Court; at least a direct motion would mean one less layer of oversight to be overcome. Unfortunately, there was normally no specific procedure under which this direct appeal would be available— as the justices forcefully reminded me later. Under Florida procedural law, there seemed to be nowhere for us to take Joe's claim of factual innocence.

The basic claim—Joe didn't do it—wasn't new. The facts in support of the claim (Tony's recantation) were brand new, but the legal claim of innocence was an argument I had made in court ten years before—in Joe's first state postconviction motion, filed in Judge McGregor's court in 1985, during Joe's first death warrant. The good news, and the fact I hoped to emphasize, was that there was now more evidence of the validity of my original conviction. This was critical because what I was really asking the courts to do was revisit their denial of that first state postconviction motion. So that's what I ended up calling the thing: an out-of-time motion to rehear and reconsider the denial of the 1985 state postconviction motion, based on new evidence. Ten years out of time is a long time, and time was ticking on death row. So, since the highest state court to deny that 1985 motion had been the Florida Supreme Court, that's where I planned to go for relief.

While Deanna was filling our car with gas, I dictated the bare bones of the motion over the phone to Laura Gillen back in Vermont. Laura would type it up and FedEx the draft to Deanna's parents' house in Wisconsin. I then called Joe from the same pay phone. Going back to court was fine with him. He told me not to worry about CCR's machinations. "CCR is just jealous of you. . . . They want the credit for the work you did on my case."

7-9-95

Dear Mike,

Hi me Mike I got that letter and stuff on C.C.R. don't these people realize I'm still in troble and why they can't help me. You come out to help when I was in troble. I'm going to write C.C.R. a letter. Lori Rosai will be here 7-13-95.

About Tall Paul I heard he died a few year's ago. He was problem in the club. I don't know if he rapet anybody. But he sure was a pan in the ass. Is Susan Cary still with us?

Do you think he will sign my warrent again Mike? You can't be writting Chiles real tuff stuff like he has to, do this or that. Remember he is Boff of Fla. But I see your mad to I love you Mike your a great guy. Can't they see I didn't rape or murder nobody. My tactoes been on my arm's for so many years before 1972. Some most covered up from other ones. The girl that was rapet is lying about me. I don't know hr for shit. Never saw her before.

What you think Chiles will do? Because of C.C.A. and you all going at it, it could get me killed. I'll write them and see what they say to me. You all worket hard to save me for years. Don't want you'es to argue now. Ok pal I'll close tell D. I said hi and sure hope I'll meet her. I'm not feeling to conterble now, Mike what you went to the Governor looks good. But do they see the bull shit the state pulled?

OK I'll close hope to hear from you soon. Lori wrote a letter a while back and said she is glad that you took my case back to. Well I'll close and tell D. I love you all.

Crazy Joe

Hi Mike,

I got a letter from Leslie Delk. She is ok, Mike. Hope she still will help you out. Let me know what you think Mike? I'll close love ya pal.

Crazy Joe

7-9-95
Dear Mike,

Hi Mike for sure & seen Lori Mike and want you to know to let her know about the bones I seen one time but not sure if human or animal. Not sure and don't want to know to be honest. I fine out that cops had more rape charges on me and witness didn't want to press charges. Mike bull shit. These cops don't want to see me get out. Fine out a guy named rat trap something like that was charged with rape on that but charges dropt. Mike I never was even picket up or charged in prison on no rape but the are I'm in here for now. Cops can do anything I can't prove shit to help me. It hurts to know that other girls where going to have rape charges on me. And I can't prove nothing all these years. Don't even know what they look like and if I see them now don't even know if I seen them before. Pal what is going on? What the cops up to, and why they wanted me so bad? Oh I hear to they wanted me in more murders what the hell they talking about? Lori I hope told you and you know about it. I try to put one thing togeather then I get more stuff trown at me. Hope the Govenor sees it bull. Mike you don't think I worry Mike I'm maybe am going crazy. Something is wrong but can't put it togeather. Over one lady cop Ralf Dilisio's wife. I know it all started from their Cap & Ralf but don't know what it is. I get feeling cops are behind it. Mike I got to watch everybody real close. Mike I got to watch out for my family sake to something is wrong Mike. I'll close. I told Lori all the truth that is all I can do. Ok now how you and D doing, you get along good with D family. Bet you do their daughter with a supper lawyer. Let me know if Lori is mad at me. Mike if it get to rough with her and she wants to pull out I'll understand. I expect more on the cops. They want me in prison the rest of my life or dead for something I didn't do something is wrong. I better if I get out head right out of Fla go to that room you got for me and get my life back to-geather. Tina [Joe's niece] ever send you the paintings, she is in Atlanta at her brothers house for a few days. She'll probley send them when she gts back. Lori didn't get hers eather. Ok I'm gone for now. Not gone, gone jut tired.

Your pal, Crazy Joe

July 11, 1995
Minneapolis, Minnesota

A few weeks ago, Nina Alvarez at ABC News asked me to send her a copy of the trial files in the Vanessa Dale Croft rape case. As had happened with Warren Holmes in May, reading the rape case transcripts only reinforced her conviction that Joe was innocent: "I'm sorry, but this rape 'victim' is a floozy and a liar. She changes her description all over the place. At trial, she says the blond guy raped her; earlier, she'd said it was the guy with the beard and without the tattoos. . . . She never said *who* slit her eyes; the first time she said her eyes were wet; later she said they were dry. . . . She'd actually seen [Joe] on TV before she identified him in the lineup. . . . And what's the story with the guy with the eye patch?"

Laura and I traded drafts daily via FedEx. I spoke with Mark Olive and others about filing directly in the Florida Supreme Court.

Olive told me, "They'll laugh you out of court."

"I *want* them to do that, and the more technicalities they trot out the better," I answered.

"I was afraid you'd say that. . . ."

Pat Doherty: "Filing in the Florida Supreme Court makes us look like fibbers, but we should do it anyway. . . . We'll whisper it in late at night. . . . Joe is right on this: if he's killed and we *didn't* file this, we'll feel like dickheads."

Lori Rozsa and Gene Miller both said we should go for it, and a social scientist and expert witness in criminal cases I spoke with offered, "If you file in the Florida Supreme Court, I'll get you the dream team for him, and I'll get them to do it for free."

Uh-huh. My "dream team" is Mark Olive, working alone.

Laura Gillen finalized our Florida Supreme Court pleading, now called an out-of-time rehearing of 1985 motion for state postconviction relief. It would be signed by Pat Doherty and me for Joe Spaziano and by Kelly McGraw *for Anthony Frank DiLisio.*

Laura got the 224-page document copied and in Federal Express. It will arrive at the Florida Supreme Court tomorrow to be filed.

7-11-95
Dear Mike,

Pal Mike you my pal your going to be my brother. Can I talk to you and hope you'll understand. I don't tell nobody in the world what to do on less it's to harm somebody. I'm from the streets understand the people. Not that I couldn't live in a nice house have nice things. Just I was told what to do hit Kicket yelled at. I didn't want that I rather have nothing. Didn't believe in cops when they tell us what we can't do and they do the same thing and call it right. I don't hate Tony because I do belive the cops done that to him. Not only him but many other people. Forget all that I want to get back to you. No Mike I don't tell people what to do, but can you please lisen to me. Your a very smart man, you put years into your law. You had to have a great dad & mom. Don't give up law because what happens to me. You can't give up on how the polations are. They don't like us little people they want all of us to put it this way kiss their ass and do what they want us to do. I don't kiss ass. You go by the book keep going Mike don't let them think you are week. I see so much bull shit on talk shows and new's bring tears to my eyes. What hurt's is I can't do nothing about it. I believe in brotherhood so much all my heart some people wonder how I can handle it. I wonder some time. You need to keep up what your doing. Law some day maybe they'll start to lisen. Don't rune your life because of me or of how polations are. You got to keep going your to smart. Wish I know half of what you know of law. Some cops want me dead because by now you know I'm an Outlaw. If regular people knew what was going on maybe they'll start to fight. Most people over most don't care one big lick. If all people in the world thought like my people we wouldn't have no more murders. We don't kill our own. I'm not no school guy read or write don't make me stupit. I don't understand lots of words and forget what I read. But I know one thing I read I'll remember. My brother, friend, is going to give it up win or lose don't sound like the Mike I know. Hope you understand me Mike. See I believe in all my heart you understand me and why I'm in the Outlaw for the brotherhood. You got a lot of brotherhood. You never was this low in life it's no good. Your to smart fight with law and paper us people need you. I got a heart of gold for people Mike as long as they don't walk on me. I'll be seeing Lori Roza Wed. See what is going on. This will be a late letter out of stamps.

Is Susan going to stop seeing me? Is all these people who was going to help me backing off because I want you for a lawyer. I'm so goofet up in the head Mike. I don't know what I'm thinking just feel they are going to kill me Mike. I was ready for the wedding. How can kill me what they know now?

Your friend, Crazy Joe

7-11-95
Dear D,

Hi me Crazy Joe. I like to ask you something. Don't let Mike give up law because of what the Polation's do. Win or lose the case he is trew. He should go on, he is a smart lawyer just they don't want to lisen. I belive you can keep him going even if they kill me I'm only one their are many other people like me. We don't have lawyers like O.J. but Mike is a smart guy in law he know's his stuff just Polations don't lisen. Not sure if I going to maek it to the wedding not sure how to think. You got a hell of a man their D you got to be a good woman. Take care my pal ok I like him a lot he tried very hard to ave me from these Polations. I hope I get a chance to hug and give you a kiss but don't know. I can't even sleep to good. I'm waiting for the Chaptalin and Sargent to tell me they are going to take me back over their. I hate that feeling. Ok you doll let me close and thank for wanting to be my friend.

Your friend,
Love,
Crazy Joe

July 11, 1995

Dear Joe:

I apologize for the shortness of this letter but Deanna and I are in Wisconsin visiting her parents.

The last time we spoke you asked me to consider filing again in the Florida courts. I now think that we should file a motion for rehearing in the Florida Supreme Court. This would be a motion filed only in the Florida Supreme Court; if it is denied, we would not take it into the federal courts. My concern continues to be that by filing anything in court we take the pressure off of the Governor.

Sincerely,
Michael

July 11, 1995
Spooner, Wisconsin

Dear Joe:

I got a telephone message from the *Orlando Sentinel* saying that they received a letter from you agreeing to an interview. Please *DO NOT* do an interview with *Orlando Sentinel*.

Sincerely,
Michael

July 21, 1995
Spooner, Wisconsin

Dear Joe:

Please excuse the delay in my getting this to you, but Deanna and I are still visiting her folks in Wisconsin. What lovely people. They're so down-to-earth, genuine, and open. I think you and your folks would like them a lot; they're a lot like your family— and like my mom. I can hardly wait to be related to them! The last two weeks on the lake have been *so* relaxing, peaceful and fun. They all send you their best.

I just received your letters today. (My law school secretary express mailed them to me here in Wisconsin.) A couple of things:

First and most importantly, my coming back into your case does not mean that others are abandoning you. Susan Cary, Lori

Rozsa, ABC, the VLRC in Tallahassee (Mark Olive, Jenny Green-burg, and the rest) are *still* working hard for you. Only CCR is out of the picture—but they weren't doing shit for you anyway.

Second, I have *some* good news. *Please don't get your hopes up,* but the Florida Supreme Court seems to be taking our motion seriously. The justices go on vacation tomorrow until mid-August, which means that they won't rule on the motion until mid-August. That *probably* means that Chiles won't sign another warrant until mid-August, at the earliest. Between now and August, I'm trying to put together a letter-writing campaign to the Governor. The Sons of Italy are going to get involved in your case. They asked me to write an article for the August 1 issue of their national newspaper—which has a circulation of four million. Lori and ABC are still investigating your case; I speak with them every other day or so. We're all trying to regroup our forces so that, *if* another warrant comes, we'll be ready to mobilize a pretty impressive army of political muscle.

Third, I don't want you to think that I'm quitting the struggle against capital punishment. No *way*. Never. Not until the last dog comes home. I'll *never* give up this fight. *Never*.

What I *am* doing is changing the arena in which I will carry on the fight. When I thought that the place to win this fight was in the courts, then I fought in the courts. I'm a lawyer, and our battleground is in court.

But now I believe that I can do more good outside of court. Sure, I'm a lawyer, but I'm also a writer—and, I have discovered over the past two months, I seem to be a pretty decent writer. What I seem to be able to do is to write about legal issues in a way that non-lawyers can understand.

Keep in mind, my friend, that of all the legal briefs I've written in your case the only one that *mattered* was the 12 page opinion piece I wrote for the *Miami Herald* on June 4.

The only way to get rid of capital punishment, I have become convinced, is to tell the stories of people like you. And not to tell those stories to judges whose principal agenda is to find some legal technicality to permit them to ignore the stories we are trying to tell them. We need to tell these stories to people who will listen to them and who, maybe—if we tell them enough *true* stories—will understand that capital punishment isn't an abstract political thing. Capital punishment is a large collection of stories.

So: I'm not giving up the fight. I am trying to change the battleground, from the court of law to the court of public opinion. I might well be wrong about all of this, and if I am, then I'll go back to being a lawyer and only a lawyer. But I have to *try* this other way.

In the meantime, I will always be *your* lawyer, until you or your family decide otherwise. I told you in 1985, during the first warrant, that I'm in this with you for the long haul. This is a marathon, not a sprint. You're not in this alone; we're not in it alone. It's a team effort, and we've put together a *hell* of a good team ("the best defense no money can buy"). With the help of God and the *Miami Herald,* we'll cross the finish line together. And alive. And free.

Take care, my friend. And write.

Sincerely,
Michael

P.S. Deanna wanted you to know that she will be writing you a long letter as soon as we return to Vermont (probably this weekend).

10

Acoustic Shadow

After the brouhaha over the weatherman's not being locked up on death row, and to show they weren't being coddled, whenever the media or the politicians came to inspect the progress of [construction of the] Death House facilities, the guards would hang an ominous black sign over the Seg Unit that read DEATH ROW. The inmates would scurry back into their cells and the guards would bolt the doors. All television sets would be turned off. The guards would stand at attention and put on their mean and ugly faces. Inmates would wear their most hardened scowls. . . . The tour group would then peek in, looking either very pleased or very scared. As soon as they departed, the cell doors were un-locked, and with a hearty laugh the inmates would go back to doing whatever it was they were doing before being so rudely interrupted.

—*Steve Thayer,* The Weatherman, *1995*

More than once during the Civil War, newspapers reported a strange phenomenon. From only a few miles away, sometimes a battle made no sound, despite the flash and smoke of cannon, and the fact that more distant observers could hear it clearly. These eerie silences were called "acoustic shadows."

—The Civil War: A Ken Burns Film, *1990*

July 23, 1995
Wilder, Vermont

If memory serves, it was Mike Farrell who came up with the idea of an open letter to Governor Chiles, signed by as many prominent people as possible, asking the governor to grant Joe clemency or pardon. It was contingency planning. If (when) a new death warrant came (meaning that Chiles had denied the clemency petition now pending), and if (when) the Florida Supreme Court summarily denied the out-of-time rehearing petition, and if (*when*) I hung tough with the decision not to take Joe's case into federal court, we'd be left with nothing to do as Joe's life trickled away. Presumably the *Herald* and others would continue investigating and writing about the case, but I'd have no control over any of that.

Conceivably, the media pressure (along with pressure from Richard Capozzola's Sons of Italy platoons) might make Chiles want to stop the noise by stopping the execution, at least temporarily. If that happened, we needed to provide Chiles with an escape hatch—a rationale for staying Joe's execution while saving face. We needed to affect the political atmosphere so that doing the right thing would also be the path of least resistance.

Until July 1995 I had never owned a TV, so I didn't recognize Mike Farrell's name when he called me out of the blue to offer any help he could provide on Joe's case. I was frazzled when he first called, and I said I'd get back with him. When I did, via fax, I misspelled his name "Ferrall." Deanna *did* know who he was—he had played the character B. J. Hunnicut on the TV show *M*A*S*H*—and I faxed him a second note apologizing for my previous abruptness. He asked me to send him the briefs and transcripts in Joe's case; after I did, I expected never to hear from him again. But to my delight, he played a critical role in Joe's case in the coming weeks.

One great perk of doing deathwork is that you get to meet some extraordinary human beings. Mike Farrell is one. Farrell is directly involved in more capital cases than most people realize, and certainly far more than I'd realized. Almost always he works entirely behind the scenes: networking, bringing different people together, lobbying gently and invisibly. He sees his job as putting other people in the spotlight (condemned prisoners, their lawyers, social scientists, political activists) while never leaving the shadows himself.

Work is the operative word. Farrell worked his tail off for Joe Spaziano (and, at the same time, for Barry Fairchild and Mumia Abu-Jamal, and doubtless others he had no reason to mention to me, which is kind of the point). And as important as his networking on the open letter was, his noodling with me about the case's facts and investigation and tactics and strategy were even more valuable to me during that chaotic time.

My personal predisposition toward solitude has meant that I possess neither the skill nor the constitution for grassroots political organizing; I delight in the *theory* of political organizing, so long as I personally don't have to organize actual groups of people I don't already know. Groups of people make my feet itch. It's probably no accident that I live in Vermont.

In Joe's case this didn't matter, however, because three organizational and networking wizards were loaded for bear and ready to rock and roll. They divided the world into three parts, one for each of our operatives. Richard Capozzola would expand his Sons of Italy mobilization to include the forty-nine other states in addition to Florida. Mike Farrell would work his awesome personal and professional network in Hollywood and beyond. Eric Freedman, a Hofstra University Law School professor and a former associate with the Paul, Weiss law firm (and a fellow traveler who I've always suspected has at least an ember of arson in his heart) would put out an Internet call for law professors to sign on to our open letter.

First we needed to create the open letter. Borrowing heavily from a superb article about Joe's case written by Colin Wentworth for *Moon* magazine, I knocked out a draft. Mike Farrell rewrote it and, as the open letter evolved over the following two weeks, our objectives became more ambitious. The letter would ask for a new trial in the Croft rape case as well as in the Harberts murder case. The letter would be directed to the Florida attorney general in addition to the governor (the attorney general is one of seven members of the executive cabinet, the clemency-granting body in Florida). Farrell thought we needed to ask for more than we expected to get, so the governor would have some wiggle room for compromise. Ask for a clemency hearing and you get nothing. Ask for commutation of the death sentence and you get a clemency hearing. Ask for absolute pardon and outright release and you get commutation of the death sentence to life imprisonment without possibility of parole. You never know. But it's certain that if you don't ask, you don't get.

When Farrell agreed to search out signatories for the open letter, he asked me to send him the trial transcripts. He said he needed to know the record so he could answer questions from potential signatories. When I sent him the "case files" (in *Orlando Sentinel* argot), he mastered them. Our many, many conversations in the weeks ahead were extremely valuable to me and to Joe (yes, they get *M*A*S*H* reruns on death row in Florida). His thoughts often clarified and sharpened my own; they also led into altogether new directions.

My fervent hope was that we would never need to publish the open letter to the governor and attorney general. We would do so only after (1) the pending clemency application had been denied, (2) a new death warrant had been signed, and (3) we had lost in the courts. Thus publishing the open letter would be a fair barometer of how desperate Joe's case had become; if we published it, then Joe was at the end of the line.

Over the next weeks, Farrell and Freedman phoned or faxed almost every day, adding a few names at a time. (I circulated the letter among my deans and faculty colleagues at Vermont Law School. Four agreed to sign: Steve Dycus, David Firestone, Bruce Duthu, and Maryann Zavez.)

STATEMENT TO GOVERNOR LAWTON CHILES AND ATTORNEY GENERAL ROBERT BUTTERWORTH IN SUPPORT OF A NEW TRIAL FOR JOSEPH ROBERT "CRAZY JOE" SPAZIANO

On August 24, 1995, Governor Lawton Chiles signed a death warrant ordering the execution of Joseph Robert Spaziano, a former Orlando biker, for a crime he probably did not commit— the 1973 murder of Laura Harberts, a young woman found dead in a Seminole County garbage dump. The electrocution is scheduled to occur at 7:00 a.m. on September 21, 1995.

We are attorneys, professors, writers, artists and lay observers of the Florida legal system. Some of us support capital punishment as a legitimate social policy in the war on crime; others of us oppose it.

Although of diverse personal, professional and political backgrounds, we are united in our conviction that the execution of Joseph Robert Spaziano, in the absence of a new trial, would offend the evolving standards of decency that mark the progress of a maturing society. [Obviously, not all of us have read the trial transcript. However, Spaziano's attorney has made the transcript and all other files available for our inspection.] Several reasons reinforce our conviction that Spaziano must receive a new murder trial; any one of these reasons demands a new trial—the combination makes a new trial a compelling moral necessity. Consider:

- There was absolutely no physical evidence linking Spaziano to Ms. Harberts' death. Spaziano's conviction was based solely on the testimony of a teenager who did not "remember" anything about Spaziano or the alleged crime until police removed him from a juvenile detention facility, dropped pending investigations on breaking and entering charges, and then "refreshed" his memory with grossly suggestive hypnosis sessions, conducted by a self-styled police "ethical hypnotist." This teenager, Anthony DiLisio, is now 37 years old. In 1995, DiLisio and his lawyer formally joined Spaziano in asking the governor for clemency and in asking the courts for a new trial on *both* the Harberts homicide conviction and on the previous, unrelated rape and mutilation of Vanessa Dale Croft, of which Spaziano was convicted in 1975—again, based in large part on the purchased testimony of Anthony DiLisio. Today, DiLisio disavows his testimony in *both* cases, saying he had been "brainwashed" by the police at the time.

- At his trial, the prosecution withheld evidence that police had better suspects in the murder.

- The prosecution offered only one piece of circumstantial evidence at trial; the prosecutor knew the evidence was false but withheld the truth from the defense, judge and jury.

- A post-conviction investigation showed that the jury had serious doubts that Spaziano was guilty, but because he was a member of the Outlaws motorcycle club—a frightening thought in the early 1970s—the jurors voted him guilty to keep him off the streets. In an effort to show mercy, they recommended a life prison sentence, but the judge overrode their recommendation and sentenced Joseph Spaziano to death in Florida's electric chair.

- Less than a decade after Spaziano's conviction, and shortly after his conviction became final on direct appeal, the Florida Supreme Court ruled that testimony gathered with the use of hypnosis cannot be used as evidence because it is unreliable and potentially harmful. The court relied on experts who said that subjects who undergo hypnosis become extremely vulnerable to suggestion and form hardened beliefs that what they "remembered" while in the trance, no matter how true or false, is absolutely accurate.

- The ruling, which came during convicted murderer Theodore "Ted" Bundy's appeals, was not retroactive. So even though the Florida Supreme Court indirectly discredited the *only* evidence used to convict Joseph Spaziano, he has been sitting on death row for 19 years.

There is a popular misconception that criminals often 'get off' on legal technicalities; Joseph Spaziano is about to be executed by one. Society, wrapped up in a frenzy of desire to exact revenge on murderers, doesn't seem to care. Despite massive evidence that he was wrongly convicted, numerous judges have disregarded his appeals as frivolous. Governor Lawton Chiles has refused to grant Joseph Spaziano a clemency hearing. Attorney General Butterworth has argued—with great success—that courts ought to use procedural devices to avoid deciding the merits of Spaziano's claim of innocence. Spaziano's appeals—an exercise in futility—are all but exhausted. The only thing between Joseph Spaziano and the electric chair is the wait. And he's scared.

General Butterworth, your office has relentlessly opposed any new trial in this case, or even any temporary stay of Spaziano's execution. In refusing to join Spaziano's (and, today, Mr. DiLisio's) requests for a new trial, you are legally correct. Florida law does not require retrial in cases involving fresh evidence, such as Spaziano's. You are legally correct—but not morally right. You can, and should, go beyond the minimal requirements of the law to permit a new trial.

It ought to go without saying that a capital prosecutor's job is not to effect as many executions as he can—by any means necessary. Such an act would be morally reprehensible; prosecutors swear to uphold the United States Constitution, which directs them to seek the truth, not stack the deck.

The police officers and prosecutors in this case had a duty to accurately record the statements of the witnesses, to fairly investigate the case, and to disclose all exculpatory evidence. Moreover, they had a duty not to prosecute an innocent man. They failed in these duties.

Whether Joseph Spaziano ought to be executed—in the absence of a new trial—is one of those choices that tests a civilization's soul. Out of all the static about "defining moments" that crowds the narrow bandwidth of modern politics and law, here—finally—is a real defining moment for a real public and a real governor. What you do in this case will tell what morality, if any, guides Florida government. The issue is life and death, and the choice is yours.

Governor Chiles and General Butterworth, this is no longer a case about the death penalty. It should not be a case about politics. It is a case about public morality, our government's commitment to human life, and about simple decency. This case tests the moral fiber and legal quality of civilization. The evidence is everywhere that more and more Floridians, even proponents of capital punishment—*especially* proponents of capital punishment—would like to know why Joseph Spaziano is being killed in *their* name. We await your answer.

Signed:

Sons of Italy Amici Lodge #2473
("All the members of this lodge are united and unanimous in requesting a new trial.")

Sons of Italy Lodge #2648

Senator George McGovern
Former Democratic Presidential candidate, 1972

Talbot D'Alemberte
President, Florida State University
Former Dean, Florida State University College of Law
Former President, American Bar Association

Stephen H. Sachs
Partner, Wilmer, Cutler & Pickering
Former Attorney General for the State of Maryland (1979–1987)
(Argued and won the leading case establishing the constitution-
ality of Maryland's capital punishment statute.)
Former U.S. Attorney, District of Maryland

Professor Michael Millemann
University of Maryland Law School
Former Chief, Civil Division and
Former Chief General Counsel
Maryland Attorney General's Office
(1979–1981)

James R. Acker
Associate Professor, State University of New York
School of Criminal Justice

Anthony G. Amsterdam
Edward Weinfeld Professor of Law, New York University
School of Law

Aris and Carolyn Anagnos

Congressman John Anderson

Congressman Tom Andrews

Dr. Maya Angelou

Ira Arlook

Edward Asner

Professor David Baldus
University of Iowa College of Law

Alec Baldwin

Professor Susan Bandes
DePaul Law School

Paul Basile
Editor, *Fra Noi*

Meredith Baxter

Hugo Bedau
Austin Fletcher Professor of Philosophy, Tufts University

Dr. Joan Willens Beerman

Rabbi Leonard Beerman

Marilyn and Alan Bergman

Rose Marie Boniello
State President, Order of the Sons of Italy, Grand Lodge of
Florida

Jackson Browne

Brad Buckner

Richard Capozzola

Erwin Chemerinsky
Lex Legion Professor of Law, University of Southern California,
School of Law

Carol Chomsky
Associate Professor, University of Minnesota Law School

Diane V. Cirincione

David Clennon

Professor Douglas Colbert
University of Maryland School of Law

Kimberly Cook
Assistant Professor of Criminology, Mississippi State University

Professor Mary Coombs
University of Miami School of Law

Phyllis L. Crocker
Assistant Professor of Law, Cleveland Marshall College of Law

Micki Dickoff
Pro Bono Productions

Professor J. Herbert DiFonzo
Hofstra University School of Law

Dominic DiFrisco
President Emeritus, Civic Committee of Italian Americans

Professor Joshua Dressler
McGeorge School of Law, University of the Pacific

Richard Dreyfuss

N. Bruce Duthu
Associate Professor, Vermont Law School

Professor Stephen Dycus
Vermont Law School

Professor Linda H. Edwards
Walter F. George School of Law, Mercer University

Nancy Ehrenreich
University of Denver College of Law

Diane G. Emery
Human Rights Activist

Shelley Fabares

Mike Farrell

Magda Finnegan
Lifelines Ireland

Professor David Firestone
Vermont Law School

Robert Foxworth

Bonnie Franklin

Professor Eric M. Freedman
Hofstra University School of Law

Michael Froomkin
Associate Professor of Law, University of Miami School of Law

Professor Linda Galler
Hofstra University School of Law

Professor Leandra Gassenheimer
Walter F. George School of Law, Mercer University

William S. Geimer
Professor of Law, Washington and Lee University

Sharon Gelman

Professor Dan Givelber
Northeastern University School of Law
Former Dean, Northeastern University School of Law

Danny Glover

Anne Goldstein
Visiting Professor of Law, University of Texas School of Law

John D. Gregory
Hofstra University School of Law

Alan Grier

Bishop Thomas J. Gumbleton

Rabbi Steven Jacobs

Dr. Gerald G. Jampolsky, M.D.

Professor Peter L. Kahn
Catholic University School of Law

Casey Kasem

Richard Kletter

Professor Stefan H. Krieger
Hofstra University School of Law

Charles S. Lanier
State University of New York, School of Criminal Justice

Piper Laurie

Jack Lemmon

John Lewis

Holly Maguigan
Professor of Clinical Law, New York University Law School

Dr. Kathleen Maguire
State University of New York, School of Criminal Justice

Ronald D. Maines
Maines & Harshman

Rabbi Robert Marx

Andrew A. Mcthenia
Professor of Law, Washington and Lee University

Gregg Meyer
Staff Attorney, South Royalton Legal Clinic

Chandler R. Muller

Denise Nicholas

Michael O'Keefe

Edward James Olmos

Gregory Peck

Deanna L. Peterson

Elizabeth Peterson

Sarah Pillsbury

Sister Helen Prejean

David Protess
Professor of Journalism

Bonnie Raitt

Jeffrey T. Renz
Assistant Professor, School of Law, University of Montana

Dr. Timothy Reynolds, M.D.

David W. Rintels

Dr. Victoria Riskin

Phil Alden Robinson

Marianne Rogers

Grant Rosenberg

Eugenie Ross-Leming

Diane Rust-Tierny
American Civil Liberties Union

Professor Jack L. Sammons
Walter F. George School of Law, Mercer University

Ed Saxon

Bruce Shapiro
Associate Editor, *The Nation*

Jonathan Simon
Associate Professor of Law, University of Miami

Robert Singer

Stacy Smith
University of Denver College of Law

Scott E. Sundby
Professor of Law, Washington and Lee University

David Tarbert
Director, Criminal Justice Clinic, Assistant Professor of Law,
Southern Methodist University School of Law

Frank Torrillo
President, Sons of Italy Lodge

Margaret Vandiver
Assistant Professor of Criminology, University of Memphis

David D. Walter
Walter F. George School of Law, Mercer University

260 / Acoustic Shadow

Professor Sidney D. Watson
Walter F. George School of Law, Mercer University

Dennis Weaver

Richard L. Wiener
Professor, Saint Louis University

Peter Yarrow

MaryAnn Zavez
Professor, South Royalton Legal Clinic

*[Affiliation is for identification purposes only and does not imply
any institutional endorsement.]*

A footnote following the open letter stated:

> Some professional journalists believe that journalistic ethics pre-
> clude professional journalists from signing this sort of statement.
> However, nationally syndicated columnists James J. Kilpatrick
> and Colman McCarthy, national publications including *The New
> Republic* and *The Nation*, and columns or editorials in every
> major Florida newspaper have publicly opposed the execution of
> Joseph Spaziano. These include *The Miami Herald, The Palm
> Beach Post, The St. Petersburg Times, The Tampa Tribune, The
> Lakeland Ledger,* and *The Gainesville Sun,* along with colum-
> nists Tom Fiedler, Carl Hiasson, Tony Proscio, Martin Dyckman
> and Tom Blackburn. The Spaziano story has been covered by
> *ABC Nightly News with Peter Jennings, The Washington Post,
> The Economist, The Nation, The New Republic, The Christian
> Science Monitor* and *Fra Noi* ("Chicagoland's Italian American
> Voice"), as well as virtually every Florida newspaper.

July 24, 1995
Wilder, Vermont

Lori Rozsa called with a question about the trial testimony of Beverly
Fink, roommate of Laura Lynn Harberts. Didn't Fink testify that Joe
came by the Harbert/Fink apartment in the afternoon? I looked up
Fink's testimony in the trial transcript. Yup: afternoon.

Rozsa had just met with Fink, and she said that she remembers seeing Joe "by the light of the full moon." Rozsa explained that this is no minor discrepancy: Fink's "whole narrative details now are based on its happening at night. . . . She now says he 'looked so evil in the moonlight.'"

Does the discrepancy matter? Once Tony DiLisio's trial testimony is excised from the equation, the evidence given by peripheral witnesses like Beverly Fink becomes magnified in importance. It was another piece of the puzzle.

July 25, 1995
Wilder, Vermont

Rumor: Governor Chiles' clemency aide reportedly said that Joe would get a new death warrant in mid-August.

> July 26
> Hi Mike,
>
> I just got your letter pal really good to hear from you. That is great that D and you had a great time. Their folks had to be happy to see who their soninlaw is going to be. My mom and Tina love you Mike. You a special guy pal. Mike the way I read the letter sounds like Chiles is going to come after me again. That is what I feel. I got an interview with Sandy or the one you told me about tomorrow, not in a good mud to talk to nobody right now. I got a letter from Lori. I told her about the Buck Knight [knife] that the cops took. But what I see to Ed Kirkland lied to me to. Couple of times on what Judge Pete Demavio [deManio] said to Ed and if they where drinking. See Ed came and seen me one time. He arged in one of my clemicie in front of Gran. I never heard of Son's of Italy. But you know what you doing. Will you send me an artical on that national newspaper. My mom probley like to see that. I don't know if she got hold of you or not but she wanted to ask you about ABC. Mike I believe in all my heart your going to be on my side. Your more than a friend pal. Your like a brother to me. Oh I sure think your a good writter to. People like all you wrote for me. I'm no good in reading law all that but what I understand sound good. Be looking forward to Deanna's letter. Let me get back to you in a second pal. I got to roul some

cigarettes. Ok I'm back just rouled up a pack of Top's. Wonder what else to say. Oh ya I thought A.B.C. lost interest in my case Mike haven't heard from them since the last time they come up. Ok I'll close really hot. Thanks Mike and Deanna. Make her a happy lady Mike. She loves you pal.

Your friend, Crazy Joe

July 28, 1995
Wilder, Vermont

Skull sessions with Warren Holmes could be as exhausting as they were intellectually energizing. Such brainstorming conversations were collaborative in an almost intimate way that defies description; not unlike an impressionist painting, these sessions can't really be explained—only experienced.

In the midst of one of our wide-ranging telephone chats, Holmes solved what had always been, for me, perhaps the principal factual conundrum of Joe's two cases, the Laura Harberts homicide and the Vanessa Dale Croft rape: Would the police (or Tony DiLisio or Tony's father, Ralph DiLisio) really have set out methodically to frame Joe for a murder he didn't commit? And, having set up Joe for capital murder, why go to the additional trouble of framing him for the Croft rape? True, the Croft rape might (and in fact did) function as an aggravating circumstance to elevate the Harberts homicide from a life-imprisonment case to a death penalty case. But did anyone really need more aggravation? Joe was an Outlaw. It was south Florida in the mid-1970s. Therefore, neither a conspiracy nor a documented method was necessary to cause a distortion (excited hounds will chase a fox—*any* fox). It was natural, but it was wrong, and *that* was threatening to the authorities.

Of course, Holmes didn't start by talking about any of that. He was calling to thank Deanna for locating, in CCR's seventeen boxes of files, the missing persons report Beverly Fink initially filed after her roommate Laura disappeared. "Boy am I glad you found that report. . . . It confirms that Beverly Fink was making up *her* testimony. . . . The more Lori [Rozsa] gets into this, the more it looks like a frame-up, pure and simple.

"Lori may well be right that the prime mover in this whole contrivance was Tony's father, Ralph. . . . The whole thing may have started with Tony's dad being jealous of Joe because Joe was sleeping with Ralph's new wife, Keppie."

"Jealous enough to get Joe executed?"

"No, not at first. Remember that 1975 letter you found from Tony's sister Angie to Joe? That letter implied that Tony and his dad, Ralph, framed Joe for the *rape*. . . . Tony was the key witness against Joe in the rape trial as well as the murder trial.

"It all makes sense if you presume that Ralph's conspiracy to frame Joe started with framing him for *rape*, not murder. Ralph thought Joe *was* a rapist; look what Joe had done to Ralph's poor wife, Keppie. Ralph framed Joe first for rape—the same crime Ralph said Joe had committed against Keppie. Since Ralph already thought of Joe as a rapist, he could rationalize framing Joe for the Croft rape. Even if Joe didn't rape Croft, he had raped other women (such as Keppie), so it's not really so wrong to set Joe up for the Croft rape. In the end, the scales balance out: Joe's a rapist and he'll go down for the crime of rape, even though Joe may not have committed this *particular* rape.

"But once Ralph had set the thing in motion, it snowballed out of his control. The police didn't want to convict Joe only of rape. They wanted to convict an Outlaw of capital murder. They wanted to send an Outlaw to the chair. So, they built on the foundation already laid down by Ralph and Tony. . . . [After all, it must have *looked* like justice to them, just as it had to Ralph and Tony . . . if you were a 1970s police officer, wouldn't *you* suspect a convicted Outlaw rapist?]

"So here's the sequence. First, Joe sleeps with Keppie. Second, Ralph finds out and confronts Keppie. Third, Keppie lies about her consensual sex with Joe, and she calls it rape. Four, Ralph decides he must avenge his wife's honor by framing the biker who raped her. Fifth, Ralph decides it would be poetic justice to frame Joe for rape; what the hell, Ralph thought, Spaziano *is* a rapist, and I know he's a rapist because he raped my wife. Sixth, Ralph uses his son Tony as Ralph's gun, the instrument of Ralph's revenge. Seventh, the frame-up for a rape becomes a dress rehearsal for the frame-up for murder. By now Ralph has lost control over the conspiracy he set in motion. The thing snowballs until Tony is the only real witness at the murder trial and only one of two at the rape trial.

"What this means is that we've been looking at the wrong time frame. We've assumed that it started with the murder frame-up and then backtracked to the crime; we've assumed that the murder was the main event and the rape an ancillary afterthought. But in fact the whole thing began with the rape case, and escalated into the murder case.

"This opens up whole new vistas for our investigation. We need to combine the chronological file for the rape into the chronological file for the murder. Ralph and Tony conspired to frame him for the rape, and they justified it by telling themselves that Joe raped Keppie; that then led into the murder. We've got to move up the time frame: It began with the rape.

"This explains, among other things, why Tony didn't mention 'bodies' during his first meeting with law enforcement: at first, he was talking only about a rape."

At the end of our phone chat, Holmes said, "We've got to the bottom of this, right here tonight." "We?" That's only half right.

Having large pieces of the puzzle fall into place—or, rather, having them put into place by Lori Rozsa, Warren Holmes, and Gene Miller—was satisfying personally. Still, it was weird knowing that Holmes's intellectual detective work wouldn't make the slightest bit of difference to the state powers with actual control over Joe's prosecutors. The new information the *Herald* was coming up with wouldn't matter at all to them, I was certain. If Tony DiLisio's recantation didn't matter to them, Beverly Fink's ever-mutating stories wouldn't matter to them.

The *Herald* thought I was being overly pessimistic. I think I was being realistic. As Joe's lawyer, I had to prepare for the worst. I'm usually pretty good at that. This time, though, I wasn't ready for what the state would throw at us.

August 4, 1995
Wilder, Vermont

I finally received a bootleg copy of the secret FDLE videotape. Deanna and I watched it together in the living room. How can Chiles' office say that there is no "recantation" on this tape? Tony's recantation of his trip to the dump could not have been clearer. He also discussed CCR's strong-arm tactics.

The video also provided some insight into the FDLE investigators working on Joe's case. The two FDLE people who interrogated Tony were the world's worst questioners—a "cluster fuck," as one colleague remarked. They mispronounced "Spaziano" for most of the tape, until

Tony corrected them. They weren't sure about the murder victim's name. They let Tony control and dominate the conversation.

I tried to phone Tony's lawyer, but phone and electrical services were dead. A hurricane had touched down in Pensacola this morning.

August 4, 1995
Dear Joe:

Again, I apologize for dashing off a quick note to you. There's a lot going on, and I need a favor.

This is the favor: I need you to write me a letter explaining, in your own words and in as much detail as you can, why the club is so important in your life. I think we need to explain to the governor—and the press—exactly why the club has been a *good* factor in your life over the past 25 years. What I've learned over the past few weeks, in discussing your case with various folks, is that most people don't understand the club at all—but that they *can* be educated. You have taught me, over our years together, how good the club has been to you and for you. Now I'm asking you to teach that same lesson to the world at large.

Second, the stay seems solid until mid-August—but after that, it doesn't look so good. So: I'm trying to mobilize public support for a new trial, by asking people to sign the enclosed statement. Deanna and I have gotten about 60 names so far. Does the statement look OK?

Third, our investigation is going well—slowly, but well. We're trying to locate Angie DiLisio (do you still have any of her letters, from 1975 or 1976?). A buddy of mine named Dr. Toni Apel, a neuropsychologist, has agreed to do a completely new neuropsych work up on your case (for free); Toni Apel is working hard for you, but he can be kind of a pain in the ass, so *please,* cooperate with him anyway. We're working on trying to identify the other human bones found at the dump site; it's beginning to look as though they are the bones of a *male*—which *really* fucks up the state's theory of the case.

Anyway, gotta run, my friend. Keep the faith. I love you.

Peace,
Michael

August 8, 1995
Wilder, Vermont

News in Florida is that Governor Chiles and his clemency aide, Mark Schlakman, *do* care about clemency and early release from prison. In fact, one Willoughby Turner Cox III, a man convicted of DUI manslaughter and serving a ten-year sentence, was released after serving a little over two years. While Cox was driving drunk, his car struck and killed twenty-six-year-old Trace Kelly. In part because of Cox's frightening history of previous crimes behind the wheel, the Florida Parole Commission had determined that he was not a deserving candidate for early release.

Why, then, was Cox sprung from prison so early? Well, it turns out that Mark Schlakman, the same person who had been telling reporters that he was in charge of Joe Spaziano's clemency case, called a member of the Parole Commission and, as the recipient of the call put it, "indicated that Cox's father (presumably Willoughby Cox II) had some connections with the governor's office." Not long thereafter, Cox the younger was a free man.

It also turns out that Cox's parents have a seasonal residence in the North Carolina mountains, and they even sold Governor Chiles some property there. So, when Chiles's clemency aide called a parole commissioner to chat about Cox's pending hearing for early release, he didn't have to be blunt. Parole commissioners don't get to become parole commissioners by being too dense to read between the lines when a lawyer from the governor's clemency department is on the phone. It doesn't matter what is said; the content of the conversation isn't the message. The call itself, more than anything that is or isn't said during the subsequent conversation, is the message.

And here I'd been telling people that clemency is dead in Florida. Silly me.

August 9, 1995
Wilder, Vermont

Cold call from Marsha Friedman, who runs a Florida publicity firm called Event Management, Inc. Friedman had found Joe's story "truly incredible." Could I use some pro bono help putting together a press release and faxing it to Event Management's media contacts? Even

though I had no clue about what she meant, exactly, she had a trustworthy voice. I thanked her and said sure. She and her folks worked
pro bono on Joe's case for the next several weeks.

August 10, 1995
Wilder, Vermont

Joe's niece Tina called: "My uncle is scared. . . . Warrant in September,
he thinks."

During the May/June death warrant, the niece and her husband
bought wood and poster sheets to make protest signs. "We'll be up
there again."

She and Joe's mom are to visit him this Sunday.

August 11, 1995
Dear Joe:

Hello, my friend. Hope you are doing well. I'm sorry that our
last letters to you were so rushed; I'm afraid we dumped some
bad news on you rather abruptly. Please know that we are trying
everything we can to prevent this next warrant from coming *at
all,* in addition to prevent it from being carried out.

One of the ways we are trying to prevent the governor from
even *signing* the warrant is by asking people to sign a statement
requesting a new trial for you; sort of a petition, but aimed at
getting signatures that the Governor will recognize and pay attention to. The first name on the list is a good friend of Gov.
Chiles, and has some pretty impressive legal credentials! There
are also a lot of non-lawyers on the list which are still names the
governor will recognize—Hollywood actors and actresses, sign-
ers, authors, political fund-raisers, etc. Remember when we told
you that Mike Farrell (B.J. Hunnicut from *M*A*S*H*) was really
interested in your case? Well, he is the one who has been working the "Hollywood" connection; he is responsible for at least
half of the names on the list.

On the legal front, we have filed a few additional motions,
which are also enclosed. The Attorney General's office responded
to our request for a rehearing, and we responded back. We also
filed a motion to make the videotape of FDLE's interview with

Tony a part of the record, and another motion to include all the press articles. They are all enclosed.

Hang in there my friend! Don't give up on attending our wedding just yet. We're doing everything we can think of!

All our love—

Mike

P.S. We just got word from Mike Farrell that Danny Glover and Harry Belafonte (singer) have also signed on to your statement! The names just keep rolling in. . . .

August 14, 1995
Mr. Martin J. McClain
Office of the Capital Collateral Representative
Tallahassee, FL
Re: Joseph Robert Spaziano
Dear Marty:

This memorializes our telephone conversation regarding FDLE's investigation of CCR's investigators' alleged misconduct in relation to Anthony DiLisio.

You told me that (1) CCR possesses no written materials whatsoever, including notes, either on CCR's meetings with Mr. DiLisio or on FDLE's interview with CCR's two investigators, in the presence of Michael Minerva (Mr. DiLisio says that, during CCR's final meeting with him, Mr. Hummell produced four alternative versions of an affidavit he demanded that Mr. DiLisio sign; I take your representation to me, on the phone, that CCR does not possess any written material whatsoever concerning its contacts with Mr. DiLisio, to constitute a denial of Mr. DiLisio's allegations on this score); (2) CCR voluntarily waived the attorney/client privilege in answering FDLE's questions regarding CCR's contacts with Mr. DiLisio; (3) the identity of the man who accompanied Mike Hummell, CCR's investigator, when he met with Mr. DiLisio was, in fact, another CCR investigator.

Thank you for following up my earlier letter with a phone call. Please treat this as a continuing request that CCR provide me with any written material in CCR's possession concerning the matter covered in my earlier letter, or any other related matters.

Sincerely,
Michael Mello

August 15, 1995
Wilder, Vermont

One of my most trusted sources: "Mark Schlakman says FDLE keeps coming up with new doubts about the conviction. . . . FDLE is saying privately that the case was botched on both sides. . . . "There is no chance of a warrant coming anytime soon."

Hope for the best. Prepare for the worst. Be ready for anything in between.

A leader in Florida's Italian American community: "I've called Chiles's people and the media. But . . . we want to hear Chiles's side. We'll wait until the end of today before giving the final go-ahead. . . . We're not willing to wait, because then it could be too late."

"Final go-ahead" for what? I wondered.

August 17, 1995
Wilder, Vermont

The significant event of the day occurred far from public view, and to this day all I know of it is contained in a four-paragraph letter written on governor's office stationery and signed by Lawton Chiles:

Office of the Governor
Tallahassee, Florida
August 17, 1995

James T. Moore, Commissioner
Florida Department of Law Enforcement

Dear Commissioner

Thank you for the assistance of your agency in the development and collection of the clemency materials regarding Joseph Spaziano. Since these materials fall within the provisions of section 14.28, Florida Statutes, and Rule 16, Rules of Executive Clemency, I request that you deliver all materials which you have developed to my clemency aide, Phyllis Hampton.

Pursuant to Section 14.28, Florida Statutes, and the Rules of Executive Clemency, these materials may not be inspected or copied.

Again thank you for your assistance in this matter.

With kind regards, I am

Sincerely,
Lawton Chiles

I would not obtain a copy of this letter until its content had ceased to be important. As of this writing, in August 2000, I still have never seen the FDLE report to which the letter refers.

August 18, 1995
Wilder, Vermont

My source close to Dexter Douglass, Governor Chiles's general counsel, ran into Douglass at a cafeteria. "We chatted about how no one bears responsibility for executions, and Douglass remarked, 'It's sort of like Nazi Germany.'" Huh?

An old friend from our Florida days said something that really touched me. He said, "You are the most beautiful writer of all of us. I don't tell you that often enough. . . . I carry your 'You are a murderer' letter to Chiles around with me, in my pocket. . . . We all need to be taking notes on what you're doing in Joe's case; when we follow the rules, they kill or clients and blame *us* for going into court under warrant [and filing at the last possible moment]."

Lori Rozsa was in Orlando, interviewing two of Tony DiLisio's sisters. The sisters both told Lori that "Ralph [their father] used Tony to get at Joe. . . . [Keppie's] affair with Joe sent [Ralph] downhill."

August 19, 1995
Wilder, Vermont

Steve Gustat, my freelance pro bono investigator: "I met with Joe yesterday, and he's a *nice* guy; I really like him. He started to cry. He's afraid of a warrant on Monday."

IN THE SUPREME COURT OF FLORIDA

JOSEPH R. SPAZIANO, Petitioner-Appellant,

v.

THE STATE OF FLORIDA, Respondent-Appellee

Case No. 67,929

MOTION FOR APPOINTMENT OF COUNSEL

1. Joseph Spaziano is sentenced to die for a murder he did not commit; he is serving a life sentence for a rape he did not commit.

2. Undersigned has represented Spaziano, *pro bono,* as lead counsel, since June, 1995.

3. CCR is disabled, by a conflict of interest, from representing Spaziano. CCR also has refused to provide logistical or other support whatsoever to undersigned counsel, as has counsel's full time employer, Vermont Law School.

4. The VLRC has been providing investigative support for undersigned counsel's attempt to unearth evidence in support of Spaziano's longtime claim that he is factually innocent. VLRC is now all but defunct; it will shut its door entirely on October 1, 1995.

5. The court's disposition of this motion will not affect counsel's representation of Spaziano. Should this motion be denied, counsel will continue as Spaziano's attorney, *pro bono,* until Spaziano is released from prison or executed.

6. Since again assuming responsibility for Spaziano's case, counsel has spent approximately 380 hrs and has accrued approximately $7,000 in out-of-pocket expenses (the June telephone bill alone was $400)—in addition to the uncompensated time spent on pursuing executive clemency. To put the matter simply, counsel is broke.

7. In a backhanded fashion, this court acknowledged the logistical difficulties facing counsel in this case. The state filed a motion to compel service of appendices. Counsel responded that any delay in service was caused by the *pro bono* nature of his representation of Spaziano. Notwithstanding counsel's explanation, the court peremptorily granted the state's motion (since withdrawn, weeks after the state received the appendices about which it complained).

8. Counsel therefore moves for appointment *nunc pro tunc,* at a rate of compensation the court deems just.

9. Counsel stresses that, whatever the court decides about this motion, he will continue to serve as Spaziano's chief counsel until this case is resolved one way or the other.

Respectfully submitted
Michael A. Mello

Monday, August 21, 1995
Wilder, Vermont

First day of the new Florida Supreme Court term.

One of my Italian American contacts called. Mark Schlakman had called her to say that "FDLE isn't close to finishing up." She was upbeat. "I think you're going to get what you want on this, Mike. . . . I take Schlakman at his word. . . . You're safe for today and tomorrow. . . . Recall your Bible: A day is a thousand years, and a thousand years is a day."

Steve Gustat updated me on the forensic investigation. As to the current status of VLRC, he said, "I have an appointment with Florida Unemployment in an hour."

My source on Dexter Douglass met with the man himself and with VLRC. Douglass "was very hostile. He said, 'You can tell Mello that he's not going to get a warrant—*today*. Mello is crazy. . . . He's threatening to sue me. He's crazy.' Sounds like you hit a nerve, Mike."

Gustat had news: "*Another* woman's dental records were compared with the bones identified as Harberts's—and that woman is *still* missing." What other woman? "Judith Turner Thompson."

11

Exquisite Chaos: The Final Death Warrant (August 1995)

I have done bad things for love, bad things to stay loved. Kate is one case. Vietnam is another.

Tim O'Brien, "The Vietnam inside Me,"
New York Times, *October 2, 1994*

It was a bad position to be in [when oxygen tank 2 exploded], exactly the kind of position that the press and the public and the news people [at NASA] would dream up when they were in the mood to ask about the poison pills. For their part, Lovell and his crewmates weren't thinking about pills . . . or anything of the sort. They were thinking about fixing the power, fixing the oxygen, fixing whatever else ailed the ship. Whether they actually could was open to question.

Jim Lovell and Jeffrey Kluger, Lost Moon:
The Perilous Voyage of Apollo 13, *1994*

August 22, 1995
Wilder, Vermont

Today I heard that Chiles's office has been putting out the word that I am mentally ill. When the governor's clemency aide made this accusation to one of my Florida colleagues, my colleague replied: "Mike realized, before the rest of us, that by playing by your rules, we maximize our chances [for a while], and then you turn around and kill our clients. For you to call him 'mentally ill' is unconscionable. He's not crazy; he's angry, and he's directed that anger at the appropriate people. I won't sit in a room with an old white man and listen to him

273

tell me I don't know anything. I won't listen to that shit. Not any-more." Later that day, I called Gene Miller to appraise him of Gov-ernor Chiles's latest line of attack. I signed my correspondence "Crazy Mike."

In one respect, I was glad that Douglass was going after me; that meant he wasn't going after Joe. One of my media sources told me to take it as a compliment and as a sign of how desperate Chiles's office was becoming. "Douglass needs a scapegoat, and you're it. I loved that you called him a murderer—that's exactly what he is. He's pissed, and he'll lash out at any source of the bother that can't fight back. He can't go after the *Herald*."

I wrote Joe:

Dear Joe:

So how are you, my friend? Things are gearing up here for an-other school year, which starts on Thursday. Where has the sum-mer *gone*?

Thank you so much for your recent letters, especially those about how much the club means to you and why. I really need to begin trying to educate the media, the governor and the court about the *realities* of the club, not the prejudices and myths about "bikers" that too many people share. At a minimum, people need to understand that it's not a crime to be an Outlaw—any more than it's a crime to be a Black Panther or a Branch Da-vidian. But before I can educate the public about the club, you need to educate me. Your letters do that very well, and I'm grate-ful to you for them.

As I hope Susan Cary discussed with you last week, I now think a warrant will *not* be coming soon. The Florida Supreme Court has decided to put our motions on hold (a very *good* sign, I think) until Chiles decides on whether to grant or deny clemen-cy. The FDLE "investigation," such as it is, is still going on; I don't think Chiles will sign a warrant until FDLE finishes its in-vestigation, if even then. I am guardedly nonpessimistic that you are safe from a warrant for the moment.

A friend of mine was *very* impressed with the "Mike and Joe on motorcycles" painting you did for me a few years ago. She made a suggestion, which I thought I would pass on to you:

Have you ever thought about doing a series of *cartoons* illustrating what it's like to live on death row for a crime you didn't commit? She thought that people on the outside would pay for such paintings by you.

Anyway, the wedding plans are chugging along. We hired a photographer yesterday, and D now has all of the pieces of her wedding dress, so soon she'll start sewing it. The second floor of our house is now divided into two rooms: the "wedding dress construction room" and the "Joe boxes war room."

Take care, Joe, and let me hear from you. D sends her love.

Peace,
Michael

August 23, 1995
Wilder, Vermont

My spies in the governor's office told me that no warrant was imminent, and that Chiles "is, absolutely, going to hold a clemency hearing; even Douglass is feeling the heat." My media spies told me that Chiles' clemency aide "told us, off the record, that a warrant would be signed near the end of this month." There were only eight days left in August, and two of them were weekend days.

August 24, 1995
Wilder, Vermont

August 24 was the first day of Vermont Law School's 1995 academic year. In the morning of the first day of each academic year, the entire Vermont Law School professional staff—secretaries, professors, librarians, switchboard operators—attends a ceremony welcoming the entering first-year law students. The ceremony takes place outdoors, on the banks of the White River, and concludes with introductions to the new students of the faculty and staff of the law school.

All this means that if you call the school during the ceremony, no one will answer the phone. If you send a fax, no one will deliver it or read it. It's the one day of the year when the place is totally empty. Everyone is at the riverside.

And that's where I was when Governor Chiles signed Joe Spaziano's fifth death warrant. I'm always the last to know. Joe learned when the warrant was read to him. I learned when I returned from the riverside.

But before Joe or his lawyer knew, the *Orlando Sentinel* knew. Chiles's office had leaked news of the warrant to the governor's favorite bulletin board. The *Sentinel*'s banner headline trumpeted that, based on the secret FDLE report (which the *Sentinel* discussed at length), Chiles would sign Joe's warrant on August 24. The headline ran across the top of the *Sentinel*'s front page: "Chiles to OK Spaziano's Death." Under the headline were two photos, one of Laura Lynn Harberts and the other of Art Harberts as he "puts flowers on the grave of his daughter."

The *Sentinel*'s story began:

> Tallahassee—Gov. Lawton Chiles today will sign a fifth death warrant for Joseph "Crazy Joe" Spaziano, the former Outlaws motorcycle gang member fighting his conviction in the 1973 torture-murder of an Orlando woman.
>
> Chiles decided to sign the warrant after the Florida Department of Law Enforcement turned up new evidence that Spaziano raped, tortured, mutilated and murdered Laura Lynn Harberts, an 18-year-old hospital clerk.
>
> Sources told *The Orlando Sentinel* Wednesday that Spaziano admitted in prison to killing Harberts and two others, and that a key witness who now says Spaziano is innocent told friends at the time of Harberts' death that Spaziano had killed her and discarded her body in a dump.

Lissa Gardner, an attorney at CCR and an old friend from the days when we both worked at CCR, told me the dates. The warrant authorized Joe's electrocution during the week of September 19–26. The prison had scheduled the execution for 7:00 A.M. September 21. Not even four weeks away.

It's ironic that we'd never gotten anyone to look at our ever-increasing body of new evidence showing Joe's innocence. But the cops now dredge up (or manufacture) new "evidence" of guilt, and it's enough to convince the governor to sign a new death warrant.

My fear was that the new "secret evidence" would provide Chiles with all the political cover he needed. Lazy reporters could simply pick it up and run with it. I prayed that the *Herald* would know enough to contextualize this new "evidence" to put it in perspective. The question was whether the *Herald* could do its own investigative reporting before Joe would be killed. I couldn't test the accuracy, credibility, or bases of knowledge of the new police informants without first knowing the identities of those informants. I tried to obtain a copy of the secret police report. So did VLRC. So did CCR. None of us succeeded.

Joyce Johns, an FSP administrator, called me a little after noon and put Joe on the phone. The guards had pulled him off the yard to read him the death warrant. Joe asked me to call his mother, daughter, niece, and ex-wife. "Damn, Mike, what do you think? Nobody cares. I figured it out. This asshole wants to kill me."

Joe's niece phoned me before I could call her. Her voice cracking with sobs, she asked, "How can Chiles *do* this? He's ruthless. I can't believe this system. . . . Please tell my uncle that I love him very much."

The news devastated Joe's mom. "Mike, they need to give him another chance. He's older and wiser. Deep in my heart, I can't see how they can execute him. I can picture him, pacing in his cell, a nervous wreck, not seeing anyone but the guards."

Joe had been read the warrant and moved to the deathwatch cells before I even learned the warrant had been signed.

Another death warrant, another press release from the governor's office:

State of Florida
Office of the Governor
The Capitol
Tallahassee, Florida

FOR IMMEDIATE RELEASE   CONTACT: Ron Sachs
August 24, 1995
GOVERNOR CHILES SIGNS DEATH WARRANT FOR JOSEPH SPAZIANO

TALLAHASSEE—Governor Lawton Chiles today signed a death warrant for Joseph Robert Spaziano—the fifth such death warrant for Spaziano for the 1973 rape and murder of Laura Harberts. Governors Bob Graham, Bob Martinez and Chiles have all signed previous warrants in this case. The Governor signed the latest death warrant after receiving the results of a two-month review of the case by the Florida Department of Law Enforcement (FDLE).

"This exhaustive review removes any doubt in my mind

about this case," Governor Chiles said. "This review upholds the finding of every court that has heard this case—Joseph Spaziano has received due process and justice demands that he now face the consequences for the crimes he has committed."

After signing Spaziano's fourth death warrant on May 24, 1995, Governor Chiles issued an indefinite stay of execution for Spaziano on June 15, 1995—after some news media reports created public doubt abut the case—and ordered the FDLE review. The Governor's action came after published reports raised questions about the testimony of Tony Dilisio [sic]—a key witness in the case.

The FDLE review of the Spaziano investigation and trial included an interview with Dilisio and interviews with other witnesses. FDLE obtained sworn statements from a number of witnesses. The FDLE probe also included the review of case files, trial records and appellate court documents.

The FDLE review of the case found substantive information that is consistent with the original story Dilisio told investigators—that Spaziano, a member of the Outlaws motorcycle gang, had taken Dilisio to see the mutilated bodies of two women on several occasions. While authorities recovered both bodies, only Harberts' remains were identified.

The FDLE probe of the case determined that police and prosecutors did not manipulate Dilisio and that he linked Spaziano to the murder victims: prior to talking to police; to the police investigating the murders; after undergoing hypnosis; during his sworn trial testimony; and to several people over the past 20 years.

The FDLE probe determined Dilisio's story has stayed consistent for two decades—and never wavered until Spaziano's execution was imminent and media reports questioned Dilisio's testimony.

FDLE also interviewed a former high-ranking Outlaw member and Spaziano associate who is an FBI informant in the Federal Witness Protection Program. This individual says that prior to Spaziano's trial for the Harberts murder, Spaziano admitted killing two women, disposing their bodies in a dump and taking a young man to see the bodies. The informant also says Spaziano was concerned that the young man would talk to the authorities.

Spaziano has been on Florida's death row since July, 1976. He also is serving a life sentence for the kidnap and rape of a 16-year old girl on February 9, 1974. The victim was raped, beaten, choked, repeatedly slashed in the chest and around the eyes and left for dead by Spaziano and a co-defendant in a remote rural location of Orange County. The victim positively identified Spaziano as her assailant. The similarities between that case and the Harberts murder were key elements that made Spaziano a prime suspect in the Harberts case.

This is the fifth death warrant Spaziano has faced in the past 10 years. Governor Graham signed the first death warrant for Spaziano in November, 1985; Governor Martinez signed two—in August, 1989 and in March, 1990; and Governor Chiles signed Spaziano's fourth death warrant on May 24, 1995.

All matters relating to a clemency review are confidential under Florida law. FDLE is making every effort to keep the identities of persons who gave statements in the review of this case strictly confidential.

A copy of the death warrant was attached to the press release.

August 25, 1995
Wilder, Vermont
(27 days to execution)

"Justice for Spaziano," the *Orlando Sentinel*'s editorial page demanded. "The judicial system has been very patient with Joseph Spaziano. It's time for him to pay for his crime. His lawyer's hollow claim and bully tactics turned out to be nothing more than another way to subvert the jury's verdict."

The *Sentinel*'s assertion that I had somehow "bullied" the Florida governor, judiciary, and police sounded especially idiotic to me on the day the *Sentinel*'s editorial was published. I was on my own. The reality was sinking in. CCR had tangled loyalties and conflicts of interest. As of yesterday, VLRC was dead. Deanna, Laura, and I would be doing this alone.

At 9:00 A.M. I faxed a handwritten note to the Florida Supreme Court clerk: "The Court should know that I have no secretary, research assistant or investigator—the latter due to the demise of VLRC." I also faxed a letter I'd received earlier that morning from VLRC:

Dear Mike:

I am writing with regard to our ability to provide you with investigative assistance on behalf of Joseph Spaziano. As you are aware, in all likelihood we will receive no federal funds as of October 1, 1995. As a result, we have to plan for the transfer of all of our cases and case files to successor counsel, and for the transfer of all property and equipment to the federal government.

Because of this situation, we have already laid off much of our staff. In order to avoid exceeding our budget and incurring potential liability, the President of our Board, Chan Muller, is instructing us to lay off most of the rest of our staff, cease taking on any new cases, and stop all investigation in pending cases. This is the only way that we can both meet our existing obligations and ensure that we transfer existing cases and case files in an orderly manner. Accordingly, I am forced to inform you that we will not be able to undertake any investigation on behalf of Spaziano.

Our entire office, and I personally, are saddened that we have to take this step, as we would much prefer to join you in proving that Spaziano is innocent. Given our financial situation, however, we have no choice.

Sincerely,
Matthew Lawry
Co-Director

Richard Capozzola was sending out three hundred letters to the Sons of Italy people. Mike Farrell was lining up additional signatories to the public statement. The *Herald* and *St. Petersburg Times* were editorializing against keeping the police report secret. The *Washington Post, Newsweek, New York Times, 48 Hours* and others were again interested in the story.

By basing a death warrant—a warrant highly likely to be carried out—on a secret police report, the governor seemed to be thumbing his nose at the press as well as at me. I was able to get a bit of media mileage out of this. As far as I knew, this was the first death warrant in history signed on the basis of a secret police report. The ACLU and the Lawyer's Committee for Freedom of the Press were considering filing lawsuits to secure access to the secret report.

August 26, 1995
Wilder, Vermont
(26 days to execution)

Gene Miller was troubled by my decision not to take Joe's case into a successive round of federal habeas corpus litigation. He asked me whether I was playing games with an innocent man's life. I said that Chiles, not I, is the game player.

Miller reminded me that the *Herald* is *totally* independent of me. Of course, I replied. Those have been the ground rules from the outset. All I've done with the *Herald* was to provide information and materials from my files, in the hope that the *Herald* would read them with an open mind and do its own homework.

Motions, motions everywhere: draft, edit, proof, fax. Motions challenging the secrecy of the police report. Motions for appointment as counsel, so I might actually be able to pay the rapidly mushrooming litigation expenses.

August 27, 1995
Wilder, Vermont
(25 days to execution)

When Joe phoned at 2:00 P.M., he said, "I woke up crazy this morning. Let me talk to my future sister-in-law." Joe and Deanna chatted for a while.

When I tried to call Joe later in the day, the deathwatch phone lines were out of order. "The whole phone system is goofed up," Joe said when we finally spoke. As an aside to a guard, Joe quipped, "I hope that chair works when I sit in it, guys."

I coughed. "Yeah, Mike, light up another one. Those things'll kill you. I'll quit if you do, Mike."

Later, I called Joe back because I wanted to talk to him about a very novel strategy that had been marinating in my head for the past few days. If anything, the strategy was even more risky than my previous decision to take Joe's case to the *Miami Herald*.

In essence, the strategy was to refuse to take Joe's case into federal court, if we lost in the Florida Supreme Court, and to tell the world that that was my strategy. The idea was to put *all* the responsibility for Joe's life in the hands of the Florida Supreme Court and that court alone. The justices couldn't pass the responsibility on to the federal courts—the buck would stop in Tallahassee.

I kept coming back to the question: How could otherwise good and decent people, such as the justices on the Florida Supreme Court, come together to kill this innocent man? Joe Spaziano's case had taught me how the legal handling of capital punishment, as it is now structured by our legal system, allows situations in which wrongful executions can be carried out.

One could point easily to the mistakes made by the various individual actors in the Spaziano story, beginning with the mistakes I made over the years as Joe's lawyer. Yet focusing on the specific mistakes of individual players in Joe's case misses the most important point, it seems to me.

Florida isn't Texas, where death walks an assembly line and judicial review is a cruel hoax. Florida is different. Perhaps more than any other state in the union, Florida has struggled mightily to make capital punishment, as a legal system, fair as well as efficient. The Florida Supreme Court justices spend a commendable, and tremendous, amount of their professional time trying to tame the wild horse of capital punishment within the rule of law, and that attitude of seriousness has trickled down to the trial judges who preside over life-or-death trials in Florida. Many Florida counties, such as Palm Beach County, demonstrate an intense commitment to ensuring that men and woman on trial for their lives will have their day in court represented by the best lawyers in the business. This our constitution demands, and no less. In postconviction proceedings, Florida death row prisoners have lawyers from a well-funded public agency (CCR) to represent them and, no matter what one might think about CCR's performance of its statutory duties in recent years, the agency provides more—much more—than the legal aid most other states make available for their death row populations; CCR's present budget of $15 million can hardly be called miserly.

And yet, even with all these honorable people working hard to see that justice is done in Florida capital cases, the "Crazy Joe" Spaziano case brought Florida to the brink of committing the most hideous sort of injustice—execution of a man for a crime he did not commit. Joe was first sent to death row in 1976. Jimmy Carter was beginning his term as president. In the decades since—during the presidencies of Reagan, Bush, and Clinton—Joe Spaziano has remained on death row.

How is this possible? How is it possible for a totally innocent man to live on death row for so long, to survive multiple death warrants, to come within days of electrocution—all in a case that couldn't stand up to two weeks of fresh-eyed scrutiny by the *Miami Herald*?

It's possible, in part, because some generally honorable actors acted less than honorably in Joe's case, in large part because Joe was an Outlaw and it was the mid-1970s in south Florida. Once the police learned that Joe was an Outlaw, he became their man; they conducted their investigation with blinders on, and they hid exculpatory evidence from Joe's defense lawyer at trial. The defense lawyer, sad to say, also dropped the ball in crucial plays, leaving a jury open to deception. A less-than-factual trial before a jury was then possible. Thanks to police and prosecution deceit, judicial badgering, and Outlaw intimidation, Joe's jury was willing to convict him, even though evidence of his guilt was flimsy. Conviction without condemnation seemed, to the beleaguered jury, a formula to satisfy conscience and the collective public. But the trial judge overrode the jury's life verdict and imposed death. From that point on the appellate courts, state and federal, properly reviewed the case only for errors by professional players. Because the jury's verdict had been seduced, the fact of guilt became an assumption. In our system, facts are supposed to be judged only by the jury. It is a great system—providing a fair jury gets facts, not fiction.

The flaws of the actors only partially explain what went wrong with the legal system in the "Crazy Joe" case. The fundamental problem, I have come to believe, is that none of these actors had systemic *responsibility* for correcting the error that had been made—that an innocent man had been found guilty. Everyone could duck the issue, and many did.

I challenge any reader to explain the route to justice for a falsely condemned man in our system. Who has the ultimate responsibility for the exoneration or for the execution of an innocent man? No one does, and that's exactly the problem. The jury was misled and badgered into finding Joe guilty of murder, even though they had valid, reasonable doubts; they recommended life, rather than death, *because* those valid yet repressed doubts had no facts to support then—yet. The trial judge was precluded by Florida law from taking account of those doubts, and so he overrode the jury's life verdict and imposed the death sentence.

Thus did the jury pitch to the judge, who ducked. The jury deferred its responsibility to the judge, who deferred it right back to the jury. Only a feeling stood between Joe and his wrongful death, and the feelings of a few good people were, in the current system, buried for the life of a whole generation.

The Florida Supreme Court deferred to the trial judge, who had deferred to the jury, who had deferred to the judge. And then the federal courts deferred to the state courts, as they are required to do under U.S. Supreme Court precedent. That left the ultimate responsibility with Governor Chiles. But then Chiles pitched it back to the courts, saying, through his clemency aide Mark Schlakman, that it was the *courts'* responsibility to guarantee that an innocent man is not put to death. So Chiles deferred to the courts, but that resulted in a deadly catch-22. And so closes the deadly circle of deflection of responsibility.

Thus I thought the key to saving Joe was to keep the responsibility for killing him squarely on the shoulders of the Florida Supreme Court and the governor. I talked to Joe about all this, and he told me to do what I felt best.

The day the fifth warrant was signed, I began drafting a memo to those people whose tactical and strategic wisdom mattered to me the most: Mark Olive (MO), George Kendall, Matthew Lawry, Jenny Greenburg, and Steve Gustat. When I began drafting the memo, I hadn't yet decided against taking Joe's case back into federal court. For me, the act of putting pen to paper clarifies what I really think or feel about a particular potential course of action. In this instance, by the time I finished writing the memo, three days after I began, I had more or less decided not to take Joe's case into federal habeas corpus.

The memo was marked CONFIDENTIAL at the top of its first page.

MEMORANDUM

DATE: August 27, 1995
TO: Pat, MO, Jenny, Matthew, Steve, and George
FROM: Mello
RE: Why I will *not* take Joe Spaziano's case back into
              federal court on a successive habeas, or into the
              state trial court on a fifth Rule 3.850 motion.

All of you are understandably skeptical about my decision not to take Joe's case into federal court. I'll try here to sort out my thought processes.

There is an undeniable legal benefit in going into every possible court to seek a stay: The system of capital punishment is random, and we might get lucky and get a stay from the federal courts—if we don't ask, we don't get. There is also a psychological benefit: we feel better, because we've done all we can do as lawyers; our client feels better, knowing that we've knocked on every legal door; the judges feel better, because they can tell themselves "the defense system worked because the defense lawyers scurried like rats from court to court, raising every conceivable issue (we chide them for doing that, but we don't mean it)"; ditto the public feels better.

So the benefits of the eleventh hour dash are clear and familiar to us; we've all been through the drill before. But every litigation decision we make—be it to go into court or not to—entails risks as well as benefits. The risks are as un-quantifiable as the benefits. The best I can do here is try to *identify* the risks as well as the benefits in choosing whether to take Joe's case into federal court under a fifth (count 'em) warrant.

First, the costs of forgoing the federal courts are minimal: to paraphrase Lincoln in 1862, for Joe Spaziano, there is no North—not on a successive habeas petition, at any rate. The "federal courts" here mean Kendall Sharp, Ed Carnes, and the Big Bill Rehnquist Court. Sharp has never granted CPC, much less a stay or an evidentiary hearing; in 13 years on the bench, Brother Sharp has not once found a single claim by a condemned prisoner to be non-frivolous—to say nothing of sufficiently potentially meritorious to justify a stay. Ed Carnes—the Alabama capital prosecutor cross-dressing as a federal appellate judge—

requires no comment. Mr. Ed wrote the Eleventh Circuit's opinion on Joe's case, and he spent more energy bitching about the page limit for my brief than he devoted to the evidence of innocence I *raised* in the goddamn brief. So we clear the Eleventh Circuit on a successive habeas petition in a 20-year-old case on which the Court granted plenary review in 1984, with no stay and no CPC. The innocence-based cert. petition I filed in November did not get a single vote for cert. And that was on a first habeas—a habeas based on pretty compelling evidence of innocence, some of which wasn't procedurally defaulted.

Our evidence on innocence is pretty powerful, but we don't have a videotape showing that Joe was elsewhere at the precise time of the murder. The videotaped alibi isn't a hypo, of course; that's what Lloyd Schlup had in his successive habeas petition. And all Schlup got out of the Rehnquist/Scalia, Thomas ("bitch set me up") court was an evidentiary hearing—and that only by a razor thin margin of 5-4, the same number of votes we'd need (5, not 4; remember *Streetman* and *Herrera*?) for a stay in Joe's case.

So the real legal test, as opposed to the black letter law, is: If you have a videotaped alibi, and you're in successor habeas status, then you might be able to scrape together five votes for a *chance* to prove your claim at an evidentiary hearing—a hearing which, in Joe's case, would occur before Judge Kendall Sharp. And a hearing before Sharp is the *most* we can expect to get out of the federal judiciary. We have little chance of getting even that, it seems to me. We don't have a videotaped alibi, or anything close. Like *Schlup,* we're a successor; unlike *Schlup,* Joe ran innocence as the centerpiece of his first habeas—and of the 13 federal judges who could have considered that evidence, none did—not a single one. In federal court, innocence is irrelevant. The Supreme Court says so, and the lower courts listen—as they're required to do.

So I think we give up little by forgoing the federal courts. Let's take their procedural default/retroactivity/abuse-of-the-writ rhetoric seriously. Fuck 'em.

On the other hand, the risks of going into federal court are great. We waste our scarce time and energy on essentially hopeless litigation before judges who don't think we belong there—

and, if the Supreme Court's pronouncements in *Teague* and *Sykes* and *McCleskey* and *Coleman* and *Parks are* the law, then those judges are right. We *don't* belong in federal court. The Supreme Court has said so again and again. Maybe it's time to start *listening* to those robed assholes.

More significantly, it seems to me, by doing the 50-yard dashes from court to court, we shift attention from Chiles and from the Florida Supreme Court. Most critically, we diffuse responsibility among Chiles, the Florida Supreme Court, and the federal courts. It's an interstitial, systemic manifestation of the Private Slovick syndrome and the *Caldwell* problem: If everyone shares some responsibility for the killing of this innocent man, then no one does.

I have long thought that diffusion of responsibility was the fundamental systemic and institutional problem with this case. The jury wasn't sure Joe was guilty, but they knew he was an Outlaw, and it was Orange County in the mid-1970s. So they split the difference, and they found Joe guilty but recommended life. The trial judge didn't know about the jury's lingering doubt about guilt, so he overrode and imposed death. So the jury shifted responsibility to the judge, and vice versa. And the same thing happened at each other sequential step along the capital assembly line. The Florida Supreme Court deferred to the jury and trial court, as principles of appellate practice dictate. And the federal courts deferred to the state judiciary, as principles of federalism command.

Finally, the judiciary (state and federal) deferred to the clemency authority of the governor—which, under *Herrera* and *Graham* they were supposed to do, no matter how idiotically unrealistic *Herrera* and *Graham* might seem to us. Finally, in 1995, the responsibility for executing this innocent man rested on the shoulders of one person: Lawton Chiles. The buck stopped there, and he knew it. That's why the *Herald's* coverage persuaded him to stay the warrant in June, I'm convinced.

And, I'm afraid, I erred in giving Chiles an out when I filed in the Florida Supreme Court. FDLE and the *Orlando Sentinel* gave him all the political cover he needed. We were back in the Florida Supreme Court, so it was the courts' problem—not his. If we lost in the Florida Supreme Court, Chiles would expect us to dash into FDC, then the 11th Circuit and the Supreme Court. With thudding predictability, the stay would be denied the night before the scheduled execution, and all of the attention—and any blame—would stick to the judges and not to Gov. Chiles. As we all know, that's the expected drill: the motherfuckers run us ragged from court to court, then they kill our clients and blame it on us for filing at the eleventh hour.

In my opinion, Joe has *some* (very little) chance of getting a stay from either of two places: the Florida Supreme Court and Chiles. If the Florida Supreme Court has any interest in doing right in this case, they have the opportunity to do so with the out-of-time rehearing motions pending before them. If the Florida Supreme Court has any inclination now—and they have never shown the slightest inclination in the eight other times Joe's case has come before them—in cutting through the procedural screens the court itself has erected to avoid even considering the evidence of innocence here, now they have the chance. I have no reason to think they will suddenly seize that opportunity. If they don't, I see no reason to give either the Florida Supreme Court or the trial court yet another chance to default and abuse us.

That leaves Chiles as our best shot at a stay. It is a very depressing thought, and I want to be clear that I do not for a moment think that Chiles will grant a stay out of any impulses of justice or fairness or decency. I keep hearing what a decent fellow Chiles is, but the May warrant, the stay (in the wake of public pressure), and the present warrant (now that the media attention has died down; remember Larry Joe Johnson?) leave me convinced that Chiles uses the killing machinery of the state according to the crass political calculus perfected by Bob Graham, the original wimp who transformed himself into a national political force, and who did so on the charred bodies of our clients.

That political calculus is, I believe, our only real chance for a stay. It's not much of a chance, but neither are the courts. It worked in June, to the amazement of us all (especially me). It may well not work again, as it wasn't supposed to work last time, either. What we must do is to maximize the pressure on Chiles.

The key to maximizing the pressure on Chiles is to eliminate any opportunity for him to pass the buck to the courts, to close off all possible escape routes. Thus, it seems to me, our chance with Chiles hinges on our ability to keep the responsibility for killing this innocent man squarely on Chiles and on Chiles alone. That's why I won't go to federal court. That's why, should we lose in the Florida Supreme Court, I won't file a new 3.850 in the trial court.

The magnitude of the pressure Chiles will face will depend, more than anything else, on our (and the media's) ability to discredit FDLE's secret, Star Chamber "process." That means getting access to FDLE's report and its underlying materials and exposing them as the product of a whitewash with a foreordained conclusion. Perhaps the combination of the report and the *Orlando Sentinel* will provide Chiles with enough political cover regardless of what we are able to ferret out. But I still think that Joe's best shot at a stay—and his only shot at any real, substantive relief—lies in my joint investigative venture with the *Herald*. The paper isn't beholden to me or to Joe of course; if they discover evidence Joe is guilty, they'd print it; they'd *have* to print it. Still, I plan to continue to treat the *Herald* as an investigative partner, giving them full and open access to my files and my thinking. By now, I trust Miller's, Holmes' and Rozsa's ability to distinguish the real, reliable evidence from FDLE's smoke screens and McCarthy-esque guilt by association.

It's terrifying to think that Joe's life is in the hands of a politician—a politician who has signed two warrants on him within three months, notwithstanding the evidence of innocence. But I believe our best shot is in keeping the responsibility on Chiles and on Chiles alone.

If Joe is killed, I want there to be no doubt that the final responsibility rests with one man, a man who must be thinking about his place in history. I want him to know that, no matter how much good he did in the Senate and in the governor's mansion, it will all be eclipsed by this; it will all be outweighed by his killing this man. Tony Proscio was right that this really *is* a defining moment for America; it will, I can only hope, be the moment for Lawton Chiles to define how he is to be remembered. This will be the ultimate measure of the grain of his character and the content of his soul. This will be in his obituary, no matter how few column inches he rates when he dies.

Wayne Gretzky (cameo star of *Mighty Ducks, II*), asked the secret of his success in hockey, said, "I always skate to where the puck is going, not to where it's been." The continuity of our litigation strategy under warrant contrasts sharply with the discontinuity of events. The "federal courts," especially *our* lower federal courts, have been packed with hacks by Reagan and Bush—suggests that perhaps we, by continuing to do the death warrant *Shinkansen* through the federal courts, are skating to where the judicial puck has been. Or maybe it's the *political* puck. Or maybe I'm just plain wrong about all of this, and maybe my wrongheadedness will cause the death of my one innocent client and close friend. Gene Miller accused me yesterday of "playing games" with Joe's life, and maybe he's right. On some level this *is* all a high-stakes game—so is Russian Roulette, and so are Pentagon war exercises in the Persian Gulf—but if it *is* all a game, then I think we need to consider changing the rules. My recent experiences with CCR convince me now—and better late than never, I guess—that Millard was right when he said at Airlie in 1986 that we risk becoming "the mask of the executioner." Better that Joe have no lawyer at all—and that the world clearly sees that he has no lawyer—than that Joe have the *illusion* of a lawyer, a hack PD office like CCR that plays by the rules laid down by the people whose job it is to kill their clients.

One final word about taking responsibility. This call is mine (and Joe's). I've been privileged to have the input and advice of many, many people far smarter than I, and for that I am deeply grateful. But the final responsibility is mine alone. I hope I'm making the right decision on this; I hope even more that we won't need to find out, because the Florida Supreme Court will grant a stay to consider the rehearing motions now pending before it. Gulp.

God help Joe. God help us.

August 27, 1995
Wilder, Vermont
(25 days to execution)

In addition to faxing my June 27 memo to its addressees, I decided to fax it to Dexter Douglass, for two reasons. First, I wanted the governor to know my reasoning in forgoing another round of federal habeas corpus litigation. Second, I wanted to smoke out the inside track between the governor's office and the *Orlando Sentinel*. *Sentinel* reporters had been swearing to me that they were not being fed inside information by the governor's office and the cops. The *Sentinel*'s exclusive access to information not even I could obtain as Joe's attorney—the secret police report, the fact that Governor Chiles would sign Joe's death warrant on August 24—suggested otherwise, at least to me.

My August 27 "confidential" memo seemed to me the perfect vehicle for testing the hypothesis that Chiles's office was indeed leaking confidential information to its newspaper of choice. So I faxed the memo to the people I wrote it for (none of whom would *ever* leak on me) and to Douglass—and to no one else.

Twenty minutes after I faxed the memo to Governor Chiles's office I got a call from the *Orlando Sentinel*. They wanted to talk about the memo.

The leaking of my memo did more than confirm that the *Sentinel* was in bed with the governor's office. It also provided a telling vignette of the simple lack of intellectual firepower of at least some of the *Sentinel*'s reporters. One of the memo's recipients was Mark Olive. One of the *Sentinel*'s reporters called Olive to confirm that the memo had been sent to him. Olive, of course, declined to say. The *Sentinel* reporter then confessed that he'd been told that Mark Olive was sometimes called "MO." The *Sentinel* reporter asked Olive, "Do you go by 'Mo'"? MO replied, "Go buy mo' of *what*? Bread? Candy?" Reporter: "Why do they call you MO?" MO: "It's my initials. M.O." Reporter: "Are you this guy's lawyer?" MO: "Which guy? Mello?" This flummoxed the breathless reporter. He oozed away.

I couldn't believe that newspaper reporters could be so baroquely clueless. Might this actually be a trick? Was the *Sentinel* setting Joe and me up? I posed these questions to other Florida reporters, and the consensus was no. As one put it, the *Orlando Sentinel*'s principal reporter on the Spaziano story "is more stupid than the average reporter. . . . [This reporter] is dumb as a brick. He's just plain stone *stupid*."

At 6:42 P.M., I received the one and only written communication I was to get from Gov. Lawton Chiles's office during 1995. This is what it said, in its entirety:

> State of Florida
> Office of the Governor
> The Capitol
> Tallahassee, Florida

Michael Mello, Esq.
Vermont Law School
Whitcomb Faculty House, Chelsea Street
South Royalton, VT

Dear Mr. Mello:

This will acknowledge receipt of your telefax received this date at 11:18 a.m.

The matters contained therein are being reviewed by the Governor and the Director of Communications and will be given due consideration.

> Yours truly,
> Dexter Douglass
> General Counsel

I heard somewhere that when Cortez arrived in the New World, he burned all his boats to assure that his men would be well motivated.

By making my August 27 memo public, I burned my boats. Having said out loud that I wouldn't be taking Joe's case into federal court, I couldn't later change my mind and, after losing in the Florida Supreme Court, run into federal court seeking a stay. I couldn't—I wouldn't—back down. If we lost in the state courts, and if the governor denied clemency, I would let them kill my friend Joe Spaziano.

There was no turning back now.

August 28, 1995
Wilder, Vermont
(24 days to execution)

The Florida Bar Association has an ethics hot line. I called it and asked for an informal opinion about what the ethical course would be for me in Joe's case. VLRC was dead, so should I bail out of the case and let it go to CCR, a law firm with conflicts of interest? Or should I do what Joe and his family wanted me to do: stay on as Joe's lawyer and just do the best I could from Vermont?

I was told, in essence, that either course of action would be ethically defensible. "You're not *required* to withdraw, if it's either you or no one." Even if I can't possibly be effective (due to the death of VLRC), I'm still not required to withdraw? "No; not if there's no one else." Ethically, I could stay in or withdraw as Joe's lawyer. I said I knew that already; rules of legal ethics often lack directive content. I said I wasn't trying to cover my professional backside; I was trying to figure out what was the right thing to do. Sorry—not their department.

It was around that time I got a phone call from "people in Geraldo Rivera's organization" (as they described themselves). These people had been "in touch with Tony DiLisio. We're trying to let Tony make a plea to the public and to Joe: have Joe and Tony speak to each other. Tony is begging us to help him do right. . . . As journalists, we'd never give Tony a dime. It would destroy his credibility."

Geraldo Rivera would devote an entire show to this grand reconciliation between Tony and Joe. "Tony wants to apologize to Joe and his family, and we want to capture it. . . . Telling his truth on this has become a *mission* for Tony." This slope was beginning to feel more and more slippery to me. Writing an op-ed column for the *Herald* was one thing; putting Joe on *Geraldo* was something of a different order of magnitude. Still, told them I'd talk with Joe about it.

August 30, 1995
Wilder, Vermont
(22 days to execution)

I fully expected the *Orlando Sentinel* to throw a temper tantrum over the salty language I used in the August 17 memo. What I didn't expect was the strongly puritanical, albeit somewhat delayed, reaction of the journalistic grown-ups at the *Herald* and *St. Petersburg Times.*

Not everyone loathed the memo. One deathwork veteran told me, "Your memo was right on. It's all true, and nobody else has the balls to say so." Another said, "I *loved* your memo. It had me rolling on the floor."

August 31, 1995
Wilder, Vermont
(21 days to execution)

My mother arrived in town, the first time she'd visited Vermont since Deanna and I became a couple. Tomorrow the three of us drive to Rhode Island for a family reunion.

IN THE SUPREME COURT OF FLORIDA
JOSEPH R. SPAZIANO, Petitioner-Appellant,
v.
THE STATE OF FLORIDA, Respondent-Appellee

SUPPLEMENT TO MOTIONS FOR APPOINTMENT AND
EXPENSES FOR INVESTIGATORS, EXPERTS, ETC.

The September 1 *Orlando Sentinel* article demonstrates that—in addition to investigation and litigation to expose the fraudulence of FDLE's super-secret "investigation"—effective representation of Spaziano must include thorough factual investigation in Chicago.

In light of the sudden death of VLRC, *pro bono* counsel is unable to conduct investigation even in Florida, much less in Chicago and in whatever state or country FDLE's super-secret sources reside. We cannot know where these super-secret witnesses are because, as with everything else about them (except what the police say they said) it's all a state secret.

The *Orlando Sentinel* is not sympathetic to Spaziano's attempts to stay alive long enough to unearth the identities and test the reliability of those alleged super-secret state witnesses, to understate the matter. The *Sentinel* sees its role as being a journalistic bulletin board for Governor Chiles and for the police: Chiles leaked to the *Sentinel* the fact that a death warrant would be signed on Spaziano on August 24; the following day, the *Sentinel* editorialized in favor of the killing of Spaziano based on secret governmental information; etc.

But even the *Orlando Sentinel* was compelled to concede that Chiles' super-secret "information" that Spaziano had murdered an Outlaw couple in Chicago in 1974 was dissolving under the most glancing of scrutiny:

> "One of the FDLE witnesses was a former Outlaw who told investigators that Spaziano admitted killing Harberts and worried that a 'young kid' who had been shown the body would go to the police.
>
> "That witness also told investigators that Spaziano had confessed to killing a Chicago biker and his girlfriend after bragging to them about Harbert's killing.
>
> *"But Chicago detectives said the 1974 shootings of Michael Dungess and Linda Noe were closed after police thought they found the killer—a biker other than Spaziano. He was not charged, but detectives could not recall why.*
>
> " 'We're trying to go back and search those records now,' Detective Anthony Biongiorno said Thursday. '*Spaziano was a suspect, but so was this other guy*' " (emphasis added).

The *Sentinel*'s editorial listed four new counts against Spaziano, all allegedly drawn from the FDLE report Chiles had leaked to that newspaper. The editorial highlighted its four points by prefacing them with "bullet" headings. The "Chicago killings" fantasy was the second bullet.

The *Orlando Sentinel*'s editorial appeared seven days prior to its news story raising doubts about FDLE's account of the Chicago episode. If a newspaper determined to see Spaziano put down on schedule can uncover evidence in seven days casting serious doubt upon information contained in its own editorial, imagine what Spaziano could discover with sufficient investigative resources.

Spaziano would be able to prove that he killed no Outlaw couple in Chicago in 1974, as he would prove he did not murder Laura Harberts or rape Vanessa Croft. He might even be able to document that FDLE's "confidential, reliable informant" is J. J. Hall.

As it is, all Spaziano can do is provide this court with news clips from a newspaper that thinks he should be killed in secret and killed as soon as possible.

Respectfully submitted,
Michael A. Mello
For Joseph R. Spaziano

September 3, 1995
East Providence, Rhode Island
(18 days to execution)

Family reunion. At dusk, we hit the road for Vermont.

September 4, 1995
Wilder, Vermont
(17 days to execution)

My house was a wreck. Life under death warrant tends to do that. While my mother was in the shower, Deanna and I frantically cleaned piles of paper from the dining room table. Table by table, room by room.

All of this mess—the mess of a desperately underresourced lawyer or no lawyer at all for a man scheduled to die in three weeks—was hauntingly familiar to Mark Olive and me. It was just this sort of counsel crisis that led the Florida legislature to create CCR in 1985. In 1985, a key player had been Sandy D'Alemberte. He understood the realities of the counsel crisis. Olive persuaded D'Alemberte to file an amicus curiae brief in Joe's case, asking for a stay until the confusion over counsel could be resolved.

D'Alemberte wanted the brief to be filed on behalf of ten prominent lawyers and to be filed in the Florida Supreme Court, and he wanted to ask the justices for a moratorium on Florida executions until resolution of the counsel crisis precipitated by the sudden death of VLRC. I was told that he understood that "the reason Mike was going off the deep end is he doesn't have any support. I've been there before, on the edge; had I not had the support, I'd have fallen through the cracks." The brief would be ready by 10:00 A.M. on Thursday, September 7.

September 5, 1995
Wilder, Vermont
(16 days to execution)

Tuesday. I teach twice on Tuesdays, and my second class gets out about 6:00 P.M. Before and after class is a tug of war between class preparation and student meetings.

At the end of the day, the Florida Supreme Court called. The justices had tentatively scheduled oral argument in Joe's case in two days, on September 7, at 2:00 P.M., in Tallahassee. Be there.

This was a good sign, the first good sign in Joe's case since Governor Chiles signed Joe's fifth warrant on August 24. On such short notice, the plane tickets would be at their most expensive; I'd need to max out my credit cards, but what the hell? Deanna booked the tickets and reserved a rental car in Jacksonville and a hotel room in Tallahassee. Basically, we would spend Wednesday getting from Vermont to Tallahassee. I'd spend Wednesday night and Thursday until 2:00 preparing for the oral argument.

But—oral argument on *what*? Stay of execution? Appointment of counsel? New trial? The court wasn't saying. "It's on all pending motions before the court; the justices just said, 'Set it up,'" I was told.

When Joe called that evening, his spirits soared when he heard that the Florida Supreme Court wanted oral argument. Don't get your hopes up, Joe, *please* don't get your hopes up. This probably means nothing.

But Joe was on fire. "Can my mom and [niece] come to the argument? I'll tell my mom to bake some granola. My mom can put you and Deanna up." He asked if we could visit him in Starke during our trip to Florida. Sure. Friday, September 8, the day after the oral argument.

Joe's niece: "He's shaved his head again; he's just not going to let them do it. He keeps joking with the guards, 'Are *you* gonna be the one who shaves my leg?'"

Oral argument notes:

This governor has chosen to abdicate his clemency responsibilities.

This abdication has systemic consequences: It means that the clemency function upon which *Herrera* were based does not exist in Florida.

Herald editorial board meeting: Leave it to the courts. (fact question? Let me depose Chiles)

This court can't force Chiles to do his job. But it can—and must—take Chiles's abdication into account in deciding whether *you* will choose to exercise U.S. discretion not to apply procedural bars to preclude evidence of innocence.

September 6, 1995
Tallahassee, Florida
(15 days to execution)

Of course, we ran late. Mark Olive faxed a draft of D'Alemberte's amicus brief. The prison bureaucracy ground forward to schedule Joe for a visit with Deanna and me on Friday, September 8.

Lori Rozsa called, sounding relieved. She, Warren Holmes, and Tony Proscio had met with Tony DiLisio in a conference room at the Pensacola airport (Tony had been accompanied by his lawyer during the meeting). Actually, it wasn't a meeting, it was a grilling, with Holmes playing the grand inquisitor role. Holmes put DiLisio through the third degree, and he passed with flying colors. "Warren walked away from Tony, firm that Tony is telling the truth now. Warren played the tough cop and leaned on him very hard." Proscio's description was similar: "Warren was merciless with Tony yesterday. Tony was rock solid. Warren insulted him, tried to lead him on . . . but Tony was solid."

The phone was ringing behind us as Deanna, my mother, and I left for the West Lebanon, New Hampshire, airport. The airline held the eighteen-seat plane until we arrived. The Philadelphia airport was stacked up, so we landed late; Deanna and I had to dash to make our connecting flight to Jacksonville and my mother had to dash to make her connection to D.C. And when our flight concluded in Jacksonville, I realized I'd forgotten the suitcase with my dress shirts and ties. Of course, I'd worn a suit and a nice dress shirt (no tie) for the plane trip from Vermont to Florida; I could wear this flying shirt for the oral argument, but I really didn't want to appear before the justices in a wrinkled shirt that smelled like an armpit.

No problem. The argument wasn't until 2:00 P.M. tomorrow, which left plenty of time to find a department store and buy a new dress shirt.

The problem was that the airline seemed to have lost the suitcase containing all my toiletries and reserve supplies of my prescription drugs. Deanna and I stood at the baggage claim conveyor belts, watching the other passengers on our flight picking up their bags. Then the awkward, awful, sinking moment when the conveyor belts stop with a buzz and a grinding of gears, and you look over the few orphan bags remaining to be claimed and, even though "many bags look alike," none of these bags looks remotely like the bag you're waiting for.

Deanna and I decided to split up. She would find the airline's baggage claims office and fill out the requisite paperwork while I located the discount rental car place and filled out *that* requisite paperwork. On our respective missions, Deanna succeeded and I failed. It turned out that United Airlines hadn't really lost our bag. As Deanna was waiting in line at the baggage claim place, an airline employee came sprinting in with our wayward bag. It had fallen off of the conveyor belt from the plane.

Meanwhile, the rental car office was nowhere to be found. Eventually, I learned that all the car rental offices had been moved out of the airport terminal, and a helpful cop told me where to catch the right shuttle. By the time I met Deanna at the appointed rendevous point, we were both stressed and exhausted. But the shuttle arrived quickly, and soon we had rented a car and were on the road.

Deanna drove the two and a half hours from Jacksonville to Tallahassee. At the hotel, we were greeted by two dozen messages—and the final version of D'Alemberte's amicus brief, which was perfect.

The only calls I returned were to Mark Olive and Lori Rozsa. Rozsa described the final days of VLRC: "It's such a sad place now. They're boxing up files; can't make long-distance phone calls or use FedEx. The Florida Supreme Court should visit *there* if they doubt you on this." I thought the *Herald* was in a unique position to write about how crippling the Volunteer Lawyers Resource Center's demise had been to my ability to represent Joe effectively. The *Herald* itself was doing a thorough investigation, but an innocent man on death row ought to have his *own* investigator, and not be forced to rely on the efforts of newspaper reporters. Or so I argued to Lori, anyway.

We had not arrived at the hotel until 11:45 P.M., and by the time we got settled, it was around 1:00 in the morning. I was far too keyed up to sleep, so instead I worked on organizing my files for the oral argument.

It was very weird, but the oral argument notes I'd made ten years earlier, during Joe's first death warrant, were still usable. We'd all been here before: Joe, the Florida Supreme Court, and I. In 1985 the facts weren't quite the same (we didn't have Tony DiLisio's recantation then), but all of my legal arguments even then were different ways of saying the same simple matter of fact: Joe didn't do it. Now, as then, Joe was under death warrant. Now, as then, Florida was in the midst of a counsel crisis.

Ever since I'd heard Richard Nixon and Spiro Agnew, in the early 1970s—when I was in high school—complaining on TV about those "liberal federal judges," I'd wanted to meet those judges. During my year clerking for Judge Vance, 1982–83, there were a few of them left on the federal bench; Judge Frank M. Johnson was one, and Judge Vance himself was another.

By the time I decided not to take "Crazy Joe" Spaziano's case into federal court, Judge Vance was dead and Judge Johnson was semi-retired—replaced by Ed Carnes. By then the Reagan/Bush-appointed federal judiciary in the South was openly hostile to the constitutional claims raised by death row prisoners, and hostile as well to the defense lawyers trying to raise those claims. The federal judges were sick of us and sicker of our clients. In other words, they were just like the state court judges during the time I was a capital public defender in Florida.

In my experience, my prosecutorial opponents—the lawyers who represented the state—were mostly irrelevant. With a few notable exceptions, such prosecutors were, by and large, lazy and not too bright. Their responses to the constitutional claims that my colleagues and I raised tended to be predictable boilerplate: "This argument should have been raised earlier—at trial, on the first appeal, or whenever." Such legal and procedural technicalities usually formed the bulk of my opponents' arguments, regardless of whether the procedural rules being invoked by the prosecutors actually applied to the case at hand. Their attitude seemed to be: "The procedural arguments are in the word processor. Might as well raise them. What the hell."

So, as I wrote my legal arguments for the Florida Supreme Court justices and prepared to make those arguments orally, I virtually ignored the counterarguments that had been raised by opposing counsel,

Assistant State Attorney General Margene Roper. Roper would argue that Spaziano is in the wrong court; he should have filed in the trial court, and he should have done it a long time ago. But Roper didn't matter. She was background noise. She wouldn't be my adversary on September 7, 1995. My real adversaries would be the seven justices of the Florida Supreme Court. They would be looking for *any* credible reason to deny a stay of execution and avoid looking at Spaziano's new evidence of innocence. The path of least resistance for the justices to follow was that argued by the prosecutor: multiple layers of procedural rules prevented the court from considering the new evidence of innocence. The easy path would be to invoke the procedural technicalities and let Spaziano die for his crimes.

My job was to persuade the justices—or, more precisely, a majority of four justices—that the path of least resistance would be to stay the execution and give me the time and resources necessary to *prove* Joe's innocence in an evidentiary hearing before the trial court. The only way to do that successfully, I was convinced, was to show the justices that this was a *real* case of total factual innocence, old-fashioned innocence. Joe Spaziano didn't commit the crime. He didn't do it. They got the wrong guy. Period. The case was subject to *very* reasonable doubt, based on the new evidence.

I knew it would be a tough sell, and I also knew that the reasons this was so were not entirely the court's fault. Over the years, the U.S. Supreme Court, as well as the Florida Supreme Court, had applied procedural default rules with a vengeance in capital cases. If the constitutional claim—a violation of the *Miranda v. Arizona* rule, for instance—wasn't raised in exactly the right way and at exactly the right time by the trial lawyer, then it was waived and couldn't be raised later. However, there was an exception to these procedural default rules: if the alleged constitutional error (the *Miranda* violation, say) might have caused the conviction of a *factually innocent person,* then the constitutional error *could* be raised and considered later on, notwithstanding the procedural default at trial.

What this means, as a practical matter in the real world of capital postconviction litigation, is that claims of "factual innocence" are raised all the time. They have to be—it is the only way around the procedural default rules. Inevitably, however, the courts, bombarded with (mostly nonmeritorious) claims of "factual innocence" in capital case after capital case, have begun to view such claims with an increasingly jaundiced and skeptical eye. The trick in Joe's case would be to snap the justices out of it, to get their attention, and to persuade them that *this* innocence claim, unlike most such claims they hear, is a *real* innocence claim. This is the needle in the haystack. This isn't just another death row lawyer crying wolf to avoid the court's rules on procedural default.

All of this had little to do with law and everything to do with the art of lawyering. It's why death warrant litigation has been likened to chess and to war. Patience is key. Start out slow. Bold steps taken prematurely are bound to fail. As in the chess opening, develop pieces slowly and systematically. Build a solid center. Don't move a piece more than once. Don't take your queen out too early. Patience is crucial. So is knowing your enemy—in this case, knowing the seven men who, at this particular moment in American history, sat on the Florida Supreme Court.

Forever, I had kept a current photo of the Florida justices within easy reach of my writing desk. In the months since I'd resumed my role as Joe's lawyer, I'd looked at that photo two dozen times.

"The Civil War and the First World War, those were the last wars where the general of one side kept his opposite's portrait in his tent," says the protagonist in Allan Gurganus's novel *Oldest Living Confederate Widow Tells All*. When a general "mapped strategy—or even when just at supper by his lonesome, he turned up his oil lamp—he studied the sly and worthy features of his counterpart. When your enemy—like ours nowadays—ceases having a nose, two eyes, one mouth, then you got troubles. You're up against a dervish and a ghost, an evil empire. Me, in my time, us in our time—we were lucky. We knew the shoe size of the opposition."

What would it take to save Joe Spaziano's life tomorrow? Four votes. Four men.

12

Checkmate

I sinned first for justice.

William Faulkner, The Unvanquished, *1938*

It is well that war is so terrible. Otherwise we might grow too fond of it.

Robert E. Lee, following the battle of Fredericksburg,
December 1862

September 7, 1995
Tallahassee, Florida
(14 days to execution)

I slipped into bed around 3:00 A.M. the morning of the argument. Not to sleep, because I knew that would be impossible—just to rest my eyes and to give Deanna some respite from the desk lamp and my pacing.

The next thing I remember was Deanna's soft return to the hotel room at around 8:30 A.M. She'd awoken at first light and taken on the mission of locating and purchasing a dress shirt and tie for me to wear during the oral argument. From the front desk she'd gotten directions to the nearest strip mall where the stores might open early and might take American Express—which was essential because we'd maxed out all our other credit cards getting to Tallahassee. The first store she encountered at the mall was a Sears—it was open and it took American Express. Deanna grabbed a white dress shirt and a handful of ties, as well as some jewelry for herself. (The jewelry she had planned to wear was in the shirt-and-tie suitcase I'd left in my Wilder, Vermont, living room.)

At 9:30, Joe's case files arrived via FedEx—good news. The bad news arrived later, as I sat in a trance at the hotel desk, looking at argument notes I had written a decade earlier and memorized during the night. Sandy D'Alemberte would be unable to argue on behalf of the amici. It was too late to even think about finding a replacement.

We had planned that D'Alemberte would handle ten minutes of the thirty-minute argument. So, a friend suggested, I should let those ten minutes pass in silence—to underscore D'Alemberte's absence: "Ten minutes of silence in court can be a very long time and be very powerful. . . . Let Sandy's brief roll over the justices like a fog: here's a group of lawyers, people the court knows, saying that what's happening to Spaziano and Mello is wrong." An unconventional idea, perhaps a bit too much so. The justices were likely already disconcerted by our unconventional litigation strategy—filing a motion for rehearing of a motion decided ten years previously. I had to prepare to argue for those ten minutes.

So I continued my preparation. I actually preferred to continue scanning my notes, as this allowed me to delay getting into my suit. I hate suits, and I avoid having to put one on until absolutely necessary. Eventually, Deanna casually mentioned that I might hit the shower soon. As she recalls: "You looked at me, kind of dazed, and said, 'Huh?' I stopped ironing and said, 'You *do* realize it's twenty to one, don't you?' [She meant the time, not my chances of winning a stay of Joe's execution.] You visibly paled. Your jaw dropped. Your eyes bugged out. You said, 'I thought it was only around eleven.' You panicked. Then I panicked. I don't remember anything after that."

I remember, though. I remember the fastest shave and shower of my life. And the matter of the tie.

Maybe it's a corollary to my fear of suits, but I have never learned how to tie a tie. As a public defender and a law school professor, I have never needed to wear ties daily to work. My father had neatly tied the half dozen ties I own, and they lived in that state in my clothes closet, awaiting those few times a year when I couldn't avoid wearing a tie. Two of those ready-to-wear ties were sitting in the bag I'd left in Vermont.

Using a diagram and trying to squelch our rising panic over the time, Deanna succeeded in tying the tie. By this time, we had only forty-five minutes until the oral argument was scheduled to begin. As

Deanna had to finish readying herself, we decided to meet at the court-house. I grabbed my notes and a few files, dashed out of the hotel, and bought the local newspapers from a street vendor as I hailed a taxicab. During the short drive to the courthouse, I read terrific pieces by Lori Rozsa and Tony Proscio in the *Miami Herald*.

At the courthouse, I signed in at the clerk's office, down the hall from the majestic rotunda that is the building's most commanding fea-ture. I paid my respects to Mr. Sid White, who had been clerk of the Florida Supreme Court since I was in elementary school. Mr. White is quiet dignity and respect personified, which is to say that, in my eyes, he is the Florida Supreme Court personified. Justices and law clerks came and went, but Sid White was my constant.

Tanya Carroll, the court's longtime "death clerk," told me that *Spaziano* was the sole case on the court's oral argument docket for the day. The format would be as follows: I would argue for twenty min-utes, the prosecution would argue for thirty minutes, and then I would have ten minutes to address the prosecution's arguments. Of course, these time limits applied only to the lawyers. The justices had all the time they wanted; they could keep us answering questions all day and night. I actually hoped that they would. It's always a good sign when the justices keep you arguing beyond your allotted time, because it in-dicates that they're interested in the claims you are trying to persuade them to accept.

After all our panic, I had twenty-five minutes until the court session began, so I went outside for a few quick cigarettes. I stayed near the outskirts of the courthouse's majestic marble steps, trying to remain unobtrusive and unseen. I'm not much for casual chitchat at any time, and at this time in particular I wanted to be alone with my Camels and my thoughts.

All of my Florida Supreme Court oral arguments have unnerved and frightened me, but the argument that would commence in less than fifteen minutes was off the charts. At least that's what my stom-ach was telling me. This would almost certainly be my last chance to argue, in person and before the ultimate justices, for a stay of execu-tion based on Joe Spaziano's innocence. In any event, this would be my last capital case. So this would be my last argument in my last case, and I would be arguing to preserve the life of a very dear friend who would die two weeks hence if I failed.

The mortal stakes for Joe didn't completely displace my awareness of my own personal and professional stakes in the argument. The justices might command me to do something that I knew my conscience forbade—to participate in an evidentiary hearing under death warrant, or to turn Joe's case files over to CCR, a law firm that Joe and I believed had a conflict of interest that precluded it from representing Joe.

I did not think it likely that the justices would dictate that I do either of those things, not during the oral argument, anyway. But I knew that if they did I could not comply, and I would have to tell that truth to the court. In any event, I would be in contempt of Florida's highest court, and would probably face immediate incarceration for an indefinite period of time, until I reversed my decision to willfully disobey the court's mandates. (A former client, Elizabeth Morgan, had been jailed for two years for civil contempt.)

This was not how I'd planned to end my career as a capital postconviction lawyer—being removed in handcuffs from the courtroom in which I had felt honored to appear more often than any other. But it was a possibility for which I needed to prepare. Thus I had a bail bondsman on standby. And, for the oral argument, I had my Florida Bar card out of its plastic compartment in my wallet—ready to give to the marshal when I resigned from the bar, which I planned to do if the justices ordered me to do something I couldn't do (such as show up and render effective assistance of counsel at an evidentiary hearing under death warrant). If necessary, Deanna would get Joe's files to the *Miami Herald*. Just in case.

About five minutes before the argument, I spread my files over the defense counsel's table, located to the right as I faced the bench upon which the seven justices would sit. The state's table was to the left. In between was a podium equipped with a light system. It shines a green light until you have two minutes left to argue, when the green is replaced by a yellow warning light. When the light turns red, that means shut up and sit down, even if you haven't finished your argument.

Actually, it's not "your" oral argument, it's the court's, and an appellate advocate must be prepared for *anything* the justices ask, to guide them down any path they wish to travel: legal questions concerning your interpretation of prior decisions; factual questions about the record in the case; questions regarding the policy implications for other capital cases affected by the judges' ruling in your case.

Still, the more questions from the court, the better. Silent arguments are the worst kind: I stand at the podium, delivering my aria, while the justices sit impassively, saying nothing and thinking God knows what. I can't address their concerns if they don't reveal them. Far better for the justices to grill me, to put me through the cross-examination wringer from hell.

So, when the justices emerged from behind the black curtain to assume the bench and I walked to the podium, I carried the notes and the outline I had prepared in 1985 and fine-tuned the previous night. If need be, I would give a speech. But I hoped that the justices would define the course of the argument through their lines of questioning. I hoped it would be a "hot bench" argument, as we say in the capital appeals biz.

It was a hot bench. Blowtorch hot. The following transcript presents the argument nearly verbatim:

BAILIFF: Ladies and gentlemen, the Florida Supreme Court. Please be seated.

THE CHIEF JUSTICE: Good afternoon. The only case on the docket is *Spaziano v. State*. Mr. Mello, you may proceed.

MELLO: Mr. Chief Justice. May it please the court. My name is Michael Mello from South Royalton, Vermont, and it is my honor, my great honor, to be representing Joseph Robert Spaziano in the proceedings before this court. There are a number of motions pending before the court and I'm not certain whether there are specific motions or specific aspects of specific motions that the court would like me to focus on but it seems to me that a large amount of paper pending before the court right now essentially boils down to four basic points. First and foremost, Joseph Robert Spaziano is innocent of the events for which he was sentenced to death 19½ years ago and for which he is scheduled to be executed two weeks from today. That was my position before this court almost exactly 10 years ago when I argued in favor of a stay of execution on Spaziano's first death warrant signed by then Governor Bob Graham. Spaziano is innocent, factually innocent, and I want to be very clear about that. All of the other factual issues in this case, all of the legal issues in this case, everything I have to say of importance about this case boils down, in my opinion, to that one basic fact. Second, if, I believe that if I had an opportunity to prove Spaziano's innocence before a jury, he would be acquitted. All I am asking for at bottom before this court right now is a stay of execution and the provision of resources to let me do my job as a capital defense lawyer. I want an opportunity to prove it to a jury. The State has been arguing on the basis of the record until fairly recently and within the past few weeks on the basis of supersecret information that supposedly reliable witnesses supposedly told FDLE [the Florida Department of Law Enforcement] that supposedly accurately reported it to the governor that they have yet more evidence of this crime and they have attempted to link Spaziano to other crimes. Well, if they've got the evidence, if it's so great, let them present it to a jury. If they wanta convict him, if they wanta kill him, let them do it the old fashioned way. What I'm asking for at bottom is a jury. Give me a jury. If they wanta kill him [noise interference].

THE COURT: As I view this, the question here at the moment is Mr. DiLisio's alleged recantations of his testimony which . . . Your contention is that this was the sole evidence upon which his conviction was based. Would not the proper remedy be at this junction to send this matter to the trial court to conduct a hearing to determine whether or not Mr. DiLisio perjured himself and gave false testimony at the original trial and then if the trial judge so found, the trial judge would then proceed to grant you that new trial in front of a jury. Now how can we as a court bypass the judge's hearing on this particular matter and just say you can have the jury?

MELLO: A couple of points, if I may. First, if the court is willing to grant a stay and remand the case to the trial court with directions that I file a 3.850 motion [in the state trial court] in this case, I will do so. And I will do so as quickly as possible. The main problem before this court right now and when we go back to the trial court, if we go back to the trial court, is I don't have an investigator. I, at this point, and since this most recent death warrant was signed, VLRC [Volunteer Lawyers Resource Center], VLRC, has ceased to exist, and I have been and Spaziano has been totally reliant upon the good graces and extraordinarily extensive work conducted by the investigative reporters at the *Miami Herald*. They've done a wonderful job, and I am incredibly grateful to them and Joe Spaziano is incredibly grateful to them, but I would really like to be able to do my own investigation, not just of Tony DiLisio's recantation. That, I think—Tony DiLisio's recantation, it seems to me, is a fairly good metaphor of everything else that's wrong with this case. When I was arguing . . .

THE COURT: . . . Has he recanted under oath?

MELLO: Yes sir, he has. As I understand, that he was under oath when FDLE interrogated him last June. He was not placed under oath in the version of the video tape of that interrogation that I have, which is sort of the other huge lurking problem in this case. If FDLE had its way, if Governor Chiles had his way, I would not have that video tape. I would have had to have answered your question . . .

THE COURT: . . . You do not have, nor have you filed with this court the matter that he has recanted his testimony under oath, do you? That is not before the court.

MELLO: Oh, I believe that is before the court. That's before the court in my motion to reopen the direct appeal to reconsider the sufficiency of the evidence point and it's before the court . . .

THE COURT: . . . and I'm saying that you don't have an affidavit from him signed by him. . . .

MELLO: That's correct.

THE COURT: Under oath . . .

MELLO: That's correct.

THE COURT: Recanting his testimony?

MELLO: That's correct. I do not have that affidavit and I cannot get that affidavit because he lives in Pensacola, is represented by counsel; I live in Vermont and Tony DiLisio doesn't like to sign things. I have the next best thing, it seems to me. What I have is a video tape or a portion of a video tape. I am now no longer certain that the version of the video tape that came into my possession, no thanks to the government, and that I provided to this court was in fact the full video tape. But according to the video tape that I have, Tony DiLisio is very, very clear and very, very emphatic that the critical, the weight-bearing beam of his testimony at trial was not true. He said that under oath. He said that to the police, which, it seems to me, is considerably more reliable than him saying it to me or signing . . .

THE COURT: . . . Did he also say that he would not sign anything to investigators that had come to him asking him to sign something?

MELLO: So far as I know, no investigator of mine has asked him to sign something. I understand . . .

THE COURT: Who's the investigator called Hummel [sic]?

MELLO: That's a CCR investigator. And according to the video tape, Mike Hummel and another CCR investigator did attempt to get Mr. DiLisio to sign an affidavit. I've never seen a copy of that affidavit. I don't know what was in the affidavit. I don't know that that affidavit exists. . . .

THE COURT: Any statement by Mr. DiLisio has under oath said that he committed perjury at the original trial. Where did he do that under oath?

MELLO: I don't think I said that he said under oath that he committed perjury at the original trial. He doesn't use the word perjury. What he has done and what he did under oath—assuming that . . .

THE COURT: When was it that he was placed under oath and gave contradictory testimony?

MELLO: I assume that he was placed under oath when FDLE interrogated him. That fact is not reflected on the version of the video tape—the bootlegged version of the video tape that I was able to get on my own, but I understand, although not from first hand knowledge, that when Florida law enforcement take formal video taped depositions of witnesses, and especially this witness, that they would have placed him under oath. His understanding was that he was speaking under oath. And when I alluded to his attorney that I would very much like a signed statement from Tony DiLisio just to have something very clear nailed down without any of the questions that had been raised by—about the veracity of the video tape, whether he was under oath, he was not enthusiastic about that idea. And the reason she said her client wasn't enthusiastic about the idea was because he said, "I've already said that under oath. I said that to the police under oath. I said it in the FDLE video tape and I said it very clear, very emphatically in the FDLE video tape." Now when I had that conversation with Kelly McGraw, with Tony DiLisio's lawyer, I hadn't—I didn't have a copy of the video tape. All I had was Dexter Douglass being quoted in the *Miami Herald* as saying, "There is no recantation on this video tape. Tony DiLisio just says he doesn't remember anything before his 21st birthday." And based on those representations, which I now know were willful misrepresentations of the truth, I tried to get Tony DiLisio to sign an affidavit. But once I got a hold of the video tape and learned that Tony DiLisio was telling the truth about the video tape—that Kelly McGraw, his lawyer, was telling the truth about what was on the video tape, that the governor's office was not, I didn't pursue the affidavit route.

THE COURT: Let me ask you too—if you had an investigator, do you think that DiLisio would talk to that investigator?

MELLO: Yes.

THE COURT: On what do you base that?

MELLO: Conversations that I have had with his attorney. Conversations—one conversation that I had directly with him at his attorneys' behest, a conversation that I was very squeamish about doing because I knew that he was represented by counsel, but he very much wants to tell the truth in this case.

THE COURT: Specifically, how are you being handicapped by not having an investigator at this point? I know, as a general thing, you would like for him to do, you know, do what investigators do, but can you be any more specific than that?

MELLO: I sure can. According to the *Miami Herald* yesterday, and the reason I keep referring to newspaper articles here is because that's my only source of information about the kind of investigation that I would like my investigator to be able to do. According to the *Miami Herald* yesterday, there is now some serious question about whether the state even identified the right remains. The state's theory at trial, and I tagged two or three dozen references in the trial transcript to this, the Altamonte dump being a dumping ground for girls. This is where the Outlaws dumped girls, and the state at least raised the very strong inference at trial that the other identified body was female as was Laura Lynn Harberts's remains. Well, it now turns out that the state knows now or may well know now, and might well have known then, that the other body was not female, that the other body was male, which kind of blows their whole scenario as fanciful, as it always seemed to me it was, of this being an Outlaw dumping ground for girls. I would like to get a forensic anthropologist in to look at those bones. I've got someone at Emory University who would love to do it if I can pay his expenses, which I can't. That's one point. I mean that . . .

THE COURT: I will pick up all your . . .

THE COURT: . . . I don't want to cut you off, go ahead . . .

MELLO: The investigation point is the critical one to me. And I would—I mean, I could go on for two or three hours about the investigation I want to do, and this is not fishing expedition stuff; this is very specific avenues of investigation that Steve Gustaff [sic], my investigator at VLRC, was working on actively when he got his walking papers and VLRC shut down.

THE COURT: Okay, let me ask you. Why—kind of a follow-up to this question—why didn't you file a 3.850 back in January instead of filing with us a motion to reopen a rehearing that was closed 10 years ago?

MELLO: A couple of reasons, one of which relates to Justice Shaw's question about resources. I didn't have the resources to put together . . .

THE COURT: . . . But of course you had the volunteer people then . . .

MELLO: They were working on the case then along with all their other cases. No one expected a death warrant to be signed, at least no one that I was talking to expected a death warrant to be signed when it was last May, and certainly no one expected a death warrant to be signed . . .

THE COURT: . . . How can you say that in the context of this particular case cause it's been here, I think, eight times, and there was a proceeding and an extensive opinion written by the Eleventh Circuit Court of Appeals and released last October. The United States Supreme Court denied cert. on that appeal in January. There was no other proceeding pending, and given those total circumstances, you had to accept that this was a primary case in which a death warrant would be signed.

MELLO: I made the mistake in January, and I have made the mistake as recently as a few weeks ago, of believing the information I was getting from the governor's office. That's why I—that was the source of the information. The information was wrong; it was a mistake for me to rely on it; if I would have—the main point here, it seems to me, is that if I messed up in not filing this as a 3.850, in not filing it in January, please don't take that out on my client.

THE COURT: What was the second reason that you didn't file . . .

MELLO: The second reason, and this is the reason that I feel a little more comfortable about than the first reason—the second reason was precisely because this case had been before this court so many times in the past, and I didn't want to file a new lawsuit, because what I was really trying to get the court to do, substantively in the papers itself, in the pleadings themselves, was to get the court to take another look at the direct appeal judgment, the sufficiency of the evidence judgment, which was based on Tony DiLisio's supposed trip to the dump with Joe Spaziano. I mean, that's not me—that's the prosecutor, that's every prosecutor up until the most recent ones. And since that was the basis— I mean, since that's really what the pleading was about, I decided to call a . . .

THE COURT: Let me ask you one other question. You make reference to conflict with CCR. What's this conflict?

MELLO: The conflict with CCR is as follows: In the FDLE video tape, Tony DiLisio accuses CCR's investigators, Mike Hummel and one of his colleagues, of essentially trying to strong-arm him into signing an affidavit that he didn't wanta sign. My understanding of the Florida Ethics Rules and of the Florida statutes on obstruction of justice and witness tampering is that those allegations, if true, and I underscore *if true,* would place Office of Capital Collateral Representative's interests in defending itself against those charges in a position directly conflicting with the position taken by the state's only real witness against their client at trial who has now recanted. CCR would be placed in the position of having to argue, and I think CCR would be in the position of having to argue when Tony DiLisio did the video tape with FDLE, he was telling the truth when he disavowed his testimony about the trip to the dump with Joe, but he really is not credible when he talked about CCR. And in fact, I understand that after—soon after FDLE's interrogation of DiLisio, FDLE went back and talked to CCR and asked them, you know, essentially, what's all this about? And it seems to me that the only ethical course of action that CCR could have done at that point, since CCR at that time still represented Joe Spaziano, was to show the FDLE the door and not to answer their questions.

THE COURT: Let me ask you this—on the matter of this particular case—DiLisio, by the recantation of testimony under oath, the testimony at trial was not the only testimony that he gave under oath. Am I correct?

MELLO: You are correct.

THE COURT: In other words, he gave testimony under oath in deposition and assuming he gave testimony under oath before a grand jury? . . .

MELLO: Yes. Grand jury, I don't know about the deposition I have. Yes sir.

THE COURT: Now, the other during the course of the case, there were two witnesses that testified that Spaziano had a relationship with the victim. Am I correct? Both her roommate and the roommate's boyfriend . . .

MELLO: Not that Spaziano had a relationship with the victim, but that Spaziano . . . I suppose it depends on how one defines relationship, but, supposedly, Spaziano had come to the apartment looking for her. I mean, that was . . .

THE COURT: . . . they both identified him at the trial, did they not?

MELLO: Well, true, but their identifications, and this did come out at trial, their identifications are pretty shaky. Their identifications were that they identified Joe Spaziano by looking at him through translucent doors, and I'm not sure how they . . .

THE COURT: . . . what you're challenging, that particular testimony at this stage, now, in addition, and this was at the time just before she disappeared. Correct?

MELLO: Correct.

THE COURT: And also at the time, at that particular time, another witness testified that Spaziano took him out to the dump together with another individual in his pickup truck.

MELLO: Took them out to the dump area to look for his stash— for his stash of marijuana.

THE COURT: Yeah, well, and Spaziano and the other individual said, "Stay there." But this was at a time, was it not, at the dump where the bodies would have been there.

MELLO: Maybe, maybe not. Those witnesses, if memory serves, and I can double check the record when I sit down, my memory of the record is that those witnesses were not real clear on the time frame. But even if those witnesses are right, all that proves is that Joe Spaziano came to—even if you believe them, and I suggest that neither of them are believable, but even if you do believe them, all they show is that Joe Spaziano had gone out to the dump area.

THE COURT: Well, basically, none of these witnesses had any relation—the witness that went out with Spaziano had no relationship with the roommate and her boyfriend?

MELLO: Right. Well, I think . . .

THE COURT: Each of these witnesses had to be wrong.

MELLO: I think that they did have a relationship. I think all of the state's witnesses in this case had a relationship, and I think that relationship is Detective George Abbgy who was desperate to nail the Outlaws. And I think he is the one who is responsible for what happened to Tony DiLisio and, to the extent that there are questions about the credibility of other witnesses and I believe that there are substantial questions, that's the common link. That's the common thread, it seems to me.

THE COURT: . . . It just answered that one question.

THE COURT: The question before you sit down, as is obvious the proceedings before us have taken a rather free form. This is the way that you have approached this case with the court, and it is obviously causing us considerable difficulty with the pleadings that you filed, the various filings that you filed with the court. But a court concern that we have is whether or not this issue could have been or should have been properly raised in a post-conviction relief motion. Now, if it had been presented in that form, and now I'm talking about the recurring issue in all of your filings focusing on recanted testimony by the witness DiLisio. Now, if it had been filed in that form in a post-conviction motion, you would have had the burden of demonstrating, first of all, that it would have made a substantial difference in so far as the outcome of the case is concerned of trial. But also, you would have carried a burden of demonstrating some good reason why this couldn't have been presented before, why it wasn't discovered before or whatever. Now, and the state, you know, would have had an opportunity to respond to that. We've got a considerable problem with the free form here of the way that this is being presented. But can you demonstrate with what you have filed with the court so far, those ordinarily two essential ingredients that would entitle you to a hearing before a trial judge to resolve those two questions that I put? Have you made sufficient allegations or statements in the pleadings that you have filed that in any way might permit this court to treat that as the claim that you are seeking or at least one of the claims that you are seeking. One, that you have discovered new evidence that clearly would make a difference in the outcome, and two, that you couldn't reasonably have discovered that evidence before that time. Could you help us with that, and am I right, is that the recurring basis for your claim here and can and where in your pleadings, or how have you demonstrated that to the court at this time?

MELLO: I believe that we have demonstrated in the pleadings and in FDLE's sworn video tape that Spaziano is entitled to a new trial. If not entitled to an order of immediate release by vehicle of reopening this court's direct appeal judgment on . . .

THE COURT: What about those two ordinary hoops that you would have to jump through to entitle you to a hearing before a trial judge on this? . . . First of all the substantial new evidence, and secondly, why that hasn't been presented to the court before?

MELLO: I can't imagine new evidence more substantial than a disavowal of the critical testimony by the witness that the trial prosecutor . . .

THE COURT: . . . That has not been filed—there are over 1,500 pages over there that have been filed in this proceeding.

MELLO: The transcript's not there?

THE COURT: Well, no, just motions and things that have been filed in this proceeding, but you have not filed in this proceeding a statement by DiLisio that his testimony was false. . . .

MELLO: I believe. . . .

THE COURT: There is nothing—you do not have any statement, any affidavit or the transcript of his stating under oath his testimony was false. Isn't that correct?

MELLO: No sir, that's not correct. I do have a transcript of him stating under oath, and as I understand him to be stating under oath to the police. . . .

THE COURT: You have not filed in this record anything that says "I swear," an oath by DiLisio, correct?

MELLO: No, I don't have him saying under oath because I have, because FDLE, because the governor's office, because the attorney general has not given me their version of the video tape. Maybe it's on their version.

THE COURT: That doesn't mean that you can't go to him and get an affidavit from him, does it?

MELLO: I live in Vermont. He lives in Pensacola. He is difficult to deal with . . .

THE COURT: The investigators that have talked to him since at least June . . .

MELLO: They are *Miami Herald* investigators who have talked to him. They are newspaper investigators . . .

THE COURT: There are CCR investigators that talked to him . . .

MELLO: He wouldn't talk to CCR, and I am as curious as you are as to why that is. He gave an explanation in the video tape why he wouldn't talk to CCR, and if his explanation is right, it's a pretty good reason. I don't have an affidavit from him and if I have to have, in order to get a stay of execution, a signed affidavit from Tony DiLisio, I do not have that today.

THE COURT: Counsel, you are way over time, but that's because we asked you a lot of questions. I'm gonna give the state, if they need it, another five minutes in addition to their 20 minutes, and I'll give you a couple of minutes for rebuttal.

MELLO: Could I just address, literally in two seconds, your last point, . . .

THE COURT: The second prong, if you will.

MELLO: I have not set out in the papers why I was not able—why my investigators in the past were not able to turn Tony DiLisio around. I don't have a good explanation for that. My investigator tracked Tony DiLisio down to Vista, California, in 1985 before the first death warrant was signed, tried to get him to talk to him, and he wouldn't. Office of Capital Collateral Representative's investigator approached him twice earlier this year, tried to get him to talk to him, and he wouldn't. Lori Rozsa of the *Miami Herald* tracked him down in Pensacola. First he slammed the door in her face, second he slammed the door on her foot, third he let her in to his kitchen; they talked for three hours, and as they say, the rest is history. I don't know why my investigators weren't able to do that. I'm not gonna . . . my investigators aren't good enough investigators . . .

THE COURT: Have you set out in any of the pleadings that you have filed at this court what you just said, that is that your investigators or Office of Capital Collateral Representative's investigators have attempted to question DiLisio on this subject, but that prior to this interview by FDLE that he had refused to cooperate with the investigators? Is that in the pleadings?

MELLO: I am not sure whether it is in the pleadings in that form. I will write it up right now and file it. I mean, that's the case, and to the extent that I can make oral motions, please treat that as one. I mean, that's what happened, and I will write it up while the state is arguing.

Normally, during the prosecutor's argument, I would listen carefully and take notes for my rebuttal. Today, however, I'd promised the justices a motion setting out the twenty-year history of Joe's lawyers' attempts to convince Tony DiLisio to admit to his perjury at Joe's trial. So I wrote the motion while Assistant Attorney General Margene Roper argued that the state ought to be allowed to kill Joe on schedule. I didn't hear her argument until I listened to it later on audiotape.

In the interest of fairness, the following passage is printed verbatim from the transcript of that argument. If you want to skip over it, however, I can summarize the state's argument in one sentence: Mr. Mello is in the wrong forum. Her voice quivering with rage, Roper argued that the Florida Supreme Court should ignore Joe's newly discovered evidence of innocence because of procedural technicalities and that the governor (and she said it with a straight face!) would grant clemency if Joe was innocent. Anyway, here it is:

ROPER: May it please the court, my name is Margene Roper; I am an assistant attorney general, and I represent the State of Florida in this proceeding. For the past 20 years, Joseph Robert Spaziano has had fly-specking review from all the courts. His case was heard by the highest court in this nation, the United States Supreme Court; he has been before the circuit court and before this court at least six times in post-conviction proceedings. Spaziano recognizes in the out-of-time motion that has been filed in this case that at this point in time he is simply out of claims, and that clemency is the proper proceeding. He indicates in his motion to this court—he addresses the court mistakenly as the Board, referring to the Board of Clemency, and he states in the introduction to his out-of-time motion that he recognizes that the claim he has may not be of the magnitude to require a court to give him relief, and he urges the Board to take action. I would submit that the Executive Branch is the proper forum in such a case for Spaziano to have gained relief. As much as Spaziano may portray this as a gateway claim to some other claim, what he has is a claim under *Herrera v. Collins,* which is a free-standing claim of innocence. I would submit to the court that Spaziano has taken that claim to the proper forum and simply because he quarrels with the result, is not an issue that can revoke the jurisdiction of this court. I would submit to this court that, historically, clemency proceedings have been private and that is a sort fact that it's ignored to the benefit of defendants. I would point out to the court that clemency was the proper proceeding. Spaziano is out of claims, but if he does have something he again wants to take before the courts, he's certainly in the wrong forum.

THE COURT: What do you say to this rebuttal? A person . . . facing execution is days away from death, all of a sudden his counsel finding out that he's without resources. He has no investigator. He doesn't have a system . . . volunteer lawyer organization that he thought he was going to have at this stage. You recognize it gets rather stressful at this point in the scenario. Everything is being, every avenue is being explored, and here is a person days from his execution date finding himself in this position. Why shouldn't he be given a continuance to see whether he can get an investigator for one thing and, is there some constitutional problem with that, or you find this . . . ?

ROPER: First of all, I think it would be a mischaracterization to say that Mr. Mello and his representation of Spaziano was without resources. CCR has represented Spaziano for quite some time. At this point in time VLRC, it's my understanding, is not defunct. They will be in existence until September 30th. The warrant runs out in this case September 26th. They are still making efforts to get funds, which may happen at this point in time, and there's no reason he can't use their investigators. CCR has a statutory mandate to handle these sort of cases. There's absolutely no reason why CCR can't assist Mr. Mello in his efforts. Mr. Mello, at this point in time, seems to be the only one who is accusing CCR's investigator of wrongdoing. It's my understanding . . .

THE COURT: There's an allegation of conflict of interests even.

ROPER: From watching the tape, your honor, I recall Mr. DiLisio concluding at the end of the tape, after he had complained about the biker appearance of an investigator, I recall him concluding that since CCR had actually helped him, at the end of that tape I didn't see Mr. DiLisio filing any charges against CCR and I know of absolutely no impending charges against CCR. I think they are characterized as wrongdoings by Mr. Mello in an effort to get separate funding by this court when there are resources available to him.

THE COURT: Is the state conceding he's entitled to counsel at this stage in the proceeding?

ROPER: I think you have to look at several things, your honor. First of all, he is represented by counsel at this stage in the proceeding. Mr. Mello . . .

THE COURT: Is he entitled to counsel at this stage?

ROPER: I would submit at this stage of the proceeding, when Spaziano's counsel is recognized, that he has no justiciable claim to bring before the courts and has sought clemency as a last resort, that further funding based on speculation would be inappropriate.

THE COURT: But he's not . . .

THE COURT: Go ahead, I'm sorry.

THE COURT: He's claiming that he has an issue that if he can show to this court that that is a valid issue, that this court should then send this case back to the trial court to make a determination as to whether or not in fact the recantation of this particular witness is in fact valid and truthful and, if so, then that trial judge should grant a new trial before a new jury. Now, the fact of the matter is, if he raises that particular issue, how can you say that he doesn't have a viable issue before this particular court?

ROPER: Because, your honor, I know of no authority to recall a mandate in a case a decade old. He is simply in the wrong forum and he should be seeking funds and whatever other expenses he may need if he can not get them from VLRC and CCR, which is doubtful, from the appropriate forum, not this court.

THE COURT: What is the appropriate forum? He already says that he can't get it from CCR because of the conflict there, and he can't get it from this particular group which is going out of existence at the end of the month, and as I looked at the new pleading that I found here, I came out a few moments ago, and apparently they are telling him, you know, that they can't help him. So what is he to do at this particular juncture?

ROPER: I think CCR has a statutory mandate to help him and one would ask what sort of investigation he needs at this point in time. He certainly doesn't need an expert . . .

THE COURT: He needs an investigation apparently and what he is telling us here today, and somebody going out there to talk to Mr. DiLisio and see if Mr. DiLisio will sign an affidavit. He apparently also needs investigators to check out what the governor's office has in a file which has apparently not been released publicly and nobody knows what's in that file other than the governor's office and perhaps the *Orlando Sentinel*—know what's in that particular file. And what he's saying is, "I need the funds to go out there and to investigate this particular matter to check all of this out." Now what is this man to do? He said, "I don't have the money to do this."

ROPER: I would submit that, your honor, at this late date in the game, on the eve of execution, that investigation should have been complete at this time. DiLisio either is or is not Mr. Mello's witness. . . .

THE COURT: . . . on that point that investigation should have been done at this particular point. The fact of the matter is that the investigation apparently has not been done. Apparently there is an allegation out there, and a very strong one, that the prime witness against the defendant in this particular case has now recanted his testimony and has said that "I did not tell the truth at the original trial." As a matter of fact, on the video tape he is talking about which is part of his particular record, he does say that the first time I ever went to that dump where the bodies were found was when the police took me there. So we now have this particular information, and remember what the U.S. Supreme Court said, death is different, and it's up to us to decide in this particular court whether or not we say we're sorry Spaziano, you cannot get any relief from us despite the fact that there appears to be evidence out there that you may be entitled to a new trial, but we can't do any of that for you because counsel didn't file the proper 3.850 motion [in the trial court] or counsel doesn't have money to investigate this matter any further and there are no other resources for him to go to. What do we do as a court? Do we sit back and say, okay, you know, counsel, you didn't do the job you should have done. You don't have the money. You should have gotten the money way back when, so it's tough, Spaziano, we're gonna electrocute you because all these things should have been done before. Now is that the state's position?

ROPER: No, that is not the state's position.

THE COURT: What is the state's position?

ROPER: The state's position is that Spaziano's counsel is in the wrong forum. He should be making these requests in the right forum. It's debatable . . .

THE COURT: Are you saying that forum is clemency? When the fact of the matter is the governor is already investigating this. The governor has a report that the governor refuses to release to anybody, and therefore the governor signs and makes death warrant. What he's saying is, give me a little time, you know, I need, I've got the evidence here. I need people to go out and investigate this proof.

ROPER: I am saying that he is, number one, before the wrong court quarreling about the result of the proceeding he himself prompted.

THE COURT: Well, what court should he be in?

ROPER: He should be in the circuit court.

THE COURT: I'll grant you that he ought to file a 3.850 in the [trial] court. But are we to tell the defendant in this case, Spaziano, you know, your attorney should have filed a 3.850, and even though we're aware of this information, that, if true, would entitle you to a new trial, we're just going to ignore all that and we're gonna let your execution proceed because your attorney didn't file the right motion?

ROPER: No, I wouldn't characterize the situation as that at all, your honor. I would say that Mr. Mello and Spaziano are seeking a stay of execution and are seeking funding from this court to further pursue litigation in another court that they should come before this court with something beyond mere speculation, something that would satisfy the *Jones* criteria, something more with a witness who has demonstrated . . .

THE COURT: Isn't that mere speculation? Do you accept the fact that this is the state's position that this DiLisio, in fact, has said that his testimony that he gave at the time of trial was not true? Do you accept that fact?

ROPER: No, I do not accept that fact.

THE COURT: You don't accept that fact at all?

ROPER: Not from the video tape that Mr. . . . .

THE COURT: I didn't ask from the video tape. The state would accept that fact—whatever . . .

ROPER: No.

THE COURT: You don't accept the fact that he has recanted his testimony?

ROPER: No, your honor, I don't. And the reason I would say to the court that that is not the case here is if you view the video tape, what Mr. DiLisio says is that he went to the dump with police. Well, that was known at the time of trial that he went to the dump with police. He was specifically asked under oath in a deposition that the police took him there. Well, of course we know he went in a police car and that's what we believe . . .

THE COURT: He says on that video tape I watched yesterday, he says specifically that the first time he ever went to that dump was with the police.

ROPER: He says specifically, your honor, that he has no recall of going there with Spaziano. That does not mean that he never went there with Spaziano. He does not recant his deposition testimony where he answered the question of whether the police took him there with the response that I show them landmarks. There is no recantation of that whatsoever. What we have here is a witness who, when asked what the police said to him, said, I don't know what they said to me. He did not know what he said after he spoke to the police. He did not know what he said at trial. The investigators on the FDLE tape asked him, would you say that the police fed you details, and he said, well, I couldn't say that they fed me details, but what I said had to come from someplace. You basically have a man who, pursuant to Mr. Mello's proffered evidence, which would include newspaper clippings, had no memory of the time of the *Miami Herald* investigation, has, according to the *Miami Herald* articles [been] fighting battles with alcohol and has no memory of his life under the age of 21 at all other than getting married, you still have the same witness who has no memory. I would submit to the court that it takes more than speculation after 20 years of litigation and flyspecking review by court upon court to stay an execution and give funds for further investigation on the basis of such speculation.

THE COURT: Let me go back to the wrong forum position that you put forth. Is the state conceding that if—that there is anything that has been filed in this court, that it had been filed in the circuit court would be a basis upon which relief could be granted in the circuit court?

ROPER: No, your honor, the state is not conceding that at all and that would be an issue for the circuit court. I am saying if more funding is being requested then in the wrong forum in the first place, then something more has to be demonstrated than the fact that this man has no memory some 20 years later. As far as filing a 3.850, it isn't necessary for this court to remand because Spaziano and Mr. Mello don't need the permission of this court in the first place to file a 3.850, and the fact that they aren't filing a 3.850 is evidence that they have the kind of evidence that is not of a magnitude to prompt court action. It's the kind of evidence that is taken to clemency and, in this case, has been taken now unsuccessfully. Now nothing is preventing them from putting such a claim to the circuit court, but since they have not done so at this point in time and considering the type of evidence proffered to this court, I would submit that a stay is wholly inappropriate and further funding at this point is wholly inappropriate, and that would be an issue for another court. It would be wholly inappropriate to fund on the basis that one of the bodies found at the dump is now discovered to be a male corpse rather than a female. That's a totally collateral issue whether the Outlaws generically dumped all sorts of bodies there. The fact remains that at trial Laura Harberts was identified by dental records, and as Justice Overton pointed out, there is other evidence. Spaziano was identified as a travelling cook looking for the victim by her roommate and her roommate's boyfriend. He was identified as that person. He was also identified as similar to the man appearing in the translucent window that night. There are also many details linking Spaziano there. There's a testimony of Mike Coppick and Mike Ellis linking him specifically to the dump, and I don't think the court should also ignore the fact that a federal district court has found this hypnosis session not to be suggestive in the least. We have quite a bit of evidence here, and I would submit that on what counsel has shown today, this court should not grant a stay of execution and certainly shouldn't grant funding when VLRC is still in operation and CCR has a statutory mandate to assist in such situations. Does the court have any further questions?

THE COURT: All right. Mr. Mello, I said I'd give you two minutes?

MELLO: How long?

THE COURT: Two.

THE COURT: Mr. Mello, let me ask you a follow-up question. The precise motion upon which you are here today in asking this court to stay this execution is a motion for rehearing of the 1985 3.850 motion.

MELLO: Two motions form the underlying—the application for stay of execution is based on the motion to reopen the first 3.850 appeal, also . . .

THE COURT: Was that the first—I want to know precisely what you're asking, what you're saying this court has a basis to re-open. Is it that first 3.850, is it the 1985 3.850, or what basis are you travelling on?

MELLO: The first one—1985 was the first 3.850. It was filed in 1985 and under warrant and decided adversely to Spaziano by this court in 1986. Also, I am asking for a stay of execution on the basis of our motion to reopen the direct appeal judgment in this case, specifically the sufficiency of the evidence determination in the direct appeal determination in this case. If . . .

THE COURT: So that would be the first direct appeal?

MELLO: Yes sir. Where the court said for the first time the evidence in this case at trial is legally sufficient because of the trip to the dump. Because of the trip to the dump with Spaziano and because Spaziano supposedly led Mr. DiLisio to the dump. Now, the second aspect of that, I respectfully suggest, was simply a misreading of the record. But the trip to the dump is—the trip to the dump with Spaziano was the heart of the state's case, and as we have been saying all along—this is not just me talking—that is the trial prosecutor who knew his case better than Ms. Roper ever will. "If we can't get in the testimony of Tony DiLisio, we absolutely have no case here whatsoever. So either we're going to have it through Tony or we're not going to have it at all." "He's the most important witness in this case, and I would submit to you that if you don't believe Tony DiLisio, then find the defendant guilty in five minutes." "Not guilty," excuse me. Finally, as to the trip to the dump, [the] prosecutor . . . [said that] that's what makes his testimony more than just idle gossip. The trip to the dump. According to the prosecutor, what makes Tony DiLisio's testimony more than idle gossip, in the words of the prosecutor, is the trip to the dump. Take out the trip to the dump and all you're left with is Tony DiLisio talking about idle Outlaw braggadocio. Braggadocio that not even Tony DiLisio believed and that Judge McGregor at the original trial held inadmissible as a matter of law when Tony DiLisio's father tried to testify about it. Finally, one final quote: from the prosecutor . . . "He took Mr. DiLisio to the Altamonte dump to view the bodies and confirm his alarming statements. At the dump site Mr. DiLisio saw the bodies of two women." Thank you.

THE COURT: Mr. Mello, the matter of your representation, and I think that, first of all, this has been a CCR case all the way along, hasn't it?

MELLO: This was not a CCR case. This has been a CCR case from January 17 until August. It was a CCR case when I was at CCR. . . .

THE COURT: Was it a CCR case when you were at CCR?

MELLO: In 1985 and 1986.

THE COURT: Isn't CCR counsel of record in the proceedings before the 11th Circuit Court of Appeals in which they rendered a decision in October?

MELLO: No.

THE COURT: That's what it shows.

MELLO: It's a little complicated. I was appointed sole counsel to represent Spaziano in the 11th Circuit. I wrote the brief. I was not able to do the oral argument for health reasons. I prevailed upon Gail Anderson at CCR to do the oral argument. She did the oral argument. By the time Judge Carnes's opinion on the 11th Circuit was issued . . .

THE COURT: But this has been—this was a CCR case originally—I mean, right—you were counsel for CCR in this case . . .

MELLO: In 1985 and 1986 . . .

THE COURT: In this case in 1985 and 1986?

MELLO: Yes.

THE COURT: And it was CCR's investigator that was still trying to get DiLisio to change his testimony in the spring of this year?

MELLO: As recently as two weeks before the May war . . .

THE COURT: So basically, your representation is as a volunteer in this particular cause?

MELLO: That's correct. Well, it is as a volunteer because, and I want to be very clear about this to the court, because Spaziano has no other attorney. CCR cannot represent him because they

have a conflict of interest. In my judgment, and more importantly, in Spaziano's . . .

THE COURT: There has been no determination by this or any
other court that there is a conflict of interest that requires an appointment of additional counsel in this case, is it?

MELLO: There has never been a determination because my understanding of the practice in that regard in the past is that those
things happen pretty informally. CCR informs me that when a
conflict arises CCR contacts VLRC and VLRC tries to find a volunteer attorney to come in and do the case. And that essentially
is what happened here.

THE COURT: Conflict cases are those ordinarily that end up with
the matter of other—where there is another defendant involving
the same incident.

MELLO: That is absolutely correct, but my understanding of
Florida's Ethics Code is that that is not the only way that a conflict of interest can come about. CCR has a directly adverse—an
interest in this case directly adverse to the interest of the witness
who is trying his best to correct a mistake, a hideous mistake,
that he made at this point.

THE COURT: How is CCR's position in conflict?

MELLO: CCR, in the course of defending itself, and as I understand, in the course of Office of Capital Collateral Representative's defending itself to FDLE when FDLE came in and interrogated Office of Capital Collateral Representative's investigators
about what happened, CCR said what you would expect CCR to
say. We didn't intimidate him. We didn't do what he describes.
And so CCR is in the position of having to . . .

THE COURT: That would be the basis of your representation . . .

MELLO: Keeps the credibility . . .

THE COURT: So CCR . . .

MELLO: That is part of the basis of my representation.

THE COURT: What you said in the brief was that it was because
Spaziano's family wanted you to represent him rather than CCR.

MELLO: That was the other part. That was—when I took the case back over in June, the conflict of interest existed, but I didn't know about it because up until, at that point, the state had been successful in keeping the video tape out of my hands. I didn't know about it then. I undertook the representation over again at the request of Spaziano, at the request of his mother and his daughter and his niece for personal reasons. And if my doing that is at all a basis for this court's denying a stay or in—if my trying to help out Joe Spaziano is gonna make it more likely that he be executed, I cannot tell you how sorry I am that I ever got back involved in this case. . . .

THE COURT: Are you asserting that CCR said we have a conflict, we want you to represent him?

MELLO: No, CCR never said that. I have not had that conversation with CCR.

THE COURT: Thank you. Thank you very much.

MELLO: May I . . .?

THE COURT: No sir. We really went over time. The governor's office—whether you've got a copy of this or not—the governor's office filed a request for leave to appear before the court on specific issues relating to congressional funding of the VLRC of Florida. Mr. Slackman, do you intend to appear? Do you wish to appear?

SLACKMAN: (Not intelligible.)

At that point, I should have stood and told the justices in a polite but firm voice: "May it please the court, I respectfully suggest that if the honorable justices doubt my representations, made as an officer of this court, that VLRC is dead today, then there are two ways in which the court can easily ascertain the truth. First, you can go to VLRC's offices yourselves. They aren't far from here, and there you can see firsthand the taped-up boxes, the cleaned-out desks, the faces of people who are losing their jobs. But don't call to set up an appointment: VLRC's phones were cut off yesterday.

"Or you can ask Steve Gustat, my former VLRC investigator, who has been my eyes and ears in Joe Spaziano's case for the past month. He's right here in court this afternoon. Steve, stand up, please. You can swear him in right now and he'll tell you, under oath, the precise status of VLRC as of this moment."

I didn't say any of this, of course. When the oral argument concluded, the court adjourned, the justices filing out, back behind their black curtain, I dashed out of the courtroom and down the hall to the clerk's office to file the handwritten motion I had written during the state's oral argument.

As I walked back to the courtroom to gather my notes and files, I noticed a phalanx of reporters waiting for me. Thus, in the majestic rotunda beneath the Florida Supreme Court's dome, I held my first and last "press conference" as an attorney for a death row prisoner. I tried to answer the reporters' questions patiently, with one exception. The *Orlando Sentinel*'s Mike Griffin was there, and I guess I sort of tore into him. Deanna told me later that Griffin's hands were visibly shaking during our exchange.

I soon gave up trying to explain why I filed directly in the Florida Supreme Court, rather than filing a Rule 3.850 in the trial court—in *that* Judge McGregor's court. *Of course* I knew that filing in trial court was the "proper" place to go initially. But had I taken that route, the trial court would have found our claims procedurally defaulted and would have made killer fact-findings against us. Then, we could have had no chance in the Florida Supreme Court. This way, we got a merits ruling out of the Florida Supreme Court—a merits ruling that the factual innocence information was important enough to require an evidentiary hearing.

I got away as quickly as I could. It was clear from Justice Overton's harping during the oral argument that I needed an affidavit from Tony DiLisio. This seemed absurd to me, given that I had already provided the court with my bootleg copy of Tony's recantation on the FDLE videotape.

13

Hell in a Very Small Place

The game was closer than the score indicated.

Dizzy Dean

Back at the hotel, after the Florida Supreme Court oral argument, I called Tony DiLisio from a very public bank of pay phones in the hotel lobby. Would he sign the affidavit about which Justice Overton seemed so preoccupied during the oral argument? "Sure, but I don't under-stand; they have the FDLE videotape; why do they want an affidavit too?" It makes no sense, but I need to humor them; will you sign one? "Of course, but I'm out here in the middle of nowhere, baby-sitting my daughter; I just put ribs on the barbecue; I have no typewriter and no notary . . ."

In the end, Tony drove to the office of his lawyer, Kelly McGraw. He and McGraw drafted a succinct affidavit, and McGraw's mother, Sally, who had gotten her notary stamp only two days before, notarized it and faxed it to my hotel in Tallahassee. I faxed it from the hotel to the Florida Supreme Court, along with yet another handwritten motion and a fax cover sheet from the Holiday Inn. This is what I faxed to the Florida Supreme Court at 8:47 P.M. the evening after the oral argument:

SPAZIANO

V.

STATE

Supplement

Immediately after oral argument in this court, undersigned counsel called Anthony DiLisio and his attorney, asking about the status of the affidavit we had discussed some time ago. Mr. DiLisio shared the undersigned's surprise that, in light of his recanted testimony to the FDLE—given under oath, to the police, and in the presence of his own counsel—the court would deem significant the technicality that Mr. DiLisio had not executed an affidavit regarding the critical aspect of his recantation—the trip to *the dump with Mr. Spaziano.*

Mr. DiLisio's reaction was immediate: He would do an affidavit, even though he did not know of an available notary, he was in the middle of preparing dinner for his child, he does not own a fax machine, and he lives in rural Pensacola.

The affidavit is attached.

Respectfully Submitted
Michael Mello

After Tony's affidavit was safely accomplished, Sally McGraw had a chance to share with me her impressions of Warren Holmes's interrogation of Tony. "Warren Holmes is a *hard-ass.* He was offensive and confrontational; two or three times I thought about stepping in and stopping it. But anyone who saw it would *know* that Tony is telling the truth now. It was so cathartic for Tony, even though it was killing *me* to see him going through it."

The oral argument had left Deanna and me on an adrenaline high. But when we called Vermont for phone messages, one was from Smitty, one of Joe's Outlaw brothers: "I have some questions regarding the pickup of Joe's body after the execution." Crash.

Joe's mom was also beginning to show the pressure—we all were. "I've been waiting for your call all day. I've been worried sick all day. Oh, God, why does he need to be so far from me, so alone. . . . In my heart, I know he'll beat this, but sometimes it just drags me down so, I don't know how to take it."

September 8, 1995
Florida State Prison, Starke
(13 days to execution)

Before driving from Tallahassee in the morning to visit Joe at the prison in Starke, I called the Florida Supreme Court to confirm that the fax of Tony DiLisio's affidavit had arrived intact. It had, and it had been photocopied and distributed to the justices. The clerk's office had no idea when the justices would issue their decision, but I could call back periodically throughout the day if I wanted. I wanted.

Around 11:00 A.M. I stopped by the Florida Supreme Court clerk's office to pick up an audiotape of the oral argument. No ruling yet. Deanna and I listened to the tape as we drove our rental car west to east across the north of Florida on I-10.

Listening to my oral argument on the rental car's scratchy sound system, it was as though I was hearing it for the first time, and in a way I was. Some points of the argument felt like a blowtorch was pointed my way. I'd remembered the justices' questions; what was new to me were my answers. I'm not aware of my own voice when I'm speaking in court, and I cringe whenever I listen to audiotapes of my oral arguments.

At the Lake City exit, we left I-10 and headed south to pick up Route 301. From a roadside convenience store, I phoned the clerk's office again. No ruling. Most of the clerk's office staff were out for lunch. The time was 1:00 P.M. I'd have to try again later.

The drill the prison put us through before we could see Joe hadn't changed much since my first visit to Joe in 1985. Florida State Prison was still Florida State Prison. Deanna and I called out our names to the guard tower, and the two tiers of perimeter gates clanked open. Once we were inside the building, our photo IDs were checked, we passed through that most sensitive metal detector I've ever encountered, and our wrists were stamped with a numerical code, changed daily, using ink visible only under ultraviolet light. Then a guard escorted us through a second set of electronically operated bars and down the hall to the colonel's office and the visiting rooms. Other guards brought Joe from the holding cells and unshackled him for our visit.

The three of us shot the breeze all afternoon. Joe and Deanna had never met in person, and I hadn't seen Joe since July 1993. We chatted about our families, his artwork, the Outlaws. Joe and I smoked cigarettes furtively. The time flew by.

At 4:56, as Joe was being shackled for his return to the deathwatch cells, Joyce Johns came in to tell me that someone from the Florida Supreme Court clerk's office was on the phone for me. I took the call in Johns's office, with Joe and Deanna waiting anxiously in the hall.

Tanya Carroll was calling to tell me that the Florida Supreme Court was issuing an opinion in *Spaziano v. State*. The case was remanded to the state trial court for me to file a state postconviction (Rule 3.850) motion. The trial judge was to hold an evidentiary hearing in seven days, next Friday. She said, "You can continue to represent him, with CCR's assistance." Most important, the Florida Supreme Court had denied a stay of execution. The evidentiary hearing would be conducted under death warrant.

By the time I got off the phone, Joe was shackled and ready to go. I stammered out the news from Tallahassee, and I told him I didn't know what it meant. We hadn't won and we hadn't lost, I said. I couldn't say for sure until I saw the court's opinion itself.

This last point wasn't true. I knew we had lost—and lost in the worst way possible. As Deanna drove us from Starke back to Tallahassee, I drafted a motion for rehearing, asking the justices to reconsider their decision to call for an evidentiary hearing but to deny a stay.

In every litigation that ends with the execution of one's client, there is a moment when possibility gives way to grief. In Joe's case, this was the moment.

I called CCR from a roadside pay phone in Starke. Would CCR do an affidavit saying the agency has a conflict of interest in Joe's case, so CCR can't cocounsel the case with me? Probably.

We rolled into Tallahassee around 8:00 P.M. Now, CCR's director, Michael Minerva, was saying he didn't see a conflict of interest. I laid it all out for him, but he still said he didn't understand it. By then I no longer believed him. Not even this amiable dunce could be *this* obtuse.

CCR's problem wasn't that it couldn't see its conflict of interest. CCR's problem was that it didn't want to risk annoying the Florida Supreme Court. Rather than risk ruffling the court's feathers, CCR was prepared to force itself upon a factually innocent man who didn't want CCR to represent him—and for good reason. The man's family didn't want CCR to represent him—also for good reason.

Worst of all, CCR's participation would provide the court with all the cover it needed to stampede Joe into the evidentiary hearing and then on to execution. Any capital appeals lawyer worth her salt knew what was coming if we took part in the hearing. The hearing would be held before Judge McGregor, who had originally sentenced Joe to death and who had denied Joe's previous postconviction motions. We couldn't possibly be prepared to put on witnesses at the hearing, or to engage in any meaningful cross-examination of the state's witnesses.

Thus unable to provide effective representation of Joe at the hearing, we would lose; Judge McGregor would rule against us. And Judge McGregor would make killer fact-findings. The Florida Supreme Court and the federal courts would affirm those fact-findings. Joe would be killed on schedule.

It was time to talk with Joe. "What are we going to do now, bro?" I told him I'd file a rehearing petition that night. He asked me to tell his niece that he was okay. *Is* he okay? "No, I'm not okay, Mike. The fucking *bastards*." I could think of nothing to say in response. "We lost. They're going to kill me, Mike, aren't they?"

No. We just needed to regroup. CCR had made my job a whole lot harder, but it was oddly liberating finally to decide—after years of defending CCR against its many critics—that now CCR was as much Joe's and my adversary as were the governor, the prosecutors, and the Florida Supreme Court. Also, I learned that Mike Hummell was the investigator CCR had assigned to prepare for the evidentiary hearing— the same investigator Tony DiLisio had accused of strong-arming him into recanting. Indeed, Hummell had been calling reporters for names and addresses he could have found in the phone book.

We only needed to change one mind. The Florida Supreme Court's opinion was close: only four justices voted to deny the stay; three voted in favor of staying the execution.

I spent the next few hours drafting the rehearing motion and noodling about it with folks by phone. The consensus was that I had no real choice: I couldn't allow the Florida Supreme Court to force me into a hearing at which I couldn't possibly be effective. There might even be an opportunity for some legal jujitsu. A friend said to me: "This is exquisite chaos. Maybe its time for all of us to stop playing the game . . . what would happen if *everyone* on Florida's death row fired CCR?"

My handwritten motion for rehearing was completed around 11:15 P.M. The hotel fax machine was down, so Deanna went through the Tallahassee Yellow Pages and found a place where we could send a fax at that hour, not far from the hotel. We then drove the rental car around Tallahassee until we found it.

My fax arrived at the Florida Supreme Court a few minutes before midnight. It said:

IN THE SUPREME COURT OF FLORIDA

JOSEPH R. SPAZIANO, Petitioner-Appellant

V.

THE STATE OF FLORIDA, Respondent-Appellee

MOTION FOR REHEARING AND RECONSIDERATION
AND STAY OF EXECUTION

On Tuesday, September 5th, at 4:30 P.M., this court notified counsel in Vermont that it had scheduled oral argument for 2:00 P.M. on Thursday, September 7th. After spending all day of Wednesday, September 6th en route from Vermont to Florida, the court granted counsel 30 minutes for oral argument. At 5:00 P.M. on September 8th, a few hours before the court knew counsel was scheduled to leave for Vermont to teach, the court issued an order—denying a stay, remanding the case for an evidentiary hearing, and "permitting" counsel to remain as pro bono counsel with the "assistance" of CCR, a law firm with a conflict of interest in this case. The "hearing" will be in the home of the *Orlando Sentinel.*

The court should be aware that counsel shall not follow the Florida Supreme Court's unreasonable commands—not when those commands deny the reality of CCR's conflict and Volunteer Lawyers Resource Center's sudden death. The state offends the federal constitution when it commands counsel to render the ineffective assistance of counsel. *United States v. Cronic,* _____ U.S. _____ (1984).

If this court intends to kill this innocent man by depriving him of the effective assistance of counsel, then it will do so without my complicity. I will not participate in a sham evidentiary "hearing" under warrant when I lack the time and resources to do the job effectively.

As the *amicus* brief set out, VLRC is dead. As counsel has told the court, I lack the funds to do a meaningful evidentiary hearing under warrant—that is part of the reason I filed in this court. If the court wants to decide whether CCR has a conflict and whether CCR can be forced upon Spaziano by this court, then the court should ask that the matter be fully briefed and argued—I should not be limited to a tiny fraction of a 30 minute argument.

I teach legal ethics, and I have no doubt that CCR *does* have a conflict. More importantly, so does Spaziano.

The state that gave the world such famous right-to-counsel opinions as *Gideon v. Wainwright* and *Argersinger v. Hamlin* perhaps ought not to treat counsel with contempt that borders on the cavalier. In any event, *Cronic* forbids court-imposed ineffective assistance of counsel.

CCR has none of the 25 banker's boxes of files in this case. Nor will CCR ever have those files, as CCR will never have the cooperation or acquiescence of Spaziano.

If it wishes to base its rulings on reality, the court must know that counsel has rejected—and it will continue to reject, until the last dog dies—the court's directive that he do the impossible.

Nor will I accept as "co-counsel" a law firm with interests adverse to my client's—a law firm my client has rejected for very good reasons.

Specifically, the court should know that (1) I will participate in no evidentiary hearing under warrant; (2) Neither Spaziano nor I will accept CCR as co-counsel in this case, since CCR refused to serve as co-counsel when I asked them to do so in June; (3) counsel lacks the funds to return to Florida for the purposes of any further court proceedings, as counsel's few remaining personal funds were spent to attend this court's 30 minute oral argument.

No valid procedural bar constitutes an adequate and independent ground precluding federal judicial review. First, Florida's default rules are discretionary and haphazardly applied. Second, the governor's abdication of his clemency function (see *Miami Herald* interview with Chiles) trumps the state's interest in procedural rectitude. We now know that the fundamental assumption of *Herrera v. Collins*—that clemency in Texas functions as a failsafe safety valve against execution of a *truly* innocent person—does not apply in Florida under *this* governor. Chiles clearly thinks it's the *court's* job, not *his* job, to prevent the state killing of innocents.

The Attorney General claimed, in Thursday's oral argument before the Florida Supreme Court, that Spaziano has "run out of legal claims." In its opinion, the court essentially agreed.

All I have is an innocent client. If I had the resources, I could prove it—without having to rely on the *Miami Herald* to do my investigation for me. I have a *videotaped police* interrogation of the state's only real witness at trial—and on that videotape that witness disavowed the testimony the trial prosecutor said was the indispensable element of his case.

If General Butterworth is correct that an innocent man in these circumstances has "run out of legal issues," then there is something very wrong with the law.

Should this court choose to hold me in civil contempt, I will waive extradition; I learned a good bit about civil contempt from my representation of Dr. Elizabeth Morgan. Should this court disbar me, I will plead guilty. Do you really think you can do anything to me comparable to what you have done to my client? What you are *about* to do to him?

In short, undersigned counsel—an experienced Florida capital appellate litigator and an ethics teacher familiar with Florida's professional responsibility commands—will not accept this court's invitation to be ineffective. If you are going to kill an innocent man without a lawyer, you will do so in such a way that the whole world will see what you are doing.

If you act as executioner of this innocent man, I will not be your mask.

Respectfully submitted,
Michael Mello
For Joseph R. Spaziano

TO: Folks . . .
FROM: Michael Mello
RE: Snatching Defeat from the Jaws of Victory
(Or How We Won in the Worst Possible Way)

Ugh. This is a hard memo to write, but I'm going to try to explain how we really *lost* in court on Friday.

First, the evidentiary hearing was ordered to address the question of Anthony DiLisio's recantation. That means the only question before the court will be this: Was Tony DiLisio lying when he testified at Joe's trial 20 years ago, as he now says he was, or is he lying *now* about lying 20 years ago? Tony will be called to the stand, and will testify quite powerfully that he was lying at Joe's trial and is telling the truth now.

Here comes the hard part. Dexter Douglass has already indicated to the media that the state intends to call some of its super-secret witnesses, and we can assume they will be used to try to discredit Tony's recantation. They will, in essence, testify that Tony was telling the truth at Joe's trial, and is lying now. We would then have an opportunity to cross-examine those witnesses and attempt to discredit their testimony—except that *we don't know who those witnesses are!*

Further, even *if* we were given the identities of those witnesses first thing Monday morning—an event which is *extremely* unlikely, given the pattern of state misconduct in this case—96 *hours* is not enough time for us to investigate those witnesses, their backgrounds, their relationship to Tony, and the validity of their testimony. In short, 96 hours is simply insufficient time to prepare *any* meaningful cross-examination of critical witnesses.

Our inability to prepare for this sham "hearing" will be the surest thing to kill Joe. If we *try*—if we rush around blindly, trying to find out what we can, however we can, and wind up doing a lousy investigation of anonymous witnesses—we go into court ill-prepared, at best, and we will be unable to discredit the state's witnesses. And if we are unable to discredit those witnesses, the judge will make a factual determination that Tony is lying now, and was telling the truth 20 years ago at Joe's trial. That ruling will be presumptively correct—which means it is *completely* unreviewable by any other court, even the Supreme Court of the US. In short, we rush this and blow it, Joe is dead. Since there is absolutely no way in which we can be prepared for a hearing in 96 hours, and given the grave consequences of a slip-shod attempt, we must prevent the hearing from happening on Friday. On this basis I have filed a motion to stay the execution and hold the evidentiary "hearing" in abeyance. We need more time.

In addition, I am an appellate attorney, not a trial lawyer. Since I learned of the court's opinion, I have been trying to find a trial attorney willing and competent to represent Joe at the "hearing" ordered by this court. As of this writing, *no* experienced, competent attorney is willing to do so under the unreasonable time constraints established by the court. I will keep looking for one.

September 9, 1995
Tallahassee, Florida
(12 days to execution)

Up at 5:00 A.M.

Deanna had two great ideas: (1) file in *Florida Supreme Court* an application for stay pending cert., a petition asking the U.S. Supreme Court to hear Joe's case; (2) get the Florida State Prison execution guidelines to reporters, so, day by day, they'll know what's happening to Joe.

We checked out of the Tallahassee hotel, drove to the Jacksonville airport, dropped off the rental car, flew to Pittsburgh and then on to West Lebanon, and then a short drive home in Vermont.

Notes made during flight:

> Idea: Contempt? What's significant here is the contempt with which the Florida Supreme Court and prosecutors treat pro bono counsel for an innocent man.

> Public Defenders are used to this sort of treatment by Florida courts. But it's unusual for Florida Supreme Court to spit on uptown lawyers like Sandy D'Alemberte, Thomas and other amici. Florida Supreme Court didn't even get right who *filed* the amicus.

> After Oct. 1, when even the Florida Supreme Court can no longer deny the reality that VLRC is dead, Florida Supreme Court will go asking Florida lawyers for pro bono help in these cases.

> Well, good luck. This is how Florida Supreme Court treats pro bono lawyers.

September 10, 1995
Wilder, Vermont
(11 days to execution)

Front-page story in *Orlando Sentinel:* "Legendary Fear of Biker Gangs Still Reigns Today." Below this headline, a summary: "Many people close to the 20-year-old murder case of Outlaws member Joe Spaziano are still terrified to talk."

The article begins: "Like ogres in a fairy tale they are part of a legend that reaches across decades to seed the sleep of innocents with nightmares." But these devils aren't mythological; to the *Orlando Sentinel* they are real: "The bikers nailed one woman to a tree. They chained another to a ceiling for an afternoon of rape and torture. They snatched teen-age girls from sidewalks, took them to dark clubhouses and raped them repeatedly." Get the gist? The sources were anonymous—because, of course, they feared retribution from the big bad bikers.

With the *Orlando Sentinel,* there was an almost delusional disengagement from reality and from facts that did not happen to coincide with the paper's middle-class, straight preconceptions of what Outlaws actually are and how they actually act. The *Sentinel* reporters and editors seemed to see all Outlaws as being like characters in Oliver Stone's *Natural Born Killers* (which was a *satire*) high on rape and murder. The folks at the *Sentinel* would have understood Stone's movie to be a documentary, not the critique of our weird television culture that it is. In any event, the *Sentinel*'s view of the Outlaws was nothing less than delusional, in my view and in my experience with the motorcycle brotherhood. In my experience, as with Outlaws, not all sociopaths wear leather and ride bikes. And, unlike the *Orlando Sentinel,* the Outlaws never broke their word to me.

At a meeting with Governor Chiles's clemency aide, CCR's Michael Minerva said that of course CCR had no conflict in Joe's case. He also joined in a general trashing of me. Finally, he said that CCR's lawyers were writing a memorandum of law to be filed tomorrow. This memo would assert, among other things, that I was emotionally unstable. The gloves were off.

But I didn't have time to waste on CCR's campaign to suck up to the governor who signed the death warrants on CCR's clients. The immediate problem was what we would do at the evidentiary hearing scheduled to be held in five days. It was obvious that I couldn't represent Joe at the hearing, even if I could find a way to get to Sanford, Florida. I'm an appellate lawyer, not a trial lawyer.

There was only one Florida lawyer I trusted to do the hearing: Mark Olive. Olive would make an unequivocally clear showing that the hearing shouldn't be taking place at all—not with only seven days' notice, no resources, and no stay of execution. The ferociously brilliant Olive wouldn't be intimidated by the court or the governor or the prosecutors.

In addition, no other lawyer could come up to speed on the labyrinthine record and history of Joe's case. Olive had supervised my work on Joe's case during the first warrant in 1985, when he and I were both still at CCR.

And I knew he would do it. Of my Florida colleagues from our old deathwork days, three people could always be counted on to come through when it was crunch time: Mark Olive, Scharlette Holdman, and Craig Barnard. Craig was dead. Scharlette was in California. Mark said he would think about representing Joe at the evidentiary hearing.

Joe's mom called to give me a pep talk. "I'm a nervous wreck, just like you, Mike." Mrs. Spaziano would visit Joe at the prison in two days. The whole family would be there in Sanford for the evidentiary hearing. "We'll all say CCR isn't Joe's lawyer. Joe doesn't want CCR. Mike Mello is his lawyer."

Smitty, one of Joe's Outlaw brothers, called to check in. Smitty had done time on Louisiana's death row for a crime he didn't commit; after his lawyers proved his innocence and secured his release from prison, he had relocated to Florida. During Joe's two 1995 death warrants, Smitty had been my greatest ally in planning logistics.

Smitty had good news: "I got [prison] approval to let Joe wear an Outlaws T-shirt when he's executed. We'll have an Outlaws tombstone, but Joe's family wants a family burial, next to his grandfather." Smitty would FedEx the T-shirt to me, and I would hand carry it to Florida when I went down to witness the execution.

Gene Miller had an idea for a trial lawyer to represent Joe at the evidentiary hearing. Warren Holmes had spent forty-five minutes on the phone with Jim Russ, "the best criminal defense attorney in Orlando," according to Miller. I was skeptical, because I'd never worked with Russ before.

As it turned out, Russ wouldn't do the hearing under warrant. Neither would Holland & Knight, Florida's largest and richest law firm (475 lawyers). Neither would Steve Bright, an experienced (and too busy) capital trial lawyer. As I called lawyer after lawyer, law firm after law firm, friend after friend, I kept hearing what I already knew: it was insane to have the hearing under death warrant. *No* self-respecting lawyer would commit to doing the impossible.

CCR would show up for the hearing, I knew. The CCR lawyers would go through the motions of "representing" Joe at a hearing not even they thought they could possibly be prepared for. CCR would go through the motions. Joe would lose the hearing. The Florida Supreme Court would affirm. The federal courts would do the same. Joe would be killed, and the entire killing machine in Florida—governor, prosecutors, judges, and CCR—would pat themselves on the back, comfortable in the pleasant illusion that Joe had had his day in court, that "the system had worked."

No. Not this time. I wouldn't allow it.

As I've mentioned, Mark Olive once told me that good law isn't what stops executions. Good facts don't stop executions. Not even factual innocence stops executions. What stops execution is *will*—the iron determination that this execution simply will not occur.

September 10, 1995
Dear Mr. Mello

My children and I are united in wanting you to represent my son Joe as his attorney.

We do not want the CCR to represent him. You have been in contact with Joe for 12 yrs. and you strongly believe in innocent. We know you will defend him with all your strength and knowledge for you have followed his case from the beginning.

Thank you,
Rose Spaziano and family

14

I'm Fired by the Court: "Crazy Michael" and "Crazy Joe"

Plenty of people who watched this spectacle [i.e., Michael Mello's actions during Joe Spaziano's August–September 1995 death warrant] concluded that Mello is reckless and maybe nuts. I can report, after dozens of hours of interviews, that his problem (if that's what it is) is that he sees the whole thing too clearly.

David Von Drehle, in his foreword to my book Dead Wrong, *1997*

September 10, 1995
Wilder, Vermont

After days of circulating rumors that I had become mentally or emotionally ill, CCR finally put its charges, and others, against me in writing. In legal papers filed in the Florida Supreme Court on September 11, and faxed to me at 5:22 P.M. that same afternoon, CCR accused me of "attempting to get a book published regarding Spaziano's case, which could place him in conflict with Spaziano's interests" (apparently referring to the book *chapter* I had sent to Gene Miller months earlier, about which CCR had been aware when the agency turned Joe's case back over to me in June) and stating that "Mr. Mello insists on being counsel for Spaziano when he concedes he cannot provide competent representation" (ignoring CCR's own claim, filed in the Florida Supreme Court earlier that same day, that CCR's caseload made it impossible for the agency to represent Joe effectively) and that "the pleadings that Mr. Mello has filed may *reflect instability affecting his ability to be counsel.*" These charges appeared over the names of CCR's director, Michael Minerva, and his two senior litigators—Martin

McClain, CCR's chief assistant; and Gail Anderson, chief of CCR's appeals unit.

Earlier on September 10, these same three CCR leaders filed, in the Florida Supreme Court, a motion for stay of Joe's execution, for a continuance of the evidentiary hearing, and for an evidentiary hearing regarding Joe's representation. The petition included the typical catalog of CCR's alleged "case overload"—the same complaints the Florida Supreme Court routinely denied summarily in cases before and after Joe's.

CCR's petition did contain an interesting item, however. In a sworn affidavit, Michael Minerva laid out why CCR had refused my repeated requests in June that CCR cocounsel Joe's case with me. This was the first I learned of CCR's reasons.

> In making this affidavit I must also address the distasteful suspicion that I or others at CCR in any way conspired with Mr. Mello or anyone else to precipitate a crisis in counsel for Spaziano in these proceedings. We did not.
>
> As outlined in the Petition, no one now at CCR was involved with Spaziano's case until May of 1994 when Gail Anderson was asked by Mr. Mello to present oral argument in the 11th Circuit Court of Appeals, which she did on June 21st. Mr. Mello resumed representation, without help from CCR, until the United States Supreme Court denied certiorari from the decision of the Eleventh Circuit affirming the denial of habeas corpus. When that occurred, CCR assumed representation, as Mr. Mello said he was unable to continue as counsel.
>
> CCR was counsel, therefore, from January 1995 until June, 1995. During that time, investigators from CCR contacted Anthony DiLisio but he did not tell them anything. Later Mr. DiLisio recanted in statements made to the press and to FDLE. The Governor then stayed the warrant and, before CCR could reinterview Mr. DiLisio or obtain the video of DiLisio's statement to FDLE, Mr. Mello asserted that he was Spaziano's sole counsel.
>
> From that time, which was June 20, 1995, until this Court's decision at 5:00 pm on Friday, September 8, 1995, CCR had nothing to do with Spaziano's case or his representation. Mr. Mello emphatically stated that he alone was counsel. Mr. Mello did not advise or consult with CCR about Spaziano's case.

Mr. Mello was not assisted by CCR after the Governor's stay for several reasons. When he reentered the case CCR was burdened with too many cases and has filed several pleadings saying so. I believe that the CCR statute does not authorize use of our limited resources if a person is otherwise represented. To be represented by CCR a death sentenced person must be "unable to secure counsel due to indigency" and Spaziano was not in that situation since Mr. Mello was declaring himself to be representing Spaziano. In June, when Mr. Mello asked for support from CCR (as co-counsel), I turned him down because I was reasonably sure we would not agree on how to represent Spaziano. Although the law authorizes me to appoint "part-time assistant capital collateral representatives . . . who shall serve without compensation. . . ."

Mainly, however, I believed that I could not accept Mr. Mello as special assistant CCR or as co-counsel when we did not agree on what to do or how to do it. We would not be able to cooperate in a way that co-counsel should and I feared that our disagreeing would not be in Spaziano's best interest. Also, VLRC was still active at that time and available to support pro bono counsel such as Mr. Mello. I thought that would be a better solution.

From the time that Mr. Mello asserted that he was sole counsel for Spaziano until the Court issued its opinion on September 8th, CCR has not been assisting Mr. Mello. We do not know what files Mr. Mello has accumulated in addition to the materials we sent to VLRC in June. We have not used the services of the Miami Herald to aid in the investigation, as Mr. Mello claims to have done. We do not even have the large stack of pleadings and other documents Mr. Mello filed in this Court that are the basis for the evidentiary hearing.

When Mr. Mello's motion for rehearing arrived in the office on Saturday, September 9th, I called the clerk of this Court, Sid White, at his home and informed him of the existence of the pleading, which had apparently been faxed to the Court after closing time on Friday the 8th. Mr. White said he would inform the Court (or the Chief Justice). I asked Mr. White for access to the pleadings filed by Mr. Mello, and for a copy of the DiLisio tape. Mr. White said he would call me if that could be arranged.

No documents or video tape have been received yet. I was able, however, to obtain a transcript of the DiLisio interview from Matthew Lawry of VLRC on Saturday, but he could not locate the tape.

Having seen the tape of Mr. DiLisio, and reviewed the transcript, it is obvious to me that even the narrow issue of Mr. DiLisio's recantation will require considerable investigation. Moreover, what Mr. DiLisio said raises issues, previously unknown and unknowable, of police misconduct, knowing use of false testimony, and suppression of favorable evidence that go beyond the recantation issue. None of this has been investigated by CCR, so we are faced with preparing this complex case from scratch with less than a week to do it all and if we fail an innocent man could die. This situation is made worse by the possibility, stated in media reports, that the State will have the advantage of using at the hearing witnesses whose identity has been kept secret from Spaziano's counsel under claim of executive privilege.

For us to go forward at this time without a stay would be to provide counsel in name only and not in substance. When life or death is the issue I cannot ethically do that.

Further affiant sayeth naught.
Michael J. Minerva

Much of this was news to me. On one score, however, CCR senior staff and I were in total agreement: CCR sure as hell wasn't working with me to save Joe's life. In fact, the CCR approach would have been, as Minerva admitted, counsel in name only. Joe deserves more than that. *Everyone* on death row deserves more than that.

What CCR filed in the Florida Supreme Court on September 10 was a subtle, face-saving offer to take over Joe Spaziano's case—against the emphatic and written wishes of Joe, his mother, his daughter, and his niece. Joe didn't want CCR—even if the pressure of time, money, and deathwatch became *nil*—and for good reason, given CCR's recent treatment of Joe's case between January and June 1995. Not a single member of Joe's family wanted CCR to get a second shot at "helping" Joe, and I sure couldn't blame them.

Until CCR's Florida Supreme Court filings on September 10, I was willing to give CCR the benefit of the doubt and to chalk up its abysmal performance in Joe's case to ineptitude and incompetence rather than malice. No longer. That CCR's attempted sabotage of Joe's case was as laughably inept as its thuggish attempts to strong-arm Tony DiLisio into recanting does not mitigate the damage CCR caused.

CCR's attack left me stunned, but it also confirmed my instinctual refusal to hand Joe's case back to CCR at the barrel of the Florida Supreme Court's contempt power. CCR had become deadly to its clients, including this innocent man.

As to CCR's claim that my actions suggested I was mentally or emotionally "unstable"—well, gentle reader, you can decide that for yourself. By now you can judge for yourself whether you've been reading a book written by a madman.

Imagine, God forbid, that your son or daughter or spouse or childhood friend is on death row in Florida. Would you entrust your loved-one's life to CCR, even if you believed him or her to be guilty of murder? And what if you knew him or her to be innocent?

September 11, 1995
Wilder, Vermont
(10 days to execution)

CCR was flailing. Michael Minerva told one person that CCR would file in the Florida Supreme Court at 9:00 A.M., telling the court that CCR could not and would not represent Joe at the hearing. The director said, "If the Florida Supreme Court forces me into a hearing under warrant, I'll resign." Meanwhile, CCR's investigators' preparation for the hearing continued making CCR the laughingstock of more than one newspaper.

Rumors: *That* Judge McGregor was off the case. Judge O. H. Eaton Jr. would be our trial judge, and he had scheduled the evidentiary hearing to commence at 10:00 A.M., Friday, September 15. But then: Judge Eaton was out of town, at a judges' conference, until Friday. I faxed the relevant paperwork to Judge Eaton's chambers. I also told the death clerk in the U.S. Supreme Court that we'd likely be heading there soon.

Sally McGraw, Tony DiLisio's lawyer's mom, needed to know whether Tony needed to be at the Friday hearing. Yes, but Tony and his counsel would need to foot the expenses themselves (eight-hour drive each way, lodging, meals), so they may want to file a motion, on *Tony's* behalf, asking the hearing to be held in abeyance (and staying the execution). Sally passed all of this on to Tony, who agreed.

I called my advisers with a question: Assuming I can keep CCR away from the hearing, should *I* show up for the hearing? The consensus was no—*emphatically* no. If MO could be there, he would. If MO couldn't be there, Joe would not have an attorney at the hearing. Counsel's chair at the defense's table would be empty.

At 11:30 A.M., I called the Florida Supreme Court. Had CCR filed anything? "Yes; didn't they fax it to you?" Nope. "The court will fax it to you now." As CCR's ninety-three-page brief arrived, my lowest expectations about CCR were met and exceeded. CCR's filing was self-defensive, self-serving, and vitriolic. CCR's bile was not directed at the governor or the court or the prosecutors. It was directed at me. CCR blamed the Spaziano crisis on me. It was a theme soon picked up by the *Orlando Sentinel, St. Petersburg Times,* and, most painful for me, the *Miami Herald.*

But those were tomorrow's disasters. I still needed to sort out who, if anyone, would represent Joe at the hearing on Friday. And, again, MO saved the day. He and Holland & Knight would represent Joe. MO needed to meet with Tony DiLisio as soon as possible.

Meanwhile, the prison was preparing Joe for his "media day," scheduled for September 12. This is the one time when a prisoner on deathwatch has the opportunity to meet with reporters. The television newsmagazine *48 Hours* would be there. Geraldo Rivera wanted to be there, but the prison wouldn't allow his satellite truck onto prison grounds; when Rivera's representatives began treating Joyce Johns like a redneck boob, I suggested to her that she tell Rivera to stay the hell away from Joe.

Gene Miller called at 12:45: *That* Judge McGregor had taken the case back over. He would preside at the Friday hearing. McGregor was trying to set up a conference call among the prosecutors and Joe's "lawyer"—CCR—to schedule the logistical details of the hearing. Miller seemed incredulous that McGregor could jump back into the case this way. I told him that under warrant anything was possible.

When I called Joe to tell him that MO and Holland & Knight were on board for the Friday hearing, he was wired. CCR lawyers had tried to visit with him the day before, but he had refused to meet with them (on my advice). CCR had, however, told Joe that CCR would be representing him at the hearing, because *someone* had to represent him. CCR also told Joe that CCR had gotten the *Miami Herald* involved in his case. Joe knew better: "A sergeant here said that's a lie; he told me not to let CCR kick Mike off my case. . . . *Everyone* here says to do what Mike tells me to do—fuck CCR."

Next I called the Sanford County Courthouse to confirm that *that* Judge McGregor would be the judge presiding over the hearing on Friday. Yes: McGregor is now our judge.

Then I heard from MO. Holland & Knight had decided there was no way they would come into this hearing under warrant—not as counsel, not as cocounsel, not as ghost counsel. The case was too hot for Florida's largest law firm.

Around this time, the Seminole County prosecutors contacted Tony DiLisio's lawyer in Pensacola. The state wanted Tony to be available tomorrow for questioning. The lawyer would try to locate him. "He's not here now, and I don't know where he is."

Rumors: According to the Orlando gossip mill, *that* Judge McGregor himself called Jim Russ to ask if Russ was Joe's attorney. When Russ answered no, McGregor said he'd call me. CCR was spreading the word that it was not Joe's counsel. A Florida Supreme Court justice had mentioned to someone in passing that I was no longer Joe's attorney. A justice had said, "There ain't gonna *be* any hearing on Friday."

Now that Holland & Knight was out of the picture, I asked Jim Russ whether *he* would represent Joe at Friday's hearing. No. "I won't go into court unprepared, and I just don't have the time to prepare adequately. . . . I'm ready to help, but not under those terms; I couldn't do it if I wasn't prepared." I couldn't blame him.

In a conference call with Russ, Gene Miller, and Warren Holmes, I repeated my earlier conversation with Russ. Holmes understood the devastating impact of an adverse ruling and bad fact-findings by Judge McGregor. "If I were saddled with bad fact-findings, that changes the risk calculation for me. . . . No judge would ever admit he was *this* wrong in a death case; you know that Gene. . . . Ego will never let McGregor change his mind; humans just don't work like that."

Holmes continued: "It's just not in human nature to go and make a 180-degree change. I agree with you, Mike; it's too risky to go to this hearing. All of my experience tells me that McGregor is incapable of changing his mind this dramatically. . . . It's just too risky for us to participate in this hearing. . . . I agree with you that we can't risk participation in this hearing."

We needed time. Already, the *Herald* had leads on other people to whom Tony DiLisio had recanted, confidentially, before he recanted on the record for Lori Rozsa in June 1995. Tony had told ministers and counselors that he'd lied at Joe's capital murder trial.

Shortly before 5:00 P.M., CCR filed additional papers in the Florida Supreme Court. Now CCR was arguing that (1) Joe was mentally incompetent to choose his lawyer (i.e., me over Office of Capital Collateral Representative), and (2) I was "unstable." Conveniently, CCR faxed to the *Orlando Sentinel* a copy of its memo calling me "unstable."

I countered CCR's filings with letters from Joe's family expressing their strong and united preference that I continue to serve as Joe's lawyer. Had there been more time, I would have laid out the solid and noncrazy reasons for Joe's and his family's rejection of CCR.

Because any evidentiary hearing in Joe's case would occur in the *Orlando Sentinel*'s backyard, I had ended our cold war as soon as the Florida Supreme Court had ordered the hearing. When I spoke with the *Sentinel*'s Mike Griffin, Griffin said he was "shocked that Judge McGregor is back on this case. . . . His memory is bad, and he was quoted in our newspaper as saying the evidence against Spaziano was 'overwhelming.'" Bingo: that sort of public prejudgment of the evidentiary hearing should disqualify Judge McGregor from presiding at the hearing.

When I told Joe that CCR was now claiming that Joe and I *both* are crazy, he couldn't stop laughing. "They're saying we're both freaks, Mike! They can kiss our crazy asses. . . . I'm looking in my mirror, and I'm seeing a bald guy with a crooked grin." Joe also said, "On the phone, CCR was trying to cut you down, but I ain't gonna sell out."

I ain't gonna sell you out, either, Joe. I love you, bro. Good night. Tomorrow should be a big day.

9-11-95
Dear Mr. Minerva,

As my attorney told you, C.C.R. is not my lawyer. I do not want C.C.R. to represent me, in any hearing. As my attorney

Michael Mello has told you, do not try to see me or write to me again. I only want you to speak to me through my attorney Michael Mello, who has been my lawyer for a long time. It can't be fair to go to court with a lawyer who doesn't know my case.

Sincerely,
Crazy Joe

September 12, 1995
Wilder, Vermont
(9 days to execution)

Today the clock stopped. The stay came down nine days before Joe's scheduled execution. It came down on September 12, 1995—Joe's fiftieth birthday.

Sid White, clerk of the Florida Supreme Court, called me at 2:30 P.M. The justices—unanimously—had just released a judgment and opinion staying Joe's execution indefinitely. The court had—also unanimously—fired me as Joe's attorney.

Joe was visiting with his mother and sister on death row when I called with the news from the Florida Supreme Court. I loved being the first one to tell him about the stay.

When I told him about the Florida Supreme Court's birthday present, Joe said, "Thank you, bro. My mom and sister were just talking about you for a long time. We love you, Mike. Let me tell the sarge the good news. Indefinite stay! That means they're looking, right, Mike? I talked to the assistant superintendent yesterday, about you and CCR, and he said I'm not crazy for wanting you as my lawyer: CCR sat down on his ass."

Still, Joe's overriding emotion was relief. I think it was more the absence of terror than the presence of anything affirmative like joy. But maybe I was just projecting my own emotional reaction onto Joe.

A usually imperturbable journalist called sounding ecstatic. "*Mazel-fucking-tov*! You scared 'em with your wildman act. You backed off the Florida Supreme fucking *Court*!"

The highest order of business was to find a Florida law firm to replace CCR as Joe's lawyer. I called Gregg Thomas at Holland & Knight and made the pitch. "Gregg, have I got a case for *you* . . ." He said he'd think about it.

When Joe's mom and sister returned home from visiting Joe at the prison, they called me. His mother was sweet, as always: "I just got through talking with Joe; you were the brains; I think Chiles is afraid of you, Mike; I think this might finally be it; he was so down last night; CCR can't kick you off the case; the whole house is in an uproar; God bless you; [his sister] had a panic attack during the visit, and Joe got worried about her."

Joe's sister cut in: "We'll make you some nice macaroni."

His mom continued: "It's the same feeling when my husband was dying; when they called he'd died, it was a release, a blessing; Joe was ready this time; guards love him."

Gene Miller's was the only other phone call we picked up that night.

Miller mentioned that Tony Proscio had written an editorial I might not like. "We just needed a tar baby, and you were convenient." That was a bit ominous, but small change compared to our celebration. Miller said: "You were fucking *brilliant*. You figured out what they were going to do, you made it impossible for them to do it, and it worked! You *did* it, and it worked."

Less than a week into Joe Spaziano's August–September 1995 death warrant, an unrelated trial in which members of the Outlaws motorcycle brotherhood were charged with racketeering came to a conclusion in Tampa, Florida. After hearing about the Outlaws for more than four months, a Tampa jury returned guilty verdicts against fourteen of sixteen Outlaw members and associates charged with various racketeering, drug trafficking, and gun charges. Two men were acquitted, and the jury deadlocked on more than twenty racketeering charges.

That Outlaws were convicted of crimes in Florida was not surprising. What was surprising, however, was the strong and public reaction of several jurors on the case. On September 1, 1995, the *St. Petersburg Times, Tampa Tribune,* and *Miami Herald* all quoted various jurors as saying that overzealous federal agents were the *real* outlaws, and the convicted Outlaws should be back on the street. The Tampa jurors claimed the government tenaciously entrapped the defendants, leaving the law-abiding jury with no choice but to follow the letter rather than the spirit of the law.

One juror, Melanie Williams, was quoted in the *St. Petersburg*

Times as saying the guilty verdicts "made me sick to my stomach," because most of those convicted were facing up to life in prison, sentences she said were way out of line for "small time hoodlums." Another juror, Charles Destro, told the *Miami Herald*, "I think the government got out of control. It went too far. We did what the law required, but it didn't feel right to us."

Patrick McNeil, also on the twelve-person jury, went further. The *Herald* reported:

> Jurors interviewed by The Herald and the Tampa Tribune said many of the convictions resulted from a literal interpretation of legal guidelines cited by the judge.
>
> "If I would have been given the right to not only judge the facts in this case, but also the law and the actions taken by the government," McNeil wrote in an open letter to the media, "the prosecutor [and] local and federal law enforcement officers connected in this case would be in jail and not the defendants."
>
> Testimony during the four-month trial revealed that federal officers lured some defendants into participating in the staged unloading of government-owned cocaine from a government-owned plane. The bait: $1,000 each for a few hours of work.
>
> The government also employed paid informants and undercover officers to repeatedly entice some reluctant Outlaws into selling small amounts of drugs and committing other crimes, according to trial testimony.
>
> "Some of the charges were legitimate, but the majority of it was trumped up," said Destro, 57, of Clearwater. "A lot of us felt outrage, but we had to go by the instructions given to us by the court."
>
> "I went home and cried," juror Kim Milyak told The Tribune. "That's how bad I felt."
>
> Jury foreman Jerry Hughes said the investigation "certainly wasn't ethical, but for the most part was legal." He said every juror harbored some concern about the government's behavior.
>
> Destro said one charge that particularly troubled him involved the sale of a quarter pound of marijuana. He said one defendant, responding to persistent requests from an undercover agent, finally served as intermediary in that sale—his role limited

to introducing the seller and buyer and handing the marijuana from one to the other.

For that, the Outlaw was convicted of possessing a controlled substance, Destro said.

In another incident, he said, an Outlaw resisted temptation despite repeated offers by an undercover agent to sell him a truckload of "stolen" cigarettes for resale.

"He kept saying he wanted no part of it and the undercover agent kept offering it to him, over and over again," Destro said. "They kept twisting his arm."

As a juror and a citizen, Destro said, he was appalled.

"If this could happen to them, it could happen to me," he said. "If the government reads this and gets mad at me, it can come after me now."

Does any of this sound familiar? Patrick McNeil, the Tampa juror who had written the open letter, contacted me through Professor Eric Freedman at Hofstra Law School. In his e-mail, McNeil wrote: "I would like to lend my support for Joseph in obtaining a new trial. During the 4½ months of the Outlaws [1995 racketeering] trial, I learned first hand what the court system will do to convict. If I can be of further assistance in your efforts, please feel free to contact me."

It's depressing to see how little had changed between 1976 and 1995. At least the Tampa Outlaws seemed to be technically guilty of the crimes charged. At least those crimes didn't carry a penalty of death.

15

"I Won't Debate My Soul with Strangers": Outlaws against All Odds

There is a time when the operation of the machine becomes so odious, makes you so sick at heart that you can't take part; you can't even tacitly take part, and you've got to put your bodies on the gears and upon the wheels, upon the levers, upon all the apparatus and you've got to make it stop. And you've got to indicate to the people who run it, to the people who own it, that unless you're free, the machines will be prevented from working at all.

Mario Savio, Sproul Plaza, Berkeley, California, December 1964

I won't debate my soul with strangers.

Andrew Hudgins, After the Lost War, *1989*

Governor Chiles's reaction to the stay was thuddingly predictable. As described by the *Miami Herald*'s Lori Rozsa:

Just as the Supreme Court was issuing its decision Tuesday afternoon, Chiles was holding a press conference across the street. He strongly criticized Mello.

"I don't think he's serving the Bar, I don't think he's serving his client," Chiles said. "I don't think he's serving justice in general with what he's doing."

But Mello said he accomplished what he set out to do—earn a stay and more time to investigate the new twists in the case. And he said he will not leave the case, though he acknowledges he needs help.

"My top priority right now is to get a major Florida law firm willing to sign on as pro bono counsel," Mello said. "We need to get that secret FDLE report. And we need to track down every piece of paper in all of the cases they've tried to pin on Joe."

Ron Sachs, spokesman for Chiles, said the Supreme Court's stay doesn't change the governor's mind about Spaziano's guilt.

"He remains convinced, unwaveringly so, about this case," Sachs said.

The *Orlando Sentinel*'s editorial reaction to the stay was also no surprise:

Justice Delayed, Again

The key issue is whether any credible evidence exists that Joseph Spaziano was wrongly convicted. If there is none, it's time justice was served.

Today is the day that justice nearly 20 years in the waiting was to be done.

It is the day on which Joseph Spaziano, an Outlaws motorcycle-gang member known as "Crazy Joe," was to be executed for the rape-murder of Laura Lynn Harberts, an 18-year-old Orlando woman.

That won't happen. Once again, as is the routine in death penalty cases, an eleventh-hour blizzard of appeals has delayed the execution. The death-row lawyers would have us believe this delay is justice served. At this point, it looks like justice delayed.

The issue is not whether the jury made the right decision in convicting Spaziano 19 years ago. It heard the evidence and found it compelling, and it found him guilty. This is no time to second-guess the jury. The issue is whether there is any credible evidence that he was convicted wrongly—and that turns on the believability of a key witness, Anthony Frank DiLisio.

In short, Spaziano's conviction has not suffered from a lack of judicial review.

Still, in response to this latest clemency request, Gov. Lawton Chiles ordered a special investigation into the case. Not only did the results corroborate Mr. DiLisio's original trial testimony, but the investigation uncovered some new facts that link Spaziano to the crime.

Those details included the record of a federal wiretap in which bikers discussed ways to force Mr. DiLisio to change his testimony. Then there are compelling interviews with former bikers.

One said he saw Spaziano drop off at the Altamonte Springs garbage dump something wrapped in cloth that was the size and shape of a human body. That occurred shortly before the victim's remains were found.

Mr. DiLisio, an Outlaw associate and admitted drug-user, told the court in the 1976 trial that Spaziano had bragged to him about raping women, cutting their breasts and killing them.

Then, Mr. DiLisio testified, Spaziano took him to an Altamonte Springs dump and showed him the mutilated bodies of two women. One of the bodies later was identified as that of Ms. Harberts. Her breasts had been cut.

In May of this year, Michael Mello, a Vermont law professor who formerly had handled Spaziano's appeals, wrote an article that was published in this and two other newspapers, arguing that Spaziano was convicted on weak evidence.

Then, as if on cue, a few weeks later, as Spaziano faced his fourth death warrant, Mr. DiLisio changed his story. After maintaining for 19 years that Spaziano had taken him to the dump to view the bodies, Mr. DiLisio announced that he had lied during the 1976 trial.

Which of Mr. DiLisio's accounts is to be believed? What's the truth? What's the lie?

Those who were present during Spaziano's trial remember Mr. DiLisio's testimony as having been unwavering, even under the menacing stares of Spaziano's biker colleagues.

Today Mr. DiLisio's credibility is not beyond suspicion. He describes himself as a lay minister—a reformed man. Yet in 1992 he pleaded no contest and served six months probation on charges of hitting a former girlfriend. In April of this year he was arrested for drunken driving.

As with all capital cases, Spaziano's conviction was appealed to the Florida Supreme Court—which found it to be legitimate. In fact, all told, Spaziano's case has been reviewed by that court four times and twice more by the U.S. Supreme Court. Twice he has been resentenced, both times—like the first—to death. . . .

[Another] biker said that when he and Spaziano were in prison together Spaziano said he was worried because he had shown two bodies to a teenager, and he was worried that the teen would go to police.

As expected, Mr. Mello pushed forward with his delaying tactics by arguing that Mr. DiLisio's change of heart warranted a review.

The court ordered that review, which was to have been held in Sanford last Friday. But Mr. Mello refused to participate—or even to turn over his client's file to a group of lawyers who specialize in appealing death-penalty cases.

That ploy forced an indefinite postponement. So Mr. Mello got what he wanted. He put off Spaziano's execution. But did he serve justice?

Hardly. Spaziano has been awaiting justice for nearly 20 years, and when Mr. Mello was given an opportunity to present what he has described as compelling evidence that his client is not guilty, the lawyer refused to show up.

That was not noticeably uncharacteristic. When this newspaper agreed to publish his original article, Mr. Mello tried to portray the *Sentinel* as supporting his effort to have Spaziano exonerated. When the *Sentinel* then examined Mr. Mello's information and found some of it to be flawed, he condemned the newspaper as working for Spaziano's execution.

What did he expect? We can't imagine that any responsible news organization would have done anything less than investigate what was being alleged.

The legal games have dragged on far too long, and no one is being served well by them. If there is compelling evidence that Spaziano was wrongly convicted, it is only fair to him that it be brought before the court. If no such evidence exists, it is only fair that justice, long delayed, be done.

But it wasn't just the state and its newspaper of choice. The *St. Petersburg Times* weighed in as well, in an editorial titled "Let the System Work":

The Florida Supreme Court was right to give Joseph Spaziano more time to prove he is not a murderer. So many questions have been raised about Spaziano's guilt that it would be unconscionable to execute him as long as there are reasonable doubts.

All he needs now is a good lawyer.

Whether intentional or not, lawyer Michael Mello's refusal to appear at a crucial hearing in the case left the Supreme Court no choice but to delay the execution, which had been scheduled for September 21.

Mello was right to ask for more time to prepare for Friday's hearing, but he was wrong to boycott the proceeding if he didn't get his way. Mello's decision was a disservice to his client that showed contempt for the very court that could save him.

The court, showing far more restraint than Mello, decided that Mello had effectively removed himself from the case. Spaziano has to find another lawyer, rely on state lawyers he has rebuffed in the past or go it alone, the court decided. Mello says he is on the case and plans to appeal, but his actions suggest that the court was right to conclude that he had removed himself.

This is not the first time Mello's emotions have overwhelmed his judgment. Last month he wrote a stinging memo, riddled with expletives, that accused Gov. Lawton Chiles's office of lying, referred to U.S. Supreme Court justices in a vulgar manner and derided federal appeals court judges.

Mello has been clashing with the state office of Capital Collateral Representative, which defends death row inmates. "Better that Joe have no lawyer at all—and that the world clearly sees that he has no lawyer—than that Joe have the *illusion* of a lawyer, a hack (public defender) office like CCR that plays by the rules laid down by the people whose job it is to kill their clients," Mello wrote in his now-infamous memo.

Spaziano might be dead if not for Mello's tireless work on his behalf, all of which he has done for free. For that he deserves a great deal of credit. But instead of fighting the CCR, he ought to work with them and get Spaziano to do the same. After all, he has admitted in motions that he has neither the money nor the expertise to handle the kind of evidentiary hearing the court has ordered.

The public deserves to know the truth about Spaziano, who has been on death row for 20 years. Spaziano deserves a fair hearing. It is time Mello stopped playing games and gave the system for which he has shown so much contempt a chance to work. It's time for Mello to stand aside.

The *Miami Herald* concurred:

Less "Panic" for Spaziano

The Florida Supreme Court yesterday found itself all but forced into a decision that it should have made willingly last week.

When the court on Friday ordered a hearing into new evidence in the murder case against Joseph "Crazy Joe" Spaziano, it allowed less than two weeks for all questions to be answered. After that, according to a death warrant that the court refused to stay, Spaziano was to be executed.

The key witness in the case, Anthony DiLisio, recently said that he lied 20 years ago when he furnished the testimony that put Spaziano on Death Row. The justices properly told a lower court to examine Mr. DiLisio's altered story and determine whether it is genuine.

But by not staying the death warrant, the court in effect imposed an unrealistic dangerous deadline. As Justice Gerald Kogan wrote in a dissenting opinion, it created an "atmosphere of panic . . . for an issue that requires calm and deliberate resolution."

The panic evidently sent some of Spaziano's lawyers off the deep end. His principal attorney, Michael Mello—who had no clerical or investigative help and was showing signs of emotional exhaustion—fell to feuding with the state agency that normally represents Death Row appeals. The result was an exchange of lawyerly insults that would have been comical—if someone's life weren't at stake.

To this the justices rightly said: Enough. They ordered Mr. Mello off the case, stayed the death warrant indefinitely, and set a new deadline of Nov. 15 for the evidentiary hearing.

Now the inquiry can proceed at a pace that befits both the complexity of the case and the gravity of the death penalty. Spaziano was convicted in 1976, when he was 30, of murdering 19-year-old Laura Lynn Harberts. The case rested almost entirely on Mr. DiLisio's lurid tale of seeing mutilated bodies and hearing

Spaziano boast of the crime. The testimony was dubious from the start, and now the witness has recanted it.

Even Nov. 15 may prove an impractical deadline. But at least there is no death warrant rushing the proceedings. That's how it should have been all along. The justices' clear desire to know the truth of this matter—which is commendable—was nearly undermined by an undue haste in pursuing it.

To Spaziano, whose life-or-death case nearly got lost in the legal pandemonium, the stay of execution came at a propitious moment. He turned 50 yesterday—two decades older than the day he came to Death Row, and now one step closer to justice.

The *Herald*'s editorial was nothing compared to a subsequent column written by *Herald* Associate Editor Tony Proscio. Proscio's column began with descriptions of Joe, Tony DiLisio, and me, who Proscio might have described as the three scumbags:

If you didn't know the players, you might have mistaken this for a romantic morality play: The tale of the Penitent Liar racing to the gallows to rescue the Wrongly Convicted Man, just as the Crusading Lawyer lunges to stay the executioner's upraised hand.

Great stuff. Standing room only. Free hankies with every performance.

Trouble is, history is a lousy screenwriter. The case of the State of Florida vs. Joseph Spaziano—the 20-year-old murder trial under examination in a Seminole County courtroom—has all the makings of a first-rate tearjerker.

The man about to be executed could well be innocent. The testimony that put him on death row is almost certainly false. And his "trial" was a mockery of the Constitution. It's an alarming story of American justice. But as a box-office blockbuster, it's got one giant problem:

The cast stinks.

The Wrongly Condemned Man, "Crazy Joe" Spaziano, is no Tom Hanks. He's a tough, scary-looking biker with a monster rap sheet and enough enemies (including several members of his own family) to overflow a medium-sized courtroom.

The False-but-Penitent Witness isn't Brad Pitt, all doe-eyed remorse and misguided innocence. He's Tony DiLisio, a fast-talking former acid-head who seems to live permanently on the edge of hysteria. Twenty years ago, as a drugged-out teenager, he succumbed to police entreaties, and two sessions of shamelessly suggestive hypnosis to accuse Spaziano, a former buddy, of torture and murder. A born-again Christian, he now admits that he was lying when his hand first rested on the Bible. Still, after days of anguished deliberation, a jury reluctantly believed his fabrication, and Spaziano headed for the electric chair.

And the original Crusading Lawyer is no Jimmy Stewart. He's an angry ideologue who writes legal briefs that read like temper tantrums, a guy who insists on referring to his adversaries (including federal appellate judges) by the unprintable names of private body parts.

These are not people you're likely to fall in love with. No one is going to become engrossed in this story for its glamour. In fact, many people seem to have missed the point of it entirely, apparently because it consists largely of small-town grotesques with often dark, imponderable motives.

What prompted this outburst? Nothing I did or Joe did or Tony DiLisio did. Rather, Proscio's bile was precipitated by an innocuous question asked of Proscio by an *Orlando Sentinel* reporter:

> All of this may explain how surprised I was when Jim Leusner, a reporter for The Orlando Sentinel, approached me last week outside Judge O. H. Eaton Jr.'s courtroom in Seminole County, during a break in the Spaziano hearing, to ask me this remarkable question:
>
> "Has The Herald lost its objectivity on this story?"
>
> Huh? *Lost its objectivity?* For what? Because its reporters and editors were somehow enthralled by the allure of these magnetic personalities? Entranced by their Gandhi-like serenity? Blinded by their charm?
>
> What element of this story, I wanted to ask him, would have caused The Herald suddenly to shed its principles? No matter how little one might think of this newspaper—and I happen to think quite highly of it—what possible motive could there be for casting ethics aside in *this* of all cases?

Who would have been the heroes of Proscio's morality play? Take a wild guess:

What he meant, I suppose, is that Lori Rozsa, The Herald's lead reporter on this story, was the first journalist to pierce through to DiLisio's conscience and hear him admit his 20-year-old lie. On June 9, Rozsa went to DiLisio's Pensacola home seeking his view of his flimsy 1975 testimony. After getting the door slammed in her face, she used the salesman's classic stratagem— she thrust her foot past the doorjamb. DiLisio soon gave in and finally told her what he previously had told only his pastor. He had lied and had sent a man to probable death.

That was dramatic (and top-notch) reporting. It demonstrated Rozsa's skill and determination. It yielded a Page One story. What it did not do is alter The Herald's interest in the case of Florida vs. Spaziano.

Well before Rozsa ever went to Pensacola—in fact, before her editor was even convinced that it was worth the trip—The Herald already had prepared an editorial saying that Spaziano's trial was a hopelessly deficient basis for executing him.

Why? Because we had read the transcripts of the trial and of DiLisio's abracadabra "hypnosis." Because we looked for corroboration, physical evidence, convincing testimony, and found absolutely none. Before the witness had recanted anything, before any Herald reporter had met him or even contemplated meeting him, keen observers of the legal system inside and outside the paper already had smelled the constitutional stench of a shamefully bad trial.

The Florida Supreme Court, intrigued by DiLisio's recantation and Rozsa's reporting, eventually ordered the current hearing. As a result, Judge Eaton is expected to decide today or sometime very soon whether he believes what DiLisio says today, or what he said 20 years ago.

Yet in all this high legal drama, the heart and soul of this horrendous matter seems to have been lost. Namely: *The case against Spaziano smelled to high heaven before The Herald ran the first story on it.* It was a phony prosecution, based on a single witness with a disastrous drug habit, several clear motives to lie, a story that took weeks (and two sessions of hypnotic suggestion) to concoct and a number of assertions that contradicted the known evidence.

Were there two bodies or one? Were they side-by-side or piled one atop the other? Were they both young, or was one of them noticeably elderly? Were they covered or in plain view? Were they in a dump or an orange grove? Did Spaziano boast of murdering them or merely hint of committing other, similar murders? All of that depends on when the teenage DiLisio was talking, and to whom. Yet the whole prosecution of Joe Spaziano rested on this one troubled kid's twisted, incredible tale.

Don't believe me. Believe the state's prosecutor at trial: "If you don't believe Tony DiLisio," he told the jury then, "the only possible verdict was *not guilty.*" Eventually jurors reached the wrong conclusion. But don't blame them: No one ever told them about the hypnosis or the contradictions.

Whether to believe Tony DiLisio is a crucial issue, but it's not the fundamental issue. The fundamental issue has nothing to do with DiLisio, or with Lori Rozsa, or with The Herald. It has to do with the electric chair, with justice and with this simple question:

Does Florida dare—does any decent society dare—to electrocute a human being based on a trial like the one they gave Joe Spaziano 20 years ago? And if so, why bother with trials at all?

That's what I should have said to Sentinel reporter Jim Leusner. Sometimes, though, the truest things don't come to your mind right away. Sometimes, you have to think things through awhile to get them right.

Sometimes, the truth can take 20 years to tell.

(By the time Proscio's column was published in the *Herald,* Proscio himself had left the newspaper and moved to New York. Proscio's slam of me personally didn't detract from the two beautiful columns he had written during Joe's two death warrants in 1995. If Proscio had to trash someone, better me than Joe.)

These quotations are extensive and somewhat repetitious. I have included them here at length because their gist is criticism of my actions, and because I want to preserve their flavor. These commentaries would not have the same impact if they were paraphrased or abbreviated.

Not all the feedback I got was negative. Syndicated columnists Colman McCarthy and James J. Kilpatrick recognized what the *Miami Herald* never has: that I had something to do with saving Joe's life in September 1995. Roger Parloff wrote a piece for *American Lawyer* titled "Fired for Saving His Client's Life":

"If this court intends to kill this innocent man by depriving him of the effective assistance of counsel," pro bono counsel Michael Mello wrote the Florida Supreme Court last September 8, "then it will do so without my complicity. I will not participate in a sham evidentiary 'hearing.'"

To stop the machinery of death from claiming his client, Mello threw himself in the gears. By refusing to show up for a hearing for which he had been given less than a week to prepare—and highlighting that, in his opinion, his client was being denied effective assistance of counsel—he shamed the court into granting a stay of execution and time to prepare properly.

For years the eccentric Mello, now a professor at Vermont Law School ["When Worlds Collide," June 1995], had written in pleadings, law review articles, and newspaper editorials that his death row client, Joseph "Crazy Joe" Spaziano, was innocent. Mello's writings were always passionate, always verbose, occasionally offensive, and never successful.

Spaziano, a member of an Orlando motorcycle gang, was convicted in January 1976 of brutally murdering Laura Harberts, an 18-year-old hospital clerk, who disappeared on August 5, 1973, and whose skeletal remains were discovered in a garbage dump 16 days later.

While the case raised numerous perplexing legal issues, the most disturbing was that—unbeknownst to the jury—the testimony of the key prosecution witness, a troubled teenage drug addict named Anthony DiLisio, consisted almost entirely of hypnotically recovered memories. Although the state supreme court later decided that hypnotically induced testimony was so unreliable as to be inadmissible per se, both that court and the federal courts refused to upset Spaziano's conviction, since his trial lawyer had never objected to DiLisio's testimony on those grounds. Indeed, his trial lawyer chose not to let the jury know that

DiLisio's testimony was hypnotically induced, fearing that the jury might give it undue credence if it knew.

While Spaziano's fourth execution warrant was pending in June 1995, DiLisio, now a born-again Christian, recanted his testimony. Governor Lawton Chiles briefly stayed Spaziano's execution to investigate the recantation, but in late August he issued a fifth warrant, claiming that a report by state investigators—which Chiles refused to make public—established that the recantation was false. Spaziano was to die September 21.

On September 8 Mello went to the Florida Supreme Court seeking a stay of execution and an evidentiary hearing concerning the recantation.

The court granted the hearing, but refused to order a stay of execution. Instead, by a 4-to-3 vote, the court ordered Mello, an appellate lawyer with very little trial experience, no associates, and no investigator, to handle an evidentiary hearing one week later, on September 15. The court also ordered the state's Office of the Capital Collateral Representative (CCR)—a public defender's office devoted to capital post-conviction appeals—to assist Mello.

Mello refused to comply.

"We would have thrown a hearing together," he says, "put on enough evidence so that [the justices could say], 'Yeah, you had your hearing,' we would have lost, the [trial-level] judge would have made killer fact-findings against us, and . . . Joe would have been dead on time and as scheduled."

In a handwritten fax sent from his motel to the supreme court on the night of September 8, Mello just said no. He wrote, among other things, that he and CCR could not provide competent assistance with just six days' preparation. Mello also pledged that he would not surrender his 25 boxes of case files to CCR or to any other attorney in time for the hearing. "If you are going to kill an innocent man without a lawyer," he wrote, "you will do so in such a way that the whole world will see what you are doing. . . . I will not be your mask."

The high court blinked. On September 12 it threw Mello off the case, but granted Spaziano a stay. Then, in January, after new pro bono attorneys at 470-lawyer Holland & Knight took over the case—and the supreme court allowed them almost three months to prepare—circuit judge O. H. Eaton, Jr., of Sanford, Florida, overturned Spaziano's conviction and granted a new trial.

"Mike Mello's responsible for Joe Spaziano's life," says H&K partner Gregg Thomas, who handled the hearing with his partner Stephen Hanlon and Orlando-based criminal specialist James Russ. Holland & Knight donated about $400,000 in lawyer time and $70,000 in costs to handle the hearing, Thomas estimates, not counting Russ's time.

The state has appealed Judge Eaton's ruling to the Florida supreme court.

Meanwhile, Spaziano is still serving life for the 1974 rape and battery of a 16-year-old girl. Mello believes Spaziano is innocent of that charge as well. But, as Mello says, "that's another story."

And an old friend from my Florida deathwork days wrote a letter I will always cherish:

Dear Mike:

This is a love letter.

I have been reading. Some comments on your writing. 1st, you are an unequaled writer, a point which bears repeating—I have always admired (envied) it. In 1985 my critique was that you wrote *law*, not (new) facts. Obviously, that (your "MO" [ha!]) and my critique has (check Harbrace on plural) changed.

You write facts now. What is remarkable is that as (normal) people age, ambition yields to self-preservation. Usually, people become more disciplined, and, concomitantly, less compelling with age—we trade passion for tactics. I think I wrote more facts in '85; I write more law in '95:'96. You wrote law in '85, but you write facts in '96.

You have moved from safety to danger. Most (i.e., me) move from danger to safety, with age. Maturity is either a beast of burden, or (rarely) liberating. My point (should I have one) is that you are becoming *younger*.

This is worth dwelling upon for a nano(sic?) second. I *still* try to kick ass, but the people around me fuckin' *caution* me, and on occasion I listen (pussy). A little. But you listen (only?) to the [traditionally] fading rads. I am beginning to think that today you do not listen at all—you trail-blaze. You are, to plagiarize Jim [Liebman], more than a "little bit retro."

Anyway, the *Miami Herald, St. Petersburg Times,* and *Orlando Sentinel*—able to agree on so little about the case of "Crazy Joe" Spaziano—finally found something upon which they all could agree: that the Florida Supreme Court was right in throwing me off of Joe's case. I happen to agree that the Florida Supreme Court was justified in punishing me for my acts of civil disobedience. The court was not justified, in my opinion, in punishing *Joe* for my actions as his attorney.

In the following pages I will discuss the matter of my civil disobedience in Joe's case. I will attempt to articulate exactly what I did, why I did it, and who I was serving.

Capital cases are all about power. Because the inherent power imbalance favors the state—the state's investigators are the police; its lawyers are flying squadrons of prosecutors; it decides when the death warrants are to be signed, and against whom; the public, the politicians, and the media are on the state's side—the best capital postconviction litigators, such as Mark Olive and Clive Stafford-Smith, have become masters in the art of legal jujitsu, using the legal system's strength against itself, reversing the polarity of the power disparity.

Until the Florida Supreme Court had decided that Joe Spaziano's innocence claim was sufficiently substantial to require an evidentiary hearing on the truthfulness of Tony DiLisio's recantation, the state possessed all the power and Joe (and I) possessed none. By virtue of my access to information, I had some influence upon the *Herald*. But influence isn't the same as power, and the *Herald* was as fiercely independent of me as it was of the courts, the governor, and the *Orlando Sentinel*. The ones with the real power wanted Joe dead, and the sooner the better. I know that the Florida Supreme Court justices took my "free-form" filings as indicia of disrespect or insolence. I intended neither disrespect nor insolence, although I was trying to shame the court into doing what it should have done a decade ago—taking a hard look at Joe's evidence of his innocence. Given that I was trying to shame the Florida Supreme Court into doing the right thing, it follows that I felt the justices *capable* of feeling shame, something of which I did not think the U.S. Supreme Court capable. (This was the core assumption underlying my "infamous" June 27 memo.) Thus, in a way, I was paying the Florida Supreme Court a backhanded compliment.

Shaming, or public humiliation, isn't a new notion; it was the impulse behind the stocks favored for punishment by seventeenth-century Puritans. Shaming penalties are once again in vogue. In Port St. Lucie, Florida, a judge ordered a woman, as a condition of her probation, to place an advertisement in her local newspaper saying she had bought drugs in front of her children. Drunk drivers in some states have to put special license plates on their cars. Men convicted of soliciting prostitutes are identified on billboards and radio shows. Shaming is seen by its proponents as addressing the needs of a public weary of crime, frustrated by the failures of the criminal justice system, and unwilling to pay for yet more prison expansion.

"The whole world is watching." That's what the antiwar protesters chanted to Mayor Daley's outlaw Chicago police during the 1968 Democratic National Convention. That's what the demonstrators chanted through the tear gas, with blood running down their faces and with broken arms and legs, as Chicago's finest beat them senseless in Grant Park, at Michigan and Balboa, even in Eugene McCarthy's suite of hotel rooms. "Your whole world is watching." That's what I had written to Florida Governor Lawton Chiles back in June 1995. It was as true of the Florida Supreme Court in September 1995 as it had been of the governor in June.

With the stroke of a word processor key, however, the Florida Supreme Court altered the operative power matrix in Joe Spaziano's case. The Florida Supreme Court had determined that Joe's innocence claim was *real*—real enough to require an evidentiary hearing. Now the only important issues were the circumstances under which that concededly necessary hearing would be held. True, the Florida Supreme Court had made it impossible for the hearing to be anything other than a sham that would enshroud Joe's execution within the ornaments of due process and the trappings of an opportunity to prove his innocence— the comfortable illusion that Joe's innocence claim had received its day in court.

But the Florida Supreme Court's validation of Joe's innocence claim had empowered me, and with power came leverage. No evidentiary hearing—not even a sham of a hearing—could take place unless Joe's lawyer at that hearing had the voluminous files in the case. CCR was more than willing to acquiesce in the fiction that it could represent Joe at the evidentiary hearing under warrant demanded by the Florida Supreme Court; CCR had done it before, and the agency would do it again; CCR would be Joe's lawyer at the hearing it couldn't possibly win, and Joe would be killed on schedule.

But not unless CCR had Joe's files. Without the files, neither the courts nor the governor could continue to pretend that the "hearing" was anything other than a mockery and a joke. The problem was that CCR didn't have the files. I had the files. In Vermont.

I had told the Florida Supreme Court, in my handwritten motion for a rehearing faxed to the court near midnight on September 8, that I refused to send Joe's files to CCR; I also said in that motion that I would defy any court ordering me to send Joe's files to CCR. Joe's files belonged to him, not to me, and certainly not to the Florida Supreme Court. Joe was my client, not the Florida Supreme Court. I would send the files to CCR *only* if requested to do so by my client or his family.

The Florida Supreme Court knew, of course, that it had the power to force me to send Joe's files to CCR, and that it could enforce that order with its power to hold me in contempt of court. The court could order me to be incarcerated indefinitely for civil contempt; it could impose monetary fines that would drive me into personal bankruptcy, guaranteeing that I would lose my house, car, and savings. The Florida Supreme Court could disbar me, eliminating my ability to practice law in Florida or any other jurisdiction; my disbarment would give Vermont Law School Dean Maximilian Kempner the pretext he needed, and for which he had long been searching, to strip me of tenure and fire me from my teaching job.

The Florida Supreme Court justices could do all these things, and more, but that would take time—more time than permitted by Joe Spaziano's impending execution date. The justices knew that, too. Perhaps, in the end, that knowledge was the reason for the Florida Supreme Court's decision on September 12 to stay the execution indefinitely, fire me from the case, order me to send Joe's files to CCR, and give the fifty-person staff at CCR two months to prepare for the evidentiary hearing. With the execution on hold, the Florida Supreme Court would have all the time in the world to coerce me into turning Joe's files over to CCR. As of the court's September 12 opinion, I had been (for the first time) under court order to send all of Joe's files "in [my] possession" to CCR. From the moment I received the court's

September 12 opinion over my fax wire, I was subject to the court's civil and criminal contempt powers for failure to comply with that court order. I knew it, the justices knew it, and they knew I knew it.

I fully expected that one day soon the Florida police (or the Vermont police at the behest of the Florida police) would show up with a warrant to search my home for Joe's files. When they didn't find the files in my house, they would take me into custody for willful contempt of the Florida Supreme Court's September 12 order regarding Joe's files. Since I had previously told the Florida Supreme Court that I would waive extradition from Vermont and voluntarily return to Florida to accept full responsibility (and punishment) for my disobedience, the court would order me to remain incarcerated in Florida until I decided to comply with the September 12 order. As I'd also told the Florida Supreme Court, that would have been a very, very long wait.

Perhaps it strikes you as odd that police may search the home/office of an attorney. They can. For me, it had happened very recently and very close to home. In June 1995, FBI and Drug Enforcement Administration agents had searched the home/office of Vermont poor-person's lawyer Will Hunter and his wife April Henzel; Hunter was suspected of (but has never been charged with) laundering drug money for one of his clients.

With this haunting image fresh in my mind, I moved all of Joe's files from my home and into my office at Vermont Law School. The government would need a warrant to search my Vermont Law School office, and perhaps the police would think twice before asking a judge for a warrant to search a law school, especially when Joe's files would more likely be located in my home office rather than my law school office; it was common knowledge that I was doing Joe's case out of my home.

Still I worried. Maybe the police wouldn't need a warrant to search my law school office. I didn't own my office at the law school; the law school owned it. All the cops would need do would be to ask Dean Kempner for consent to rifle through my office in search of Joe's files. The dean would happily give his permission. Later, in court, I could challenge the validity of the dean's consent, and therefore the legality of the search, but by then the damage would have been done. CCR would have Joe's files. His life would be in their cowardly and incompetent hands.

The only way I could keep Joe's case away from CCR was to find a law firm willing to take over the case—and to send Joe's files to the new firm rather than to CCR. The trick was to find a law firm before the Florida Supreme Court sent the marshals to my house in Vermont.

As insurance, I decided to send all of Joe's files to the *Miami Herald*. The *Herald* had had open access to the files for months anyway, so I wouldn't be giving the paper anything it didn't have already.

If the Florida Supreme Court wanted to play hardball to get Joe's files to CCR, its lapdog law firm, then let them fight it out with the *Herald*. It's not easy for the state to obtain a warrant to search a lawyer's office; it's even harder for the state to get a warrant to search a *newspaper*'s offices. The First Amendment—freedom of the press and all that.

Like the *New York Times* and *Washington Post* in the Pentagon Papers case in 1971, the *Miami Herald* would have the spine to resist any efforts by the state to push it around. More important, the *Herald* had the resources to make that resistance effective and expensive to the government. Florida's flagship newspaper possessed the firepower to hire the state's best and most experienced law firms specializing in the First Amendment. The government might at the end of the day succeed in forcing the *Herald* to disgorge Joe's files, but it would have to fight like a wildcat for every page. It would take sweat and money and time. Lots of time.

Soon after I'd sent Joe's files to the *Herald*—based on the word of Gene Miller and Lori Rozsa that only they and Warren Holmes would have access to the files, and that they would send the files only to the lawyer I designated, or back to me, regardless of any directives to the contrary from the Florida Supreme Court, the governor, the attorney general, or anyone else—the *Herald* persuaded the law firm of Holland & Knight to take over Joe's case. Holland & Knight was Florida's largest and richest law firm, a powerhouse firm that was to other Florida law firms what the *Herald* was to other Florida newspapers. My trust in Gene Miller, Lori Rozsa, and Warren Holmes was vindicated—and in spades. When I asked Miller to send Joe's files on to Holland & Knight, it was the most natural thing for the *Herald* to do. It felt like keeping Joe's case inside the family, in a way: the *Herald*'s general outside counsel on First Amendment and other matters was, of course, Holland & Knight.

An aging French aristocrat was asked one day to describe his most vivid memory of the Reign of Terror. "I survived," he answered without pause. Whenever it occurs to me that the Florida Supreme Court didn't disbar me or worse for my action in late 1995, I think about that Frenchman's neck intact.

When the Florida Supreme Court kicked me off Joe's case on September 12, the justices cited my "flagrant disregard of this court's procedures and directions." The court was correct.

I'm not sure I would characterize my actions during Joe's fifth death warrant as *flagrant* disregard of the court's procedures and directions, but the label isn't unreasonable in this instance. I had consciously disregarded the procedural rule that, as an initial matter, I should have filed in the state trial court, rather than in the Florida Supreme Court. I also had made a conscious decision that I would not allow the court to compel me to accept CCR as cocounsel—against the reasonable wishes of my client and his family. In addition, I had consciously decided that I would neither show up at the scheduled evidentiary hearing nor send Joe's files to CCR. I believed that under Florida law, Joe's files belong to *him*—not to me or the Florida Supreme Court or CCR.

I expected the court to hold me in contempt. In September 1995 I didn't need to research the law regarding contempt of court. Years earlier I had worked on Elizabeth Morgan's case. For two years, Dr. Morgan had been incarcerated in the District of Columbia jail for civil contempt, for refusing to produce her young daughter for court-ordered unsupervised visitation with the child's father. Dr. Morgan remained in jail for almost two years, until an act of the U.S. Congress ordered her freed.

I learned from Dr. Morgan's case that most of the important rules of law don't apply to civil contempt cases: there is no right to trial by jury; there is virtually no due process of law; trial judges' orders of contempt are almost never overturned on appeal. This is why it took literally an act of Congress to get Dr. Morgan released from jail.

Civil contempt is beyond the reach of law because it is *civil,* not criminal. Its purpose is to coerce compliance with court orders (in Dr. Morgan's case, to produce her daughter for visitation; in my case, to send my Spaziano files to Office of Capital Collateral Representative), not to punish. That's the theory, anyway. During Dr. Morgan's two years in the District of Columbia jail, I often wondered whether it mattered that she was there for purposes of "coercion" and not as punishment. It seems to me that the District of Columbia jail is pretty much the same in either case.

On September 12, 1995, however, the question wasn't so much whether the Florida Supreme Court would hold me in civil contempt. The question was what would the justices *do* about it? Would they send marshals to my home in Vermont to search for and seize Joe's files? I half expected the answer was yes.

By 1995 it had become clear—if it was not clear already—that the expected role of capital postconviction defense lawyers is to enable the legal system to speed up executions. How *ought* we postconviction defense attorneys respond to this state of affairs? What ought we do— and what ought we *not* do?

For myself, the question of what we ought not do is the easiest to answer. To paraphrase the Hippocratic oath, *first,* we *ought* not to do any harm. We ought not to accept the new rules laid down that require us to enable the state to kill our clients. We should resist. Such resistance can take at least two possible forms. Capital postconviction lawyers of conscience *could* refuse to participate in the machinery of death, or they could sabotage the smooth operation of the machine. Often acts of civil disobedience appear to violate the ethical regulations governing the conduct of lawyers. Such acts, however, are justifiable for the achievement of a higher priority—such as justice or life itself. We can be the spanner in the works, the steel spike in the tree trunk. We can, with respect to the system, insist on substance over form, truth over protocol. Any lawyer contemplating such civil disobedience should keep in mind, however, the ultimate fate of the spanner and the steel spike: the tool of repair will suffer more immediate wear and tear than the system to which it is applied. The machine may stop for a little while, but eventually it will be repaired. The machine will be fired up again. Spanners, forced to gap hard, opposing pressures, can be broken. Spikes that find a soft entry may endure. It is not a game; it is very demanding.

The operational limits of the sort of civil disobedience I mean must be marked out by the moral conscience and strategic prudence of the individual lawyers who choose the path of civic resistance. Some lawyers might limit their civil disobedience to acts of passive resistance and quiet subversion. Other lawyers might resist with more overt but nonviolent means. Still others might choose to disable the machinery of death by any means necessary—including violence.

Mapping out the limits of one's range of acceptable civil disobedience implicates both moral and strategic considerations. For me, in Joe Spaziano's case in 1995, moral and strategic concerns led me to implement civil resistance under the following necessary conditions.

First, delay of execution at any cost was what my client wanted. Not all clients do. Some condemned people decide—not necessarily irrationally, in my view—to acquiesce in their own execution by waiving further appeals. The wait to be killed at some indefinite time in the future can become worse for some people than the actual killing itself, and some condemned souls decide to "volunteer" for execution. How lawyers should respond to such death wishes is hotly contested among lawyers who specialize in deathwork. My own belief is that I should honor my client's decision to volunteer for execution, assuming the client is mentally competent to make the choice. But Joe Spaziano was no such volunteer. He fiercely wanted to live, and he wanted me to fight as hard as I could to keep the state from killing him.

Second, in preventing the state from executing my innocent client, I would limit my civil disobedience to nonviolent means. For me, eschewing violence was a tactical, not a moral, judgment call. I do not believe that nonviolence is always a necessary condition for legitimate civil disobedience. I would have applauded the partisans who dynamited the railroad tracks to Auschwitz, even though a German soldier or two might die in the explosion. A state that uses violent killing (the way Florida does) as an instrument of social policy seems to me to lack the moral credibility to demand nonviolence from its civic resistors. Nevertheless, I engaged only in nonviolent civil disobedience, but I did so regardless of whether or not I had to violate civil or criminal law in the process. Because I was pursuing justice, and for other reasons, I did not commit my unlawful acts in silence, or shielded from view. I frankly, openly, and honestly engaged any relevant parties, privately or publicly. Frankly, I was willing and ready to accept punishment and other possible consequences of my unlawful action. I expected to have to do so. At a minimum, I expected to be disbarred. I also expected to be held in civil and criminal contempt of court—offenses that typically are punished by incarceration in jail or prison. Further, I expected to lose my job as a tenured member of the Vermont Law School faculty.

I considered these to have been acts of civil disobedience or civil resistance. My personal belief is that, in virtually all instances of civil disobedience, the actor's willingness to accept punishment for the law's violation is a necessary condition for the disobedience to be deemed legitimate.

At the time of my actions in Joe Spaziano's case, in August and September 1995, the Florida Supreme Court had not decided whether accepting punishment is an essential element of legitimate civil disobedience. The court did resolve this issue fourteen months later, when it decided the appeal of Paul Hill, a minister who shotgunned an abortion doctor and his armed escort to death in Pensacola, Florida. Ironically, during my brief stint as Paul Hill's appellate lawyer, I had tried to file a Florida Supreme Court brief arguing that willingness to accept punishment isn't *always* a condition of legitimate civil disobedience.

Paul Hill asserted that his killings were "justifiable homicide" because he was preventing a greater evil (of abortion) from occurring. The Florida Supreme Court rejected this argument, adopting the reasoning of a Pennsylvania trial judge:

> To accept appellant's argument would be tantamount to judicially sanctioning vigilantism. If every person were to act upon his or her personal beliefs in this manner, and we were to sanction the act, the result would be utter chaos. In a society of laws and not of individuals, we cannot allow each individual to determine, based upon his or her personal beliefs, whether another person may exercise her constitutional rights and then allow that individual to assert the defense of justification to escape criminal liability. We recognize that, despite our proscription, some individuals, because of firmly held and honestly believed convictions, will feel compelled to break the law. If they choose to do so, however, they must be prepared to face the consequences. Thus, such private attempts to circumvent the law with the aim to deprive a pregnant woman of her right to obtain an abortion *will not be tolerated by this Court.*

I agree, at least in the context of my actions in Joe's case. For example, in my handwritten September 8 rehearing motion, I offered to waive extradition and return to Florida in the event the court wished to hold me in contempt. I was more than willing to pay the personal costs of my "unlawful" actions. I believed—and strongly—that both my conscience and the ethical norms and values of the legal profession required me to violate the law in order for me to be able to provide minimally effective representation to an innocent man on the brink of execution on a fifth death warrant.

Thus, when the Florida Supreme Court punished my civic resistance by throwing me off Joe's case, the justices were, in my opinion, justified. Of course, I was saddened at being fired and trashed by a court before which I had practiced respectfully and reasonably for fourteen years. I had hoped—wrongly, it turned out—that the justices knew me well enough to understand that my extreme actions during Joe's fifth warrant were driven by the extremity of the situation in which Joe and I found ourselves.

The Florida Supreme Court's September 12 opinion sent the unmistakable message that the justices (*all* the justices) thought I was treating the court disrespectfully. In reality, the fact that I was in the court at all—as opposed to federal court, as set out in my "infamous" June 27 memo—evinces my respect for the court as a whole and for the justices individually. I had faith they'd do the right thing in Joe's case. At the end of the day, that faith proved justified: the Florida Supreme Court stayed the execution indefinitely and gave Joe's new lawyers, Holland & Knight, four months rather than seven days to do the right thing.

Yeah, at the end of the day. But September 12, 1995, was one of the longest days of my life. At the end of it, I was never so happy to be living in Vermont rather than Florida, teaching school rather than trying to stay the hand of the Sunshine State's executioner.

In retrospect, my "game of chicken" with the Florida Supreme Court (to use Mike Radelet's phrase) was probably unnecessary. Trial Judge O. H. Eaton Jr. almost certainly would have granted a stay of execution.

He wouldn't have blasted us through a sham evidentiary hearing under warrant, as I'd feared in September 1995 (and as other state trial judges did in Jerry White's case and Philip Atkins's case in December 1995 and as Florida trial judges have done in countless other death cases). He wouldn't have made killer fact-findings. In the end, he would have mandated a new trial.

Thus what I did in September 1995 was unnecessary.

But I couldn't have known that at the time. In the blast furnace of Joe's August–September death warrant, Judge Eaton was still an unknown quantity. Of the dozens and dozens of Florida state trial judges who had in my many years of deathwork denied stays and ordered evidentiary hearings under warrant and made killer fact-findings, I'm not sure a single one of them would have done what Judge Eaton did in January 1996: ordered a new trial for the infamous Outlaw "Crazy Joe" Spaziano. During the chaos of Joe's fifth warrant, I couldn't have known that the luck of the draw would give us a trial judge of singular courage, independence, and determination.

On the other hand, had I acquiesced in the evidentiary hearing under warrant, I'm not sure that we'd even have gotten Judge Eaton as our judge. Recall that during the five days prior to the September 15 hearing scheduled by the Florida Supreme Court, Judge Eaton was out of town—at a judges' conference. He planned to return on September 15, the day of the hearing. The other Orlando and Seminole County trial judges were also at that same conference.

Which state trial judge *wasn't* away at the conference? Judge Robert McGregor—*that* Judge McGregor, who had presided over Joe's 1976 trial, and who had summarily denied stays of execution for Joe Spaziano every chance he got. During Joe's 1985 warrant, McGregor had denied a stay; ditto in 1989; ditto in 1990.

Maybe Judge McGregor would have recused himself based on his comments in the *Orlando Sentinel* suggesting he had prejudged the outcome of the hearing. Maybe. Litigating under death warrant creates its own universe of bad craziness. I'm not at all certain that McGregor would have disqualified himself under the hydraulic pressure of the warrant in Joe's by-then high-profile case, with his hometown newspaper (the *Orlando Sentinel*) and his governor baying for Joe's blood. Maybe McGregor would have resisted the monstrous pressure and done the right thing. But I wouldn't bet on it. I wouldn't bet Joe's life on it.

There is one decision I don't regret in the slightest, not even with the benefit of 20/20 hindsight. I'm *glad* I disregarded Florida's procedural requirement that I file Joe's case in the trial court rather than directly in the Florida Supreme Court. Had I filed initially in the Seminole County trial court, this is the best-case scenario of what would have happened:

Judge McGregor would have been our judge— and since McGregor would never have shot off his mouth to the *Orlando Sentinel* about his prejudging the case (without a little prodding), he would have had no need to recuse himself from the case. If he had not *publicly* prejudged the case, *that* Judge McGregor would surely have summarily denied the stay, forcing me to appeal to the Florida Supreme Court. The Florida Supreme Court would have heard oral argument, possibly denied a stay, and ordered an evidentiary hearing. So the case would have been sent back to the Seminole County trial court, the honorable Judge McGregor presiding. Next, Judge McGregor would have held the evidentiary hearing under warrant, and the sand in Joe's egg timer would have continued running out. With only weeks left, I feared a corpse for a client. Additionally, since I would have been out of time and resources, my only witness would have been Tony DiLisio. The prosecutors would have gleefully defamed Tony's recantation, using their secret information—which I couldn't rebut, lacking the necessary time and resources. Predictably, McGregor would assert that the 1976 trial (over which *he* had presided) was not a miscarriage of justice, because he would refuse to credit Tony's recent recantation. McGregor would write a "fact-finding" stating that Tony's recantation was unreliable. I could then have appealed to the Florida Supreme Court, but the justices would have been obligated to do exactly what the rules of appellate practice tell them to do—defer to the trial court's "facts found" following an evidentiary hearing. Judge McGregor, being the trial court *and* the fact finder, would be affirmed. Stay denied. Big surprise.

Next, I could file a federal habeas petition in federal district court. For reasons of efficiency, the case would have gone to Judge G. Kendall Sharp, as it did the previous time around. Tragically, Judge Sharp would be forced by law to do what procedural rules require *him* to do—defer to Judge McGregor's "fact-findings." Stay denied. So, it would mean moving on to the Eleventh Circuit Court of Appeals, where, for reasons of efficiency, the case would have been assigned to a panel directed by Judge Ed Carnes, the former Alabama capital prosecutor. Judge Carnes would do exactly what *his* procedural rules told him to do—defer to Judge Sharp's deference to the Florida Supreme Court's deference to Judge McGregor's "fact-findings." Stay denied. Predictably, I would go to the U.S. Supreme Court, asking the justices to decide Joe's case. But, of course, they would say no, because under their *Herrera* reasoning, *factual* innocence isn't an *issue* in a federal habeas proceeding, because it is an issue of fact. And the fact finder would already have decided what facts were worth finding. Stay denied.

Finally, I would have no choice left except to apply for executive clemency, based on factual innocence. But Governor Chiles would conveniently continue to maintain that innocence and guilt are matters for the *courts* to decide, and this case had received painstaking judicial review over the past nineteen years, by a bazillian judges, yadda, yadda, yadda. Clemency denied. Stay denied. Joe electrocuted. Maybe we could all go out for coffee afterward.

This hypothetical scenario is not far-fetched. So, the next time you read about some lawyer making an appeal for his client based on legal technicalities, remember: he might not have anywhere to bring his facts, but they'll hear his technicalities.

It's a great system, but, like all systems, it is dependent upon its operators.

16

The Police Detective, the Psychic, and the Skull

So Eichmann's opportunities for feeling like Pontius Pilate were many, and as the months and the years went by, he lost the need to feel anything at all. This was the way things were, this was the new law of the land, based on the Führer's order; whatever he did he did, as far as he could see, as a law-abiding citizen. He did his *duty,* as he told the police and the court over and over again; he not only obeyed *orders,* he also obeyed the *law.*

Hannah Arendt, Eichmann in Jerusalem:
A Report on the Banality of Evil, *1963*

On September 12, 1995—the same day the Florida Supreme Court stayed Joe's execution, fired me as Joe's lawyer, sent Joe's case to CCR, and gave CCR two months to prepare for the evidentiary hearing on Tony DiLisio's recantation—the chief justice of the Florida Supreme Court issued an order assigning Judge Robert McGregor to preside over Spaziano's evidentiary hearing. *That* Judge McGregor would be calling the shots again.

However, recently Judge McGregor had made comments to reporters indicating that he had prejudged Joe's evidentiary hearing. On September 11, 1995—three days after the Florida Supreme Court's order for the evidentiary hearing and one day before the court granted Joe an indefinite stay and fired me from the case—the *Miami Herald* reported on an interview with Judge McGregor, quoting him as saying Tony DiLisio "was surely a key witness, laying it at Spaziano." The *Herald* also quoted McGregor's opinions regarding DiLisio's trial testimony: "The defense did their best to belittle the testimony of the youngster. I didn't see any suggestion that the kid was making it up."

Nice, but not enough to disqualify McGregor from presiding at the evidentiary hearing on the truthfulness or falsity of DiLisio's June 1995 recantation. According to the Code of Judicial Conduct, a judge "shall not, while a proceeding is pending or impending in any court, make any public comment that might reasonably be expected to affect its outcome or impair its fairness." Judge McGregor's comments in the *Herald* may not have been enough.

However, the *Orlando Sentinel* came to Joe Spaziano's rescue. On July 2, 1995, the *Sentinel* quoted Judge McGregor's opinion of Joe's trial: "All of the pieces fell in place. . . . There weren't any inconsistencies that made me suspicious of somebody else . . . or pointed the finger in anyone else's direction except Spaziano." And: "The largest—and most compelling piece, McGregor acknowledged, was Tony DiLisio." This article was about DiLisio's recantation. The *Sentinel* had interviewed Judge McGregor in order to give him an opportunity to comment upon the recantation.

And then the smoking gun. On August 24, 1995, in yet another article on Tony DiLisio's recantation, the *Orlando Sentinel* reported: "Judge McGregor remembers evidence at the murder trial as overwhelming."

Based on Judge McGregor's public comments about the case in *Orlando Sentinel* and *Miami Herald* articles, Joe's attorneys filed a motion asking Judge McGregor to recuse himself from the hearing. After consulting with his chief judge, McGregor removed himself from the case.

Because the Florida Supreme Court had stayed Joe's execution, the disqualification motion could be filed, considered, and decided without the hydraulic pressures added by a death warrant. Had the evidentiary hearing occurred under warrant, I have no doubt that Judge McGregor would have presided. I also have no doubt McGregor would have disbelieved Tony DiLisio's recantation. McGregor's fact-findings would have been affirmed by the Florida Supreme Court. Joe would have been executed on schedule at 7:00 A.M. on September 20, 1995.

Tony DiLisio's recantation in 1995 won Joe a stay of execution, but it raised many troubling questions, not the least of which was whether or not it was enough to win Joe a new trial.

The Florida prosecutors, police, governor's office, and even the *Orlando Sentinel* wondered why DiLisio waited twenty years, until the eve of the execution, to change his story. They claimed that it was because Tony was afraid of the Outlaws, or because he had been pressured by Spaziano's lawyers or the *Miami Herald*. They even claimed that it could be because Tony wanted the publicity, or that he was just plain flaky.

As the *Herald*'s Lori Rozsa reported, however, Tony DiLisio himself, once the state's star witness, gave the answer to these inquiries. He stated that if he were going to recant out of fear, he would have done so years before—the only person or thing he fears now is God. The idea that DiLisio desired publicity was equally ludicrous, because the *Orlando Sentinel,* in cooperation with the state, had destroyed the quiet family life that he had so clearly worked for by publicizing every flaw in his life, from his divorce problems to his financial difficulties. And if the state thought that Tony was a flake in 1995, imagine the Tony DiLisio of twenty years before, when he was a scared, drug-addicted teenager who was the star witness in a capital murder trial.

DiLisio's claims were good, but they needed corroboration. The search was on to see if Tony had confided any of what he told Rozsa to another person. He had, to Elmer Leidig, who had served as Tony DiLisio's counselor for years previous to his recantation. Tony had told Leidig that "he was done wrong as a child, that he did wrong."

Leidig also stated that Tony had said that "he testified to something that wasn't true, and it had bothered him all this time." Leidig remembered Tony telling him that the false testimony involved hypnosis, and that the police officers had suggested things to him. "He said that there was a man accused of killing a girl and taking her to a dump," Leidig said. "Tony said somebody said that the man took him to the dump, but he didn't. The police took him there." DiLisio had told Leidig all this well before he recanted to Rozsa.

Leidig said that he had advised Tony to come forward with his story. He told Tony that although telling the truth might be difficult, in the end it is the best way. But DiLisio didn't come forward right away because he believed that others had also incriminated Spaziano. He was wrong, of course; he was the only witness linking Spaziano to the crime. The prosecutor at the time of trial admitted that he did not have a case without Tony DiLisio's testimony.

Leidig told Rozsa in October 1995 that he still visited DiLisio twice a week. He claimed that "Tony is heart-bound that something will occur to prove to them that he's telling the truth. I'd like to see somebody in authority talk to him and believe him."

Tony's nickname among the Alabama death row prisoners to whom he ministered—his *nom de row,* so to speak—was Brother Nitro. Brother Nitro's 1995 recantation won Joe Spaziano a stay of execution. Brother Nitro's recantation, plus Pastor Leidig's corroborating testimony, might be enough to win Joe a whole new trial.

As discussed earlier, in June–August 1995, the Florida Department of Law Enforcement prepared a secret report for Governor Lawton Chiles regarding the testimony of Tony DiLisio. Based on this report, Governor Chiles determined that Joe Spaziano should be executed, even though the report contained at least one factual error and was based on the testimony of witnesses with motivation to lie. The report was the result of two months of investigation regarding DiLisio and his recantation. Based on the findings, the governor concluded that DiLisio was lying now but had told the truth nineteen years ago when he testified that Joe had committed the murder of Laura Lynn Harberts.

I never did succeed in extracting from the government the secret police report upon which Governor Chiles based his decision to sign Joe's fifth death warrant. The only piece of the cops' secret handiwork I have ever seen is the videotape of FDLE's interrogation of Tony DiLisio. And the governor's chief lawyer, Dexter Douglass, lied about what that videotape actually contained.

Once again, the *Miami Herald* had the investigative resources to do what I couldn't. Lori Rozsa investigated the asserted facts set out in the secret police report. The *Herald* published her findings on October 14, 1995:

Chicago

One finding upon which Governor Chiles based his decision was an inference that Spaziano was a suspect in an unsolved Chicago murder. On December 31, 1974, Mike Dungress, 29, and Linda Noe, 23, were both shot in the head in their apartment in Chicago. Dungress was a former member of the Chicago branch of the Outlaws, and Noe worked at a Bathhouse.

Patrick Camden, of the Chicago Police News Affairs Bureau, reviewed a synopsis of the file but refused to release it. He did state that Spaziano was never mentioned in the file. Homicide detectives identified Michael Wax as the suspected killer because of an heroin deal gone bad. Police closed the case in 1982, even though Wax was not prosecuted because the informant refused to testify. They labeled the case "cleared exceptionally." Chicago detectives say that they are convinced that Wax killed Dungress and Noe. There were no other motorcycle gang murders at the time.

The FDLE Report had this to say about Chicago: An informant claimed that Spaziano confided in him that while he was on the run in Chicago he partied with an Outlaw member and his wife. While drunk, he confessed that he had killed some people. Once he had sobered up and realized what he had told them, he was afraid they would talk so he went back and killed them.

Governor Chiles, after reading the Report, stated that "[w]ell it just happens that we checked in Chicago, there's a couple of unsolved murders up there at the time. And that was something that kind of came in as I said later, so I guess it's a chain of a lot of events to a subjective decision that I have to make." The Chicago authorities said that if anyone from Florida ever inquired about the case, they didn't know about it. When the governor's general counsel was pushed on this issue, he claimed that "We gave no weight to that [Chicago] in our consideration of the case."

This secret informant is Ralph "Lucifer" Yannotta, an ex-biker turned government informant. Yannotta was a former member of the Pagan and then Outlaw motorcycle gangs who went to jail in 1974 for murder. In 1978 he became a government informant against other Outlaws charged with crimes. He testified in three trials against the leader of the Outlaws in the 1970s, "Big Jim" Nolan, who was charged with the murder of three Hell's Angels. His first trial resulted in a hung jury, his second in a mistrial, and his third in an acquittal. "Big Jim" is now serving time on a federal racketeering charge. Yannotta claimed that he had participated in "death detail" on the Hell's Angels murders and had helped to hogtie the three men and drown them with cement blocks.

Defense attorneys who knew Yannotta called him a "classic jailhouse snitch— he made whatever statements the police wanted to hear." Charles White, the attorney for Jim Nolan, claimed that Yannotta was not a credible witness because he had lied to the court before, at his own trial, and he had been forced to admit to this. "He had good reason to cooperate. His story got better and better at each trial." White said. "He was a diabolical person who could not be called a credible man." He had been implicated in five murders, but through his bargaining with prosecutors, he entered a witness protection program and was paroled in 1994.

Yannotta claimed that not only had Spaziano confessed to the Chicago murders, but that he also admitted to the two garbage dump murders while they were in jail. He claimed that Spaziano told him that he had taken an 18-year-old boy to the dump, and he was afraid that the boy would talk to police. However, by this time DiLisio had already given the police statements and testified against Spaziano at his rape trial.

Tony DiLisio

There is much deliberation in the FDLE Report on the fact that DiLisio reported his story on being taken to the dump by "Crazy Joe" to more than the police. To them, it seems to add an element of veracity to his statement. However, DiLisio does not deny that he bragged to many people, including the police. "Sure, I was bragging about it," he says now. "I thought it was cool. It made me look like a big man, so I told it to everybody. I had everybody conned." His high-flying status even led to a romance at the detention center where he was confined. "I thought it would really impress her, talking about bodies and cops and murder." The girl gave birth to DiLisio's first child, Toni Marie DiLisio, though they never married. "It worked," claimed DiLisio.

Another aspect of DiLisio's story was the allegation that Spaziano had raped his stepmother in an assault that Tony himself prepared by telling Spaziano when she would be home alone. Tony DiLisio, other family members and people who worked with Keppie DiLisio and with Spaziano told the FDLE that they were actually having an affair, and that Keppie had made the rape charge only after her husband discovered the affair. Keppie reported the rape to police several months after the alleged attack and then dropped the charges. This never made it into the Report. Keppie denies the allegations of an affair.

The FDLE also claimed that members of the DiLisio family had been threatened and attacked, and that a thirteen year old friend of Tony's was raped in retaliation for his testimony against Spaziano. Family members deny the claim that they have been threatened. The Report does not identify who made the threats, who was threatened or how these threats were carried out. Tony DiLisio says that he does not know anything about a friend being raped. The source of both of these pieces of information has been kept secret.

There are also interviews with people who state that they believe that Tony DiLisio is telling the truth now. These interviews are not in the Report. One of these people is Reverend Frank Brim of the Worldwide Ministry for Restoration, Inc. in Pensacola. DiLisio was a member of his church and Brim claims to know him well. He describes DiLisio as an "obsessive, compulsive liar who doesn't have a good record for telling the truth." But he lies, Brim says, if it benefits him, and Reverend Brim is at a loss to explain how this recantation benefits Tony DiLisio.

"That's what frightens me," Brim says. "I'm convinced that this prideful man has come forth and admitted to this dreadful lie because he has finally come face to face with something he is not sure he can live with, that is, the wrongful death of Joe Spaziano."

In 1976, Judge Robert McGregor had sentenced Joe Spaziano to the electric chair based on more than the testimony of Tony DiLisio, a hypnotized and drug-crazed teenager. He also depended on the testimony of Laura Lynn Harberts's roommate, Beverly Fink, and Fink's boyfriend, Jack Mallen. Once again, it was Lori Rozsa and the *Herald* who unearthed the real story.

Prosecutor Claude van Hook argued at the time that Fink's and Mallen's testimony was important because it provided an eyewitness

link between the defendant and Harberts. But the *Herald* demonstrated that the record showed a different story. Spaziano was not mentioned—nor was anyone even resembling him—by either the roommate or the roommate's boyfriend for nearly two years. Fink and
Mallen did not tell the story of Harberts being terrified of a strange
dark-haired man until after they knew that Joe had been accused of
her murder.

Harberts and Fink, both eighteen, had lived together for four months
when Harberts disappeared on August 5, 1973. Fink reported her
missing two days later. The police asked Fink about Harberts's current
boyfriends. The police report states that "Laura dated very few men,
and Miss Fink checked on the ones she knew." Fink said nothing about
any unusual encounters or frightening episodes.

The first police report and follow-up report were more or less routine
missing person reports, but that changed with the police's August 27,
1973, interview with Fink, which occurred six days after two bodies
were found and dubbed the "Dump Murders" in headlines and on the
evening news. The police wanted to know anything that might give
them a clue to the killer's identity. They wanted to know what Harberts's current dating status and pattern were, and whether or not she
had seemed scared lately.

Fink claimed that "she'd take spells, sometimes she'd go out every
night, and sometimes she'd go for a week at a time and she wouldn't
go out with anybody." She named seven men that Harberts had gone
out with: Ben "Black" Peterson, "Don," "Warren," "Kenny," Jim
Davis, John Lackey, and Joe Suarez. She asserted that Harberts had
definitely been scared once. She was afraid of a couple she had met two
weeks previously, Walter and Ann Garris; the Garrises lived in a trailer
in Orlando.

The Garrises had frightened Harberts with talk of group sex, and
they refused to take her home at one point after a trip to Rock Springs.
Jack Mallen, then twenty-one, also knew about Walter and Ann
Garris. He believed that the couple made "good suspects" because
they were "weird," and Harberts had gone with them on at least one
outing before she disappeared. Fink claimed that Ann Garris had
called Harberts at 4:00 A.M. a few days before she disappeared, and
another witness told the police that he had seen Harberts and Ann
Garris at an ABC liquor lounge around the time she disappeared.

When investigators George Abbgy and James Martindale questioned Walter and Ann Garris, the couple claimed that the group sex conversation was "just a dream." They soon dropped out of sight, and the murder investigation fell apart. There was no mention of a frightening encounter with a stranger the night before the disappearance, and the police did not deem any other leads worthy of pursuit.

Two years later, after the police had obtained Tony DiLisio's hypnotized testimony that "Crazy Joe" had shown him the two bodies, the police went back to Fink and Mallen. This time, their story was different. They testified that one summer afternoon in 1973, a dark-haired, threatening-looking man had come to the apartment. They claimed that man was Spaziano, who told them that he was a traveling cook and that he was looking for Harberts. Fink claimed that he was wearing a white muslin shirt with a scarf around his neck and he was five feet, nine inches tall. Mallen claimed that he was five feet five. Spaziano is five feet, two inches tall. He stated to his lawyer that he had never seen Harberts, never worked as a cook, never posed as a cook, and never wore a white muslin shirt.

Fink and Mallen both testified that the traveling cook came back a second time in the early morning of August 5, the day that Harberts disappeared. Fink testified that Harberts was asleep on the couch. Mallen said that Harberts was awake, and the three were chatting and drinking. There was a knock at the door, and Harberts asked Mallen to answer it. Mallen testified: "She did not want to see this person. She was obviously scared."

No one ever opened the door. Mallen spoke to the man through the door, which had a frosted glass panel, and asked him to go away. He testified at first that he could see nothing but the silhouette of a man, but under questioning by the prosecutor, he went on to describe the man anyway—short and stocky, with bushy hair. He even described the jacket the man was wearing as a blue denim Levi's jacket. Spaziano was short and slender.

Both Fink and Mallen identified Spaziano as the "traveling cook." Fink testified that she had picked Spaziano out of a photo lineup several weeks before the trial. Mallen said that the police asked him to identify the person on trial the day before the trial began.

There still remained another burning question: Why hadn't Fink and Mallen mentioned this menacing stranger in their original statements?

Why would they wait two years to tell anyone, and why would Harberts go out with a man she was petrified of just fourteen hours before? No one at the trial ever asked those questions.

When Fink was interviewed in 1995, she added new details to her 1976 testimony. She claimed that Mallen wasn't there when the traveling cook showed up the first time, and that he had arrived at night, not in the afternoon. She was sure that the man at the door late that night (a door that she now said was open) was Spaziano, and Harberts was terror-struck by his appearance. She also claimed that she told the police about the traveling cook in 1973. She couldn't imagine why they left it out of their report. Mallen refused to discuss these contradictions, stating only that "Spaziano's a dirtbag. He deserves to be fried."

The initial police investigation into Joe Spaziano, Outlaw, was based in large part on a tip from a psychic. Once again, Lori Rozsa and the *Herald* were responsible for bringing these facts to light.

As the *Herald* learned, George Abbgy told Spaziano in an interrogation that he was the prime suspect in the double murder investigation because a "woman put me on to you. She described you to a letter. Anne Gehman. She reads minds." This was never mentioned by Abbgy in the police reports, but prosecutor Claude van Hook knew about the psychic connection.

Gehman remembered her involvement in the "Crazy Joe" case well. Abbgy had asked her to help him. He had at first been a little skeptical of her abilities, Gehman said, but she won him over with personal details of his parents, "who were in the spirit world."

Well-known in the community of Cassadaga, Gehman was the youngest medium certified by the National Spiritual Association of Churches. She was a practitioner of psychometry, the alleged ability to divine facts concerning a person by touching an object belonging to that person. "Every little molecule carries a memory with it. It might be called an aura. It plays back like a movie."

Gehman also helped to solve the Ted Bundy case, she claims. She told police, after touching a locket and sweater belonging to Kimberly Leach, Bundy's last alleged victim, that the girl was dead, where her body was, and that a man named Brady had killed her. She was only off on the name. She didn't testify in that case, either.

In the Spaziano case, Gehman was asked to touch an object, which she immediately identified as the skull of Laura Lynn Harberts. Pathologists never identified a cause of death for Harberts, and they never identified the body partially buried beneath Harberts's.

Gehman rode around in the police car with Abbgy and the skull and told him where the body was found, how Harberts was murdered, and where he could find the killer. She told Abbgy, "You will find this person in Chicago. He will be arrested in Chicago on a simple charge. Other people are involved, like a gang, or several people."

Spaziano was arrested in Chicago on a disorderly conduct charge on April 25, 1976. This was six months after Tony DiLisio initially spoke to the police and told them that Spaziano bragged to him that he raped women and black people and cut them up. He also told the police he had seen Spaziano with a man with a "patch on his eye" at the dump with the bodies. Gehman told the police at the time that the killer had dark hair and a "lazy eye, one side of his face was different from the other."

Before Gehman gave the police these details, a map of the dump had appeared in the local paper, as had mug shots of Spaziano. Gehman claims that she hadn't seen them.

In Gehman's analysis, the question still remains about the whereabouts of the "accomplice." Twenty-two years later, Rozsa reported, Gehman added this to her analysis: "He has a patch over his left eye, and he limps on his left leg. I have a feeling he is in the Miami area. I see a little place, very smoky, close to the water. It's a little hangout place. I see some bikers. He has a fire-engine red motorcycle, with gold lettering. There's a smell, like pizza. There's something sexual, like an adult type thing. Something off and warped sexually." She is positive that Spaziano is guilty and wishes that Abbgy had allowed her to testify.

The posttrial investigation, you may recall, contained evidence that Tony DiLisio's testimony was not the only critically false information given to the jury. As mentioned previously, Beverly Fink testified that Harberts had received a telephone call from someone named Joe just before the time of her disappearance. The state implied and argued that the telephone call must have been from Joe Spaziano. Although Spaziano argued that the call may have been from another Joe, the jury clearly believed that the caller may have been Spaziano. It was, on the face of it, an incriminating piece of circumstantial evidence. Yet we now know from recently disclosed police files that at the time of the trial, the police had determined that the caller was not, in fact, Joe Spaziano, but a man named Joe Suarez. Suarez, it is now known, had occasional liaisons with Laura Harberts. At trial, the state failed to disclose these facts. In addition, Joe Suarez denied to the police that he had been with Harberts on August 5, 1973. Yet, based on an undisclosed documented interview with Suarez, the police were able to conclude that he *was* with her on the night of her disappearance. It wouldn't take Perry Mason to explain why Suarez didn't want to get involved. And Joe Suarez was not the only police suspect in line ahead of "Crazy Joe" Spaziano. Spaziano was not the *original* suspect for these crimes, or even the *best suspect*. That honor fell to one Lynwood Tate.

Lynwood Tate was an aspiring fireman who drew police attention as they sought the person(s) who brutalized Laura Harberts. As they investigated, they discovered that Tate had a history that was far more than coincidentally linked to the victim, and to sexual violence. An Orlando woman told police that Tate had raped her, and police also learned that he had been arrested in Atlanta for a series of rapes and abductions there. In connection with Harberts, the police found receipts showing that Tate had opened a bank account in Orlando around the time of her disappearance. Eleven days later, Tate applied for a job at the hospital where Harberts worked. Another witness told police he had seen Tate and two women, two months before the crime, at the dump where the bodies of Laura Harberts and another individual were later found.

The Florida investigators tracked Tate to Athens, Georgia, and stayed for a week, interrogating, hypnotizing, and polygraphing him. When he failed the polygraph, Abbgy concluded that "everything indicated strongly that Lynwood Tate did commit the murder of Laura Lynn Harberts and the other unidentified female." He remained the prime suspect until 1974, when the DiLisio family entered the picture.

During the investigation of Harberts's murder the state believed that her killer was Lynwood Tate, but none of the documents suggesting Tate's guilt were made available to the Spaziano defense team or to the jury. Tate was given several polygraph tests about his role in the killing, which he failed. He was a known rapist, and all of the investigators involved concluded that Tate had committed the murder. Tate told the investigators "on several occasions" that "he didn't know whether he committed the murder" and "that if he did, he would like to know it." At one time, "an indication was made [by Tate] that there was a possibility that he may have done this and did not know it." Most important, the police located an eyewitness, William Enquist, who positively identified Tate as the individual he observed at the scene of the crime with several women near the time of the killing. None of the documents containing *any* of this information were disclosed. The defense lawyers weren't told, even though disclosure of such information is expected. In the interests of justice, it is a common practice—often a required one—for justice professionals to share critical facts. This practice is intended to assure that what happened at Joe Spaziano's trial doesn't happen—that juries and judges won't be served only select pieces of the evidentiary puzzle.

The state also failed to disclose the contents of an interview with Tony DiLisio conducted in October 1974 (about six months before the first disclosed interview). Although only police notes confirm this interview (as opposed to a transcript or tape), it appears that this was the first police interview with DiLisio where the subject of the murders in the dump arose. The police notes indicate that all Spaziano had ever (allegedly) said to DiLisio was, "Man, that's my style." The notes do not indicate that Spaziano admitted to the murder or that he gave any other information to DiLisio. Of course, six months later, in DiLisio's first recorded statement, the story had changed radically.

In the fall semester every academic year I teach a seminar on capital punishment at Vermont Law School. The class is a bit legal philosophy, a bit legal history, a bit social science, a bit politics, a bit cultural studies, a bit other. Because I believe my law practice background provides my teaching with extra depth and texture, I try to use my own death-work stories to make various points I want to communicate to my students during the semester.

On the first day of class, I typically use one of my old cases to illustrate the various stages of the capital punishment assembly line: trial, direct appeal, state postconviction, federal habeas corpus, executive clemency. When this class began in August 1995, my mind was very much on Joe Spaziano's case. It seemed natural to use Joe's case to illustrate for my students how the legal machinery of death works.

The seminar met every Tuesday afternoon, and I gave the students weekly updates on what had transpired in the case since the class last met: the death warrant, the death of VLRC, the Florida Supreme Court oral argument and the court's September 8 and September 12 opinions, my being fired by the Florida Supreme Court, the ethical dimensions of my war with CCR and with the Florida Supreme Court. *Peyton Place* meets *L.A. Law*.

Given that we ended up spending much of each class talking about Joe's case anyway, my students approached me with a proposition. As I was still Joe's lawyer for purposes of seeking U.S. Supreme Court review of the Florida Supreme Court's actions during the August–September warrant, and as the demise of VLRC meant that I had no resources, why not convert the seminar into a clinic? Our class project for the semester would be to conceptualize, research, write, and file the petition for U.S. Supreme Court review. It would be a win-win-win situation. Joe would get a first-rate petition to be filed, I would get help in creating that petition, and my students would get the experience of translating the theories and doctrines they'd been learning in law school into a real-life case with a real-live client.

We agreed to do it, but I had one ironclad condition. They were not simply going to be my research assistants, living in the law library, finding cases, and checking citations. If this was going to work as an educational experience, I wanted them involved every step of the way, from deciding the questions to be presented to crafting the arguments to drafting the document we would end up filing. The course would have two basic texts: the seminar materials I had prepared over the summer and the bible of U.S. Supreme Court advocacy, Stern, Gressman, and Shapiro's book *Supreme Court Practice*.

The petition for U.S. Supreme Court review of a case is a different animal from the appellate briefs that law students (and most practicing attorneys, for that matter) are used to creating. Typically, a brief argues why you should have won in the lower court. By contrast, a review petition is a request, to an appeals court, that that court select your case as being worthy of the court's time and energy. You're not arguing, "We should have won in the court below"; you're arguing, "You should decide to decide my case; it raises important enough legal issues to be worthy of your time." The U.S. Supreme Court gets thousands of such requests each year; they grant less than 3 percent of them.

In essence, we would be a twelve-person law firm. Rules of professional ethics and responsibility, such as the lawyer's duty to maintain confidentiality, would apply to the project. Every law firm needs a name, so in honor of the ongoing O. J. Simpson murder trial, we decided to call ourselves the BDNMCB Law Firm: "The Best Defense No Money Can Buy."

All of the students worked closely with one another on this semester-long project, but two students in particular emerged as natural-born leaders. Tanja Shipman and Elyse Ruzow were my field marshals.

I hope the seminar students learned as much from me during our joint venture as I learned from them. By the beginning of the semester, I had sketched out and drafted my vision of the review petition. I expected that the students would fine-tune my arguments and beef up my legal research, but that the essential contours of my draft would remain unchanged. In fact, what we ended up filing was vastly and fundamentally different from my original draft. It was also better—*much* better.

We worked throughout September and early October on the petition. The Court's page limit for a review petition is forty pages. The petition we filed was eighty-seven pages, but we thought Joe's case was important enough to justify the extra length. Along with the petition and its appendices, we filed a motion to exceed the Court's page limit.

October 15, 1995
Vermont Law School, South Royalton

My capital punishment seminar students and I had been talking about the effectiveness-of-counsel dimensions of Joe's case from the outset of the semester. By the time the U.S. Supreme Court denied our motion for our petition to exceed the page limit, we had decided to jettison the counsel issues in favor of presenting the secrecy issues more fully and completely. But when Governor Chiles signed Jerry White's death warrant (one day after the Court denied our page-limit motion), we thought we should revisit the issue of raising the matter of CCR's ineptitude and malice in Joe's case, along with the Florida Supreme Court's actions in firing me and forcing Joe's case on CCR (the latter became moot when Holland & Knight agreed to take Joe's case over from me). As White's case disintegrated over the following weeks, it became clearer and clearer that the dangers I had predicted during Joe's August–September warrant were going to actualize in White's case. We had to raise these matters in our petition for U.S. Supreme Court review in Joe's case.

Still, what about the page limit? Our petition had been more than twice the page limit, and it had only really dealt with the secrecy issue.

The students came up with the answer. The Court's rules limit the number of pages permitted in each petition, not the number of *petitions* one can file. We could file two separate petitions, one on secrecy and the other on counsel; we'd then get forty pages per petition.

Clever idea, but surely we couldn't circumvent the page limit by filing multiple petitions for review of the same lower court judgment. The students pointed out that in Joe's case there really were *two* judgments— or at least two different *opinions*, one issued on September 8 (dealing with secrecy) and the second on September 12 (dealing with counsel; firing me and sending Joe's case to CCR). Two opinions, two judgments. Two judgments, two petitions for review. We decided to do it.

We divided the class into two groups. All students would work on both petitions, but each group would have primary responsibility for only one petition or the other. Elyse Ruzow would organize the Petition 1 Group, addressing secrecy. Tanja Shipman would organize the Petition 2 Group, focusing on counsel.

October 16, 1995
Vermont Law School, South Royalton

Two seminar students, Elyse Ruzow and Brian Marsicovetore, and I spent most of the day working on the petitions for U.S. Supreme Court review. Elyse came up with a lovely new theory: the *prosecutor* has a duty to get any exculpatory information from the FDLE investigation and from the governor's office. This would solve one of our petition's principal conceptual problems: by characterizing what we're after as something other than clemency material, the state can't invoke the "clemency" exception to its general duty to turn over all evidence indicative of innocence. Elyse and Brian researched in the library; Laura Gillen word-processed; I edited in my office.

October 17, 1995
Vermont Law School, South Royalton

Laura turned both petitions around several times. Elyse, Doug Gould, and Katie Clark noodled and edited. I gave up in the early evening and went home to crash.

Elyse worked on the petitions until 3:00 A.M. By the time she finished, most of the legal research, logic, and policy holes had been filled.

Our first "question presented," as it's called in the Court's nomenclature, focused on the legality and constitutionality of the government's use of the secret FDLE police report. Generally, the rule is that criminal trial prosecutors must hand over to the defense any exculpatory information possessed by the state; under the "*Brady* rule," if the police or the prosecutors possess material evidence tending to show that the defendant might be innocent, the government must fork it over to defense counsel.

This rule has been around for a long time, at least since the *Brady v. Maryland* case was decided by the Warren Court in 1963. More recently, the Burger Court and now the Rehnquist Court have diluted the strictness of the *Brady* rule. The modern Court also has not been inclined to extend the *Brady* rule beyond the factual context in which it originally appeared: exculpatory information that comes into the government's possession before trial or during trial. Thus, had the secret FDLE investigation occurred prior to Joe's 1976 trial, the prosecutor clearly would have been required to hand over to Joe's defense lawyer any exculpatory information obtained by the police in the course of their investigation—the videotape of Tony DiLisio's recantation to FDLE agents, for instance.

The problem, of course, was that the FDLE's investigation of Tony DiLisio's recantation didn't occur until *after* the time of Joe's 1976 trial for the murder of Laura Lynn Harberts. Given that the secret police probe happened nineteen years after the trial, we had a set of very important questions for the Supreme Court: *Shouldn't* the *Brady* duty (that government officers must turn over all innocence-indicating information) extend to information that comes into the government's possession many years after the trial? *Isn't* the *Brady* rule an ongoing obligation of the government, or does the *Brady* obligation (and government integrity) end when the trial ends? What difference does it make if, as in Joe's case, the police investigation is ordered by the government? While it is admittedly true that "separation of powers" doctrine precludes the courts from meddling in executive functions (such as clemency), if the government's *Brady* obligation continues after trial, how can the police, the law, or even public officials withhold exculpatory evidence from a person the state intends to execute? Is not exculpatory evidence *itself* available to the courts? The governor is, after all, still free to give or withhold clemency, as he sees fit. No one would be arguing against the governor's authority to grant or withhold clemency. We would be arguing against his right to withhold critical evidence.

Joe's case would present the justices with an excellent opportunity to decide these important questions of federal constitutional law. This was so because the unique facts of Joe's case framed the constitutional questions with unusual clarity. Here, the governor clearly had ordered a police investigation into a crucial aspect of Joe Spaziano's claim of factual innocence—the believability of Tony DiLisio's reported (in the *Miami Herald*) recantation of his critical testimony at Joe's 1976 trial. Equally clearly, the governor had mandated that the police investigation remain secret from Joe and his lawyer—although not secret from the *Orlando Sentinel,* the cops' and governor's newspaper of choice. Equally clearly, the governor invoked his clemency authority as the basis of his secrecy mandate. Equally clearly, Governor Chiles had relied on the secret probe as the basis of his decision to sign Joe's August–September death warrant.

But most clearly and most important, the secret police investigation had generated information that was *exculpatory,* that tended to show that Joe was factually and totally *innocent.* The only aspect of the FDLE investigation I had been able to obtain on my own, no thanks to the government, was the FDLE videotape that included Tony DiLisio's recantation. My bootleg copy of that tape showed the state's own star witness recanting the testimony that the prosecutor himself told Joe's jury was the linchpin of his case against Joe—"Ladies and gentlemen of the jury," the prosecutor told them, "if you don't believe Tony DiLisio, you must acquit the defendant in 5 minutes." A Florida Supreme Court justice had interpreted DiLisio's videotaped testimony as a recantation. On the videotape Tony took it all back. It doesn't get any more exculpatory than that.

Thus Joe's case would present the U.S. Supreme Court justices with interesting and important questions of constitutional magnitude. Further, those questions did not concern legal technicalities. The state possessed evidence that showed it was very possibly trying to kill a man who in fact was totally innocent. At issue was whether Lawton Chiles, or anyone else, had a right to withhold such crucial information. These seemed to me fairly important legal issues, issues worthy of the Court's attention.

As I've mentioned, the justices grant only a tiny fraction of the thousands of petitions for Supreme Court review filed every year. I hoped that Joe Spaziano's case might be one of the select few.

October 19, 1995
Vermont Law School, South Royalton

Elyse, Doug Gould, Brad Powers, and Laura Gillen finalized the first petition and assembled and photocopied the voluminous appendices. When they had shipped the whole mess to the U.S. Supreme Court via FedEx, they turned their attention to mapping out the second petition.

Gene Miller called: the evidentiary hearing had been rescheduled to begin January 8, 1996. Judge Eaton ruled yesterday. Thus Holland & Knight and Jim Russ would have a total of four months to prepare for the hearing that the Florida Supreme Court had originally ordered me to prepare in seven days. We were making progress.

October 20–26, 1995
Vermont Law School, South Royalton

The capital punishment seminar students and I conceptualized, crafted, researched, wrote, rewrote, reconceptualized, rewrote again, edited, argued about, and, at last, finalized the second petition requesting the U.S. Supreme Court to grant plenary review in Joe's case.

When we finally got the second petition into FedEx, it was something of a letdown. Waiting for courts to act is always harder than working frantically to create petitions to be filed in those courts.

17

The Fires of Jubilee:
Florida's Malfunctioning Electric Chair

People who wish to commit murder better not do it in Florida, because we might have a problem with our electric chair.

Florida Attorney General Bob Butterworth, following the fiery botched execution of Pedro Medina, March 25, 1997

If you really want the least painful, most accurate method, it would be the guillotine.

Representative Victor Christ, chair, Florida House Justice Council, March 26, 1997

The only electrical appliance older than the electric chair is the lightbulb.

Steve Thayer, The Weatherman, *1995*

December 5, 1995
Wilder, Vermont

Sometimes I really hate being right. I especially wanted to have been wrong about CCR. As events proved, I wasn't wrong. Today Jerry White was executed.

On Friday, October 13, 1995, Governor Chiles signed two death warrants: one for Jerry White and one for Philip Atkins. White didn't have a lawyer. He had been represented by a volunteer, pro bono attorney, but his lawyer didn't have the resources to represent him under warrant.

Thus, under the precepts of the Florida Supreme Court's September 12 opinion in Joe Spaziano's case, White's case would go to CCR.

But CCR said it couldn't represent White because of its already-crushing caseload—just as CCR had told the Florida Supreme Court that it was too overworked to take on Joe's case. In Joe's case, the Florida Supreme Court ignored CCR's claims of overwork and forced the agency to represent Joe. In White's case, the Florida Supreme Court also ignored CCR's claims of overload and forced the agency to represent White at an evidentiary hearing under warrant. In White's case, as in Joe's, CCR accepted the Florida Supreme Court's edict and was willing and ready to represent a condemned man at a hearing under warrant—circumstances that the agency *itself* said precluded it from rendering effective assistance of counsel.

What happened next to Jerry White was exactly the scenario I was afraid would play out in Joe's case when the Florida Supreme Court demanded I participate—with no resources—in the evidentiary hearing under warrant; that was why I boycotted the hearing, which caused the court to fire me (but also to stay Joe's execution). CCR "represented" Jerry White under warrant. It threw an investigation together and presented its half-baked evidence to the state trial judge at the evidentiary hearing. The judge ruled against White, and he made killer fact-findings. These fact-findings are, as a practical matter, almost entirely insulated from subsequent appellate review; because trial courts decide facts and appellate courts decide law, appellate courts defer to trial court findings of fact—especially when those findings are made by the trial judge following an evidentiary hearing, even though the hearing took place under the crushing pressure of a death warrant. Even though CCR complained loudly that the hearing was a frenzied sham, the appellate courts didn't care: a hearing is a hearing, and you got yours. So CCR dashed impotently from court to court, and in the end it was to no avail. White got his hearing. End of story. Then White was electrocuted.

It wasn't that Jerry White's case had no constitutional defects or that CCR's factual investigation uncovered nothing of use. White's trial lawyer was a racist, which was a problem because White was black; at one point White's attorney had referred to how fast "jungle bunnies" can run. White's trial lawyer also was an active alcoholic; he confessed his alcoholism in a letter to Governor Chiles. White's prosecutor signed an affidavit that he was worried about defense counsel's drinking history; every day of the trial the prosecutor smelled his opposing counsel's breath for booze and, although he didn't smell any, he noted that White's lawyer seemed "confused." Furthermore, the state had withheld exculpatory evidence. And so on the Friday before the week when White and Atkins were executed, a friend at CCR called me to vent. "Why aren't these idiots raising racism as an issue? With O. J. and the Million Man March and charge of prosecutorial racism, now is the time to raise hell and go to the media. But Marty [White's lawyer] ignores it all. . . . All the people here know how to do is come up with reasons why CCR *can't* do them. 'It's not the way we do things at CCR.'" Even with CCR's flaccid effort, Jerry White came within only one vote of winning a Florida Supreme Court stay; he lost by a vote of four to three, the same margin by which Joe was denied a stay by the Florida Supreme Court's September 8 opinion.

In White's case, CCR was able to do a good enough job to create the illusion that White received the effective assistance of counsel—but not good enough to win. CCR caved to the Florida Supreme Court's dictates and ostensibly served as White's last lawyers, but then CCR didn't have the guts to raise and fight for at least one potent constitutional issue: racism in Florida's criminal justice system. At a time when most of America was talking about and pondering the racial aspect of O. J. Simpson's murder trial, CCR was too timid to raise hell about the role of racism in Jerry White's case.

In other words, in Jerry White's case CCR did exactly what it was ready and willing to do in Joe Spaziano's case. After issuing a few desultory whimpers, CCR caved in to the Florida Supreme Court's edict that CCR serve as White's lawyer. CCR also acquiesced by participating in the evidentiary hearing under warrant. That acquiescence led to Jerry White's death as surely as did Governor Chiles's signing of White's death warrant. When the trial court made his posthearing factfindings, the die was cast; White was as good as dead. The deadly factfindings meant that no appellate court would intervene to stop the execution. And no court did.

Even in the midst of the Spaziano firestorm, I hoped against hope that my harsh judgment about what CCR had become was wrong— that CCR hadn't in fact devolved into a hack public defender officer that was in bed with the governor who signs the death warrants on its clients. But the mess in the White case demonstrated that I wasn't wrong in Joe Spaziano's case. In Jerry White's case, CCR fulfilled my lowest expectations about what CCR had become: a component in the machinery of death, the executioner's mask. And White's execution wasn't the end of it—it was only the beginning. Today Jerry White was electrocuted. Tomorrow Philip Atkins—whose case CCR also acquiesced in taking on, participating an evidentiary hearing under warrant—will be executed.

The history of botched electrocutions is as old as the chair itself. The electric chair was the brainchild of Thomas Alva Edison. Prior to its first use—in 1890, at Auburn Prison in Auburn, New York, on a man named William Kemmler—Edison sent his electric chair around the country to show the dangerousness of a competitor's version of a device used to generate electricity. Dogs, cats, and an orangutan were strapped into Edison's chair and electrocuted, all to show the power of electricity.

The first electrocution of a man was botched. Still, the device steadily gained in popularity as a relatively "humane" alternative to hanging. The youngest person killed in an electric chair, executed in South Carolina in 1944, was a fourteen-year-old African American boy; his arms were so thin they kept slipping out of the chair's restraining straps.

States without centralized death rows resurrected Edison's idea of the traveling chair. In Louisiana, for example, a portable electric chair was carried on the back of a flatbed truck from parish to parish, depending on who needed executing where. In the early 1930s, one occupant of Louisiana's portable electric chair was an African American man named Willie Francis. Perhaps the tarp covering the chair on its journeys had sprung a leak, or perhaps the ride over Louisiana's unpaved back roads had jostled loose one of the chair's electrical wiring connections. Whatever the reason, the chair didn't kill Willie Francis, although it shocked him and scared the hell out of him. After several unsuccessful attempts to electrocute Francis, the chair was declared broken, and Francis was taken back to jail.

After the portable chair was repaired, the Louisiana officials wanted to try it again on Willie Francis, but his lawyers argued that that would constitute "double jeopardy" in violation of the U.S. Constitution. Four justices of the U.S. Supreme Court agreed, but that fell one vote shy of mattering for Francis. With Justice Felix Frankfurter casting the deciding vote, the Court decided that Louisiana could kill Francis in its now-repaired electric chair. Louisiana did exactly that.

Steve Thayer, in his lovely novel *The Weatherman,* describes how a botched execution resulted in the abolition of capital punishment in Minnesota almost a century ago:

> It was a homosexual from England who put an end to capital punishment in Minnesota. His name was William Williams, a twenty-seven-year-old steamfitter who had immigrated to America. By all accounts he was a mean, ugly bastard. Williams and sixteen-year-old Johnny Keller became lovers and traveled about the northland looking for work. But Johnny tired of the travel, and tired of Williams, and returned to his mother's home in St. Paul. Williams soon followed.
>
> On the night of April 12, 1905, Williams went to Johnny's home. Johnny's mother angrily sent him away. Williams returned after midnight with a gun. He was drunk and enraged. First he shot Johnny Keller's mother in the back; then he shot Johnny twice in the head as he slept in bed. Williams reported the killings himself but denied he had done the shooting. The jury didn't believe him. They found him guilty of first-degree murder. The judge sentenced William Williams to hang by the neck until he was dead. At the time of sentencing the judge couldn't know how long that was going to take.
>
> William Williams's last meal was prepared by the sheriff's wife. He was given a shave and a haircut. He prayed with his priest. He shook hands and said good-bye to all of his jailhouse friends. Then at the stroke of midnight on February 13, 1906, William Williams, his hands cuffed behind his back, was led from his cell at the Ramsey County Jail. He took the long walk.
>
> They crept down the iron stairway to the sub-basement, where the scaffolding had been erected. The death chamber was cold and damp and smelled of mildew and fresh dirt. Thirty-two witnesses, mostly reporters, stood in a semicircle below the gallows. The deputies left Williams alone at the foot of the gallows steps. Without hesitation he climbed the thirteen stairs that led to the rope. The Ramsey County sheriff was waiting for him. The sheriff read the sentence. In a soft, almost inaudible voice

Williams made a final statement, proclaiming his innocence right up to the end of his rope. "This is legal murder," he said. "I am accused of killing Johnny Keller he was the best friend I ever had and I hope to meet him in the other world. I never had improper relations with him. I am resigned to my fate. Good-bye."

A black hood was placed over his head. The noose went around his neck. The sheriff descended the steps to the lever.

Public executions have always been an inexact science. When the sheriff sprang the trap door, the prisoner fell through it all right, but the rope stretched eight inches and his neck stretched four inches, and Williams's toes hit the floor. The knot slipped behind his neck, slowly strangling him as he tiptoed about. After a few minutes of this dance macabre the sheriff ordered deputies to mount the gallows and pull on the rope, lifting the feet off the floor. But ten minutes later Williams was still alive, still thrashing about. So the sheriff climbed back up the thirteen steps and helped pull on the rope while a deputy stood below and pulled on Williams's feet. Williams returned the indignity by emptying his bowels: the last supper. The stench was sickening. Reporters scribbled furiously. Finally, at 12:46 A.M., fifteen minutes after he had dropped through the trap door, the Ramsey County police surgeon declared William Williams was dead. And so was the death penalty in Minnesota.

December 6, 1995
Wilder, Vermont

Philip Atkins was executed twenty-four hours after Jerry White was killed.

The usually unflappable Mike Griffin of the *Orlando Sentinel* wanted to talk with me about Jerry White. "I've witnessed a dozen executions, and it was a sound I've never heard before."

"Jerry White screamed" when he was electrocuted, Griffin told me. "It was a muffled scream," but nevertheless clearly a scream. None of the reporters who witnessed White's execution had ever heard anything like it before.

There was something else new. After White's execution, Griffin said, "there was a rhythmic banging on the bars of the prison. . . . That's another thing [none of the reporters had] ever heard before."

By 1995, after sixteen years of Florida executions, the prison personnel had the routine down pat. The prison's execution protocols were codified in 1979 and revised in 1983; that codification exists in a "confidential" document reproduced in the appendix to this volume. It contains a detailed set of assignments, procedures, and stage directions. The execution guidelines, originally typed on a manual typewriter on pages designed to fit inside any standard three-ring binder, are written in the language of bureaucratese.

I have long thought that perhaps the most important institutional function of such execution guidelines is to provide a rote ritual and so make each execution as sanitized, bureaucratized, and depersonalized as possible. By focusing on doing one's job as part of the institutionalized and bureaucratic whole, one perhaps can forget that one is playing a part in the strapping of a healthy, adult human being into a chair specifically designed, invented, and tested to kill that healthy, adult human being. Perhaps the routinization and the ritual are designed to obscure the basic and inescapable fact that executions are about killing people. Executioners kill people.

However, the spell cast by the executioner's protocols might be broken if the about-to-be-executed prisoner reminds the observers that he *is* a human being. By screaming, for example. For this reason Jerry White's muffled scream might be an event of significance. Or maybe not. Did the scream signify that White was in pain caused by the machinery of electrocution? Electrocution is a constitutionally acceptable method of execution precisely because it is assumed to cause instantaneous unconsciousness and therefore painless death. Had the electric chair malfunctioned? Does one about to be executed have a constitutional right to killing machinery that is functioning properly?

The possibility that malfunctioning machinery caused White's execution to be botched was not a matter of only academic concern. Recall that Atkins was scheduled to die, in that same electric chair, twenty-four hours after White was electrocuted. For this reason CCR had, only hours before Atkins's execution, been in court arguing that the state could not, consistent with the U.S. Constitution, execute Atkins in an electric chair that malfunctioned only twenty-four hours previously. His counsel argued that Atkins himself had heard White scream (the deathwatch cells are just down a hall from the electric chair). Hearing White scream had terrified Atkins for his last twenty-four hours on earth.

CCR must have understood the futility of its endgame legal arguments in the Atkins case. After all, a few years earlier the electric chair had seriously malfunctioned, and the electrocution of Jesse Tafero was unquestionably botched. Some member of the execution detail had mistakenly used an inferior-quality sponge (as noted previously, a wet sponge is used to help conduct electricity from the apparatus into the shaved-bald head of the executee). When the switch was pulled on Tafero, the cheap sponge didn't conduct the two thousand volts into his head—he sponge burned rather than conducted. Jesse Tafero's head burst into flames. Tafero wasn't electrocuted, he was burned to death.

The next scheduled occupant of Florida's electric chair was a woman named Judy Buenoano. Buenoano's lawyers claimed that she had a constitutional right not to be burned to death. The state countered that the prison had fixed the sponge problem; the chair should work fine for Buenoano. The courts ruled in the state's favor, but Buenoano's execution was stayed on grounds independent of the earlier botched electrocution.

Incidentally, Jesse Tafero was likely innocent. Jesse and his common-law wife, Sonia "Sonny" Jacobs, were condemned to die for shooting and killing a law enforcement officer. Jacobs's death sentence was vacated by the Florida Supreme Court on direct appeal; Tafero's was upheld. Jacobs was resentenced to life imprisonment, and Tafero moved ever closer to the electric chair.

A few years ago, Micki Dickoff, a childhood friend of Jacobs and now an independent producer in Hollywood, got back in touch with her long-lost girlhood pal. Jacobs and Tafero had always proclaimed their innocence, and when Dickoff and her partner, attorney Christie Webb, began digging into the old records of Jacobs and Tafero's trial, they became believers. Over the next few years, Dickoff and Webb worked with Jacobs's pro bono lawyers. They were able to prove that Jacobs couldn't have shot the police officer—the only hypothesis that fit the evidence was that a man named Rhodes, a companion of Jacobs and Tafero, must have fired the fatal shots. Rhodes had cut a deal with the prosecution; in exchange for his testimony against Tafero and Jacobs, he got off with a comparative slap on the wrist.

The evidence that Dickoff and Webb unearthed got Jacobs released from prison. She now lives with Dickoff and Webb in California.

That same evidence also vindicated Jesse Tafero, and it should have won his freedom as well. But the new evidence came too late—Tafero had already been burned to death by the state.

Jerry White was executed on December 6, 1995. The next day, I heard from one of my friends at CCR. "Jerry White was a total nightmare. . . . I felt like I was part of the problem; I've never felt that way before. . . . No pun intended, but I felt so *white* around Jerry that day; the whole system just felt so racist."

CCR even botched the final details. West Palm Beach Public Defender Dick Jorandby, my boss for my first two years as a capital public defender, had been asked by CCR's director to drive up to Starke to witness the execution. Jorandby drove from West Palm Beach to Starke, but when he arrived he found that his name wasn't on the prison's list of designated witnesses. Why not? Because CCR had neglected to put his name on the list.

"I'm still innocent" were Pedro Medina's last words. The daughter of the woman Medina allegedly murdered was convinced he was innocent. Three justices of the Florida Supreme Court had concluded that Medina's claim of factual innocence was sufficiently substantial to require an evidentiary hearing.

On March 25, 1997, moments after saying those last words, Pedro Medina was strapped into Florida's electric chair to be electrocuted. But as twenty-four hundred volts of electricity surged into his body, blue and orange flames up to a foot long leapt from the right side of his head, filling the execution chamber with smoke. According to Associated Press reporter Ron Ward, who witnessed the execution, "The smell of burnt flesh filled the witness room (separated from the death chamber by Plexiglas) and lingered." The *Washington Post* reported that, as witnesses gasped, a maintenance supervisor wearing electrical gloves patted out the flames while another official opened a window to disperse the smoke.

The state doctor in attendance said that he thought the death had been instantaneous and painless. A report later released by Governor Chiles's office said that the twenty-four hundred volts that killed Medina did so instantly, before the flames appeared, and that he had not suffered from the flames.

An investigation by the Department of Corrections found that the flames engulfing the head of Pedro Medina were caused by a corroded copper screen in the chair's headpiece. But the *New York Times* reported that a report prepared for Governor Chiles by two engineers and made public on April 11, 1997, concluded that the accident occurred because one of the sponges placed under the headpiece, used to help conduct the electricity and to offset the heat generated, was dry and caught fire. The report recommended that only one sponge should be used, and that should be dipped in saline solution.

In other words, Medina's botched execution had been caused by human error—much as human error regarding sponges had caused flames and smoke to rise from the head of Jesse Tafero seven years earlier. The Tafero fire was caused by the use of a synthetic sponge, a poor conductor of electricity even when dipped into saline solution. The sponge used in Medina's case appeared to be a natural sea sponge, according to the Associated Press. Jesse Tafero was later proven to have been innocent. In 1997, Pedro Medina maintained his own innocence until the end.

Medina's claim of factual innocence was strong enough to persuade three justices of the Florida Supreme Court to dissent from that court's denial of an evidentiary hearing into the credibility of Medina's newly discovered evidence of his total factual innocence of the capital murder for which he was about to be put to death. Like Spaziano, Medina lost by the narrowest of margins in the Florida Supreme Court—four votes to three; the three dissenters would have stayed Medina's execution until an evidentiary hearing could be held to explore his claim of innocence. A few hours after Medina's botched execution, I spoke by phone with a good friend in Florida. Sounding shell-shocked, my friend said of the execution, "They burned him alive . . . after losing by only one vote in the Florida Supreme Court . . . fucking *Chiles*."

Did Medina's four-to-three loss on a factual innocence claim offer any portent of the justices' thinking about Joe Spaziano's case? There was no way for anyone outside the court to know for sure. It was like reading tea leaves, but, in the absence of any reliable information, tea leaves would have to do.

On the one hand, perhaps the court's rejection of Medina's innocence claim foreshadowed what the court intended to do in Joe's case. The Florida Supreme Court's initial denial of a stay of Joe's August–September death warrant was a four-to-three split, the same lineup as in Medina's case. Maybe Medina's loss was the handwriting on the wall.

On the other hand, the Medina and Spaziano cases could be distinguished. In Joe's case, the justices unanimously agreed that a hearing was needed on the innocence evidence; they disagreed only about the need for a stay of execution to make the hearing less frenzied. In Medina's case, the four-justice majority did not think Medina was entitled to a hearing in the first place. And Joe had won in the trial court; this was an appeal by the prosecution to reverse Judge Eaton's order for a new trial. Medina had lost in the trial court.

In fact, maybe Medina's four-to-three loss in the Florida Supreme Court was a *good* omen for Joe's case. If the court was divided on Joe's innocence claim—three to three, for instance—perhaps a bit of horse trading was going on behind the justices' veil of secrecy. Maybe the justice with the crucial swing vote, the tie-breaking justice, had decided to split the difference by breaking the tie in Joe's favor but against Medina. In this way neither of the two voting blocs got everything it wanted; the trio of justices *in favorim vitiae* wouldn't succeed in saving Joe's innocence claim *and* Medina's innocence claim, but then the trio *in favorim mortis* wouldn't succeed in rejecting Joe's innocence claim and Medina's innocence claim. Each voting bloc would thus leave with some, but not all, of what its members wanted. This sort of vote trading may not happen explicitly, but it happens quietly, I am convinced.

Of course, I couldn't know what Medina's case portended for Joe's case, if anything at all. For me, trying to read the tea leaves allowed me to banish from my mind's eye, for minutes at a time, the image of Medina saying his last words—"I'm still innocent"—just before his face mask burst into flames. For some reason I also couldn't clear the words "the fires of Jubilee"—a phrase associated with Nat Turner's rebellion—from my mind.

For a long time after Pedro Medina's botched execution, I couldn't stop thinking about those people who believed in Medina's innocence as strongly as I believe in Joe's. The *New York Times* reported that a day after the execution, Medina's supporters at the First Presbyterian Church of Cape May in New Jersey, where Medina lived briefly after arriving from Cuba during the Mariel boatlift, waited for the body to be released to the church member who sponsored him. "Our hearts are breaking," said Kathryn Stoner-Lasala, the church's pastor. "The State of Florida has burned a man at the stake."

At the time of Medina's execution, 377 inmates lived on Florida's death row. Leo Jones was scheduled to die in Florida's electric chair next, then Gerald Stano. Medina was the thirty-ninth man to die in Florida's electric chair since capital punishment was approved by the U.S. Supreme Court in 1976.

The day before Pedro Medina's botched execution was my fortieth birthday.

The clock was ticking for CCR. My refusal to allow CCR to take over Joe Spaziano's case was based on the agency's track record of incompetence and cowardice. I didn't trust the agency to fight for Joe's life and to stand up to the governor and the Florida Supreme Court. As with Jerry White, CCR would have done the evidentiary hearing under warrant and before Judge McGregor. They would have lost the hearing. Joe would have been executed. The script would have been the same as it was for Jerry White.

The chain of events leading up to White's execution—the sham evidentiary hearing under warrant, the four-to-three loss in the Florida Supreme Court—didn't surprise me, but it did seem to surprise CCR. White's muffled scream seemed to bother CCR, too.

Events occurring outside CCR's cloistered preserve must have made the agency nervous. A commission chaired by former Florida Supreme Court Justice Parker Lee McDonald concluded that CCR was guilty of a pattern and practice of unethical behavior and recommended that CCR, in its present form, be abolished. Then the prison *really* botched the electrocution of Pedro Medina, a CCR client.

When I first argued for CCR's abolition, in 1995, I never thought it could happen anytime soon. The agency and its patron, Governor Chiles, seemed as entrenched as ever. But things can change in Florida with tremendous speed.

My critique of CCR's ethics received support from a surprising source. In 1985 I was allied with Governor Bob Graham and Attorney General Jim Smith—two politicians who built their public careers upon the electrocuted corpses of my clients—in arguing for the creation of CCR. In 1995 I found myself allied with the McDonald Commission in its call to abolish CCR and replace the agency with an alternative model of providing death row prisoners with legal aid. The Commission for Review of Postconviction Representation was created by Governor Lawton Chiles, the state senate president, and the speaker of the state house of representatives. It was charged with reviewing Florida's system of providing postconviction counsel for death-sentenced inmates in the hope of trimming the average time it takes for death sentences to be carried out. The commission, chaired by Parker Lee McDonald (who loathed CCR from soon after it was created in 1985), included several members of the legislature.

The McDonald Commission and I agreed on two propositions, although we approached them from entirely different frames of reference. First, we agreed that CCR had engaged in a long-standing pattern of violations of Florida's rules of professional responsibility. Second, we agreed that CCR ought to be replaced.

The McDonald Commission found that CCR's "reputation has been tarnished" by "many unethical tactics and abuses." But where I fault CCR for tepid and inept representation of its clients, the commission concluded that "CCR has engaged in abusive public records requests and dilatory litigation tactics, including the failure to reveal adverse legal representation to the court."

The McDonald Commission and I agreed that CCR's ethical abuses were of such a magnitude that the agency should be abolished. "The commission finds that based on CCR's lack of institutional integrity, [the Florida legislature] should consider other models of postconviction representation," the commission wrote in its report. In addition, the commission's report included a section captioned "Additional Recommendations to Improve the Administration of Justice in Florida." The first such recommendation was as follows: "The Commission Strongly Encourages the Florida Bar and the Florida Supreme Court to Strictly Enforce the Canons of Ethics and Professionalism in Death Penalty Cases." The commission explained:

> The Commission is disturbed by the credible information demonstrating litigation abuses committed by the office of the Capital Collateral Representative. The Commission urges the Florida Supreme Court and all other state courts to require all attorneys to comply with the Canons of Ethics, regardless of the nature of the case. No justification exists to allow any attorneys to violate the rules binding on the legal profession.

The botched execution of Pedro Medina, the Florida Supreme Court's rush to kill Joe Spaziano and Jerry White, and the McDonald Commission's scathing attack on CCR's ethics and integrity must have been unsettling to the agency. The case that blew CCR apart, however, was Gerald Stano's. Stano was the death row prisoner who I had thought, in the mid-1980s, might have been the man who actually murdered Laura Lynn Harberts in 1973.

Actually, the Stano land mine was wired directly to Joe Spaziano's case. From 1993, when I reentered Joe's case, to September 1995, when the Florida Supreme Court "fired" me from Joe's case, CCR had assisted me in my representation, from Vermont, of Joe Spaziano. That wasn't a problem for me, and it wasn't a problem for CCR. It was a problem for Gerald Stano, and understandably so.

Until the mid-1980s, Stano had been represented by Mark Olive, with logistical and resource assistance from CCR. The problems began when Stano filed, in court, a handwritten "Motion to Declare Conflict of Interest with the Office of Capital Collateral Representative." The reason: "CCR was now attempting to place the blame for the murder of Laura Lynn Harberts. . . . Now, the office charged with defending Mr. Stano [i.e., CCR] is attempting to *FRAME* him for this murder solely due to the infamous tag of Mr. Stano being labeled a 'serial killer.'" Stano continued:

> The defendant would now formally plead of this honorable Court to in effect, order the office of C.C.R. to immediately relinquish their custody of any, all case files, records pertaining to Mr. Stano's capital, non capital cases.
>
> And to order the director Michael Minerva, and any-all other members at the office of C.C.R. to appear before his honor for a full and in-depth Judicial inquiry in to the allegations of C.C.R.'s attempting to frame the defendant for the aforementioned murder.

A few months later, Governor Chiles signed a death warrant on Gerald Stano, or, more precisely, on one of Stano's two capital murder convictions and death sentences, in two different Florida counties, one case in Volusia County and the other in Brevard County. In a letter to CCR's director, Michael Minerva, the governor's office described what happened next:

State of Florida
Office of the Governor
Tallahassee, Florida

Mr. Michael Minerva
Capital Collateral Representative

Dear Mr. Minerva:

I am writing in response to our telephone conversation this afternoon regarding the Stano execution. In our conversation, you informed me that CCR cannot competently represent Stano in the Brevard county case based on the April 29, 1997, execution date. You informed me that the only way for CCR to provide Stano competent representation is by contracting with Mr. Mark Olive [to serve as Stano's attorney]. However, Mr. Olive is not able to work with CCR because he is representing Stano in the Volusia county cases. You informed me that the circuit court in Volusia county held that CCR has a conflict with Stano. Consequently, Mr. Olive cannot contract with CCR without Stano waiving the conflict. You reiterated that CCR has no one available to handle Stano's case, and that without a stay you cannot designate someone to represent him. Finally, you indicated that if a stay is not granted, you will inform the court to appoint someone else to represent Stano, and will resign your office.

I have spoken to General Counsel Douglass, and he has instructed me of the Governor's position. The Governor will not grant Mr. Stano a stay of execution. Mr. Stano procedurally exhausted review of his conviction and death sentence in the state and federal courts on July 6, 1995, almost 12 years after his conviction. The Governor signed Stano's third death warrant in this case on March 11, 1997. Neither Mr. Olive nor our agency took any action in Stano's Brevard conviction from July 6, 1995, to March 11, 1997. The Florida Constitution charges the Governor with the duty to carry out the law. Because Mr. Stano has exhausted court review of his death sentence, the Governor has the duty to implement the lawful death sentence.

The courts are the proper forum to hear your concern that CCR cannot competently represent Mr. Stano during this death warrant. Any further pursuit of your concerns, which we feel were misdirected to the Governor, should be taken up with the Attorney General.

The Governor expects you to comply with your statutory and ethical duty of representing Mr. Stano to the best of your ability.

Sincerely,
Thomas Crapps
Assistant General Counsel

Minerva abruptly resigned as director of CCR, three months before his term would have expired. CCR was bankrupt; the agency had already run through its $5 million annual budget for 1996-97—and there were still three months left in the fiscal year. According to an article by Mary Smith Judd in the *Florida Bar News,* Minerva had protested the Florida Supreme Court's "refusal to relieve the CCR staff from representing serial killer Gerald Stano, saying conflicts were created during the office's representation of Joseph Spaziano, when the possibility was raised that Stano had committed the murder for which Spaziano was convicted."

The logic of Minerva's resignation letter echoed my September 1995 reasons for refusing to participate in the Spaziano/DiLisio evidentiary hearing. "Without time and resources to do the job right," Minerva wrote to Governor Chiles, "I am unwilling to lend the appearance of fairness to the death penalty process." Words I could have written. Very close to words I *did* write two years previously, in September 1995— words that caused Minerva and his fellow travelers to inform the Florida Supreme Court that my possible mental or emotional "instability" may have rendered me unable to continue to serve as Joe's counsel.

And Minerva's one-time allies, Governor Chiles and Chiles's general counsel, Dexter Douglass, wouldn't even let Minerva cut and run with some semblance of dignity. The governor refused to accept Minerva's resignation. Douglass was quoted by the *Florida Bar News*'s Judd as saying the governor's lawyer was "'quite shocked' by the resignation, especially in light of CCR's claim to be bankrupt. 'His letter did not indicate they were supposedly out of funds,' Douglass said. 'Very rarely do we have agency heads of any kind resign when they're out of money,' he said. 'They stick around to explain and help raise funds to carry through the end of the fiscal year.'"

The CCR ship that Minerva jumped was foundering. The McDonald Commission recommended sweeping change to publicly funded capital defense—the dissolution of CCR and the creation of regional offices, the whole system being more closely governed by judges and legislators (and therefore political pressures, given that Florida legislators and state court judges are elected). Two bills dismembering CCR swept easily through both houses of the Florida legislature. They became law without even requiring the governor's signature. CCR had ceased to exist. Whether it would be replaced by something worse for death row was another open question.

The signs so far do not inspire confidence. In a front-page story published in the *National Law Journal* in December 1998, expert death penalty reporter Marcia Coyle wrote:

> After his state lawyers neglected and misrepresented his case for more than five years, death row inmate Jeffrey Muehleman was ready to go it alone. "These guys," he told a trial judge, "could get me killed quicker than I could get myself killed. That's about the bottom line of it."
>
> Agreeing, Florida Circuit Court Judge Crockett Farnell, in a blistering October opinion, lambasted the lawyers for incompetence and deceit and threw them off the case.
>
> Robert Peede also sensed something very wrong about the lawyers the state of Florida had provided to pursue his postconviction appeals. He turned to his pen pal for a decade, a soft-spoken Virginia woman who discovered that his lead lawyer, a former prosecutor, had been suspended once and publicly reprimanded another time. Of the two assistants who would argue Mr. Peede's case to the Florida Supreme Court on Dec. 2, one had been out of law school one year; the other had earned his license just weeks before argument.

Saddest to me was how far CCR had fallen since it first opened its doors on October 1, 1985, amid so much hope and fear: fear that it could become just another functionary in Florida's legal machinery of death, and hope that we—Scharlette Holdman, Mark Olive, and the rest—could, by sheer power of will, prevent that devolution from happening. Until Holdman and Olive were forced out by the bureaucrats who came to control CCR, they did. For a brief moment in the mid-

1980s, CCR was the best capital postconviction defense organization in the world.

Call it the revolt of the lab rats. The Florida legislature and governor created CCR to speed up executions. Give 'em lawyers and we can kill 'em faster, the logic went, because then the capital punishment assembly line will operate more smoothly. We were the grease.

Actually, we were more like lab rats. Today offices like CCR are commonplace in capital punishment states, but back then we were the first, and we were making it up as we went along. We had no models and no reservoir of experience from other states upon which to draw. It was all a big experiment, and we were the lab rats. But we were lab rats with law degrees and a mission to make CCR into a dangerous law firm. We altered the experiment.

We altered the experiment by refusing to behave as lab rats. I don't know quite how to describe this, but for me the test-pilot phrase "pushing the outside of the envelope" comes close. Tom Wolfe, in *The Right Stuff,* writes that "the 'envelope' was a flight test term referring to the limits of a particular aircraft's performance, how tight a turn it could make at such and such a speed, and so on. 'Pushing the outside,' probing the outer limits, of the envelope seemed to be the great challenge and satisfaction of a flight test."

Of course, I'm no test pilot. Test pilots risk their lives every day on the job. But at CCR we risked other people's lives—and not strangers'—with our tactical and strategic decisions. When test pilots screw up, they die. When I screwed up at CCR, my clients died.

It takes courage to push the outside of the law's envelope every day, day in and day out, and the reason CCR worked in the early days was the courage of Scharlette Holdman and Mark Olive.

At the end, it wasn't even clear to all that CCR was in as dire financial straits as it claimed. The majority leader of the Florida Senate told one newspaper that the agency was not broke, and may have had $1 million left of its $5 million 1996–97 budget. Florida's auditor general reported that the agency had roughly $169,000 left, and was in line to receive $86,000 in federal reimbursements. The agency could "squeak by" until the end of the fiscal year, the auditor general said.

CCR didn't have money for expert witnesses, travel expenses, and the like, but its staff would receive their pay on time. The agency had money in a separate salary account, and would meet the May and June payrolls, Martin McClain told the *Florida Bar News*. If ever there was a sparkling metaphor for CCR in the age of Michael Minerva and Martin McClain, that is it.

Winter 1995
Wilder, Vermont

Lori Rozsa told me that Holland & Knight will be asking for more time to prepare—another two months. "Your decision to boycott the hearing has been vindicated here at the *Herald*. Of course, not in *print*, but in our hearts. . . . You and Tony would have been slaughtered at that hearing under warrant." So that's why the firing was okay with them. I guessed Christmas would be better for me, too—better for me and "Crazy Joe."

Today, Lori told me she found Miller's account of the evidentiary hearing in the Pitts and Lee case sad. "It's depressing. Gene had so much in Pitts and Lee, and they *still* lost the evidentiary hearing in Marriana." And the state trial judge made posthearing fact-findings. And the Florida Supreme Court deferred to those fact-findings and upheld the convictions and death sentences of Pitts and Lee, even though the hearing itself was a circus. (Almost literally: Joe McCawley, the Florida cops' ubiquitous "ethical hypnotist"—who hypnotized Tony DiLisio for the police in Joe Spaziano's case—actually held an in-court session, in which he hypnotized a key witness. This was within a few months of when McCawley hypnotized Tony DiLisio so he could "remember" his trip to the dump site with Joe Spaziano—the trip that Tony recanted for the first time in 1995.)

November 7, 1995
Wilder, Vermont

The phone company disconnected my dedicated fax line at home, because I couldn't pay the $1,600 bill from September. I'll pay it off in monthly installments over the next year and a half.

November 27, 1995
Wilder, Vermont

Letter from the U.S. Supreme Court: the Court granted the state's motion for ten extra days within which to file responses to our two petitions for the court to review Joe Spaziano's case.

Just like the state. Delay, delay, delay.

December 19, 1995
Wilder, Vermont

Gene Miller called: "My ace reporter Lori is in the hospital having her baby. The last thing she said to me was, 'At least I'll be able to be at the hearing.'"

Gregg Thomas had been asking me to attend the evidentiary hearing at Holland & Knight's expense. He wanted me to be his "media liaison," and I flatly refused. Not having to deal with institutions like the *Orlando Sentinel* was one of the best things about no longer being Joe's lawyer in the Florida courts. And newspapers were as sick of me as I was of them; the *Miami Herald* and *St. Petersburg Times,* as well as the ever-predictable *Orlando Sentinel,* had all editorialized in support of my firing by the Florida Supreme Court.

Gregg Thomas also said he wanted me there at the hearing so we could strategize and noodle. And he emphatically told me that I was still Joe's appellate lawyer. By far the most likely outcome of the hearing would be a loss, killer fact-findings, and a new death warrant within twenty-four hours. I promised Gregg that if that happened I wouldn't leave him hanging out to dry.

Still, I told him that I wouldn't be at the hearing. The reason had little to do with him or the case. The reason was that Deanna and I were getting married on December 30. Since we couldn't afford a honeymoon, the closest facsimile thereto would be a trip to Florida for the honeymoon. A round-the-clock marathon with lawyers and witnesses and investigators and reporters and banker's boxes of documents didn't seem the best way to start my life as a married person, but Deanna was willing. I am a very fortunate guy.

Every year around Christmas/Hanukkah/Kwanza time, there pops up some unscheduled, poignant juxtaposition between executions and the holiday season. In 1995 there were two. I heard of one through Jenny Greenburg, a friend at VLRC, who happened to be in Governor Chiles's office when Jerry White was electrocuted. In the midst of the electrocution, Christmas carolers began singing right outside the office. Eventually, an aide closed the door.

The second happened on the grounds of Florida State Prison. Some well-intentioned folks set up a nativity scene—facing the electric chair. After receiving several complaints, the prison ordered the nativity scene removed. I haven't been able to determine if the decision had to do with the issue of separation of church and state. Perhaps the holy family was an embarrassment, or wasn't on the approved list of observers.

December 30, 1995
Wilder, Vermont

Deanna and I were married this evening, in Rollins Chapel, a stone chapel on the grounds of Dartmouth College. She made her own gown, and bride and dress lit up the room with their radiant beauty. Her sisters Elizabeth and Norma were bridesmaids; my best man couldn't be Joe, for obvious logistical reasons, but his spirit was well represented by my best men who were able to share the moment corporally as well as spiritually: Jeff Robinson, Mark Olive, and Mike Millemann. Deanna's father gave her away; my mother gave me away. For both of us, it was our first marriage, and our last.

It had been a king-hell of a year of wildly improbable juxtapositions. Between the death warrants and the writing and the teaching, somehow Deanna had created a magnificent dress and an equally magnificent wedding, both planned and carried out to the last exquisite detail.

And so we were married. And Joe was alive to witness it, albeit in absentia.

Gregg Thomas
Holland & Knight
Tampa, Florida
via fax

Dear Gregg:

Many thanks for sending me the "to do" list and the chronology. Just a few random thoughts:

First, I continue to believe very strongly that you need to bring the rape case into this evidentiary hearing, for making-the-record purposes if for no other. The obvious hook is that Tony DiLisio was the key to both prosecutions. Atmospherically, the presumptive validity of the rape conviction makes it easier for judges, being human beings (sort of), to minimize the power of our challenges to the homicide. The obvious flaws in the rape case were what got Warren Holmes (and thus Gene Miller and thus the *Herald*) to take our arguments about the murder case seriously. Also, as Lori Rozsa has shown, the rape case set-up was central to the Harbert-case set-up. The key to both set-ups seems to have been Ralph DiLisio, and his primary agenda (at least initially) was to set Joe up for the rape, since Ralph had convinced himself that Joe had "raped" Keppie. Further, in terms of Joe's practical realities (*i.e.*, actually getting him out of prison sooner rather than later), we need to attack *both* convictions; that's why I spent so many pages on the rape case in my clemency application and principal Florida Supreme Court filing. Finally, and most importantly, this will likely be Joe's one and only evidentiary hearing. I've been trying to get an evidentiary hearing for ten years, since the first 3.850 filed during the first warrant. Even if Judge Eaton won't allow testimony on the rape case, you need to proffer everything we have, it seems to me.

Second, might we argue that the recent death of Tony's father was the catalyst and condition precedent to his recantation? *Tony* believes his father was the key to his perjury, and he might well be right. But even if he isn't, his belief on this score goes to show (1) why he waited so long to recant, and (2) all of my "due diligence" couldn't possibly have made any difference, and this explains why it *didn't* make any difference.

Third, Warren Holmes and Lori Rozsa suggested to me some time ago that Pitts and/or Lee might make dynamite witnesses at the evidentiary hearing. I agree. Holmes also thought Pitts or Lee would be willing to testify at Joe's evidentiary hearing. Even if Eaton won't let them testify, just having them present in the courtroom would send some powerful messages. Here is living, breathing, corporeal proof that rogue cops in Florida do (and have) sent innocent "outsiders" (Blacks and Outlaws; Jent and Miller, too) to death row. And it wouldn't hurt to remind folks that the one and only other time Gene Miller and the *Herald* championed a claim of innocence was two decades ago. And, in that lone instance 20 years ago, the *Herald* was right.

Fourth, you might want to think about using Mike Radelet and/or Hugo Bedau to (1) provide historical, institutional and systemic context for Joe's innocence claim, and (2) underscore the rarity with which Radelet and Bedau, the national experts on death row innocence, go on record in individual cases. As you know, Radelet and Bedau wrote an affidavit for me in Joe's case about a year ago. (Radelet was [mis]quoted in this Sunday's *New York Times* as saying that he's only gone on record in two cases: Rolando Cruz, where I represented them in the Illinois Supreme Court as *amici curiae,* and Parris Carriger in Arizona [scheduled to be killed tonight at one minute past midnight. Just like the movies].) He assured me on Sunday that he was misquoted and that he'd be happy to testify at Joe's evidentiary hearing.

Fifth, and relatedly, Bill Geimer wrote an affidavit in Joe's case contextualizing Juror Lena Lorenzana's affidavit that Joe's jury voted for life because of lingering doubt about Joe's guilt. Bill was the senior author of the only published study of why Florida juries recommend life. He found that lingering doubt about guilt was the single strongest reason given by the jurors he interviewed (69%).

Sixth, what ever became of Steve Gustat's investigation into the possibility that the second set of bones at the dump site were male? Steve and I had spoken of bringing in a forensic anthropologist to nail this down. Lori was also working this angle. You could get it into evidence to rebut Tony's many pre-trial statements that both bodies he "saw" at the dump "with Joe" were female.

Seventh, do you plan to call Lori, Warren Holmes, Gene Miller, and/or Tony Proscio as witnesses? Lori would provide the facts of Tony's first recantation to her, in June, as well as the pastor's account of Tony's recantation to him two years earlier, while Tony was going through his divorce. Holmes and Proscio can describe Holmes' grilling of Tony not long ago.

Eighth, I would like you to make a record concerning (1) Joe's longstanding wish that I be his appellate lawyer; (2) Joe's wish that CCR *not* be his lawyer, *and why*; (3) the fact that I (and not Office of Capital Collateral Representative) will be Joe's appellate counsel in any proceedings that might occur subsequent to the hearing; (4) the lawlessness and factual wrongness, of the Florida Supreme Court's fiction that I "effectively withdrew" from Joe's case by refusing to participate in the evidentiary hearing on 96 hours notice and with no resources—when it has taken Florida's largest law firm four months to prepare for that hearing

(Florida's ethics rules—or any other state's, so far as I know—do not provide for a court's unilateral finding of constructive withdrawal in blatant disregard of the reasonable wishes of the client, his family, and his lawyer). If we lose the hearing and we (or I) end up back in the Florida Supreme Court under warrant, I want the record on these matters to be crystal clear. I will be (and am) Joe's appellate counsel, whether the Florida Supreme Court and CCR and governor and attorney general like it or not.

Ninth, you need to make a record concerning why Joe, in 1975, would have had no memory of his whereabouts on a specific day two years earlier—notwithstanding his absolute innocence of the 1973 homicide. Dr. Toni Apel was eager to testify on this score—under warrant. I'm certain she still is, and I'm equally certain she'd make a dynamite witness for us. If not her, then you need to find another neuropsych to make the record on this critical question of why Joe has no alibi for the time of the murder.

Tenth, do you plan to call Joe as a witness? This would be risky, for obvious reasons, but I think the benefits outweigh the dangers. (I also see this as Joe's, not our call, here as at trial. We give him the information he needs to make an informed decision on his part, but the judgment call itself is his.) Lori and other reporters have grilled Joe on the hard questions, and he has done very well. I think he would do as well in court. But apart from the strategic reasons for calling him, I believe there is another reason as well. The most likely scenario, even if the hearing goes perfectly for us, is that we'll lose. (Does Eaton have the guts to say that three governors, two AG's, FDLE, the Florida Supreme Court, the FDC, the Eleventh Circuit and the U.S. Supreme Court have been so wrong about this case for so long? And you thought *The Player* was a movie about Hollywood.) If we lose on January 10, a warrant will come on January 10 or January 11. We don't be able to stop the killing this time. So: I think it's important that Joe has the opportunity to tell the world, in open court and under oath, that he didn't kill Laura Harberts, and that he didn't rape Vanessa Croft. This has nothing to do with the law. But this case has *never* had much to do with law. It took me 10 years to appreciate that fact.

Eleventh, you might want to consider getting all the facts Lori has written about into the record, perhaps by presenting those facts as things you'd prove if given the time and investigative resources. That's how I tried to get Lori's study into the Florida Supreme Court record.

Finally, at the risk of beating a dead horse on points that are probably moot anyway (and of mixing metaphors), I have to register my continuing objection to your decision to use Jim Russ, rather than Mark Olive, to do the trial work. I'm sure Russ is a fine stand-up lawyer, but why you would forgo someone of Olive's capital postconviction experience and skill remains utterly incomprehensible to me. Your decision to freeze out the media is not so incomprehensible to me but, in my view and for what it's worth, equally wrong.

Anyway, I hope this is of some use to you. Thanks again for sending me some of the recent paperwork. Please keep in touch.

Sincerely yours,
Michael Mello

The key to our winning the evidentiary hearing, Warren Holmes believed, was to persuade Judge Eaton on two points. First, how and *why* did Tony DiLisio lie in 1976? Second, how and *why* did Tony recant in 1995? "In other words, we need to *contextualize* both the original lie and the recantation, to show why each happened when it did. . . . If we can't do that we're fucked, Mike."

This was the primary reason Holmes believed that doing the hearing under warrant would have been a disaster. "What's Eaton gonna do? Listen to who? Listen to Tony, a totally obnoxious kid, and just say he *believes* him? Fuck no. . . . If we're limited to the issue of Tony's credibility, we lose. Period.

"The rape case is inseparable from the murder case; you just can't understand the latter in isolation from the former. . . . In the whole course of the rape case, Tony *never* mentioned any bodies; that's key. . . .

"If this judge doesn't know *both* cases *cold,* we're dead."

On January 17, 1996, the U.S. Supreme Court denied both of Joe's petitions for review. The decisions were unanimous. The justices gave no explanation—just a one-line statement that they had declined to review Joe's case.

This marked the end of my role as Joe's lawyer. It also signified the conclusion of my travels as an attorney for people condemned to die. Hereafter I would write about capital punishment rather than live it.

I knew I was leaving Joe's case in good hands. Still, I fully realized Joe might lose the evidentiary hearing. A new death warrant would be signed that same day. Jim Russ or Holland & Knight or CCR would dash from court to court, desperately seeking a stay. But there would be no stay. If he lost this one, Joseph "Crazy Joe" Spaziano would be killed in his twentieth year on death row, still proclaiming his innocence—an innocence I believed in and longed to vindicate.

My actions in September 1995 thus would have bought Joe nothing more than an additional five months of life on death row. Was it worth it? Hell, yes. Over the years, Joe and I had marked the passage of time by Christmases. My actions September past had bought Joe another Christmas. That alone made the whole thing worth it to me.

My actions had also bought him one last chance for justice. The odds of his seeing that justice were minuscule, really too infinitesimal even to be measurable, even for me. But with Jim Russ and Holland & Knight on his side, Joe would be meeting his would-be executioners on a level playing field—for the first time ever.

It was worth it. We were hungry, and we *wanted* this thing.

18

Judgment Day

It is a great brotherhood, which to a condition of life arising out of the midst of danger, out of the tension and forlornness of death, adds something of the good-fellowship of the folk-song, of the feeling of solidarity of convicts, and of the desperate loyalty to one another of men condemned to death—seeking in a wholly unpathetic way a fleeting enjoyment of the hours as they come. If one wants to appraise it, it is at once heroic and banal—but who wants to do that?

Erich Remarque, All Quiet on the Western Front, *1929*

I can crash a plane better than anyone.

Gene Ryack (played by Mel Gibson), Air America, *1990*

January 8–15, 1996
Wilder, Vermont

The evidentiary hearing on the believability of Tony DiLisio's recantation began on January 8, 1996. Joe's star witness was DiLisio himself, who testified under oath that his 1976 testimony that sent Joe to death row was false. The prosecution subjected DiLisio to savage cross-examination, but his testimony was bulletproof. Then the state brought in a parade of witnesses in an attempt to discredit DiLisio. Even Joe's brothers (his blood brothers, not the Outlaws) testified against him.

I didn't go to Florida for the hearing. I wanted very much to go, but I was still a lightning rod for criticism about Joe's case, and it was best for me to keep a low profile during this round. I remained in Vermont and got daily bulletins about the hearing from Lori Rozsa and the folks at the *Miami Herald*.

Because I was dependent on secondhand information about how the hearing was going, I had a chance to reflect on how differently the *Herald* and the *Orlando Sentinel* were reporting the story. As the hearing progressed, the *Sentinel*'s jihad against "Crazy Joe" Spaziano became more and more hysterical and shrill. Headlines screamed, "Spaziano's Life Hinges on Whether Judge Believes Witness's Latest Story," "Witness's Brother Doesn't Believe His Story," "Don't Let Him In': Friends Recall Victim Being Afraid of Spaziano." One story included the running head "Is recantation a sham?"

As the hearing seemed to be going Joe's way, the *Sentinel* became truly desperate. The headlines track the newspaper's accelerating descent:

"Former Outlaw: Spaziano Enjoyed Killing," January 8, 1996; front page (This article began, "The first time Willie Edson laid eyes on Joe Spaziano was through the sight of an M-1 rifle.")

"Edson: Spaziano Kept Bag of Teeth," January 8, 1996

"Spaziano Brothers: Joe Said He Killed a Nurse," January 9, 1996; front page

"DiLisio's Facts Wobble," January 10, 1996; front page

"Spaziano's Former Girlfriend Contradicts Dilisio's Story," January 12, 1996; front page

"Stepmother Disputes DiLisio's New Version," January 13, 1996; front page

"Brother Against Brother: Michael Spaziano Takes Stand to Testify Against 'Crazy Joe,'" January 14, 1996; front page

"Witness After Witness Disputes DiLisio's Story," January 14, 1996

Needless to say, the *Miami Herald*'s coverage of the hearing was quite different. This raises a larger, and fascinating, question about the media's role in covering the criminal justice system generally and Joe Spaziano's case in particular. Why did the *Herald* and the *Sentinel* view the same hearing, the same witnesses, and the same trial transcripts and court files so differently?

David Barstow, writing in the *St. Petersburg Times,* provided a thoughtful analysis of the difference in coverage. Different reporters had different takes on the credibility of the players involved, especially the believability of Tony DiLisio's recantation. The *Herald* put Tony DiLisio through relentless cross-examination by the inestimable Warren Holmes; Holmes had worked with the *Herald* on Gene Miller's major miscarriage-of-justice cases, and Miller correctly considers Holmes "a man with a ruthlessly logical mind" and a "superb homicide investigator," according to Barstow's story. At the end of Holmes's third degree, DiLisio held up. The *Sentinel,* by contrast, thought that the most significant aspect of DiLisio's recantation was that Tony was not forthcoming about his own past sins of drunk driving and domestic violence. Tony had said he had been "Christian and clean" for more than ten years; the *Sentinel* knew he had been arrested twice for DUI and for hitting a former woman friend.

Further, Barstow pointed out that access to information influenced the coverage. Once the *Sentinel* began trashing Joe, I decided—wrongly, I now believe—to quit talking to reporters from that paper (I was working so frantically on Joe's case that I couldn't justify taking the time to talk with them anyway); similarly, the police stopped speaking with the *Herald* reporters. Thus perceptions that the newspapers were pursuing their own separate agendas widened the split in their coverage of Joe's case. "With key sources taking sides, perception becomes reality," Barstow noted.

Issues of turf also explained the different coverage. Laura Lynn Harberts was killed, and Joe Spaziano was tried, convicted, and condemned, in the *Orlando Sentinel*'s territory. The *Sentinel,* a local newspaper, had been virtually unknown outside Florida until it came to national prominence in the mid-1970s by "exposing" the sins of the local biker gang, the Outlaws. When the *Miami Herald* scooped the *Sentinel* in the *Sentinel*'s own backyard in its coverage of Joe's case, the Orlando newspaper adopted an oppositional mind-set; whatever the *Herald* said, the *Sentinel*—out of competitiveness or professional jealousy or both—said the opposite.

Although there is some measure of truth in all these observations, it seems to me that the underlying explanation for the difference in the two newspapers' coverage is simpler. It is largely a matter of experience versus naïveté, appreciation of nuance and subtlety versus obtuse prejudice, and intelligence versus lack of intelligence. In other words, the *Herald* had Warren Holmes, whose instincts guided Gene Miller, Lori Rozsa, and the rest of the *Herald*'s team. The *Sentinel* didn't. It really is as simple as that.

By having Warren Holmes as a guide into the nether world of cops and killers and courts and prosecutors, the *Herald* had an inestimable advantage over the *Sentinel*. Holmes possesses three indispensable and irreplaceable qualities: frighteningly accurate instincts, a wealth of experience as a cop and investigator, and, perhaps most important, independence. Unlike the cops and governor's aides who leaked selected information to the *Orlando Sentinel*, Warren Holmes had no initial stake in believing Joe's claims of innocence. To the contrary, Holmes's (and Gene Miller's) skepticism about such claims is the stuff of legend. Holmes moved methodically, objectively, and slowly. At first, his reading of the trial files convinced him that the *Herald* ought to conduct its own investigation into the case. Only after later testing Tony DeLisio's believability in the crucible of his own withering interrogation did Holmes become persuaded—strongly but always provisionally—that DiLisio was telling the truth in his recantation.

Warren Holmes was the *Herald*'s Ariadne. Holmes's experience, instincts, and ruthless and relentless objectivity and insistence on facts, facts, and more facts provided the *Herald*'s team with the context they needed to sort out which facts were significant and which were unimportant. When Holmes read a transcript, he knew what red flags to look for. A good example is Joe McCawley, the self-styled "ethical hypnotist" who Holmes believed had implanted false memories in a key witness in the Pitts and Lee case, a *Herald* triumph from the mid-1970s. When Holmes saw that McCawley had hypnotized Tony DiLisio at the behest of the local police, he was immediately alert to that fact's significance.

Whereas the *Herald* had Holmes and Miller, the *Orlando Sentinel* had a gaggle of reporters who diligently pored over files and talked to witnesses, but who lacked the experience and analytic skills to distinguish what was important from what was not. The *Sentinel*'s team was led by an amiable dunce named Mike Griffin. Griffin, a reporter in his mid-thirties, brought to his task a palpable fear and loathing of the Outlaws. In his *St. Petersburg Times* piece, David Barstow noted:

At times, Griffin felt he had to set the record straight. He thought the *Herald* painted too rosy a picture of Spaziano and his fellow Outlaws. Griffin, 34, grew up in Orlando, and he remembered well the fearsome reputation of the local Outlaws in the '70s. There were tales of gang rapes and killings, and he recalled his parents keeping him inside at night when women's bodies began turning up in local dumps. After Spaziano was arrested for one of the "dump murders," the newspapers were filled with Spaziano's violent exploits.

When Griffin wrote that Spaziano lived "a misfit's life of spontaneous brutality and murder," he says he was trying to counter the *Herald*'s depiction of Crazy Joe as a clownish charmer—"the most popular guy on death row."

"I was aiming that at his supporters, and I include the *Miami Herald* in that," he says.

And then there was the cozy relationship among the *Orlando Sentinel,* the police, and the governor's office. Mike Griffin swore to me that the cops and the governor's office were not leaking confidential information to the *Sentinel.* How, then, did the *Sentinel* know about and print the news that Governor Chiles was going to sign Joe Spaziano's fifth death warrant on August 24, 1995? How else could the *Sentinel* have known this before Joe or his lawyer knew? How else could the *Sentinel* have known on August 24 the contents of the "secret" police report that provided Governor Chiles the political cover he needed to sign that death warrant on that day? How else could my "infamous" August 27 memo have gone from my fax machine to Chiles's fax machine to the *Sentinel*'s fax machine without missing a beat? And how about what John Gordy, the head of the secret police investigation, told the *St. Petersburg Times*: after Gordy stopped speaking to the *Herald,* he did not "end his relationship with the *Sentinel.* If anything, Gordy talked even *more* openly with the *Sentinel* reporters. He fed them information."

Thus Griffin's representations that the *Orlando Sentinel* was not in bed with the police and the governor's office are transparently false. He is either a liar or a fool. It is no small irony that Griffin disbelieves Tony DiLisio's recantation because Tony lied about Tony's past sins.

To this day, the *Orlando Sentinel* reporters say that I quit dealing with them because I thought they were "biased." But that isn't at all accurate. I can deal with bias—no one was more "biased" against believing Joe's innocence claim than Warren Holmes, Gene Miller, and Lori Rozsa at the *Herald*. I didn't freeze out the *Sentinel*'s reporters because they were biased. I froze them out because they were inept and stupid and unable to digest simple facts; because they couldn't understand why Mark Olive might be nicknamed "MO." If they couldn't grasp these simple things, how could I hope they'd understand genuinely complex and subtle matters—such as whether Tony DiLisio's recantation ought to be believed? The sad answer is that they couldn't.

The hearing ended on January 15. Gene Miller and the *Herald* people seemed certain that Joe would win a new trial from Judge Eaton. I wasn't so sure. I reminded Miller that Pitts and Lee had also gotten an evidentiary hearing and that they'd lost. Trial judges are elected in Florida, and it would require an especially courageous judge to go against the local newspaper (the *Sentinel*) and mandate a retrial. And I had no doubt whatsoever what would happen in the wake of a loss in the hearing before Judge Eaton: the governor would sign a new death warrant in a matter of days, and this time not even the *Miami Herald* would be able to keep Joe from the electric chair.

To me, the outcome of the hearing was very much in doubt. A credulous reader of the *Orlando Sentinel* might well conclude that no judge with half a brain would believe Tony DiLisio's recantation and order a new trial for Joe Spaziano. When Seminole County Circuit Judge O. H. Eaton Jr. did exactly that, the *Sentinel* went apoplectic.

January 22, 1996
Wilder, Vermont

Gene Miller called with the news: On January 22, 1996, we won. Following a weeklong evidentiary hearing, Judge Eaton ordered a new trial in Joseph Spaziano's case. The best defense of Judge Eaton's decision is Eaton's own reasoning. The judge's opinion thus requires quotation here in full (except for the legal citations):

IN THE CIRCUIT COURT OF THE EIGHTEENTH JUDICIAL CIRCUIT IN
AND FOR SEMINOLE COUNTY, FLORIDA
CASE NO. 75-430-CFA
STATE OF FLORIDA,

Plaintiff,

vs.

JOSEPH R. SPAZIANO,

Defendant.

ORDER VACATING JUDGMENT AND SETTING TRIAL DATE

On September 12, 1995, the Supreme Court of Florida entered an order treating two out-of-time motions for rehearing as a successive Rules of Criminal Procedure 3.850-3.851 motion based upon newly discovered evidence of the recantation of the testimony of a significant witness and remanded the case to this court for consideration of that issue. By separate order dated October 12, 1995, the Supreme Court directed this court to commence an evidentiary no later than January 15, 1996. The hearing commenced on January 8, 1996, and was completed on January 15, 1996. At that time the matter was taken under advisement.

The Issue

The issue to be decided is whether, due to the newly discovered evidence of the recanted testimony of Anthony DiLisio, the defendant is entitled to a new trial.

The Law of Newly Discovered Evidence and Recanted Testimony

In order to prevail on newly discovered evidence the defendant must prove:

1. the evidence has been discovered since the former trial;

2. the evidence could not have been discovered earlier through the exercise of due diligence;

3. the evidence is material to the issue;

4. the evidence goes to the merits of the case and not merely impeachment of the character of a witness;

5. the evidence must not be merely cumulative; and

6. the evidence must be such that it would probably produce a different result on retrial.

In determining whether a new trial is warranted due to recantation of a witness's testimony, a trial judge is to examine all the circumstances of the case, including the testimony of the witnesses submitted on the issue. Moreover, recanting testimony is exceedingly unreliable, and it is the duty of the court to deny a new trial where it is not satisfied that such testimony is true. Especially is this true where the recantation involves a confession of perjury.

Findings of Fact

Trial judges are taught to determine the credibility of a witness and the weight to be given to testimony by considering the demeanor of the witness; the frankness or lack of frankness of the witness; the intelligence of the witness; the interest, if any, that the witness has in the outcome of the case; the means and opportunity the witness had to know the facts about which the witness testifies; the ability of the witness to remember the events; and the reasonableness of the testimony considered in light of all of the evidence in the case. Additionally, trial judges attempt to reconcile any conflicts in the evidence without imputing untruthfulness to any witness. However, if conflicts cannot be reconciled, evidence unworthy of belief must be rejected in favor of evidence which is worthy of belief. These principals have been applied here, although it has not always been easy.

The crucial testimony at the trial of this case in 1976 came from the mouth of Anthony DiLisio. It was he who provided the only evidence of the cause of death of the decedent and it was he who supplied the jury with the evidence connecting this tragic event to the defendant. Without his testimony, there simply is no corroborating evidence in the trial record that is sufficient to sustain the verdict—not even any evidence from the medical examiner who performed the autopsy.

DiLisio now testifies that he did not tell the truth during the trial and provides a complicated explanation of the events which led up to his trial testimony. This testimony is credible and is corroborated by other evidence to a significant extent.

DiLisio testified that he and his five siblings lived in a dysfunctional family ruled by his father, Ralph DiLisio, who physically abused them. DiLisio tried to please his father but he never succeeded. His father owned a boat dealership known as Maitland Marine and DiLisio frequented the business as a young teenager.

Ralph DiLisio started an affair with a younger woman

employee named Keppy *[sic]* who seduced DiLisio when he was fifteen and with whom he had frequent sexual intercourse for about two and one half years. His father and Keppy ultimately married. DiLisio had sex with her for the last time on their wedding day. It was during this time that DiLisio started using drugs including marijuana, hash and alcohol.

The defendant worked at the marina and DiLisio knew who he was. There is a conflict as to just how close their relationship was but none of the witnesses who testified were able to establish a fast friendship.

Not surprisingly, Keppy began to have a sexual relationship with the defendant. Ralph DiLisio found out and became angry. At some point Keppy accused the defendant of raping her. It was about that time that Ralph DiLisio asked his son if the defendant had told him that he mutilated women. DiLisio testified that the defendant never said anything like that to him. But the idea was planted in his mind.

DiLisio's mid-teenage years included several brushes with the law. He ran away from a drug treatment center in a stolen car with two other juveniles and ended up in Volusia House. It was there that Detectives Abbgy and Martindale, who were investigating the homicide in this case, approached DiLisio for information. After being encouraged by his father to cooperate with the police, he agreed to be hypnotized in order to refresh his memory.

The detectives induced DiLisio to cooperate by inferring that his cooperation would get him out of Volusia House and would result in several serious criminal charges being dropped. They also supplied him with bits of information prior to the hypnosis session. He was scared. He went along with the police in an effort to please them and his father.

After the first hypnosis session was over, DiLisio did not think the police believed he cooperated. In fact, he "recalled" very little during the first session. It was then that the police took him to the scene of the homicide. A second hypnosis session was scheduled the next day.

Tapes of the sessions are in evidence as are the transcripts. The hypnotist does not give the listener confidence in his abilities. The defense experts who testified about the sessions and procedures agreed. One of them gave the hypnotist a "double f" and the other rated his skill level at "zero." It is plain from the testimony of these two distinguished experts that the reliability of the procedure used should be seriously doubted and that the information which was produced as a result was unreliable. Both experts agreed that hypnosis cannot improve recall beyond that which can be recalled through conscious efforts and that is exactly what the hypnotist thought he could do. It is most likely that the crime scene depicted by DiLisio is a scene that he created for the purpose of pleasing the police and his father. One of the experts even pointed out that the actual crime scene did not match DiLisio's depiction in several material respects.

The State called several witnesses in order to attack DiLisio's testimony and destroy his credibility. Many of these witnesses had major credibility problems themselves. One of the witnesses, a murderer in the Federal witness protection program, testified that he and the defendant were in prison together after the defendant was sentenced to life for rape but before the trial in this case. The witness heard the defendant express concern over a young boy whom he had taken to see some dead bodies. The reliability of that statement is questionable. If the statement was made, it is likely that the defendant was discussing the testimony he had learned DiLisio was going to give at trial. That is the only way to reconcile the testimony with DiLisio's version of the events without rejecting it as being untruthful.

Another witness, Bill O'Connell, was a counselor at the Volusia House and knew DiLisio while he was there. He stated that DiLisio was having trouble sleeping and told him that he had taken the police to a grave site. However, that statement, if made, does not agree with other credible evidence in the case unless it was made after DiLisio had developed his testimony for the trial. The same is true of the statement Annette Jones says DiLisio made to her and the statement DiLisio says he made to Sandy Vehman.

Conclusions of Law

In the United States of America every person, no matter how unsavory, is entitled to due process of law and a fair trial. The defendant received neither. The validity of the verdict in this case rests upon the testimony of an admitted perjurer who had every reason to fabricate a story which he hoped would be believed. The courts of this country should not tolerate the deprivation of life or liberty under such circumstances. A fair trial requires a determination of the truth by an informed jury. The verdict of an uninformed jury results in an unfair trial. An unfair trial is an unlawful trial because it produces an illegal result.

The evidence of recantation in this case is newly discovered evidence which could not have been discovered earlier through the exercise of due diligence. It is material evidence which goes to the merits of the case. It is not cumulative evidence and it would probably produce a different result on retrial. As Justice Kogan stated in his concurring opinion remanding this case to this court:

> Today we are presented with a grossly disturbing scenario: a man facing imminent execution (a) even though his jury's vote for life imprisonment would be legally binding today, (b) with his conviction resting almost entirely on testimony tainted by a hypnotic procedure this Court has condemned, (c) with the source of that tainted testimony now swearing on penalty of perjury that his testimony was false, and (d) without careful consideration of this newly discovered evidence under the only legal method available, Rule of Criminal Procedure 3.850 or 3.851.

That careful consideration has now been given and the validity of the Judgment and sentence has been found to be so questionable that it cannot stand.

IT IS ADJUDGED:

1. The Judgment rendered on January 23, 1976, and the sentence entered on June 4, 1981, are vacated.

2. This case is set for trial during the trial period commencing March 25, 1996, with docket sounding on March 12, 1996.

ORDERED at Sanford, Seminole County, Florida, this 22nd day of January, 1996.

O. H. Eaton Jr.
Circuit Judge

The new trial order was held to be in abeyance while the state appealed Judge Eaton's new trial judgment in the Harberts homicide case. (So much for the state's loud and frequent demands for "finality" in death cases.)

Some might say of Spaziano's new trial order: The system worked. "In fact, it was lawyers and reporters who worked. The legal system did its powerful best to kill," Colman McCarthy wrote in February 1996. In the same week that Joe Spaziano won a new trial, Delaware hanged a man and Utah executed another man by firing squad.

That Same Day
Wilder, Vermont

It took me a while to absorb the magnitude of this unqualified victory for Joe. This was a whole new trial—a whole new trial without the prosecution's false testimony of Tony DiLisio. Not just a temporary stay. Not just a resentencing. This was a whole new trial. Deanna tells me that I spent that first day after I received the news wandering around the house mumbling, "New trial. New trial. New trial."

Of course, this didn't mean Joe was a free man. At the new trial, he could still be convicted and sentenced to die. Also, he was still underneath the Croft rape case conviction. But those were tomorrow's worries. One step at a time.

Today had been a giant step. New trial.

That Same Day
Wilder, Vermont

I couldn't speak with Joe today, but I could speak or fax to everyone else. And I did: my mother, Mike Farrell, Mark Olive, Mike Radelet, Margaret Vandiver, the Sons of Italy folks, David Von Drehle, Jeff Robinson, Mike Millemann, Colman McCarthy, James J. Kilpatrick . . . everyone.

By the end of the day, my adrenaline had dropped and reality had set in. Surely the state would appeal Judge Eaton's new trial order. There was still the rape case to take out. There was work to do.

Still, I took a while to be grateful—for this day and for those people and institutions who made this day possible.

The *Miami Herald* saved Joe's life. But for Gene Miller, Warren

Holmes, and Lori Rozsa, Joe would have been killed in 1995. Tony DiLisio's recantation saved Joe's life, and the work of James Russ and Holland & Knight at the evidentiary hearing won the new trial. They won this day.

Further, without the inadvertent cooperation of the *Orlando Sentinel* and Governor Lawton Chiles generally and the governor's general counsel, Dexter Douglass, particularly, Joe Spaziano never would have won a new trial—or at least would not have won a new trial until many, many years in the future. To be sure, all the critical help Joe's case received from these quarters was entirely inadvertent. Still, without the assistance Joe got from the *Sentinel* and its gubernatorial patron, my first and last client would still be languishing on Florida's death row.

Without the *Orlando Sentinel,* we would have possessed no grounds to recuse *that* Judge McGregor from presiding over the evidentiary hearing. Had we not been armed with Judge McGregor's quotes in the *Sentinel* about his belief that the evidence of Joe's guilt was "overwhelming," McGregor never would have disqualified himself from the case. With McGregor as the judge running the show at the evidentiary hearing, there would have been no new trial order. With Judge McGregor out of the picture, Joe had a shot at a new trial and therefore a chance of freedom. Not a guarantee. A chance.

However, it is to Dexter Douglass, Governor Chiles's right-hand man, that Joe truly owes his shot at freedom. At virtually every critical stage of the drama unfolding between May and September 1995, Douglass's advice to Chiles—which the governor followed unerringly, by all accounts—seemed almost intended to maximize my odds of winning for Joe the ultimate goal I thought wasn't remotely possible in May 1995: a new trial with a chance of release from prison. Even if helping me was not Douglass's intention, it certainly was his effect.

Douglass and Chiles's greatest gift to Joe was the signing of the August–September death warrant—and their basing that warrant on the secret police investigation into the credibility of Tony DiLisio's recantation. Had the governor just let it alone—not granting clemency, but also not signing a death warrant—Joe's case (and his life) would have remained in limbo indefinitely. Eventually, the Florida Supreme Court would have dismissed the out-of-time rehearing I'd filed there; then I would have filed in Judge McGregor's court, where the case would have languished until he'd dismissed it without an evidentiary hearing, which I would have appealed on the slow track, which the Florida Supreme Court would eventually have sent back to Judge McGregor, who would have eventually held the hearing and eventually ruled against Joe and made deadly fact-findings, which I would have appealed to the Florida Supreme Court, which would have affirmed, which I would have taken into federal district court (Judge G. Kendall Sharp) via a habeas corpus petition, which Judge Sharp would have denied, which I would have appealed to the Eleventh Circuit Court of Appeals (Judge Ed Carnes), which the court would have denied, which I would have taken to the U.S. Supreme Court, asking for plenary review, which would have been denied. Some future governor would then have signed Joe's death warrant, and he would have been executed. Even if, by some twist, the state trial court would have ordered a retrial, that wouldn't have happened until years and years down the road.

In short, but for the August–September warrant, there is no way Joe would have won a new trial in early 1996. Most likely, there would have been no new trial decision at all—ever. If a new trial mandate would ever have been issued, it would have been issued only many years in the future.

Similarly, the August–September warrant spurred the *Miami Herald* to dig deeper into the Harberts murder case and, more important, into the Croft rape case as well. Newspapers like the *Herald* always have many vastly different priorities competing for extremely scarce (and getting scarcer) resources devoted to investigative reporting, an intensely labor-intensive enterprise. Perhaps the *Herald* would have maintained its high-priority level of investigative reporting on Joe's case even without its feet being held to the journalistic fire by the warrant—but the warrant guaranteed that it would.

Another Chiles/Douglass gift to Joe was the executive decision to keep the police report secret. This government-in-the-darkness tactic gave me—for the first time since the May–June death warrant was signed—a genuine constitutional question worthy of the attention of the U.S. Supreme Court, and as a bonus, the secrecy converted a case concerning the death penalty (which the Florida Supreme Court, the U.S. Supreme Court, and the citizenry in general are sick of) into a case concerning the First Amendment and freedom of the press (which the Florida Supreme Court, the U.S. Supreme Court, and the citizenry in general care very deeply about). For the first time in my memory, a coalition of First Amendment advocates and deathworkers began to form. That nascent alliance did not evaporate when the Florida Supreme Court stayed the August–September death warrant.

The explicit governmental seediness of trying to kill a possibly innocent man on the basis of secret evidence suddenly made it easy for me to sell Joe's case to the national media. Blood lust, vengeance, and cover-up are so, well, *ungubernatorial,* don't you think? The secret report gave me a sound bite, which gave me a lure with which to snag the attention of busy reporters and news organizations. No sound bite could capture the depths of the injustice of executing Joe Spaziano, but "They're killing an innocent guy based on secret evidence they won't turn over even to the guy's pro bono lawyer" caught people's attention. Given this bite, savvy reporters could elicit public concern, and that concern provided a forum for education.

In general, the August–September death warrant electrified a national media that had by then more or less lost interest in Joe's case. The governor's stay of his May–June warrant had cut short a burgeoning interest on the part of the *New York Times, Newsweek,* the *Washington Post,* and all the major TV networks. "Innocent man who has been languishing on death row for nineteen years is still languishing there" lacks the attention-grabbing cachet of "Innocent man set to die in twelve days." The second warrant gave Joe's story legs it would not have had otherwise.

The Chiles/Douglass tag team also made ordinary people—many people—take a second and harder look at an issue they had long thought settled: Is capital punishment a wise social policy? This gift to death penalty abolitionists was huge. It seemed to me that virtually all thoughtful capital punishment supporters really didn't believe, down deep in their stomachs, that we could ever, *ever* execute innocent people in this country of ours. I'm not saying that learning about Joe's case has converted death penalty supporters into death penalty abolitionists; rather, Joe's case made many people revisit and rethink one of their most cherished assumptions about capital punishment: that it is always executed upon the guilty. My exhibit A on this score is James J. Kilpatrick, previously a true believer in the death penalty. Kilpatrick wrote in his magnificent column on Joe's plight that cases like Joe Spaziano's in Florida and Joe Giarratano's in Virginia have shaken the pillars of his faith in capital punishment. If Kilpatrick ever becomes a convert to abolition (and I think he is close now), I think his reasoning might run something like this: if an innocent like Joe can be executed, then perhaps a machinery of death invented, operated, and imposed by fallible humans might not be such a hot idea.

Through their actions, Chiles and Douglass also induced folks to make what, for optimistic death penalty abolitionists, may be the most important change in thinking: a shift in frame of reference from thinking about capital punishment as an abstract moral or policy issue (easy question for most Americans—they're for it) to thinking about capital punishment as a legal system (much tougher). Once people really understand that we execute innocent people (or at least we try like hell to), they may take a longer look at who else we are killing in all our names: retarded people, crazy people, people who were children when they committed their capital crimes, and, most universally, run-of-the-mill killers. In order to execute the occasional Ted Bundy, we must have a legal system that runs the risk—the *real* risk—of killing the occasional Joe Spaziano.

Douglass and Chiles made my life as Joe's lawyer easier. By dissembling publicly about the contents of the FDLE's videotaped interrogation of Tony DiLisio, Douglass highlighted, in a straightforward and easy-to-understand way, the dangers of government secrecy. Ditto as to Douglass's statement that the interrogation lasted an hour and forty-five minutes—twice as long as my bootleg tape of the interrogation. That gave me an easy and irrefutable answer to any questions (including those raised by the Florida Supreme Court justices) about why this or that wasn't on the tape (Tony's being placed under oath, for example). All I had to say was that maybe that information was on the portions of the videotape not on my bootleg version; if someone would compel the government to give me *its* version of the videotape, then we'd know for sure.

Perhaps the governor's and the *Orlando Sentinel*'s greatest contribution to the overturning of Joe's murder conviction was the pressure they put on the *Miami Herald* to keep digging ever deeper into the factual history of the case. As wildly wrong as the *Sentinel* got that history, the fact remains that the Orlando newspaper knows more about Joe's case than any other newspaper save the *Herald*. For the *Herald*, there was nothing absolute about historical truth; the *Herald*'s conclusions about the factual basis of Joe's innocence were never more than estimations based upon what the best available evidence told the *Herald* at any given time. For the *Herald,* all facts always were provisional, contingent, and subject to reexamination based on the discovery of new evidence by others—the *Orlando Sentinel,* law enforcement, or the governor's office. Thanks in part to the energy of the *Sentinel* reporters, the *Herald*'s interpretations of its historical facts and conclusions were constantly being tested against new information, however outlandish.

Although the *Sentinel*'s new information scared the hell out of me at the time—because I feared that the *Herald*'s reporters might lose the will or the investigative resources necessary to debunk them—I now see that the *Sentinel*'s oppositional mind-set kept the *Herald* sharp. At every turn, the *Herald* tested the *Sentinel*'s new stuff and found it lacking. Reexamination as a means of refining—how would the founding fathers view that? This process of continuous reexamination only served to reinforce Warren Holmes's and Gene Miller's original instincts that Joe was indeed innocent. Without the *Sentinel*'s endless irritations, the *Herald*'s investigation would have had to struggle to remain vital and not degenerate into dogma. You see, reexamination is not only a cheap defense tactic; it is a haven of honest people who want to determine what is *right.* It helps us get at the truth, and it takes time.

On this score the *Orlando Sentinel*'s contribution to Joe's innocence claim was, of course, entirely inadvertent. The *Sentinel*'s goal was to kill Joe Spaziano. If he was not to be electrocuted for Laura Harberts's murder, then by God the newspaper would pin *some* murders and rapes on him. Relying on secret sources, the *Sentinel* tried to do exactly that. The newspaper intimated that he killed a couple in Chicago. He killed a Michigan woman. He committed a series of previously unsolved rapes. When all else failed, the paper focused on his being an Outlaw—a member of a group hated rabidly by the boys and girls who work at the *Sentinel.* I mean, what the hell, he had to be guilty of something, didn't he? So execution was just *indicated.*

If you think all this is far-fetched, remember Richard Jewell. For eighty-eight days in 1996, Jewell was the most-watched man in America. Everywhere the former security guard went, the FBI and news cameras followed. Why? Because secret police sources had told the *Atlanta Constitution* that Jewell was the prime suspect in the July 1996 bombing of Centennial Olympic Park. He "fit the profile" of a lone bomber. Jewell was eventually cleared by the FBI, but the damage had already been done. He'd been tried and convicted by his hometown newspaper. He was guilty on account of our suspicion, so we found that the evidence confirmed our belief.

I'm not saying that the *Orlando Sentinel* didn't have the freedom and the right to publish all the garbage it printed about Joe and his case, because it did. I'm a First Amendment absolutist.

Still, for all its malice and ineptitude, the *Orlando Sentinel* performed a service in Joe's case. It was a service not unlike that provided to responsible historians by Holocaust deniers. As Raul Hilberg, author of *The Destruction of the European Jew*, told Christopher Hitchens, if Holocaust deniers "want to speak, let them. It only leads those of us who do research to re-examine what we might have considered as obvious. And that's useful for us."

Useful, but not indispensable. When good faith is applied by informed, intelligent writers, the results are spontaneous. The principal reason for the high quality of the *Miami Herald*'s investigation into Joe's case, for example, was unrelated to the *Orlando Sentinel*'s coverage. The sources of the *Herald*'s integrity and objectivity were internal. In particular, the ferocious skepticism of the *Miami Herald*'s people themselves was what kept the *Herald* on its toes. No truth was sacrosanct to them; they treated each new piece of evidence dredged up by the *Sentinel* or the police as yet another opportunity to test the validity, completeness, and reliability of what they already knew. Here, as with so many other aspects of the *Herald*'s investigation into Joe's innocence claim, all roads lead to Warren Holmes—the *Herald*'s Cynic, follower of the pre-Socratic Greek sect whose motto could have been, "Question everything."

In short, Douglass, Chiles, and their publicists at the *Sentinel* were largely responsible for Joe's winning a new trial. But for them, Joe would still be rotting on death row, without any chance of freedom. But this troika brought that previously unimaginable goal within reach. Thanks, guys. We couldn't have done it without you.

Almost from the day Judge Eaton ordered a new trial for Joe, the Florida police began scrambling to find anything they could to throw against Joe. Over the spring and summer of 1996, a pattern emerged.

First, the police would concoct some new "evidence" against Joe. Second, they would leak their new stuff to the *Orlando Sentinel,* and the *Sentinel* would publish a breathless news story based on the cops' new evidence. Third, the *Miami Herald* would actually *investigate* the cops' new discoveries and, invariably, prove that the new evidence was either nonexistent or laughably unreliable. Then the cycle would repeat itself.

Sometimes the *Sentinel* was not the shill for the cops' new discoveries—necrodentistry is one example. In a November 1996 *Herald* story, reporters John McKinnon and Lori Rozsa described the theory:

> Call it necrodentistry.
>
> Seeing the original murder case crumble in a Seminole County courtroom, Central Florida police are trying to link Spaziano to another unsolved murder. They now say the diminutive biker could have yanked the teeth from one corpse and put them in a second victim's jaw.
>
> That might explain why the teeth don't match. . . .
>
> A second skeleton found at the dump in 1973 along with Harberts was never identified.
>
> Earlier this year, Seminole County deputies Ray Parker and Ralph Salerno reinterviewed witnesses from the original Harberts investigation.
>
> They took a statement from a woman who knew Spaziano then. She said that in the spring of 1973, she saw Spaziano at Daytona Beach with "a young girl" riding on the back of his motorcycle. The girl asked her to hold her purse "for safekeeping," according to the Seminole County sheriff's office. The girl didn't pick up her purse after the motorcycle ride. Five days later, she said, Spaziano showed up at her door "and demanded the purse."
>
> She turned it over, but not before peeking inside for the identification. She told Salerno and Parker that she remembered only that the girl was from Ann Arbor, Michigan.
>
> Two months ago, Seminole police asked forensic anthropologist Dr. William Maples to examine the unidentified remains.
>
> They had been examined before. In 1973, Lawrence Angel of the Smithsonian Institution's Department of Anthropology concluded that the body was that of a white female 16 to 21, about five feet five inches; slender build. She had crooked lower teeth and two fillings in her upper teeth.

According to a 1996 press release from the Seminole sheriff's office, Maples concluded that the girl was 15 to 16 years old, five feet, seven inches, 110 pounds and had crooked teeth.

Based on Maples' description, a police artist drew a sketch of what the girl might have looked like. Seminole police asked Ann Arbor police and TV stations for help in identification.

Deputies in Washtenaw County, where Ann Arbor is, came up with an unsolved missing persons case from 1970, three years before the Daytona Beach motorcycle ride.

In April 1970, Cynthia Coon, 14, disappeared on her way to school. She was five feet four inches and weighed 100 pounds.

She "looked a little bit" like the police artist sketch, Seminole sheriff's spokesman Ed McDonough said.

Dental records could establish an identification—the skull of the skeleton had crooked teeth and fillings, easy to match.

But they didn't match. Cynthia Coon had never been to a dentist in her life. Her father, Dr. William Coon, a pathologist, said "she had straight teeth," no fillings.

How to reconcile that?

McDonough said Spaziano "had the habit of removing teeth from his victims." Those found in the skeleton "probably weren't her teeth. The could very well be someone else's teeth."

Maples said that if anyone had tried to adhere teeth from one body into the jaw of this body, it would have showed.

"If the corpse had fillings in places where there should not be fillings, there is a problem." Maples said.

Seminole police want the Coon family to give a blood sample for DNA testing. The family has not consented.

McDonough still sees Spaziano as a suspect. "He was the type that removed teeth and put them back in other victims," McDonough said. "He was very sick that way."

On April 1, 1996—April Fools' Day and Law Day—Orlando attorney Jim Russ filed a postconviction motion for a retrial of Joe Spaziano's conviction for the 1975 rape of Vanessa Dale Croft. At the Seminole County hearing, Tony DiLisio testified, in open court, under oath and subject to cross-examination by the prosecutors, that he lied at *both* Joe's 1976 murder trial and 1975 rape trial. As to his testimony at the 1975 trial for the rape of Vanessa Dale Croft, Tony testified in 1996:

Q: And when you went there to Orlando to testify at that trial where Joe Spaziano was on trial, did you testify truthfully or falsely?

A: Falsely.

Because Holland & Knight had backed out of the rape case, Russ, his associate Tad Yates, and his inestimable paralegal, Lori Lakeman, were on their own. And because Holland & Knight had refused to litigate the rape case as part of the firm's challenge to the murder case, Russ's postconviction motion in the rape case had to be filed in Orange County rather than Seminole County. The Harberts murder (and trial) occurred in Seminole County; the Croft rape (and trial) occurred in Orange County.

Filing in Orange and not Seminole County meant that Judge Eaton would not decide Joe's challenges to the lawfulness of his rape conviction. That fact alone radically diminished Joe's chances of winning that challenge. One could hardly expect *two* judges of the fearlessness, independence, and courage of Judge Eaton to pop up.

As it turned out, the motion was assigned to Orange County Judge Dorothy Russell. Russell was a former prosecutor who seemed to take special glee in torturing Jim Russ and his clients. When she denied Russ's motion to disqualify her based on her palpable bias, the outcome became a foregone conclusion.

On September 17, 1996, Judge Russell rendered her decision. Predictably, she denied the motion for retrial. Not quite predictably, the way she went about denying the retrial motion was silly—there really is no other word for it.

It was silly in two respects. First, Russell denied the motion without conducting an evidentiary hearing. Yet she also made credibility determinations about Tony DiLisio's testimony at the *Seminole County* evidentiary hearing on the Harberts homicide case. Judge Eaton—based on DiLisio's live testimony in his court, in his presence—had concluded that Tony's recantation was truthful. Judge Russell—based on nothing more than her reading of the cold transcript of Tony's testimony in Judge Eaton's court—reached the opposite conclusion. Russell found DiLisio's recantation not to be credible, explaining, "This court finds, under the circumstances as we know them today, that DiLisio's recantation is inconsistent, incredible, and unreliable in its entirety, and does not constitute a sufficient basis to entitle Spaziano to a new trial."

The second silly aspect of Judge Russell's rationale had to do with her bias. If Russell's denial of the retrial motion wasn't enough to demonstrate her bias, the tone of her opinion eliminated any doubt: "This court finds that an evidentiary hearing in Orange County would result in a colossal waste of time and resources for everyone concerned."

The tone of Judge Russell's opinion echoed that of the prosecutor's office from whence she came. In the state's principal response to Joe's new trial motion, the prosecutor complained that "twenty-one (21) years [after the rape trial], in 1996, Spaziano has mustered the unmitigated gall to ask this court to allow him to reopen those [Croft's] wounds and bring her back to the Courthouse again." The state begged Judge Russell to "avoid a repeat performance of the spectacle served up by Spaziano in Seminole County and spare the taxpayers of Orange County suffering the same fate as the victim herein (i.e., Vanessa Dale Croft, the rape victim)" and asserted that "this matter should be resolved by this court as expeditiously and cost-effectively as possible."

Thus did the Florida prosecutors manipulate Judge Russell into "protecting" Vanessa Croft by ignoring Joe Spaziano's claim of factual innocence—a claim based on evidence so compelling that the Florida Supreme Court unanimously mandated that a hearing be held. Joe won that hearing because Judge Eaton investigated and determined that it was not the *wounds* being examined, but the *evidence* as to who inflicted them.

The *Orlando Sentinel* ate up the fiery rhetoric of the Orlando prosecutor and Judge Russell. Indeed, one must wonder whether the *Sentinel* was the intended audience for the state's barbs aimed at Joe Spaziano. Joe's defense counsel received the prosecutor's brief (quoted above) four days *after* the local *Orlando Sentinel* ran a story about it.

Attorney Russ would appeal Judge Russell's decision. In the meantime, the Florida Supreme Court geared up to decide the state's appeal of Judge Eaton's retrial order in the Harberts homicide case.

When the Florida Supreme Court's black curtain parted on December 4, 1996, and the justices emerged to assume their seats on the bench, the atmosphere in the courtroom couldn't have been more different from when I had orally argued sixteen months before, on September 7, 1995. When I had walked up to the podium that day, Joe's prospects could hardly have looked bleaker. He was scheduled to die in two weeks—on a fifth death warrant. The governor and his allies at the *Orlando Sentinel* were basing the warrant on the still-secret FDLE police investigation—including linking Joe with a series of other rapes and murders. In more than nineteen years, no judge on any court, state or federal, had ever evinced the slightest interest in Joe's long-standing claims of factual innocence. From Vermont, I was representing Joe pro bono, with no resources, no help from the recently defunct VLRC, and with the active opposition of CCR and its pals in the governor's office. CCR and the governor's office were spreading rumors that I was "unstable" if not outright crazy.

What a difference eighteen months can make. When Jim Russ walked up to the Florida Supreme Court's podium to argue in support of Judge Eaton's new trial order—Holland & Knight was conspicuously absent from defense counsel's table that day—his position of strength could hardly have been greater. There was no death warrant, and Russ wasn't asking the justices to stay Joe Spaziano's imminent execution. Russ wasn't asking Florida's highest appellate court for a hearing and an opportunity to prove the truthfulness of Tony DiLisio's recantation. He'd already had that hearing, before Judge Eaton, and he'd won.

Joe Spaziano had won in trial judge Eaton's court, and he had won in the best possible way for him. Judge Eaton had held a full and fair hearing at which all sides were given free reign to present all their appropriate witnesses and to cross-examine the other side's witnesses. The prosecutors, drunk as ever on hubris and arrogance, had had their crack at ruining Tony DiLisio on the witness stand, under oath. They couldn't. At the end of the day, Judge Eaton decided that he believed Tony's recantation to be truthful. He had explained his reasoning in an impeccably crafted opinion founded on justice and the highest principles of our nation's legal history. Thus Judge Eaton's new trial order was virtually bulletproof, immune to any realistic possibility of reversal by the Florida Supreme Court, despite the state's appeal.

The state's appeal. Those three little words describe the transformation that had occurred between my September 7, 1995, oral argument and Jim Russ's December 4, 1996, oral argument. In capital defense circles, it was like a dream come true. For once, it was the *state* that was asking the Florida Supreme Court justices to overturn a respected trial judge's decision in Joe's case. For once, the state had the burden of persuading the justices that the lower court had erred. For once, the state was considered the guilty one, while the defense was clean and freshly laundered.

In the practice of law in the appellate courts, the party arguing reversal of the lower court's judgment argues first. In every single one of the previous oral arguments in Joe's case, his lawyer went first. Today, the prosecutor argued first.

There's an old appellate advocate cliché: When you don't have the facts, argue the law; when you don't have the law, argue the facts; when you don't have either the facts or the law, yell loudly, jump up and down, and flail your arms. Yelling, jumping, and flailing were all the state's attorney had left to offer, and he proceeded to do all three with a vengeance. He also trashed Judge Eaton, personally.

According to John McKinnon's analysis of the oral argument, which appeared in the *Miami Herald,* the prosecutor "fired off a blistering attack" against Judge Eaton. "In a desperate bid to save the state's crumbling case, [the prosecutor] told the state supreme court that Circuit Judge O. H. Eaton, Jr. had twisted facts to fit his view that Spaziano deserves a new trial." The state labeled one of Judge Eaton's conclusions in the case "ridiculous"; others were called "absolutely absurd." McKinnon described the scene: "Chopping the air with his hand, even pounding the lawyer's lectern, the drawling, red-haired [prosecutor] came across more like a fire and brimstone evangelist than an appellate attorney. And Eaton was the sinner he was preaching against."

The attack on Judge Eaton earned the state a "momentary advantage, however," according to McKinnon. Jim Russ "appeared to be caught flat-footed by [the prosecutor's] nitpicking attack. Russ complained that he had come to argue the legal issues, not to retry the facts—something that the high court isn't supposed to do anyway." At the end of his oral argument, "Russ stumbled briefly again. Hurriedly trying to recap the court's legal test for new trials, he mixed it up. 'Well, I've turned it around,' he said in frustration. 'You wrote it. You know it.'"

McKinnon also noted that "Justice Ben Overton went out of his way to commend Russ and Spaziano's other lawyers from Holland &

Knight, who worked without fees. The only way the courts can operate is to have proper representation on both sides, Overton said." Justice Overton, I could not help recalling, was the judge who had hammered me so relentlessly during my oral argument in September 1995. It hurt to remember that day. I decided to rejoice in this one instead.

A few weeks after the oral argument, the Florida Supreme Court awarded Jim Russ its prestigious Tobias Simon Pro Bono Service Award, based in part on Russ's work on Joe Spaziano's case. It was a crowning moment. The award is coveted in large measure because its namesake, Florida ACLU attorney Tobias Simon, was a tireless opponent of capital punishment and a genuine lion in the seemingly endless war to bring equal justice to Florida's most disadvantaged residents—African Americans. When Jim Russ was honored in the name of Tobias Simon, it was, to me, a spiritual victory. This award has been given to several Florida lawyers for their arduous, often-resented representation of the Sunshine State's most hated criminals. Jim Russ thus joins the honored company of Craig Barnard, as he should.

In 1975, Tony DiLisio's testimony sent Joe Spaziano to prison for raping Vanessa Dale Croft. One year later, DiLisio's testimony sent Joe to death row for the murder of Laura Lynn Harberts. In the spring of 1995, Tony DiLisio took it all back. He took back the very testimony that had, nineteen years earlier, sent Joe Spaziano to death row for a crime he didn't commit. It was all a lie.

Why did it take Tony DiLisio so long to recant? It sure wasn't for want of trying by Joe's lawyers and investigators. For me, the reason doesn't really matter. What matters is that it did take nineteen years. Had Joe been executed at any time during those years—on his first death warrant in 1985, or his second in 1990, or his third in 1992— DiLisio's recantation would have come too late. Too late to save Joe's life, I mean.

Why did it take Tony nineteen years to recant? Only Tony himself knows the true answer to that question. Perhaps Tony heard a beating, telltale heart.

19

To Bedlam and Partway Back

But the war in Vietnam drifted in and out of human lives, taking them or sparing them like a headless, berserk taxi hack, without evidence cause, a war fought for uncertain reasons. . . . Certain blood for uncertain reasons. No lagoon monster ever terrorized like this.

> *Tim O'Brien*, If I Die in a Combat Zone:
> Box Me Up and Ship Me Home, *1973*

1-8-97

Dear Mike,

Sure hope your right next Christmas be home ☺. I'll be at your place ☺. . . .

You feel things are going to be ok Mike? Yes I worry a bunch, I don't know what they'll pull next. I don't trust cops at al.

Sure is a drag in here got no money no stamps no T.V. now radio. They say I can buy a radio here, but no income. At less over at U.C.I. everybody was looking out for me. I even started to do up cards.

I sure hope your all right about the F.S.C. [Florida Supreme Court]. I'm right in the cell next to the cell when I first come on death roul 20 years ago.

Well not to much more to say Mike just waite to see what happens. I'll close and love you all.

Your Friend Always
Crazy Joe

P.S. Can you send me a book of stamps I really need them ☺. I'll make it up to ya.

2-2-97
Dear Mike & D

Hi you all, sure wish Mike we could work on the book to-gether. See I was plaining on doing it with you myself. So you can see and meet the people to do a much better job. Oh I received the stamps thanks a hole bunch. Now back to the rest I like to get movies made of the story mike. Lisen Mike shouldn't be much longer let's see what Jim, and Holland & Knight do. I still haven't heard if they got the book I done. Lori Rozsa was suppose to send it to them but I never heard nothing. Mike I don't even remember what letter you was talking about. I know lots of stuff I said was between us. But I know to what you do will be right. I got so many problems I can't think so mad I'm back in these cells in this place. I was hopping never to see F.S.P. again. Mike I wanted to work with you on everything I do. That is why I'm going to be happy to sit around with you and D. and paint your place up ☺. I told my lawyers already. I want to do the 2 books I got already once I get out and I get an agent. And we work together Mike. I'm 51 stone broke I got to do some-thing. I have no T.V. or radio right now I misset the supper Bowl I can't paint got nothing Mike but like they said Holland & Knight believe this is going to be my year. Ya sure what I see it. The Government wants me dead. They lie, sheat, and steal polu-tions people go for it. I believe my story will show people some-thing is very wrong with the sistuum every. Why me I wonder, and maybe this is what I'm for. Nobody but you and my daugh-ter and Tina and lawyers and Lori Rozsa know me. I want to sit on a Harley and have that freedom again. Let me close Mike love you all D. you take care my bro, Mike ☺.

Love you All
Crazy Joe

P.S. Write Soon. Wish I can call you to come pick me up ☺.

A few weeks after Judge Eaton ordered a new trial in the Harberts homicide case, in January 1996, the prison moved Joe from death row to the general prison population. In general population, Joe could hang out with his Outlaw brothers who were also incarcerated at Florida State Prison. He was given a job outside the walls (but inside the razor-wire fences) picking up trash. He began a cartoon autobiography of his twenty years in prison for crimes he didn't commit.

And he could call me on the telephone pretty much anytime the prison phone was free. During the first fourteen years of our friendship, Joe had been able to call me only when he was under death warrant. For the first time, he could ring me up to chat about things other than his scheduled date with death. No one at the prison gave an explanation for the decision to move Joe from death row to general population.

And then, just as suddenly and inexplicably, Joe was sent back to death row. In December 1996, one day after the Florida Supreme Court heard oral arguments in the state's appeal of Judge Eaton's new trial order, the prison moved Joe back. He was the only man on Florida's death row who didn't have a death sentence. Just in time for Christmas.

Why the move, and why then? Prison officials gave no explanations, so all we could do was speculate. Maybe the move back to death row had been a bureaucratic screwup. Maybe the original move *from* death row had been a bureaucratic screwup. Or maybe officials had gotten some signal through the prison grapevine—or thought they had—that Joe was going to lose the Florida Supreme Court appeal. If that happened, then the governor would immediately sign a new death warrant on Joe. That would be the end. Joe would be electrocuted. Neither the *Miami Herald* nor Holland & Knight nor Jim Russ would be able to save him.

Thus Joe would spend Christmas 1996 in the same place he had spent the Christmases of 1995, 1994, 1993, 1992, 1991, 1990, 1989, 1988, 1987, 1986, 1985, 1984, 1983, 1982, 1981, 1980, 1979, 1978, 1977, and 1976. He was entering his third decade on death row for crimes he never committed.

In a December 6, 1996, letter to Deanna and me, Joe began by writing:

Well they got me locket up on [Administrative] Confinement, they took me out of population, no [disciplinary violation] no

trouble . . . and [they] don't know what to do with me. . . .
Nobody knows what is going on. . . .

I'm on death row but no death sentence. Really Mike it's a
bummer. I had a good job and happy and now back to this.
What they want out of me. . . .

Well, if you can fine out what is going on and let me know
I can sure be OK. Right now I'm not to good of a mude really
pisset. OK bro let me close and love you.

Your friend, Crazy Joe

My death row pen pals didn't know much either. On of my correspondents wrote, in a letter dated December 13, "They snatched him
out of [general] population and brought him back here to the north-
east unit and locked him up." In a letter dated December 15, 1996, another of my pen pals wrote: "Sure pissed me off to learn [that Joe had
been returned to death row]. He's been back now for just over a week,
they're keeping him in one of the high security cells on lower D-wing,
'The Disciplinary Floor,' but supposedly has all his personal property.
Of course they're listening, watching all movements, conversations.
Damned rednecks."

April 17, 1997
Vermont Law School, South Royalton

When the news came, I was teaching my 9:55 A.M. legal ethics class.
After class, I chatted briefly with Emily Kucer and then headed up to
my office. From there I called home for phone messages. There were
two, one each from Lori Rozsa and Gregg Thomas. The content of
both was the same: this morning the Florida Supreme Court had affirmed Judge Eaton's new trial order in Joe's capital murder case. The
court's decision was unanimous. This was the end of the line for Joe's
1976 conviction for the capital murder of Laura Lynn Harberts. Before
the state could execute Joe for her murder, they would have to prove to
a new jury—without the benefit of Tony DiLisio's damning testimony
from 1976—beyond a reasonable doubt that Joe Spaziano murdered
Laura Lynn Harberts. Judge Eaton's new trial order seemed to be final.
The 1976 capital murder conviction no longer existed.

Even had Tony DiLisio not recanted his crucial trial testimony, the
prosecution couldn't use Tony this time around: the police had hypno-

tized Tony twice before he implicated Joe, and in a trial held now that hypnosis would render Tony's testimony inadmissible as a matter of law. Without DiLisio's testimony, the 1976 prosecutor said at the time, "we'd absolutely have no case here whatsoever." Today, the state still had nothing beyond Tony. Today, as in 1976, there was still no physical evidence linking Joe to the crime. Today, as in 1976, no cause of death could be determined for Harberts. The capital murder case of *State of Florida v. Joseph Robert Spaziano* was, for all practical purposes, concluded.

The state could still delay the inevitable retrial by seeking U.S. Supreme Court review, but the word making the political rounds in Tallahassee was that this was the end of the line for the appellate prosecutors. Under Florida's procedural rules, the state had two weeks to ask the Florida Supreme Court to put its decision on hold to give the state time to seek U.S. Supreme Court review. Then the state would have ninety days—until August 15, 1997—to decide whether or not to retry Joe Spaziano for the 1973 murder of Laura Lynn Harberts.

After getting the news, I spent hours on the phone, with Miller and Lori Rozsa and Deanna and Mike Farrell. Reporters called, asking for my reaction. I told them I'm ecstatic, delighted, overflowing with joy. These weren't exactly lies, but they weren't exactly the truth, either. I *should* feel ecstatic. I want to feel ecstatic. But all I really feel is relieved, relieved that they won't kill him, at least not anytime soon. He might well walk out of prison a free man. I'm happy about that.

What I'm not is surprised. I'm not surprised that the "system" finally "worked." But, then, I wouldn't have been any more (or less) surprised had the Florida Supreme Court ruled the opposite way and reversed Judge Eaton unanimously; in that event, Governor Chiles would have signed Joe's death warrant by the end of the day, and Joe would have been executed twenty-eight days hence. An affirmance of Judge Eaton and a chance for freedom, or a reversal of Judge Eaton and certain death within a month—neither outcome would have surprised me.

For a week, I tried to write Joe a letter. Nothing came. Finally, I wrote him a poem, the first poem I've ever written.

Why wasn't I more joyful about all this?

MEMORANDUM

TO: Gene Miller, *Miami Herald*

FROM: Michael Mello

DATE: May 15, 1997

RE: Filing a Motion to Preclude Death as a Possible
           Punishment on the Retrial: Bringing the Croft
           Case Before Judge Eaton (Reprise)

Please pardon the abruptness of this memo; I'm still in the midst of end-of-semester chaos, and this memo was written on the fly.

I remain convinced that we ought not abandon hope of getting the Croft rape case before Judge Eaton as part of the Harberts homicide case. Now that the Florida Supreme Court mandate in Harberts has issued, there is no danger whatsoever that the Croft rape case might somehow endanger Judge Eaton's new trial order in Harberts. Of course, the best time to have done this would have been *before* the Croft 3.850 had been filed in Orange County, and certainly before the rabid Judge Russell had ruled, dismissing the 3.850 and making her killer factfindings. But it's still not too late, I'm convinced.

In a fall 1995 letter to Gregg Thomas, I attempted to set out the intimate connections—factually, logically and legally—between the murder case and the rape case:

> First, I continue to believe very strongly that you need to bring the rape case into this evidentiary hearing, for making-the-record purposes if for no other. The obvious hook is that Tony DiLisio was the key to both prosecutions. Atmospherically, the presumptive validity of the rape conviction makes it easier for judges, being human beings (sort of), to minimize the power of our challenges to the homicide. The obvious flaws in the rape case were what got Warren Holmes (and thus Gene Miller and thus the *Herald*) to take our arguments about the murder case seriously. Also, as Lori Rozsa has shown, the rape case set-up was central to the Harbert-case set-up. The key to both set-ups seems to have been Ralph DiLisio, and his primary agenda (at least initially) was to set Joe up for the rape, since Ralph had convinced himself that Joe had "raped"

Keppie. Further, in terms of Joe's practical realities (*i.e.*, actually getting him out of prision sooner rather than later), we need to attack *both* convictions; that's why I spent so many pages on the rape case in my clemency application and principal Florida Supreme Court filing. Finally, and most importantly, this will likely be Joe's one and only evidentiary hearing. I've been trying to get an evidentiary hearing for ten years, since the first 3.850 filed during the first warrant. Even if Judge Eaton won't allow testimony on the rape case, you need to proffer everything we have, it seems to me.

To those factual and logical connections we now have one more: The rape conviction was *the* reason Judge McGregor gave for overriding the sentencing jury's 10–2 or 9–3 verdict of life imprisonment. Joe's sentencing jury didn't know about the rape conviction, Judge McGregor did. The judge imposed death—and the Florida Supreme Court affirmed—death on the basis of the rape case. No rape conviction, no death sentence—because in Florida, under the so-called *Tedder* rule, the jury's "recommended" sentence of life over death must almost always be followed.

Thus, without the rape conviction, Judge McGregor wouldn't have overridden the jury's life recommendation. If he *had* overridden it, the Florida Supreme Court almost certainly would have reversed—as it has done in more than 80% of the jury override cases it has decided.

This allows us now to file a motion to preclude death as a possible punishment on the retrial. The state's only credible response will be *for them* to bring the rape case into the murder case: Without the rape conviction, they have no grounds for asking Eaton to override the 1976 jury recommendation of life. Once the *state* brings the rape case into the murder case, the validity of the rape conviction becomes fair game for us—especially since (1) in his 1996 testimony, Tony recanted his rape case testimony as well as his murder case testimony; and (2) Judge Eaton believed the recantation.

One possible problem: All of this assumes that the 1976 jury recommendation of life remains in force at the retrial. Holland & Knight could research this point easily; the only case I know of off the top of my head is one decided in 1991. In that 1991 case, the Florida Supreme Court held that double jeopardy barred re-subjecting a defendant to a death sentence when the jury in the initial trial recommended life imprisonment. Citing the Florida Constitution's prohibition against double jeopardy, the court explained that "when it is determined on appeal that the trial court should have accepted a jury's recommendation of life imprisonment pursuant to *Tedder*, the defendant must be deemed acquitted of the death penalty for double jeopardy purposes."

The 1991 case isn't directly on point, but it's promising. Again, Holland & Knight can nail this research down quickly and easily.

Filing a motion to preclude death as a possible punishment has at least two tactical and strategic benefits, besides the obvious one that it might actually be granted. *First*, it might spook the state into thinking that it won't get a death-qualified jury at the retrial on guilt/innocence. Death-qualified juries are notoriously more prone to convict than "normal" juries (Joe's 1976 murder trial is a good example). Given that the state had next to nothing in 1976, and it has even less today the possibility of losing a death-qualified jury on retrial might tip their scales.

Second, the state might see through our not-so-subtle attempt to leverage *them* into introducing the Croft case into the murder retrial—in their feared and loathed Judge Eaton's court. The state might figure that the *risk* of getting the rape case before Judge Eaton is high enough to convince them to drop the murder case (under cover of the grand jury motion [I have not received a copy of the motion itself] for instance)—by dropping the murder case, they know they'll at least keep the rape case in Seminole County, even though they might lose Judge Russell. (The state has *gotta* think that *any* judge in Orange County would be better than Judge Eaton. I sure as hell would.)

May 21, 1997
Wilder, Vermont

The current president of the Florida Outlaws is a man called Fuzzy. His hair and flowing beard are graying, but he moves like a cat. Although powerfully muscular, he has about him the quietude of a man comfortable in his own skin. He has a *presence* in a room. When I first met him, he was wearing a black T-shirt, jeans, and a .45 sidearm on his belt. His voice is gravelly, and his eyes miss nothing. He is one of the most trustworthy men I've encountered in my travels through life, and I've come to think of him as my friend.

Fuzzy, an ex-Marine who saw active combat in Vietnam—when I was still in elementary school in Virginia—and who has a lightning-quick mind, is a unique combination of intensity and serenity. The Outlaws choose their leaders carefully and well, and all the ones I've dealt with over the years, from Wildman and Rocky in the mid-1980s to Fuzzy today, have always been judicious—sometimes too judicious, from my perspective—in the information they've passed on to me. Because that information almost always comes to them from third parties (and thus is hearsay), to be reliable it must satisfy two criteria: (1) the information must come from a person who is trustworthy and credible, and (2) that trustworthy person must have a direct basis of knowledge of the facts he or she is reporting.

So when Fuzzy phoned me to say that he'd received information that Joe was in imminent danger of being killed, I took it very seriously. The tip reached Fuzzy through Speedy, another Outlaw incarcerated at Florida State Prison in Starke, where Joe was currently housed. I'd worked with Speedy before; I knew he wouldn't pass this story on to Fuzzy, and Fuzzy, in turn, wouldn't pass it on to me, unless both men had checked it out first.

This is what Speedy told Fuzzy: A very large and muscular fellow who calls himself Q hates the Outlaws; indeed, while in prison, Q had stabbed to death an Outlaw called Funky Tim. Q himself had later been stabbed by an Outlaw in retaliation for Q's murder of Funky Tim. After being stabbed, Q had been moved to the administrative confinement part of Florida State Prison, not far from where Joe was housed. The concern was that, if Joe and Q were released into general population in that area of the prison, Q would bait Joe into fighting by trashing the Outlaws. Joe, unaware that this was a set-up, would defend the honor of his club, and Q would kill him.

The best way to provide Joe with some life insurance against this Q was to let the prison bureaucracy know that we knew what was going on, or at least that we suspected he was planning something. We decided that Fuzzy would call Lori Rozsa at the *Miami Herald* and tell her what we'd heard. I would write to Joe.

My writing Joe would serve two purposes. First, it would give Joe a heads-up if he wasn't already aware of what was happening. Second, prison officials would read my letter before it reached Joe, so they would know that we know.

My letter to Joe went out the next day.

June 3, 1997
Wilder, Vermont

Summer break. My law school classes were over. Grades were in. The class of 1997 had graduated and its members were studying for the bar exam.

I was writing this book. At 5:30 P.M., I got a call from Rosie Merrill, a longtime friend of Joe's, now living in Kentucky, who was helping me pull together press coverage of Joe's 1976 murder trial. At the end of our conversation, Rosie asked, as she always asks, whether it looked as though Seminole County would reindict Joe for the capital murder of Laura Lynn Harberts. Usually, I'm noncommittal, but today I felt optimistic. I assured Joe's friend: "The one thing we can count on is that the Seminole County prosecutor will wait until the last possible minute to decide. We'll hear at 4:55 P.M. on August 15. But all the signs coming out of Florida government are good. I think it's over."

Less than a minute after I got off the phone with Rosie, the phone rang again. It was Lori Rozsa, sounding somber and asking if I'd heard. I hadn't. "This afternoon, the Seminole County grand jury indicted Joe for the capital murder of Laura Lynn Harberts. We didn't even know the grand jury was *sitting*." Because grand jury proceedings are secret and ex parte—the defense is excluded, with power neither to present its own witnesses nor to cross-examine the state's own witnesses— neither the *Herald* nor Joe's lawyers knew what evidence the prosecutors had fed to its grand jury. Judge Eaton would preside over the retrial; although he would be moving into the civil trial division on July 1, he was taking the Spaziano case with him.

But the indictment meant that, although the 1976 capital murder conviction was history, the case was far from over. Rozsa wanted to know, did I have any reaction, that could be published in a family newspaper, to the day's events?

Reaction? You bet. This was a wonderful gift from the state of Florida: Joe would finally get his jury, a real jury this time, a jury that would hear all the exculpatory evidence that the state succeeded in keeping from the 1976 jury. Give Joe a real trial and a real jury. That's been my plea for fourteen years: give me a jury. If the prosecutors want to kill this innocent man, then let them do it the old-fashioned way. Let them prove to a jury that they have proof of Joe's guilt beyond a reasonable doubt.

Only through retrial can Joe prove his innocence once and for all. Absent a jury verdict of acquittal, the cops and the prosecutors could and would complain to the press that the defendant had gotten away with murder, that his clever defense lawyers had gotten him off on some "legal technicality."

After twenty-one years on death row and five death warrants, Joe would finally get a real trial. At that trial Joe would be represented by James Russ and Company. If the state wanted to try to frame him again, this time the whole world would be watching. The *Miami Herald* would see to that.

I was delighted. Let's rock and roll.

June 4, 1997
Joseph Spaziano
No. 049043
Union Correctional Institution
Raiford, Florida

Dear Joe:

Yesterday was one of those days I really miss being able to talk with you by phone. I know that the indictment must have left you with that snakebite feeling.

But, what I wish I could say to you in person, is that the indictment is a *good* thing, a *very* good thing, especially if James Russ can convince Judge Eaton to dismiss the case—for lack of evidence—or preclude death as a possible punishment (see my enclosed memo to the *Miami Herald*'s Gene Miller).

Such a dismissal by Judge Eaton, or an acquittal by a jury, is the only real way to vindicate your innocence. Had the state simply decided not to retry you, they would have whined that you got away with murder and that I got you off on some "legal technicality." This is a lot of crap, of course, but it's what the Florida cops and prosecutors always argues about innocent men and women they've sent to death row. They argued it in James Richardson's case. They argued it in the Jent and Miller case. They argued it in Sonia Jacobs' case. They'd argue it in your case.

The only thing that will shut them up is a decisive decision—by the trial judge or jury—that they simply don't have the evidence that you had anything whatsoever to do with the death of Laura Lynn Harberts. Yesterday's indictment was a gift, because it sets the stage for a dismissal by the judge or an acquittal by the jury.

A decision against retrial would not have the same cleansing effect. The clouds the state has put over your total innocence will only be dispelled when the legal system makes its decision out in the open, with the whole world of Florida watching. Then you will be able to walk out of Florida prison in a way that will do justice to your total innocence.

It was an interesting coincidence that you were indicted less than a week after the United States Supreme Court gave the green light for Paula Jones to sue President Bill Clinton for sexual harassment. Paula Jones' claims were initially ridiculed because she was seen as "trailer trash" not entitled to her day in court. You were indicted 23 years ago—because you're an Outlaw. In *Jones v. Clinton*, it took the United States Supreme Court to reaffirm the rule of law: Even "trailer trash" are entitled to their day in court. In *Spaziano v. Florida* it was Judge Eaton who reaffirmed the rule of law and said: Even Outlaws get their day in court.

Stuart Taylor, the journalist who convinced his peers to actually look at Jones' *evidence*, her facts, wrote: "Like water on stone the steady drip, drip, drip of fact and evidence wears away at the ideological biases and knee jerk first reactions that we all bring" to the culture wars. Taylor continues: "Felix Frankfurter, when asked whether a supreme court justice ever changes his mind, liked to say: 'If he's any good, he does!' The rest of us, too."

"Facts are what happened; law is the set of rules you apply to that evidence," Taylor also writes. In your case, the state has no facts. And the law is that without facts—a *lot of* credible and believable and substantial facts—you are not guilty. At the conclusion of any remotely fair trial, you will be acquitted.

Grand jury proceedings aren't designed to be fair to the citizen-accused; that's not their function. So please don't be troubled by the fact that the Seminole County prosecutor was able to convince his captive grand jury to indict you, or that the *Orlando Sentinel* will scream for your blood in an effort to poison the local atmosphere and make a fair trial impossible. Florida prosecutors own their grand juries; grand juries hear only what the prosecutors want them to hear; your lawyers aren't even *present* and they sure aren't allowed to put on any evidence to prove your evidence or cross-examine the state's "evidence." Small-town grand juries in Florida do whatever their local prosecutors tell them to do. They'd indict a ham sandwich for capital murder if the prosecutor asked them to. And why not? They only hear the state's side of the story; the ham sandwich's defense lawyer isn't even allowed in the grand jury room. And if it happens to be an *outlaw* ham sandwich, well, then . . .

The trial will be much different. The playing field will be level, and Russ will be there to ensure that it stays that way. You'll win a real jury trial, Joe.

It's what we've been asking for all these years: Give us a *real* trial. Give us a jury.

Anyway, hang in there, my friend. Take care and please write.

Peace,
"Crazy Michael" Mello
Professor of Law

6/6/97
Dear Mike,

Yes Mike I just got your letter and made me feel so much better bro. I figure this is what was going on on what you said but wasn't for sure. But sure I feel much better. Mike I love you bro. I'm ready to sit by that fire you D. and me and maybe have some marshmellows. Then I got to go visit Marynoel and my grand-kids for a coupl weeks but I won't set foot in Cali on less I got a couple of my body guards. [California, where Joe's daughter was living, is the home of the Hells Angels.]

I wanted to ask you is Vermont right next to New York City? I'm not exactly sure whre it is. And take it, it is really cold tehir. Well I better fine me a good woman to keep me warm.

Hey Mike I know you at one time was worried about James Russ but you feel much relax now and see he is great. I like te guy like you Mike he's very strong in the head serious guy, you know what I mean. He aint a guy to smile much. He knows what he's doing and tryes to do it and talk to me for my best interest. I'm very relaxed around him.

I wish Holland and Knight would help him on the rape case.

Well let me get the hell out of here tell D. I send my love. Is she pregnant yet? Get to it bro. I like to be there when she ahs Mike junior. Hay I'll be honest when you'es have a baby I will spoil them.

Love you,

Get to it D

I'm pumped up again, bro, if I get out and have no identification, no birth certificate, no social security number, I got shit. How will I be able to get a license? Let me know what I have to do for ID.

Ok I'll close
Bro. Crazy Joe

6/9/97

Dear Crazy Mike,

Hi pal sure can't waite to read your book. I see it is going to be a hit by the introduction. So glad we meet Mike, so glade. I'm so proud to know you and you believe in me with all your heart, I do you to your a friend a good friend that wouldn't sell me out. Let me become a peace of bacon. . . . you understand me more than anybody. I'm tired of Fla. I'm ready to come home bro. Well let's see, I just let somebody read your introduction they say you written is super. The way you put words.

I wrote to Dawn [Siebert, my student research assistant] but she never answered me so I'll hold on maybe she'll write again. Yes Mike I sure like to see the rought, rought, rought draft. I didn't know you was hearing from Fuzzy my brother. But ya that is great. I like that Crazy Mike. Ok Mike let me close.

Love you all
Crazy Joe

P.S. July 28 my trial starts

So the government of Florida had decided to try yet again to send Joe Spaziano to death row and to execute him for the murder of Laura Lynn Harberts. Could anyone—including me—have really expected otherwise? Two decades ago, the state framed him for murder and rape. Then, for more than nineteen years, the Florida courts deployed an army of legal technicalities to avoid even *considering* the ever-accreting evidence of Joe's innocence. Only in 1995, shamed by the *Miami Herald*'s investigation, did the Florida Supreme Court—ever so grudgingly—stay Joe's execution and order an evidentiary hearing on Tony DiLisio's recantation. And in 1997, when Judge Eaton's retrial order gave the justices no excuse to reverse him, the Florida Supreme Court affirmed the retrial order. Grudgingly, again.

Even then, some of the justices could not resist taking shots at Tony DiLisio. Justice Wells's concurring opinion bemoaned the rules of appellate procedure that constrained him to affirm Judge Eaton's retrial order. And Justice Overton wrote a concurring opinion in *Spaziano* asking the Florida legislature to enact a law extending the statute of limitations for perjury, so that any future lying witnesses might be deterred from coming forward as DiLisio did in 1995. The Florida legislature obliged Justice Overton by enacting just such a statute.

This, then, was the sum and substance of the Florida government's understanding of who was to blame for the miscarriage of justice in Joe Spaziano's case: the problem was Tony DiLisio's 1995 *recantation*. Not the original perjury itself. Not the cops who manufactured that perjury by hypnotizing DiLisio and pressuring him to bear false witness against Joe Spaziano. Not the Florida courts who condoned the miscarriage of justice for two decades. Not the governor who signed Joe's fifth death warrant under cover of a secret and fraudulent police report. To date, the one and only legal legacy of *Spaziano v. Florida* is this: an extended statute of limitations for perjury, aimed at deterring recantations like Tony DiLisio's in 1995.

All of this makes me think of another death case, one in which I was marginally involved years ago. While the events in Joe Spaziano's case were still unfolding, I received a phone call from Mike Radelet, a friend and colleague with whom I'd worked on that other case.

"Before you decide to retire from deathwork, you should know that Rolando Cruz walked [off death row and out of prison] yesterday. . . . The prosecutor put on the state's case, and when they were done the judge blew up at them. After haranguing the prosecution for not hav-ing a case worth shit, the judge turns to the defense lawyer and asks sweetly, 'Does counsel for the defense have any motions to make?' after a stunned silence, Cruz's lawyer says, 'Uh . . . umm. . . . Move for judgment of acquittal?' Granted! The judge slammed down the gavel and said, 'Case dismissed. Call the next case!' And that was that."

Rolando Cruz had been thrice condemned to die for the savage rape and murder of a ten-year-old girl, and thrice the Illinois Supreme Court had thrown out the murder convictions and sent Cruz's case back for new trials. The Illinois Supreme Court, a court not known for its solici-tude for the constitutional claims raised by death row prisoners, al-ways found a legalistic rationale for throwing out Cruz's murder con-victions and sending the case back to a jury to try again. I suspect that the court's real reasons remained unstated: the justices kept hoping that one of Cruz's juries would acquit him, because the state's case against Cruz was almost laughably gossamer. The Illinois Supreme Court didn't have the visceral fortitude simply to acquit Cruz, and they didn't have the visceral fortitude to affirm his murder convictions and allow the state to kill him. So the justices kept sending Cruz back for retrials, hoping that at some time, some trial judge or jury would have the courage to do what the Illinois Supreme Court didn't: acquit Ro-lando Cruz and set him free. Now one had.

If the Illinois Supreme Court justices didn't have doubts about Cruz's guilt, they would have been in a minority among those who have studied the case's history. One prosecutor resigned her job rather than work on Cruz's prosecution. Even the ordinarily rabid *Chicago Tribune* (whose parent company, incidentally, also owns Florida's *Orlando Sentinel*) had raised questions about Cruz's guilt.

Cruz's case had been my dress rehearsal for raising Joe Spaziano's innocence claim in Florida. I had signed on as counsel in a friend of the court brief filed in the Cruz case during its last trip up the ladder to the Illinois Supreme Court. My clients in *Cruz* had been Professors Hugo Bedau and Michael Radelet, the nation's two leading scholars of inno-cence and capital punishment. The first goal of our short brief (which was written mostly by Mike Radelet, as I recall) had been to situate Cruz's innocence claim within its historical, cultural, and institutional context—to demonstrate that innocents have in fact been sentenced to death and executed in the United States. The brief's second goal was to argue that courts, not governors or other politicians, should possess primary responsibility for identifying and correcting miscarriages of justice. If the courts rely on executive clemency to weed out claims of innocence, then the inexorable result will be the execution of people who are innocent.

The Rolando Cruz saga didn't conclude when Cruz was acquitted of a crime he didn't commit. After an intensive investigation, several DuPage County, Illinois, prosecutors and sheriff's deputies were indicted for obstruction of justice in framing Rolando Cruz.

Any chance the cops or prosecutors in Joe Spaziano's case will be prosecuted, or censured, or even mildly reprimanded? Don't hold your breath. But with the state's new perjury statute, Florida is safe from recanters like Tony DiLisio.

June 10, 1997
Wilder, Vermont

In the end, Joe Spaziano's life was decided by one word: "affirmed." With that single word of legalese, issued by three judges of Florida's intermediate appellate court (the Fifth District Court of Appeals, or Fifth DCA), the Florida judicial system upheld state trial judge Dorothy Russell's summary dismissal of Joe's postconviction challenge to his 1975 conviction and life sentence for the rape of Vanessa Dale Croft.

In the lexicon of appellate litigators, this kind of summary affirmance of a trial court's judgment is called a per curiam affirmance, or PCA. Per curiam because it is a summary disposition; there is no opinion or explanation for the court's decision—or, rather, the simple word *affirmed* is the totality of the court's "opinion." It's called a per curiam *affirmance* because that's what it does: affirms the judgment of the trial judge, in this case Judge Russell's summary dismissal of Joe's challenge to the Croft rape conviction.

I learned of today's PCA at about 3:45 P.M., when I got a phone call from the *Orlando Sentinel*'s Mike Griffin. As always, Griffin broke the bad news gently. Then I called the *Herald* to confirm. It was true: PCA by the DCA.

Next I called Fuzzy. His reaction: "This is retaliation for Joe's beating the murder case. This means that he'll *never* walk out of Florida prison, even if the indictment in the murder case miraculously evaporates." A bit paranoid, you think? Well, consider the alternative, rival hypothesis: maybe the judges just blew off the appeal; maybe they didn't bother to read or understand the briefs. Fuzzy's explanation makes as much sense to me as anything else I can come up with.

It was a shitty day for Outlaws all over, Fuzzy told me. Earlier today, a federal indictment was unsealed charging seventeen Chicago-area Outlaws with RICO racketeering crimes; nine of the seventeen were charged with six murders between 1992 and 1995. Other alleged crimes included drug dealing, attempted arson, and bombings in attacks on the Outlaws' archrivals, the Hells Angels.

On the West Coast, the news was that another American outlaw—lowercase o—was faring somewhat better in the criminal justice system. Elmer "Geronimo" Pratt, a former leader of the Black Panther party during the late 1960s, was released on bail after serving twenty-seven years in a California prison for a murder conviction he always claimed was concocted by the FBI as part of its attempt to exterminate the Panthers. Shortly after noon, Pratt was freed on $25,000 bond by the same Santa Ana judge who two weeks before had overturned Pratt's conviction on the ground that prosecutors withheld crucial evidence at his original trial, a trial that kept him behind bars for more than a quarter century (at the time of Pratt's trial, California did not have a capital punishment system that passed constitutional muster).

There is a quirky sort of symmetry to the day's events. Joe Spaziano, an Outlaw, will die in prison for crimes he did not commit. Geronimo Pratt, a different kind of outlaw—albeit one equally feared and loathed by law enforcement and most of mainstream America during the relevant time frame for both cases, the social and cultural tumult of the late 1960s and early 1970s—walks free after twenty-seven years of imprisonment. Both outlaws, in their own ways; both illegally imprisoned, although for marginally different periods of time.

On one point Fuzzy was most certainly correct: this was the end. Sure, there would be motions to be filed: a motion for rehearing in the DCA, arguing forcefully that Croft wasn't just a noncapital rape case, it really was a *capital* case, because without the Croft rape case there would have been no death sentence in the Harberts murder case, since without Croft the murder trial judge would have followed the sentencing jury's verdict of life imprisonment; another motion in the murder case to make the validity of the rape conviction an issue in the murder case. It wasn't over yet. There would still be some sound and fury, from the *Herald* and, I hoped, from Jim Russ as well.

But, in the end, Fuzzy was right. The DCA's PCA of Judge Russell meant that Joe would never walk out of prison a free man. Important battles remained, but as of today the war was over.

We'd lost. We'd all lost.

MEMORANDUM

DATE: June 10, 1997
TO: Gene Miller
FROM: Michael Mello
RE: Rehearing of 5th DCA's Summary Affirmance in Spaziano Rape Case

Thank you again for asking my thoughts on where James Russ and Holland & Knight go from here. I would proceed aggressively on two fronts, one of which you and I have previously discussed in some depth: making the validity of the rape conviction a prominent feature of the ongoing murder case before Judge Eaton in Seminole County. In my view, the DCA's decision today means that this *must* happen, and soon—ideally before the status conference scheduled for this Friday, the 13th.

Equally important, Russ & Co. need to file a motion for rehearing in the district court of appeal. Rehearings are always a long shot, and here it will be especially so: The appellate court simply blew this case off, not even deeming it worthy of a 20-minute oral argument per side. What the rehearing needs to do is get their attention. To have a shot at snapping the judges out of their rubber-stamping torpor, I believe that the rehearing must possess five essential elements—four substantive and one atmospheric, affect and tone related.

First, the rehearing must show that this isn't just another run-of-the-mill rape case. For all the reasons you and I have discussed, the rape case was an indispensable component to the capital murder case: No rape case, no murder case, and certainly no death sentence in the murder case—*the* reason Seminole County Judge McGregor overrode the sentencing jury's 9–3 or 10–2 recommendation of life imprisonment was the Orange County rape case.

The rehearing needs to make this crystal clear: No Orange County rape conviction in Croft, no Seminole County death sentence in Harberts.

Second, the rehearing needs to lay out *why* the murder case and rape case are so inextricably intertwined, factually, logically and historically. Here (with permission), I would lift much of Lori's "*Ticking*" story from May 18 (from "Era of Motorcycle Gangs" to the end). Also, my memos to you and to Gregg Thomas might have some usefully "plagiarizable" language.

Third, and related to one and two, the rehearing needs to underscore the fact that the Florida Supreme Court—after full briefing, oral argument, and the discipline of crafting an opinion for a *unanimous* court (recall Earl Warren's efforts to get a unanimous court in *Brown v. Board of Education*)—reached a reasoned conclusion diametrically opposed to Russell and the District Court of Appeal (DCA) on the central issue in both cases: the believability of Tony DiLisio's recantation. Also, the DCA's summary disposition makes today's ruling unreviewable by the Florida Supreme Court—resulting in a hopeless conflict between two trial courts in two separate Florida counties on a crucial credibility issue with life or death consequences for Joe Spaziano. What is *Eaton* supposed to do with the Florida Supreme Court opinion *and* today's DCA opinion? Are *both* opinions "law of the case" in Eaton's court?

Fourth, I believe the rehearing ought to address and refute the state's (and Russell's) alternative basis of argument: That even without Tony DiLisio's testimony, the evidence against Joe was sufficient. Here, I'd argue (a) that the prosecutor at trial emphasized (in closing argument and elsewhere), and the prosecutors on appeal and in Federal habeas corpus (on the tattoo issue) all stressed the importance of DiLisio's testimony, and (b) if you take away DiLisio, all the state has is Croft, a witness who flunked a polygraph, failed to pick Joe out of a lineup, offered ever-changing descriptions of her assailants and the nature and location of the attack, etc. There must be some limit to Russell's (and the DCA's) power to, Stalin-like, perform retrospective plastic surgery on the actual trial record in an actual case.

Fifth, I believe that this rehearing needs to be fiery—in direct proportion to the outrageously cowardly action by the DCA in blowing this case off with a one-word dispositional order. Florida's highest court has now agreed with Judge Eaton that Joe Spaziano has spent the past two decades on death row—and survived five death warrants—for a murder he might not have committed at all. The state robbed Joe Spaziano of his adulthood—and damn near his life—based on the police's hypnotism and manipulation of a screwed-up teenage doper who hated Spaziano. And now, the state intends to try him again—this time on even less evidence than the first time around in 1976.

The *least* the Florida DCA owes Joe Spaziano is an oral argument and an opinion articulating the reasons for its strange affirmance of Judge Russell's even stranger opinion summarily denying the Rule 3.850 Motion for postconviction relief. No evidentiary hearing in the trial court. No argument in the DCA. No opinion in the DCA. What the hell kind of "due process" is that?

I know that passion is not favored in appellate practice in Florida. I didn't use it myself in the 12 years I practiced capital appellate law in Florida, until the spring of 1995. But passion—and other professional risks as well, such as writing the June 4, 1995 *Viewpoint* for the *Herald*—seemed to me necessities driven by the extremity of the situation: a man about to be killed for a rape and murder he didn't commit. Because the Florida Supreme Court justices knew me to be a reasonable and professional attorney, with a long track record as such before that court, my passion got their attention. My actions earned me the never-ending contempt of the Florida Supreme Court and virtually every Florida lawyer with whom I had ever worked in the past (with the lone exception of James Russ, who sent me a very nice letter in January, 1996), but it also worked. The reason it worked is the same reason the Florida Supreme Court didn't report me to the bar: I believe they understood, on some level, that I believed my extreme actions were necessitated by the extremity of the situation I—my client, actually—faced.

I've only been involved in one successful rehearing motion in Florida. It was a long time ago, in 1983; I had just started working at Dick Jorandby's West Palm Beach Public Defender office, under the supervision of the late Craig S. Barnard. The Florida

Supreme Court had recently affirmed, by a vote of 4-3, the death sentence of Tommy Randolph, one of Craig's clients. The Florida Supreme Court opinion was an outrage; on the critical point, the one-vote majority opinion simply ignored Craig's main argument. Since I was the new kid on the block, I was assigned to write the rehearing.

The more I wrote the angrier I got at the court's sleight of hand. With the self-righteous ire that only a newly-minted lawyer can have, my draft rehearing ended up arguing that the Florida Supreme Court's opinion in *Randolph* was, essentially, lawless—lacking in those qualities of principled neutrality that are at the core of law and lawfulness. My draft became known, around the office, as the "What is a court, anyway?" rehearing.

To my surprise, Craig didn't tone it down much, even though its tone was decidedly un-Craig Barnardesque (see David Von Drehle's book). Rather, precisely because it would be so out of character for him to file such a brief in "Craig's court" (as we all called the Florida Supreme Court), he thought it might get the justices' attention. And it did. The rehearing changed one vote, making it 4-3 in favor of a life sentence for Tommy Randolph.

Anyway, the point (and there is one, I'm pretty sure) is that Craig pulled it off in *Randolph* because he was Craig—the consummate reasonable man and sane lawyer. Similarly, Russ—or, better, Phillip Hubbart [the Miami lawyer Gene Miller got to represent Joe in the rape case litigation]—might be able to pull the same off on this DCA rehearing. In the spring of 1995 I decided to pony up all the credibility chips I had for Joe's case—my innocent man. I could think of no more worthy client upon whom to spend them.

Come to think of it, I still can't.

Joseph Spaziano
No. 049043
Union Correctional Institution
Dear Joe:

It's Friday the 13th, and as I write this you and Jim Russ are appearing before Judge Eaton for the status conference. Deanna says that Friday the 13th is always her lucky day, and that she'll try to send some your way today.

God knows, you could use some good luck. More than a decade ago, I promised never to bullshit you, and I'm too old and cranky to start now. The DCA's summary affirmance of the rape case is very, *very* bad news. It doesn't necessarily mean that Russ will *never* be able to knock out the rape conviction, but I think it does mean that it's going to be a long haul to get you out of prison, even if Russ slam-dunk wins the murder case. It also means that Holland & Knight will continue to avoid the rape case like the plague; according to the *Orlando Sentinel*, Gregg Thomas is now out of the murder case, which make me wonder whether the law firm intends to dump the murder case, too.

As I presume Russ has explained to you, he has several possible options in the rape case. *First,* he can file for rehearing in the DCA. *Second,* he can seek Florida Supreme Court review, a very long shot. *Third,* he can seek United States Supreme Court review, also a long shot. *Fourth,* he can file a *habeas corpus* petition in federal district court, and then appeal its denial to the 11th circuit.

Fifth, and while he's doing one-through-four, he can (a) make the rape case an issue in the murder case, before Judge Eaton; and (b) continue to investigate—and to help the *Miami Herald*'s investigation—of the rape case. They'll need a major investigative breakthrough to justify another 3.850 postconviction motion—something like Vanessa Dale Croft's finally recanting her trial testimony and telling the truth about the *total* lack of any involvement whatsoever by you in whatever happened to her back in 1974. Gene Miller, the *Herald* editor, is trying to get a first-rate investigator, an old colleague of his, to approach Ms. Croft.

All is not lost. We've been in tighter spots together, bro. This ain't over yet.

So: When are you going to get me on that Harley? I've been writing about Harleys for weeks now. I think I'm ready.

Peace,
Michael ("Crazy Mike") Mello
Professor of Law

6/14/97

Hi Mike & D.

Well I just came back from Sanford, Russ ask the Judge if I don't want to attend all these hearing and stuff, I don't want to be at the county jail, I rather be back here. The trial has been put off till the end of October or beginning of November. Keep this to you but if you can talk to either Sheilla [a lawyer at Holland & Knight] or Harlon [Stephen Hanlon] and let me know in your own words why they are backing off my case. Now remember don't let nobody know only talk to them personally ok. Russ don't want me to tell nobody but I have to let you know. Not this personally the hole H&K. What I heard they are getting a little [tired] of helping me. I'm going to send Sheilla a letter after I write you to send you the first book I done. OK hold it for me Mike. I know if I wasn't an Outlaw and had the money to pay them I'll have them. But if it is because they are pressured because of the clients they have in their business I understand. Please let me know Mike in your words what they said. I am looking forward for your response Mike. And to let me know what you feel on this new trial. I think I know OK. Love you Mike & D. Now I sit out these next 4 or 5 months. Let me know you received the book OK. The second one Lori Roza has in good hands. OK I'll close and get a letter to Sheila. OK Crazy Mike.

Your Friend
Crazy Joe

P.S. 6-15-97

Hi Mike & D. The letter don't go out tonight to bro. I'm so depresset really bad. Best thing happened since I've been back is I got a letter from Dawn and Mike Radelet. Shit Mike I can't prove I didn't do no murder or that rape they are talking about. You know they turned me down on that appeal on the rape case don't you? James tried to explain to me the next step on it but Mike my head is so messet up. He told me you called him. Is Lori Rozsa and the Miami Herald still with me. Do you know if Lori is going to be at the trial. Hope H&K don't hate me and backet off because they don't believe me. I wrote Sheila and Stephen a letter to write me and give me some info on why. I in a way understand their company under pressure. I told them to send you the book to hold for me. First time you see it Mike they going to kill me legally murder me. I got your letter and Mike R. letter and the state lied once they will do it again. I need a book of stamps bad Mike, can you send me a book. Now about Dawn it sure was nice to hear from her. She seems like a nice person. She is in Seattle, Wa. She has her first case the 24. Juvenile case sure hope she wins. Thank Crazy Mike for your believing in me. I hope and think I'm going to have a fair trial I hope. So many people lien on me. Don't know as yet who the new ones will be. My head keeps going in circles. I go back 22 years when I went thru the same thing back then. Well I'm going to close. Love you all and you for sure are my best friend. So happy we meet and I'm lucky to be still alive today if wasn't for you. Tell D. I'll be a little late to get the place painted up but if things go right won't be much longer. You got faith in James, Mike? Do you feel he'll win this case. Please write me, ok, so I can get my head right again.

Love you bro,
Joe

No man was more responsible for bringing "Crazy Joe" Spaziano to the brink of death in 1995 than Dexter Douglass, Florida Governor Lawton Chiles's general counsel. He supervised the sham police investigation into the truthfulness of Tony DiLisio's 1995 recantation. He publicly lied about the contents of that investigation. He persuaded Governor Chiles to keep the police investigation secret. And he persuaded Chiles to sign Spaziano's fifth death warrant in August 1995.

In June 1997, opportunity knocked once again for Dexter Douglass. The Florida Constitution requires, at regular intervals, the formation of a Constitution Review Commission. The Constitution Review Commission is charged with reviewing the Florida Constitution and recommending any amendments, which are then decided upon by the voters in the next general election. In June 1997 Governor Chiles appointed a thirty-seven-member commission. It included the current and former chief justices of the Florida Supreme Court, two former speakers of the Florida State House of Representatives, the current and former Florida Senate presidents, the immediate past chair of the ABA House of Delegates, a former Florida bar president, and business and civic leaders. To chair the Florida Constitution Review Commission, Governor Chiles chose Dexter Douglass.

20

An Absence of Malice

The plane banked and headed out over the China Sea, toward Okinawa, toward freedom from death's embrace. None of us was a hero. We would not return to cheering crowds, parades, and the pealing of great cathedral bells. We had done nothing more than endure. We had survived, and that was our only victory.

Philip Caputo, A Rumor of War, *1977*

In the summer of 1995—during the eye of the storm after the May–June death warrant but before the August–September death warrant—I did something I typically do when a capital case seems to be slipping away. I reread every piece of paper I had on Joe's case, looking for something, anything, that might help when the next death warrant came—as Joe and his family and I knew it would come, even though we didn't know exactly when.

I didn't find anything we could use in court. But I did find something. I found a letter Joe had written—twenty summers earlier, to one of his Outlaw brothers. I knew I must have read it before, probably in late 1983 when I first became involved in Joe's case as a Florida public defender. Back then, I most likely skimmed the letter and returned it to its file. I was "thinking like a lawyer," and because Joe's letter to Chris wasn't germane to Joe's case, I disregarded it and forgot about it.

This is what Joe wrote to his brother in 1975:

Dear Chris,

Well brother you all probley know by now what happen. Well I got to let you'es know. About the State Witnesses. I am mad

479

and I know my brother are mad. At all of this. Well what I want to say, is forgive him. For he does not know what he do. Could you understand that. He knowe's I am not the guy. So that saw I can say. Is forgive him for he doe's not know. His day will come.

Let Tom read this letter. My Attorney neede's some more money he is working on my peal on my first case. He wante's $2,000 more dollar. Call him personaly please Tom and see what he saide's. If I shell die *Brother's*. I will die an *Outlaw*. There will be brother hood forever. Remember I love you all. And remember what I said, he does not know what he do. I will be a 1% forever.

Love
Joe
A.O.A
Brotherhood

P.S. I still have a shot.

During my years as Joe's lawyer, we had often discussed Tony Di-Lisio. Or so I thought. In 1996 I realized that we had never really had a conversation about Tony, because I had been doing all the talking. Joe didn't contradict me, and into his silence I read agreement.

I had assumed that Joe hated Tony as much as I did. As it turned out, however, Joe didn't despise Tony at all. Joe saw Tony as an instrument—a denuded instrument of the state's determination to destroy the Outlaws by any means necessary. Joe saw Tony as a victim of the criminal justice system, as Joe was himself.

The question of Tony's responsibility came up because of Geraldo Rivera, of all people. Rivera wanted to televise the first meeting in twenty years between Joe and Tony. Tony wanted to apologize to Joe in person, and Rivera wanted to capture the moment on national TV.

Although Joe wanted to do it, and although I believed that Tony's remorse was genuine, I thought it was risky. I was afraid Joe might be less than gracious when he was actually in the same room with the man whose perjury had kept him on death row for a crime he did not commit.

But the problem was with me, not Joe. I was projecting. The more Joe and I talked, the clearer it became to me that Joe bore no malice toward Tony. I loathed Tony. Joe did not.

And he never had, at least not in the thirteen years I have known him. I realized this when, in 1995, I went back and reread the letters Joe had written to me. In letter after letter Joe expressed anger at the cops and the courts—but not at Tony. About Tony—to whom Joe often referred as "that kid"—Joe was bewildered and frustrated. "Why did Tony lie at the trials?" Joe asks time and again. "When will he tell the truth?" About Tony, Joe *was* frustrated and confused. But he was not angry.

It had been right there all along in the letters. I had read right past it, superimposing upon Joe's words my own anger at Tony. I think I did so because I believed that had I been in Joe's position, I would have hated Tony. But this conceit violated one of my cardinal rules: I must remember that I can never imagine what my clients' lives are like. I can't imagine what it is really like to live on death row. I can't imagine what their prior lives had been like—lives that had brought my clients into the community of the condemned. And, finally, I could not imagine why Joe didn't despise Tony DiLisio. I couldn't understand it. I could only respect it and honor it.

August 1, 1997
Wilder, Vermont

Today's *Orlando Sentinel* headline: "Will His Own Words Haunt Spaziano?" The front-page article began: "The two-year murder investigation [of Spaziano] has turned up one witness who has repeatedly implicated the tattooed biker in the killing of an Orlando woman: Spaziano himself. . . . Investigators say the Outlaws motorcycle gang member confessed or bragged about the killing to at least eight people, including family members, fellow bikers, inmates and even a jail nurse."

The *Sentinel* did concede that "in compiling Spaziano's tales of bloody bravado, investigators have so far assembled little more than a circumstantial case" and that "the state's case may rest on a rogue's gallery of witnesses. Many have criminal records of their own—and three are convicted murderers." Translation: most of the state's witnesses are jailhouse snitches who have every incentive to sell their manufactured testimony in exchange for favorable treatment by the authorities in their own troubles with the law.

But what about the nurse? What's *that* all about? As with the witnesses produced by the FDLE during its secret investigation during summer 1995, this state's witness is not one I've ever heard about before.

When the FDLE leaked its secret report to the *Orlando Sentinel* in 1995, and when the newspaper breathlessly presented the police findings, the case against Joe Spaziano looked pretty strong. But when the *Herald* put the cops' evidence under a microscope, the case against Joe collapsed—as the original 1976 case against him had collapsed. Then, as now, the government's case was based on the hearsay testimony of snitches and informants—testimony that is notoriously unreliable.

Will the state's surprise nurse pan out? At this moment, I can't know. Stay tuned.

August 2, 1997
Wilder, Vermont

One of Joe's old friends in the Outlaws called me with a true story of the FBI.

An Outlaw leader needed his potato farm plowed. Problem was, he was in prison at the time. So he wrote a letter to his wife: "It's time to dig up the backyard for the potatoes." The Outlaw knew his mail was read by prison personnel, and he also knew that the prison routinely forwarded to the FBI copies of Outlaws' mail. And he knew that the FBI was somewhat preoccupied with "breaking" Outlaw "codes."

In this case, the FBI cipher breakers concluded that "potatoes" meant guns. Law enforcement descended on the Outlaw's home and presented his wife with a warrant to search the backyard for the buried guns. The agents dug and dug and dug. No guns. No potatoes, either.

Of course not. Now that the FBI had tilled the Outlaw's soil, it was time to plant those potatoes.

August 4, 1997
Wilder, Vermont

Lori Rozsa called: "It took about ten minutes of research to learn that the nurse [the state's new star witness, according to the *Orlando Sentinel*] was, back in 1981, married to a Seminole County Sheriff's deputy. This makes her sixteen-year silence, before coming forward about Joe's 'confession,' even more suspect, don'tchathink?"

Sure do. Also, the nurse's husband is now a private investigator in

Florida. In many states, obtaining a PI license requires character references from local law enforcement officials. Might this nurse's suddenly recovered memory be the product of some favor called in by her husband's former colleagues in Seminole County law enforcement, in their present desperation to send Joe Spaziano back to death row for the murder of Laura Lynn Harberts?

August 5, 1997
Wilder, Vermont

Gene Miller faxed me the state's witness list. It includes the predictable array of jailhouse snitches now in the federal witness protection program or in federal or state prison. It also includes Joe's mother, Rose; his sister, Barbara; and two of his brothers, Michael and Tommy. According to the state's list, Joe's sister and brothers are to testify about "statement(s) of defendant." In other words, the state plans to send Joe back to death row based on things he allegedly said to his siblings.

The state's witness list also includes one Joseph Suarez, DVM, of DeBary Animal Clinic. Could this be *the* Joe Suarez, the sex offender who called Laura Lynn Harberts on the night before she disappeared— the same Joe Suarez who was an early suspect in the Harberts homicide? And today he's a *veterinarian*?

Also on the witness list are Tony DiLisio and the *Miami Herald*'s Lori Rozsa. Go figure.

August 19, 1997
Wilder, Vermont

Gene Miller called. Lori Rozsa has met with Tony DiLisio's wife. Seems the Florida police have been leaning on her and leaning on her parents. Hard.

The obvious goal of the police's meetings with Mrs. DiLisio, as she described those meetings to Rozsa, was to terrify her—to make her frightened, not just of Joseph Spaziano but of her husband, Tony, as well. The police told her about horrific crimes they said Spaziano and his Outlaw colleagues had committed and would commit against Mrs. DiLisio and her family, if given the chance. On one visit, the cops insisted on checking out her car for bombs. To protect herself from Outlaw terror, Mrs. DiLisio armed herself with an aluminum baseball bat, which she carried with her for a time.

Mrs. DiLisio also described the marital advice she received from the Florida police. How, the police demanded, could she have married a man like Tony DiLisio? Didn't she know Tony's "role model" was the monster Spaziano? Didn't she know that Tony was on the Outlaw's payroll? Didn't she know that her husband might even be an Outlaw himself? And so on.

Mrs. DiLisio's only crime was to have married the man the Florida police had used as their instrument of destruction of "Crazy Joe" Spaziano. What kinds of pressure must those selfsame police be bringing to bear upon those people truly within their dominion and control—criminals turned state's witnesses, people desperate for a deal, any deal, to make their own lives a bit easier. One man on the state's witness list has been arrested more than fifty times. He plans to testify that Joe Spaziano "confessed" to him about the murder of Laura Lynn Harberts.

August 30, 1997
Wilder, Vermont

Gene Miller called. At a hearing yesterday on James Russ's twenty-five pending motions, Judge Eaton moved Joe's capital murder trial back six months, from October 1997 to April 1998. The judge also authorized Russ to hire, at state expense, two investigators to help him test and respond to the ongoing two-year police investigation of the Harberts homicide—the police investigation that had begun with the secret FDLE investigation during summer 1995, an intensive investigation that has cost the Florida taxpayers roughly $180,000 to date. By contrast, Miller estimated that Russ would be able to spend $12,000 for his own investigators.

The prosecution also requires the delay, Miller said. Seems that the government has lost the dental records of Laura Lynn Harberts—the only link between Harberts and the remains found in the Seminole County dump site in 1973. No link, no conviction.

For Joe, the delay means six more months on death row. Six more months of legal limbo, neither a convicted murderer nor a vindicated innocent man. It means another Thanksgiving on death row, Christmas on death row, New Year's Day on death row, Valentine's Day on death row. And another birthday, on September 12, Joe's fifty-third, his twentieth celebrated in Florida's maximum security prisons.

January 19, 1998
East Providence, Rhode Island

We buried my father today. He drowned six days ago in Narragansett Bay.

February 21, 1998
Wilder, Vermont

Gene Miller called. Those wonderful folks in Florida law enforcement, those boys who brought us necrodentistry, a psychic fondling a human skull in the front seat of a police car, and Tony DiLisio, are at it again. Now they have found a former exotic dancer who claims, more than two decades after the alleged event, that Joe Spaziano bit off a portion of her breast and ate it in her presence. Uh-huh.

March 31, 1998
Wilder, Vermont

Today Florida carried out its fourth execution in eight days. Today it was Daniel Remeta, a pen pal of mine. Yesterday it was Judy Buenoano, the first woman executed in Florida since the time of slavery. Last Monday it was Leo Jones. Last Tuesday it was Gerald Stano—the man who, long ago, I had thought might have committed the crime that landed Joe Spaziano on death row.

This is an election year in Florida. The front-runner in the governor's race is one of George Bush's sons. In Texas, the nation's leader in executions these days, another of Bush's sons has been governor for four years. The Florida Bush, if elected, promises to bring the Texas execution stats to Florida. The *Los Angeles Times* has called this the Battle of the Bushes.

April 1, 1998
Wilder, Vermont

Seems that the state has objected to Judge Eaton's appointment of co-counsel for James Russ, and Florida's intermediate appellate court has sided with the state on this point.

7/16/97

Dear Crazy Mike,

   Well Mike sure sounds like you was busy. I haven't heard of this Ted Kaczynski case. He ain't the one who supposed to have killed in Atlanta, your friend is it?

   . . . I know he [James Russ] is a hard guy. He even thinks places we bugged when we talk. He don't trust nothing. He got mad went off on him where I was seeing him, he grabbed the note from the guard hard said he don't want no press cop's no-body to talk to me, he was pissed the Orlando Sentinel tried to talk to me. Is this Italian American group really going to help me or is it a front Mike? Lori Rozsa and Linda my xwife looked trew old files to fine out where I was Aug. 1973. I can't put down any people trying to help me Mike. I do know James Russ ahs got his ways and makes a point in the court room. I love all ya, you understand me buddy. I don't think James will leave me on the hang no way he told me he will work on my case till the day he dies. I believe him I have to. Too many big time people are helping me so they all will do their best. I seen them work and loved it. Look Mike I'm still alive ☺ ok bro. I'll close love you pal, oh no hold up, how is D doing, she ok. You working on get-tin her in the way PRENICK ☺.

Love ya,
Crazy Joe

August 11, 1998
Wilder, Vermont

Gene Miller called: the retrial has now been postponed indefinitely. No trial date will be set until September—around Joe's fifty-third birthday and the third anniversary of the Florida Supreme Court's decision stay-ing his fifth death warrant.

21

Life Itself

Often in a true war story there is not even a point, or else the point doesn't hit you until twenty years later, in your sleep, and you wake up and shake your wife and start telling the story to her, except when you get to the end you've forgotten the point again. And then for a long time you lie there watching the story happen in your head. You listen to your wife's breathing. The war's over. You close your eyes. You smile and think, Christ, what's the *point*?

Tim O'Brien, "How to Tell a True War Story," Esquire, *1987*

October 2, 1998
Wilder, Vermont

James Russ called. The prosecutor in the Laura Harberts murder case has offered Joe Spaziano a deal. Under the deal, Joe would plead nolo contendere, or no contest, to second-degree murder and receive a sentence of twenty-five years: time served plus two more years. Because of his conviction in the Vanessa Dale Croft rape case, Joe would not be released from prison. In theory, he would be eligible for parole in two years.

But he would get his life back. Under the plea offer, Joe could not be sentenced to death: the state of Florida could not kill him. No sixth death warrant. No more time in the deathwatch cells. No more final countdowns, first by weeks, then days, then hours, then minutes, to the date and time certain when Joe Spaziano would be killed in Florida's electric chair for crimes he did not commit.

Equally important, Joe would not plead *guilty*. He would not stand up in court and testify (falsely) that he murdered Laura Harberts. Joe would plead *no contest*. It's called a best-interest plea, and under it Joe would continue to maintain his innocence—his total factual innocence—of murder and rape.

Russ had met with Joe about the prosecutor's plea offer. Joe's reply was instant and emphatic: Hell no. No way he'd plead anything but "innocent" to crimes he didn't commit.

Russ was concerned that Joe didn't really understand the ramifications of turning down the plea. Russ thought that, because Joe and I have known each other forever, I might be better able to make certain that Joe understood what he was giving up (certain life) in rejecting the plea offer. I agreed to fly to Florida to meet with Joe.

However, before heading for Florida, I felt I needed to touch base with the folks at the *Miami Herald*. Before talking intelligently with Joe about the consequences of rejecting or accepting the plea offer, I needed to know how Gene Miller, Lori Rozsa, and the *Herald* would respond if Joe accepted the plea bargain. So I called them. I began by telling Miller and Rozsa that I was speaking with them on condition that they not publish anything about the plea offer until Joe had had a chance to consider and decide whether to accept or reject it. I made certain they understood that premature publicity about the offer could well cause the prosecutor to withdraw it.

They understood. They promised, as representatives of the *Herald*, not to publicize the plea until Joe had decided on it. Then they broke their word.

Why did I tell the *Herald* about the plea offer? Two reasons. The first is what I said above: I wanted to know, before meeting with Joe, whether the newspaper would bail out of investigating the Croft rape case if Joe took the plea. Miller answered this question with a resounding yes: if Joe accepted the deal, the *Herald* would drop its coverage of his case. Joe needed that piece of information if he was going to be able to think through the plea offer and talk it through with me.

The second reason I told the *Herald* was more of a chess move. I knew that a strong force against Joe's taking the plea would be his not wanting to let down the *Herald*. I also knew that if the *Herald* did betray my confidence and try to pressure Joe into rejecting the deal, the *Herald*'s treason would make it much easier for Joe to decide to take the plea.

October 6, 1998
Wilder, Vermont

Today the *Miami Herald* published an article headlined "State Offers Plea Bargain to Spaziano." Lori Rozsa wrote the story. Gene Miller acquiesced in its publication.

I don't know why the *Herald* burned its source (i.e., me) by publishing a story that the paper's editors knew might cause the life plea offer to be withdrawn. Neither Miller nor anyone else at the newspaper has to date given me a satisfactory explanation. This was the reason Miller gave me: "We're a newspaper. It was an accurate story. Our job is to print accurate information, and that's what we did. We've been hearing rumors about a plea offer since July. All you did is confirm what we'd heard."

I do know that Miller fiercely opposed Joe's taking the plea. Miller said I needed to tell Joe, in no uncertain terms, that if he accepted a plea, the *Herald* would drop coverge of his case. Miller knew—because I told him—that publicizing the plea offer might well sabotage it.

By disclosing the plea offer to the *Herald*, I had screwed up. Royally. My goal had been to keep Joe's options open—to take the plea or not—until he could make his own decision. The *Herald*'s story could well have caused the prosecutor to withdraw the plea offer. I couldn't know how badly I'd screwed up until I met with Joe. I would do that on October 8.

I flew from Vermont to Jacksonville, Florida, on Wednesday, October 7. I rented a car and drove to the Holiday Inn near the Jacksonville airport. I was scheduled to meet with Joe for three hours on Thursday, October 8.

October 8, 1998
Florida State Prison, Starke

I'd asked for a wake-up call at 7:00 A.M., and when it came I ordered a room-service breakfast of eggs, bacon, sausage, toast, grits, coffee, and Florida orange juice. I called Deanna and Fuzzy, just to check in and make sure that nothing had changed. Nothing had.

On my hotel bed, I organized my notes, and then I organized them again. This was not a social visit. Joe and I needed to cover a lot of ground, and I wanted to make sure we got to it all. I also didn't really know what Joe wanted to do about the plea offer, so I had to be prepared for anything.

At 11:00 A.M. I climbed into my rental car and headed to I-10, then to Route 301. I parked the car in the prison parking lot, got buzzed through the perimeter chain-link and concertina-wire fence, went through the metal detector from hell, picked up my guard escort, and walked to the visiting room.

Joe was waiting in a holding cell. Once I was in the visiting room, Joe was brought in and his handcuffs and shackles removed. He held out his hand to shake mine, and we both smiled.

Our visit took place in one of the cubicles near the colonel's office, just Joe and I, alone in the small room. We snuck cigarettes.

For the first hour of our visit, Joe was adamant that he would never take any plea. We drafted a public statement that he would issue, explaining why no plea could ever be acceptable to him.

Then we talked about the *Miami Herald,* and the center of gravity of the conversation shifted. Much of Joe's resistance to the plea was his fear that the *Herald* would feel let down. But now that the *Herald* had burned us, the newspaper had rendered itself irrelevant to Joe's decision. With the *Herald* out of the equation, Joe really listened when I reiterated the benefits of accepting the plea. Notwithstanding the *Herald*'s assertions to the contrary, any capital retrial of Joe Spaziano in Florida was a risk—even though he was as innocent today as he was twenty-two years ago. Joe Spaziano simply couldn't trust Florida's criminal justice system not to malfunction—again.

The second hour of our visit was the polar opposite of the first. Joe said he was ready to take the plea. I believed him. I believed he understood and accepted what he would be giving up in taking the plea—a chance to prove his innocence before a Florida jury. I also believed he understood and accepted what he would be receiving in taking the plea—life. Life itself.

Sitting across that metal table from Joe, in the small visiting cubicle in Florida State Prison, I believed Joe understood all these things. I believed, but I wasn't sure. I needed to be sure. So I took the copy of the prosecutor's plea offer, which had remained on the table between us during our meeting, and I wrote at the bottom, "Subject to the additions set out in this document, I accept this offer." Then I drew a line.

Under the line, I printed Joe's name. I handed the paper to him to sign. He did.

Joe's signature on the plea offer had no legal significance whatsoever. It didn't bind him to accept the deal. I had him do it because I wanted to watch his face while he signed. Then I was sure.

October 9, 1998
Outlaws Clubhouse, Jacksonville, Florida

There was one other piece of unfinished business that I needed to take care of before I left Florida. When Joe and I met yesterday, I told him, based on phone conversations with Fuzzy Miller, the president of the Florida chapter of the Outlaws, that the club would not object to Joe's decision to take the plea. Still, I wanted to be certain. When Fuzzy invited me to meet him at the Outlaws' clubhouse, I accepted on the spot.

The Outlaws were, as usual, gracious and indulgent hosts. The visit turned immediately into a working session. With Fuzzy's help, I wrote up a letter to Joe and a draft of a memorandum of plea agreement. Fuzzy invited me to spread my paperwork over the clubhouse bar, which I did in short order. He also allowed me to take over the clubhouse phone and fax machine. Thus, for most of the afternoon, the Outlaws' clubhouse was converted into my mobile law office.

As always, I wrote in longhand, on yellow legal pads. Throughout the afternoon, I faxed the drafts back and forth to Laura Gillen in Vermont, who word-processed the documents and faxed them back to me at the clubhouse. By the end of the day, I had a draft plea agreement and a final version of a letter to Joe. (I used my hotel as the address on the letter, lest the prison censors intercept it, as they might have done had I used the clubhouse as my return address.) Here is the letter:

Michael Mello
Room 1205
Holiday Inn—Airport
I-95 at Airport Road
Jacksonville, Florida
October 9, 1998

Joseph Spaziano
No. 049043
Florida State Prison
P.O. Box 181
G-13-16
Starke, FL 32091

Dear Joe:

So, let's chat.

As always, it was terrific meeting with you yesterday. As always, the three hours flew by way too fast. It was wonderful seeing you not under warrant, dressed in something other than death row orange, and looking very good in body, mind and spirit.

I was especially glad to be able to talk with you in person about the prosecution's September 15, 1998 plea offer. You made the right decision in accepting the plea offer, Joe. It was important to me that we discuss, in person, the pluses and minuses of your accepting or rejecting this plea offer (Jim Russ tells me that this is their final offer, he's in the best position to know and I trust him). I had to see for myself that you know—really *know* that the decision whether to even consider, much less to accept, a plea is yours and yours alone to make. It's not my decision to make. It's not the *Miami Herald*'s decision to make. It's not the Club's decision to make. You should, *if you want*, discuss the plea with anyone who really cares about you and who can keep your communications with them confidential.

But, in the end, it must be your decision to make. Anyone who cares about you will respect and honor and understand and support any decision you make. The people who don't care about you—the politicians who use your case to score cheap political points, and the newspapers who use your case to sell papers—don't matter to me at all. They can take their opinions and go straight to hell, so far as I'm concerned.

Joe, I'm proud of you for deciding to accept this plea. I'm especially proud of you for not bending to the *Miami Herald*'s pressure to reject the plea and go to trial. It took real courage for you to decide to take the plea.

It makes me very sad that the *Miami Herald* chose to betray my confidences by publishing an article about the plea offer. They knew I gave them that information on condition that they keep it confidential until you had had a chance to consider and decide on the plea offer. It makes me even sadder that, in publishing the article when they did, the *Herald* deliberately attempted to sabotage the plea offer (they knew that the plea offer might well be withdrawn if the *Herald* made the offer public) and that the *Herald* put pressure on you to reject the plea and risk a trial at which, even though you are totally innocent, you might have been sentenced to death again. The *Herald* certainly knows that innocent people can be and have been sentenced to death in Florida.

It's ironic that, by burning me and pressuring you, the *Herald* made the arguments in favor of taking the plea much stronger. With the *Herald* out of the equation, the plea decision seems to me fairly straightforward.

The plea will have six substantive provisions. First, you plead [no contest] to the lesser included offenses of second degree murder in the Laura Lynn Harberts case. You cannot be sentenced to death for the Harberts case, nor can your plea in Harberts serve as an aggravating circumstance in any future prosecution. Second, you continue to maintain your total factual innocence. This is what is called an "*Alford*/best interest plea." That means you do *not* admit or confess to killing Ms. Harberts. In fact, you *couldn't* admit to that. Such an admission would be perjury, since you did not kill Ms. Harberts or anyone else. Third, the agreed-upon sentence would be 25 years. You have already served 23 years for a murder you did not commit. That's far more than enough. Fourth, the sentence for the murder would run concurrent with the sentence you have been serving on the Vanessa Dale Croft rape case. That would make you *eligible* for parole [in two years]. You would also continue to fight the rape case in court. Fifth, you would be transferred back to UCI and placed back into general population, as you were in 1996. Sixth, prior to entering the plea, prosecutor would exercise good faith efforts to ascertain whether there are any plans by either the Orange County or Chicago authorities to institute prosecutions for homicides allegedly committed by you in the early 1970s, and he will report his findings to Jim Russ.

As I wrote to you earlier, and as we discussed yesterday, I see two main reasons to take this plea. First, taking the plea should mean that you would never again face a death sentence. You need Russ to get this nailed down in the plea agreement itself, but removing you from the possibility of a death sentence is the strongest argument in favor of accepting this plea. And it's a strong argument. Any retrial means the *possibility* of another death sentence. True, the prosecution's case is falling apart, and they seem to know it—the fact that those people, who have tried so hard to kill you for the last 22 years, have even *offered* you a plea shows to me how weak *they know* their case to be. Still, any trial is a risk; they didn't have any real evidence against you in 1976, either, and look what they've managed to do to you. The *Herald* is certain you won't be sentenced to death again, or even if you are, the sentence would be thrown out on appeal. But you're still an Outlaw; the *Orlando Sentinel* is still there; Florida is still Florida. It's not the *Herald*'s life that's on the line if you turn down this plea. It's your life.

The second argument in favor of taking the plea has to do with the kind of prison time you would likely be serving in the future. The prison would probably put you back into general population. In fact, they never should have taken you *out* of general population. The fact that they did makes me wonder whether the prison is trying indirectly to pressure you into taking the plea: the prison has made your life hell, giving you a taste of limited "freedom" by putting you into general population for a while, then they yanked you back into hell, and now they're offering you a deal to return to relative freedom. Maybe it's just coincidence that the prison has put psychological pressure on you, and so the prosecutor's offer looks much more attractive to you right now. Maybe it's coincidence. Still, I have to wonder.

The reasons not to take a plea (and Russ tells me he's convinced that this is their final offer) are also worthy of serious consideration. First, even if you don't technically confess to killing Laura Lynn Harberts, and even if you later say that you only pled [no contest] to get out from under a possible death sentence, the outside world will *perceive* that you have admitted guilt for killing Ms. Harberts and that your claims of innocence all these years were just lies. *Any* plea will smack of an admission of guilt that you murdered Ms. Harberts. That's exactly how the *Orlando Sentinel* will see it—which brings me to the second argument against taking this plea.

The second reason is because, in my opinion, taking this plea might mean spending the rest of your life in prison. This plea only resolves the Harberts murder case—it does not resolve the Croft rape case or the other homicides in Orange County and Chicago the state is trying to frame you for. In my view—Russ may disagree with this, and you need to talk with him about it—they would never parole you on Croft if you accept this plea. And you'd probably not win anything on Croft in the courts, in part because the *Miami Herald* would drop your case if you took this (and maybe any) plea.

Third, there is the *Miami Herald*. Lori Rozsa might understand why you might take this plea, but the rest of the newspaper would not. They have devoted three years of hard work, and a lot of their institutional credibility, into proving your innocence. They would see any plea as an admission of guilt, and that would make them feel betrayed. I'm not saying this should influence your decision: It shouldn't. But I do think you need to understand that this would be a consequence of your accepting *any* plea and especially *this* plea. Gene Miller told me to be certain to tell you that if you took a plea, the *Herald* will drop the Croft case. We need to assume the *Herald* will carry through on its threat.

Anyway, it was wonderful seeing you. You did the right thing. For me, the most important thing for you to understand is that I love you and I will honor, respect and understand the decision you have made. This is about *your* life.

Peace,
Michael ("Crazy Mike") Mello

I also had a working draft of the plea agreement. I would edit it on the plane ride home tomorrow.

Still, I knew that the plea deal might well fall through. Joe was anguished over this deal, and he might change his mind. I certainly couldn't blame him if he did.

October 13, 1998
Wilder, Vermont

I received a letter from Joe: he's at peace about accepting the plea deal.

October 16, 1998
Wilder, Vermont

Three letters from Joe today, each written on three consecutive days. The first letter said he was okay with the plea deal. The next day, after thinking about it all night, Joe wrote that he couldn't take the plea deal. The following day, Joe wrote that he'd take the plea deal.

October 20, 1998
Wilder, Vermont

Letter from Joe: no plea deal.

October 22, 1998
Wilder, Vermont

Letter from Joe: he'll take the plea deal.

October 26, 1998
Wilder, Vermont

Letter from Joe: no plea deal.

November 2, 1998
Wilder, Vermont

Letter from Joe: no plea deal.

November 3, 1998
Wilder, Vermont

Letter from Joe: no plea deal. But James Russ was coming to meet with him.

November 6, 1998
Vermont Law School, South Royalton

Gene Miller left a message on my home answering machine at 9:30 A.M.: last night, Joe was transferred from Florida State Prison to the Seminole County courthouse. A hearing before the judge in the Laura Harberts murder case was scheduled for 1:30 P.M. Did I know what was going on?

I didn't. To try to find out, I called James Russ's office. His assistant told me that Russ was in but was "unavailable" to take my call.

At 12:45 P.M., I was scheduled to participate in a debate on capital punishment. The audience consisted of about a hundred high school students. I decided to scrap my prepared remarks and talk about Joe's case and about what might be happening in the Florida courthouse as I was speaking. Joe's case is a perfect vehicle for exploring capital punishment as a legal system because it illustrates most of what's wrong with America's legal machinery of death: the political pressures on police to solve horrible crimes, to target unpopular citizens, and to manufacture evidence; the refusal of the legal system to admit it when it has made mistakes; and the diffusion of responsibility among juries, state judges, federal judges, and governors, with the result that no one actor bears the ultimate responsibility for the killing that takes place in the state's name. The death penalty warps our legal system in all these ways. Perhaps the ultimate deformity is an innocent man pleading no contest to avoid execution for crimes he did not commit. As it turned out, I sat down from the podium at exactly 1:30 P.M.—when court was convening at the Seminole County courthouse.

In Florida, Joe Spaziano was entering a "continuing to maintain innocence" plea of no contest to the second-degree murder of Laura Lynn Harberts. The plea agreement provided that Joe would be eligible for parole in two years.

The plea agreement included a notarized affidavit by Joe Spaziano in which Joe staunchly maintained his total factual innocence:

"MAINTAINING MY INNOCENCE/BEST INTEREST" STATEMENT OF
JOSEPH ROBERT SPAZIANO
STATE OF FLORIDA
COUNTY OF SEMINOLE

I, JOSEPH ROBERT SPAZIANO, having been duly sworn, make the following statement under oath.

a. I maintain my total factual and legal innocence of the crimes charged in the June 3, 1997, superseding indictment filed in this case. I swear that I did not kill Laura Lynn Harberts.

b. I am pleading nolo contendere (no contest) after fighting for my life and freedom for more than twenty-three (23) years because I want to live. I want to share life with my daughter and three grandchildren. I hope and pray that someday I shall be released from confinement and be free to do so.

c. I am pleading nolo contendere (no contest) because, although I did not commit the crimes charged in the June 3, 1997, superseding indictment filed in this case, my lawyers advise me that I may again be convicted of murder in the first degree and sentenced to death or to life in prison without the possibility of parole for twenty-five (25) years. I understand there are prosecution witnesses who say I confessed to the crimes charged in the June 3, 1997, superseding indictment filed in this case. I swear that I have never confessed to anyone to the crimes charged in this June 3, 1997, superseding indictment, but I realize that I can't prevent others from accepting the testimony of these prosecution witnesses. These are some of the reasons why I have for twenty-three (23) years, and now, continue to maintain my innocence.

d. The decision of choosing life over death is stark reality for me. I have lived under the specter of death for more than twenty-three (23) years for a crime I did not commit. I have had five death warrants issued against my life. I have spent weeks on phase one of death watch, in cells only a few paces away from the electric chair. I have come within days of being electrocuted until a court issued a stay of execution, never knowing when I would be put to death. I do not want my daughter and three grandchildren to live under the threat and fear of my death by electrocution. I do not want my daughter and three grandchildren to experience the hurt and damage of my death in the electric chair. These are some of the "best interests" which I acknowledge.

e. This sworn statement constitutes some of the reasons underlying my acknowledgment that, while maintaining my innocence, I feel that this plea of nolo contendere (no contest) to be in my best interest. My statement is further submitted to notify and assist the trial court in fulfilling its judicial responsibilities.

JOSEPH ROBERT SPAZIANO

SUBSCRIBED AND SWORN TO before me
this 5th day of November, 1998.

Notary Public
Personal knowledge

As Joe entered the no-contest plea, his twenty-eight-year-old daughter sat in the audience. Joe stood in ankle chains before the judge. During the brief exchange with the judge, Joe answered, "Yes, sir" and "Yes, your honor" and "Yes, I do" when asked if he wanted to enter a no-contest plea.

It was over.

But it wasn't over. One chapter was over: the state of Florida would not kill Joe Spaziano for another man's crimes. Another chapter was opening: Joe was still imprisoned for other men's crimes. Now we would focus on invalidating the rape conviction.

March 13, 1999
Wilder, Vermont

Joe's lawyers have filed a habeas petition in the Florida Supreme Court on the Croft rape case. Also, the *Miami Herald* has published a gigantic story, by Lori Rozsa, attacking the rape conviction. I knew Gene Miller didn't mean it when he said that, if Joe took the plea, the *Herald* might drop its investigation of the case. Miller's too honorable for that.

Miller and I talked about this book manuscript. Miller thought the book couldn't be published until after the retrial—readers want an ending. But I disagree. I'm not even sure what counts as an "ending" in a story like this. Anyway, this book should end in uncertainty.

Uncertainty was the hallmark of my years as Joe's lawyer. Uncertainty has been the hallmark of Joe Spaziano's odyssey through America's criminal justice system.

This story will have no ending. Or perhaps this story ended in January 1976, when Tony DiLisio took the witness stand to lie at the behest of cops willing to send the Outlaw Spaziano to death row by any means necessary.

22

Why the "Crazy Joe" Case Matters

"Judge Haywood," said Janning.

It's coming, thought Haywood. Now it comes.

Janning looked at him, finally blurting out the words. "The real reason I asked you to come. I want to know. I want to hear from a man like you. A man who has heard what happened. I want to hear—not that he forgives, but that he understands."

Haywood looked at Janning, sympathy welling up in him. He felt impotent, wanting to say something to this man but unable to. Understand, said Haywood to himself. I understand the pressures you were under. From my own experience here I understand that. But how can I understand the death of millions of men, women, and children in gas ovens, Herr Janning? How can I understand that? How can I tell you I understand it?

Janning looked at Haywood, sensitive to what he must be feeling. He spoke finally. It seemed almost as though he were reading Haywood's mind.

"I did not know it would come to that. You must believe it. You must believe it."

Haywood stood staring at the man before him. Then, almost without thinking, he said the words, as though he were speaking to a child.

"Herr Janning. It came to that the first time you sentenced to death a man you knew to be innocent."

Janning stared at Haywood, unable to take in the enormity.

> *Abby Mann,* Judgement at Nuremberg:
> The Trial of Four Nazi Ex-Judges, *1961*

April 1, 1999
Wilder, Vermont

Last week the trial began for the gaggle of former Illinois prosecutors and police officers charged with framing Rolando Cruz and sending him to death row for crimes he did not commit. This prosecution is a first in American history. The Cruz story, and other similar stories, have caused political leaders in Illinois to rethink capital punishment itself.

June 15, 1999
Wilder, Vermont

The jury in the Cruz case acquitted all the defendants. But the outcome isn't important; what matters is that the case was tried at all.

July 4, 1999
Wilder, Vermont

The Florida Parole Commission has denied Joe parole in the rape case. The commission recommended that Joe be paroled in sixty-one years—in the year 2060, when he will be around 115 years old.

August 19, 1999
Wilder, Vermont

The federal court of appeals has given Joe permission to file a second habeas corpus petition in the rape case. Such permission is rarely granted these days. It's the first good news in the rape case since Tony DiLisio recanted his crucial testimony in that case. Now, for the first time, Joe has some hope of invalidating the rape case—of walking out of prison a free man.

Meanwhile, the United States recently executed its five hundredth prisoner since executions resumed in 1977. Almost every year these days a new record is set for numbers of executions. The demographics of death row suggest that the executions will continue to climb in coming years.

October 13, 1999
Wilder, Vermont

I got a letter from Joe today. He just started working as a cook in the prison mess hall. He sounds upbeat. He's back to painting and drawing again.

December 1, 1999
Wilder, Vermont

I received a wonderful, hand-illustrated Christmas card from Joe today. There were elves, and each letter of "Merry Christmas" was decorated with a different-color design.

While addressing my own card to Joe, it hit me that I'd forgotten to send him a birthday card. Damn.

December 23, 1999
Wilder, Vermont

The afternoon before the last Christmas Eve of the twentieth century, I received an overnight U.S. mail package. It was from my friend Fuzzy Miller, president of the Florida Outlaws.

The package contained a book of photographs by Michael Upright, a member of the Outlaws. The book is titled *One Percent*.

The photos, all in a stark black and white, are beautiful and haunting. But what I will treasure is Fuzzy's inscription, written with a black felt-tipped marker, in his flowing hand, on the title page: "To Crazy Mike (Mellow hell), the one not afraid to buck the system! Fuzzy, 1%er, O.F.F.O. [Officer of the Outlaws]."

January 7, 2000
Wilder, Vermont

Yesterday, in a special session, the Florida State Legislature passed a bill replacing the electric chair with lethal injection. Now Florida's living dead will have a choice between "Old Sparky" and a state-induced drug overdose.

The lesson of the "Crazy Joe" case isn't that innocent people are condemned to die. Of course they are—it's inevitable. The law of averages and the inherent fallibility of legal institutions created and administered by human beings create a vacuum in which some innocent people are bound to be imprisoned and executed.

Between 1972 and the end of 1995, 313 executions were carried out, but more than 1,500 inmates exited death rows after their capital sentences were vacated by appellate courts, 72 condemned inmates had their death sentences commuted to prison terms through executive clemency, and 98 inmates died in prison without inconveniencing the state by living to resolve their situations. Today, about 3,600 people remain as death row inmates.

These figures were compiled by Professors Michael Radelet and Hugo Bedau, the nation's leading experts on releases from death row because of doubts about guilt. In a study published in 1996, Radelet and Bedau identified "68 cases of death row inmates later released because of doubts about their guilt. With 313 executions in the U.S. between 1970 and the end of 1995, one death row inmate is released because of innocence for every five inmates executed." The doubt noted here does not concern the severity of the crimes committed; rather, this is doubt as to whether particular incarcerated persons even *did those crimes*. Should anyone in such a situation be *terminated*?

Between 1973 and this writing (August 2000), eighty-four people who had been on death row in the United States have been found to have been wrongly convicted and released from prison or acquitted. These are their names:

Walter McMillian, convicted and sentenced to die in Alabama in 1988, released from prison in 1993

Randal Padgett, convicted and sentenced to die in Alabama in 1992, released from prison in 1997

Robert Cruz, convicted and sentenced to die in Arizona in 1981, released from prison in 1995

John Knapp, convicted and sentenced to die in Arizona in 1974, released from prison in 1987 (later reincarcerated on another charge)

James Robinson, convicted and sentenced to die in Arizona in 1977, released from prison in 1993

Jonathan Treadway, convicted and sentenced to die in Arizona in 1975, released from prison in 1978

Jerry Bigelow, convicted and sentenced to die in California in 1980, released from prison in 1988

Patrick Croy, convicted and sentenced to die in California in 1979, released from prison in 1990

Troy Jones, convicted and sentenced to die in California in 1986, released from prison in 1996

Anthony Brown, convicted and sentenced to die in Florida in 1983, released from prison in 1986

Willie Brown, convicted and sentenced to die in Florida in 1983, released from prison in 1988

Robert Cox, convicted and sentenced to die in Florida in 1988, released from prison in 1989

Andrew Golden, convicted and sentenced to die in Florida in 1991, released from prison in 1993

Robert Hayes, convicted and sentenced to die in Florida in 1991, released from prison in 1997

Sonia Jacobs, convicted and sentenced to die in Florida in 1976, released from prison in 1992

Anibal Jaramillo, convicted and sentenced to die in Florida in 1981, released from prison in 1982

William Jent, convicted and sentenced to die in Florida in 1979, released from prison in 1988

David Keaton, convicted and sentenced to die in Florida in 1971, released from prison in 1973

Wilbert Lee, convicted and sentenced to die in Florida in 1963, released from prison in 1975

Ernest Miller, convicted and sentenced to die in Florida in 1979, released from prison in 1988

Anthony Peek, convicted and sentenced to die in Florida in 1978, released from prison in 1987

Freddie Pitts, convicted and sentenced to die in Florida in 1963, released from prison in 1975

Juan Ramos, convicted and sentenced to die in Florida in 1983, released from prison in 1987

James Richardson, convicted and sentenced to die in Florida in 1968, released from prison in 1989

Bradley Scott, convicted and sentenced to die in Florida in 1988, released from prison in 1991

Delbert Tibbs, convicted and sentenced to die in Florida in 1974, released from prison in 1977

Larry Troy, convicted and sentenced to die in Florida in 1983, released from prison in 1988

Shabaka Waglini (Joseph Green Brown), convicted and sentenced to die in Florida in 1974, released from prison in 1987

Earl Charles, convicted and sentenced to die in Georgia in 1975, released from prison in 1978

James Creamer, convicted and sentenced to die in Georgia in 1973, released from prison in 1975

Henry Drake, convicted and sentenced to die in Georgia in 1977, released from prison in 1987

Gary Nelson, convicted and sentenced to die in Georgia in 1980, released from prison in 1991

Robert Wallace, convicted and sentenced to die in Georgia in 1980, released from prison in 1987

Joseph Burrows, convicted and sentenced to die in Illinois in 1989, released from prison in 1994

Perry Cobb, convicted and sentenced to die in Illinois in 1979, released from prison in 1987

Rolando Cruz, convicted and sentenced to die in Illinois in 1985, released from prison in 1995

Alejandro Hernandez, convicted and sentenced to die in Illinois in 1985, released from prison in 1995

Verneal Jimerson, convicted and sentenced to die in Illinois in 1985, released from prison in 1996

Ronald Jones, convicted and sentenced to die in Illinois in 1989, released from prison in 1999

Carl Lawson, convicted and sentenced to die in Illinois in 1990, released from prison in 1996

Steven Smith, convicted and sentenced to die in Illinois in 1986, released from prison in 1999

Darby Tillis, convicted and sentenced to die in Illinois in 1979, released from prison in 1987

Dennis Williams, convicted and sentenced to die in Illinois in 1979, released from prison in 1996

Larry Hicks, convicted and sentenced to die in Indiana in 1978, released from prison in 1980

Charles Smith, convicted and sentenced to die in Indiana in 1983, released from prison in 1991

Jerry Banks, convicted and sentenced to die in Louisiana in 1975, released from prison in 1980

Shareef Cousin, convicted and sentenced to die in Louisiana in 1996, released from prison in 1999

Curtis Kyles, convicted and sentenced to die in Louisiana in 1984, released from prison in 1998

Johnny Ross, convicted and sentenced to die in Louisiana in 1975, released from prison in 1981

Kirk Bloodsworth, convicted and sentenced to die in Maryland in 1984, released from prison in 1993

Lawyer Johson, convicted and sentenced to die in Massachusetts in 1971, released from prison in 1982

Sabrina Butler, convicted and sentenced to die in Mississippi in 1990, released from prison in 1995

Clarence Dexter, convicted and sentenced to die in Missouri in 1991, released from prison in 1999

Roberto Miranda, convicted and sentenced to die in Nevada in 1982, released from prison in 1996

Thomas Gladish, convicted and sentenced to die in New Mexico in 1974, released from prison in 1976

Richard Greer, convicted and sentenced to die in New Mexico in 1974, released from prison in 1978

Ronald Keine, convicted and sentenced to die in New Mexico in 1974, released from prison in 1978

Clarence Smith, convicted and sentenced to die in New Mexico in 1974, released from prison in 1976

Timothy Hinnes, convicted and sentenced to die in North Carolina in 1986, released from prison in 1989

Samuel Poole, convicted and sentenced to die in North Carolina in 1973, released from prison in 1974

Alfred Rivera, convicted and sentenced to die in North Carolina in 1997, released from prison in 1999

Gary Beeman, convicted and sentenced to die in Ohio in 1976, released from prison in 1979

Dale Johnson, convicted and sentenced to die in Ohio in 1984, released from prison in 1990

Clifford Brown, convicted and sentenced to die in Oklahoma in 1982, released from prison in 1986

Charles Gidders, convicted and sentenced to die in Oklahoma in 1978, released from prison in 1981

Richard Jones, convicted and sentenced to die in Oklahoma in 1983, released from prison in 1988

Robert Miller, convicted and sentenced to die in Oklahoma in 1988, released from prison in 1998

Adolph Munson, convicted and sentenced to die in Oklahoma in 1985, released from prison in 1995

Gregory Wilhoit, convicted and sentenced to die in Oklahoma in 1987, released from prison in 1993

Ronald Williamson, convicted and sentenced to die in Oklahoma in 1988, released from prison in 1999

Neil Ferber, convicted and sentenced to die in Pennsylvania in 1982, released from prison in 1986

Jay Smith, convicted and sentenced to die in Pennsylvania in 1985, released from prison in 1992

Jesse Brown, convicted and sentenced to die in South Carolina in 1983, released from prison in 1989

Michael Linden, convicted and sentenced to die in South Carolina in 1979, released from prison in 1981

Warren Manning, convicted and sentenced to die in South Carolina in 1989, released from prison in 1999

Randall Dale Adams, convicted and sentenced to die in Texas in 1977, released from prison in 1989

Clarence Brandley, convicted and sentenced to die in Texas in 1980, released from prison in 1990

Muneen Deeb, convicted and sentenced to die in Texas in 1985, released from prison in 1993

Ricardo Guerra, convicted and sentenced to die in Texas in 1982, released from prison in 1997

Frederico Macias, convicted and sentenced to die in Texas in 1984, released from prison in 1993

Vernon McManus, convicted and sentenced to die in Texas in 1977, released from prison in 1987

John Skelton, convicted and sentenced to die in Texas in 1982, released from prison in 1990

Benjamin Harris, convicted and sentenced to die in Washington in 1985, released from prison in 1997

The numbers for Florida are especially troubling because Florida has had more erroneous capital convictions than any other state; indeed, no other state comes close. Radelet and Bedau identified eighteen such Florida cases—followed by seven in Illinois; six each in Texas and Georgia; four each in New Mexico and Arizona; three in Louisiana; two each in California, North Carolina, Ohio, Pennsylvania, and South Carolina; and one each in Alabama, Indiana, Maryland, Massachusetts, and Mississippi. Behind each of these numbers is a name and a history. To repeat the names of the innocent freed from death row in Florida as of this writing: Anthony Brown (on death row 1983–86), Willie Brown (1983–88), Robert Cox (1988–89), Andrew Golden (1991–93), Robert Hayes (1991–97), Sonia Jacobs (1976–92), Anibal Jaramillo (1981–82), William Jent (1979–88), David Keaton (1971–73), Wilbert Lee (1963–75), Ernest Miller (1979–88), Anthony Peek (1978–87), Freddie Pitts (1963–75), Juan Ramos (1983–87), James Richardson (1968-89), Bradley Scott (1988–91), Delbert Tibbs (1974–77), Larry Troy (1983–88), and Shabaka Waglini (1974–87). The Radelet/Bedau data do not include two men: Joe Spaziano, who has not yet been released from prison, and Jesse Tafero, who was executed (and whose electrocution was botched) on May 4, 1990.

Nationally, one in five scheduled executions has been adjudicated as dubious. In Florida, nineteen out of thirty-eight—half of those marked for death—have been, upon reconsideration, excused from their appointments with the executioner. Such ratios and percentages might be of negligible concern in the measurement of some government errors. But do they inspire confidence that this governmental system is capable of forming principled decisions as to whether particular citizens have lost their moral entitlement to life? A decision as to whether a human being will die is not a matter of pork barrel waste or misallocation of office space. Once punishment is administered, it cannot be remedied.

Reasonable minds can disagree about the details of Radelet and Bedau's data; one can quibble about whether or not this or that particular death row prisoner is indeed innocent. But the data really do nothing more than quantify the commonsense notion that all people, even those in government positions, make mistakes. Anyone who has ever waited for a letter to arrive in the U.S. mail, or who has had the sublime pleasure of dealing with the IRS or INS, knows that the government makes mistakes because *people* make mistakes. Even when our government is deciding life or death, it can make mistakes. We knew that before the "Crazy Joe" case.

The Florida cases noted above share several common characteristics, none of which ought to sound unfamiliar to any close observer of the Sunshine State's machinery of death. First, most of the accused individuals were in some sense "others," members of discrete and insular minorities marginalized and despised by Florida's dominant culture (white, male, affluent). Pitts, Lee, and Brown were African Americans. Jent, Miller, and Spaziano were bikers. Second, all were from the lower socioeconomic strata of society; none were products of the affluent classes. Third, and closely related to the preceding point, all had lousy and/or howlingly underresourced defense attorneys at their trials. Fourth, cops or prosecutors or both succeeded in hiding from their defense lawyers important evidence suggesting their innocence. Fifth, when their postconviction lawyers and investigators finally were able to unearth that evidence of innocence (and more, much more), the prosecutors deployed an arsenal of legal technicalities to persuade the courts not even to consider the newly discovered evidence of total factual innocence (by asserting that the innocents had found the new evidence too late, or they'd filed in the wrong court at the right time, or in the right court at the wrong time, or whatever). In every single case, the state denied—loudly and publicly—that the defendant was innocent at all, even in the face of overwhelming evidence to the contrary—physical evidence or a credible confession by another to the crime.

With thudding predictability, the state fought tooth and nail to keep these individuals on death row, and, when the courts ruled otherwise, the state actors screeched that these people were all *getting off on some legal technicality,* that they were getting away with murder.

For myself, this last point, the state's lack of humility in the face of an irrevocable penalty—prosecutors' utter inability or unwillingness to admit that perhaps they might have been wrong, that a legal system created and administered by fallible human beings might have made mistakes in the cases of these few of the hundreds of people who have been sent to Florida's death row—is breathtaking. It is this governmental arrogance, even in the face of facts and impending electrocution, that ought to give capital punishment proponents pause.

Nothing about any of the five factors I have cited has changed much over the two decades Joe Spaziano has lived on Florida's death row for other men's crimes. People whom the majority culture deems "other" are still more likely to be sentenced to die and to be executed. Virtually all men and women on death row are and were poor. Most had lousy lawyering and investigating at the trial level. Cops and prosecutors still hide evidence of innocence from capital defendants and their attorneys. The state still possesses its arsenal of legal technicalities to preclude reviewing courts from even considering newly discovered evidence, and capital prosecutors still employ that arsenal with a vengeance. Joe Spaziano's case illustrates all of these things.

Yet, perhaps saddest of all, Joe's case illustrates the state's hysterical denial that mistakes can be made, and that the confluence of those mistakes can land a person on death row for a crime he did not commit. When confronted with Tony DiLisio's recantation, the government ducked, covered, and lied. The government ordered a fraudulent police "investigation," then kept that investigation secret, and then lied about at least one crucial aspect of its secret probe—saying that DiLisio didn't recant during his videotaped interrogation by FDLE. Anyone who thinks that the state's actions during May–September 1995 constitute a good-faith exploration into Joe's factual innocence claim is, in my opinion, either hopelessly naive or hopelessly ignorant.

If Joe Spaziano ever breathes free air again, he will do so despite the combined might and power of Florida's governor, prosecutors, and law enforcement personnel. He will receive no apology from the state that robbed him of at least two decades of his life. To be sure, many state actors—including more than a few of Joe's guards from across the decades—will cheer. But that cheering will be silent and unofficial. Official Florida will say that Joe and his lawyers and the *Miami Herald* got away with murder. Those cops who framed him in 1976 will receive no official censure for framing this innocent man. They won't be indicted for obstruction of justice. To the contrary, they will receive the very public sympathy and support of official Florida, and, of course, the *Orlando Sentinel.*

In Florida, the state government wants to speak with a single voice to "Crazy Joe" Spaziano. That one voice will deliver a simple message: Just be glad we didn't kill you—at least we didn't strap you into our periodically malfunctioning electric chair.

At least.

Because of my experiences with Joseph Spaziano's case, a few people have asked me for thoughts on "working" the news media. My only thought is that you *cannot* work the media, at least not in a capital postconviction case. What you can do is provide specific reporters with information, so long as the information is true, accurate, and complete. Here are my observations on taking a capital case to the media:

1. Choose your reporters carefully and according to two criteria: Do they do their own homework? and Do they have open minds? Ironically, reporters who are willing to take your word, uncritically, for what the raw, primary documents in the case say are not reporters with whom you want to be dealing. If they do not ask you the hard questions, they will not ask the prosecutors the hard questions either, and the prosecutors always have better sound bites; they also have grisly crime-scene photos. So, the more skeptical the reporter, the better. If he or she supports capital punishment as a public policy, all the better.

2. Your client had better really be innocent, and you had better be able to prove it. You should know that if you run a fraudulent innocence claim in the media and you are found out—and you will be found out, trust me—then the media will slaughter both your client and you, as they should. Also, you will make it significantly harder for others to

convince the media that their clients are innocent, even if they are. You must be prepared to live with the fact that, by poisoning the media atmosphere within which such claims must be raised, your fraudulent innocence claim will likely contribute to the killing of innocent people in the future.

3. Tell the truth, omitting and embroidering nothing, including, especially, the evidence that hurts your client. If you have chosen the right reporters, you will not be able to fool them—so don't even try.

4. Legal technicalities do not matter in media coverage, regardless of whether those technicalities work to your client's benefit or to the prosecution's. The qualified good news is that in this venue, unlike in court, you will be able to tell the whole story. The legal technicalities that preclude courts from hearing newly discovered evidence bearing on actual innocence do not apply in this forum. By the same token, the exclusionary rule does not apply, either; the state is as free as you are to tell *its* whole story. And, although at trial your client need not testify in his own defense, here you had better have a provable alibi, or a damn good reason for not having one. The trial is over; your client lost; *you* now have the burden of upsetting a presumptively valid murder conviction and death sentence.

5. Open *all* your files to your reporters, and keep them open. Resist the temptation to purge. If you are working with the right reporters, they will find you out if you try to hold anything back, and they will nail you and your client.

6. Be willing to say, in writing and on the record, that of your X number of death row clients (you must give a number, and it had better be fairly high), *this* is the one, the only one, whom you believe in your bone marrow to be entirely innocent. Be ready to live with the consequences such a public statement will bring from your former clients and their families, who will feel, quite justifiably, that you have sold them down the river in favor of your one current client. Grievances may be brought against you, and you may be sued for malpractice. Be prepared.

7. Be ready to give up any future representation of death row clients. You possess only a finite amount of credibility capital and, by the time this case is over, you will be deficit spending at an order of magnitude that only the Pentagon might understand. This only works *once*. If you take on any future clients, they will, and rightly so, demand that you do for them what you did for this one client.

I remain guardedly nonpessimistic that, in the end, the United States will reject capital punishment. This will happen, I am convinced, not because of rational arguments. It will come because, in our collective stomach, we decide that our fallible government ought not be in the business of deciding who dies.

Abolition of capital punishment will come because of a collection of stories told and retold—stories like "Crazy Joe" Spaziano's. It won't be soon, and it won't be sudden. But eventually, after the stories have piled up over years, it will come, as the abolition of slavery came. That took a civil war, and the war was sparked by John Brown's doomed raid on Harper's Ferry in 1859. Looking back, we can see how Brown's raid—and his execution—provided the spark. Someday, we will look back on capital punishment, and, most likely, we will be able to identify such a spark. I don't know what that spark will be, or whether anyone will recognize it as such when it occurs. But, I believe, it will come.

This is the end of this book, but it is not the end of Joe's story. Joe isn't yet free. Until he is, we will write as many new chapters to his story as it takes.

The letter I'd been dreading finally arrived. It was postmarked three weeks previously, but, since it originated on Florida's death row, the delay wasn't unusual. The letter was less than half a page long, written in careful but somewhat loopy longhand, on wide-lined notebook paper.

It wasn't from Joe. It was from Butch Sireci, one of my old clients from my time in Florida as a capital public defender. We'd fallen out of touch since 1987, when I left Tallahassee and CCR for D.C. and private law practice. It was the letter I'd been dreading since Gene Miller first asked me in May 1995 to write an op-ed piece on why I believed

Joe Spaziano to be innocent—the most clearly innocent of my former clients.

Dear Mike,

Greetings from an old acquaintance!! I hope this finds you well, and in the Best of spirits these days!

Mike, if you are the one and the same who knows me from the time you spent with the West Palm Beach, Fla. Public Defenders office—I would like to ask you a couple of questions, now that I have concrete proof of my innocence!!

I look forward to hearing from you soon!! Thank you, for your time and Patience!!

Sincerely,
Butch

I didn't know what to write in reply. I still don't.

Appendix

Execution Guidelines
for the State of Florida

Confidential
Foreword

The documents enclosed herein are considered very sensitive because of the subject matter and certain security requirements that could create serious problems if compromised.

Their distribution is very limited and intended for the exclusive use of the designated recipient and should not be loaned, reproduced, or made public without the authority of the undersigned or higher level authority.

———————————————

R. L. Dugger,
Superintendent
Florida State Prison

This document contains a summary of the most significant events which will occur during the final days preceding a scheduled execution. It will be used as a management guideline by the Superintendent to assure that operational functions are properly planned with the staff who have been designated responsibilities.

It is our purpose to carry out the intent of Florida Statute, Chapter 922, and we believe this guideline coupled with Florida State Prison Institutional Operating Procedures Number 34 and 65, as well as Post Orders 100, 101, and 102, are consistent with the intent of Florida Law. These guidelines may be modified as appropriate for differing circumstances surrounding individual Death Warrants, particularly in accordance with the designated day of execution within the active week of the Death Warrant.

Index
Effective May 1, 1979
Revised November 1, 1983

1. Execution Guidelines for Week of Active Death Warrant
2. FSP Institutional Operating Procedure #34, Staff Responsibilities and Special Procedures for Inmates with Death Warrants
3. FSP Institutional Operating Procedure #65, Outside Security Procedures
4. FSP Special Post Orders for Death Watch Supervisor, Grille Gate Monitor and Cell Front Monitor (Special Post Order Numbers 100, 101, 102)

Execution Guidelines for Week of Active Death Warrant

Execution day—minus five (5)

1. Execution squad identified
2. Media and official witnesses escort identified
3. Support personnel for entrance and other check points identified
4. Medical support staff for execution identified
5. Electrician tests all execution equipment to include emergency generator and telephone
6. Superintendent briefs all CO 111 and above regarding execution activities

Execution day—minus four (4)

1. Security Coordinator notified
2. Assign Death Watch Spv. & Cell Front Monitor
3. Inmate personally re-inventory all property and seal property for storage
4. Institution Chaplin notified to visit daily
5. All visiting changed to non-contact
6. Telephone check of outside line by ASO
7. Establish communications with DOC Attorney for consultation as required
8. Establish notification list and contact staff in event of significant legal change (G. Georgieff)
9. Schedule meeting for crowd strategy pursuant to FSP 10P no. 65 by Security Coordinator
10. Designated electrician tests all execution equipment to include emergency generator
11. Measure inmate(s) for clothing
12. Inmate specifies in writing funeral arrangements
13. Specifies recipient of personal property in writing
14. Execution squad drill

Execution day—minus three (3)

No activities—Monitor

Execution day—minus two (2)

1. Execution squad drill
2. Asst. Supt. Operations tests telephone
3. Electrician tests equipment

Execution day—minus one (1)

1. Execution squad drill
2. Asst. Sup. Operations tests telephone
3. Electrician tests equipment to include emergency generator
4. Waiting area for execution set up by Asst. Supt. Operations
5. Electrician makes up ammonium chloride solution and soaks sponges
6. Condemned inmate orders last meal
7. Chief Medical Officer prepares certificate of death = cause "legal execution by electrocution"
8. Official witness list finalized by Central Office (12 + 4 alt.)
9. Executioner contacted and liaison set up for execution day
10. Asst. Sup. Programs confirms funeral arrangements with family
11. Information office arrives to handle media inquiry
12. Security Meeting held
13. External Death Watch Observer identified
14. Designated media pool observer identified by Information Office (twelve)

Execution Day

4:30 A.M.: The Food Service Director will personally prepare and serve the last meal. Eating utensils allowed will be a plate and spoon.

5:00 A.M.: The Administrative Assistant or designate will pick up executioner, proceed to the institution, enter through Sally Port and leave the executioner in the Waiting Room of the Death Chamber at 5:00 A.M. A security staff member will be posted in the chamber area.

6:00 A.M.: A. Beginning at 5:30 A.M., the only staff authorized on Q-1-E are:
1. Observer, designated by the Secretary
2. Superintendent
3. Assistant Superintendent for Operations
4. Chief Correctional Officer IV
5. Death Watch Supervisor
6. Second Shift Lieutenant
7. Chaplain
8. Grille Gate Monitor
9. Cell Front Monitor

Any exception to the above designated staff must be approved by the Superintendent.

B. The Assistant Superintendent for Operations will supervise the shaving of the condemned inmate's head and right leg.

C. Official witnesses will report to Florida State Prison's Main Gate no later than 5:30 A.M., be greeted by two designated Department of Corrections escort staff, security cleared and moved to the staff dining room where they will remain until later escorted to the witness room of the execution chamber.

5:50 A.M.: Authorized Media Witnesses will be picked up at the media onlooker area by two designated Department of Corrections staff escorts. They will be transported to the Main Entrance of Florida State Prison, as a group, be security cleared and then escorted to the Classification Department where they will remain until later escorted to the witness room of the execution chamber.

6:00 A.M.: A. The Assistant Superintendent for Operations will supervise the showering of the condemned inmate. Immediately thereafter he will be returned to his cell and given a pair of shorts, a pair of trousers, a dress shirt, and socks. The Correctional Officer Chief IV will be responsible for the delivery of the clothes.

B. Switchboard operator will be instructed by Superintendent to wire all calls to Execution Chamber from Governor's Office through switchboard.

C. The Administrative Assistant, or designate, three designated electricians, a physician, and a physician's asst. will report to the execution chamber for preparation. The Administrative Assistant or designate will check the phones in the chamber. The electrician will ready the equipment and the Physician and Medical Technician or Physician's Assistant will stand by.

6:30 A.M.: The Administrative Assistant or designate will establish phone communication with those officials designated by the Superintendent.

*6:50 A.M.: A. The Asst. Superintendent for Operations will supervise the application of conducting gel to the right calf and crown of the condemned inmate's head.

B. The Superintendent will read the Death Warrant to the condemned inmate.

C. Official witnesses will be secured in the witness room by two designated Dept. of Corrections staff no later than 6:50 A.M.

D. Authorized media witnesses will be secured in the witness room by two designated Dept. of Corrections staff no later than 6:50 A.M.

E. Beginning at 6:55 A.M., the only persons authorized in the witness room are:

12 official witnesses
4 alternate witnesses
1 physician
1 medical technician
12 authorized media representatives
4 designated Dept. of Corrections staff escorts

Any exception to the above designated persons must be approved by the Superintendent.

* See Execution Guidelines Appendix "A" if two inmates are to be executed.

6:56 A.M. A. Beginning at 6:56 A.M., the only staff authorized in the execution chamber are:

   Observer, designated by the Secretary
   Superintendent
   Asst. Superintendent for Operations
   Correctional Officer Chief IV
   Administrative Assistant or Supt. Designate
   Chaplain (Optional)
   Two (2) Electricians
   One (1) executioner
   One (1) physician
   One (1) Physician's Assistant

Any exception to the above designated staff must be approved by the Superintendent.

  B. The Superintendent, Asst. Superintendent for Operations, and Correctional Officer Chief IV will escort the condemned inmate to the execution chamber. The Adm. Asst. or designate will record the time the inmate entered the chamber.

  C. The Asst. Superintendent for Operations and Correctional Officer Chief IV will place the condemned inmate in the chair.

  D. The Superintendent and Asst. Superintendent for Operations will secure back and arm straps and then forearm straps.

  E. When the inmate is secured, the Asst. Superintendent for Operations and Correctional Officer Chief IV will remove the restraint apparatus and then secure lap, chest, and ankle straps. The anklet will then be laced and the electrode attached.

7:00 A.M. A. The Superintendent will permit the condemned inmate to make a last statement. The Supt. will then proceed to the outside open telephone line to inquire of possible stays.

  B. The electrician will place the sponges on the condemned inmate's head, secure the head set and attach electrode.

  C. The Assistant Superintendent for Operations engages the circuit breaker.

  D. The electrician in the booth will activate the Executioner Control Panel.

E. The Superintendent will give the signal to the Executioner to turn the switch and the automatic cycle will begin. The Adm. Asst. or designate will record the time the switch is thrown.

F. Once the cycle runs its course the electrician indicates the current is off. The Adm. Asst. or designate will record the time the current is disengaged.

G. The Assistant Superintendent for Operations then disengages the manual circuit behind the chair.

H. The Superintendent invites the Doctor to conduct the examination.

I. The man is pronounced dead. The Adm. Asst. or designate records the time death is pronounced.

J. The Administrative Assistant or designate announces that the sentence has been carried out, and invites witnesses and media to exit. "The sentence of _____ has been carried out. Please exit to the rear at this time."

K. The official witnesses and media pool will then be escorted from the witness room by the designated Department of Corrections staff escorts.

7:20 A.M. to 7:30 A.M.

A. O/S Lieutenant notified by ASP to bring in ambulance attendants.

B. The inmate will be removed from the chair by ambulance attendants under the supervision of the Assistant Superintendent for Programs.

C. The ambulance will be cleared through Sally Port by escorting officer.

D. Admin. Asst. or designate will return the executioner and compensate him.

Post Execution

    A.   The physician must sign the Death Certificate.

    B.   The Superintendent will return the Death Warrant to the Governor indicating execution has been carried out.

    C.   Superintendent will file a copy with the Circuit Court of Conviction.

    D.   Classification Supervisor will advise Central Office Records by teletype.

Distribution

    A.   The Administrative Assistant will make distribution of this document to all involved, instruct those staff as to the confidentiality of this schedule, and explain individual roles, as necessary.

Execution Guidelines Appendix "A"

In the event of two executions, on the same date and approximate time, some modifications to procedures will be necessary.

6:30 A.M.   1.   All procedures from Execution Day—Minus Five (5) through Execution Day 6:30 A.M. will be the same, except that they will be duplicated for the 2nd condemned inmate where necessary or appropriate.

6:50 A.M.   2.   Beginning Execution Day—6:50 A.M. the following modification will be in effect if two inmates are to be executed.

A. The Assistant Superintendent for Operations will supervise the application of conducting gel to the right calf and crown of the #1 condemned inmate's head. The #2 inmate will stand by in his cell.

B. The Superintendent will read the Death Warrants to the #1 and #2 condemned inmates.

C. Official witnesses for execution #1 will be secured in the witness room no later than 6:50 A.M.

D. Authorized media witnesses for execution #1 will be secured in the witness room by two designated Department of Corrections staff no later than 6:50 A.M.

E. Official witnesses and media witnesses for execution #2 will remain in the Staff Dining Room and Classification Department respectively until transported for execution #2 at the designated time.

F. Beginning at 6:55 A.M. the only persons authorized in the witness room are:

    12 Official witnesses
    4 alternate witnesses
    1 physician
    1 medical technician
    12 authorized media representatives
    4 designated Department of Corrections staff escorts

Any exception to the above designated persons must be approved by the Superintendent.

6:56 A.M.   A.   Beginning at 6:56 A.M. the only staff authorized in the execution chamber are:

> Observer, designated by the Secretary
> Superintendent
> Asst. Superintendent for Operations
> Correctional Officer Chief IV
> Administrative Assistant or Supt. Designate
> Chaplain (Optional)
> Two (2) Electricians
> One (1) Executioner
> One (1) Physician
> One (1) Physician's Assistant

Any exception to the above designated staff must be approved by the Superintendent.

    B.   The Superintendent, Asst. Superintendent for Operations, and Correctional Officer Chief IV will escort the condemned inmate to the execution chamber. The Adm. Asst. or designate will record the time the inmate entered the chamber.

    C.   The Asst. Superintendent for Operations and Correctional Officer Chief IV will place the condemned inmate in the chair.

    D.   The Superintendent and Asst. Superintendent for Operations will secure back and arm straps and then forearm straps.

    E.   When the inmate is secured, the Asst. Superintendent for Operations and Correctional Officer Chief IV will remove the restraint apparatus and then secure lap, chest, and ankle straps. The anklet will then be laced and the electrode attached.

7:00 A.M.   A.   The Superintendent will permit the condemned inmate to make a last statement. The Superintendent will then proceed to the outside open telephone line to inquire of possible stays.

    B.   The electrician will place the sponges on the condemned inmate's head, secure the head set and attach electrode.

    C.   The Assistant Superintendent for Operations engages the circuit breaker.

    D.   The electrician in the booth will activate the Executioner Control Panel.

E. The Superintendent will give the signal to the Executioner to turn the switch and the automatic cycle will begin. The Adm. Assistant or designate will record the time the switch is thrown.

F. Once the cycle runs its course the electrician indicates the current is off. The Adm. Asst. or designate will record the time the current is disengaged.

G. The Assistant Superintendent for Operations then disengages the manual circuit behind the chair.

H. The Superintendent invites the Doctor to conduct the examination.

I. The man is pronounced dead. The Adm. Asst. or designate records the time death is pronounced.

J. The Administrative Assistant or designate announces that the sentence has been carried out, and invites witnesses and media to exit. "The sentence of _____ has been carried out. Please exit to the rear at this time."

K. The official witnesses and media pool will then be escorted from the witness room by the designated Department of Corrections staff escorts.

7:20 A.M.

A. Media witnesses for execution #2 brought around by transport to Death House entrance and stand by.

B. Official witnesses for execution #2 brought around by transport to Death House entrance and stand by.

C. Media witnesses and official witnesses from execution #1 to also witness #2 join others in standby vehicle after exiting witness chamber.

D. Remaining media witnesses and official witnesses depart institution via transport through Sally Port Gate.

E. Executed inmate removed from chair, placed on stretcher, and deposited in hallway outside execution chamber by Administrative Assistant (or designate), physician, physician's assistant, and two electricians.

F. Superintendent, Assistant Superintendent, Correctional Officer Chief, Official Observer, return to Death Watch Cell area.

7:30 A.M.   A.   The Assistant Superintendent for Operations will supervise the application of conducting gel to the right calf and crown of the #2 condemned inmate's head.

B.   Official witnesses for execution #2 will be secured in the witness room no later than 7:30 A.M.

C.   Authorized media witnesses for execution #2 will be secured in the witness room no later than 7:30 A.M.

7:36 A.M.   Beginning at 7:36 A.M. the only staff authorized in the execution chamber are:

    Observer, designated by the Secretary
    Superintendent
    Asst. Superintendent for Operations
    Correctional Officer Chief IV
    Administrative Assistant or Supt. Designate
    Chaplain (Optional)
    Two (2) Electricians
    One (1) Executioner
    One (1) Physician
    One (1) Physician's Assistant

Any exception to the above designated staff must be approved by the Superintendent.

7:38 A.M.   A.   The Superintendent, Asst. Superintendent for Operations, and Correctional Officer Chief IV will escort the condemned inmate to the execution chamber. The Adm. Asst. or designate will record the time the inmate entered the chamber.

B.   The Asst. Superintendent for Operations and Correctional Officer Chief IV will place the condemned inmate in the chair.

C.   The Superintendent and Asst. Superintendent for Operations will secure back and arm straps and then forearm straps.

D.   When the inmate is secured, the Asst. Superintendent for Operations and Correctional Officer Chief IV will remove the restraint apparatus and then secure lap, chest, and ankle straps. The anklet will then be laced and the electrode attached.

7:40 A.M.   A.   The Superintendent will permit the condemned inmate to make a last statement. The Superintendent will then proceed to the outside open telephone line to inquire of possible stays.

B.   The electrician will place the sponges on the condemned inmate's head, secure the head set and attach electrode.

C.   The Assistant Superintendent for Operations engages the circuit breaker.

D.   The electrician in the booth will activate the Executioner Control Panel.

E.   The Superintendent will give the signal to the Executioner to turn the switch and the automatic cycle will begin. The Adm. Assistant or designate will record the time the switch is thrown.

F.   Once the cycle runs its course the electrician indicates the current is off. The Adm. Asst. or designate will record the time the current is disengaged.

G.   The Assistant Superintendent for Operations then disengages the manual circuit behind the chair.

H.   The Superintendent invites the Doctor to conduct the examination.

I.   The man is pronounced dead. The Adm. Asst. or designate records the time death is pronounced.

J.   The Administrative Assistant or designate announces that the sentence has been carried out, and invites witnesses and media to exit. "The sentence of _____ has been carried out. Please exit to the rear at this time."

K.   The official witnesses and media pool will then be escorted from the witness room by the designated Department of Corrections staff escorts.

8:00 A.M.   A.   Outside Lieutenant notified by Asst. Supt. for Programs to bring in two ambulance attendants.

8:15 A.M.   A.   The second inmate will be removed from the chair by ambulance attendants under the supervision of the Asst. Superintendent for Programs.

B.   The first inmate will be removed from the hallway, by ambulance attendant under the supervision of the Asst. Supt. for Programs.

C.   The ambulance(s) will be cleared through Sally Port by escorting officer.

D.   The Administrative Assistant or designate will return the executioner and compensate him.

Post Execution

    A.   The physician must sign the Death Certificate(s).

    B.   The Superintendent will return the Death Warrant(s) to the Governor indicating execution has been carried out.

    C.   Superintendent will file a copy with the Circuit Court of Conviction.

    D.   Classification Supervisor will advise Central Office Records by teletype.

Distribution

The Administrative Assistant will make distribution of this document to all involved, instruct those staff as to the confidentiality of this schedule, and explain individual roles, as necessary.

Florida State Prison
Institutional Operating Procedure Number 34,
Staff Responsibilities and Special Procedures
for Inmates with Death Warrants

34.01   Authority

A.   Florida Statutes, Chapters 945.21 and 922

B.   Rules of the Department of Corrections, Chapters 33-3 and 33-15

34.02   Purpose

The purpose of this operating procedure is to designate staff responsibilities and establish uniform property, privilege and facility guidelines for condemned inmates with signed death warrants.

34.03   Receipt of Warrant, Housing and Security Assignments

A.   Upon receipt of the warrant which authorizes execution, the Superintendent or his delegate will inform the inmate and permit him to make a phone call.

B.   After the condemned inmate is informed of the signed warrant he will normally be transferred to Q Wing, first floor, east side. Exceptions will be authorized only by the Superintendent, Assistant Superintendent for Operations, or Correctional Officer Chief IV for good and valid reasons.

C.   Correctional Officers will be assigned to the Q-1-E housing area in a manner consistent with Special Post Orders 100, 101, and 102 which set forth the guidelines for the Death Watch Supervisor, Grille Gate Monitor and Cell Front Monitor.

34.04   Region II Institutional Notification, Security Coordinator Notification, and Advisement of Law Enforcement Agencies

A.   Upon determination of the execution date and time, the Regional Director, Superintendents of Union Correctional Institution, Reception & Medical Center, Baker Correctional Institution, Lawtey Correctional Institution, and the Security Coordinator may be advised by Florida State Prison's Superintendent or his delegate. Should circumstances develop which necessitate it, Control Force activities will be coordinated by the Security Coordinator. Formulation of security personnel will be at the discretion of the Security Coordinator.

B. The following law enforcement agencies also may be notified by the Superintendent or his designate.

   1. Union County Sheriff's Office
   2. Bradford County Sheriff's Office
   3. Florida Highway Patrol—Troop Command—Lake City
   4. Florida Department of Law Enforcement—Gainesville
   5. Florida National Guard—St. Augustine

34.05   State Issued Property and Possession Limit

A.   State Issued Property (Possession Limits):

   1. Standard issue of clothing
   2. One bed
   3. One mattress
   4. One pillow
   5. Standard issue of bedding
   6. One toothbrush
   7. One tube of toothpaste
   8. One bar of handsoap
   9. All Death Row inmates will be issued a lock razor consistent with FSP 10P #86, Section 86.03
   10. Two towels
   11. One washcloth
   12. Two pair of undershorts
   13. Toilet tissue, as needed
   14. Stationery, Six (6) sheets
   15. Envelopes, Three (3)
   16. Religious Tracts as distributed by the Inst. Chaplain, Maximum possession, Ten (10)
   17. Writ Paper, as needed, to be distributed from Library. Notary services are available by signing FSP Form #40 which is available every Sunday and Wednesday in the housing areas. Preparation of legal documents will be handled consistent with FSP 10P #4, Section 4.05.
   18. Authorized medication, as prescribed by staff physician. All empty containers must be discarded.
   19. Administrative Remedy Forms (DC-77 or DC-77A) as needed.
   20. One black & white television (Provided by Inmate Welfare Fund)

34.06   Bank Coupon Withdrawals

Condemned inmates will be permitted to make bank coupon with-drawals every Thursday. Withdrawals will be limited to a maximum of $20.00 per withdrawal. FSP Form #133 will be submitted to the housing officer each Sunday for processing. The total coupon posses-sion amount at any time may not exceed $25.00.

34.07   Canteen Privileges

Canteen privileges to include purchasing and possession limits will be as specified in Special Post Orders #100, 101 and 102. Glass, aerosol, and metal containers *will not* be allowed after the warrant has been signed.

34.08   Disposition of Unauthorized or Contraband Items

Contraband items found in the possession of condemned inmates will be confiscated and disposed of in accordance with FSP 10P #66. Excess property items will be stored in accordance with the provisions of Special Post Orders #100, and 101.

34.09   Package Permits

Package permit privileges will be suspended for inmates with active Death Warrants. Any package already mailed will be received and stored with the inmate's other property on Q-1-East, with the excep-tion of consumables.

34.10   Library, Law Library Services, Periodical Subscriptions

A.   The condemned inmate may request in writing to the librarian and receive legal materials from the law library. Such exchanges will be very carefully inspected by the librarian and Death Watch Supervisor. There will be no exchanges or communica-tion with inmate legal clerks and the condemned inmate.

B.   The inmate may continue to receive periodical subscriptions but may not order new subscriptions. Periodicals, newspapers, etc. will not be allowed to accumulate and during the final week only two periodicals and two newspapers may be retained by the inmate.

34.11   Diet

Three (3) meals per day will be fed to all condemned inmates. Special dietary instructions for medical reasons will be followed.

34.12   Recreation

Recreational activities for inmates with death warrants will be suspended.

34.13   Television and Radio Privileges

Television and radio privileges will be the same as routinely provided, except that during the time a death warrant is active the television/radio will be located outside the inmate's cell.

34.14   Personal Phone Calls

Should the condemned inmate request personal or legal phone calls they will be considered on an individual basis by the Assistant Superintendent for Operations or Superintendent. The Assistant Superintendent for Operations or Superintendent will coordinate all approved calls with the Security staff assigned to Q-1-E.

34.15   Clothing

When Florida State Prison's Administration is made aware that a Death Warrant has been signed, the Clothing Room Supervisor will be contacted. Within a reasonable period, the inmate will be measured for a suit. A suit coat, slacks, dress shirt, undergarments and socks will be procured by the Clothing Room Supervisor and provided to the condemned inmate on the morning of the scheduled execution. Should the inmate's family offer to provide a suit and dress shirt, it will be permitted.

34.16   Visiting—Social, Religious, Legal, Media

Visiting and interviews for inmates with death warrants will be in accordance with Florida Statute 945.21 and Department of Corrections Rules, Chapter 33-3.04 and 33-15. Additionally, the following circumstances shall apply:

A.   Social Visits

    1.   *Only* those members on the *approved* visiting list will be allowed social visits with the condemned inmate after a death warrant is signed.

    2.   All social visits will be non-contact and held in the Maximum Security Visiting Park, any two days, Monday–Friday, 9:00 A.M. to 3:00 P.M.

    3.   All social visits will be in accordance with FSP 10P #72.

4. Social visiting will be allowed two days per week between the hours of 9:00 A.M. and 3:00 P.M. and will be held Monday through Friday.

5. During the time of an active death warrant social visits at one time may be flexible as circumstances permit.

6. Abuse of the visiting park by the inmate or his visitors may result in restriction or suspension of social visiting privileges.

7. A final contact visit for the condemned inmate may be authorized by the Superintendent based upon the individual circumstances of the condemned inmate and visitor or visitors. The Superintendent, Assistant Superintendent for Operations, and Correctional Officer Chief IV will determine the security conditions of the visit. Search and security procedures shall be the minimum deemed necessary in order to maintain security. The contact visit will be supervised by not less than two Correctional Officers physically present in the visiting room. Selection of these Correctional Officers must be approved by the Superintendent, Assistant Superintendent for Operations or Correctional Office Chief.

B. Religious Visits

1. Priests or ministers of the inmate's recorded and recognized religious faith may visit the condemned inmate at the same time under the same circumstances as social visitors.

2. There may be a special provision for cell front visiting between the condemned inmate and his personal minister or priest as approved by the Superintendent immediately prior to the execution. The condemned inmate's personal minister or priest will not be permitted to accompany him to the execution chamber. This service will be provided by the Institutional Chaplain if the inmate so desires. The personal minister or priest may witness the execution from the witness room.

C. Legal Visitors

1. The attorney of record or other licensed attorney approved by the attorney of record, the inmate, or his family, may visit with a condemned inmate after the

death warrant is signed. Also, a paralegal aide in a previously established employer/employee relationship with an attorney representing the inmate may visit with him after the death warrant is signed. However, all attorneys or paralegal aides must be cleared in advance before attempting to visit the condemned inmate.

2. Visit, as specified above, may be contact type and will be conducted in the interview room provided for that purpose.

3. Normal hours for legal visits are Monday through Friday, between the hours of 8:00 A.M. and 4:30 P.M. The Superintendent or his designee may authorize a visit to occur on any day, and at any time.

4. During the time of an active death warrant legal visits will normally be non-contact and held in the maximum security visiting park or other location as specified by the Superintendent, Assistant Superintendent for Operations, or Correctional Officer Chief IV.

D. Media Interviews

1. Media interviews with all death row inmates with death warrants will be scheduled through the Assistant Superintendent for Operations and will continue as usual on Tuesday, Wednesday and Thursday, between the hours of 1:00 P.M. and 3:00 P.M. (except holidays), until the warrant becomes active. Thereafter #2. and #3. below apply.

2. A death row inmate with an active death warrant may be scheduled for an individual interview with the media representative of his choice, at a time and date specified by the Superintendent within 48 hours prior to the scheduled execution.

3. A final group media interview for a condemned inmate will be granted with the inmate's permission, within 48 hours prior to the scheduled execution in accordance with Department of Corrections Rule 33-15.

4. Telephone interviews with media representatives will not be permitted.

34.17   Citizen and Media Witnesses

Florida State Prison's Superintendent will assure that twelve (12) citizens as required by Florida Statute, Chapter 922.11 and twelve (12) media representatives, as outlined in Department of Corrections Rule 33-15, .01 and .02 witness the execution. Department of Corrections staff members will be designated by the Superintendent to coordinate the citizen and media witnesses to and from the witness chamber.

34.18   Key Personnel Duties Prior, During and Subsequent to an Execution

A.   Superintendent

1.   Assure that procedures described in this operating procedure either personally or by delegation carried out.
2.   Set the day and time of the execution.
3.   Designate Department of Corrections staff members to coordinate the citizen and media witnesses to and from the witness chamber.
4.   Read the death warrant to the condemned inmate just prior to execution.
5.   Just prior to the execution, the Superintendent will allow the condemned inmate to make his last statement.
6.   Order the executioner verbally or by gesture to proceed with the execution.
7.   Cause to be announced to the witnesses that the sentence has been carried out.
8.   Return the warrant to the Governor's Office.

B.   Assistant Superintendent for Operations

1.   Assume the duties of Superintendent in the event the Superintendent is detained.
2.   Coordinate the security of the condemned inmate(s).
3.   Coordinate approved visits and phone calls with assigned security staff.
4.   Supervise the condemned inmate's property inventory, storage and release to the authorized party.
5.   Supervise preparation of the condemned inmate for execution in the cell area and execution chamber.

C.   Assistant Superintendent for Programs

1.   Two physicians and one medical technician to be present at execution.
2.   Supervise removal of the body from the execution chamber.

3.   Coordinate the release of the condemned inmate's body to the authorized recipient or coordinate burial at State expense in the event no one claims the body.

D.   Administrative Assistant or Superintendent's Designate

1.   Coordinate and supervise the movement of the executioner to and from the execution chamber, compensate and aid in maintaining the Executioner's anonymity while at the institution.

2.   Establish and maintain communications with the State Officials or courts which are designated by the Superintendent. The communications will take place from the execution chamber.

3.   Announce the completion of the execution to the witnesses.

4.   Ensure blinds are raised at all times.

E.   Correctional Officer Chief IV

1.   Aid the Assistant Superintendent for Operations with his duties as defined in 34.18 (B).

2.   Properly prepare the condemned inmate for execution. The inmate's crown will require shaving, and he will be dressed in white shirt and slacks (no shoes). The suit coat will not be worn during execution but will be placed on the body at the conclusion of the execution.

3.   Provide security arrangements for the movement of the condemned inmate from his Q-Wing cell to the execution chamber in compliance with the schedule set by the Superintendent.

F.   Chaplain

1.   Offer increased chaplaincy services to the condemned inmate and his family.

2.   Accompany the condemned inmate to the execution chamber if the inmate so desires.

G.   Maintenance Personnel

1.   The Maintenance Supervisor will be responsible for assuring that the execution apparatus is functioning properly at the scheduled time of execution.

2.   During execution, two Department of Corrections Maintenance employees will be posted in the execution

chamber. Each will assure that after the inmate is seated, the apparatus is properly connected.

H. Medical Personnel

1. One Medical Doctor and a Medical Technician or additional Physician will be present during the execution.
2. Two minutes after the electrical current ceases the Medical Doctor will examine the body for vital signs.
3. The Medical Doctor will pronounce the inmate dead, and he and the Medical Technician or Physician will then assure that the proper documents are recorded.

I. Security Coordinator

1. The Security Coordinator will have the responsibility of determining if Confrontation Control Forces should be formed. If circumstances develop which necessitate their formulation, the Security Coordinator will coordinate their activities.
2. The Security Coordinator will also be responsible for advising and maintaining contact with law enforcement agencies as specified in Section 34.04 (B) of this Operating Procedure.

J. Department of Corrections Information Director

1. Coordinate "media releases" for the Department.
2. Aid in supervising and coordinating media interviews with the condemned inmate.

34.19   Disciplinary Action

Regardless of an inmate's status he remains subject to disciplinary action for violation of rules and regulations.

Disciplinary Reports may be written on inmates with death warrants, however, processing will be postponed.

34.20   Violations

Inmates, visitors, or personnel who violate the provisions outlined in this Operating Procedure may be subject to disciplinary action or other actions as may be deemed appropriate.

_____

Superintendent

Florida State Prison
Institutional Operating Procedure Number 65,
Outside Security Procedures (Executions)

65.01   Authority

A.   Florida Statutes, Chapter 922, 944-09 (2E) and (4)

B.   Department of Corrections Rules 33-3.09

65.02   Purpose

The purpose of this operating procedure is to outline the outside security procedures to be followed prior, during and subsequent to
executions.

65.03   Receipt of Notification

A.   Upon being advised of the execution(s) date and time, the following law enforcement agencies may be notified by the
Administrative Assistant or the Superintendent's designate.
1.   Bradford County Sheriff's Office
2.   Union County Sheriff's Office
3.   Florida Highway Patrol—Starke Office
4.   Florida National Guard (St. Augustine)
5.   Florida Department of Law Enforcement (Gainesville)

65.04   Command Post

A.   The Main Command Post may be located in the Florida State
Prison Administration Building Conference Room. Once established, it will remain operational until the execution is over and
the debriefing is concluded.

B.   An Auxiliary Command Post at Union Correctional Institution's
Administration Building Conference Room may be utilized
should any circumstances arise which would dictate its use.

65.05   Control Force

A.   Notification
1.   Civilian demonstrations will normally be the responsibility
of law enforcement agencies. The Security Coordinator
will remain aware of the civilian activities and the effect of
these activities on the inmate population.
2.   Should circumstances develop, Control Force activities will
be coordinated by the Security Coordinator. Formulation

of security personnel will be at the discretion of the Security Coordinator.

3. The Security Coordinator will determine the need and number of confrontation teams to be on ready and standby status. The implementation of the confrontation teams will normally be deployed by the Department of Corrections Security Coordinator.

4. Once the need and number of Control Force Teams have been determined, the Security Coordinator will contact the Superintendent of institutions from which Control Force Teams have been selected. Selection will be accomplished through close coordination with the Superintendent of each institution.

B. Assembly Areas

1. Three squads of Department of Corrections Control Force Teams will be ready and assembled at the FSP Administration Building under the command of a Correctional Officer Chief IV.

2. Two squads will be ready and assembled at UCI's Training Building under the command of a Correctional Officer Chief II.

3. The Florida Highway Patrol will assemble their confrontation squad(s) at the designated place.

4. Additional control force teams may be placed on standby status as the need and situation dictates. If placed on ready status, they will report to the RMC Training Building for briefing and deployment.

65.06 Intelligence

A. The Department of Corrections' Security Coordinator has been designated to seek and coordinate pertinent intelligence information on any person(s) or group(s) which may be present. Intelligence information will be gathered from the following agencies:

1. Federal Bureau of Investigation
2. Florida Department of Law Enforcement
3. Florida Highway Patrol
4. Florida Sheriffs
5. Local law enforcement agencies

6. Other agencies as the Security Coordinator deems necessary and appropriate.

B. The Department of Corrections' Security Coordinator will be responsible for compiling all intelligence information received prior to and after issuance of a death warrant.

65.07 Security Briefing and Selection of Law Enforcement Representative

A. Briefing

After a death warrant is issued, the Department of Corrections' Security Coordinator, upon authorization of the Assistant Secretary for Operations, may assemble all concerned Department of Corrections personnel and outside law enforcement agencies and conduct a briefing.

The following areas will be covered:
1. Dissemination of intelligence information
2. Determination of personnel needed and strategy
3. A discrete designation of agency and personnel responsibilities.

B. Selection of Law Enforcement Representatives in Command Post
1. During the meeting described in Section 65.07 (A) of this policy, selection of law enforcement representatives to represent the various law enforcement agencies will be determined in order that all agencies involved will have a representative available in the command post during decision making processes that involve their particular agency. This will enable all agencies to be familiar with that portion of the operation they are involved with and assist in other areas where possible.
2. Only those individuals selected during this meeting will be authorized to enter the command post. All other persons entering must have the permission and consent of the Department of Corrections' Security Coordinator or his designate.
   a. Each agency who has responsibility as outlined above will be allocated appropriate operating space in the command post.
   b. Each agency officer in charge will determine which of their personnel man the command post.

    c. Each agency will be responsible for equipping his key field staff with communications equipment which will be operated on a common frequency to the command post.

C.   Security Assignment

    1.   During the meeting described in Section 65.07 (A) of this policy, security needs will be determined and security assignments will be made. Some areas to be considered for assignment are:

        a. Visitor check points:

            1. Alpha: The archway on Highway 16, South, Bradford County, Starke side.

            2. Bravo: Highway 16 and main entrance to Florida State Prison.

            3. Charlie: Highway 199 at State property line and Pine Grove Cemetery.

            4. Delta: The archway on Highway 17, West, Union County, Raiford side.

            5. Echo: Intersection Highway 16 and Rivergate Road, Union County.

            6. Foxtrot: Florida State Prison landing strip and taxi junction.

        b. Designation of check point personnel:

            1. All check points will be manned by a state trooper and/or a deputy sheriff and a Department of Corrections' Correctional Officer for identification.

        c. Screening Responsibilities:

            1. All traffic by land or air will be screened by personnel appointed in Section 65.07 C. of this operating procedure. Occupants will be inquired as to their destination and purpose for travel through state prison property. All vehicles permitted to enter may be issued a color coded pass card as described below. The driver of any vehicle may be required to produce the pass card issued upon request by Department of Corrections and law enforcement officials.

                a. Official visitors and state employees—blue card and Department of Corrections identification card, printed "staff" or "official visitor."

   b. Local residents and traffic passing through—white card, printed "through traffic."

   c. Observers—any person desiring to assemble in the designated onlooker areas—red card, printed "observer."

   d. Press—yellow card, printed "press."

d. Traffic Control

   1. Florida Highway Patrol Troopers and Deputy Sheriffs will be dispersed at infrequent intervals on State Road 16 and 199 to insure vehicles and persons keep moving to their destination or color coded designated areas.

   2. Coded communications will be disseminated by the command post to appraise field staff of general conditions existing at intermittent intervals. These codes are:

      a. Condition Green—Boundaries are not in jeopardy. Conditions appear normal.

      b. Condition Blue—Impending problems, command staff should contact command post, confrontation appears possible or designated boundary in jeopardy.

      c. Condition Yellow—A confrontation has taken place or a boundary has been exceeded.

   3. Pilots will be expected to fly their craft in airspace areas outside the perimeter marked by blue flags which will be spaced at intervals circling the compound area.

e. Designated Observer's Areas

   1. Four areas will be properly marked and designated:

      a. Two (2) observer areas will be located south of the Poultry Farm road on the east side of Highway 16. The boundaries of these areas will be clearly defined by red flags. Observers will not be permitted to breach the designated boundary.

   2. One (1) press area will be located to the south of the vehicle parking area. The press area will be clearly defined by yellow flags. Press will be permitted to enter observer areas on the east side of Highway 16. Guidelines may be distributed to all visiting press and observers.

3. One (1) vehicle parking area for observers and press will be clearly designated by white flags. All observers and press will depart their vehicles and proceed to the onlooker or press area.

    f. Crowd Monitoring

        1. Uniform and civilian dressed officers from all law enforcement agencies and Department of Corrections may be assigned special duties to monitor the observer areas and make reports to the command post.

        2. Video tape equipment may be utilized to monitor the observer areas as directed by the command post.

D. Each agency will appoint a coordinator to insure security assignments are properly disseminated to authorized personnel outside the command post. Additionally, they will insure that instructions received from the command post are properly carried out and keep the command post informed of problems they encounter or observe.

E. Security Assignment Deployment

    1. Security assignments will be made as outlined in Section 68.07, A.B.C., and D. If additional requirements arise, representatives in the command post will coordinate their assignment.

    2. Requirements for security staff other than those previously described in this operating procedure will be determined by command post representatives.

    3. During the meeting described in Section 65.07, A. of this operating procedure, a decision setting the date and time security assignments begin will be determined. A roster of all assignments and relief will be established during or immediately at the conclusion of the meeting.

65.08   Logistic and Support

A. There may be many items during this entire procedure. Some items will only be utilized by certain groups. Others may be used by all attending. Following is a list of items predetermined to be needed. It may be determined at any time that additional logistic and support items are required. It will be the responsibility of the representatives in the command post to obtain the additional needed items if at all possible.

    1. Lighting (All)

    2. Water (All)

  3. Toilets (Observers and Press)
  4. Engineering Tape (mark observer, press and parking)
  5. Coffee and food (Staff)
  6. Emergency lighting (All)
  7. First Aid Station (All)
  8. Garbage pickup (All)
  9. Helicopter (Security Department)
  10. Communications Equipment (Security Department)
      a. Walkie Talkies
      b. Mobile units
      c. Radio for command post
  11. Automobiles (Security Department)
  12. Transfer Bus (needed by Security Dept. for transferring possible civilian violators)
  13. Farm Equipment (Security staff)
  14. Flex-a-cuffs (Security Department)
  15. Flashlights (Security Department)
  16. Megaphones (Security Department)
  17. Photographer with camera (Security Department)
  18. Wall map and hand out map (Security Department)

65.09   Debriefing

After the sentence of law has been carried out and all persons have departed state property, a debriefing will be conducted by the Department of Corrections' Security Coordinator. All Department of Corrections and law enforcement personnel assigned to implement this policy will be debriefed.

_____

SUPERINTENDENT

Florida State Prison

Special Post Order #100, Death Watch Supervisor

I.   Introduction

The duties and responsibilities of this post are that of observation and supervision of all activities concerning a condemned inmate(s) during pre-execution (Death Watch) monitoring. His duties are the general supervision and control of other security personnel assigned to monitor the condemned inmate during the time under death warrant to include preparation of the condemned inmate(s) prior to execution.

II.   General Duties and Responsibilities

This officer must be a Correctional Officer III or higher. He reports directly to the Superintendent, Assistant Superintendent for Operations or the Correctional Officer Chief IV. He will normally assume the Administrative Shift work schedule but may be required to work different hours as needed. During off duty hours he will remain on standby status unless relieved by the Correctional Officer Chief IV.

III.   Specific Duties and Responsibilities

A.   Immediate Action

1.   Upon notification of your assignment (normally when a death warrant reaches active stage), prepare to assume the duty schedule reflected above.

2.   Your post will be the first floor area leading into Q-1-East, or the Administrative Office area. You will assume authority of all personnel assigned to pre-execution monitoring (Death Watch).

3.   You will review the post orders for the Grille Gate and Cell Front Monitor to become familiar with all functions of subordinates.

4.   There may be two (2) Cell Front Monitors per shift assigned if there are more than two (2) condemned inmates awaiting execution, otherwise there will be one per eight hour shift and one relief.

5.   You will ensure that the condemned inmate upon reaching active death warrant status personally inventories and packs away all items he is not permitted to retain. The inmate, yourself, and one witness will sign the property

inventory. The inmate will be permitted to retain a copy of the inventory. The sealed property will be retained in storage on Q-1-E until ordered removed or surrendered to the inmate's designate.

6. You will ensure that all significant information is entered on the Supervisor's Log (long day book). All Persons Entering Q-1-east for Any Purpose, Will Sign in and Out, and you will keep a record of same. Form DC-36 will be maintained by the regularly assigned Grille Gate Monitor. Form 1038 will be annotated at fifteen minute intervals by the Cell Front Monitor.

7. You will prevent unauthorized traffic from entering the Q-1-East area. (See Special Post Order 101.)

8. You will ensure that sufficient clothing in the inmate's size is retained in the Q-1-East area to accommodate exchange each time the condemned inmate leaves his cell.

B. Subordinate Personnel

1. The Grille Gate Monitor and the Cell Front Monitor will be a Correctional Officer I or II who reports directly to you.

2. Ascertain the phone number and address of all subordinate personnel in order that they may be contacted after hours.

3. Subordinate personnel reporting to you will be in accordance with the number of condemned inmates on Death Watch:
    a. One inmate = one (1) Grille Gate Monitor per shift + one (1) relief = four (4)
    b. Two inmates = one Cell Front Monitor per shift + one (1) relief = four (4)
    c. More than two inmates = two Cell Front Monitors per shift + two reliefs = eight (8).

4. Cell Front Monitors and Grille Gate Monitors will be assigned hours as reflected in Appendix "A."

5. Ensure that all orders and instructions are read and understood by all subordinate personnel.

C. Routine Security Measures, Checks, Logs

    1. Maintain, or cause to be maintained (by Grille Gate Monitor), a "Supervisor's Log" (long day book) of activities.

    2. Personally supervise the feeding of *all* meals during your shift. Ensure that no inmates are utilized in the feeding of any meal during an active death warrant.

    3. Keep all unauthorized personnel out of the Q Wing first floor area unless he is housed there.

    4. Ensure that the security of the Q-1-East area is reported to the Control Room each half hour during active death warrant.

    5. Do not permit anyone to enter the condemned inmate's cell except by order of the Superintendent, Assistant Superintendent for Operations, or the Correctional Officer Chief IV. The only exception is a life threatening emergency.

    6. Ensure that the condemned inmate is handcuffed behind at any time he leaves his cell. He will remain handcuffed until he is returned to his cell. (He may be handcuffed in front while in the Maximum Security Visiting Park).

    7. Any time the inmate is moved, he will receive a double escort.

    8. At least one (1) officer will always remain in the Q-1-East area (Grille Gate Post) even if it is temporarily vacant.

    9. Ensure that the Q-1-East area is kept clean and orderly.

D. Property Items

    1. The condemned inmate may be permitted only the following items in his cell after his death warrant becomes active:

Bedding	Clothing
One mattress	One pair trousers (blue)
One pillow	One t-shirt (orange)
One pillow slip	One pair undershorts
One blanket	One pair socks
Two sheets	One pair shower slides
Toilet Articles	Comfort Items
One towel	One TV located outside cell (on stand)
One bar soap	One radio located outside cell (on stand)

One deck cards

One Bible

One book, periodical, magazine, newspaper (exchanges allowed)

2. Items not mentioned such as cigarettes, lighter, toothbrush, toothpaste, etc., will be distributed to the inmate as
needed and immediately returned if not consumable.

E. Telephone Calls, Interviews, Visits

1. Normally, the inmate will receive telephone calls from a
special extension plugged in at his cell location. When not
in use you will personally ensure its security.

F. Emergencies and Other Contingencies

1. If any employee is taken hostage he is without authority,
regardless of rank.

2. Ensure that fire extinguishers are readily available and in
serviceable condition. In all cases of fire, you are to consider the safety and accountability of all personnel and inmates in your area.

3. In the event of self-inflicted or other injury, take immediate and decisive action and contact the medical clinic immediately to send a physician.

4. Personally supervise the dispensing of any medication on a
single unit dosage basis.

5. Immediately notify the Correctional Officer Chief IV,
Assistant Superintendent for Operations, or Superintendent in the event of a medical emergency.

IV. Summary

This post order cannot cover every possible contingency. Apply good
judgment when decisions are necessary and time permitting, clarify
doubtful or unusual circumstances with the Correctional Officer Chief
IV, Assistant Superintendent for Operations, or Superintendent.

Do Not Discuss These Duties and Responsibilities with Anyone
Without Specific Authorization from the Correctional Officer Chief IV,
Assistant Superintendent for Operations or the Superintendent.

_____   _____

Colonel R. R. Music   R. L. Dugger, Superintendent

Next Review Date:

Florida State Prison

Special Post Order #101, Grille Gate Monitor

I.   Introduction

The duties and responsibilities of this post are in effect immediately upon notice of a signed Death Warrant and remain in effect until the warrant is stayed or the execution is carried out.

At the signing of a Death Warrant, the officer assigned this post will assume his duties. He is the only officer assigned to Death Watch monitoring until the warrant becomes active. Any temporary additional assistance needed will be provided by the appropriate shift supervisor or Correctional Officer Chief IV. This is a temporary post manned at the direction of the Superintendent, Assistant Superintendent for Operations, or the Correctional Officer Chief IV.

II.   General Duties and Responsibilities

This officer must be a Correctional Officer II or higher level officer. He reports directly to the Correctional Officer Chief IV, Assistant Superintendent for Operations, or Superintendent, at the beginning of pre-execution monitoring until relieved or until the execution is stayed or carried out. He will assume the shift schedule ordered by the Correctional Officer Chief IV as reflected by Appendix "A" attached. This officer essentially performs both the functions of Death Watch Supervisor and Grille Gate Monitor stationing himself behind the locked grille gate station entering Q-1-East.

III. Specific Duties and Responsibilities

A.   Immediate Action

1.   Upon notification by the Correctional Officer Chief IV or Assistant Superintendent for Operations, you will assume your duties and responsibilities as described herein and your Shift Supervisor will be alerted of your assignment.

2.   Begin maintenance of Death Watch Supervisor's log ensuring the recording of significant detailed information.

3.   Identify available security personnel through Shift Supervisor to assist with moving all condemned inmate(s) to Q-1-East. Personally supervise collection and movement of all inmate property items to Q-1-East.

4.   Identify assigned Death Watch personnel through the office of the Correctional Officer Chief IV or Assistant

Superintendent for Operations. Have the Control Room notify assigned personnel to report as scheduled.

5. The condemned inmate(s) will be escorted to the Asst. Superintendent for Operations' Office by the Correctional Officer Chief IV or his designate. When the inmate(s) leaves his cell, immediately confiscate all of his property and take it to the Death Watch area (Q-1-E) and lock it in the storage closet on Q-1-East. At the same time vacate Q-1-E-4, Q-1-E-5 and Q-1-E-6, making these cells clean and sterile of any items.

6. Retrieve Q Wing Key #27, 173, and Key 4, 5, 6 from the Control Room and follow key control memorandum (attached).

7. Personally inspect the cells mentioned in #5 above.

8. Notify the Correctional Officer Chief IV, Asst. Super-intendent for Operations, or the Superintendent when the cells are ready.

9. The condemned inmate will be escorted to the Q-Wing area and housed as follows after strip searching and ex-changing his clothing:

   a. If there is only one condemned inmate, house in Q-1-E-5, leaving 4 & 6 vacant.

   b. If there are two condemned inmates, house in 4 & 6 leaving 5 vacant.

   c. If there are three condemned inmates, house in 4, 5, and 6.

10. When the inmate returns, carefully and thoroughly inspect his property in his presence at his cell front. Surrender *all* the property to him with the exception of contraband items. Contraband items will be confiscated and the in-mate provided a receipt.

11. Begin the pre-execution monitoring schedule.

12. Familiarize yourself with these orders (with attachments) and those of your subordinates.

13. Your duty station will be the locked grille gate leading into Q-1-East. You will keep the keys in your possession except when needed by authorized persons.

14. During pre-execution monitoring the following persons are authorized to enter the Q-1-East area:

a. Superintendent

b. Asst. Superintendent for Operations

c. Asst. Superintendent for Programs

d. Correctional Officer Chief IV

e. Shift Supervisor or Asst. Shift Supervisor

f. Officers to assist in routine functions (i.e. showers, escort, shakedown) as authorized by Death Watch Supv. or Confinement Lieutenant

g. Confinement Lieutenant

h. Any medical or security personnel you deem appropriate in an emergency situation.

i. Prison Chaplain

15. You are responsible for the cleanliness of your area as well as the cell area during pre-execution monitoring.

B. Subordinate Personnel (Active Death Warrant)

1. The cell front monitor(s) will be a Correctional Officer 1 who reports directly to the Grille Gate Monitor. This post will not be filled until the Death Warrant becomes active.

2. The duty schedule for the cell front monitor(s) will be the same as reflected by Appendix "A."

3. The required number of cell front monitors will be determined by the number of inmates on Death Watch. The following circumstances will apply.

a. 1 or 2 condemned inmates = 1 monitor

b. 3 condemned inmates = 2 monitors

4. Obtain from each of the subordinate personnel his home phone number or location where he can be reached. In the event of unplanned absence, the Correctional Officer Chief IV, Asst. Superintendent for Operations, or Superintendent should be contacted to arrange a substitute. No annual leave or compensatory leave will be taken by personnel on this assignment except in emergency circumstances.

5. Ensure that proper logs are maintained by subordinates and review and initial them prior to your duty relief. Do not forward copies of the log entries unless requested.

C. Routine Security Measures, Security Checks and Logs

1. Keep an accurate chronological log of your activities.

2. Keep a sign in/out for every person who enters the grille gate or Q-1-East area for any reason.

3. Personally supervise the feeding of all meals. During active Death Warrant status no inmates may assist in the preparation or delivery of meal trays.

4. Ensure the inmate(s) is checked to determine his well being at least once per hour.

5. Maintain close surveillance of subordinate personnel.

6. Keep all unauthorized personnel out of the Q-Wing first floor area to include inmates, other employees or visitors.

7. Report the security of your post to the Control Room every thirty minutes.

8. Do not permit the inmate to leave his cell except by order of the Superintendent, Asst. Superintendent for Operations, or Correctional Officer Chief IV. The only exception is a life-threatening emergency.

9. During pre-execution monitoring do not permit any inmate access to Q-Wing, first floor, unless he is housed there, cleaning up or feeding. During active death warrant do not permit any inmate access to Q-Wing, first floor, unless he is housed there.

10. Form DC-36 will be maintained on the condemned inmate(s) by the regularly assigned Grille Gate Monitor. This log will be separate from other logs and will be a part of his permanent record.

11. Movement of Inmate: Personally ensure that the condemned inmate is handcuffed (behind him) at any time he leaves his cell. The handcuffs will not be removed when he is receiving no contact visits or media interviews, but may be placed in front.

12. When a condemned inmate is moved he will be escorted by two experienced officers designated by the Shift Supervisor.

13. While moving condemned inmates with signed death warrants, it will not be necessary to lock down all other inmate traffic. However, during active death warrant status, lock down of all other inmate traffic will be necessary.

14. Every effort will be made to avoid authorization of movement for two condemned inmates at the same time and

scheduling of social or legal visits will be handled accordingly. In the event it becomes necessary, the Q-Wing telephone visiting space may be utilized where surveillance of Q-1 East can be maintained simultaneously.

15. When the condemned inmate is moved from his cell, he will be searched and placed in different clothing. The same clothing may be reused until soiled so long as it is thoroughly inspected before reissuing it to him.

16. During pre-execution monitoring condemned inmates may enjoy routine canteen privileges to include those allowed in the Maximum Security Visiting Park. However, procedures must remain consistent with the provisions of III.D. 3.

17. Visiting—Unless otherwise directed, all visiting, except legal, will be non-contact and held in the Maximum Security Visiting Park.

18. Escort for visiting during pre-execution monitoring will be provided by two experienced Correctional Officers assigned by the Shift Supervisor.

19. Supervision of visiting for condemned inmates in pre-execution monitoring will be designated by the Shift Supervisor until the warrant becomes active and then all supervision will be assumed by the Death Watch Supervisor.

20. An accurate log of pertinent information to include names of each visitor, time of arrival and departure of each visitor and the inmate will be maintained by the officer assigned to supervise visiting. He will otherwise follow the spirit and intent of FSP 10P #72, Visiting Guidelines for the Maximum Security Visiting Park. The visiting hours and persons authorized will be determined by the Superintendent or Asst. Superintendent for Operations. Additionally, only one condemned inmate may utilize the Maximum Security Visiting Park at the time.

21. During all pre-execution monitoring the condemned inmate(s) will remain handcuffed while in the Maximum Security Visiting Park but may be in front during visit.

22. Visiting—Active Warrant—Unless otherwise directed, all visiting (legal, social, religious) will be non-contact and held in the Maximum Security Visiting Park.

23. Escort for the visiting and other movement from Q-1-East during an active warrant will be designated by the Death Watch Supervisor.

24. An accurate log of pertinent information to include names of each visitor, time of arrival and departure of each visitor and the inmate will be maintained by the Visiting Park Supervisor. He will otherwise follow the spirit and intent of FSP 10P #72, Visiting Guidelines for the Maximum Security Visiting Park with the following exceptions:

    a. The number of persons authorized and the visiting hours will be in accordance with specific instructions is-sued by the Superintendent or Asst. Superintendent for Operations.

    b. Allowable canteen items will be products in accordance with D.3.

D. Property Items and Privilege

1. Until the Death Warrant is active the condemned inmate may retain those property items brought with him to Q-1-East in his cell (excepting contraband items).

2. At the time the warrant becomes active the inmate must reinventory his property in the presence of the Death Watch Supervisor and pack and seal all property items ex-cept those listed below:

Bedding	Clothing
One mattress	One pair trousers (blue)
One pillow	One t-shirt (orange)
One pillow slip	One pair undershorts
One blanket	One pair socks
Two sheets	One pair shower slides
	One sweatshirt
Toilet Articles	Comfort or Personal Items
One towel	One television located outside cell
One bar soap	One radio located outside cell on stand
	One safety razor or shaving powder, issued only when needed
	One deck cards

One Bible

One paperback book, periodical, magazine, newspaper (exchange allowed)

One ballpoint pen

One pencil

One legal pad

One ream legal paper

3. The inmate may order and purchase with canteen coupons the following items while in death watch status:

    a. Canned colas (opened by officer and served in paper cup)

    b. Candy bars

    c. Cookies, crackers, potato chips

    d. Tobacco products (except matches)

    e. Heated sandwiches

    Note: All orders and deliveries inspected and delivered by officer. This includes removal of non-transparent candy wrappers, and sandwich wrappers. Care should be taken, however, to avoid handling of the contents except with napkin, tissue, etc.

E. Telephone Calls, Interviews

1. You may expect the condemned inmate to receive authorized telephone calls, media or other interviews while in pre-execution monitoring status.

2. Specific instructions for each interview or phone call will be given by the Superintendent, Asst. Superintendent for Operations, or the Correctional Officer Chief IV, and will be logged (no exceptions). You will ensure supervision of each phone call or interview.

3. You must ensure that the inmate receives a careful strip search after each interview to include an exchange of clothing and slides.

4. You must clear the interview/phone call area of all other inmate traffic.

5. Normally, the inmate will receive telephone calls from a special extension plugged in at his cell location. When not in use you will personally ensure its security.

F. Emergencies and Other Contingencies

1. If any employee is taken hostage he is without authority regardless of rank.

2. Ensure that fire extinguishers are readily available and in serviceable condition. In all cases of fire, you are to consider the safety and accountability of all personnel and inmates in your area.

3. In the event of self-inflicted or other injury, take immediate and decisive action and contact the medical clinic immediately to send a physician (if doctor not on site, the ranking medical person).

4. Personally supervise the dispensing of any medication on a single unit dosage basis.

5. Immediately notify the Correctional Officer Chief IV, Asst. Superintendent for Operations, or Superintendent in the event of medical emergency.

IV. Summary

This post order cannot cover every possible contingency. Apply good judgment when decisions are necessary and time permitting, clarify doubtful or unusual situations or circumstances with the Corr. Officer Chief IV, Asst. Supt. for Operations, or Superintendent.

Do Not Discuss These Duties and Responsibilities with Anyone Without Specific Authorization from the Corr. Officer Chief IV, Asst. Supt. for Operations or Superintendent.

_____   _____
Colonel R. R. Music   R. L. Dugger, Superintendent

Florida State Prison

Special Post Order #102, Cell Front Monitor

I.   Introduction

The duties and responsibilities of this post are in the direct supervision and monitoring of a condemned inmate's activities during the final days of pre-execution monitoring (Active Warrant).

This is a temporary post to be manned at the discretion of the Superintendent, Asst. Superintendent for Operations, or the Correctional Officer Chief IV.

II.   General Duties and Responsibilities

This officer may be a Correctional Officer I or higher ranking officer. He reports directly to the Grille Gate Monitor. He is posted in the area directly in front of Q-1-East 4, 5, and 6. He must remain alert on his post at all times maintaining direct observation of the condemned inmate. He may converse with the condemned inmate utilizing discretion in emotional areas. He will assume the assigned schedule as reflected in Appendix "A."

III.   Specific Duties and Responsibilities

A.   Immediate Action

Upon notification of your assignment, notify your shift supervisor for relief of your normal post.

Follow the instructions of the death watch supervisor and/or grille gate monitor and assume your assigned shift unless otherwise notified.

B.   Subordinate Personnel

None

C.   Routine Security Measures, Security Checks and Logs

1.   Maintain FSP 1038 "Officer Observation Recap of Condemned Inmate" at fifteen minute increments. (Copy attached). Give Form 1038 to the Grille Gate Monitor at the end of your shift.

2.   Closely observe the condemned inmate's activities and immediately report to the Grille Gate Monitor or Death Watch Supervisor any unusual circumstances or activities.

3. Ensure that all eating utensils and trays are not allowed to remain in the cell when not in use.

4. Remain posted at the cell front but do not hesitate to enter the condemned inmate's cell if circumstances warrant it.

5. The cell door key(s) will remain in the possession of the Grille Gate Monitor except as needed.

6. You may converse freely with the inmate but avoid opinionated or inflammatory statements. Do not discuss your personal feelings regarding the Death Penalty. Do not make promises to the inmate. All requests by the inmate not covered herein will be referred to the Superintendent, Asst. Superintendent for Operations, or the Corr. Officer Chief IV.

7. Do not leave your post unless properly relieved.

8. Visually inspect and thoroughly examine all items permitted into or out of the inmate's cell. Examine carefully all clothing sent to you from the Clothing Room.

9. Do a very thorough strip search of the condemned inmate any time he enters or exits his cell.

10. Exchange the inmate's clothing and slides any time he enters or exits the cell. The same clothing may be reused until it becomes soiled.

11. The condemned inmate will be handcuffed any time he is authorized to be removed from his cell.

12. Ensure that all post orders are being followed. It is expected that all Cell Front Monitors conduct themselves in a professional manner. A calm, mature atmosphere should be maintained.

13. You will be responsible for the daily cleanliness of your area and the cell areas. Normally the day shift will be responsible for sweeping and mopping the entire area, however, you will ensure that the area remains in a state of cleanliness and trash containers are emptied during your tour.

D. Property Items

1. The condemned inmate may be permitted only the following items in his cell:

Bedding	Clothing
One mattress	One pair trousers (blue)

One pillow	One t-shirt (orange)
One pillow slip	One pair undershorts
One blanket	One pair socks
Two sheets	One pair shower slides

Toilet Articles	Comfort Items
One towel	One TV located outside cell (on stand)
One bar soap	One radio located outside cell (on stand)
	One deck cards
	One Bible
	One book, periodical, magazine, newspaper (exchanges allowed)

2. Items not mentioned in #1 such as cigarettes, lighter, toothbrush, toothpaste, etc., will be distributed to the inmate as needed and immediately returned if not consumable.

3. Personally supervise and approve any exchange of items to or from the condemned inmate's cell. Any variation from the approved list of items in #1 and #2 must be approved by the Superintendent, Asst. Superintendent for Operations, or the Corr. Officer Chief IV.

E. Telephone Calls, Interviews, Visits

Follow the instructions of the Death Watch Supv. or Grille Gate Monitor in each specific incident.

F. Emergencies and Other Contingencies

1. If any employee is taken hostage he is without authority regardless of rank.

2. Fire extinguishers are readily available for your use at the Grille Gate Monitor station. In all cases of fire you are to consider the safety and accountability of all personnel and inmates in your area.

3. Notify the Grille Gate Monitor immediately in the event of a self-inflicted or other injury.

4. In a life-threatening emergency, take decisive action to include leaving your post to enter the condemned inmate's cell, if necessary.

Colonel R. R. Music   R. L. Dugger, Superintendent

Index

Abbgy, George, 103, 392; Tony Di-
Lisio and, 436; Ann and Walter
Garris and, 391; Anne Gehman
and, 393; investigation by, 19,
27; Outlaws and, 316; on Lyn-
wood Tate, 394
ABC News, 260, 261–62; Croft rape
case and, 241; on Tony DiLisio,
220; investigation by, 245
Abgney, Otha Lee: testimony of, 14
Acker, James R.: open letter and, 254
ACLU: and secret police report, 281
Alford/best interest plea, 493
Alibis, 32, 513
Altamonte Springs dump, 9, 212,
359
Alvarez, Nina, 218, 220; Croft rape
case and, 241
Amicus briefs, 170, 299, 304, 341
Amsterdam, Anthony G., 46, 88,
150; on court watchers, 139;
open letter and, 254
Anagnos, Aris and Carolyn: open
letter and, 254
Anderson, Gail, 171, 172, 180, 328,
346; *Miami Herald* and, 175;
oral argument and, 161–62; stay
and, 207

Anderson, John: open letter and, 254
Andrews, Tom: open letter and, 254
Angelou, Maya: open letter and, 254
Antiterrorism and Effective Death
Penalty Act (1996), 148, 219
A.O.A. *See* Association of Outlaws
America
Apel, Toni, 212; neuropsychiatric
workup by, 265; testimony by,
425
Appeals: direct, 41, 42, 252, 327,
395; waiving, 377
Appointment of counsel, motion for,
271–72, 294–96
Argersinger v. Hamlin, 338
Arlook, Ira: open letter and, 254
Asner, Edward: open letter and, 254
Association of Outlaws America
(A.O.A.), 174
Atkins, Philip, 379; death warrant
for, 402; execution of, 404, 405,
407–9

Baldus, David: open letter and, 254
Baldwin, Alec: open letter and, 254
Bandes, Susan: open letter and, 254
Bard, Rich: editorial by, 195
Barkett, Rosemary, 85–86, 88, 94,

107, 144; dissent by, 145; *Parker*
case and, 145

Barnard, Craig S., 56, 57, 63, 74,
76, 104, 105, 106, 107, 110,
150, 179; brief by, 49, 51; federal
constitutional law and, 46–47;
Francois case and, 71; hypothesis
of, 99–100; ninety-day grace
period and, 71; Spaziano and,
45, 48; *Randolph* case and, 474;
Sullivan case and, 95

Barstow, David, 430; on Griffin,
431–32

Basile, Paul: open letter and, 254

Baxter, Meredith: open letter and,
255

BDNMCB Law Firm: "The Best Defense No Money Can Buy," 397

Bedau, Hugo, 468; open letter and,
255; study by, 423–24, 504, 509,
510; testimony of, 116

Beerman, Joan Willens: open letter
and, 255

Beerman, Leonard: open letter and,
255

Belafonte, Harry, 268

Bergman, Marilyn and Alan: open
letter and, 255

Best interests, 493, 497–99

Biker gangs. *See* Motorcycle
brotherhoods

Biongiorno, Anthony, 295

Blackburn, Tom, 260

Blackmun, Harry, 141; on factual innocence, 139; *Herrera* case and,
142; *Spaziano* case and, 168, 186

Board of Clemency, 89, 320

Boniello, Rose Marie: open letter
and, 255

Boyd, Justice, 107, 110, 111; on
guilt, 182; Scharlette Holdman
and, 108

Brady rule, 399–400

Brady v. Maryland, 167, 399

Brainwashing, 24, 26, 251

Brennan, Justice: dissent by, 64

Brim, Frank: Tony DiLisio and, 389

Broner, Johnny: Harberts murder
and, 14

"Brother Nitro." *See* DiLisio,
Anthony Frank

Browne, Jackson: open letter and,
255

Buckhout, Robert, 27, 103; on hypnosis sessions, 28–29

Buckner, Brad: open letter and, 255

Bundy, Theodore "Ted," 1, 44, 52,
57, 71, 135, 252, 392, 443; execution of, 3, 91

Bundy case, 80, 195–96; hypnosis
and, 25, 68–69, 110; psychic
and, 392

Burger Court, *Brady* rule and, 399

Burr, Richard, 45; *Sullivan* case and,
94, 95, 96

Butterworth, Robert, 339; death
penalty and, 253; on Medina
electrocution, 402; open letter to,
250–53; *Spaziano* case and, 252

Camden, Patrick, 387

Capital punishment, xx, 4, 31, 91,
104, 413; abolishing, 46, 88,
406–7; as abstract moral/policy
issue, 443; assembly line, 419;
debate on, 1, 442, 497; human-
ization of, 225; as legal system,
xxii, xxiv, 170, 282; as liberal/
conservative issue, 2; madhouse
of, 160; Norman Mailer on, xix;
mitigating circumstances and,
113; moral issue of, xxii; opposition to, 1–2, 245–46, 502, 511,
514; as public policy, 512; ran-

domness of, 285; seminar on, 395–96; statute, 46, 112; support for, 83; vacating, 503, 504–9; writing about, 427

Capozolla, Richard, 249, 280; open letter and, 255; *Spaziano* case and, 225, 248

Carnes, Ed, 158, 285, 300, 328, 441; appeal to, 159; criticism of, 163–64; on habeas rules, 164; *Hitchcock* case and, 165; on mitigating circumstances, 166; motion denial by, 163, 167–68; on probable cause, 164–65; procedural rules and, 381; review by, xxi–xxii; *Spaziano* case and, 286

Carroll, Tanya, 105, 305, 334

Cary, Susan, 172, 239, 243, 244, 274

CCR. *See* Office of Capital Collateral Representative

Cells; death row, 98–99; deathwatch, 90, 99, 118, 277, 334, 408, 487; holding, 90–91, 334, 490

Certificate of Probable Cause, 165

Certiorari petitions, 42, 140; page limits for, 176; stays of execution and, 341

Chemerinsky, Erwin: open letter and, 255

Chicago murders, 295, 386–87

Chiles, Lawton, 154, 218, 220, 222, 231, 236, 298, 342, 354, 400; CCR and, 175–76, 413, 414; Chicago murders and, 387; clemency and, 198, 233, 248, 252, 266, 275, 358; Constitution Review Commission and, 478; *Cox* case and, 266; criticism of, 281, 361; death penalty and, 253, 443; death warrants by, 176, 180, 186, 219, 229, 230, 238, 250, 261, 275–79, 291, 297, 386, 397,

402, 404, 415, 432, 457, 477; Dexter Douglass and, 225; FDLE and, 223, 226; inadvertent cooperation of, 440, 441, 445; letter from, 210, 269–70; letter to, 214–17; Medina execution and, 410, 411; Minerva and, 417; open letter to, 247–48, 250–53, 267; *Orlando Sentinel* and, 287, 289, 291, 294; override and, 152; personal attack by, 273–74; pressure on, 228, 239, 248, 284, 287–90, 371; secret police report and, 276, 289, 386, 295, 401, 450; *Spaziano* case and, 205, 213, 221, 386; stays of execution and, 207, 210, 357–58, 368, 382; stroke for, 232–33; videotape and, 309

Chomsky, Carol: open letter and, 255

Chris (Outlaw), 58; letter to, 479–80

Cirincione, Diane V.: open letter and, 255

Civil contempt, 339, 372; threat of, 375, 376. *See also* Contempt of court

Civil disobedience, 370, 379; acts of, 377–78; contemplating, 375–77

Civil law, learning, 134–35

Clark, Katie: petition work and, 399

Clemency, 62, 198, 232, 233, 261, 275, 321, 323, 326; applying for, 153–57, 159, 175–76, 214–15, 216, 219, 221, 250, 271, 279, 358, 382; denying, 44, 292, 400; example of, 266; executive, 55, 59–60, 214–15, 271, 382, 395; granting, 43, 319–20, 398, 400; hearing on, 249, 252; innocent and, 338, 382; proceedings/ privacy of, 320; problems with,

266; purpose of, 196; Spaziano on, 61; support for, 219, 248

Clennon, David: open letter and, 255

Clients: lawyers and, 119–20, 122, 125; representing, 120

Cobb, Perry, 506

Cocounsel, 347, 351; CCR as, 375; problems with, 338

Code of Judicial Conduct, 384

Colbert, Douglas: open letter and, 255

Collins, LeRoy: death warrants by, 216–17

Commission for Review of Post-conviction Representation, 414

Contempt of court, 372, 375. *See also* Civil contempt

Convictions, 42; erroneous, 504–9

Cook, Kimberly: open letter and, 255

Coombs, Mary: open letter and, 255

Coon, Cynthia, 447

Coon, William, 447

Coppick, Mike: testimony of, 326

Coppick, William: testimony of, 17

Court files, 228, 237, 250, 376; battle over, 372–74; transferring, 306

Coyle, Marcia: on CCR, 418

CPC, 286; denial of, 148

Craig Barnard Hypothesis: testing, 99–100

Crapps, Thomas: letter from, 416–17

Credibility issue, 340, 359, 435, 437, 440, 448, 514

Criminal justice system: commitment to, xi; racism in, 403–4, 410

Crocker, Phyllis L.: open letter and, 255

Croft, Vanessa Dale, 19, 22, 49, 55, 202, 262, 295; identification problems for, 10–11; Outlaws and, 134; polygraph for, 207,

215; rape of, 5, 6, 9, 13, 20, 188, 251; skepticism about, 8; Spaziano and, 10–11, 12; testimony of, 6–8

Croft rape case, 439, 470; investigating, 488, 499; new trial in, 249; resolving, 495; sentence for, 493; trial files on, 241

Cruel and unusual punishment, 94, 139

Cruz, Rolando, 424, 506; framing of, 469, 502; release of, 467–68, 469

D'Alemberte, Talbot "Sandy," 297, 298; amicus brief by, 299, 304, 341; Leonel Herrera and, 141; open letter and, 253

Daniel, Larry, xxiv

Dante: admonition of, ix

DCA. *See* Fifth District Court of Appeals

Death chamber, 90–91, 93; staff at, 91

Death clerks, 2

Death penalty, 99, 362; imposing, 42, 47; legal system and, 497; life sentences and, 121; moral issue of, xxii; opposition to, 93, 100, 101, 442

Death penalty cases, 31; appealing, 360; judiciary's treatment of, 176

Death row, 4, 104; cells on, 98–99; described, xxvi, 48, 53, 54, 98, 481; media investigation of, 181; mistakes on, 225, 511; public defender office and, 83; transfer to/from, 90, 118, 207, 454–55

Death row inmates: backgrounds of, 127; described, 247; judicial contempt for, 177; lawyers and, 125; number of, 504; public defenders and, 119–20; released, 504–9; representing, 514

Death sentences, 45, 55, 104, 455; commutation of, 165, 249; imposing, 41, 46; innocent people and, xix; plea agreement and, 494

Death warrants, 48, 60, 99, 103, 104, 128, 479; end to, 487; holding off, 172, 442; litigating under, 44, 289–90, 297, 300, 306, 302, 335, 343, 349, 380, 404, 405, 426; press release about, 277–79; pressure of, 63, 124–25, 150, 267; secret police report and, 280; signing, xxii, 84, 86, 89, 118, 121–23, 137, 144, 145, 176, 183; 186, 208, 216, 229, 230, 238, 250, 275–79, 284, 291, 307, 312; 370, 386, 477; surviving, 169, 226, 227, 228

Deathwatch, 350, 498; first phase, 92; leaving, 207, 208; second phase, 92, 200, 201; transfer to, 104

Deathwatch cells, 99, 334, 408; moving to, 90, 277; transfer from, 118, 487

Deathwork, 88, 96, 104, 224, 369, 377, 380; First Amendment advocates and, 441–42; teaching about, 395–96; world of, xxiii–xxiv, 3, 87, 149

Delays, 169, 358, 360, 377, 420; postconviction process and, 83; reducing, 83

DeManio, Peter, 11–12, 261

Destro, Charles, 355, 356

Diamond, Bernard, 27, 103, 107; hypnosis and, 74; tape analysis by, 29

Dickerson, Sandra H., 224, 232, 261

Dickoff, Micki, 409; open letter and, 255

DiFonzo, J. Herbert: open letter and, 256

DiFrisco, Dominic: open letter and, 256

DiLisio, Angie, 263, 265

DiLisio, Anthony Frank "Tony," 23, 70, 73, 103, 233, 262; affidavit from, 331–34; CCR and, 176, 180, 193, 211, 223, 268, 314, 318, 321; clemency and, 219, 221; credibility of, 101, 183, 224, 316, 358, 359, 385–86, 400, 428, 430, 431, 433, 437, 440, 448, 472, 477; criticism of, 340, 467; drug abuse by, 21–22, 29, 436; dump visit and, 327, 328, 333, 359, 424; Keppie DiLisio Epton manipulation of, 23; evidentiary hearing and, 349–50, 351, 384; FDLE and, 215, 221, 235–36, 264–65, 310, 313–14, 319, 333, 346, 386, 443; framing conspiracy and, 263, 264; hypnosis of, 24, 26–29, 66, 74, 101, 103, 166, 188, 196, 200, 205, 365, 367, 391, 420, 431, 436, 467; importance of, 20, 472; investigation of, 192, 395, 430; locating, 46, 146, 186, 187, 318; lying by, 65, 103, 220–23, 308, 310, 317, 319, 339–40, 362, 364, 386, 389, 435, 481, 500; nickname of, 386; prehypnosis statement of, 28, 221–22; recantation by, xxii, 208, 218–20, 223, 234, 236, 238, 264, 300, 309–10, 314–16, 321, 324–25, 328, 331, 333, 339–40, 348, 349, 352, 359, 360, 363, 365, 368, 370, 381, 383–86, 399,

420, 423, 426, 430–32, 434,
440, 450, 452, 456–57, 466,
469, 502, 511; Joseph Spaziano
and, 51, 206, 209, 217, 242,
313, 315–16, 366, 393, 480,
484; Gerald Stano and, 58, 61;
testimony of, 6, 11, 17–25, 30,
102, 166, 182, 183, 196, 224,
235, 251, 261, 278, 324–25,
327, 359, 362–63, 367–68, 385,
389, 393, 400, 428, 435, 437,
439, 447–48, 452, 456–57, 459;
videotape and, 220, 267–68, 311,
323, 347, 348, 399; witness list
and, 483
DiLisio, Irene, 21
DiLisio, Keppie Epton, 11, 21, 423,
435–36, 459; Croft rape and, 10;
Lori Rozsa and, 483; Joe Spaziano and, 22, 23, 262, 263, 264,
270, 389; testimony of, 484;
Tony DiLisio and, 23, 436
DiLisio, Ralph, 21, 240, 262, 423;
Keppie Epton DiLisio and,
435–36; Spaziano and, 22,
263, 264, 270, 458
Direct appeal, 41, 42, 252, 327, 395
Disbarment, threat of, 372, 375, 377
Disciplinary Floor, 456
DNA testing, 447
Documentary Institute, 224, 232
Doherty, Pat, 135, 213, 214, 219,
220–21, 227, 229, 242; clemency
and, 221; on filing/Florida Su-
preme Court, 241; memo to, 285
Dostoyevski, Fyodor, 91
Double jeopardy, 405, 460
Douglass, Dexter, 218, 221, 236,
270, 272, 291, 311, 416; briefing
by, 222; Lawton Chiles and, 225;
clemency and, 233; Constitution
Review Commission and, 477,

478; court records and, 231;
criticism by, 274; death penalty
abolitionists and, 443; inadvertent cooperation of, 440, 441,
445; letter from, 292; Michael
Minerva and, 417; publicity and,
229–30; secret witnesses and,
340; Spaziano case and, 223;
videotape and, 235, 386
Dressler, Joshua: open letter and, 256
Dreyfuss, Richard: open letter and,
256
Drug Enforcement Administration,
search by, 373
Due diligence, 423, 434
Due process, 278, 371; denial of,
164, 473; executions and, 139;
right to, 437–38
Duthu, N. Bruce: open letter and,
250, 256
Dyckman, Martin, 207, 260; call to,
200; editorial/column by, 195
Dycus, Steve: open letter and, 250,
256

Eaton, O. H., Jr., 364, 369, 425,
471, 472, 474, 475; cocounsel
and, 485; criticism of, 451; Croft
rape case and, 423, 458, 459,
460; Tony DiLisio and, 365, 448,
450; evidentiary hearing and,
349–50, 426; investigation by,
448, 449; new trial order by, 380,
412, 433–38, 439, 445, 449, 450,
454–57, 462, 463, 466, 484; petition and, 401; Spaziano case
and, 464, 473; stay of execution
and, 379
Editorials and op-ed pieces, 354,
360–64; writing, 190, 191, 194,
195, 200, 245, 260, 279–80,
293, 514

Edwards, Linda H.: open letter and, 256

Ehrenreich, Nancy: open letter and, 256

Eighth Amendment, 166, 167

Electric chair, 93, 96, 97, 121, 402; development of, 405; location of, 98; malfunction of, 408; replacement of, 503

Electrocutions, 103; botched, 405–7, 409; constitutional challenge to, 64, 94; described, 90–91, 93; fear of, 498; first, 405; witnesses for, 202. *See also* Executions

Eleventh Circuit Court of Appeals. *See* U.S. Court of Appeals for the Eleventh Circuit

Ellis, Michael: testimony of, 17, 326

Emery, Diane G.: open letter and, 256

Enquist, William: on Tate, 395

Epton, Keppie. *See* DiLisio, Keppie Epton

Equal protection: executions and, 139

Ervin, Richard, 105, 107, 110; oral arguments and, 118

Ethics rules, 314, 329, 378–79, 414, 425. *See also* Legal ethics

Event Management, Inc.: press release by, 266–67

Evidence: circumstantial, 393; credibility of, 437; exculpatory, 145, 164, 176, 253, 283, 399, 400–401, 404, 463; mitigating, 112, 144, 164; newly discovered, 438, 510, 511; physical, 251, 510

Evidentiary hearings, 147, 301, 331, 346, 347, 349–50, 361, 362, 417, 440–41, 459; CCR and, 383; conducting, 335; criticism of, 367, 368, 372; under death warrants,

305, 335, 379, 380, 404, 405, 423, 426, 427; Tony DiLisio and, 384; forgoing, 375

Exculpatory evidence, 176, 399, 400–401, 463; disclosing, 253; discovering, 145; withholding, 164, 283, 404

Execution dates, 43, 44, 89

Executioners, 91; compensation for, 93; protocols for, 408

Execution guidelines, 91–92, 341, 517–63

"Execution Guidelines for Week of Active Death Warrant," 91–92, 520–32

Executions, xx, 3, 71, 88, 170, 208, 485 botched, 402, 405–7, 409, 411–13, 415, 509–10; changing method of, 96–97; delaying, 377; described, 92–94; holiday season and, 421; nonconsensual, 84; number of, 502; protocols for, 408; public, 407; reasonable doubt and, 361; rites of, 96; scheduling, 43, 44, 89; volunteering for, 377. *See also* Atkins, Philip; Bundy, Theodore; Electrocutions; Herrera, Leonel; Innocent persons; Stays of execution; White, Jerry

Execution squad, identifying, 92

Executive clemency, 395; applying for, 55, 59–60, 214–15, 271, 382

Fabares, Shelley: open letter and, 256

Fact-findings, 331, 381, 435; appellate review and, 403; killer, 336, 379, 421, 441, 458

Factual innocence, 381, 450; claims of, 139, 141, 238, 301–2, 410, 411, 495; clemency and, 382;

evidence of, 219, 237, 238; maintaining, 488, 493, 497–99. *See also* Innocence
Fair trial, right to, 437–38
Family dysfunction, 37–38, 127
Family history: gathering information on, 121–22, 124
Farnell, Crockett: on CCR, 418
Farrell, Mike, 268, 439, 457; open letter and, 247–50, 267, 280
Faulkner, William, 87, 149–50, 303
FBI: Richard Jewell and, 444–45; Outlaws and, 482; search by, 373
FDLE. *See* Florida Department of Law Enforcement
FDLE Report, 270, 276; Chicago murders and, 387; Tony DiLisio and, 388
Federal habeas corpus, 41, 45, 48, 141, 281, 395, 472; avoiding, 284, 285, 291; filing, 381; limiting, 219. *See also* Habeas corpus petition
Fiedler, Tom, 260
Fifth District Court of Appeals (Fifth DCA), 425, 469, 470, 472; appealing to, 288; criticism of, 473; Croft rape case and, 474, 475; PCA of, 471
Fink, Beverly: Laura Lynn Harberts and, 52, 390; Joe Spaziano and, 391; testimony of, 15–16, 260–62, 264, 389–93
Finnegan, Magda: open letter and, 256
Firestone, David: open letter and, 250, 256
First Amendment, 374, 445; deathworkers and, 441–42
Florida Bar Association: ethics hot line of, 293; problems with, 195–96; *Spaziano* case and, 191

Florida Clearinghouse on Criminal Justice, 83–84
Florida Constitution: clemency and, 233; reviewing, 477–78
Florida Constitution Review Commission, Douglass and, 477, 478
Florida Department of Law Enforcement (FDLE), 231, 425; botched case and, 269; CCR and, 268, 329; Lawton Chiles and, 223, 226, 287; Tony DiLisio and, 206, 207, 215, 221, 235–36, 264–65, 310, 313–14, 319, 333, 346, 386, 389; investigation by, 218–19, 222, 227, 234, 236, 274, 398, 399; new evidence by, 276; *Orlando Sentinel* and, 482; review by, 277, 278; secret report by, 228, 289, 294, 295, 296, 308, 358, 386, 484; videotape and, 211, 212, 215, 220, 223, 235–36, 264, 267–68, 309, 311, 313–14, 317, 331, 332, 399, 400, 443, 511; witnesses by, 482
Florida Ethics Rules, 314, 329
Florida Outlaws. *See* Outlaws
Florida Parole Commission, 266, 502
Florida State Legislature: CCR and, 87; lethal injection and, 503; public defender office and, 83
Florida State Prison (FSP), 64, 230, 233; death chamber at, 90–91; death row at, 98; described, 52–54; execution guidelines by, 341; mail from, 48; Outlaws at, 455, 461; Tony Spaziano at, 31, 454, 497; visiting, 334, 490–91
"Florida State Prison Institutional Operating Procedure Number 34," 533–41
"Florida State Prison Institutional

Operating Procedure Number 65," 542–48
"Florida State Prison Special Post Order #100, Death Watch; Supervisor," 549–52
"Florida State Prison Special Post Order #101, Grille Gate Monitor," 553–60
"Florida State Prison Special Post Order #102, Cell Front Monitor," 561–63
Florida Statutes. *See* Section 14.28; Section 922.11
Florida Supreme Court, 44, 118, 129, 299, 301, 341, 353, 360, 443; appeal to, 43, 48, 125, 126, 238, 284, 381, 455; *Bundy* case and, 68, 252; capital cases and, 113, 114; CCR and, 336, 344, 346, 348–49, 403, 413; civil contempt and, 376; court files and, 372, 373, 376; Croft rape case and, 458, 459; Tony DiLisio and, 333–34, 472; direct appeal and, 42; double jeopardy and, 460; FDLE investigation and, 236; firing by, 370, 375, 379, 383, 415, 421, 424; habeas corpus petition and, 145; *Hill* case and, 378; hypnosis issue and, 252; innocence claim and, 371–72; *Medina* case and, 410, 411–12; oral arguments before, 118, 161–62, 300–301, 305, 334, 338–39, 396; postconviction motions before, 238, 239, 241, 244, 248, 274, 380, 401, 475; pressure on, 287, 288, 292; *Randolph* case and, 474; recess for, 63, 86; sentences affirmed by, 84; shaming, 370–71, 373, 379; *Spaziano* case and, 30, 160, 191, 237, 282, 334–35, 441, 449–50, 451, 457; Joe Spaziano on, 453; stay of execution and, 117, 123, 144, 372, 379, 383, 466, 486; vacation for, 229, 245

Foreshadowing, distortion by, xxiii
Fourteenth Amendment: violation of, 30, 167
Foxworth, Robert: open letter and, 256
Framing, 262–64, 466, 469, 502
Frankfurter, Felix, 405–6, 464
Franklin, Bonnie: open letter and, 256
Freedman, Eric M., 356; open letter and, 249, 250, 256
Freedom of the press, 374, 441
Froomkin, Michael: open letter and, 256
FSP. *See* Florida State Prison

Gainesville Sun: Spaziano case and, 260
Galler, Linda: open letter and, 257
Garbage Dump Murders, 9–10, 390, 432
Garris, Ann, 391; Laura Lynn Harberts and, 16, 390
Garris, Walter, 17, 391; Laura Lynn Harberts and, 16, 390
Gassenheimer, Leandra: open letter and, 257
Gehman, Anne, 392, 393
Geimer, William S.: affidavit by, 424; open letter and, 257
Gelman, Sharon: open letter and, 257
Gillen, Laura, 155, 159, 190, 220, 222, 239, 241, 242, 279; Gene Miller letter and, 183; petition work and, 398, 399, 401
Ginsburg, Ruth Bader: *Jacobs* case and, 143

Givelber, Dan: open letter and, 257
Glover, Danny, 268; open letter and, 257
Goldstein, Anne: open letter and, 257
Gordy, John, 432
Gottlieb, Karen, 179, 180, 181, 187
Gould, Doug: petition work and, 399, 401
Graham, Bob, 67, 216, 219, 277, 287; CCR and, 413; clemency and, 60, 62, 196, 261; death warrants by, 63, 65, 68, 86, 89, 99, 121, 144, 279, 307; political calculus of, 288; postconviction motions and, 215
Grand juries, 465
Grassroots organization, 249
Greenburg, Jenny, 218, 245, 284, 285, 421
Gregory, John D.: open letter and, 257
Grier, Alan: open letter and, 257
Griffin, Mike, 221, 222, 223, 231; criticism of, 431; on Tony DiLisio, 228, 432; on Robert McGregor, 352; on *Miami Herald,* 432; news flash from, 225; *Orlando Sentinel* and, 432–33; on Outlaws, 432; press conference exchange with, 331; Russell dismissal and, 469; *Spaziano* case and, 228; videotape and, 220; on White execution, 407
Grisham, John, 91
Guilt, doubts about, xix, 114, 115, 182
Guilt/innocence phase, 100–101
Gumbleton, Thomas J.: open letter and, 257
Gurganus, Allan, 302
Gustat, Steve, 218, 284; investigation by, 272, 312, 424; memo to, 285; on Spaziano, 270; VLRC and, 330–31

Habeas corpus petition, 43, 48, 55, 146, 164, 167, 441; constitutional claims and, 141; filing, 145, 475, 502. *See also* Federal habeas corpus
Hall, J. J., 296
Harberts, Laura Lynn, 55, 99, 202, 250, 262, 276, 277, 279; dental records of, 14, 484; disappearance of, 13–14, 38, 51, 124, 201, 390, 391–92, 393; Beverly Fink and, 260–61, 390; identification of, 326; murder of, 5, 6, 14, 19, 20–21, 32, 100, 101, 295, 367, 386, 399, 456–57, 462, 464, 466, 483, 484, 488; psychic and, 393; remains of, 272, 278, 312, 359, 392; Tony Spaziano and, 19, 146; Gerald Stano and, 415; Joe Suarez and, 394–95; Lynwood Tate and, 394
Harberts murder case, 470; plea in, 493, 494–95, 497; retrial of, 30, 249
Hardee, JoAnn, 10, 11
Hells Angels, 8, 131, 132, 465; murders of, 387–88; Outlaws and, 470; postwar America and, 9; Joe Spaziano and, 38, 39, 40, 197
Herrera, Leonel, 139; certiorari grant for, 140; execution of, 141, 143; innocence claim of, 140; oral argument for, 142; representation for, 141; stay for, 140
Herrera case, 286, 287, 297, 320; factual innocence and, 141, 381
Hiasson, Carl, 260
Hidden memories, recovering, 24, 25

Hilberg, Raul, 445

Hill, Paul Jennings, 1, 175, 183, 378

Holding cells, 90–91, 334, 490

Holdman, Scharlette, 81, 88, 99, 104, 106–8, 110, 111, 150, 343; CCR and, 86, 418, 419; Clearing-house and, 83–84

Holland & Knight, 343, 353, 454, 455, 460, 471, 476; Croft rape case and, 448, 475; evidentiary hearing and, 401, 420, 421; *Miami Herald* and, 374; new trial order and, 440, 450; pro bono work by, 369, 451–52; representation by, 350–51, 379, 459; *Spaziano* case and, 368–69, 397–98, 427; Spaziano on, 466

Holmes, John, Jr., 92

Holmes, Warren, 192, 206, 343, 424, 444, 445; advocacy by, 189; court files and, 228, 374; Tony DiLisio and, 193, 204, 298; on Eaton/evidentiary hearing, 426; innocence claim and, 433; inter-rogation by, 333, 430; on Robert McGregor, 351–52; *Miami Her-ald* and, 431; Gene Miller and, 186; new trial order and, 439–40; on Pitts/Lee, 423; qualities of, 431; rape case and, 422, 458; skepticism of, 187–88; skull ses-sions with, 262–64; *Spaziano* case and, 188, 194, 195, 198–201; trust in, 289

Hoover (undercover cop): Croft and, 10

Horkan, Tom, 105, 106, 107, 109, 110, 173, 199; clemency and, 162; Florida Catholic Conference, 162, 218

Hubbart, Phillip, 474

Hughes, Jerry: criticism by, 355

Hummell, Mike, 268, 313–14; Tony DiLisio and, 186, 212, 310, 336

Hypnosis, 136, 166, 183, 200, 206, 278; audiotapes of, 66, 184; criti-cism of, 24–27, 29–30, 68–69, 74, 101, 103, 110, 112, 113, 167, 176, 180, 188, 196, 205, 251–52, 364, 366, 367, 436–38, 473; cross-examination and, 30; described, 26–27; police, 69, 103, 188, 251

Identification, problems with, 466

Inmates. *See* Death row inmates

Innocence: claims of, 179, 238, 302, 371–72, 412, 433; defining, xix; evidence of, 510; proving, 512–13. *See also* Factual innocence

Innocent persons, 463; clemency and, 338; execution of, xix, 139, 141, 142, 143, 283–84, 469, 513; freeing, xix

Investigations, 121, 125, 280, 322–23; conducting, 122–23; independent, 227; limiting, 122; postconviction, 88–89, 251; pre-sentence, 145

Investigators, paying, 294–96

Italian-American Association, *Spazi-ano* case and, 225

Italian Americans: Lawton Chiles and, 269; *Spaziano* case and, 225

Jacobs, Steven: open letter and, 257

Jailhouse snitches, 481, 482, 483

Jampolsky, Gerald G.: open letter and, 257

Johnson, James, 106–7, 110, 111

Judd, Mary Smith: on Michael Minerva, 417

Judicial review, 83, 282

Juries, death-qualified, 460
Jurors: affidavits by, 116, 424; contacting/questioning, 100; criticism by, 251, 284, 354–55
Jury overrides, 46, 144, 168, 284, 471
Justice: delaying, 358; miscarriages of, 143; pursuing, x, 377
Justine, Jerry, 63, 66, 103; described, 26; Tony DiLisio and, 30, 46, 180, 186, 187; hypnosis tapes and, 27

Kahn, Peter L.: open letter and, 257
Kasem, Casey: open letter and, 257
Kendall, Carson: testimony of, 15
Kendall, George, 146, 284
Keppler, Mike: death chamber staff and, 91
Kilpatrick, James Jackson, 367, 439; capital punishment and, 443; editorial by, 201, 260; Gene Miller and, 192; *Spaziano* case and, xxii, 442–43
Kirkland, Edward, 56, 70, 71, 74, 82, 105, 113, 261; deposition by, 10; executive clemency, 59–60; tapes and, 27; trial files of, 106
Kletter, Richard: open letter and, 257
Kogan, Gerald, 144; concurring opinion by, 438; dissent by, 145, 362; on guilt, xix; *Parker* case and, 145
Kozinski, Alex, 97, 98
Krieger, Stefan H.: open letter and, 257
Krop, Harry, 33–34, 107
Kucar, Emily, xvi

Lakeland Ledger: and *Spaziano* case, 260
Lanier, Charles S.: open letter and, 257

Last meal, 92
Laurie, Piper: open letter and, 257
"Law of Newly Discovered Evidence and Recanted Testimony, The," 434
Lawry, Matthew, 171, 218, 280, 284, 285, 348
Lawyers: appellate, 340–41, 451, 473; clients and, 119–20, 122, 125; condemnation by, 127; death-row, 358; defense, 465, 510; delays by, 358; postconviction, 25, 26, 119–21, 169, 170, 306, 308, 376, 414, 510; role of, 119
Lawyer's Committee for Freedom of the Press: secret report and, 281
Legal ethics, x, 120, 125, 338, 396, 397; questions about, 293; teaching, 215. *See also* Ethics rules
Legal system, 484; death penalty and, 497; failure of, xxii
Leidig, Elmer: corroboration by, 385–86
Lemmon, Jack: open letter and, 258
Lethal injection, 96, 97, 503
Letter-writing campaign, 245. *See also* Open letter
Lewis, John: open letter and, 258
Life imprisonment, 47, 99, 100, 123, 129, 166, 249, 470; death penalty and, 121; doubts and, 115
Litigation: death warrant, 302, 305, 335, 379, 380, 404, 405, 423, 426, 427; expenses, 281; piecemeal, 215; postconviction, 176, 301–2; stages of, 41, 42 (exhibit)
Lock down, 90
Lorenzana, Lena: affidavit by, 424

Maguigan, Holly: open letter and, 258
Mailer, Norman, xix

Maines, Ronald D.: open letter and, 258

Mallen, Jack: Beverly Fink and, 15, 16; on Laura Lynn Harberts, 52; testimony of, 16–17, 389–92

Malpractice suits: preparing for, 513

Mann, Abby, 501

Marshall, Thurgood, 64, 94

Martindale, James, 391, 436

Martinez, Bob, 138, 216, 277; death warrants by, 144, 145, 279

Marx, Robert: open letter and, 258

McCarthy, Colman, xxii, 260, 367, 439

McCawly, Joe, 212; hypnosis by, 27, 200, 420, 431

McClain, Martin J., 180, 345–46, 420; criticism of, 229; letter to, 211–12, 268–69; oral argument and, 161; *Spaziano* case and, 214

McDonald, Parker Lee, 111, 114; CCR and, 413, 414; jury override and, 144; *Parker* case and, 145

McDonald Commission, 414; CCR and, 413, 415, 418

McGovern, George: open letter and, 253

McGraw, Kelly, 209, 220, 242; affidavit and, 332; clemency and, 219; Tony DiLisio and, 311

McGraw, Sally, 332, 333, 349–50

McGregor, Robert, 100, 101, 108, 109, 112, 123, 165, 349, 350, 441; death penalty and, 99; on Tony DiLisio, 327, 383, 384; evidentiary hearing and, 383, 413; fact-findings by, 336, 351, 381, 384; Mike Griffin on, 352; Warren Holmes on, 351–52; jury override by, 471; legal technicalities and, 238; mental evaluation and, 124; mitigating circumstances and, 166; postconviction

motions and, 102, 111, 117–18, 238, 335; recusing of, 384, 440; James Russ and, 351; sentencing by, 389; *Spaziano* case and, 21, 384; stays of execution and, 105, 380, 381

McKinnon, John; investigation by, 446–47; on oral argument, 451; on Overton, 451–52

McNeil, Patrick: criticism by, 355–56

Mcthenia, Andrew A.: open letter and, 258

Media, 229, 350, 457; Lawton Chiles and, 248; distrust of, 180; poisoning, 512, 513; post-conviction cases and, 370, 512–13; public defenders and, 178–79; *Spaziano* case and, 442, 462; technicalities and, 513; treatment for, 178–79

Medina, Pedro, 402, 410–13, 415

Mello, Deanna L. Peterson, 175, 190, 191, 209, 222, 232, 233, 237, 239, 240, 144, 246, 261–62, 275, 279, 281, 294, 297, 298, 299, 303–6, 421, 422; death warrant and, 297; editorial by, 195; Farrell and, 248; open letter and, 258; oral argument and, 333, 334; plea bargain and, 489; public support and, 265; on videotape, 264

Merrill, Rosie, 462

Meyer, Gregg: open letter and, 258

Miami Herald, 175, 234, 298, 305, 367; bulletins from, 429; capital punishment and, xx; CCR and, 181, 350, 351; Lawton Chiles and, 274, 338, 357–58; court files and, 231, 306, 373; coverage by, 232, 429; criticism by, 421; criticism of, 180, 228; Croft rape

case and, 495, 499; on Ralph Di-
Lisio, 21; Tony DiLisio and, 204,
220, 311–12, 318, 352, 365, 366,
385, 400, 430; editorials in, 178,
195, 245, 293, 362–64, 473; on
Fink/Mallen testimony, 390; firing and, 370; Harberts murder
and, 13, 441; Holland & Knight
and, 374; Warren Holmes and,
431; investigation by, 189, 190,
216, 232, 248, 289, 308–9, 318,
325, 339, 347, 386, 389, 392,
443–46, 466; jurors in, 354, 355;
Robert McGregor and, 383, 384;
memo to, 294, 458; new trial
order and, 439, 463; on oral argument, 451; plea bargain and,
488–90, 492–95; relations with,
246, 281; resistance by, 374;
secret police report and, 280;
Spaziano case and, 1, 3, 20, 160,
180, 181, 184, 186, 187, 191–95,
198, 199, 201, 206, 217, 222,
260, 281, 283, 350, 351, 432,
444, 512; stays of execution and,
210; VLRC demise and, 299
Millemann, Michael, 155, 159, 254,
422, 439
Miller, Fuzzy, 460–61, 466, 470,
491, 503; plea bargain and, 489;
on retaliation, 469. *See also*
Outlaws
Miller, Gene, 207, 219, 274, 290,
343, 345, 351, 401, 431, 444,
457, 463, 474, 485, 486; advocacy by, 189; contacts by, 181–82,
185, 192; court files and, 228,
229, 237, 374; Croft rape case
and, 422, 423, 424, 458, 475;
Tony DiLisio and, 204; editorial
by, 190, 191, 194, 195; framing
conspiracy and, 264; habeas
corpus litigation and, 281; on

Warren Holmes, 430; innocence
claim and, 433; investigation
and, 185; letter to, 182–83, 186,
195–96, 458, 471–72; on Robert
McGregor, 350; new trial order
and, 433, 439; Pitts/Lee and,
420; plea bargain and, 488, 489,
495, 497, 499; on Tony Proscio,
354; Lori Rozsa and, 201, 421;
on James Russ, 484; skepticism
of, 179, 187; *Spaziano* case and,
180, 184, 186, 187, 193, 194,
199; stay and, 209; support from,
241, 289; witness list from, 483
Milyak, Kim: criticism by, 355
Minerva, Michael J., 214, 268, 335;
affidavit by, 346–48; CCR and,
342, 345–46, 349, 416, 418,
420; letter to, 210, 352–53,
415–17; resignation of, 417; on
Spaziano case, 342, 346; *Stano*
case and, 416
Miranda rights, 139, 301
Miscarriages of justice, 143, 468–69
Mitigating circumstances, 144; capital sentences and, 113; nonstatutory, 112, 114, 164, 165,
166; statutory, 145, 166
Moore, James T.: letter to, 269–70
"Motion for Rehearing and Reconsideration and Stay of Execution," 337–39
Motorcycle brotherhoods, 4–5, 8–9,
82, 131, 200, 354; preconceptions of, 342; Spaziano and, 38,
39, 114, 197. *See also* Hells
Angels; Outlaws; Pagans;
Warlocks
Muller, Chandler R., 280; open letter
and, 258

National Law Journal, xxii, 418
Necrodentistry, xxiii, 446–47

Nicholas, Denise: open letter and, 258
Ninety-day grace period: end of, 65–66, 68, 71
No contest plea, 488, 497–99
Nolo contendere. *See* No contest plea

Obstruction of justice, 314, 512
O'Connell, Bill, 437
Office of Capital Collateral representative (CCR), 52, 81, 100, 102, 110, 136, 160, 174, 191, 276, 314, 514; *Atkins* case and, 409; budget for, 282, 419–20; caseload at, 87, 88, 125, 346; clemency and, 219; as cocounsel, 375; conflict of interest for, 271, 313–14, 321, 335, 338, 415; court files and, 306, 372–75; creation of, 83; criticism of, 150, 178, 235, 245, 290, 352, 404–5, 413–15, 418, 450; Croft rape case and, 207; Tony DiLisio and, 180, 193, 205–6, 211, 223, 268, 314, 318, 321; dissolution of, 413, 414, 417, 418–19; ethics of, 413–14; evidentiary hearing and, 350, 372, 383; FDLE and, 268, 329; Florida Supreme Court and, 336, 344, 346, 348–49, 403, 413; investigation by, 213, 234, 318, 319; *Miami Herald* and, 181; oral argument and, 161; pressure tactics of, 223; problems with, 170, 195–96, 234, 328, 329–30, 336, 337, 343–49, 361, 368, 396, 425; *Spaziano* case and, 170, 192, 209, 212, 227, 230, 239, 293, 320, 338, 342, 346–51, 371–72, 383, 397, 398, 413, 424; *Stano* case and, 415, 417; statutory duties of, 282; support from, 326, 347; training session for,

149; *White* case and, 402, 403, 404, 410; working at, 84–87, 89, 99, 137, 282–83
O'Keefe, Michael: open letter and, 258
Olive, Mark, 81, 99, 105, 106, 108–10, 128, 150, 159, 217, 220, 241, 242, 245, 422; admiration for, 129; call from, 195; capital postconviction work of, 369, 370, 426, 433, 439; CCR and, 86, 416, 418, 419; Tony DiLisio and, 187; Leonel Herrera and, 140, 141; memo to, 285, 291; oral arguments and, 111, 117, 118; representation by, 342, 343, 350–51; *Spaziano* case and, 107; Stano and, 415, 416; on stopping executions, 344
Olmos, Edward James: open letter and, 258
Open letter, 247–53, 260, 280; signatories of, 253–60
Oral arguments, 161, 297, 300, 305–7, 332, 333, 337–39, 396, 451, 452, 471, 473; audiotape of, 334; preparing, 303, 304–5
"Order Vacating Judgment and Setting Trial Date," 434–38
Organic personality syndrome, 33–34
Orlando Outlaws. *See* Outlaws
Orlando Outlaws clubhouse, 129–30, 131, 134
Orlando Sentinel, 221, 222, 225, 232, 322, 400; CCR and, 350, 352; Lawton Chiles and, 287, 289, 291, 294, 432; clemency and, 219; court files and, 228, 231; criticism by, 421, 431; criticism of, 360, 465; death warrant news and, 276; on Tony DiLisio, 385, 433; editorial in, 195, 200,

279–80, 358–60; FDLE and, 294, 482; firing and, 370; front-page story in, 341–42; Mike Griffin and, 432–33; on Laura Lynn Harberts's disappearance, 13–14; inadvertent cooperation of, 440, 443–45; interviewing with, 244; Robert McGregor and, 380, 384, 440; memo and, 293–94; on Outlaws, 5, 8, 130, 342, 430; plea agreement and, 494, 495; press conference and, 331; Tony Proscio and, 364; Dorothy Russell's dismissal and, 469; secret police investigation and, 276, 450; *Spaziano* case and, 191, 228, 291–92, 295, 350, 429, 444, 445, 446, 481, 512; on state's witnesses, 482; on Gregg Thomas, 475; videotape and, 220, 236; on White execution, 407

Outlaws, 22, 64, 175, 200, 206, 263, 274, 283; Abbgy and, 316; breaking codes of, 482; charges against, 354, 356, 470; chivalry of, 130–31; crimes against, 355–56; Vanessa Croft and, 8, 10; described, 5, 9, 127, 132; Tony DiLisio and, 385, 428, 480, 484; dumping by, 312, 326; FBI and, 482; fear/loathing of, 342, 431; fights with, 128, 131; at Florida State Prison, 455, 461; Mike Griffin on, 432; Hells Angels and, 470; leaders of, 461; letters from, 107; *Orlando Sentinel* and, 430; plea agreement and, 491, 492; police and, 82, 131, 133; relations with, 130, 342; Joe Spaziano and, 5, 32, 38, 40, 121, 122, 146, 174, 182, 183, 197,

201–3, 223, 227, 242, 243, 251, 265, 283, 287; visiting, 129–30, 131, 491; Yannotta and, 387. *See also* Miller, Fuzzy
Overton, Ben, 326, 331, 332, 451–52, 467

Pagans, 9, 387
Page limits, 176, 177; problems with, 397, 398
Palm Beach Post, Spaziano case and, 260
Paludan, Phillip Shaw, 119, 131–33, 211
Pancake, John, 193
Pardons, 233, 248
Parker v. Dugger, 145, 166
Parloff, Roger: on *Spaziano* case, 367–69
Parole, 266, 502
PCA. *See* Per curiam affirmance
Peck, Gregory: open letter and, 258
Penalty phase, 101
Per curiam affirmance (PCA), 469, 471
Perjury, 435, 438, 467
Perkins, Paul, xvi
Personal history, gathering, 120–21
Peterson, Deanna L. *See* Mello, Deanna L. Peterson
Peterson, Elizabeth, 237, 422; open letter and, 258
Petition Groups, 398
Pillsbury, Sarah: open letter and, 258
Plea agreement, 495, 497–99; accepting, 491, 492–93, 496; death sentence and, 494; mulling over, 487, 488–89, 490; Outlaws and, 491, 492
Political environment, 229, 249, 288
Postconviction cases, 43–46, 104; media and, 370, 512–13; myster-

ies of, 46; power and, 370; strategy for, 120

Postconviction lawyers: evidence and, 510; professional distance and, 119–20; resistance by, 169, 170, 306, 308, 376, 414; work of, 25, 26, 120–21, 376

Postconviction motions, 102, 103, 117–18, 121, 123, 144, 145, 238, 239, 242, 316; denial of, 335; filing, 124, 335

Postconviction process, 41, 87, 169, 176, 301–2, 319, 418; delays and, 83

Postponements, indefinite, 360. *See also* Delays

Potter, Mark, 232; on Chiles/FDLE, 226; Tony DiLisio and, 218

Prejean, Helen: open letter and, 258

Press release, pro bono, 266–67

Prisons: control room, 54; "grand central station," 54; visiting, 52–54, 490. *See also* Death row; Florida State Prison; Union Correctional Institution

Prison personnel, 67, 408

Probable cause, 165

Procedural detail, x, 176–77, 238

Professional responsibility, 119–20, 125; violation of, 414

Proscio, Tony, 260, 289, 305, 365, 424; criticism by, 366; Tony DiLisio and, 298; editorial by, 354, 363–64; on *Spaziano* case, 1

Protess, David: open letter and, 258

Psychiatric evidence: gathering, 121–22, 124

Psychic, and Spaziano investigation, 392

Psychological tests, 33, 34

Public defender office, 128, 230; criticism of, 290; death row and, 83; Florida State Legislature and, 83

Public defenders, 1, 4, 230, 300, 304, 361, 479; appellate, 129; clients and, 119–20; problems with, 404; reporters and, 178–79

Public humiliation: vogue for, 371

Punishment: accepting, 378; coercion and, 375; erroneous, 509–10

Racism, prosecutorial, 403–4, 410

Radelet, Michael, 92, 93, 109, 208, 379, 439, 467, 468, 476, 477; study by, 423–24, 504, 509, 510; testimony of, 116

Raitt, Bonnie: open letter and, 258

Reasonable doubt, 301, 463; executions and, 361; guilt and, 114, 115

Rebuttals, 319, 320

Recantation, 381, 469; evidence of, 438

Rehearings: motion for, 244, 248, 336, 337–39, 347, 378, 473–74; thoughts on, 471–73

Rehnquist Court, 143, 169, 285, 286; *Brady* rule and, 399

Renz, Jeffrey T.: open letter and, 258

Resentencing, 102, 165, 359, 409

Resistance, 169, 170, 374, 376

Responsibility, 397; placing, 228, 239, 248, 284, 287–90; professional, 119–20, 125, 414

Retrials, 30, 102, 249, 463, 464; denying motion for, 448

Retribution, code of, 132–33

Reynolds, Timothy: open letter and, 258

Ridlon, Ian, xvi

Rintels, David W.: open letter and, 259

Riskin, Victoria: open letter and, 259
Rivera, Geraldo, 293, 350, 480
Robinson, Phil Alden: open letter and, 259
Roen, Sam, 18–19
Rogers, Marianne: open letter and, 259
Roper, Margene, 327; answer briefs and, 158; *Spaziano* case and, 301, 319–26
Rosenberg, Grant: open letter and, 259
Ross-Leming, Eugenie: open letter and, 259
Rozsa, Lori, 208, 217, 220, 239, 240, 243; bulletins from, 429; case files and, 228; on Chiles/stay, 357–58; clemency and, 221; court files and, 229, 237, 374; criticism of, 228; Croft rape case and, 423, 458, 499; Tony DiLisio and, 202, 204–6, 270, 298, 318, 352, 366, 385; Keppie Epton and, 483; FDLE report and, 226; Fink testimony and, 260–61, 262; framing conspiracy and, 264; on Anne Gehman, 393; on Harberts murder case, 13; innocence claim and, 433; investigation by, 232, 244–45, 386, 389, 392, 425–26, 446–47; Fuzzy Miller and, 461; new trial order and, 440; plea bargain and, 488, 489, 495; skill/determination of, 365; *Spaziano* case and, xxii, 192–95, 198, 199–201, 223; on state's witness, 482; stay and, 207, 357–58; support from, 201, 241, 289; Lynwood Tate and, 218; "Ticking" story of, 472; on VLRC demise, 299; witness list and, 483
Rule 3.850 motion, 45, 105, 106, 108, 111; considering, 475; denying, 473; described, 42–43, 44; filing, 102, 289, 308, 312, 313, 324–27, 335, 423, 458, 459
Rule 29-1, 165
Rules of Executive Clemency, 270; Rule 16 of, 269
Russ, James, 343, 426, 454, 455, 465, 471, 473, 474, 486, 487; award for, 452; cocounsel for, 485; Croft rape case and, 448, 475, 476; hearing and, 401; McGregor and, 351; motions by, 484; new trial order and, 440, 450, 463; plea bargain and, 488, 492, 494, 495, 496, 497; postconviction motion by, 447, 448; pro bono work by, 369, 451–52; *Spaziano* case and, 427, 452; Spaziano on, 466, 477
Russell, Dorothy, 460, 471; criticism of, 473; Croft rape case and, 449; fact-findings by, 458; motion denial by, 448, 449; postconviction challenge dismissal by, 469; refuting, 472; James Russ and, 448
Rust-Tierny, Diane: open letter and, 259
Ruzow, Elyse, 397, 398, 399, 401

Sachs, Stephen H.; civil law and, 134; open letter and, 254
St. Petersburg Times: CCR and, 350; criticism by, 421; editorials in, 195, 360–62; firing and, 370; on Mike Griffin, 431–32; investigation and, 216, 227; jurors in, 354–55; memo and, 294; secret police report and, 280; *Spaziano* case and, 191, 199, 200, 260, 350, 430
Salerno, Ralph, 446

Sammons, Jack L.: open letter and, 259

Sapolsky, Robert: on electric chair/ lethal injection, 96

Saxon, Ed: open letter and, 259

Schlakman, Mark, 222–23, 284, 330; clemency and, 266; on FDLE, 269, 272

Schlup v. Delo, 142–43, 163, 167, 286

Search warrants, 140, 373

Secret police report, 276, 289, 386, 400, 401, 450, 484, 511; challenging, 281, 399; death warrants and, 280; obtaining, 277

Section 14.28 (Florida Statutes), 269, 270

Section 922.11 (Florida Statutes), 89

Separation of powers, 400

Shaming penalties: vogue for, 371

Sharp, G. Kendall, 285, 286, 381, 441; rebuke by 147–48

Shaw, Leander, 110, 312

Shipman, Tanja, 397, 398

Simon, Jonathan: open letter and, 259

Singer, Robert: open letter and, 259

Sireci, Butch, 85; death warrant for, 127; letter from, 514–15; stay for, 128, 134

Sixth Amendment, violation of, 30

Smith, Stacy: open letter and, 259

Smith v. Balcom, 115

Sons of Italy, 249, 261, 280, 439; open letter and, 253; *Spaziano* case and, 225, 245, 248

Spaziano, Joseph Robert "Crazy Joe": affidavit by, 497–99; artwork of, 56, 64, 65, 70, 75, 152, 154, 157, 158, 334; auto accident, 32–39, 40; brain damage/ paralysis for, 32–36, 38; Chicago murders, 295, 386–87; conviction of, 5–7, 12, 14, 20–21; described, 18–19, 31; family life of, 31–32, 37–38, 39, 191, 197; D.R. (prison disciplinary infraction), 66–67, 69; Hells Angels, 38–39, 197; innocence of, xx–xxi, 499–500; letters from, 49–51, 55–63, 65–67, 69–82, 136–39, 150–51, 153, 157, 158, 170–72, 217–18, 224–25, 230–33, 239–43, 261–62, 352–53, 453–56, 465–66, 476–77, 479–80, 486; "Maintaining My Innocence/Best Interest" Statement, 497–99; meeting, xxiv, 26, 47–48, 54–55, 64; psychiatric evaluation, 33, 124; self-image of, 35–36. *See also* Death warrants; Outlaws

Spaziano, Linda, 212, 486; marriage to, 39–40; on rape conviction, 12–13

Spaziano, Mary Noel, 12, 77, 82, 114, 465

Spaziano, Michael, 483

Spaziano, Robert (Bobby): on Joe/ accident, 36–37

Spaziano, Rose, 12, 58, 483; Joe and, 31–32; letter from, 344

Spaziano, Tommy, 36, 67, 483

Spaziano v. Florida, 457, 467

Stafman, Ed, 125, 126, 136, 151, 170–71, 234; CPC application and, 148; motion by, 159; *Spaziano* case and, 146

Stano, Gerald, 55, 60, 62, 70, 413; CCR and, 234, 417; confession by, 51, 52; death warrant for, 415, 416–17; Tony DiLisio and, 58, 61; execution of, 415, 485; Harberts murder and, 52, 415

Stays of execution, 98, 102, 105, 112–13, 123–24, 127–28, 140, 146, 207, 209–10, 297, 301, 305, 307–8, 318, 324, 342, 360–63, 372; certiorari and, 341; Lawton Chiles on, 357–58; denial of, 117, 216, 381, 382, 383; dissenters for, 411–12; granting, 26, 144, 353, 367, 368–69; indefinite, 353, 362, 379; motion for, 252, 327, 337–39, 340

Stevens, John Paul, 174; dissent by, 168; *Jacobs* case and, 143; *Spaziano* case and, 47

Strategies, 120, 377; high-risk/low-risk, 227; mapping, 302; novel, 281–82, 289–90, 304

Students: petition work by, 397–98, 400–401; as research assistants, 396

Suarez, Joe, 17, 212, 215, 483; arrest of, 13; Harberts and, 15, 16, 390, 394

Suicide watch, 81, 92, 160

Sundby, Scott E.: open letter and, 259

Tactical issues, 120, 122

Tampa Tribune; on FDLE report, 226; jurors in, 354, 355; *Spaziano* case and, 260

Tarbert, David: open letter and, 259

Tate, Lynwood, 13, 212, 215; Laura Lynn Harberts and, 394–95; interview of, 218; polygraph for, 394

Technicalities, 117–18, 252, 382, 401, 466; dealing with, 241; getting off on, 176, 463, 511; invoking, 238; media and, 513; procedural, 237

Tedder rule, 166, 459

Testimony: hypnotically refreshed, 24–25; recantation of, 434, 435; tainted, 438

Texas Court of Criminal Appeals, Leonel Herrera and, 140

Thayer, Steve, 226, 247; on botched executions, 406–7; on electric chair, 402

Thomas, Gregg, 353, 369, 456, 458, 472; amicus brief by, 341; evidentiary hearing and, 421; letter to, 422–26; murder case and, 475

Tillman, Herb, 12

Tino, Tina (Joe's niece), 241, 267, 454

Torrillo, Frank: open letter and, 259

Trebilcock, Bob, 190, 195

Trial stage, 41

Trial transcripts, 4–5, 100, 228; investigation and, 231; mastering, 48–49

True Police, on Croft/Harberts cases, 18–19

Twenty-fifth Amendment, clemency and, 233

UCI. *See* Union Correctional Institution

Union Correctional Institution (UCI), 208, 217, 453; prison-within-a-prison at, 98; transfer to, 493

U.S. Court of Appeals for the Eleventh Circuit, 44, 57, 129, 234, 328, 381, 425; appeal to, 43, 95, 125, 145–46, 159, 288, 441; brief to, 49; clemency and, 154, 155, 157, 158; filing with, 169; habeas corpus and, 163, 286, 346; hypnosis issue and, 167; opinion by, 164–65, 169, 313; oral argument and, 161,

346; *Spaziano* case and, 286;
whimsical doubt and, 115
U.S. Senate Judiciary Committee,
testimony before, 137
U.S. Supreme Court, 142, 323, 370;
appealing to, 288, 441; capital
punishment and, 4, 413; cert in,
43; clemency and, 154; FDLE investigation and, 236; *Herrera*
case and, 140; *Hitchcock* case
and, 144; hypnosis issue and,
136; opinions by, 139; petition-
ing, 168–69, 426; review by, 44,
396; *Spaziano* case and, 401,
441
Upright, Michael, 503
United States v. Cronic, 337, 338

Vallely, James: diagnosis by, 33–35
Vandiver, Margaret, 439; editorial
by, 195; open letter and, 259
Van Hook, Claude, 229; on Fink/
Mallen testimony, 389–90; psychic and, 392
Vehman, Sandy: Tony DiLisio and,
437
Vermont Law School, 137, 175, 190,
271, 275, 377; capital punishment seminar at, 395–96; court
files at, 373; open letter and, 250
Videotape, 323, 324, 330, 339, 348;
bootleg version of, 443; contents
of, 386; FDLE and, 209, 211,
212, 215, 223, 235–36, 264,
267–68, 313–14, 317, 331, 332,
399, 400, 443, 511; *Orlando
Sentinel* and, 220, 236; recantation on, 220, 264; requesting
copy of, 347
Visits, final, 92
VLRC. *See* Volunteer Lawyers Resource Center

Volunteer Lawyers Resource Center
(VLRC), 245, 272, 329; death
row prisoners and, 128; demise
of, 279, 280, 293, 294, 297, 308,
312, 320, 330–31, 337, 341, 396,
450; funding for, 330; investigative report by, 271; lawyers from,
171, 172; Lori Rozsa on, 299; secret evidence and, 277; Ed Stafman and, 146; support from,
322, 326, 347
Von Drehle, David, xxiv, 2, 183,
199, 345, 439, 474; *Bundy* case
and, 195–96; on Scharlette
Holdman, 84

Walker, Barbara Spaziano, 197, 483;
on accident, 36; on family life,
37–38; on motorcycle club, 39
Walter, David D.: open letter and,
259
Washington Post, xix, xxiv, 198,
260, 374; on Medina execution,
410; Gene Miller and, 192; *Spaziano* case and, xxii, 280, 442
Watson, Sidney D.: open letter and,
260
Weaver, Dennis: open letter and, 260
Wehner, Charles: testimony of,
14–15
Wells, Charles: concurring opinion
of, 467
Wentworth, Colin, 249
West Palm Beach Public Defender's
Office, 25, 46, 94, 473, 515;
interview with, 45; Krop/Vallely
and, 33; litigation strategies/
constitutional theories at, 85
White, Jerry, 379; death warrant for,
397–98, 402, 403, 404; evidentiary hearing for, 403; execution
of, 3, 402–8, 410, 413, 415, 421;

scream of, 407, 408, 413; racism and, 404; trial lawyer of, 403–4

White, Sid J., 107, 109, 110, 111, 138, 305, 347–48, 353

Wiener, Richard L.: open letter and, 260

Williams, Melanie: criticism by, 354–55

Wilmer, Cutler & Pickering, 125, 134–37

Witnesses, 202, 481, 482, 483, 484; anonymous/investigation of, 340; assembling, 92–93; credibility of, 435; media and, 93; tampering with, 314

Witness protection program, 278, 388, 437

Yannotta, Ralph "Lucifer," 387, 388

Yarrow, Peter: open letter and, 260

"You are a murderer" letter, 214–17

Zavez, MaryAnn: open letter and, 250, 260

Zinker, Leonard: Spaziano examination, 32–33

Michael Mello is professor of law at Vermont Law School. He is the author of *USA vs. Theodore Kaczynski, Dead Wrong,* and *Against the Death Penalty.*

Mike Farrell is an actor and president of California Death Penalty Focus.

1993–94
Brief and oral argument in Eleventh Circuit; denial of habeas corpus petition affirmed by Eleventh Circuit; application for review in U.S. Supreme Court

May 25, 1995
Miami Herald conditions its involvement in Spaziano's case on Mello's writing an op-ed piece for the paper, explaining why he believes Spaziano is innocent

June 14, 1995
Florida Departmen[t] Law Enforcement (FDLE) officers que[s]tion DiLisio, who repeats his recanta[tion]; interrogation videotaped

1992
Federal habeas corpus petition filed in federal district court

Early May 1995
Mello approaches *Miami Herald* about Spaziano's case; *Herald* says it will consider the matter

June 9, 1995
Tony DiLisio recants to a *Miami Herald* reporter

1993
Habeas petition denied; appeal to Federal Court of Appeals for the Eleventh Circuit

May 24, 1995
Fourth death warrant signed; execution scheduled for 7:00 A.M., June 27, 1995

June 11, 1995
Miami Herald runs front-page story on DiLisio's recantation

January 1995
U.S. Supreme Court denies petition for plenary review

June 4, 1995
Mello's op-ed piece appears in *Miami Herald* and other Florida news-papers; *Herald* agrees to investigate Spaziano's case

June 15,
Governor
Spaziano'[s]
orders FD[LE]
secret inv[estigate]
believabil[ity]
recantatio[n]